N.C.EDSALL
1970

ARTHUR JAMES BALFOUR

Arthur James Balfour (1848–1930), aged 29

Portrait by George Richmond

ARTHUR JAMES BALFOUR

THE HAPPY LIFE OF THE POLITICIAN
PRIME MINISTER
STATESMAN AND PHILOSOPHER
1848-1930

By

KENNETH YOUNG

LONDON
G. BELL AND SONS, LTD

Printed in Great Britain by
The Camelot Press Ltd., London and Southampton

FOR
PHYLLIS,
WITH LOVE

CONTENTS

ILLUSTRATIONS

PREFACE

rthur Balfour once remarked that he was more or less happy when being praised and not very uncomfortable when being abused, but 'I have moments of uneasiness when I am being explained.' He had, however, few such occasions for disquiet—fewer still since his death in the early spring of 1930. Apart from the two-volume life by his niece, Blanche Dugdale, which came out in 1936, there has been no biography at all, and singularly few studies of him. Yet he spent 50 years in politics, 32 of them as a Minister of the Crown, nearly four as Prime Minister. Indeed, 35 or 40 years ago it must have seemed to young and old alike that Balfour had always been in the public eye and the forefront of the political scene; for the man who was Lord President of the Council as late as 1929 had been Chief Secretary for Ireland—then a key post—as early as 1887. For half a century the cartoonists had been drawing the long, elegant legs and the precarious pince-nez; several generations of humorists (less inhibited then) had poked fun at 'Pretty Fanny' and 'Prince Arthur', the 'delicate product of Cambridge culture'; at the politician who 'never read the papers'; at the 'philosophic doubter' incapable of making his mind up on the claims of tariff reform and free trade, and at the 'enervated aristocrat' they pictured drifting gracefully through social upheaval, wars and the defeat of his party. During his lifetime, his partiality for detective stories and for tennis were as familiar to the public as the 'Balfour Declaration' and his ability to lecture on difficult philosophic themes from a few words written on the backs of long envelopes. Some of his *bon mots* were famous: 'Everything is now permissible, even orthodoxy'; 'History never repeats itself; historians repeat each other'; 'If there is no future life, this world is a bad joke; but whose joke?' A generation and more of public speakers were nourished by his throw-aways: 'Conservative prejudices are rooted in a great past and Liberal ones in an imaginary future.' Parliamentarians through 30 years were tickled by his intellectual felicity:

'There are those', (he said during one Irish debate) 'who talk as if Irishmen were justified in disobeying the law because the law comes to them in foreign garb.   I see no reason why any local colour should be given to the Ten Commandments.'

His wit could shoot forth a polished aphorism, as when he said of Comte's Positivism: 'It may encourage us to die with dignity, it hardly permits us to live with hope.'   It could take on a more literary tone as it did when he said of golf: 'Care may sit behind the horseman, she never presumes to walk with the caddy.'   It could bite and sting: 'Mr. Gladstone was formerly as ready to blacken the Irish Members' characters as he is now ready to blacken their boots.'   It was not only the Commons who got the benefit of his verbal agility.   In New York in the 1920s he was being shown the latest skyscrapers by his guide who, having expatiated upon these marvels, added: 'And, Lord Balfour, the whole building from roof to cellars is fireproof,' to which Balfour was heard to murmur: 'What a pity!'   Some of his very best remarks were confined to Cabinet papers; during the struggle between his Cabinet and Curzon, then Viceroy in India, he observed that Curzon was claiming for the Indian viceregal government that dominance which 'would raise India to the position of an independent, and not always friendly, power'.

The froth of cartoonists, the jets of wit, have a high evaporation rate, and sometimes when they vanish it is disconcertingly revealed that there was nothing much beneath.   A public face gradually grows into its mask; take the face away and the mask is left in its fixed stare, until the mask, too, fades and crumbles.   Nobody tries to 'explain' because there seems nothing to be explained.   With Balfour, however, the opposite is true: when the froth evaporates, it is not nullity but complexity that remains, and it is that complexity that has inhibited explanation.   'His subtle nature', Russell Kirk wrote of Balfour in that brilliant exposition, *The Conservative Mind*, 'will not be explained here and, for that matter, no one has attempted it.'

Balfour's nature was certainly subtle and so was his brain—he had a superb intelligence.   But the main difficulty in understanding him arises from a change in us rather than an opacity in him.   He was a whole man, born in such circumstances and with such a temperament that he was able to develop all his nature and enjoy doing so.   This is not common; and it is even less common today than in the nineteenth century.   He was born luckily and lived happily: the sequence is familiar to few living persons.   Of course, he had personal sorrows; he had neither wife nor child; he could on occasion feel ill-used though the feeling did not last long; he could be angered; he could be depressed. But at the the very heart of his being was a great calm whither he could retire at will: *che sera sara, tout passe*—such expressions are called to mind; yet the calm was nourished from deep sources and by a capacity for contemplation whose quality we may glimpse in such celebrated passages in his philosophical works where he writes of mutability and of the transience of man and his universe: 'The energies of our system will decay, the glory of the sun will be dimmed, and the earth, tideless and inert, will no longer tolerate the race which has for a moment disturbed its solitude. Man will go down into the pit and all his thoughts will perish. The uneasy consciousness, which in this obscure corner has for a brief space broken the contented silence of the universe, will be at rest. . . .' These are not just fine words; they are very close to the inner man; they describe, in part, the source of his calm as well as the temper of his philosophical speculation.

It may, of course, be said that the capacity for extracting solace from such contemplative gifts would be much reduced in a man struggling for existence in a mean house in a back street surrounded by squawking children and a nagging wife. This may be so, though it cannot be taken as proven, and in any case is no kind of criticism of Balfour. It is true that there was nothing that Balfour wanted that he could not have, nothing that he wanted to do that he did not do. His wants were subtle, refined and interlocking; they could be so because they did not include food and warmth, status in society, the best education—towards these he had no need to strive for he was born to them. He was a Cecil, his mother being a sister of the great Lord Salisbury; his father was a Scottish laird (descended on the maternal side from the Earls of Lauderdale), ultimately of Saxon or Danish extraction; from him at 21 Balfour inherited estates and investments estimated at £4 million. Eton and Cambridge, and the great houses of the Victorian aristocracy at almost its highest point of power were wide open to him, and wel-coming. Moreover he was an agreeable young man, tall and hand-some, though sometimes languid, with notable eyes—not large, but often shining with humorous or sympathetic interest, less frequently half-abstracted as though regarding some absorbing inner landscape.

Balfour loved Society, or rather that section of Society which in the late nineteenth century demonstrated a distaste for the cruder pursuits of the upper classes—the deep-drinking after a hard day's hunting, the more vulgar satisfactions of the flesh—and preferred instead the graces of conversation in which beautiful women as well as amusing men were equal partners. This Society—it came to be called 'The Souls'—could be frivolous, it could play word-games such as 'Clumps' (a sort of early 'Twenty Questions'), it could just have fun; it preferred tennis to shooting, it rode bicycles rather than horses; but it sparkled with ideas; it was open to the speculations of science and the new in music and literature and art; although in the main composed of members of the aristocracy, it welcomed intellect even if embodied in those who, like Wells, were the sons of drapers, or, like the scientist Sir Oliver Lodge, of potters. In such circles Balfour found both recreation and admiration.

The distinction and rarity of his mind stood out, as well as his natural wit and (something often overlooked), his sheer sense of fun: 'real "funniness" ', wrote Lady Betty Montgomery, 'which made one laugh oh! so heartily when it came on one so suddenly'.

But the house-parties in the green afternoons of Victorianism at Longleat, Panshanger, Taplow or Stanway, were not long hours of chat; they provided for retreat in private sitting-rooms and in such sitting-rooms during those long unhurried week-ends Balfour often devoted himself to speculation and the writing of philosophy, later to the composition of Cabinet memoranda, and sometimes to love. Balfour had a need for retreat. There was in him always the pattern of advance-and-withdraw, of the scratch and the caress, of the Society man and the solitary. The pursuit of philosophy in itself (which began, he tells us, as early as his years at Eton) was an expression of his downbeat mood just as the cut-and-thrust and business of parliamentary life expressed the upbeat. Systole and diastole, they were for most of his life in exquisite balance and harmony. 'When I'm at work on politics, I long to be in literature, and *vice versa*,' he once told John Morley. It was the secret of his superb balance; when the one became boring and unpleasant, he took refuge in the other. When he was a very young man, he told his mother he wished to devote his life to philosophy; she dissuaded him, telling him that if he did so by the time he was 40 he would have nothing left to say in philosophy. It was, however, a long time before he committed himself completely to the hazards of politics; and he continued to write philosophical studies throughout his life. But philosophy never became a mere hobby. Others have had hobbies; Balfour had separate passions. Which of them ruled? In the end, no doubt, it was politics; as Austen Chamberlain wrote; 'At least from the time when he became Chief Secretary for Ireland (when he was 39), politics became his ruling passion to which in the measure which their pursuit made necessary, he was prepared to, and in fact did, subordinate all others.'

Two such passions perhaps precluded a third; there is in the mature Balfour no such passion for women as we find in some other Victorian and Edwardian politicians. It has been said of the Cecils that their sexual drive is generally low-powered. Yet the view that Balfour was in this respect a cold man is not entirely true. The Society in which he found his true home, the 'Souls', was not notably a-sexual; the opposite is more nearly correct—'What', it was jestingly said, 'shall it avail a man if he gain the whole world, and lose his own particular Soul?' Very early in life, Balfour fell deeply in love with May Lyttelton, the sister of a Cambridge friend and a niece of Gladstone; she died before an engagement could be announced. This left a searing wound on Balfour that was perhaps never entirely healed during the almost 60

years of life that remained to him.   But within the *ambiance* of the
'Souls', where he became the cynosure of female eyes, there were
affaires, and in particular a long-lasting one with another man's wife—
an *affaire* that threatened more than once to become public property
and even to lead to the divorce court.   But after the first flush of
passion, it was Balfour who became the pursued rather than pursuer,
though the friendship persisted to his death.   This was the third
passion; it was, however, one that Balfour kept strictly in check and it
remained subservient to the other two.

The result of this delicate balancing of aim and desire was that
Balfour became a man so integrated as to seem polished, but he was
not self-polished as Maynard Keynes implied when he said of him in
the 1920's: 'He is the most extraordinary *objet d'art* our society has
produced.'   If he appeared languid and his languour, in turn, a pose,
it was partly because of his having been regarded as delicate in early
life; he was made to rest a great deal at his prep school and his eyesight
(until fashion permitted him to wear spectacles at Cambridge) prevented him from normal boyish games; it was partly, also, that he knew
how to conserve his energies, sleeping well, and seldom rising before
noon, though, like his friend Winston Churchill, he did much business
in bed.   He was detached, yes, but this was a genuine detachment
from the struggle either for life or position, and this meant that he
could not be panicked nor pushed into decisions before he had examined them.   There was certainly something donnish in his outlook.
His mind was naturally inclined to lucidity, preferring, as his prep
school master early observed, principles rather than isolated facts.
This bred in him an intellectual coolness which Cambridge increased;
this could and did in his young manhood sometimes emerge in an
ungraceful *froideur*, a minor intellectual *hubris*, but this did not persist.
He was a reasoning man, but a good deal of his philosophy is devoted
to casting doubt on reason—'We know in part and therefore we know
wrongly. . . .   Our intellectual progress is scarcely to be discerned, so
minute is the parallax of Infinite Truth.'   Any tendency to *hubris* was
counteracted not only by a philosophical scepticism, but by a considerable understanding of and respect for the processes of science: even
the great Rutherford once remarked to him, after his address to the
British Association, that he admired the scope of his scientific knowledge, and Rutherford's official biographer adds that 'It is noteworthy
that this philosopher quickly understood the importance of the work of
the physicist.'

The pose of Balfour is as mythical as his coldness.   Cynthia Asquith,
who knew him from her childhood upwards, regarded him rather as
enthusiastic, even impassioned.   He could certainly be feline in political relationships, not least in the early part of his career when, having

decided on politics as a *métier,* he discovered that though reputations may be made in the House, office is quite as likely to come through operations back-stage: if this is a criticism it is not of Balfour, but of politics in general.   But he was a man who could also weep—over the death of those he loved, over the appalling slaughter of the war in the trenches; and about such emotional outbreaks, as of his closest personal relationships, he was not flamboyant but secretive.   His real friend-ships were few, but they were deep; and to such friends his loyalty was impregnable, his sympathy without limit.   His feelings were not on the surface; once stirred they emerged in action, whether it was the consolation of the bereaved or the plight of the Jews.   His attitude to the Jews is, indeed, one that reveals more of him than almost any other public matter with which he was concerned. Here one observes how often it was an intellectual proposition (the uniqueness of the Jews in history, the grand idea of a re-established Jewish nation) that first stirred him, and how emotional force was then attracted to it.   For Balfour was no Semitophile; he had talked to Cosima Wagner during one of his musical pilgrimages to Bayreuth, and he doubted whether any increase in Jewish immigration was good for Britain.   Yet he used his immense political skill and (by then) vast influence to put the British Government behind Chaim Weizmann.   The Balfour Declara-tion, though a Cabinet decision, remains part of his political achieve-ment; but still it carries different undertones and a different psycho-logical atmosphere from his other achievements.   Balfour's acts in this connection were in a sense the conscience-money paid by a wealthy, happy man to the poor and downtrodden for whom otherwise there was no hope.   His own country had, indeed, its poor and down-trodden; but for them there *was* hope—not least the hope of education, and one of the great personal successes of Balfour, the politician, was in this field.   The Education Act of 1902 he carried through in the teeth of every kind of opposition, risking at every turn the downfall of his government.   Balfour's tenacity in pursuit of an objective once he had determined upon it on intellectual grounds was terrier-like.   Undeter-mined, however, as he was for example over the merits of free trade versus protection, he resembled more the eel than the hound.   This eventually led to his rejection by the Conservative party and his resignation of the leadership in 1911.   His lack of fervour for a cause in which he did not believe may be a criticism of him as a politician; it is surely in his favour as a man and as a statesman.

To achieve the objects which he regarded as essential for his country, he would spare neither pains nor effort; he would work like a demon and use his skill in political manœuvre like a Renaissance prince: the organisation of defence (the Committee of Imperial Defence was largely his creation); the furtherance of education, technology and

science; the reorientation of Commonwealth relationships—to these he
devoted hours of toil and the best endeavours of a keen, capacious brain
and a mind with a genuine quality of vision. But many of his aims,
by their very nature, were not susceptible of publicity; they could not
catch votes; and his often-mentioned ability to see both sides of a
question was a positive weakness in a politician. Moreover, he was
never on terms of intimacy nor even acquaintance with the rank-and-
file of his party either in the House or in the country. Party organisations bored him as they did his uncle Salisbury and later Winston
Churchill. He could not simulate bonhomie though his manners to
high and low were perfect; it was only King Edward VII who, somewhat over-sensitively, complained that he often felt that Mr. Balfour
was condescending towards him.

On the other hand, he was a party man through and through. His
great horror was the thought that somehow his party would be split,
as Peel split it, and he would go to extreme lengths to avoid such an
eventuality. Yet it was Balfour who persisted in cleaving to a Coalition Government after the First World War, partly because he believed
that Lloyd George's drive was as necessary in the dangerous early years
of peace as it had been in the desolate days of the war. For Lloyd
George he had from the first a personal liking—the liking, perhaps, of
opposites; without him, and Maurice Hankey, he doubted whether
the war would have been won. Balfour and Lloyd George were ideal
partners in the last years of the war, and Balfour's calm, poise and
enormous capacity for handling the sheer business of political office
('In business', wrote Morley, 'he is absolutely without atmosphere')
were an ideal balancing factor to Lloyd George's roughshod dynamism
and soaring vision. As Humbert Wolfe, then a civil servant, wrote:
'Balfour and Lloyd George—a pylon with its dynamo.'

But Balfour remained a true, bred-in-the-bone Conservative. He
was aware of the social evils in Britain, but he distrusted 'self-constituted physicians . . . gentlemen who think that they pay Providence
a compliment by assuming that for every social ill there is a speedy and
effectual specific lying to hand; who regard it as impious to believe
that there may be chronic diseases of the body politic as well as of any
other body. . . . Of two evils it is better, perhaps, that our ship shall
go nowhere than it shall go wrong, that it should stand still than that
it should run upon the rocks.' He had an utterly realistic awareness
of how exactly government really runs. He wrote brilliantly in *The
Foundations of Belief* of precept and prescription and 'Authority'—the
Burkeian bases of Conservatism. He saw no point in opposing what
was bound to come; and it was he who, to the distress of more dogmatic
Conservatives, decided that when opposition to the Lloyd George
budget of 1909 turned into a full-blown crisis of the Constitution, that

BJB

it was necessary to admit defeat rather than to lay the way open to tampering with the very foundations of the State. He disbelieved in Randolph Churchill's version of 'Tory Democracy'; on the other hand, he had no personal sympathies with the business men and the captains of industry who transformed the Conservative party from 1911 onwards. As he hinted in his lecture on Decadence at Newnham College, he suspected that there was beginning some 'process of social degeneration' when increasing numbers of men would lack an object in life, when life itself would descend to a monotone, when there would be an extraordinary passion for sameness. Such a world we, indeed, now inhabit. That did not mean that Western civilisation would cease from its onward movement; it meant only that such a movement would become less and less pleasant for the individual. He doubted whether the process could be halted; he knew there had been one ice-age, his friend George Wyndham reported him as saying, and found no reason to suppose there might not be another. Meanwhile, here and there, it might be possible to delay and to ameliorate. The great division between the happy and the unhappy was that between the well and the ill, between the non-destitute and the destitute: these could be ameliorated and perhaps eventually reduced to minute proportions but not by any political doctrine; only science, technology and production would avail: 'You must have production before you can have distribution. . . . The problem is not to equalise down but to equalise up.'

But in any case, seen against the immeasurable vistas and intolerable ages of the universe, most things were relative; man proposes but God disposes. Not even philosophic thought could expect any kind of permanence: 'I don't very much care whether there is an appreciation of my philosophy. . . . All that any man's thought is, is a contribution greater or less to the stream of thought of his own time, which flows on and turns into the thought of the next generation. There is a fashion in thought as impermanent as a fashion in dress.' Meanwhile, a man must do what he can with the gifts of mind and heart with which he has been endowed but expect neither great success now nor great glory in the future: 'Imperishable monuments and immortal deeds, death itself, and love stronger than death, will be as though they had never been'—these words had, indeed, been preceded by the proviso 'so far as natural science by itself is able to teach us'; yet so moving and emotive are they that there is no doubt they were deeply felt. For the rest, there were the pleasures of the mind, of conversation and wit in country houses; there was golf in the peace of North Berwick, the sea sparkling in the sunshine; there were the ever-changing prospects of politics, the exciting new world revealed by science, there were young people and young ideas, and always there was the solace of music, particularly the music of Handel for which very early Balfour discovered a passion—in his twenties he financed a performance of *Belshazzar* at the Albert Hall, in his eighties it was Handel whose music poured from the great horn of the gramophone in his sitting-room at his brother's house in Woking where in 1930 he died.

But what then of religion? If the universe was to go down to the pit and the earth left as cold and cheerless and uninhabited as it once was before, what of men's belief in God and hopes of a future life? It was the problem Balfour pondered through all his philosophical works from *A Defence of Philosophic Doubt* (1879) to *Theism and Thought* (1924); always he argued for God and usually he won, but it was certainly a near thing in *Philosophic Doubt*. Even at Cambridge, however, he had what someone described as 'a queer kind' of belief in Christianity; all his life he was interested in psychical research for if it could be proved that life went on after death, then that much of Christian belief was nearer proof, but he was never convinced by such research: on the other hand he believed in personal survival though, as he told Conan Doyle, his beliefs were older than scientific psychical research 'and do not depend on it'. He told someone else: 'I deem it at least as certain as any of the hundred-and-one truths of the frame-work of the world, as I conceive the world. It is no mere theological accretion, which I am prepared to accept in some moods and reject in others.' The bitterness of the death of those we love, he told Lady Desborough, was not in the thought that we had parted with them for ever but rather that, until we die also, we shall never again see them smile or hear their voices: 'The pain is indeed hard to bear, too hard it seems sometimes for human strength. Yet measured on the true scale of things it is but brief; death cannot long cheat us of love.'

There seems little doubt that he was a believer; there is no doubt at all that he was a practising Christian, attending church every Sunday unless politics interfered and holding family prayers when he was at home in Whittingehame, East Lothian. If the connection between science and religion was hard to establish by reason and logic, it was the worse for reason and logic; and they, as he knew, are not the whole world. Faith, too, existed as indubitably as they did; neither the inner world of man nor the visible universe itself were wholly comprehensible either by science or by the reasoning powers of man. There were more things in heaven and earth than naturalism imagined.

Such was Arthur Balfour: in politics a realist, in private life at once a contemplative and a lover of Society; a man with a great capacity for work who gave to the superficial observer the impression of a dilettante trifler; a religious man with a mind as sharp as a butcher's knife. It has been said of him that he was a man born out of his time, that he would have been happiest in the late eighteenth century and certainly, as he wrote himself, he had no sentiment of allegiance to the middle third of the nineteenth century, to Landseer and the revival of Gothic, to 'the windy prophesyings of Carlyle, nor the thin lucidity of Mill'. He has been compared with Lord Halifax the 'Trimmer' and the third Earl of Shaftesbury whose 'system' is best displayed in Pope's *Essay on Man*. The pages that follow show how shallow such comparisons are. He was quite *sui generis*, fitting into no common mould—the aristocrat who hated hunting and shooting and preferred the middle-class games of golf and tennis; the Victorian intellectual who could not stomach Browning and much preferred the then unfashionable Jane Austen; the politician who ruled the House of Commons for 15 turbulent years but whose public speeches seldom swayed a crowd and were sometimes a disaster.

Yet Balfour, despite his wholeness, had his Achilles's heel. On his death-bed, and for the first time in his life, he became worried about money. He had always lived well though not in any sense extravagantly. But he had over some years poured money into a semi-scientific scheme which constantly went wrong and proved impracticable. He had paid little or no attention to his financial advisers who warned him of declining fortune. On his death-bed he asked his heir whether he would be able to eat on what was left. It was not quite so bad as that, though Whittingehame House was abandoned, his great library sold and his London house in Carlton Gardens off Pall Mall disposed of. What had caught up with Balfour was not so much a lifelong distaste for finance and economics as that wind of change first blown into English Society through the Radical budgets of his friend, Lloyd George, along with the decline of Britain from her leading position as a producing power, and the defeat of the great landowners by the great industrialists. It was the latter, in particular, that lay behind the relegation of Balfour from the leadership of the party in 1911.

What then of his achievements in the field of his 'ruling passion'? Only two British Prime Ministers since Lord Salisbury have been major influences upon world polity: Lloyd George and Winston Churchill, both significantly wartime leaders. Balfour does not rank with them. The work he did in Ireland was a great achievement; but it was largely erased by what followed. In education, as we noted, he laid an important foundation stone; his constant stress upon technology and science as 'the great engine of future progress' was wise and helpful; his work for defence (some of which even now cannot be detailed) was a sound skeleton upon which others put the flesh. Again his vision in plotting the new relationships within the Commonwealth at the conference of 1926—it was embodied in the Statute of Westminster in 1931—has now been overtaken by realignments and novel situations; his hopes of an 'Anglo-Saxon Federation' have not yet been realised.

This is no more than he would have expected; what he said of philosophy would apply no less to politics. Yet this is to take a God-like view of history where it is not politicians, but inventors, scientists and poets who are the great and lasting influences: it is Shakespeare not Burleigh who remains a potent influence from Elizabethan times upon the minds of men now living. Politicians and statesmen in modern times cannot be measured by such standards, much less in the ever faster swirl of events in the twentieth century. But Balfour has claim to a longer influence than most leading politicians in the last 80 years because he so constantly looked ahead, so constantly built for the future rather than allowing himself to be sidetracked by the immediate; ironically enough had he done so he might have remained in power longer than he did. He may have loved power and office—most politicians do, otherwise they would be farmers or dons—but he did not love them sufficiently to work more arduously for them than for what he believed to be the things essential for the future safety and prosperity of his fellow-countrymen. He was essentially a statesman not a politician. His influence, and it became enormous, was heavily on the side of the civilised life; in the day-to-day decisions of Ministerial office, as in his larger policies, he was for the light. He preferred happiness himself and believed that many others would, given the opportunities. But he never forgot that, in the poor, fallen state of our nature, there are some who unwittingly prefer catastrophe, misery and destruction. Politics after all, at bottom, is the struggle for existence, as Wallace Stevens pointed out. Of this Balfour was always aware: it made him not a cynic as some have thought but a realist. His influence would be thrown into the scales on the side of life, but it would be foolish not to recognise that in the end death might win, not least because man's powers are finite, the universe's infinite. *Ce qu'on voit est toujours moins important que ce qu'on ne voit pas*—Bastiat's words are as true in politics as in science, in history as in statesmanlike planning.

Material—something approaching half a ton of it—for a life of Balfour is to be found in the British Museum in London and at Red-cliff, Whittingehame, near Haddington in East Lothian. Some of this material was seen, and some of it sorted, by Balfour's sole biographer, the late Mrs. Blanche Dugdale, Balfour's niece. At that time all the material was at Whittingehame. It was subsequently divided into the personal and the political-cum-philosophical; the former was retained at Whittingehame, the latter sent to the British Museum. The division was not well made: much of the personal has gone to the British Museum, some of the political remains at Whittingehame. Only within the last two years has the material at the British Museum been catalogued; and about a third of this has been barred to the historian by the Cabinet Office and other Government departments on so-called 'security' grounds. Some of the material still at Whittinge-hame would, no doubt, be brought under the same ban were it ever to be sent to the British Museum. Balfour died in 1930. The United States Government is already making available 'top secret' material from the war of 1939–45. From the historian's point of view, owners of political papers cannot be too strongly urged in present circumstances to keep control of their property for once it is handed to the British Museum authorities they are not even allowed to give permission for historians to see their own property.

Happily, in the case of Balfour, the arbitrarily imposed gaps are easily closed from other sources, both published and unpublished. What follows in the body of this work may be taken as substantially complete. Much of it has not previously been published; Mrs. Dug-dale, writing within a few years of her uncle's death, was inhibited by many factors, political and personal, which no longer apply; and she was, moreover, writing a 'family' life rather than an historical and political biography. She made no attempt to integrate Balfour's philosophy into his life; the philosophy was dealt with in an appendix only and by Professor Pringle-Pattison.

Thus, I have had a fair field and a very great deal of unpublished material to go at, much of it throwing new light not only on Balfour himself, but on the political history of his times as well as on other politicians. I have received the greatest assistance, kindness and hospitality from the Earl and Countess of Balfour during my visits to Whittingehame. Without their unfailing helpfulness, the book could not have been written; though, of course, for the interpretation of Balfour that emerges in the book they are in no way responsible.

Other sources of material are to be found in letters in private hands, in biographies of coaeval and near-coaeval politicians, authors, scient-ists and prominent members of Society, and in the memories of those still alive who knew Balfour though, naturally, those who knew him intimately in his heyday are decreasingly few. Among those whose conversation with me proved especially useful are Lord Hankey, Lady Ruth Balfour, the late Lady Cynthia Asquith and the late Sir Henry T. Tizard.

Not least I wish to thank my wife, to whom this book is dedicated, for her suggestions and her patience in listening as the tale of Arthur Balfour unfolded, and to my five small children for the peace they allowed me and the joy they give me.

KENNETH YOUNG

London—Brighton—Headingley
February 20, 1962

ACKNOWLEDGEMENTS

To Her Majesty the Queen for permission to consult Balfour's correspondence with Queen Victoria, King Edward VII, King George V, and other members of the Royal Family.

To the Earl of Balfour for permission to consult Balfour papers stored at Redcliff, Whittingehame, East Lothian, and to the Earl and Countess of Balfour for advice, assistance and hospitality during the years of preparation; also for permission to reproduce a number of portraits and photographs.

To Lady Violet Benson for permission to consult Balfour's correspondence with the Countess of Wemyss.

To the Trustees of the British Museum for permission to consult the Balfour papers there.

These are the principal sources of unpublished material I have used. Acknowledgements of already printed material is made in the Notes. But I should wish to thank also the undermentioned for information, advice and other assistance: Lord and Lady Traprain, Lord Beaverbrook, the late Sir Henry T. Tizard, Lord Hankey, the late Lady Cynthia Asquith, Lady Ruth Balfour, the Earl of Birkenhead, Sir George Thomson, F.R.S., Sir Colin R. Coote, Mr. Peter Montgomery, Mr. Lawrence Burgiss, Capt. Alan Graham, Capt. A. L. Kennedy, Professor Asa Briggs, Professor Bonamy Dobrée, Mr. J. F. Hearn, Mr. Robert Rhodes James, Mr. A. Lane-Roberts, Mr. Kenneth Hopkins, to Mr. S. L. Dennis and Mr. M. H. Vazvill, of G. Bell & Sons, and to Mr. and Mrs. Adams of Hove for secretarial work.

BRIEF BIOGRAPHY

ARTHUR JAMES BALFOUR

1848 Born at Whittingehame House, East Lothian, eldest son of James Maitland and Lady Blanche Balfour

1861 Eton College

1866 Trinity College, Cambridge

1874 M.P. for Hertford

1879 *A Defence of Philosophic Doubt*

1885 President of the Local Government Board

1886 Secretary for Scotland

1887 Chief Secretary for Ireland

1891 First Lord of the Treasury, Leader of the House of Commons

1895 *The Foundations of Belief*

1902 Prime Minister

1905 Resigns, defeated at the election of 1906

1908 'Decadence': Henry Sidgwick Memorial Lecture

1909 'Criticism and Beauty': Romanes Lecture

1911 Resigns from leadership of Conservative party

1914 'Theism and Humanism': Gifford Lectures, Part I

1915 First Lord of the Admiralty

1916 Secretary of State for Foreign Affairs; given O.M.

1919 Lord President of the Council (until 1922)

1922 Order of the Garter
      Created Earl of Balfour and Viscount Traprain

1923 'Theism and Thought': Gifford Lectures, Part II

1924 Chairman of the Medical Research Council

1925 Lord President of the Council

1926 Chairman of the Committee of Dominion Prime Ministers

1928 Prince of Wales proposes his health at 80th birthday lunch

1929   Baldwin Government resigns; Balfour hands over seals of office

1930   March 19, dies at Fisher's Hill, Woking; buried in family ground at Whittingehame, East Lothian. Earldom passed to brother Gerald, Viscountcy to Gerald's son, R. A. L. Balfour (the present Earl)

Balfour's published works include, as well as those mentioned above: *The Immediate Problem of Philosophy*: a lecture delivered to the Edinburgh Philosophical Society (1880); *The Pleasures of Reading*: an address (1888); *Lies and Replies*: exposure of some Gladstonian fallacies (1892); *Essays and Addresses* (first edition 1893; third edition 1905 includes studies of Berkeley, Handel, Cobden, Progress, the religion of humanity, the nineteenth century, the new theory of matter, etc.); *Economic Notes on Insular Free Trade* (1903); *Speeches on Fiscal Reform* (1906); *Questionings on Criticism and Beauty* (1908)—the lecture printed from verbatim reports, as distinct from the revised and improved lecture referred to in Brief Biography; *Arthur James Balfour as Philosopher and Thinker: A Collection of the more important and interesting passages in his non-political writings, speeches, and addresses, 1879–1912*, edited by Wilfrid M. Short (1912); *The British Blockade* (1915); *Essays, Speculative and Political* (1920)—includes 'Decadence' and 'Criticism and Beauty', also studies of Bergson, Francis Bacon, the presidential address to the Society of Psychical Research in 1894, and briefer articles and introductions to Treitschke and Zionism; *Opinions and Arguments from Speeches and Addresses, 1910–1927*—on the Irish question, Socialism, science and industry, the League of Nations, Zionism, Eton, etc.; *Familiar Beliefs and Transcendent, Reason* British Academy Lecture (1925); *Chapters of Autobiography*, unfinished, ed. Blanche Dugdale (1930).

1

THE SILVER SPOON

1848–1869

The name Balfour, which even now is more commonly found north of the Border than in England, originally derived from a small hamlet of that name on the banks of a stream, the Or, in Fifeshire. The place-name itself is Gaelic, deriving perhaps from 'Baile findh Or', meaning the place below or 'under' the Or (as in Ashton-under-Lyne); or it may come from 'Baile fuar', which means the cold town. 'Or' itself is an obsolete Gaelic word for water, though it is thought to have an even older, pre-Celtic root.

But the Balfours themselves were not Celts. They trace their descent from Siward, a Northumbrian who was one of the Saxon or Danish immigrants welcomed into the Lowlands in the eleventh century by King Duncan I and his successors. They settled in Fifeshire and adopted the name Balfour in the next century. Some of them became sheriffs of the county. In due course, the family spread into other parts of Scotland and even to the Orkneys. But the Fifeshire branch which concerns us was founded by Peter Balfour, who, in the latter part of the fourteenth century, married Eva Sibbald who lived at Balgonie. The family was later known as the Balfours of Balbirnie. The estate of Balbirnie, Fife, from which the family took its name, was bought by George Balfour in the seventeenth century.

It was, in turn, a comparatively late shoot from the Balfours of Balbirnie that produced the Balfours of Whittingehame in East Lothian, to which Arthur James Balfour belonged. It was, in fact, A. J. Balfour's grandfather, James, who founded the Whittingehame family. James Balfour, born at Balbirnie in 1773, was the second son of John Balfour, then the laird. Since it was James's elder brother Robert—

later a lieutenant-general and a Knight—who would inherit Balbirnie, James was sent to India in 1793 to seek his fortune as a 'Writer' (i.e. a clerk) in the East India Company. This was a not unusual practice in those days for second sons of country gentlemen. The family had had one previous connection with India: James's uncle William had served on the Madras Board of Revenue.

James Balfour rose swiftly in 'John Company's' service. Within three years, he was Assistant Under-Secretary in the Public Commercial and Revenue department of the Madras Presidency and, by 1800, he was Deputy Commercial Resident. This promotion by no means satisfied his ambitions, as his letters home reveal. But on August 30, in the same year as his promotion, he was suddenly suspended from the service. It appears that, being fond of riding, he had accepted the present of a fine Arab horse from a local potentate, and this, in the more stringent conditions prevailing in the Company after the Clive reforms, was regarded as a major misdemeanour.

This setback in James Balfour's career, however, made his fortune. After two years in England, he returned to India, this time not as a clerk, but with a contract in his pocket from the Admiralty for supplying the British Navy with provisions while they were in Indian waters. How the contract got into his pocket is not clear. It had previously been held by the Hon. Basil Cochrane who had apparently not greatly exerted himself. James Balfour did, and within a decade he had made a fortune of some £300,000, more than £1½ million in present-day values. He returned to England for good in 1812, though he remained on the list of purveyors until 1815.

James Balfour's portrait, with its high, narrow forehead, shrewd eyes and long, thin lips bespeaks the legendary canny Scot, and it is well within the tradition that having made a substantial fortune he should wish to found a family of a no less substantial kind—of a kind, preferably, that would show that a second son was as good as, if not better than, a first. So, on January 19, 1815, he married Lady Eleanor Maitland, daughter of James, eighth Earl of Lauderdale. Though the earldom had had its greatest moments in the seventeenth century, the family was connected with some of the most aristocratic lineages in Scotland. The Balfours of Balbirnie, landowners and 'upper gentry', had not previously sported a title.

But James Balfour did not stop there. He already had a house in Grosvenor Square, London. In 1817, he bought the 10,000-acre Whittingehame estate in East Lothian from the Hay family, kinsmen of the Earls of Tweeddale. In 1824, to his elder brother's chagrin, he somehow acquired Balgonie, part of the family's ancient estate; and in 1839 he bought Strathconan in Ross-shire, with its deer forest, salmon river and large shooting-lodge. He became a local dignitary,

Deputy-Lieutenant, Justice of the Peace; he sat as M.P. for Anstruther Easter Burghs, and later for East Lothian.

It was, however, Whittingehame that preoccupied him. This is not surprising. The estate is in one of the most beautiful settings of Lowland Scotland. Its central feature is a steep and wooded glen with a stream at the bottom; the soil is reddish and fertile, and the foliage has a luxuriance suggesting a much more southerly clime, although it lies among the gently-contoured foothills of the Lammermuirs. From its high points can be seen to the north the shimmering expanse of the Firth of Forth, only some seven miles distant at its nearest approach where it laps against the sea walls and harbour of the small town of Dunbar.

Upon the western bank of Whittingehame's central glen, James Balfour began in the early 1820s to build a fine new house, and by 1827 it was ready for occupation. It was larger and grander than any house for miles around—larger and grander in particular than Balbirnie House recently reconstructed by James's brother, Sir Robert. The architect of Whittingehame House was Robert Smirke, whose best-known memorial is the British Museum with which he was, indeed, occupied during this same period. Smirke belonged to the Greek revival school of architecture, and it may have been he who insisted that the local red sandstone of East Lothian was unsuitable for his style and conception. It was almost certainly James Balfour himself who proposed as a substitute the light grey stone of his native Fifeshire—the same stone used by his brother in rebuilding Balbirnie. The vast quantities needed were brought over the Forth from Fifeshire by boat, and hauled up the hills to the site by draught oxen and horses.

The Fifeshire stone was an excellent choice: Whittingehame House, though not architectually exciting, stands in its clearing pleasant and cool, its comparative paleness asserting its dignified remoteness from the warm-coloured, rather squat, farmhouses and factor's house of the estate. Today it is empty. Owing to rising costs and falling incomes, it was vacated shortly after the death of Arthur James Balfour in 1930, and has since been used intermittently for, among other things, a home for refugees from Hitler, and a Glasgow remand school. The present earl occupies the factor's house, about a mile away to the north.

James Balfour's offspring began to appear before Whittingehame House was ready for occupation. James and Lady Eleanor, his wife, had five children in all, the first dying in a fire in infancy. The next two were both sons: James Maitland Balfour, who became the father of Arthur James, and Charles, who later succeeded to Balgonie and bought an estate in Roxburghshire called Newton Don. The last two were daughters, one of whom married Lord Fitzroy, seventh Duke of Grafton.

The heir, James Maitland Balfour, was born on January 5, 1820. He was educated at Eton and Trinity College, Cambridge. Perhaps there, too, we may detect the rivalry of James and his brother, Robert. Robert had sent his eldest son, John, to Eton, the first time a Balfour had been educated there; James went one better by adding Cambridge, again a new departure in the family.

James Maitland Balfour was a handsome, dashing and athletic young man whose charm, however, was liable to sudden dissipation by bad temper. He enjoyed London life; but he also inherited some of his father's prudence; at any rate, he wisely became a director of the North British Railway at the height of railway expansion. In 1841, he was elected an M.P. and sat for Haddington Burghs until 1847. He spent much time and money on reorganising the East Lothian Yeomanry Cavalry, equipping it with uniforms and commanding it until his death in 1856.

When James Maitland Balfour was 23 he married a girl of 18, Lady Blanche Mary Harriet Gascoigne Cecil, second daughter of James, second Marquess of Salisbury. This was, indeed, going one better than the Balbirnie Balfours. The Salisburys, from the time of Queen Elizabeth's William Cecil, had been one of the most powerful families in Britain and, after a slight eclipse in the eighteenth century, were shortly to produce one of the most distinguished of Queen Victoria's Prime Ministers, Robert Cecil, the third Marquess. He, the 'great' Lord Salisbury, still at this time Viscount Cranborne, was Lady Blanche Balfour's brother and the uncle of her children.

Lady Blanche's first offspring were girls, one of whom died at birth, the other two being Eleanor Mildred, known as Nora, and Evelyn. When James Balfour, their grandfather, died in 1845, no male heir had yet appeared. But on July 25, 1848, Lady Blanche was delivered of her first son. He was named Arthur James—James after his father, and Arthur after the Duke of Wellington, Arthur Wellesley, who, it appears, was an intimate friend of Lady Blanche's mother. As two pamphlet writers put it in the year Arthur Balfour (for so he was always called) became Prime Minister: 'The Duke of Wellington gave the Balfour babe his first name and his blessing. Lord Salisbury's mother and he were great friends. To Apsley House she would frequently repair for sweet converse with the hero of Waterloo, who was quite a *persona grata* in the Cecil circle. His letters to her had reached the "Ever yours affectionately Wm." stage before she found that repose in a higher realm which the eccentric habits of her lord rendered impossible in this.' (The habits of the second Lord Salisbury do not concern us; but it is worth remarking that the levity of such comments on a Prime Minister's antecedents is hardly conceivable today.)

Following the coming of Arthur in 1848, Lady Blanche gave birth to one more girl and four more boys: Cecil Charles (1849), Alice (1850), Francis Maitland (1851), Gerald William (1853) and finally Eustace James Anthony in 1854. 1854 was, however, a year of ill-omen. Some five months before the birth of his last son, James Maitland Balfour had broken a blood-vessel during a paroxysm of coughing. It was the first indication of tuberculosis of the lungs. From this time until his death two years later, he was, in varying degree, an invalid, and it was now that Lady Blanche showed what metal she was made of. At first medical advice from the best sources was sought; but when nothing much improved her husband, Lady Blanche took to nursing him herself, devoting herself to the task with unremitting, self-denying passion.

In 1854-5, she took him to winter in Madeira, and the elder children, including Arthur, accompanied their parents, as they did in the following year. Of these trips, as of his father's death in Madeira in 1856, Arthur Balfour remembered little: 'I cannot in the least recollect his personality,' he afterwards wrote in his autobiographical fragments; and, apart from some tiny incidents, all that remained in his mind of Madeira were 'visions of transparent seas; of a precipitous coast-line and strange vegetation. . . .'

The death of James Maitland Balfour plunged his widow, Lady Blanche, into such grief that her brother-in-law, Charles Balfour who was with her and the children in Madeira, feared for her reason. It is recorded that, during her husband's last days, Lady Blanche said to someone who attempted to divert her thoughts by news of the outer world: 'What is all the world to me if my husband is dying?' For some weeks after she returned to Whittingehame, she lay ill and distraught. But, in due course, she recovered, and it was said that never again did she lose that iron self-control that was so marked a feature of her character as a widow and a mother.

II

One of Arthur Balfour's earliest distinct memories dated from the year of his father's death, 1856. He remembered standing in the cardroom of the Turf Club—a predecessor of the present one—watching through the window the fireworks display in celebration of the ending of the Crimean War. This was in March, 1856, when the Treaty of Paris was signed, and the Balfour family were presumably on their way back from Madeira to Scotland.

The world the seven-year-old boy briefly glimpsed around him in the London of that time was that of Victorianism at its noonday height. He saw a world peopled by men with heavy beards, dressed in frock coats, coloured waistcoats and a diminished form of the cravat; the

women wore voluminous skirts that had not quite ceased to be crino-
lines, nor had yet become bustles. It was a world, for the young heir
of Whittingehame and nephew of the Salisburys, of dignified, but by no
means drab adults, surrounded by multitudes of servants, of great
houses, considerable splendour and a warm sense of all being for the
best in the best of all possible countries; and beyond all that, he would
be aware of a Queen upon her throne, herself still visible to her people
with the Prince Consort at her side, and Lord Palmerston her Prime
Minister. At Hatfield House, the home of his mother's family, which
Balfour remembered visiting from his earliest years, he could see the
whole of England's historic past laid before him. But history never
stirred Balfour. What pleased him more as a seven-year-old boy,
whose brothers were all younger than himself, were the lively young
Cecils who, though technically his aunts and uncles, were in fact very
much his own age, being his grandfather Salisbury's offspring by his
second marriage to Lady Mary Sackville-West.

During the two years following his father's death it was, however,
Whittingehame that Arthur Balfour saw most of, and it was his mother
who dominated his life, and that of his brothers and sisters. 'Dominated'
is not too strong a word. Lady Blanche, once her grief had spent
itself, became not merely the *châtelaine* of a great estate—building
cottages, planting trees, keeping the business affairs strictly in her own
hands—but the head of her family, at once mother and father combined. The bride of 18, the mother of nine children (one of whom died
at birth) became almost over night a widow of the most powerful
character and remarkable gifts. There had, indeed, been sharp eyes
which had observed the potentialities in her even before her husband's
death. Lady Victoria Talbot, daughter of the eighth Earl of Shrewsbury,
wrote to her friend, Lady Waterford, in 1854:

'In Blanche there is such a wonderful power of command and duty that
to know her slightly you would think she was a healthy-minded, happy
wife, a mother of children, doing all the good she could, and consequently at peace with God and man. But you could never suspect the
intense funds of feeling, dashing and flashing and bursting and melting
her at times to pieces. And she looks so quiet, and pure and almost
cold, aye cold; about as cold as Hecla under its crust of ice. She is a
glorious character.'

That power of command and sense of duty now took control of her
children's rearing and education. The smart French furniture of the
main rooms of Whittingehame House was put into dust-covers; some
rooms were closed altogether; and the whole life of the house was centred
on the nurseries and the schoolrooms. Lady Blanche's love for her
children was not demonstrative, but it was all-embracing and practical.
When, for instance, her whole brood were stricken with diphtheria,

then with typhoid and later with whooping-cough, she nursed them herself, and for nine weeks of one illness was never out of her dressing-gown, being on duty night and day. The early Victorian era, even in the wealthiest houses, was not noted for its attention to sanitation and drainage; cess-pools were primitive, water often tainted; regular baths were not thought a necessity, any more than they had been in the days of Queen Elizabeth. Happily for the Balfour children, Lady Blanche had excellent, far-seeing ideas on the subject of health. She did not believe in such drastic, and then almost universal, remedies as brimstone and treacle, castor oil, liquorice and Gregory powder. Her eldest daughter, Nora (later the wife of the Cambridge philo-sopher, Henry Sidgwick), recorded that: 'My mother's ideas on the physical care of children were advanced for her day: she believed in good nourishment, cod liver oil, open windows, plenty of time in bed and no over-work.' For colds and fatigue, she dosed her children not with ferocious purgatives, but with port wine. The wisdom of her methods must surely be acknowledged, for she lost not one of her children (apart from the daughter who died at birth); and that, a century ago, was something of an achievement.

As her family of eight grew out of babyhood, Lady Blanche herself taught them to read and write, but she did not stop there. She was for her times remarkably well educated. She had read widely; she knew what words meant; as Dr. Robertson, Minister of Whittingehame parish from 1865 to 1918, wrote in his memoir of her: 'A slipshod word or thought would never serve with one who went so thoroughly into whatever she spoke about: so that in conversation with her one had to use all one's mind.' She was familiar with much of the best English writing. Arthur had not long been able to read when she introduced him to the works of Lord Macaulay; and he later recorded that he at once became 'his fascinated admirer. His style delighted me. I thought his dialectics irresistible. His gifts of narrative carried me away; the things he wrote about invariably interested me; in short he supplied much of the mental nourishment I desired, in the exact form that best suited my very youthful appetite.' True, Balfour added in his autobiographical fragments, Macaulay has his critics who say that 'brilliancy is but a surface quality'. But—'I am not an impartial judge. My feelings are too deeply concerned.'

In due course, Balfour was introduced to Milton and Dryden; but it was *Lycidas* not *Paradise Lost*, *Absalom and Achitophel* rather than *The Hind and the Panther*, that attracted him. The 'family idol' was Jane Austen: 'My mother's enthusiastic admiration was shared by most of her children.' An examination of the shelves at Whittingehame would show, he said, that the Jane Austen volumes were worn and dirty, which indicated the age of their earliest readers. It may be noted that

CJB

Lady Blanche's enthusiasm for Jane Austen was not common in those days; to that generation *Pride and Prejudice* and *Mansfield Park* seemed dated. Few of the great Victorian novelists, except Trollope, speak of having read her. But for Lady Blanche, who hated slipshod words, Jane Austen's precision of language and economy of structure had an obvious appeal.

Partly, perhaps, for the same reasons, Lady Blanche admired French writers, particularly novelists. This was not yet the era of Podsnappery when other countries could be considered a 'mistake', nor of moral 'sniffery', though as early as 1849 *Blackwood's Magazine* had announced that it would review no more French novels 'until a manifest improvement takes place'. Lady Blanche early set her children on the road to French literature by taking 'the most exciting French novel she could find'. She did not bother their heads with grammar. Instead she 'sought by the aid of translations, excisions and explanations, to make her youthful audience grasp the general trend of the narrative, and ultimately without much difficulty to follow its details. She chose *Monte Cristo* for her first experiment. . . .'

Upon Latin, Greek and mathematics, she set less store. Governesses for the girls and tutors for the boys she considered sufficient for those subjects, which is perhaps why Arthur said he 'never acquired sufficient mastery of the classics to enjoy them as literature'. Nevertheless his brother, Gerald, who later received the same tuition, became a classical don at Cambridge. Arthur, however, in a House of Commons that contained many excellent classicists, such as Gladstone, Rosebery, and Asquith, never turned a classical quotation. Instead, he had a grasp of the principles of science unequalled among his political peers, and for this, too, Lady Blanche was responsible. Like her brother, later Lord Salisbury, she had herself been interested in scientific experiments, and had watched him in his private laboratory at Hatfield. Her younger son, Francis ('Frank'), indeed, turned out to be a scientific genius; when he was 29, Cambridge University created for him a chair of Animal Morphology—he was one of the first geneticists, the very first to dissect a chicken embryo; the great Charles Darwin himself told him in 1881 that 'You will some day be the chief of the English biologists.' Arthur was not a practical scientist, yet the thread of science ran through all his life, in his writing and in his political career, in his friendships with Rayleigh (who married his sister Evelyn), Oliver Lodge, and J. J. Thomson, emerging finally in the powerful support he gave to research when he became Lord President of the Council in the last decade of his life: science, to him, was the main 'engine' in the advance of civilisation.

But the eager intellect of Lady Blanche ministered as much—or more—to the souls of her children as to their minds. She might love

French literature; she also believed that man could only be saved from his inborn and illimitable wickedness by baring his soul before God and calling upon Christ in His infinite mercy to save him. She might, as Balfour wrote, have sufficient breadth of mind never to treat science as 'dangerous to the higher life', as many Victorians did; she was nevertheless convinced that upon the purity and uprightness of a man's conduct in this world depended his future in the next. Escaping Hell Fire was a constant preoccupation.

Lady Blanche was, in fact, an Evangelical Christian of a strict type. Like the Wesleyans, of whom the Evangelicals were a counterpart within the Church of England, she had a horror of vestments, candles, incense and all sort of 'papistry'—a dislike that Balfour shared throughout his life. She did not think that outward show of religion mattered in the slightest, and for that reason she brought up her children as members of both Church of England and of Scotland.

What was important for her was the inner eye of conscience which ought to subject each action and every passing thought to scrutiny. Discipline was transferred from an outer authority to an inner, which was a great deal more difficult to resist except at the cost of a burden of guilt. This led to introspection, a marked feature of mid-Victorian life, as may be observed in such published journals as those of Hurrel Froude, Macready, Mark Pattison and Anne Clough. Evangelicalism had, however, its other, its out-giving side. In Lady Blanche's young days it was this aspect of the movement that affected, particularly, members of the upper classes. It instilled into them the idea that they had a duty to their inferiors, not only before God but before man. This was the age of district-visiting and schemes of philanthropy, ranging from the formation of linen clubs to the founding of Mechanics Institutes. It was also the age of inquiries into child labour, working hours, public health and even prostitution, to which a 60-page article was devoted in the *Westminster Review* as early as 1850.

Evangelicalism, not yet hardened into complacency or the hypocritical materialism Dickens attacked, was the spearhead of that movement which, as G. M. Young wrote, sought 'to induce some modicum of cleanliness and foresight, to find some substitute for savage sport and savage drinking, to attract the children to school and the parents to church, to awaken some slight interest in books and the world beyond the end of the street . . .' It may well be that it was this 'sensibility to human suffering', as Bagehot called it, replacing the 'unfeeling obtuseness of the early part of the century', that saved England from the extreme forms of revolution that raged across Europe in the year of Arthur Balfour's birth, 1848.

Certainly, as reflected through his mother, it had the profoundest effects on Balfour himself. It was reflected in small ways and large.

During the distress in Lancashire in 1862–3, Lady Blanche dispensed
with several servants and put their wages to the Famine Fund; meanwhile, two Lancashire mill-girls were imported to do the roughest
work.   Cooking and other chores were done by the Balfour children
—Arthur himself being the boot-cleaner-in-chief. (The curious
economics implicit in this discharging of servants did not apparently
occur to Lady Blanche.)   More profoundly, Arthur Balfour reflected
his mother's teaching in that sense of duty that drove him into politics
at first against his will, in his lifelong preoccupation with the problem of
aligning religion and the naturalistic philosophy of Victorian science,
in his sobriety in a by no means sober age, in his dislike of 'savage
sport' (and his preference for tennis and golf).

Lady Blanche's direct guidance of her children ceased only with her
death.   Even when, as an undergraduate, Balfour expressed a wish that
he should make over his inheritance to one of his brothers and devote
himself entirely to the study of philosophy, she gave him, he later
wrote, a 'tremendous rating', telling him that the wish to shirk the
responsibilities of his position was an example of poorness of spirit;
and, adds another member of the family, when Lady Blanche 'condemned, she spurned; when she made up her mind, she did not change
it'.   But if she condemned Balfour's wish for a life of a philosopher, she
added a shrewd practical reason for doing so: 'Do it and you will find
that you have nothing to write about by the time you are forty.'

When Balfour in his autobiographical fragments wrote of his indebtedness to many men, statesmen, philosophers and friends, he
added, 'But all my debts to them, compute them how you will, are as
nothing to what I owe to her love, her teaching, and her example.'
This is a touching tribute and, as far as Balfour himself was concerned,
it was no doubt true.   But Lady Blanche was a woman of iron.   Her
régime was intelligent and also rigorous, and her sense of morality and
duty had a psychologically penetrating quality that did not suit all her
children alike.   For Arthur its severity was mitigated in ways we shall
shortly observe; for some of his brothers and sisters, it proved too much.

In his autobiographical fragments, he said that it was largely
through the working of his mother's spirit that the 'close-knit community
of our family life remained unbroken by her death'.   This was not
quite true.   Younger members of the family later noticed that the three
sisters obviously hated each other and were unanimous in affection
only to Arthur, Frank and Gerald—the three sons who did well in the
world.   Gerald, however, never concealed his dislike and fear of his
mother.   The youngest brother, Eustace James Anthony, though a
gifted painter and a considerable architect, married unhappily and
drank himself to death.   Another brother, Cecil Charles, though no less
gifted, was wayward, ill-mannered, even criminal: as a young man, he

forged a cheque with Arthur's name, was bought out of the entail of Whittingehame and banished to Australia. There he, too, shortly died of drink. Nor could Alice Balfour be described as entirely well-orientated. She never married and hated men; she was full of repressed grudges and secret sorrows; she was a hoarder and had an over-weening jealousy of Arthur's friends and, when she became his house-keeper at Whittingehame, never made them welcome there. In countless small ways, she contrived to make life difficult for her relations. Yet Alice also had a talent for painting and natural history, she loved animals and children and—here the compelling sense of duty had its beneficial side—she devoted much time to the welfare of the tenants and, among other good deeds, founded a nursing association in East Lothian.

These were some of the 'casualties' left in the wake of Lady Blanche's mental and spiritual juggernaut. Arthur escaped severe damage by being 'delicate', and officially remaining so until middle life. 'In what', he later wrote, 'from a medical point of view my "delicacy" exactly consisted, I have not the least idea.' One of its symptoms, however, is suggested by the fact that when Balfour was asked in later years for his memories of his childhood, he replied that he could only recall 'having very tired legs after walking'. This probably indicates the nature of his 'delicacy': he tired easily, which meant that he could rest while the others worked, go into retreat when it suited him, and thus not take the full brunt of the régime. His eyesight also was bad. The two combined offered a loophole of escape. Of course, this 'delicacy' affected his scholastic studies as well, which is perhaps why he was a late-developer in the academic field—but also perhaps why he was eventually able to develop at all.

That he was thus cushioned against the régime may have bearing on the fact that he alone in that strict household retained a natural gaiety. A private 'Family Record', written mainly by the present Countess of Balfour from the memories of Alice Balfour, stresses Arthur's high spirits as a child, his sense of the comical, and his 'ex-travagant' behaviour. He is said to have, on occasion, fallen on his knees before his mother's companion, Miss Emily Faithfull—daughter of a former vicar of Hatfield—and to have serenaded her, to her great confusion, with a song called 'Thou art like a flower'. The other Bal-fours were not renowned for their sense of humour. Arthur's natural gaiety was never entirely lost.

It would be incorrect to over-emphasise the defects of Lady Blanche's régime; it had, as we have seen, many positive and uncommon virtues. Yet it is not without significance that in old age Balfour's comment on his departure at the age of 10 to a private preparatory school in the south of England was that it proved 'an unmixed blessing, though accompanied by all the pains of family separation'.

III

Lady Blanche's decision to send Arthur away to school was perhaps hastened by the fact that the latest of the tutors employed at Whittinge-hame constantly remarked that his late pupils, the Percys, were much cleverer than the Balfours whom he found 'unteachably stupid'. Balfour also recalled that this man was in the habit of pulling his ears during the Latin lesson.

Balfour arrived at the Grange School at Hoddesdon, Hertfordshire —no great distance from Hatfield—on May 13, 1859. The school was small and was probably chosen because its headmaster, the Rev. C. J. Chittenden, was the brother-in-law of Lady Blanche's companion, Miss Faithfull. Chittenden was, it appears, an excellent teacher, clear in his instruction and kindly in his manner. He loved music, and it was probably from him that Balfour gained that intense love of music that filled no small part of his leisure throughout his life. It seems that the piano interested Balfour less than the concertina—or it was, perhaps, easier to learn to play. The instrument was not then exclusively the perquisite of religious revivalists: Sankey and Moody were not yet known. Balfour, at any rate, took to the concertina, and was sometimes, during his holidays at Whittingehame, discovered lying in bed playing it, as he was to play it at many musical evenings in his young manhood.

Chittenden was also an 'ardent admirer of Tennyson' as was natural in 1859, but this taste his pupil never shared. Balfour preferred the poetry of Pope, then by no means universally admired. This love of Pope he long retained; 'his passion for Pope' surprised even so 'advanced' a young woman as Lady Cynthia Asquith sometime round the turn of the century, for even then the eighteenth-century poet was still out of fashion.

But Chittenden's great merit in his pupil's eyes, apart from the fact that he took an intelligent interest in science, was that he was always ready to answer questions about things in general, 'asked by an inquisitive and doubtless rather tiresome pupil'. For this reason Balfour acknowledged a debt to him 'greater certainly than any I owe to other teachers of my boyhood'.

If the pupil was impressed by the master, the master was no less impressed by his pupil. Chittenden later described Balfour, aged 11, as 'a peculiarly attractive boy, with a look of bright intelligence when he was well'. His health, he noted, was far from robust. He seemed to lack vital energy, and he was often abstracted. His delicacy was such that he was required by doctor's orders to lie down in the afternoon when he felt 'languid'. On such occasions 'he liked to have the organ softly played in the hall below'. He was always fond of music, but athletic games he only 'endured'.   Instead, he preferred walking with his master while his fellows were playing cricket and football.

Balfour here emerges as something of a namby-pamby, a hot-house flower.   It is true that his lack of interest in games was partly due to his poor eyesight, and glasses were not considered the thing among his school-mates at that time.   When later at Cambridge, he could openly use spectacles, he at once became interested in games, notably 'royal' tennis.   Nevertheless, there *was* a feminine streak in his character; it emerged again at Cambridge in his predilection for blue china in his rooms.   This seemed to some of his fellow-undergraduates rather affected and, because he was also somewhat fastidious in his habits, he received the nickname of 'Pretty Fanny'.   Later still, when he first entered the House of Commons, observers thought there was about him 'a distinct flavour of effeminacy'.   Nor did he ever marry.

But there was never any suggestion of the homosexual about Balfour: his heterosexual proclivities may have been low-powered but, as we shall see, they were certainly present.   He was not a man who needed to assert his masculinity to prove that it existed; but neither did it occur to him to conceal the 'femininity' which is part of every masculine character, as a certain masculinity is part of the female character.   Indeed, in him the two components were very finely balanced to give both sides of his nature full play.   The femininity itself became visible early because of his physical delicacy which, in turn, was due to his psychological situation as a fatherless child under the influence of a dominating mother.

At Grange School he was accepted for what he was and generally liked for his good humour and unselfishness.   He was often withdrawn into his own thoughts, and his school-fellows teased him on this account. Some of them, travelling one day by railway with the headmaster, observed on stopping at a station called Ponder's End that it would be a good place to leave Balfour as he was always pondering.   When his leg was pulled, he would join in the laughter—and then shut up his assailant by 'some witty repartee'.   Both the abstractedness and the witty repartee remained part of his character, as generations of political opponents were to discover in the House of Commons.

Chittenden showed considerable insight into his pupil's mind.   He soon discovered for instance that to teach him it was best to lead him first towards general principles rather than to try and get him to remember isolated facts.   Once he was given a principle which explained a number of instances that had appeared unconnected, 'his satisfaction would amount (judging from appearances) to a feeling of pleasure'. He had the ability, uncommon in a boy, of spotting inconsistencies in a number of connected facts; and 'his interest in anything he learned varied in proportion as it gave room for reducing chaos to order'.

He did not care much for mathematics, though his love for logical progression gave him some interest in Euclid as in Latin prose.

History attracted him while he sat under Chittenden, but history exclusively in its political, social and economic aspects. He lacked 'historical imagination', and had no enthusiasm for antiquity as such. Later at Cambridge, it was not the history of philosophy that concerned him, but its uses in solving the problems of contemporary life and thought. Balfour was not a natural scholar, as was his brother Gerald; he always preferred to go by himself, and to read as he willed.

Holidays from the Grange School were spent partly at Hatfield House, more usually at Whittingehame, where he had a library, a great estate and the seashore near at hand to explore. Occasionally, there would be visits to neighbouring families such as the Wemyss—a family later to play an important part in his life—at Gosford House, Longniddry, East Lothian. Occasionally, too, Balfour's uncle Robert, afterwards Lord Salisbury, would visit Whittingehame, for he was one of the trustees of the estate during Balfour's minority. Sixteen years separated uncle and nephew; yet even in these early days uncle spoke to 'nephew as a man speaks to a man, and not as a man speaks to a boy. He permitted no flavour of patronage, no tactful manipulation of the subject-matter, to mar the impression of conversational equality. If he asked a question it was not in the spirit of a teacher. He assumed reciprocal comprehension; he looked for an intelligent response. . . . That he should have thought it worth while to converse with me as he did, opened out prospects full of interesting possibilities, and encouraged me if I could to explore them.'

Meanwhile, Lady Blanche continued her enlightened education of her children in English and French literature; and Arthur joined in with his younger brothers and sisters on his holidays from the Grange School, as he continued to do until he became an undergraduate. But it was scarcely an orthodox academic education, and, as we have seen, even at his preparatory school Arthur Balfour's interests did not lie in a specifically scholastic groove.

Thus it was that when, after three years under Chittenden, he went in 1861 to Eton he did not succeed in taking Remove. He was placed lower down the school in the Upper Fourth, and put in Birch's House, Birch later being succeeded by the Rev. Francis St. John Thackeray. He does not seem to have made any close friends at Eton, though he fagged at one period for a young man called Henry Charles Keith Petty-Fitzmaurice who, as the Marquess of Lansdowne, was later to be a close friend and political associate. He appears not to have known Lord Randolph Churchill, though Eton shook to his escapades from 1863 onwards, nor a fellow-Scot, Lord Dalmeny—later Rosebery—who was a year his senior.

Indeed, Balfour was something of a solitary at Eton. He was excused early school on doctor's orders, and thus seldom took part in the hearing of those lessons he and his fellows had been instructed to learn by heart. He was still considered insufficiently robust for football, and his eyesight still prevented his enjoying cricket (Etonians, like Grangeians, considered it 'not done' to wear glasses). Nor did he make much mark in the class-room. He had no gifts for languages (except for the French learned at his mother's knee, and French counted for little in the Eton of those days); he disliked grammar, and the weekly task of writing Latin prose he detested almost as strongly as he detested the weekly task of writing Latin verse. He was not, in short, as he himself summed it up, 'a hero among my fellows, nor the subject of hopeful speculation among my teachers'.

There was in the latter respect, however, one never-to-be-forgotten exception. When Balfour reached the Upper Fifth of the school, he came under a master called William Johnson, better known to the outer world as William Cory, poet, scholar, historian, eccentric, and remembered still for his translation of Callimachus's epigram on Heraclitus of Halicarnassus—'They told me, Heraclitus, they told me you were dead . . .' Cory, on an occasion memorable for Balfour, set an essay on a subject outside the ordinary curriculum for the terminal examination known as 'Collections'. What the subject was is forgotten, but Balfour, greatly to his surprise, was proclaimed second in merit among all the competitors. Cory announced that he would have been first had not the poor quality of his other papers made that impossible.

Balfour never forgot this fleeting triumph, for it came at a time when regular scholastic failures had begun to discourage him and make him feel unsure of himself. It was partly as a result of these failures, partly their cause, that Balfour turned to such extra-curricular studies as contemporary philosophy, and the relation between science and religion. He said when he was 80 that these matters had 'been continuously in mind—I've worked at them on and off—well, since I was at Eton. No really *before* Eton I began muddling about with those ideas.' The 'ideas' were those posed by certain works of science and natural history that seemed to challenge the authority of the Bible and some basic principles of the Christian religion. Among them were Sir Charles Lyell's *Principles of Geology*, published in three volumes between 1830 and 1833, which showed that the world must be far older than the accepted date of the Garden of Eden, and Charles Darwin's *Origin of Species* (1859), which challenged the literal rendering of the first chapter of Genesis. In 1860, there had been a famous debate at the British Association meeting between Samuel Wilberforce, Bishop of Oxford, and T. H. Huxley, anatomist and agnostic, on the question whether man was evolved from animals. Meanwhile, the Bible itself had come under severe attack, particularly from German scholars, on both historical and textual grounds.

It was towards the end of his time at Eton that these matters suddenly impinged on Balfour's young mind, and he began to realise that the implications of 'the elementary science text-books and the Leyden jars' posed for him, as for almost all his and several subsequent generations, problems that were at once cosmological and personal. Personal in Balfour's case, as in so many others, because they seemed to undermine the foundations of that faith instilled with so much certainty and so powerfully at his mother's knee. For Lady Blanche herself there had, indeed, been no problem. The conflict between 'a religious view of the Universe and a naturalistic one . . . never tempted her to discourage scientific study; she never treated it as dangerous to the higher life; she never took refuge in bad science when good science appeared to raise awkward problems. On the other hand, she never surrendered her own convictions as to the inestimable value of her central religious beliefs.'

There, indeed, in the happy symbiosis of science and religion, is Balfour's own attitude in miniature—a point of view, as he said, that appealed to him when his mother first formulated it and which, he wrote when he was 80, 'after more than 60 years' reflection, appeals to me still'. Its appeal, however, was stronger when he was 15 and when he was 80 than when he was 20 or 30. It may be said of Balfour as it was said of his uncle, Salisbury, that 'he read Strauss and Renan, Comte and Thomas Huxley, but continued to worship Christ'. There are, however, hints that he did not come to the latter without considerable doubts and self-questioning, and his first philosophical study, *A Defence of Philosophic Doubt* (1879), though attempting, on behalf of religion, to call scientific philosophy in doubt, is a curiously ambiguous work.

These, then, were the ideas he was 'muddling about with' at Eton, and it was the possibility of having more time for free speculation in such matters that made him anxious to proceed to the university. It was no doubt, in part, to them that he referred when he wrote that 'the most valuable things I learned at Eton were not the things I was taught'. To some extent, no doubt, his interest in speculation—where 'there were *no* accepted authorities', no agreed methods or conclusions —was a form of compensation for his lack of success as measured in the school lists. It was only much later that he said, 'I had, indeed, no great difficulty in maintaining an average position among my contemporaries. But I had no great desire to do more.'

However dissatisfied he was with his achievements at Eton, he never criticised his school. Indeed, as Lady Cynthia Asquith records,

Balfour's devotion to Eton was 'scarcely rational'. It is true, of course, that time tends to cast a rosy hue over early experiences, yet there is genuine feeling behind the remarks he made in 1920 when his portrait at Eton (by G. Fiddes Watt) was unveiled. He sought to put into words the essence of the Etonian experience, 'that peculiar virtue, some unforgettable grace', and found it above all in 'that corporate feeling which more and more seems to me to be the essential virtue of this institution: something inseparably associated, I agree, with the chapel, the playing-fields, the school yard, the river—all the material facts with which we are so familiar'.

IV

Balfour left Eton in the summer of 1866 at the age of 18. Briefly, we glimpse him in Italy and touring Florence with his sister Nora, and George Eliot's *Romola* as a guide-book. In September, he is closeted with a tutor of trigonometry, required for matriculation; and at the beginning of October, 1866, having successfully negotiated the preliminary examination, we catch sight of him riding in a fly from Cambridge station towards Trinity College where a quarter of a century earlier his father had studied. As the fly passed the Fitzwilliam Museum, Balfour felt that that building was the 'symbolic gateway into a new life. I was greatly moved . . .'

He entered Trinity College as a 'Fellow-Commoner', a rank or status that was shortly afterwards abolished. It was a mediaeval survival, entitling its possessor to wear a blue-and-silver gown, to dine at High Table in Hall, and to sit there on a chair instead of on a bench. Educationally speaking, the Fellow-Commoner was exactly on a par with other undergraduates, except that his parents paid larger fees. Balfour's father had been a Fellow-Commoner; so was Balfour's uncle and exact contemporary, Lord Sackville Cecil, with whom he entered Trinity College. These were probably the reasons why it was decided that Balfour should have this privileged rank. But it was not Lady Blanche's doing: she, as her son said, 'had no natural liking for "privilege" nor for the appearance of privilege, least of all in a form that verged so closely on the ludicrous'.

Nevertheless, being a Fellow-Commoner brought one inestimable advantage to Balfour: it meant that he could enjoy not only converse with his contemporaries and more official relations with his tutors, but also the unbuttoned talk of his seniors at High Table. Among these seniors were some of the most distinguished scholars of the nineteenth century. Dr. William Whewell, a celebrated Master of Trinity, philosopher and historian of the inductive sciences (and the man who first minted the word 'scientist'), died as a result of falling from his horse in the year Balfour arrived in Cambridge, and was succeeded by W. H. Thompson, late Professor of Greek, better known perhaps for his caustic tongue than for his academic output, which was small. H. A. J. Munro, who had produced his still-celebrated critical edition of Lucretius in 1864, and later became Professor of Latin, was an amiable and kindly figure; and as contrast, there was C. W. King, an eccentric expert on engraved gems.

Somewhat naturally, it was the younger generation of dons with whom Balfour found himself more nearly on easy terms, among them Joseph Pryor and Percy Hudson, both for a time his tutors. F. W. H. Myers, poet and essayist, was also a don at Trinity at this time, and it was possibly through him that Balfour first became interested in psychical research. When the Society for Psychical Research was founded, Myers became its first secretary. Though that did not take place until 1882, Myers was early interested in a subject already in the air in the late 1860s. In 1871, Sir William Crooks, the physicist, published his articles about his experiments with Home, the American medium, but his challenge to the Royal Society to take notice of such inquiries was not taken up. Nevertheless séances and experiments with the planchette rapidly caught on in fashionable society as well as in more serious quarters. From 1875 onwards, Balfour arranged séances with various mediums at his home in London at No. 4 Carlton Gardens, S.W.1. The part that spiritualism played in his psychological development will be mentioned later. It may be noted now that the matter had a philosophical as well as a personal importance to him: if the existence of a world beyond death could be demonstrated, it would bridge the gap between the intuitionist and empiricist positions, and provide the sole empirical 'proof' of religion. Balfour, though he was President of the Society for Psychical Research in 1896, was never convinced by spiritualistic phenomena; other members of his family were less exacting in their attitude.

Myers's influence on Balfour was, perhaps, countered by another Fellow of Trinity, John Strutt, Senior Wrangler in 1865, and only some six years older than Balfour. Strutt, who later became the third Lord Rayleigh, was a brilliant physicist whose most celebrated discovery was in the realm of chemistry: it was he who first proved the existence of the gas, argon. He became one of the famous Cavendish Laboratory professors, a Nobel prizewinner, and later Chancellor of the University. As an experimenter, he was noted for his immense care and caution— he was distinctly reserved towards allegedly psychic phenomena— and it was from him that Balfour gained real insight into the methods and aims of the physical sciences. Strutt and he became friends, and later relations; in 1871, Rayleigh married Evelyn, the best-looking of Balfour's sisters. For several weeks each year, No. 4 Carlton Gardens

became their London home, and they constantly visited Whittingehame.   The intimacy thus cemented was life-long and immensely
productive in a wider field.   Not merely did Balfour keep *au fait* with
scientific movements through his brother-in-law—and even on one
occasion helped an experiment of his by recording the readings of a
magnetometer—but when Rayleigh in later years originated the idea
of the National Physical Laboratory, it was Balfour who, as First
Lord of the Treasury, helped it into being and, in the last decade of his
life, as Lord President of the Council, was responsible for its workings
and financing.

The strongest influence of all upon Balfour's mind when an undergraduate was, not unnaturally, exerted by someone under whom he
studied directly for his Tripos: this was Henry Sidgwick.   Balfour had
chosen to read for the Moral Sciences Tripos, a very recent institution
which included philosophy and political economy. 'Chosen' is perhaps not the correct word.   He had, indeed, very little choice.   He
did not know enough Latin and Greek to study classics; he was no
mathematician—and at that time mathematics was a required prelude
to the Classical Tripos.   The new Moral Sciences Tripos provided a
means by which philosophy could be offered for an Honours degree
without a classical background; and it was clearly towards philosophy
that Balfour was tending at Eton.   The decision, he tells us, was
clinched by his reading, almost on the eve of his departure for Cambridge, J. S. Mill's *System of Logic* (1843), and his more recent attack on
the late Sir William Hamilton's neo-Kantianism: here, Balfour felt,
was something to grip on, to pursue further, and the proper person to
aid his pursuit was Henry Sidgwick.

Sidgwick, a Yorkshireman, was one of the outstanding scholars of his
generation. Some ten years older than Balfour, he had been elected to
a Fellowship of Trinity College in 1859; a decade later he resigned
his Fellowship because he believed a shift in his religious views no
longer enabled him honestly to subscribe to the religious tests then
demanded of Fellows. (It was, incidentally, his resignation that led
to the abolition of the tests two years later, in 1871.) He afterwards
became Professor of Moral Philosophy, and published influential books
on ethics, political economy and politics. He, too, was deeply interested in psychical research; he, too, married a sister of Balfour, Nora,
and helped establish Newnham Hall (later College), of which his wife
became secretary and principal.

His influence upon Balfour's development was both wide and deep.
Balfour, for instance, cared 'not a jot' for the history of philosophy, and
was interested only in 'the clash of beliefs held by modern men about the
universe': Sidgwick before him had said he hated 'the history of
philosophy even more than any other history; it is so hard to know

what any particular man thought, and so worthless when you do know it'. Even Balfour's later well-known ability to see both sides of every question, which so infuriated his political colleagues, had earlier been observed with similar fury by Sidgwick's philosophical colleagues: they attributed it to the constitutional lack of passion in a Cambridge don.

Sidgwick in his twenties had been a follower of Mill and the Positivists, though never a whole-hearted one. By the end of Balfour's first term at Cambridge, Sidgwick was, however, writing to a friend: 'Take notice that I have finally parted from Mill and Comte—not without tears and wailings and cuttings of hair.' Balfour himself had never accepted Mill, apart from, for a time, his political economy. In his view, Mill had failed to deal with the key problems in philosophical positivism—the problem of the 'external world' and of 'causation'; and his failure seemed to Balfour to shatter the whole foundation of empirical positivism.

By the time Balfour was one of the students, a small group, sitting in Sidgwick's private rooms, and listening to Sidgwick's stammering delivery, the philosopher was turning his attention to the idealistic way of looking at the universe, principally represented in Britain by the work of Sir William Hamilton, Professor J. F. Ferrier and Hutcheson Stirling (whose The Secret of Hegel, as a wit complained, was only too well kept by its author). Here Balfour could not follow him; though a Scot, like the three philosophers just named, he had no taste for idealism; and, indeed, one of his essays written on the subject of Ferrier's Institutes of Metaphysics (1854) was rejected by Sidgwick as too flippant: 'The subject', remarks Balfour, 'was the universe, and doubtless he was right.'

Sidgwick, though a stimulating philosophical writer, never entirely made up his mind, and certainly never promulgated a complete system of speculation. He hovered between intuitionism and utilitarianism to such an extent that John Maynard Keynes, the economist and Fellow of King's College, Cambridge, was rather brutally but not extravagantly to sum up his position by saying: 'He never did anything but wonder whether Christianity was true and prove it wasn't and hope it was.' This could never be said of Balfour, at least after his first book; but Balfour consciously worked within a narrower scope and made no claims to answer the larger philosophical questions. Nevertheless, it is not too much to say that, for years after leaving Cambridge, Balfour's mind, philosophically speaking, ran in parallel with that of Sidgwick: it is significant, for example, that a few months after the appearance of A Defence of Philosophic Doubt in 1879, Sidgwick was reading a paper to the Metaphysical Society—which Balfour joined in the year of its dissolution, 1880—in which he, too, attempts to show that the fundamental premises of science are themselves the concern of philosophy.

Sidgwick, however, was no mere director of studies: it was through him that Balfour first tasted the wine of complete intellectual freedom of which perhaps Cambridge alone was the source in the middle of the nineteenth century. Sidgwick had belonged to the group called the 'Cambridge Conversazione Society', better known as 'The Apostles' because it was limited in membership to 12 men in residence. It had been founded in 1820 by a few undergraduates at St. John's College who were interested in 'higher philosophy'; to it had belonged such men as F. D. Maurice, Tennyson, Arthur Hallam, R. C. Trench and Monckton Milnes, later Lord Houghton, who said that he was as 'proud of being an "Apostle" as he was of being an English gentleman'. The Apostles met weekly over anchovy toast and tea, and discussion followed. Where it differed from a thousand other such university groups was that, in a university and at a time when lip-service at least was required to Church of England theological orthodoxy, its discussions were absolutely unfettered. As Sidgwick put it: 'The freedom both of subject and handling was absolute; and not only did no one ever dream of violating this freedom or suggesting any limit to it, but every member would have regarded this as an attack on the ark of the covenant.'

Sidgwick describes the Apostles as intimate friends who, in their devoted pursuit of the truth, 'were perfectly frank with each other, and indulged in any amount of humorous sarcasm and playful banter'. 'Absolute candour' was the only duty; inconsistency with previously expressed opinions did not matter; there was no proposition, however well established, that a member had not the right to question or deny. The gravest subject could be jestingly treated, and the Apostles understood that both suggestion and instruction could often be gained from what was, in form, a joke.

Membership was kept more or less secret, so that we do not know whether in fact Balfour belonged to the Society. It is probably doubtful whether he did. But, in some ways, he is unmistakably close to the spirit of the Apostles: his undogmatic attitude, willingness to consider every point of view, and open-minded breadth and capacity for absorption—these belong to the true atmosphere of the 'Cambridge Conversazione Society', an atmosphere Balfour first breathed in through Sidgwick.

Thus was Balfour's mind emancipated, and it now took on those characteristics which were to remain an essential part of the mature man, both in politics and in private life. There was, indeed, a yet deeper layer in his nature, a sort of personal (not philosophical) intuitionism, that we no more than glimpse at a later stage. Furthermore, there was another side to the 'apostolic' outlook: if it was agreeably undogmatic, it was also somewhat cool, with a suggestion of *surtour point de zèle*, even of superiority to the common mass (though the latter was carefully concealed). All these we may trace also in the company nicknamed the 'Souls', of whom Balfour was acknowledged leader, and in the Bloomsburyites. But if, as J. M. Keynes suggested, the Apostles sometimes gave the impression that they had 'a mission to enlighten the world on things intellectual and spiritual', then Balfour there parted company with them: 'mission' is the last word one would use of him.

A contemporary of Balfour at Trinity College, Walter Durnford, observed that Balfour 'in the rather prim society of the High Table held his own with the dons, some of them men of undoubted genius . . .' But what of his relationships with his fellow undergraduates? Years later, when he was opening the extension to the Edinburgh University Union, he said: 'I know from my own experience—now rather an old experience—that it is our contemporaries who make our most useful critics; it is even our contemporaries who make our most useful teachers. . . .'

Balfour had acquaintance in several sets of undergraduates, and some of them used to meet in his rooms (at the corner of New Court adjoining the Library) on Sunday evenings to discuss men, books, and his claret. Among them were the Hon. Hugh Elliot, Arthur Kinnaird (later Lord Kinnaird)—known to his friends as 'kidney bean'—and Reginald MacLeod (later the MacLeod of MacLeod). It was perhaps after such a discussion—Balfour's claret was said to be excellent—that Balfour got into his only recorded scrape. One night he was walking down Jesus Lane with Kinnaird and Elliot when it was suggested that the bell of a certain Dr. Ransome should be pulled in order to annoy the don who, it appears, was then in bad odour with undergraduates. 'A. J. B.', Elliot recalled, 'put out his hand as if to pull the bell, though he did not touch it, nor as a matter of fact intended to ring it. As he stretched out his arm a policeman, who was concealed behind a door-way, sprang out and charged him with ringing the bell. A. J. B. denied the accusation and, as the best way of testing the truth, proposed that we should wait and see whether the door was answered. As it was not, the policeman rang the bell himself when the door was at length opened. But the inmates of the house declared the bell had rung twice.'

Next morning Balfour appeared before the magistrates, was told by the chairman (the Mayor of Cambridge) that if he did not regulate his conduct he would one day find himself in prison, and was fined £1.

Kinnaird accompanied Balfour on an adventure of a different kind in the long vacation of 1867. Accompanied by MacLeod, they sailed in Rob Roy canoes down the coast of Skye and across the 16 miles of ocean to Rum. This was more than adventurous: it was positively

1. James Balfour (1773–1845) grandfather of A.J.B.

2. James Maitland Balfour (1820–56), aged 17: father of A.J.B.

Portrait by George Richmond

3. Lady Blanche Balfour (1825–72),
aged 22: mother of A.J.B.

Portrait by James R. Swinton

4. Whittingehame House, nr. Haddington, East Lothian

dangerous as someone pointed out to Lady Blanche before the expedition started. Her reply to this was both wise and perceptive: 'Would you', she said, 'have me spoil a character?' In fact, disaster was avoided and, as Balfour said, 'It was well because it ended well.'

The Balfour who undertook this rough and hazardous voyage was, let it be said, the 'delicate' youth, unable to play games and required to rest each afternoon: clearly the mental freedom of Cambridge was being reflected in physical freedom. Indeed, at Cambridge he took to physical exercise with all the gusto of a formerly deprived person. His game was 'royal' tennis which he played with 'a kind of aesthetic rapture; and I verily believe', he afterwards wrote, 'that in those days I extracted as much concentrated joy from a two hours' game as physical exercise is capable of giving in the time'. Balfour 'haunted' all three courts available—the 'Old' court dating from Charles II's reign, one at Parker's Piece, and one behind the 'Backs'. He thought later that the time he devoted to tennis was 'scandalous', but it completed his physical emancipation. It also led to acquaintance of quite another variety, not least with George Darwin, the son of the celebrated evolutionist. In due course, Balfour met Charles Darwin, then composing his larger bombshell *The Descent of Man*, and found him both sympathetic and charming.

Still another section of his contemporaries came into Balfour's view through his interest in music. At home, his opportunities for hearing music were small; Cambridge had excellent organists, well-trained choirs and many fine amateur players, including one of his tutors, Percy Hudson, a 'cellist. There was a good deal of chamber-music, some symphony concerts and a little opera. Mendelssohn's reputation was declining; Wagner's star had not yet risen, though Brahms's was beginning to; and the stable fare was Schumann, Schubert, Beethoven, Bach and Handel. For Handel, he had a particular fondness for the rest of his life.

Of the friends Balfour made through a mutual love of music, the most important was Spencer Lyttelton. Lyttelton belonged to a famous family, and was one of eight brothers, all of whom played cricket for Eton against Harrow and for Cambridge against Oxford. Balfour's greatest friend among them was eventually to be the youngest, Alfred, at this time still in the lower school at Eton. With Spencer, Balfour took several trips abroad—to Spain, Greece and Egypt—during Easter vacations at Cambridge. The Lyttelton family were connected with the Gladstones, Lady Lyttelton, their mother, being a Glynne and the sister of Catherine, wife of W. E. Gladstone, the Liberal leader.

It was against a background of Lytteltons and Gladstones that Balfour passed much of his early manhood after he came of age; it was a

D<small>JB</small>

Lyttelton sister and a Gladstone daughter who precipitated the intense emotional experience of the next period of his life. However, despite his intimacy with Spencer Lyttelton, it was not until after he left Cambridge that he first visited the home of the Lytteltons, Hagley Hall, Stourbridge in Worcestershire.

Philosophy, conversation, music, tennis, friends—'my life at Cambridge', Balfour said, 'was a period of almost unmixed satisfaction'. But in view of Balfour's subsequent career, there is one striking omission: there is no mention of the Cambridge Union, where budding politicians could try their luck with speech-making and stand up to criticism from their coaevals. Balfour, in fact, never spoke at the Union; he did not even attend the debates. He disregarded politics and even had a contempt for them, according to his friend, Durnford, who added in his memoir: 'I do not think we had any idea that there was the stuff in Balfour which would make him one of the foremost politicians of our time.'

Some part of this disdain for politics may have been due to his uncle Lord Salisbury, who in 1867, when Balfour was 19, resigned his office as Secretary of State in Lord Derby's government rather than agree to the Reform Bill. The language of his speech of resignation was despairing, condemnatory and bitter: he said that the monarchical principle was dead, the aristocratic principle was doomed and democracy was triumphant. He foresaw 'government by grocers' and wanted no part in it. He did not believe that government and politics could in future be taken seriously by men of intelligence. Salisbury, who had been the *enfant terrible* of the Conservative party, was *terrible* still; and, of course, he was wrong. All the same, his attitude may have weighed with his nephew.

Yet, for all that, one feels that Balfour's disdain of politics at this time was inherent rather than acquired. He felt that the world contained more serious matters than politics knew of, not least the contemporary problems of philosophy and the development of the physical sciences. There is little doubt that he would have preferred to stay at Cambridge, to exchange his Fellow-Commonership for a Fellowship, and to spend his life within the walls of Trinity College.

So, indeed, he might have done, but for one fact: when in November 1869, he sat for his Tripos examinations, he took only a Second Class, though a good one. 'Henry Sidgwick was disappointed', he remarks, 'and certainly I should have preferred a First myself.' Sidgwick told him that he believed that his comparative lack of success was due, not to the quality of his work, but to its quantity. Balfour all his life wrote slowly, and preferred to polish and alter endlessly before submitting his work to other eyes. This was not possible in the examination room. Moreover, he had not made a great show of working.

He said: 'I was never taught anything I did not want to learn. I was not required to produce essays on subjects about which there was nothing I desired to say, nor to attend lectures I did not wish to hear.' This was no doubt pleasant, but obviously not enough to get a First. Friends thought he was not a great reader—though he was the sort of man who might wish to appear more nonchalantly study-free than he really was —but believed he had 'a wonderful facility for picking other people's brains': his ability to listen to others and extract their meaning and experience was a life-long trait. But the general consensus of opinion seems to have been well put by the writer who sketched Balfour's life in 1902 when he became Prime Minister: 'No contemporaries have come forward to testify to Mr. Balfour's intense appetite for work at the university. To this day he is held up at Cambridge as a comfortable example to undergraduates who propose to exert themselves after their thirtieth birthday.'

Balfour himself afterwards asserted that his Second was 'in no sense a discouragement', and he went on to explain that the Tripos examination was 'but an unimportant episode', for he had already planned his 'future speculative activities' before it took place. It is amusing to observe that in later speeches on the subject of education he frequently insists that a university ought not to be principally an examining organisation. All the same, Balfour retained a deep love for Cambridge and a close relationship with the university, through his brothers-in-law, Sidgwick and Rayleigh, and through his brothers Gerald and Frank, both of whom became dons. He received an honorary degree and in 1902 an honorary Fellowship; in 1919, he succeeded Rayleigh as Chancellor.

In the July of his Tripos year, Balfour had come of age and entered into his inheritance of Whittingehame and Strathconan. At Whittingehame, the bonfires had blazed, the church bells rung out, and wines flowed freely for guests and tenants. His two trustees, Lord Salisbury and his other uncle (his father's brother) Charles Balfour of Newton Don, made speeches to which Balfour replied: it was only the second time he had ever made a speech, the first being at a tenants' dinner one Christmas at Hatfield House. On his final return from Cambridge at the end of the year, Balfour set himself to learn all he could of his possessions and how best they might be improved. His first act had a certain symbolical significance: he levelled down one of the terraces at Whittingehame House, thus turning what had been a dark basement into a place where light and air easily penetrated.

But if light entered the lower quarters, gloom now pervaded the main apartments. Lady Blanche had been stricken with heart disease and was dying slowly and with considerable suffering. For some years she lay immobile in her bedroom and the house was hushed. Few of the children remained at home. Balfour spent much time with his mother, but until she died in May, 1872, at the early age of 47, the interests and social pursuits, natural to a young man in his position, were centred either in London or at the country homes of his friends. In 1870 he bought the house at No. 4 Carlton Gardens, S.W.1, and there entertained considerably; this house, which he retained throughout his life, now became the base for his entry into the upper reaches of Victorian Society.

2

LOVE AND FRIENDSHIP

1870–1879

At 21 Arthur Balfour was something over six feet tall, lissom and graceful in movement, though giving the impression of lounging indolence. His face was oval with a short, straight nose and a very slightly projecting upper lip on which the philtrum, the channel running down from nostril to lip, was unusually long. Early in his manhood he grew a moustache, at first quite luxuriant and swept back, later much narrower, but always effectively disguising the assertiveness implied in the lip it covered. The chin was well-moulded, neither too strong nor too weak, the forehead high and comparatively wide—though the head itself was not large—and the brown hair, parted then in the middle, was brushed back in some profusion to cover the tips of the ears and to proliferate towards the nape of the neck. The sideburns grew downwards towards the jawbone.

It was, however, the eyes that seemed to hold a secret. Not notably large, they were luminous and expressive; there was something about them sad and contemplative; they bespoke at once intelligence and sympathy, in the latter respect somewhat belying their owner's slight air of indifference. They were eyes in which women could find warmth and receptiveness; at the same time, they looked inwards, too, as though regarding a strange landscape of quiet but absorbing interest.

This, then, was the young man, handsome, charming and rich, who moved into Society in 1870. The few doors that might have been closed to him as a simple Scottish laird were opened wide to the scion of the Cecils, and he was soon a welcome guest at such houses as Panshanger (Earl Cowper), Latimer (Lord Chesham)—where the three daughters introduced him to lawn, as distinct from 'royal', tennis—, Taplow (Lord Desborough), Wilton (Earl of Pembroke), Ashridge (Earl Brownlow) and Stanway (Earl of Wemyss, also a near neighbour at his other house, Gosford in East Lothian). With many members of these and other families, Balfour quickly became friends, meeting them constantly in the country, in London, at balls and entertainments, and inviting them in his turn to Strathconan, Whittinge-hame and No. 4 Carlton Gardens. At Devonshire House, Holland House and other great aristocratic rendezvous of the upper social life, Balfour encountered such notable hostesses as Lady Waldegrave and her rival, Lady Molesworth, and he mingled with the racing, the shooting and the hard-drinking sets. But to these sets he never belonged. He had no interest in horses (though at this time he sometimes rode in the Park with his sisters and friends) and less in guns, though deer-stalking at Strathconan had a certain appeal; he preferred conversation to drink, and music or philosophy to either.

He made considerable acquaintance in the world of the arts. Through Lady Airlie, an early friend of his mother, Balfour was introduced in 1871 to the painter, Edward Burne-Jones, and became a frequent visitor to his house and studio at Hammersmith. Burne-Jones, then on the threshold of his fame as an ally of the Pre-Raphaelites, was lively and amusing despite the fact that his pictures concentrated on 'wan women' and mythological subjects. Balfour commissioned him to design a series of pictures for the long drawing-room walls at No. 4 Carlton Gardens, and Burne-Jones chose to illustrate the Perseus legend; the designs in some cases were still, however, unfinished at his death 28 years later. Other of his pictures, including the 'Wheel of Fortune', hung on the walls at Carlton Gardens until the house was sold after Balfour's death.

Although Balfour had no special interest in the pictorial arts, he was also a frequent visitor to Frederick Leighton's studio in Holland Park. Leighton, the first painter to be made a peer (the day before he died), was an uninspired artist, but a scholar and man of the world. It was at his house, some years later, that Balfour first met George Wyndham and his sister Mary, both to play important parts in his life.

Music had become one of the ruling passions in Balfour by this time. He attended the Philharmonic Concerts at the Crystal Palace, oratorios at Exeter Hall, chamber and orchestral concerts at St. James's Hall. At Carlton Gardens, he installed two grand pianos and, from time to time, the Handel Society rehearsed there. In 1873, he instigated, and financially guaranteed, a performance in full of Handel's *Belshazzar* at the Albert Hall. For the music of Handel, Balfour had a decided affinity and knew much about it, as he showed some years later in a discriminating essay on the composer in the *Edinburgh Review* in January, 1887. He found in Handel's music a majesty, a sense of unforced glory and an unequalled power of expressing in choral compositions every shade of dramatic emotion.   Nothing in it was to him frigid or dull; he was enamoured both of Handel's copious gift of melody and of his soaring religious emotion: 'In the age of Voltaire and of Hume, Handel produced the most profoundly religious music the world has yet known.   In the age of Pope and Swift, Handel conceived works whose austere grandeur has never been surpassed.'   Speaking of composers, Balfour said that he reserved his enthusiasm not for the innovators and 'heralds of a new order of things', but 'for those who have brought to the highest perfection a style which, because perfected, must have been probably in the main inherited,—who have pressed out of it every possibility that it contained,—and who leave to their successors, if these needs must attempt the same task, no alternative but to perform it worse.   Of such was Handel.'

This is an essay that reveals its author as much as its subject—as Balfour intimated by adding: 'The writer is obliged to confess to a degree of affectionate devotion to the great composer which is not possible, or, I had almost even said, which it is not desirable that the majority of readers should show.'   What it reveals of Balfour is his profound love of classical form in the arts (an inherited style whence 'every possibility' has been 'pressed out') combined, however, with a spirit that soars triumphantly, grandly, into the empyrean.   It has been said of Balfour that he had a coldly classical mind. It is not entirely true: he loved a regularity of form with emotion bursting through, almost but not quite leaving that form in broken pieces.   Of music's effect upon him we catch a glimpse in the diary of Mary Gladstone who, at a Crystal Palace concert in the early 1870s, noticed that on his face as he listened was 'appreciation so keen and intense as almost amounted to pain'.

If music in this period was the key to his innermost feelings, it was also the key that opened the door to his most intimate friendships. Spencer Lyttelton, his musical friend from Cambridge, introduced him to his home at Hagley, Stourbridge, in 1870.   There he met not only the 12 Lyttelton children, but also the seven young Gladstones, for Catherine Gladstone, after the death of her sister, Lady Lyttelton in 1857, had in some measure mothered the Lytteltons, too, and the families were constantly together at Hagley, Hawarden, London, or at the seaside.   They were a vigorous, boisterous group, full of jokes and energy and they stimulated the gaiety, inherent in Balfour but overlaid at this time by the excessive sobriety of Whittingehame and worry about his ailing mother.   Mary Gladstone, the third daughter and fifth child of the Liberal leader, kept a journal whose entries for this period are full of references to Balfour 'laughing immoderately', or to him and his brother, Eustace, and sister, Nora, 'overpowered by laughter as usual'.   She describes a party after the Eton-Harrow match at Lords on July 15, 1871: 'Ate with the Balfours.   Mr. Balfour had invited everyone he knocked up against right and left, till the party swelled to a gigantic size.   Spencer (Lyttelton) and I were jammed up at the end of the carriage, ten others inside, five on the box, and others about the wheel and the steps.   Our host was in mad spirits, shouting choruses between acts, hatless, with a handkerchief round his head, hair flying all over the place.'

A month later Balfour hauled all his new friends off to Whittinge-hame, where Mary Gladstone records on August 8, 1871: 'Big party— Gladstones, Lady Raleigh, Strutts, Lord Aberdeen, Lord Polwarth, 4 brothers Balfour.   With stupendous and unheard of energy we sang glees and "Round about the Starry Throne" (how I need scarcely remark) and at 11.45 p.m. started off on a walk to the garden, guided about in total darkness by the four brothers, pushed up hills, supported down dales. . . .'   Next day they dined out of doors—'one of those uproarious meals which can only take place in the presence of our host!'—followed by another 'perilous midnight walk to the garden'. By day they rushed down the glen ('Mr. Balfour singing "How vain is man" '), to picnic on the seashore, 'the meal a triumphant success, especially the fire, and afterwards building a sand castle at which we all worked like ants and made the "Sea look a fool" '.

When it rained they sat indoors and, with no less gusto, composed limericks.   A verse from one of them, preserved among Balfour's papers, is worth quoting if only because it indicates the proper pro-nunciation of the name of his estate:

> 'There was an old person of Whittingehame
> Who was forced by hard fate to sit in jam,
>   When her friends cried "Alas",
>   She but said "Let that pass",
> This collected old person of Whittingehame.'

Another collection of limericks, composed by Balfour and Mary Gladstone during this first visit to Whittingehame, is interesting since, as well as bringing in local place-names, it introduces some of the favourite expressions—they are underlined—of Balfour in conversation. These include 'mildly but firmly', 'drivelling', 'must draw the line', 'let that pass', 'but no matter' and 'that's a detail'.

Other diversions were ghost stories; Mary Gladstone often refers to 'interesting talk on ghosts and mesmerism . . . telling ghost and robber stories.   Mr. Balfour told the most thrilling.'   The 'robber' stories refer probably to the *romans policiers* of Emile Gaboriau, popular at that time, among them being *L'Affaire Lerouge* and *Le Dossier No. 113*.   These were almost the first detective stories to be written, and thus early Balfour developed a taste that he was never to lose for this kind of fiction.

The party also went to church and sat under Dr. Robertson, the Whittingehame minister. Mary Gladstone observed: 'The Service very funny indeed, but rather good prayers and sermon, the singing bad, very, but painstaking. . . . After dinner Mr. B. read prayers and we sang "Abide with Me".' (The 'funniness' of the service probably consisted in the fact that it was conducted strictly according to the Prayer Book without any hint of ritual. The young Gladstones had been brought up as High Church.) Balfour, when at Whittingehame, always read Sunday evening prayers in the large dining-room, with guests, family and servants sitting round the walls, the only light coming from two candles on a small table in the centre of the room where Balfour sat. He read slowly, without dramatic emphasis, but bringing out every shade of meaning, and he chose himself one chapter from the Bible, frequently from Isaiah, the Psalms or St. Paul's Epistles. Afterwards there would be music, Handel, Bach, Beethoven, glees and hymns accompanied by Mary Gladstone on the piano and by Balfour himself on the concertina or, as the friends called them, 'the Infernals'.

So life and gaiety returned to Whittingehame in 1871 after a long absence. What Lady Blanche thought of it can only be surmised. But the inheritance was now Balfour's; he was the master. Moreover, whatever might be thought of Gladstone's politics or his brand of religion, he was undeniably a devout churchman. He could scarcely have been bettered as the herald of a new order. Curiously enough criticism of the 'new' Balfour came, not from his seniors, but from one of his own generation. In the summer of 1870 when Balfour first went to Hagley, one of the Lyttelton girls named Mary, though always known as May, confided to her diary: 'Music and madness on the part of Mr. Balfour.' And later: 'Morning and a good part of the afternoon sadly frittered away over music. Mr. Balfour dangles about and does nothing to an extent that becomes wrong. . . . Mr. B. went at 8.30, rather glad though I like him very much, only I feel about ten years older than him.' May Lyttelton was actually a few years younger, scarcely 20, but she was a serious-minded, educated girl who, like other Victorian sisters, had read parallel with her brother, Spencer, when he was at Cambridge, and could hold her own in philosophical disputation. She was a tall girl with clouds of shining hair and brown eyes set wide apart; full of vitality, responsive, eager, she was a striking figure and perhaps the outstanding personality of the Lyttelton children.

It was in describing a party at Hawarden Castle, the Gladstone home near Chester, in the same year that her journal begins to focus more closely on Balfour. On December 10, 1870, she notes the presence of John Strutt, Balfour's Cambridge friend—they were known by now as the 'Cambridge inseparables'—Frederick Max-Müller, the Oxford philologist and mythologist, and Lord Edmond Fitzmaurice, and then observes: 'Mr. Balfour (Spencer's friend) is certainly clever and very unlike other people—which may be affectation and conceit—poetical; good countenance, flighty and visionary.' For many years, Balfour was to give a first impression of conscious superiority, but it did not usually last long. At Hagley next month, when Balfour was again a visitor, May Lyttelton has slightly altered her views. There was a discussion of 'metaphysics and nonsense' followed by amusing talk about Miss Austen's novels, 'Mr. B. being a suggestive and clever person though condemned as affected by most of the others.' A few days later she has quite altered her mind, for she refers to 'Mr. Balfour (who is neither affected nor conceited)'.

During the next two years, Balfour saw a great deal of May Lyttelton. He himself kept no diary, but she frequently refers to his coming to lunch ('How we have lived and died with him these last few days!'), or urging her to attend the Handel festival with him, or meeting accidentally at Professor John Tyndall's lectures on Sound, or waltzing with her at the Northumberland House ball, and appearing at the Waverley Ball 'in white wig and embroidered coat'. So much, indeed, was Balfour with her in these months, that one of her brothers, Neville, later a General, observed that he was not certain that he liked 'this friend of Spencer's— he seems to do nothing but hang around the girls'.

He was, however, equally often with the Gladstones, with no Lytteltons present. Mrs. Gladstone referred to him at this period as 'that very pretty quaint boy, tall and funny', and the G.O.M. himself, then Prime Minister, observed to his wife that 'I really delight in him, no more and no less'. In October, 1872, Mr. and Mrs. Gladstone and Mary were again Balfour's guests, this time at Strathconan, his Highland estate. Gladstone was due to return to London for a Cabinet meeting on the 11th, but was so much enjoying his stay that he put off his departure until the last possible moment. The party set off to accompany him on foot to the nearest station, Ach-an-Alt, some five miles away. It was necessary at one stage to cross a loch by boat, and the boatman was so old and the wind so strong that it took much longer to get to the other side than was anticipated: 'Conceive, then, my feelings', Balfour wrote, 'when, looking westwards up the Strath, I saw our train approaching with ill-timed punctuality.' Gladstone, though physically vigorous, was well over 60 and, as Balfour leaped out of the boat and splashed towards the shore, the seriousness involved in the possible postponement of a Cabinet meeting flashed across his mind. Happily, his frantic waving caught the engine-driver's eye, the train stopped, and the Prime Minister was put safely aboard. 'As the train ran slowly out of the station', Balfour observed, 'I saw with intense thankfulness a pair of wet socks hanging out of the carriage window to dry . . . I had at least not inflicted upon my distinguished visitor the added horrors of a cold in the head.'

Balfour found Gladstone an easy and interesting conversationalist, 'though he knew nothing of any philosophy later than Bishop Butler, nothing of science worthy of mention, little of modern theology except through the Tractarians'. As a talker he required 'a fair field', but 'he was natural, tactful, and, if need be, eloquent, totally without pretension and totally without spite'. In the 1870s, the two became as friendly as their difference in ages and outlook allowed. They met often in London for dinner, Gladstone's town house being No. 11 Carlton Gardens, a few yards away from Balfour's. During some repairs to No. 11 in 1876, Gladstone actually lived for a brief period at No. 4. Often, when the Prime Minister (as he was until 1874) and the future Prime Minister conversed, Mary Gladstone noticed a look on 'Mr. Balfour's face of intense, eager interest, his whole attitude such a transformation of his usual indolent postures'. There is little or no record of their discussing politics: the subject that so aroused Balfour's interest on this occasion was terminable annuities. Sometimes the subject was a good deal less serious. On one occasion at a party of Gladstones and Balfours, the Prime Minister 'under strong family persuasion, took the bass part in an old glee, which was by no means solemn. The first lines, I think, run as follows:

> "Mein Heer Van Dunk
> Though he never was drunk,
> Sipped brandy and water gaily . . ."

It is set to music which reflects the unpretentious vigour of the verse, and it includes a rollicking solo assigned to the bass, and on this occasion sung by the Prime Minister with admirable spirit. The audience unfortunately was very small and intimate. . . .'

In the early part of the 1870s, the relationship between Balfour and the Gladstones had become so close that there were many observers who thought that the interest of the young man-about-town must be more in the daughter than in her famous father. Nor was it only casual eyes who believed they caught sight of romance in the making. Gladstone himself wrote to his wife on one occasion from No. 11 Carlton Gardens, observing: 'Mr. Balfour breakfasted here. I thought he rather lingered, even when I was obliged to show signs of moving. That is all I can say. We were three only': the third being Mary.

No doubt it would have been a suitable match in many ways, though it might have had a curious effect on political history. Mary herself by this time was certainly in love with Balfour. Years later she admitted as much in a letter to Lavinia Talbot, and even asked Lavinia to tell Balfour so. By then Mary had married the Rev. Harry Drew. Lady Horner, who knew of this letter, recorded that it surprised her very much: 'I had never thought it possible that anyone could wish to acknowledge an unrequited attachment, but Mary said she felt it was a great waste to have given love without its ever being realised.' She adds that Lavinia did tell Balfour: 'I believe he was neither impressed nor embarrassed by this, which must have been almost as disconcerting as his previous coldness.'

Balfour possessed considerable attraction for women, and was never less than charming to them. It was perhaps this general charm that deluded Mary, or it may even have been that at one stage he was attracted by her. But the reason why he did not respond in the obvious manner was that, as early as 1872, he had fallen in love with someone else, in fact with May Lyttleton.

As we have seen, May had not only physical comeliness but also mental powers on a level with Balfour's own. When they first met, May had her doubts about him which she confided to her diary, and Balfour may well have hesitated, not wishing to risk a rebuff. Then his mother died, and he was for some months greatly occupied with business affairs at Whittingehame. In those months, May had met, and swiftly fallen in love with, a handsome and brilliant young man, Rutherford Graham, son of the earliest Pre-Raphaelite painter, William Graham, and brother of Frances, later Lady Horner and herself an intimate of the Balfour group. May and Rutherford became engaged, but her father, Lord Lyttelton, insisted that the young man should do a year's hard work before the marriage. This, however, was not to be. During the probationary period, Rutherford Graham died.

May Lyttelton was greatly grieved by his death, and it was some time before, gradually, her intimacy with Balfour revived. Her sister, Lavinia, who had married Edward Talbot, Warden of Keble College, Oxford, and later Bishop of Winchester, became the confidante of both. Indeed, in the tragic events that followed, the Talbots were Balfour's mainstay and remained always his intimate friends.

By the beginning of 1874, it seemed as though the renewed friendship would shortly blossom into marriage. Yet Balfour still hesitated, partly perhaps because of deep-buried psychological reasons, partly because of an uncertainty about his innermost self which he referred to as 'the *feeling* of frivolity'. He seems at this time to have had a sense of the unreality of life and an inability to come to grips with the business of living. Philosophical work he found some sort of safeguard against the feeling of frivolity, but not a complete one. The truth was, perhaps, that he did not know what he was going to make of his life, but was not the sort of rich man who is temperamentally prepared to drift.

At this point, the Salisburys, his uncle and aunt, came to his rescue —or provided a welcome distraction. Dining one day with them at their London home, Arlington House, they suggested to him that he should enter politics. Balfour no doubt had vaguely considered that some day in the future he might well follow in the footsteps of his father and grandfather and become an M.P.; the prospect, however, did not greatly attract him and, certainly, there seemed to be no urgency about it. Politics, in any case, lacked interest to him.

Salisbury, however, had by now thrown off his 'a-curse-on-both-your-houses' attitude to party affairs, and indeed was shortly to become Secretary of State for India. Moreover, he had a definite and immediate proposal for his nephew. An election was in the offing, and the Conservative Member for Hertford (in which constituency Hatfield lay) was retiring: would Balfour care to take his place? In this matter at least, Balfour showed no sign of indecision. He agreed and at the election of January, 1874, after one speech, a little canvassing and the composing of an electoral address, he was duly returned as a Member in Disraeli's last Parliament. He was 26. But having entered the House, Balfour attended only occasionally, and did not open his mouth there, publicly, until two and a half years later, having in the meantime made a leisurely trip round the world.

Power and politics had not yet exercised their charms upon him, even though the business of being elected may have provided some excuse for irresoluteness in the affairs nearer his heart. Fate itself, however could not be thus easily turned aside or delayed.

On December 23, 1874, Balfour called for tea at the Lytteltons' London house in Portland Place, and found May alone. She was practising 'like mad' the Bach E minor fugue from a *Suite de Pièces* Balfour had lent her on a previous visit. A few days later they met again at the Cheshams' Christmas house-party at Latimer. May's sister, Lavinia, afterwards recalling that May told her of the party, wrote, 'I began to think something was really coming, and I recollect telling Edward one evening that a "je ne sais quoi" had happened which made me speculate more than I ever had before.' The Gladstones, too, who saw May shortly afterwards, described her as 'glowing with happiness'.

There may well have been an understanding between them then, and, as subsequent events suggest, a proposal and even an acceptance. But no engagement was ever to be announced. In February, 1875, while at home at Hagley, May fell ill of typhoid fever. She lay for some weeks between life and death, as Mary Gladstone wrote in her diary: '(Though she was) quite torpid, the change in her face when she saw me was wonderful, and yet though she smiled so beautifully, still very different. When I came near, she said, "Oh, this is fun. Did you think I shouldn't see you, silly old thing", and going on saying "O, what a break! . . ." She said, "You see, I'm not so very much better".'

It is Mary Gladstone who also describes the last scene of all on Sunday morning, March 21, 1875: ' "She left off breathing and was no more." All was quiet and peaceful. Lavinia and Lucy had said hymns to her. Mamma' (Mrs. Gladstone, her aunt, who had been nursing her) 'whispered "God be with you, darling", to which she believed she answered "yes".'

Balfour, it seems, had not visited her during her illness, believing perhaps that her condition was not as grave as it was and that visitors were bad for her. It was May's brother, Edward Lyttelton, who wrote to him on the day of her death. Balfour replied immediately and, though his letter has not been preserved, we may gather something of its tenor from Edward's reply. Balfour had enclosed a ring and asked him to put it in her coffin. It was a ring, Lavinia Talbot understood, that had belonged to his mother. Edward wrote: 'I have done as you asked. It was not possible for me to see it with my own eyes, as the coffin was lying in the Rectory where a servant is ill with fever and we are not allowed to go in; but I gave it to an old servant who took the greatest care to see it put in and the coffin closed afterwards. There were no undertakers near so it is all safe. I have told no one about it except Edward Talbot and his wife, as I was a little puzzled at first.'

Thus the engagement ring went with May to her grave. Balfour's grief may be imagined; Lavinia Talbot recorded that the death 'staggered him to the last degree. He has told me he walked for hours about the London streets—where, he never knew. He came to Hagley the day before the funeral': and during the service broke down completely.

This fact, indeed, could not be hidden; yet the secrecy with which Balfour asked for the ring to be put into the coffin, and a promise he extracted from Lavinia and her husband never to tell the others of his attachment, have a curious and revealing psychological tone. Always in his personal affairs, Balfour carried a reasonable decorousness to the point of almost shamefaced secretiveness—in great contrast to his extremely insecure habits as a Minister of the Crown and repository of numerous State secrets.

Partly, no doubt, he did not wish to attract sympathy, for, as Lavinia Talbot wrote, 'if really moved, he could not restrain tears, and that would have been dreadful to him'. To the Talbots alone did he reveal the wounds caused by May's death. For, all his life, unless ill or later abroad, he spent the anniversary of May's death with this couple, and through them became interested in Keble College, after Lavinia had told him: 'May was bent on interesting you in all the work and life here.'

In the weeks following May's death, Balfour seems to have lapsed into something like despair. There are no further references to the 'feeling of frivolity'. He asked Lavinia to copy out the extracts about himself in the diary May kept, and this copy, now brown with age, is in a black satchel with a lock along with other letters from the Lyttelton mourners among his private papers. But the bulk of his correspondence with the Talbots was burned on his instructions after his own death, 55 years later.

Not perhaps surprisingly, there is some evidence that soon after May's death, Balfour's interest in spiritualism, or at any rate, psychic research, which as we have seen was first aroused at Cambridge, increased. Campbell Homes notes in *Facts of Psychic Science* that as early as 1875 Balfour was investigating materialisations in a series of séances with Miss Wood and Miss Fairlamb. Some of these took place at No. 4 Carlton Gardens, which after 1873 was also the London home of Rayleigh and his wife, Balfour's sister Evelyn. There were séances there with Mrs. Jencken and Mrs. Guppy and with Slade—Browning's 'Sludge'. Conan Doyle, a later acquaintance of Balfour, said in a letter to a newspaper (*The Times*, March 29, 1930) that he believed that Balfour 'even had some undeveloped psychic gifts of his own and that he obtained some results in an experiment in crystal-gazing. Andrew Lang mentions the fact in one of his books.' Balfour, somewhat later, shared expenses with Henry Sidgwick in an 'engagement' with the 'girls' and with the once celebrated Albert Snow, 'the poetical medium', who afterwards asked Balfour for more money than had been agreed upon. There is, however, no evidence that Balfour got in touch with May (though a quarter of a century later a message purporting to come from the recently dead Salisbury was delivered to him at a séance at Carlton Gardens).

In August, 1875, shortly after Parliament rose from the summer recess, Balfour escaped from accustomed scenes and sought relief abroad. His companion was May's brother, Spencer Lyttelton, who two years before had joined him in a trip to Cairo and to Greece, lasting about six weeks.

Of this round the world tour, we know only what his companion recorded in his diary. Balfour was ill and 'comatose' for most of the Atlantic crossing; neither of them cared for the garish advertisements which disfigured New York; and Balfour objected to travelling by Pullman coach to Chicago because he had no head-rest. San Francisco, on the whole, bored them and they hated the dust, but the Big Trees, which they drove out to see, and the Yosemite Valley interested them, and were the only features of the whole tour that Balfour afterwards spoke of with any enthusiasm. In New Zealand, they travelled somewhat roughly and seem usually to have been wet to the skin. Near Christchurch, however, Balfour suddenly bought a stock-run, and at Canterbury gave £50 to the Archdeacon for 'some good purpose'.

It was invested and on the proceeds a gold medal, called 'The Balfour Medal', awarded annually to the boy at Christ's College who, as the Archdeacon wrote to Balfour, 'shall pass the best examination in the four Gospels and Acts of the Apostles in Greek, or in some portion of them, and in the Book of Common Prayer, or some portion of it'.

From New Zealand they passed to Australia, Balfour again being very seasick, and from Melbourne to Sydney he travelled overland alone. They then sailed for Singapore, and Spencer Lyttelton notes: 'A. J. B.'s servant got very drunk on voyage.' When this occurred again while they were staying at Government House with Sir William Jervoise, Balfour gave the man his ticket home, subsequently, however, re-engaging him, only some while later to find that the man had enlisted.

In Singapore, Balfour received news of his sister Nora's engagement to Henry Sidgwick and decided to cut short his tour, omitting a visit to India, and to return home. The reason for this was that Nora had acted as *châtelaine* of Whittingehame since his mother's death, and other arrangements would have to be made; but it may be also that Balfour had become tired of jogging round the world, and felt able once more to face his life at home.

No outward appearance suggested that Balfour was a changed man when he returned to England in the spring of 1876, but changed he was. We no longer hear of gay parties; we hear, indeed, of 'music', but 'madness' is no longer coupled with it, as it had been in May Lyttelton's diary. Balfour was more serious in outlook, and even more reserved about his deepest feelings. He had given his heart to May, hesitantly and even secretively, and the end had been disaster— with the possibility of his deepest feelings being uncovered and commented upon. It is certain that never again was he to allow himself to undergo that mixture of romantic and sexual experience usually called 'falling in love'. There were to be many friendships with women, some perhaps involving a certain passion, one at least being an *affaire*. But nothing seems to have tempted him towards marriage.

Undoubtedly, however, his tour had given him fresh impetus for life, but life in its more serious aspects: philosophy and politics. From his return in 1876, he began work on the book that was to appear four years later under the title of *A Defence of Philosophic Doubt*. He saw much of Sidgwick and corresponded with him; through him he met many of the most distinguished thinkers of the time, not least that brilliant cross-section in the Metaphysical Society, to which Balfour himself was elected, however, only in 1880 shortly before its demise. Among them were Archbishop Manning and the Archbishop of York (Thomson), Gladstone, Fitzjames Stephen, F. D. Maurice, Martineau, Seeley, Froude, Mark Pattison, Huxley, James Hinton, Bagehot, Frederic

5. Lady Blanche Balfour, as a widow, aged 32

6. Eleanor (Nora) Mildred Balfour, eldest sister of A.J.B., later Mrs. Henry Sidgwick

Portrait by H. T. Hudson after J. J. Shannon

7. Gerald William Balfour, aged 60: brother of A.J.B. and later 2nd Earl of Balfour

Portrait by Fitzroy Watt

8. Mary (May) Lyttelton, aged about 23

Harrison and others.   Many of them became acquaintances of Balfour, and with some of them he came into closer relations in the Synthetic Society, the successor of the Metaphysical, of which he himself was a founder member and later president.

Balfour by no means gave up his life in Society; but its general tenor in the latter part of the 1870s is probably better conveyed by a letter which he wrote to Edward Talbot from Whittingehame on January 2, 1878:

'You ask for news of what we have been doing at Whittingehame: but I will not drag you through the details of that painful three days which is annually given up to the horrors of a shooting party.   Since that scourge has been withdrawn, I have been left in tolerable peace. There is, as there ought to be at this time of year, a family gathering of unusual dimension.   All my brothers are here and the Sidgwicks. . . . The result is what you might expect from the component causes.

'Every man retires for a quarter part of the day to his respective den, emerging at meal times like a giant refreshed and prepared to argue at any length or on any side of any question.   To enumerate all the subjects which have been exhaustively discussed would be impossible.   But I may mention among others, contemporary politics in all its branches, the theory and practice of shaving (this with great minuteness much to Alice's disgust), a large number of mechanical and other scientific problems, wine (this with more energy than knowledge), Transcendental Philosophy, Art, and the London Markets —price of copper and so forth. . . .

'At present this house is a "Temple of Research".   Gerald and Cecil are not doing much—but Frank, though he supposes himself to be taking a holiday, is I believe preparing his book for the press (in the smoking-room), Eustace (in the billiard-room) is drawing the illustrations for *his* book, Henry Sidgwick is finishing his article for the Encyclopaedia and writing a paper for the Metaphysical Society in *his* sitting-room, while I, in mine, am working very hard at my "immortal work", though not, I am sorry to say, making much way with it: still it is a great thing to get *some* quiet time before the hurry and bustle of London and Politics.

'If I add to this that Alice is groaning over the iniquities of the household in her "boudoir" while Cecil is reading through the City articles in the Library and Gerald strumming on the P.F. in the drawing-room, I shall have exhausted both the party and the house. . . . I am at this moment grumbling bitterly about having to be in town on the 17th.   What between Society and the House and Ctte., spare time seems utterly to vanish: however it can't be helped.'

It was indeed a remarkable family, and we may note here how it had developed.   Frank, after a highly successful Cambridge career in

EJB

science, was already a Fellow of the Royal Society, and the book he was working on was to make him the acknowledged world authority—at 28 —on comparative embryology.   He was, in Arthur's eyes, the most brilliant member of the family.   The book Eustace was illustrating—a work on architecture—was to achieve less fame, and Cecil's study of the City, instead of leading to financial triumph, led him into dubious paths.   Gerald, however, was already a Fellow of his college, Trinity, Cambridge, and shortly became university lecturer in Greek.

Yet there is something a little donnish, a little rarefied, about it all when the eldest of the family was still only in his early thirties. Strangers might already find the atmosphere rather hard to breathe in, and in later years the tendency developed.   It was perhaps somewhat over-intellectualised; they did not go in much for personal chaff or personal remarks; and when they laughed it was usually at finding something irrational in behaviour or speech.   They were deeply interested in each other's opinions; they would have found each other's emotions embarrassing.   Emotion, indeed, one suspects—not least in Balfour himself—was banished to a dark corner; and dark corners there certainly were.   The marriage of Nora and Henry Sidgwick was, in a sense, typical.   Sidgwick was sexually impotent; no wonder that years later Nora remarked that she had had a 'grey life', and that she liked winking because 'it is the least tiring expression of emotion'.

If emotion was taboo, the sharp criticism of opinions, the quick pointing out of illogicalities, the ruthless pressing home of argument, were *de rigueur*: they were to serve Balfour well, not only as a critical philosopher, but as a sharp-tongued, quick-thinking debater in the House of Commons.   It was in that assembly, to which he had been elected in 1874 and in which he made his maiden speech in 1876, that he perfected a style of wit which was to make some of his *bons mots* famous.

II

'When in the spring of 1876', Balfour wrote in his *Chapters of Autobiography*, 'I had returned from the Antipodes, Lady Salisbury made no secret of her opinion that my third session should not be allowed to close without overt sign of activity.'   So at 8 p.m. on August 10, 1876, he rose to his feet for the first time in the House of Commons and passed some unexceptionable remarks on Indian silver currency.   The occasion for this 'maiden speech' was carefully chosen so as to make it as obscure and unnoticed as possible.   It took place, during the Committee stage of the Indian Budget debate, when the House could be counted upon to be ill-attended.   No party issue was raised and no division expected.   'I desired', wrote Balfour, 'security not success'; and in that, at least, he succeeded, his brief speech causing scarcely a ripple of interest in the House's 'friendly and silent solitude'. It was a year before he spoke again.

This reluctance to speak, this total lack of parliamentary ambition, was temperamental and personal; but it was also partly due to the calm that persisted during the first two years of Disraeli's last ministry. Gladstone had relinquished the leadership of the Liberals to Lord Hartington (later the Duke of Devonshire), a talented but inexperienced politician. Sir Charles Dilke, the Radical, was still rising rather than risen, and his friend, Joseph Chamberlain, entered the House for the first time only in 1876, and was there introduced by John Bright, already past his zenith. The Conservative ministry, though 'distinctly able', was not exactly inspiring. Disraeli himself was feeling his age, and later went to the Lords as the Earl of Beaconsfield, but he was still quite capable of snatching an unexpected victory and, indeed, was shortly to proceed to the greatest triumph of his career. Lord Derby, by now an incapable figure, was Foreign Minister; and at the Exchequer was Sir Stafford Northcote, a country gentleman with a capacity for hard work but lacking in forcefulness. Gathorne-Hardy (later Lord Cranbrooke) was, indeed, a first-class debater, and Richard Assheton Cross, formerly a Lancashire bank manager, was an excellent framer of domestic legislation. Apart from Lord Salisbury, who had conquered his repugnance to Disraeli and returned to the India Office, the most promising member of the ministry was Sir Michael Hicks-Beach who, as Ensor remarks, 'though he never became Prime Minister, had certainly more capacity for that or any other high office than many whose luck has carried them to the summit'.

The years 1874–6 were, as we know now, the calm before the storm; but that calm was undeniable and by no means merely due to personalities in the House. For one thing, the great domestic, 'democratic' reforms were over; the extension of rural franchise, the County Councils Act, the Local Government Act were, indeed, still to come, but they all in some measure stemmed from the breach in the walls of the old order made by Disraeli's franchise reform Act of 1867—the same Act that had driven Salisbury from the Cabinet, crying, 'When labour gives law to capital, Trades Unions rule supreme, democratic parliaments contrive a graduated income-tax, the poor voting supplies and the rich finding ways and means,' then chaos was come again.

The Act had had other effects. Since it roughly doubled the electorate and enfranchised working-men and the lower middle-classes in the growing urban areas, it meant that votes now had to be wooed and won. Hence, the formation of federated parties. The Conservatives had called theirs' 'The National Union of Conservative and Unionist Associations', intended, according to Disraeli, 'not as a confederacy of nobles, not as a democratic multitude; [but as] a party formed from

all the numerous classes in the realm—classes alike and equal before
the law'.   To it was added, in 1870, the Conservative Central Office.
Both these organisations had done much to ensure a Conservative
majority in 1874.

Behind Government was Monarchy and Monarchy so strong that in
1872 Disraeli, always a barometer of public opinion, could make the
Queen a focus of the new Imperialism promulgated in his famous
Crystal Palace speech, could even speak of her without much ridicule as
'Gloriana . . . the Fairy Queen'.   Yet only 18 years before, the monarch
had been so bitterly attacked in the press that the Queen had threatened to abdicate, and only a year or two before, the English Republican
movement reached its peak, partly because of the Queen's prolonged
withdrawal from public life after the Prince Consort's death; 50 Republican clubs existed in the larger towns; Dilke and men such as the
economist, Henry Fawcett, could openly propagate anti-Royalist ideas.
Then the illness of the Prince of Wales, and an attempt to assassinate the
Queen, suddenly swung public sympathy in favour of royalism; and
republicanism, as an effective force, vanished from politics.   But from
this point, also, may be dated the decline in the sovereign's personal
powers, though this was as yet hardly evident.

It was true, though scarcely observed by politicians, that certain deep
and adverse developments were taking place beneath the surface.
Britain, for instance, was beginning to be an industrial rather than an
agricultural nation.   Wheat-growing began its long decline in 1872;
there was a slump and serious unemployment in 1878, aggravated by
unfavourable weather in the following year.   Increasingly, food had to
be imported for a growing population; increasingly, there were demands
for the revival of a protectionist tariff, now under the name of 'fair
trade'.   For the moment, industrialism supplied the answer, largely
because Britain still led the world in technological skills; but a quarter
of a century later the gap between Britain and her industrial rivals had
almost closed.

If the calm was, therefore, temporary, it was also comparative.
Occasions were not lacking for the exchange of parliamentary acerbities,
and such a bright young man as Lord Randolph Churchill, second surviving son of the Marquess of Blandford (later the seventh Duke of
Marlborough), who had entered Parliament in the same year as
Balfour, had already made his presence felt before going off to Ireland
as his father's secretary when the Duke became Viceroy.

Balfour, however, was not to be roused; the murmurings of 'Home
Rule', the early threats of Parnell—the Englishman who led the Irish
Party—left him apparently unmoved. In 1877, he proposed one or
two amendments to the Universities Bill, also in the committee stage,
and supported a proposal that degrees should be granted to women.

He was opposed by A. J. Beresford Hope (his uncle by marriage, and M.P. for Cambridge), and by Lord Edmond Fitzmaurice who observed that it 'was disgusting to hear so much' about women inside the House of Commons. A year later, in March, 1878, with an Eton acquaintance, Lord Francis Hervey (M.P. for Bury St. Edmunds), he drafted what he called his 'Burials Bill'. This was intended to avoid Nonconformist objections to being buried in parish churchyards controlled by the Church of England, without affecting the proprietary rights of the Church. But the Noncomformists themselves were cool towards it; they were after bigger game, to wit, to turn all the ancient endowments of the English Church to secular uses. Thus, a Bill which removed a small grievance was not to their taste, for it removed a portion of their ammunition for the larger struggle.

This was pointed out to him by Beresford Hope; and, therefore, Balfour who, as he afterwards said, was not at this time much moved by theories of 'political dynamics', submitted his draft Bill to his other uncle, Lord Salisbury, who remarked: 'A very good Bill—if men's minds were in a temper to take good bills.' He added: 'If you bring it in, you will find yourself probably well protected from the curse which attaches to those of whom all men speak well.'

When the Bill came up for Second Reading, it was talked out to the extent of 14 columns of *Hansard*—there then being no closure—by Beresford Hope himself; and his other uncle's forecast came true, for during a debate on a Ground Game Bill at the same period, a Conservative, noting Balfour's lack of interest in game, remarked that Balfour 'cares a dashed deal more for a dead dissenter than for a live rabbit'. Summing it up some 40 years later, Balfour commented: 'Thus approved by one uncle, then talked out by another, my first humble attempt to improve my country's laws was quietly destroyed!'

Balfour's final, still unwilling, word in his first Parliament took place in May, 1878. But before this occurred the political calm had been ruffled, and then rudely broken, by the intrusion of foreign affairs. One major result of the subsequent changes was that Lord Salisbury succeeded Lord Derby as Foreign Minister; one minor result—though major for his fortunes—was that Balfour became his uncle's Parliamentary Private Secretary, a position that had, as he said, 'neither responsibilities nor emoluments', but which brought him into close contact with public affairs and the seats of power.

The world situation that brought about this small, but vital, alteration in Balfour's status may be summarised briefly. The Ottoman Empire was tottering to its end with malignant side-effects in the shape of massacres of its subject peoples; Russia, moreover, was ready to step in where the Turks withdrew. Neither the massacres nor Russia's eagerness were pleasing to Britain. In 1876, Salisbury was sent to

represent Britain at the Conference of Constantinople. He presented a
scheme to Turkey to prevent the dissolution of the Ottoman Empire
and thus to stem Russian designs—designs which, had they been
successful, would ultimately have threatened India. His scheme was
both dubious and unacceptable, and war broke out in April 1877 between Russia and Turkey, the only happy result being that Salisbury,
as his biographer says, discovered in Constantinople that 'international
politics had gripped him with a hold never again to be loosened'.

In due course, the Turks were defeated and the Russians were
marching towards Constantinople. There was confusion, not to say
fright, all over Europe, and particularly in Britain. British naval
forces were moved towards the Dardanelles, and some entered the Sea
of Marmora. At the Treaty of San Stefano, between Russia and Turkey, the triumphant Russians dictated their terms—the establishment
of a Bulgarian principality, and the aggrandisement of all Russia's
Balkan protégés at the expense of Turkey. The Turkish buffer in
Europe was gone except in name.

In this emergency, Beaconsfield (as Disraeli now was) realised what
had long been obvious, namely that his Foreign Minister, Lord Derby,
who had been at least partly responsible for the unfortunate Zulu war
and the Afghanistan misadventure, was quite incapable not merely of
conducting foreign policy but even of conducting himself. Beaconsfield had shrunk to the last from insisting on anything to which Lord
Derby would have refused his assent, and Derby consistently refused to
take any decision at all. Long afterwards Balfour told Lord Esher
that the 'tension between Lord Derby and Lord Salisbury was at one
time most acute, and the two men's characters were exceedingly hostile.
Lord Derby being a "glorious philistine" and Salisbury a "glorious
Bohemian".' Much earlier, only two years after Derby retired, Salisbury was very frank about his predecessor, as Balfour recorded in a
private memorandum. Salisbury said: 'Why Lord Derby resigned is
obvious enough. Why he did not do so before is the only problem
which requires solution. I suppose it was too great an effort even to
form a decision which would for ever relieve him of the necessity of
deciding anything again. The scenes in the Cabinet towards the end
of his official connection with it must have been highly curious. The
issues of peace and war trembling in the balance: Lord Derby, between
overwork, alchohol and responsibility, in a condition of utter moral
prostration, doing as little as possible and that little under compulsion.'

Salisbury, in fact, succeeded Derby only just before the point of no
return, in March, 1878. The evening following his appointment he
withdrew to his house at Arlington Street and composed—without any
data from outside sources—a despatch that has been rightly noted as
having altered the face of Europe. Sent out as a Circular Note, it was

in effect an ultimatum to Russia: either the San Stefano Treaty was discussed as a whole at a Congress of European powers, or Britain would go to war with Russia. Russia accepted but, before the Congress could begin, and while great events were brooding, Balfour rose to make his last small contribution in that House of Commons. On Tuesday, May 21, 1878, Gladstone was fulminating against the Government's moving Indian troops to the aid of British Forces in the Mediterranean. He sat down suddenly in a depleted house, and it was left to the Parliamentary Private Secretary to reply. Mary Gladstone was in the House and noted in her diary: 'Mr. Balfour had to answer, poor man, there being no one else. It was funny watching him —much emphatic gesture—too much.' Perhaps the gesture was meant to make up for the deficiencies in knowledge; at any rate, *Hansard* prints nothing now worthy of mention.

The Congress of Berlin opened on June 13, 1878. But before Salisbury left England with his chief, Beaconsfield, and his P.P.S., he made some preliminary understandings with Bismarck (who was to preside over the Congress) and with Count Schouvaloff, the Russian ambassador in London. Unfortunately, the confidential memorandum embodying these understandings was leaked to a newspaper. As further preliminaries were to be discussed (involving the British acquisition of Cyprus), Salisbury ordered that the ciphering and deciphering involved should be carried out by his private secretaries alone: 'My help', Balfour recorded, 'was also required and gladly given; but I have to add that though goodwill was admittedly not lacking, I earned no praise from my colleagues either for the speed or the accuracy of my amateur performances. Still I can truthfully claim to have played a part, however small, in the acquisition of Cyprus. . . .'

Balfour spent a month in Berlin with his Chief. His personal involvement with the deliberations was no more than that of an amanuensis; but he used his eyes and his ears. He realised, as did his uncle, that Beaconsfield, though still shrewd, was failing, though not probably quite to the extent that Salisbury suggested in a letter to his wife: 'What with deafness, ignorance of French, and Bismarck's extraordinary mode of speech, Beaconsfield has only the dimmest idea of what is going on, understands everything crossways, and imagines a perpetual conspiracy.' The successful result of the Congress was hailed in Britain as a triumph of 'Peace with Honour'; yet Balfour realised that the restoring of territory to Turkey was storing up trouble for the future. In the shorter view, however, it was favourable to the interests of the British Empire, for after all, he later wrote, 'Pan-Slavism was dead. Turkish domination in Eastern Europe was dead or dying, Russia, when not occupied with her internal troubles, was seeking expansion elsewhere; and the fighting elements in the Balkan States found it more to their taste to fight with each other than to look for quarrels further afield.'

It was a somewhat cynical, at any rate realist, summary of the situation. Just as Balfour had learned from his experience with his 'Burials Bill' that 'perfect schemes' were not necessarily acceptable in the devious parliamentary game, so now he discovered that diplomacy did not begin or end round a conference table and that altruism played singularly little part in it. But he also found out that, even when great matters are at stake, social life continues, and is even more splendid. The 'festal ceremonies' in Berlin may have bored Salisbury; they fascinated his nephew, even though at his first State banquet he had to appear in borrowed clothes, held together by pins, his luggage having gone astray. One of the public prints of the time records—or perhaps just assumed—that this put 'Lord Salisbury at death's door through immoderate laughter at his nephew's predicament and appearance'.

Balfour found the hospitality of Lord Odo Russell (later Ampthill) attractive and kind, and it was at one of Lord Odo's parties at the Embassy that Balfour met and briefly talked to Bismarck himself. The subject was not the Eastern Question. 'Are you', asked Bismarck, 'a descendant of the Balfour of Burleigh who plays his part in Sir Walter Scott's *Old Mortality*?' Balfour disclaimed such honour; but expressed his gratification that Bismarck was acquainted with the Scottish novelist. 'Ah,' replied the Prince, 'when we were young we all had to read Sir Walter. He was considered so very proper.'

That was the extent of his conversation; yet it may have been this actual face-to-face meeting with the maker and ruler of modern Germany that first turned Balfour's thoughts to the question of defence which was to occupy him all his life. Germany's defeat of France in the war of 1870 had radically altered the balance of power in Europe, mainly because of one simple fact: Britain disposed of no more than 110,000 troops while, during the war, Prussia and her associates had mobilised 475,000 men with adequate reserves. Germany, in fact, had seized the ascendancy in Europe. Despite Cardwell's army reforms in the 1860s, there was immense opposition to increases in Service estimates. Increases there would eventually have to be; meantime Britain would depend on diplomacy, and Lord Salisbury's ultimate achievement was triumphant diplomacy—without any very strong military 'teeth'.

Such intimations, if they came, were quickly overlaid by more immediate events, both political and personal. Beaconsfield and Salisbury returned to England and were hailed as the saviours of peace. But the popularity of their Government did not last long. Grievances about agricultural distress, the threat of Parnellism, the unhappy issues of the Zulu war and Afghanistan—all these provided ammunition for a revived Gladstone who began his first, highly successful Midlothian Campaign at the end of 1879.

For Balfour the end of the 1870s marked a closer political relationship with Lord Salisbury; gradually the nephew became the eyes and ears in the Commons of the uncle in the Lords, and began to understand that political influence was not necessarily achieved by speeches in the House of Commons, though it had there to be maintained. But he was by no means yet decided that politics was to be his life work; if he had been defeated in the election next year, 1880, he was determined—now that his mother was no longer there to advise him against it—to leave politics for philosophy. Indeed his final decision to pursue a political career was not taken until some seven years later. Music, social life, Whittingehame and the publication of *A Defence of Philosophic Doubt*—these were still his major pursuits when Disraeli's last Parliament drew to an end. Moreover, it was towards the end of 1879 or early in 1880 that a new, personal relationship began which was to last all his life. It may, or may not, have been chance that made him stop his never to be completed *Chapters of Autobiography* with this sentence: 'It was, I believe, at Sir Frederick Leighton's studio that I first met Mrs. Percy Wyndham, her son George and her daughter Mary.'* George and Mary Wyndham, both considerably junior to Balfour in age, were to become the closest and most intimate of his friends. His association with George was, in addition, to have a political side which ended in disaster; but the friendship never faltered. With Mary, who married Hugo Charteris, Viscount Elcho, later Earl of Wemyss, Balfour in due course entered into the most intimate of all human relationships.

* The additional brief chapter, or notes, on "America, 1917" was in fact written earlier and was left unrevised and unfinished

3

THE WORLD OF THOUGHT

A Defence of Philosophic Doubt, 1879

In the 1870s nothing blended more easily in Society than a young aristocrat with a desultory politician. The mixture remains fairly credible when one adds to it the land-owning laird, the ardent tennis-player, the music-lover and even, perhaps, the psychical researcher. But Balfour went a step further and in so doing put himself well above the ruck of rich young men; for while not yet 30 he published a large book of philosophy which is no mere *jeu d'esprit* or superficial study furbished up in a few weeks. Whatever its ultimate merits, *A Defence of Philosophic Doubt* demonstrates a remarkable mastery of technical method and outlook. Indeed readers totally unacquainted with the serious speculations of professional philosophers may even now find this bulky work rather hard-going; they may react in somewhat the same way as did John Morley, the Liberal journalist and politician who, as editor of *The Fortnightly*, printed an extract from it in advance of publication. Morley, though happy to print it, told Balfour that 'he could not understand a word of it'—though, in fact, it contains a frequent felicity of phraseology, and is intellectually clear and precise.

What Balfour ironically called his 'immortal work' appeared in 1879 and it had taken him over three years to write, though, as he said, he had been toying with some of its ideas even before he went to Eton. Its title had originally been *A Defence of Philosophic Scepticism*. It was changed to its present title at the suggestion of Lord Salisbury, not, Balfour tells us, because of 'considerations of philosophic propriety, for to these, I imagine, he was completely indifferent'. Salisbury's point was that, as more people would hear of its title than would read its contents, it would be better to avoid the word 'scepticism' which to the ordinary person might suggest doubts about religion rather than philosophic doubts about science. Despite the change, however, there were those who misinterpreted his aim—not entirely without reason, as we shall see—and it afterwards provided much ammunition for political opponents. As late as 1925, in his last essay in philosophy, *Familiar Beliefs and Transcendent Reason*, Balfour had to note that certain philosophers still regarded him as a 'doubter who rejoices in his doubts; a philosophic nihilist who prefers any kind of intellectual chaos to what he conceives to be the ill-founded dogmatism of existing modes of thought'.

Balfour was not a born 'professional' in philosophy. He cared 'not a jot', for the history of philosophy, as was noted above. 'Dead systems', he wrote, 'seemed to me of no more interest than abandoned fashions. My business was with the ground-work of modern beliefs.' Conversely, he believed that almost all philosophy, not least his own, would date. The most useful philosophy was *ad hoc*, and the best gift philosophers could have was 'the instinct which tells them where, along the line of contemporary speculation, that point is to be found from which the next advance may best be made, and that speculative faculty which is as much a natural gift as an aptitude for mathematics or a genius for poetry'.

He goes further still and, in his *Essay on Berkeley*, positively denigrates the gift for philosophy. 'Philosophy is nearly as likely to be done well in early as in later life.' (He is writing this at 33.) 'It is wholly independent of experience and nearly independent of book learning. It needs neither profound knowledge of human nature, nor that superficial acquaintance with the ways of mankind which goes by the name of "knowledge of the world".' Something so denuded would be unlikely, one might suppose, either to interest or to have any effect upon its readers and the world at large; and this may have been Balfour's true opinion in his more realistic moments. It is not after all very far from the view of such Existentialist philosophers as Jaspers and Heidegger who assert that traditional philosophy is remote from life, a game, an irrelevant mental exercise.

It is, however, in total contradiction to Balfour's view of an 'advance' being possible and of philosophy's necessity to be topical. In the *Defence*, which he states in the preface is 'a piece of destructive criticism', he specifically foresees his work having 'effects'. He says: 'If it [i.e. 'the path of my argument'] seems to run through a somewhat uninteresting region, and to lead to no desirable goal, yet it, or something like it, must, I believe, be traversed before intellectual repose is finally reached. . . . If speculations which do nothing but destroy seem to be, as indeed they are, unsatisfactory even from a speculative point of view, the reader must recollect that definite and rational certainty is not likely to be obtained unless we first pass through a stage of definite and rational doubt.'   Again we are reminded of Jaspers: 'The plunge from the rigidities, which were deceptive after all, turns into the ability to stay in suspense; what seemed abyss becomes the space of freedom; the seeming nothing turns into that from which true being speaks to us.'

Balfour then continues: 'To judge, then, of the true bearing of arguments like those contained in the preceding chapters, we must look not merely at the arguments themselves, but also at the general habits of thought which prevail at the time of their publication.   We must consider not only the nature of the agents, but the nature of the material on which it is to act.'   Thus, philosophy *can* affect action: 'It is plain that a sceptical attack, especially if it deals with the system which happens at the moment to be in favour, may have considerable consequences—consequences, at least, quite as considerable as any considerations, which are addressed merely to the reason, are ever likely to produce.'

By 'sceptical attack' Balfour did not mean any such sweeping doctrine as that of Professor H. L. Mansel, Dean of St. Paul's for two years before his death in 1871—he is referred to in a footnote in a later edition of the *Defence*—which demonstrated the 'permanent and essential' incapacity of the human mind to prove anything that is believed. Balfour had no inclinations towards sceptical systems that led to doubts whether man's perceptional equipment allowed him to know anything but himself.   His scepticism acted by subjecting certain claims to the test of logic, coherence and ordinary reason.   Man, he says, is incapable of proving much of what he believes, but this incapacity may cease at any time and indeed has often done so.

To what, then, is his sceptical instrument directed, what is 'the nature of the material on which it is to act'?   Balfour, no less than ourselves, lived in an age widely recognised as being transitional, an age in which, as he said in his lecture 'The Immediate Problem of Philosophy' (1880), 'old forms of belief decay, and new forms of belief spring up'. The engine of change was science, and in particular the Darwinian theory of evolution and natural selection.   In addition, there were Lyell's geological discoveries that tended to show that Geology was incompatible with Genesis; and there were textual and historical criticisms of the Bible.   But what really caused the furore was the development from the Darwin theory of the idea, not so much that men were descended from monkeys, as that the adaptation of animals to become man could have originated by natural means and that there was no need to invoke a special act of creation for him.   It was not so much Darwin's revelation of certain laws governing evolution that put the rationalist cat among the theological pigeons as the belief that this implied that evolution was either random or rigidly deterministic, or worse still proceeded blindly and not in accordance with divine plan. All these seemed to upset the widely-held argument from design, first popularised by William Paley in his *Natural Theology* (1802), and more subtly the argument, still common, that a universe which includes the regularities that we call scientific laws, laws which have resulted in nebulæ, electrons and intelligent animals, must have had a Designer.

There is, indeed, and remains, a certain core of Darwinism that is not easily reconcilable with Christian, or possibly with any, moral standards. But this was not the precise case at issue in the nineteenth century. Balfour accepted the theory of evolution in the biological field, as did many others, even churchmen such as R. W. Church, Charles Kingsley and Cardinal Newman (though they confined their adherence to private letters). What Balfour could not accept were some of the philosophical systems and ideas built upon Darwin's back, theories which sought to use the new developments in science to bolster various forms of naturalism, realism and materialism, claims that the new science, like Donne's 'new philosophy' 250 years before, called 'all in doubt'.

Thus, the *Defence* belongs to the mid-stream of Victorian thought, which on the one extreme included the rantings and thunderings from the pulpit, on the other the subtler responses of Newman, Bergson and others. It is, in a refined sense, a polemical book—a piece of 'destructive criticism' could scarcely be otherwise—and it was written, as Balfour said elsewhere, at a time when 'the pretensions of Science are greater even than its triumphs'. But it did not make mere debating points; it is written in the spirit of the Metaphysical Society whose members were much more deeply concerned to find common ground between Science and Religion than to argue to win. One may say of it what Professor A. W. Brown says of the Society that, by the very nature of its critical and inquiring spirit 'no problem is ever "solved"; every "solution", or every compromise, brings new insights and new questions'.

Balfour underlines this when, towards the end of the *Defence*, he writes that if discrepancies between the one faith and the other can be swept away by concessions, well and good. But if, as appears more likely, 'consistency can only be purchased by practically destroying one or other of the conflicting creeds, I should elect in favour of inconsistency—not because I should be content with knowledge which being self-contradictory must need be in some particular false, but because a logical harmony obtained by the arbitrary destruction of all discordant elements may be bought at far too great a sacrifice of essential and necessary truth'. Truth, after all, is always emergent; watertight systems merely delay its emergence; life flows—and we shall see later how interested Balfour became in the 'flux' philosophy of Bergson.

After what has been said about Balfour's deep interest in practical science, it cannot be supposed that he is writing against science as such, nor even against its causative presuppositions or its assumption that there is an independently existing external world. His chief aim is to show that science has no more claim to a rational foundation than have other beliefs which, nevertheless, most people hold no less firmly, not least religious beliefs, 'from which we would not, if we could, be freed'. This is a somewhat dangerous line of argument, and it led him into deep and self-revealing difficulties, as will be clear from a more detailed consideration of the *Defence*.

II

Balfour begins by seeking to disengage the grounds of belief from their causes, 'to distinguish them from what simulates to be ultimate and to exhibit them in systematic order'. Many people, he thinks, fail to keep in mind the distinction between the causes of antecedents which produce a belief, which is a matter of psychology or history, and the grounds or reasons for a belief, which is a matter for philosophy. 'How came I to believe this?' never answered the question 'Why ought I to believe this?' It is never a final answer to say of any particular belief that 'it is innate, connate, empirical or, *a priori*, the result of inheritance, or the product of the association of ideas'.

The 'most ordinary view of scientific philosophy' is that science makes statements about the laws of phenomena founded entirely on observation and experiment which are also the evidence of scientific truth. The most general propositions of the course of nature, it is claimed, may be proved in the same way. Balfour takes as example J. S. Mill's *System of Logic* (1843). To this work, Balfour tells us elsewhere, he was referred when he first asked for a philosophical theory of modern science: 'the shock of disillusionment remains with me to the present hour'. Balfour could, he tells us, have forgiven Mill had he admitted that 'when all had been done that could be done to systematise our ordinary modes of experimental inference, the underlying problem of knowledge remains unsolved'. But Mill, like the English empirical school he headed, seemed to hold that the fundamental difficulties of knowledge did not begin until the frontier was crossed dividing physics from metaphysics. To Balfour himself, the problem of knowledge began with the convictions of common sense. Balfour expanded on the need for a theory of knowledge in his 1880 lecture on 'The Immediate Problem of Philosophy': 'We still find ourselves face to face with great controversies as to whether this subject or that subject is one about which knowledge is possible, without having any rational assurance that we possess anything which can be described as connected knowledge at all.'

The *Defence* disposes effectively of Mill and proves that 'pure empiricism is not at present a tenable system'. One example of Balfour's
method is this: discussing the law of universal causation, he denies the
right of the empirical philosophers to say that this law is 'the uncon-
tradicted result of observations extending through centuries'. For,
says Balfour, 'the fact that mankind has been observing, or doing anything else, for centuries, cannot be to any of us a matter of direct
observation or intuition. It must, therefore, be an inference from
experience; the only experience it can be inferred from is the immediate
and limited experience of each individual; this, therefore, either at one
remove or two, is the only possible empirical foundation for the law of
causation, or any other general principle. This argument does not
show, of course, that empirical philosophy is false; but it does show,
beyond question, that it is not plausible.'

In the Second Part, Balfour turns to the 'premises which, if not
ultimate from a philosophic point of view, are at any rate ultimate from
the scientific point of view—i.e. those on which science depends, but
which do not depend on science'. Here, he tells us, he seeks to suggest
doubt, not to establish scepticism; to show that our 'natural convictions
may be right, but they must be shown to be right . . . and where proof
is necessary, scepticism is possible.' He instances optical illusion, as
when a knife in water appears to be bent. Perception assures us that
it is so; reflection shows us that it cannot be so because it is inconsistent
with the order of nature as revealed to us by science. Yet 'unless there
exists a persisting universe, the order of nature, as revealed to us by
science, is a dream. If, therefore, the existence of such a universe is
given us merely in perception, we can assert that a particular object is
transient only by a mediate inference from an authority whose immediate verdict is that it is persistent.'

We should not, therefore, acquiesce too easily in our 'natural convictions'; 'the subject-matter of science is not a thing that should too
readily be taken for granted'. Of this, philosophy ought to be the
judge. But in these days, he asserts, 'Whenever any faith is held
strongly and universally, there is a constant and overpowering tendency
to convert Philosophy, which should be its judge, into its servant.'
Speculation needs destructive criticism; the bias given to thought in
the days of the Schoolmen 'was not a whit more pernicious to the cause
of impartial speculation' than the current scientific creed.

After referring briefly to Hume's two-edged sword—his scepticism
which applied equally to science as to religion—he turns to transcendentalism, noting that Hume's relation to Kant had been hammered out by Green and Caird. The language used by Kant is often
misleading since it suggests sometimes that 'the business of transcendental speculation was not to justify beliefs but to account for their existence';

but, in fact, transcendentalism does attempt to establish a creed, it does seek to show that 'the trustworthiness of far-reaching scientific postulates is involved in simple experiences which everyone must allow to be valid'.

Balfour's argument here need not be followed in detail.   Referring to a passage from Kant's *Critique*, he comments: 'This proof, it will be observed, is transcendental, i.e. its method of procedure is to show that an experience which we certainly have is impossible, unless the thing to be proved be admitted.'   But, on the other hand, he does not carry us with him today when he doubts whether many people, 'whatever their perplexities, can find intellectual satisfaction in such a formula as this: "The universe is the process whereby spirit externalises itself, or manifests itself in an external world, that out of this externality, by a movement at once positive and negative, it may rise to the highest consciousness of self." '   His comment, though pithily expressed, will not command universal agreement: 'The great body of mankind certainly prefer a contradiction which they do not see, to a reconciliation which they do not understand.'

His references to Kant's 'great obscurity' will, however, be generally applauded; it is still true, as Balfour observed 80 years ago, that this obscurity results in his critics being as 'likely to be attacked for not understanding his arguments as for not having answered them, a proceeding by which what was intended to be a philosophic discussion is suddenly converted into a historical one'.

Balfour then reviews three 'popular philosophical arguments'—the argument from general consent, from success in practice, and from common sense—but warns his readers that their insufficiency to 'furnish a basis of philosophic certitude' cannot be legitimately demonstrated: 'It is as impossible to prove that a belief is *not* to be accepted as one of the ultimate data of knowledge, as to prove that it *is* to be so accepted.' This is a question for each man's individual judgement; the philosopher can only see that a man's decision is 'really given on the main question at issue'.   He himself believes that 'men ought not to give up on speculative grounds the belief in "the uniformity of nature, or any other great principle" '.   But because these principles work in practice is no ground for believing them to be even approximately true.   Certainly, it gives 'no reasonable encouragement' to the compromise between theoretical scepticism and practical faith, for 'if scepticism proves anything, it proves that experience proves nothing'.

Nevertheless, says Balfour—it is the first direct statement of his own personal beliefs—he himself accepts that compromise.   But before proceeding to expatiate on this compromise, which in a sense is at the root of his work, Balfour deals with the authority of consciousness and original beliefs as they emerged in Mill's studies of Reid and Hamilton, in psychological idealism ('in the form in which Berkeley left it'), in Herbert Spencer's 'Proof of realism' and 'the test of inconceivability'. It was, he remarks, reserved for Spencer—despite his extraordinary range of information and his ingenuity in framing suggestive hypotheses —'to elaborate a theory which can pretend to justify the assumption neither of the man of science nor of the theologian, and which will satisfy the requirements neither of the ordinary man nor of the philosopher'.

It is not until he comes to Part Three, which opens with a brilliant chapter on 'Science as a Logical System', that he returns to personal statement. According to science, he says, the real world can be neither perceived nor imagined. For example, the sensation of coloured light, science tells us (or, rather, told Balfour in the late 1870s) is produced by material particles vibrating with a certain rapidity. The varieties of colour are the result of differences in rapidity and combination of these vibrations when they reach the eye. But no one can see these particles. Moreover, the particles themselves must be regarded as colourless since their colour is 'merely the effect produced on our particular organism by their rapid periodic motion acting through space by means of the diffused ether'. No one can imagine 'uncoloured vibrating atoms'. We are compelled 'by the laws of imagination, to confound the effect with the cause before we can picture to ourselves the cause at all'.

But 'unless appearances are to be trusted, why should we believe in Science? If Science is true, how can we trust to appearances?' Science claims to be founded on experience—and the experience must be that of the immediate knowledge of objects given in perception. Thus, science's conclusions contradict its premisses: it claims that appearances are real and then demonstrates that they are unreal, so that it must be regarded as incoherent and confused. This, says Balfour, though a very obvious argument, is one to which he does not know of any reply.

Nevertheless, in spite of the defectiveness of science in its premises, inferences, general relation of its parts and the mutually inconsistent proofs of its doctrines given by philosophers and scientists, everyone has 'an implicit and indestructible confidence' in its truth—which, Balfour says, he shares. He adds that this conclusion will embarrass only those who believe that we must make the strength of our beliefs vary exactly with the strength of the evidence on which they exist.

But, then, if scepticism about the pretensions of science means only the intellectual recognition of the want of evidence but not the consequent unbelief, what is its point and value? Balfour replies that, firstly, 'impartial scepticism' is always beneficial when 'any faith is held strongly and universally', for such a faith always leads to bias, and bias blinds us to the illimitable possibilities of the universe and the partialness of all claims to certainty: 'It was so formerly, when Theology ruled supreme; it is so now that Science has usurped its place. The bias of the Schoolmen was no worse than the bias of Science.'

Secondly, philosophy should be the judge not the handmaiden of faith, particularly so in an age which so strongly holds the 'principle that Science is the one thing certain, that everything which cannot be proved by scientific means is incapable of proof and that everything which is inconsistent with Science is thereby disproved'. Certainly, 'The vast extension of Science in recent times, its new conquests in old worlds, the new worlds it has discovered to conquer, the fruitfulness of its hypotheses, the palpable witness which material results bear to the excellence of its methods, may well lead men to think that the means by which these triumphs have been attained are above the reach even of the most audacious criticism.'

Thirdly, such 'sceptical uneasiness' leads to 'an intellectual dissolving view' which, however uncomfortable, is correct: 'The multitude of beliefs which, in obedience to a mechanic and inevitable law, sway for a time the minds and actions of men, and are then for ever swept away to the forgotten past, giving place to others, as firmly trusted in, as false, and as transitory as themselves, form a spectacle which is not only somewhat melancholy in itself, but which is apt to suggest uncomfortable reflections as to the permanent character of the convictions we ourselves happen to be attached to.' This is as true of Comtism as of Hindoo cosmogonies, of men of science as of the Indians whose superstitions they analyse and classify.

III

From the point of view of Balfour himself, this is one of the most interesting passages in the book. Whenever Balfour considered mortality and transience, his words took wing, as they did again in one of the most celebrated chapters of *The Foundations of Belief*:

'Man, so far as natural science by itself is able to teach us, is no longer the final cause of the universe, the Heaven-descended heir of all the ages. His very existence is an accident, his story a brief and transitory episode in the life of one of the meanest of the planets. Of the combination of causes which first converted a dead organic compound into the living progenitors of humanity, science, indeed, as yet knows nothing. It is enough that from such beginnings famine, disease, and mutual slaughter, fit nurses of the future lords of creation have gradually evolved, after infinite travail, a race with conscience enough to feel that it is vile, and intelligence enough to know that it is insignificant.

'We survey the past, and see that its history is of blood and tears, of helpless blundering, of wild revolt, of stupid acquiescence, of empty aspirations. We sound the future, and learn that after a period, long compared with the individual life, but short indeed compared with the divisions of time open to our investigation the energies of our system will decay, the glory of the sun will be dimmed, and the earth, tideless and inert, will no longer tolerate the race which has for a moment disturbed its solitude. Man will go down into the pit, and all his thoughts will perish. The uneasy consciousness, which in this obscure corner has for a brief space broken the contented silence of the universe, will be at rest. Matter will know itself no longer. Imperishable monuments and immortal deeds, death itself, and love stronger than death, will be as though they had never been. Nor will anything that is be better or be worse for all that the labour, genius, devotion, and suffering of man have striven through countless generations to effect.'

Such passages are sometimes quoted to show that Balfour, in his heart, had neither faith in the future nor hope in the consolations of religion. They do not, as they stand, show anything of the sort. The last extract, for example, is preluded by the phrase 'so far as natural science by itself is able to teach us'.

Nevertheless, the very power and vision that emerges in these passages suggest that Balfour is deeply moved by such thoughts. One senses in them a strong contemplative sense, a half-poetical, half-mystical feeling that bears comparison with Thomas Traherne's 'Centuries'. It appears again when Balfour describes (see p. 133) the swelling hills of his native Lowlands; and, in a slightly different form, when he is moved by music or the contemplation of the achievements of Francis Bacon which evokes from him such typically 17th-century phrasing as 'the chance harvests of empiric invention'.

There have been, indeed, those who believed that at the heart of this man, who could be a witty socialite and, as we shall see, an occasionally somewhat devious politician, lay a contemplative core. J. G. Piddington noted that: 'A.J.B. arrived at more conceptions by intuitive processes than he himself ever realized, and what he put down to intellect was really intuition.' Margot Tennant, the daughter of the Scottish landowner, Charles Tennant, and later the wife of Herbert Asquith, who knew Balfour well from the latter years of the century until his death, wrote: 'Anyone who has read his books will perceive that his faith in God is what has really moved him in life: and no one can say that he has not shown passion here. Religious speculation and contemplation were so much more to him than anything else that he felt justified in treating politics and society with a certain levity. . . .' Lady Oxford and Asquith (as she became) was not always the most reliable of witnesses and this particular quotation contains certain doubtful conclusions; all the same, her testimony is worth weighing.

What is not, however, always understood—and she herself confuses this issue—is that contemplation is not confined to those who profess a religion, nor does it even always assume a belief in God, or at least in a God of the Christian sort.   In later days, Balfour certainly came to have a deep, powerful faith, not merely in an amorphous Divinity, but in a personal God—'whom', as he said, 'men can love, a God to whom men may pray'.   But, at the time he wrote the *Defence*, such a belief was intellectual rather than a living thing 'distilled through all the needful uses' of his life.   For the argument of that book brings him to the point where not only science but religion also are shown as lacking rational grounds of conviction.   The sole practical foundation for our convictions about both depends on their 'claims on belief' and these can only be described as 'a kind of inward inclination, or impulse, falling far short of—I should perhaps rather say, altogether differing in kind from—philosophic certitude, leaving the reason therefore unsatisfied but amounting nevertheless to a practical cause of belief, from the effects of which we do not even desire to be released'.   It is not far distant from Hume's 'strong propensity' to believe.

He then wrote the sentence that some of his earliest critics pounced upon: 'If Religion is thought to stand in this respect on a level with Science (a point which it has not been my business to discuss), the same remarks, *mutatis mutandis*, may properly be applied to it. . . . Religion is, at any rate, no worse off than Science in the matter of proof.'

It is true that he speaks of 'the passion for some living share in that Faith which has been the spiritual life of millions'; it is also true that he brings religion back into the scheme of things because of 'our need for religious truth, rooted as it is in the loftiest region of our moral nature'. Yet the feeling remained that religion had been locked out of the *Defence*, accidentally argued away, and it was this—combined with the disbelief that the cool idol of Society that Balfour became could be deeply religious—that caused such remarks as H. G. Wells's: 'Lenin believed in the dogmas of Marx about as much as Balfour believed in the Holy Trinity.'

The real position was a good deal more complex.   It seems to have been as follows: Balfour had a strong contemplative sense from early years, perhaps due to his delicate health and need for long periods of quiet alone.   At the time he wrote the *Defence* this sense had not merged with a more orthodox faith in a Christian God; in the next few years it did so merge; but not until many years later was the logic of his intellect able to absorb it and place it in perspective.   God certainly comes into *The Foundations of Belief*, his next full scale work published in 1895; yet even so there is an interesting letter from Balfour to Professor A. S. Pringle-Pattison—a philosopher friend he made as a result of the *Defence*—and dated as late as February 7, 1924, in which Balfour writes: 'In *The Foundations of Belief* the relation of my methodological doubt to my constructive conclusion was not made clear; and it was not made clear because I had not worked it out in my own mind with sufficient fullness and precision. It is a rather melancholy reflection that it has taken me more than 40 years to fill up the gap.'

'The truth is', wrote Pringle-Pattison, summing up Balfour's philosophy after his death, that in the *Defence* Balfour 'was not yet in possession—not yet at any rate in conscious possession—of a really constructive principle.' But that a 'constructive principle', in a personal sense, already existed there is little doubt. A letter referring to this early period of Balfour's life from an unnamed friend is relevant. The writer says: 'When I look back on the troublesome and most critical time of our making up our minds whether we could intellectually accept Christianity or not, in our vast ignorance it was a grand support to us to know that in your case faith in the Creed was compatible with clearness of thought.' But to the ordinary reader of his philosophy the existence of such faith was not evident; it was obscured, paradoxically enough, by Balfour's intellectual clarity and logic. In him, his mental powers and his religious insights did not lie easily together; and in one sense, all his philosophising was an attempt to make them cohere.

Technically speaking, the *Defence* aligns its author with the tradition of Hume; but in spirit it is imbued by Pascal's maxim that the Heart has reason which Reason knows not. It is not, indeed, far distant from the Roman Catholic doctrine of *credo quia impossible*, nor from some of the writings of Newman. His philosophical writings, wrote Professor Clement C. J. Webb in his address to the British Academy after Balfour's death, 'may indeed be said to have had all one theme: the importance of attending not only to the rational grounds but to the non-rational causes of belief'. Webb believed that Balfour had rendered important service to English thought by his persistent emphasis on 'the antecedents of belief which are, not, properly speaking, reasons'; and this at a time when depth psychology had not yet brought all reasoning under suspicion of being merely rationalisation of irrational impulses. Webb also compared Balfour with the eighteenth-century, third Earl of Shaftesbury, who was also a critic of a dominant philosophy closely allied with the scientific movement of his time. Like Shaftesbury, too, Balfour was to be deeply concerned with aesthetic experience (see below p. 323 ff.).

To what extent did Balfour the philosopher influence Balfour the politician? As we shall see, *The Foundations of Belief* contains a section on 'Authority' which has political bearings. But it is only in a very general sense that effects may be traced—the subtly critical mind that wrote the *Defence* looked with equal critical subtlety on, for example, the tariff controversy of later years; and no doubt enabled Balfour always to see both sides of any question, which is not particularly valuable to a politician. There was, however, no question of his activities as a statesman being governed by his philosophical principles —if he would have admitted the word; and in this matter he is in strong contrast to his near-contemporary and fellow Scotsman, R. B. Haldane, later Lord Haldane of Cloan (1856–1928) who once represented East Lothian in Parliament. Yet, obviously, the philosopher and the politician were one and the same man, and certain attitudes, as we shall see, were common to both. At the same time, one of the reasons for Balfour's writing philosophy at all was that it represented a withdrawal from the immediate present, as it had done when he began the *Defence* after the death of May Lyttelton. Though it solved none of life's problems, it enabled him to meet them with greater equanimity. It was at once a relief and a relaxation from politics; and it is significant that when, under pressure, he resigned the leadership of the Conservative party in 1911, he plunged at once into the preparation of *Theism and Humanism*.

IV

A Defence of Philosophic Doubt was published in an edition of 1,000 copies at the author's expense by Macmillan, and—so much for its effects on 'action'—it caused scarcely a ripple on the surface of intellectual life. It was only after the remarkable success of *The Foundations of Belief*, that it came steadily into demand and was re-issued in 1920. It was, however, favourably reviewed by Professor Edward Caird in *Mind*, and Professor Hans Vaihinger, of Halle University, dealt with Balfour's cool and indeed, scathing references to Kant in *Kommentar Zu Kants Kritik der reinen Vernunft* (2 vols., 1881–92). Professor Frederick Pollock of Trinity College, Cambridge, wrote an amusing letter to Balfour in July of the year of publication pointing out that, though Balfour was no transcendentalist, he had managed to be 'more Kantian than Kant'. For 'Kant admits the validity of the speculative reason for *science*, but for things above science calls in the *Practical Reason* which can't say *it is* but only *I am certain*. You seem to deny the competence of the Speculative Reason *in toto*,—and make both Science and Religion equally affairs of the Practical reason.' Balfour's reply is not extant.

Balfour's book brought him both new respect and endless witticisms in the Society circles in which he moved. It also brought him, as mentioned above, a new friend in the person of Professor Andrew Pringle-Pattison (formerly Seth), then a young philosopher at Glasgow University. Balfour shortly afterwards endowed for three years a 'Balfour Lectureship' in extra-mural philosophical studies to which Pringle-Pattison was appointed. Though they never became intimate personal friends, they criticised each others works and never lost touch, even when Balfour was immersed in affairs of State.

4

POLITICIAN'S PROGRESS

1880–1887

The seven years from 1880 to 1887 were the most crucial and formative period in the adult life of Arthur Balfour. He began them as a man of 32, still undecided as to the proper field for the exercise of his talents, still indeed dubious of the talents themselves, except in the world of academic speculation. He ended them as a chief Minister of the Crown, his future clearly set in the region of politics. But one cannot point to a particular date or event as being decisive. It was only gradually during the seven years that he found himself being interested by, and then capable of playing a part in, the parliamentary duelling and the cut-and-thrust of debate. It was only tentatively and slowly that he learned that politics is as much a matter of back-stage manœuvrings and private meetings as of speech-making.

Somewhere, too, in the course of these seven years, he began to feel the pull of ambition, and the detached, dilettante attitude, natural to him when he first entered the House of Commons, gave way to personal involvement—even to pique, anger, a certain devious cunning. By the end of the period, the languorous detached air was even more noticeable, but it was now more a mask, a *persona*, than a reality, and eventually it became almost a trade-mark. Twenty years later, by another convolution, the politician had assimilated himself to his mask.

Looking back now on the Parliament that assembled in the spring of 1880, one may well feel that it was ideally adapted to the slow maturing of the political gifts of such a man as Balfour. In the first place, his party had been soundly beaten at the election which followed the dissolution on March 8. Beaconsfield had miscalculated. He had dissolved on the strength of two successful by-elections, and had made the general election a vote of confidence in the Conservative foreign policy and the need to deal decisively with the growing Irish Home Rule movement. The result astonished him; it was, as Lord Salisbury wrote to Balfour on April 10, 1880, a 'hurricane' that swept Beaconsfield and his party into the wings, and it seemed to him to 'be inspired by some definite desire for change'. It was, in reality, the rising gale of Radicalism; and it was because Radicalism was so poorly represented in Gladstone's subsequent Cabinet that this sweeping Liberal victory was eventually frittered away.

More than 100 Conservatives lost their seats; but Balfour was not among the vanquished. Even for him, however, there was no question of a walk-over as there had been in 1874. His opponent at Hertford was Edward Bowen, a Harrow Schoolmaster (and author of *Forty Years On*) who, though not formidable as a speaker, was supported by those who were, those who, as Balfour remarked, like their great model found 'in the brutalities of which the Turkish irregulars had been guilty in 1876, conclusive reasons why their hearers should vote against Lord Beaconsfield in 1880'. So Balfour had to work hard at his electioneering, but in due course he was returned by a majority of 164. Then—the Hertford result being declared early—he went off to speak in Midlothian where Lord Dalkeith was engaged in 'a gallant but hopeless' struggle with Gladstone.

En route to Scotland, Balfour called at Hatfield House where, in the absence of Salisbury, Beaconsfield had his campaign headquarters. Beaconsfield hoped Balfour's success was a good augury, though the other available results were not encouraging: 'I recall him', wrote Balfour, 'standing at the north door of the house looking down the avenue—a strange, almost a picturesque figure, dignified and calm, though not, I thought, unmoved.'

A few days later when the extent of the defeat was revealed, Balfour again talked to Beaconsfield, this time in Downing Street, and reported to his uncle that the defeated leader 'did not take a despairing view of our case, though he said we should never return to power in his time'. (Nor did they: Beaconsfield died a year later.) He went on to talk to Balfour of the importance of managing the House of Lords, the need to avoid conflict 'unless something substantial is to be gained thereby', and of his own decision to continue active in politics.

A few weeks after Balfour's talk with the leader, a young lady remarked to him how much she wished she could hear Beaconsfield's conversation. To this Balfour rather cruelly replied that she had no need to meet him to hear his conversation: 'You have only to imagine a brazen mask talking his own novels.' This is the first tart remark of Balfour on record: it is not the last. His ability to sting was another aspect of his character; if scarcely an amiable one, it became a great strength in debate.

When the House of Commons reassembled on April 29, Gladstone was Prime Minister, and supporting him were Hartington, Chamberlain, Dilke, Harcourt and Bright. It was in appearance a strong team, and the Conservative leaders (with Beaconsfield and Salisbury in the Lords) were obviously no match for them. The Conservative rank-and-file were depressed and bewildered. Moreoever, the future was by no means clear: Beaconsfield was old and often ill—there was no obvious candidate to take his place as leader of the party. Sir Stafford Northcote, the leader in the Commons, certainly had prior claims but evoked little enthusiasm. He had been a good minister; he had also many years before been Gladstone's secretary and, it was said, had never lost the habit of deference to him. He was a good financier, but a bad speaker. He was genial but, as Rosebery said, entirely without the necessary 'spice of devil'. Balfour himself spoke of him as a scholar and a gentleman, a man of wide experience and urbane manners, 'but no more a match for Mr. Gladstone than a wooden three-decker would be for a Dreadnought'.

What was true of Northcote was true in some degree of others on the Opposition front bench. R. A. Cross (later Sir Richard Cross) and W. H. Smith were, Balfour later wrote, excellent heads of departments and able Cabinet ministers, but the fall of the Government meant that 'they were transferred, through no fault of their own, from duties which they performed with credit to duties which they really could not perform at all'. Winston Churchill, in the life of his father, Lord Randolph, refers to them, indeed, as 'the ancient and dreary wreckage of the late Administration'.

These views were echoed by a section of the press. On December 1, 1880, the periodical *Vanity Fair* commented: 'The Conservative Party, together with its old name of Tory, has lost its old spirit and energy . . . Lord Beaconsfield . . . has been surrounded and hindered by the worn out old relics whose only notion of leading the Party has been to prevent anybody else leading it. (They are) one and all convicted incapables, yet they give themselves the airs of heaven-born Leaders. . . . The superannuated oligarchy of Sir Stafford Northcote, Sir Richard Cross, . . .'.

Here, then was opportunity enough for a young man with his parliamentary way to make; and the new House had not been long in session before the young man appeared. But it was not Arthur Balfour: it was Lord Randolph Churchill, duly re-elected for Woodstock, who knocked loudest on the door of opportunity. He intervened in the debate which arose out of the question whether a newly-elected member, Charles Bradlaugh, could properly be allowed to sit since he was an atheist and free-thinker. Seizing his opportunity, Churchill kept the House in uproar for days whenever the Bradlaugh question arose, much to the mortification of Gladstone and the pleasure of the Conservatives.

In this he was supported by two older Conservative members, Sir Henry Drummond Wolff and John Eldon Gorst (later Sir J. E. Gorst). Unlike the brilliant, moody, erratic Churchill, they were not spurred on by feeling themselves 'still at 31 obscure'. Wolff, M.P. for Portsmouth, who had first seen the possibilities of the Bradlaugh affair, was 49, 'a diplomat', Balfour later wrote, 'by profession, a man of the world by temperament and training, with a great aptitude for amusing and being amused. . . . Without being a great speaker, he had a quick eye for the possibilities of a Parliamentary situation and a tongue ready enough to turn opportunities to account.' Others spoke of his being 'as cunning in politics as in diplomacy'.

Gorst, M.P. for Chatham, was 45 and he had been in the House since 1866. But he nourished a strong sense of grievance. He had been appointed by Disraeli in 1869 to establish a new Conservative party machine throughout the country; neglecting his practice at the Bar he had done so with resounding success, and Disraeli ascribed the Conservative victory in 1874 as in large part due to Gorst's efforts at the Central Office and National Union. Unfortunately, he was given no place in the Government he had done so much to bring into power, partly because he was a somewhat difficult man who never bore fools gladly. This smouldering sense of ill-treatment is what gave an edge to his speeches and certainly did not endear him to the leaders of his party. Balfour spoke of him as being 'a good mathematician, a good lawyer and an experienced organiser . . . so I always understood, he had before my time done good work for the party.' He had 'more force than charm, but was clear and incisive if somewhat cynical. . . . He was often unanswerable, but not so often persuasive.'

It was these three men—Churchill, Wolff and Gorst—who now joined forces to hammer and hamper the Government wherever possible, and even as early as the Bradlaugh incident to embarrass the official Leader of the Opposition, too, for Northcote himself sympathised with Gladstone in his difficulties over Bradlaugh and would would have done little to harass him further. During the Bradlaugh debates, Balfour never spoke. He is described at this time as 'a superior young man, genteelly devoid of passionate convictions . . . without ambitions or the necessary energy to stimulate it. . . . He reclined on the front Opposition bench below the gangway, his legs characteristically stretched out in front of him, with his eyes half closed in the serenity of philosophic contemplation. . . .'

It, therefore, occasioned some flippant comment when, while a resolution by Wolff was being put to the House, it was observed that Balfour rose and went into the same division lobby as Wolff, Gorst and Churchill. Thus was born what was shortly to be dubbed 'The Fourth Party'. Undoubtedly, it was Balfour's membership of this fiery little group of sharpshooters which first brought him clearly into the public eye, and which also gave him the confidence to get on his legs, and attack and counter-attack. The group was, of course, never a party in the technical sense; its objects were to distract and damage the enemy and to awaken their friends—and few of the friends, at least those on the front Opposition bench, much cared for the process. But in so far as the four stuck together, defended each other under attack (from in front or behind) and concerted their efforts, they were reasonably safe from the fate usually reserved for the individual rebel.

None of his three colleagues became close personal friends of Balfour —their tastes and backgrounds were too divergent—but he enjoyed their company and, for a time, worked closely with them. Some idea of the little group's usual methods may be gathered from this account by St. John Brodrick, later the Earl of Midleton and a close colleague of Balfour. It should be remembered that at the time of which Midleton speaks the closure had not yet been instituted:

'To waste time, some respectable M.P. would be put up to advocate an arguable proposition quite at variance with the Government's proposal. Randolph Churchill would enforce it by a philippic castigating the Government in advance for wasting time if they even attempted to oppose it. This, as intended, brought up Gladstone with an impassioned harangue of twenty minutes proving the fallacy up to the hilt. The ball was then fairly rolling, and Balfour would develop a few selected points on which he was still in doubt. With good management the amendment would run for many hours, and about 4 a.m. the Opposition would go to bed delighted to have used up an hour of Government time on two lines of the Bill, and with the consciousness, if it were accused, that the Government must parade again at mid-day, while they could saunter in at their ease to resume guerilla tactics with the certainty of having squeezed some other nefarious Bill out of the Government programme.'

The tactics were effective. It would be reasonable to claim that when the historian (Ensor) states that 'never in the modern era has a triumphant House of Commons majority achieved so little', it was partly a result of the efforts of 'The Fourth Party'.

At first, Balfour did not possess the nimbleness and brilliance of Churchill in these wrecking tactics; but he learned. He first cooperated with the group in the debates concerning the Employers' Liability Bill, introduced early in the session of 1880. Churchill thought the Bill should go much further than it did in extending the employers' liabilities when injury was caused by defective machinery, incorrect orders, or negligence by supervisors. This seemed to Churchill to be consonant with what he had already christened 'Tory Democracy', and which he regarded as a development of Disraelian principles.

Balfour at first did not agree, or perhaps had not made up his mind; but later he joined his group in the attack, and eventually went farther than any of them by suggesting an amendment to the Bill to extend its provisions to cover domestic servants: the proposal was negatived by an overwhelming majority, but not before all three colleagues had joined in with a number of small points. When the Government protested at the waste of time, the group at once pointed out that the welfare of domestic servants was an important matter, and the Government was pilloried for considering it beneath their notice. When a Government speaker remarked that the zeal for the working classes was a new-found virtue in the Conservative party, and had not been apparent in the conduct of the late Government, it was Balfour who tartly replied that the late Government had not been formed from Members below the gangway, and that if it had the claims of the working classes would no doubt have been met.

It is not necessary to describe all the pies in which 'The Fourth Party' had its fingers during the year 1880—the close examination of the Estimates, for instance, or the exploitation of the Government's growing Irish problems. But there is one revealing picture of Balfour in the House at this date, drawn by Sir Henry Lucy, the diarist of successive Parliaments. He says that on August 20, 1880, 'The Young Men below the gangway' put Balfour up to move a resolution that the House was still 'inexpediently' in session on unimportant matters:

'The Member for Hertford is one of the most interesting men in the House. He is not a good speaker, but he is endowed with the rich gift of conveying the impression that presently he will be a successful Parliamentary debater, and that in the meantime it is as well that he should practise. He is a pleasing specimen of that highest form of culture and good breeding which stands to the credit of Cambridge University. He is not without desire to say hard things of the adversary opposite and sometimes yields to the temptation. But it is ever done with such sweet and gentle grace and is smoothed over by such earnest protestations of innocent intention that the adversary rather likes him than otherwise.'

Lucy then adds a curious note about the reactions of Balfour's uncle, A. J. Beresford Hope, the Member for Cambridge. Balfour is 'ever within sound of the encouragement of his chuckle. . . . When Mr. Balfour is on his legs, Mr. Beresford Hope does not trust himself to look at him, but his whole being is suffused with a sense of his presence. . . . He watches over him as a hen hovers round its last surviving fledglings . . . and the tall slim young man looks down on him with a fond smile.' Beresford Hope had clearly changed his attitude since the days when he opposed the 'fledgling's' early stumblings towards speech in the House.

'The Fourth Party', which made the name of Churchill and helped to put Balfour on the political map, was of course, as Balfour wrote to his uncle on September 29, 1880, not a party at all—'it has no organisation, no Leader and no distinctive principles'. Its policies were concerted *ad hoc* over cheerful dinner-parties given by its members; and, though the four often acted together, there were times, even in the first flush of success in 1880, when they disagreed. Balfour, for instance, found himself having to sit for many weeks in between Gorst and Churchill, who had quarrelled, and while both were prepared to speak to him, they would not speak directly to each other.

Balfour himself, from the beginning, reserved the right to act on occasion as he thought fit, rather than at the behest of his three colleagues. He wrote to Wolff, who with Gorst was inclined to view 'The Fourth Party' as more of a permanency than a temporary ginger group, that he would not publicly admit that the 'Party' existed at all: 'We must always assert that the name is a joke and a device of the enemy to sow dissension in the Conservative Party. So shall we be able to preserve our independence, in spite of all the front benches in the world. . . . What I never can get you to understand is that what we should aim at—for our own sakes and that of the party at large—is the largest possible amount of real independence and the smallest possible appearance of it.'

As was recognised by his colleagues, and as Wolff wrote in his memoirs, Balfour's position was somewhat different from theirs because of his family ties with one of the Conservative party's leading politicians, Lord Salisbury. He went certainly at least as far as they did in criticising Northcote's supine leadership in the Commons; he was never at any time willing to go so far as to split the Conservative Party. At a meeting of the Party at the Carlton Club on August 20, 1880, it was, indeed, Balfour who voiced the general dissatisfaction with Northcote, though he managed to do it in such an ingenious way that Northcote's name was not actually mentioned. Privately he wrote to Salisbury confessing that he had never 'disliked doing anything more'. In fact, as far back as July 6, 1879, while the Conservatives were still in power, he had written to Salisbury telling him that 'already there is a large amount of discontent which Northcote's method of conducting business has aroused. But since there is no possible outlet to this in action, since there is neither an alternative Leader, nor an alternative policy on the larger questions of the day, which any Conservatives would dare to support, I suppose the discontent will end in words and

perhaps in a certain difficulty in getting men to inconvenience themselves to please the Government.'

During 1880 such letters increased in number and in critical vehemence. On August 25, 1880, he wrote to Salisbury: 'The condition of
our Party is even more unsatisfactory than it was when you were here.
We are trampled on by the Government, but we make no sign. We
have no organisation. We have no Leader—or rather our Leader
[Northcote] is (and what is worse is very commonly thought to be) a
source of weakness, rather than of strength.'

The complaint's substance, he added, was 'not that Northcote is a
great deal away from the House, but that when he is there his object
seems to be to discredit the actions of the Independent Members—
however legitimate they may be'. Balfour himself, for instance, had
brought forward a motion intended to bring home to the Government
the fact that they would be opposed when they tried to force important
Bills through at a time of year when criticism was impossible: 'It will
give you some idea of Northcote's notions of leading an Opposition if
I tell you that when I went to see him on the preceding Tuesday
to ask him if it would be convenient for him to be there to support me,
he told me that he should probably be absent and if there should
probably take up his parable against me.'

Balfour says that Disraeli had told him that Northcote had complained that Independent Members (i.e. backbenchers) never consulted him; if that is true, Balfour adds, 'it arises from the fact that
nobody has any confidence as to the motives which may prompt his
advice. He appears to have a real dislike to doing anything which
may annoy the Government—or which may modify the very excellent
opinion which they now entertain about him!'

To this, Salisbury replied more sympathetically in private to Balfour
than he would have done in public where he behaved always with
circumspection and loyalty to Northcote. He wrote now: 'I am afraid
that the efficiency of our Party will decay and that we shall not recover
the confidence of the country. For it is the central figure of a party in
the Commons to which constituencies are wont to look, if their confidence is asked for that Party.' But he could see no remedy for the
situation. Beaconsfield also sympathised, but counselled caution and
the avoidance of any break with Northcote who represented 'the
respectability of the Party'; 'I', he added, 'was never respectable
myself.'

Northcote had complained to Beaconsfield. This was hardly
surprising. The stage was rapidly being reached when as Balfour
wrote to Salisbury on May 14: 'It would be a pity if our people below
the gangway get into the habit of thinking that Northcote having
voted one way is sufficient reason for their voting the other.'

'The Fourth Party' did not conceal their scorn for Northcote. Privately they jeered at him as 'the Goat'. They also deeply offended Cross and W. H. Smith by referring to them as 'Marshall and Snelgrove'. 'The Fourth Party' suspected that there might have been deeper reasons for Northcote's antagonism towards them. Gorst wrote in a letter to Balfour in 1880: 'The Goat is trying to dissolve the Fourth Party. I often fancy the Goat has his eye upon a possible coalition with the Whigs. In some quarters this is spoken of as the next political combination.'

Balfour repeated the idea in a letter to his uncle on September 29, 1880, attributing it, however, to Wolff: 'Wolff has always asserted that Northcote's hostility is owing to a scheme he is cherishing of forming eventually a junction with the Whigs. But, putting aside the fact that Wolff always suspects everybody of everything, I fail to see how the present action of Members below the gangway can either help or hinder any such political combination. I can hardly believe Northcote to be such a fool as to think that the Tory Party can purchase the future support of the Whigs by showing present incapacity to resist the Radicals.'

To this Salisbury, holidaying at the Châlet Cecil at Puys near Dieppe, replied on October 5, 1880: Northcote 'may hope by adopting a moderate attitude to win over Whig rank and file to become Tories; and this, if Gladstone is violent, is not an unlikely occurrence. I think these tactics so far, are wise. . . . If there is any feeling in his [i.e. Northcote's] mind against the Fourth Party (which I have no ground for believing) it is probably due to the great impudence with which Wolff talks about him. . . .'

But if Balfour's attitude to Northcote was as unequivocal as that of Churchill himself, that did not mean that he accepted and underwrote all other of Churchill's attitudes. For example, in September, 1880, while Balfour was on holiday in Ross-shire, Churchill wrote asking that he should suggest to his uncle that he should address Churchill's constituents at Woodstock when he visited Blenheim in November. Balfour passed the letter to his uncle, but added that 'The proposal strikes me as a cool one; and if you do not feel inclined to accede to it, you have only to let me know, and I will get you off in a manner that will cause no awkwardness. . . . What Randolph says about your speaking to his constituents being an honour to the "Fourth Party" may really be an argument against your doing so. Northcote certainly dislikes us.'

Balfour, in other words, was anxious to avoid involving his uncle with Northcote in controversy since this would probably have resulted in a serious taking of sides throughout the party. In the end Salisbury did address the meeting at Woodstock—*and* paid tribute to Northcote's leadership. Churchill, on the other hand, avoided reference to North-cote, and instead praised Disraeli. But to have Salisbury, one of the party leaders, on the same platform at all with Churchill, the party rebel, implied some sort of unity; so at any rate Beaconsfield preferred to believe when, reporting on a party meeting at his house on February 10, 1881, he boasted that he had been able 'to weld into homogeneous action all sections of the Conservatives'. He indicates the diversity of these sections by describing their extremes: 'Lord Randolph at the head of his Bashi-Bazouks, and the respectable Mr. Walpole and Company, who view Lord Randolph with more repugnance than they do the Fenians, equally attended the meeting at my house.'

Nevertheless, by the end of the year 1880, during which Balfour had carved a small niche for himself in the Commons and, more important, had come closer into the political confidence of his uncle Salisbury, it was clear that fundamental realignments of power within the Con-servative party were about to take place. Churchill, in six months, had become the outstanding figure at the younger end of the party and his name was known throughout the country. Northcote, the leader in the Commons, had at the same time lost prestige, while Salisbury remained roughly in the same position—admired by many but by some elders still regarded as too intransigent in principle and too scathing in speech. But now the issue of the future leadership of the Conservative Party began to loom; and in April, 1881, when Beaconsfield died, it became the question of the hour.

Beaconsfield had indicated a few months before that he would prefer Salisbury to succeed him in the Lords: 'One of my dreams', he wrote to Salisbury on December 27, 1880, 'was that in February (1881) I should be sitting behind you in the House of Lords and that you would be leading H.M.'s Opposition.' In due course, Salisbury was elected unanimously to that position—but in the Lords only. In the Com-mons, Northcote remained leader, the Queen having written to him confidentially on May 15, 1881, that she was 'anxious to say that *she* will look upon Sir Stafford Northcote as leader of the great Con-servative party, though it may not be necessary to *announce* this now.'

The position was, therefore, that Salisbury and Northcote would lead the party as a sort of duumvirate with equal powers, leaving the office of 'Leader of the Conservative Party' vacant. Thus, as Balfour wrote, 'neither the practice of the Constitution, nor party loyalty, debarred any Conservative from endeavouring to obtain a position' left in so equivocal a state. It was Churchill's ambition to gain that position, a laudable one no doubt and not, in view of his swift successes, an impossible one. Balfour in later years saw in it nothing to criticise. But he himself would naturally not support him; quite apart from his ties with Salisbury and his personal ambitions, which were clearly hitched to his uncle's star, he and many others in the party, as in the country, began to have increasing doubts as to Churchill's fitness for supreme power. He was brilliantly volatile in criticising Liberal blunders; but he was unreliable in his attitudes. It was not only Liberals, such as Edward Hamilton, who condemned his unscrupulousness; it was not only Hartington who was astounded when, having attacked Churchill as 'vile, contumacious and lying', satisfaction was demanded of him privately by a most dubious go-between, Captain O'Shea—an Irish M.P. and husband of Parnell's mistress. As for 'Tory Democracy', many Conservatives saw this as 'the wolf of Radicalism in the sheepskin of Toryism'.

Events were to show Churchill's grave lack of judgement, both in private and political life, just as they were also to show his astounding attraction for the lower middle-class voter, newly enfranchised and open to the most flagrant demagoguery. Thus, those who have criticised Balfour for gradually detaching himself from association with Churchill and his eventual open opposition to him, have closed their eyes to Balfour's sound reasons for so doing. They have pointed to Balfour's 'waspish' comments on Churchill in private letters to his uncle; they have scarcely considered that Churchill's conduct gave more than adequate cause for them. That loyalty to Salisbury and personal ambition also entered into the matter is no doubt quite true: neither quality, surely, can be condemned out of hand. The Irish M.P., F. H. O'Donnell, summed up the situation reasonably when he wrote: 'Drummond Wolff started the Fourth Party; Gorst made it; Churchill led it; Balfour adorned it. Balfour was a member of the Fourth Party in the body, while always communing in the spirit with the Conservative Front Bench. . . . With all his judicious reluctance, he was a good comrade to the Fourth Party without ceasing to maintain his succession to more permanent honours.'

Towards the end of 1880, the periodical *Vanity Fair* asked 'The Fourth Party' to pose for their famous cartoonist 'Spy' (Leslie Ward). Balfour, who was at Whittingehame, was dragged down to London at the insistence of Wolff, but warned him that 'I shall be haggard and ghastly of hue from the effects of a night journey; but that will be taken to be a consequence of the anxiety and labour which my Parliamentary efforts on behalf of my country have forced me to undergo'— and he added—'of the pain which the behaviour of my colleagues has so often inflicted.'

'The Party' met at Spy's studio and joyfully posed themselves in their typical, though somewhat exaggerated, House of Commons attitudes. But it was their last meeting in the old gay spirit of the Four Musketeers. Until as late as 1885, the four often acted together in the Commons; but gradually the ways divided, Churchill moving

GJB

upwards, Balfour veering towards the centre of Conservatism, while
Wolff and Gorst were eventually left high and dry.

II

From 1881 to the fall of Gladstone's Government in 1885, Balfour's
story is of his increasing independence as a Commons speaker and of
his involvement in such important debates as those on the Irish question
and the closure, of his behind-the-scenes activities in connection with
Churchill's bid for the Conservative leadership, and of his ever closer
relationship with Salisbury.   During this period, the prestige of the
Liberal Government, swept in by a 'hurricane' victory, gradually
declined, both as a result of its internal schisms and of its ineptitude in
the Sudan and in foreign affairs generally.

As a speaker in the House, Balfour tended in the beginning to, as
Lucy put it, 'gently purr', though in debate he was quite capable of
scratching.   It was not until May, 1882, that he showed his ability to
speak with power and force when he rose during the Kilmainham
debate and attacked Gladstone: 'This was the first speech he had ever
made', wrote Winston Churchill in his life of his father, 'that commanded general attention, or gave any promise of his future distinction.'   Since Balfour was in a few years to be a leading actor in the
Irish Tragedy, of which the Kilmainham debate was a brief scene,
some general background must be sketched.

The 'Irish situation' had begun to dominate home politics during
Disraeli's last Government and was increasingly to do so in the next
forty years.   Salisbury's aphorism that 'politics is Ireland' was no
piece of empty wit, and Beaconsfield, it was said, had died with the
word 'Ireland' on his lips.   The origins of the problems went back to
Cromwell and, indeed, as readers of Edmund Spenser will recall,
long before him.   Basically—but only basically—the situation was
simple.   Cromwell had driven a large Roman Catholic population
into the West with the cry 'Hell or Connaught', but the land they
farmed was insufficient in good years and the cause of famine in bad.
The later large-scale emigrations, often in intolerable conditions, to
America were insufficient to relieve matters at home, where priest-
ridden poverty, illiteracy and near-starvation were rife.   Successive
Governments tampered with the problem, often only to exacerbate
matters through ignorance.   The main needs were land reform, drastic
social measures, and firm Government; but they were seldom considered because of vested interests, lack of money, or difficulties of other
sorts.   Measures of coercion alternated with periods of weak acquiescence; violence came and went; and agitators of all sorts added fuel to
the flames.

Moreover, there were underlying influences which were not always evident to the naked eye. Much of agricultural Ireland was owned by absentee English landlords; the northern area round Belfast was largely industrial. The landlords and the Ulstermen tended to be Protestant; the Irish labourers and tenants were Roman Catholics. Americans had fingers in the Irish pie. When the movement in Ireland for Home Rule began in 1870, Englishmen tended to see it as an offensive attempt at break-away from the Empire. Currents and cross-currents, in which religion, self-interest and national pride were inextricably mixed, combined to make Ireland as hard to understand as it was difficult to govern.

At the same time, Ireland was represented in the House of Commons, and in 1878 found a leader of genius in the person of an Englishman of the land-owning upper classes, Charles Stewart Parnell, who entered Parliament in 1875. Already among the Irish members were revolutionary Fenians. In 1879, during a severe agricultural depression, the Irish National Land League was formed; and henceforward, Irish obstructiveness in the Commons was paralleled by destructiveness in Ireland itself—the burning of property, the maiming of cattle, and assaults on human beings.

Disraeli's last Government had sought to use coercive methods to pacify the country. Gladstone after 1880 turned the other way, but failed to bring in immediate relief measures. Boycott and murder followed, and Gladstone resuscitated the methods of coercion. With them, however, he gave a measure of land reform which went far towards providing tenants with the 'Three F.'s' they sought—fixity of tenure, fair rents, free sale. But Parnell, the Irish parliamentary leader, realising that this was a concession to violence, stood out for still more. In the Commons, he deliberately got himself expelled, and continued to agitate the tenants against taking advantage of the offered measures. Eventually he was imprisoned in Kilmainham gaol.

For a time this suited him well, personally as well as politically. It also pleased the Irish American extremists who were financing the insurrection, and whose aims went a great deal further than reform or redress; and Parnell's orders to the tenants to pay no rent till the Government had restored the people's constitutional rights were obeyed. 'Captain Moonlight', who commanded the forces of disorder and violence, took over. But six months later Parnell, perhaps through jealousy of his lieutenant, who was ready to compromise, and of the Irish Member, Captain O'Shea—by whose wife Parnell had had a child—opened secret negotiations with Joseph Chamberlain, the Radical leader and President of the Board of Trade, and with Gladstone. It was agreed, though not in writing, that Parnell and two other agitators should be released on the understanding that he would call off the 'no rent' campaign and stop the outrages; the Government, in turn, would bring in a Bill to smooth over the question of the arrears of rent now owing as the result of the campaign.

At once W. E. Forster, Gladstone's Chief Secretary for Ireland, resigned. 'Either,' he said, 'the release is unconditional or it is not. If unconditional, I think it is at the present moment a surrender to law-breakers. If conditional, I think it is a disgraceful compromise.' St. John Brodrick describes the scene when Forster vindicated his resignation: 'Rising, behind the Front Bench from which he had during many nights faced the untiring Irish guerillas, a tall, rude, unkempt figure, he demanded from Captain O'Shea, who had been Gladstone's inter-mediary with Parnell, the full text of the agreement on which the suspects were to be released. Captain O'Shea read the letters which had passed, giving Parnell's undertaking to give the Land Act fair play and check agitation.

' "Read on," said Forster.

' "That is all," said O'Shea, on which Forster, producing a paper, read Parnell's pledge to the Government to use the forces which had raised the agitation in Ireland to bring it to an end, and himself to support the Government measure to the end of the Session.'

Thus the dubious compact was revealed; when Gladstone rose to reply his position was gravely weakened.

It was at this point that Balfour leapt in to press the weakness home in a speech full of biting contempt for the Government's ineptitude and inconsistency. He said that, despite Forster's revelation, Gladstone had insisted there was no treaty. But this was obviously untrue. 'The Government', Balfour said, 'had not entered into a contract; no, they have only given the Hon. Gentlemen behind them something they very much desired, and the Hon. Gentlemen have, on their part, given the Government something they very much desired. . . . I do not think any such transaction can be quoted from the annals of our political history. It stands alone in its infamy. The Government has been degraded by treating on equal terms with men whom they have asserted to be steeped to the lips in treason. . . . They had negotiated in secret with treason, and, almost worse than all, it appeared that one of the things the Government had, in their own words, reasonable grounds for believing, was that they would obtain the Parliamentary support of men they had put in prison for the gravest crime.'

In this speech there was real fire, though—or perhaps, because—it was made extempore. It was a speech which moved Balfour a further step up the political ladder. But, of course, it interrupted the friendly relations with Gladstone (though not, as we observe from her diary, with Mary Gladstone). Although Gladstone could scarcely deny the gravamen of the charges, he was deeply wounded. After all, to be accused of lying and infamous conduct might still cause a certain stir even in these days, when honour is a shield less brightly burnished. Writing to Balfour on some semi-official matter a year later, on February 19, 1883, Gladstone still felt that 'we are without doubt at present sharply divided. But I have not lost and shall not readily part with the pleasant recollections of other days.' Balfour himself seems to have had some qualms whether, however true the charges were, it was fitting for a young man so to berate the celebrated and aged Prime Minister, the Grand Old Man. In a letter, presumably intended for someone in the Gladstone circle—though whether ever despatched or not is uncertain—Balfour says: 'I am sorry that the word "infamy" should have slipped out in the heat of a debate. *The reason*, I am sorry to say, is not that I think it is inapplicable, or that I think that Gladstone has any right to complain of it, but that I am of the opinion that very violent words should be excluded from debate. . . . I must add that Gladstone's attitude seems to me very strange in the matter. I understand that he thinks an old friend should not have attacked so vehemently. Now this is in itself a position which, whether right or wrong, is capable of defence. But it seems to me wholly inconsistent with the character of his reply to my speech. No man should claim *both* the privileges of considering himself injured by an attack *and* the privilege of replying to that attack with a violence which greatly surpassed it.'

It may be added that Gladstone's Kilmainham bargain did not immediately alter the course of Irish events. A few days after the release of Parnell, Lord Frederick Cavendish, Chief Secretary for Ireland, was assassinated, along with the Under Secretary, in Phoenix Park, Dublin. Parnell, it appears, was genuinely horrified, and from then until the end of the Gladstone Parliament he sought—despite some dynamite outrages in London—to make the Land Act work. But coercion continued, and Parnell became increasingly cool in his allegiance to the Liberals, particularly when Churchill in his speeches was offering—though without his Party's permission—a discontinuance of the repressive measures should the Conservatives return to power. As a result, when Chamberlain and Gladstone approached Parnell about the possibility of his agreeing to a scheme of devolution, involving County Boards and a National Council, Parnell felt strong enough to refuse to talk.

Balfour came into the public eye again when he intervened in the debate on the closure, by which the Speaker could propose the ending of a debate if a bare majority of the House, there being at least 400 members present, agreed. The Conservatives, equally aware of the delaying tactics of Parnell, amended it to read that a debate should be closured only by a two-thirds majority. Churchill opposed both;

Balfour supported his party's amendment; and the clash between the two former colleagues was the outstanding feature of the debate.   The clash was observed with particular satisfaction by Northcote.

Balfour also made two other noteworthy speeches, one on the London slums (an evil in which Salisbury showed commendable interest), and one on Highland poverty in which he had a particular concern because of his own Highland estate at Strathconan, Ross-shire.   He pleaded for large-scale emigration as the only answer to poverty in this once overcrowded part of Scotland.   (He himself had carried out improvements by foregoing rents, but such was the diminution of his income, that in 1884 Strathconan had to be let on lease, and when the lease ended the estate was sold.)

These and other parliamentary activities combined to make many observers see in Balfour a 'coming man'.   One result was that in 1884 he was asked by East Manchester to stand at the next election for that constituency; since Hertford was due to be swallowed up in the next redistribution of seats, he accepted, and thus began his long connection with Lancashire.

In 1884, Balfour was personally concerned in the manœuvres and negotiations that followed upon the franchise reform Bill, forced upon Gladstone by the Radicals of his party.   The Bill, first mooted in 1884, was intended to bring two million more voters on to the register by extending the franchise to householders in the county constituencies, and to Ireland on the same terms as England; at the same time, the plural-member system was to be abolished.   In principle, Salisbury opposed the Bill but, after it had easily passed through the Commons, was chary of killing it directly in view of popular agitation in which such sinister phrases as 'Peers against the People' had been heard.

Balfour himself had from the beginning been in favour of allowing the Bill to pass; and, speaking one night in Edinburgh on the same platform as Churchill, dissociated himself from Churchill's attack on the Bill.   But he did observe that certain difficulties were likely to arise. Obviously, it would occasion a redistribution of seats: 'A suffrage Bill, satisfactory in itself, might be eminently unsatisfactory if yoked to an unfair Redistribution Bill.'   It would also be useless if a fair redistribution Bill did not become law until after an election under the new franchise Bill had taken place.

What guarantees, therefore, would the Government offer on the matter of redistribution?   At first, Gladstone was up in arms, regarding such a question as a 'threat' and telling the Queen, who had remonstrated with him over his strong language, that Salisbury in the Lords and his 'nephew and private secretary' Balfour—though Balfour had ceased to be the latter in 1880—had threatened to kill the Bill 'in language alike violent and boastful'.

Gladstone was intransigent in refusing to couple franchise and redistribution; so in due course the franchise Bill was thrown out by the Lords. The Queen again intervened and sought to pacify the Liberals, some of whom began openly threatening to abolish the second chamber. Gradually attitudes softened, and it was Balfour himself who made the first tentative suggestion to Gladstone of consultation. The problem, he said, was whether a Conservative pledge to pass the Bill through the Lords '*is* or is *not* to precede an agreement with regards to the provisions of the Redistribution Bill'. If the pledge came first it would, would it not, he wondered, be possible 'for the House of Lords to be committed to the Reform Bill, and subsequently to find that no common understanding with regard to Redistribution could be arrived at by the two parties?'

Gladstone's reply, taken down by Hartington and passed to Balfour and thence to Salisbury, was: 'We should receive a request [for consultation] in a spirit of trust and, assuming that the intention was to come to an agreement, should not ask for the "adequate assurance" beforehand.'

The result was now a foregone conclusion, and after discussions between Gladstone, Hartington, Salisbury and Hicks-Beach, both Bills were passed into law. The upshot was interesting. The abolition of the plural-member system resulted in Ireland in Liberals and Conservatives being swept away (except in Ulster) and, since the Irish Party would always have a majority over the other two, Parnell heading a much larger contingent than the population warranted. In England, the measure stopped the Liberal party running Whigs and Radicals in double harness, one of each per contest, and hastened the decline of Whiggism. As Balfour himself remarked: 'Mr. Chamberlain' (who had first pressed the measure on the Government) 'will make Whiggism an impossibility and an anachronism.'

But the Reform Bill of 1884 had still another effect, one yet more revolutionary, for, as Ensor says, 'the historic *communitates* ceased to be, as such, the basis of the House of Commons. The individual for the first time became the unit and numerical equality ("one vote, one value") the master principle.' Democracy indeed, and democracy with a sting. Only a year before the Bill was passed, Joseph Chamberlain, President of the Board of Trade—the Radical business man who had been the uncrowned King of Birmingham before entering the Commons—had had this to say, and it was the first time a Minister of the Crown had so openly given a call to class-war: 'Lord Salisbury constitutes himself the spokesman of a class—of the class to which he himself belongs, who toil not neither do they spin; whose fortunes—as in his case—have originated by grants made in times gone by for the services which courtiers rendered kings, and have since grown and increased, while they have slept, by levying an increased share on all that other men have done by toil and labour to add to the general wealth and prosperity of the country.'

In view of such statements, and the anti-aristocratic feeling whipped up in the country at this time by the Radicals, it might be supposed that the Conservatives gave way over the Reform Bill because of fear of consequences.   For there is, indeed, a matter of principle involved. There was, and is (though it is no longer historically possible) a case against universal suffrage, which Salisbury himself hinted at when he deplored the 'placing of a great empire under the absolute control of the poorest classes'.   Yet both Balfour, and more reluctantly Salisbury, accepted the enlarging of the franchise and the destruction of 'the historic *communitates*'.   Were they then departing from Conservative principle?

Balfour himself, referring to this particular Bill many years later, defined Conservatism as being 'averse to changes—inclined to continuity'.   But he also added, 'I saw no point in resisting what was bound in logic to come.'   Certainly where changes were coming he preferred astute delay; it gave time for tempers to cool and for thought to take over from passion; it prevented those sweeping, doctrinaire changes whose appearance is so speciously beneficial and whose working out is so commonly maleficent.   Few revolutions achieve the aims on their banners; but all revolutions achieve something, and it is usually the unpleasantly unexpected.   As George Saintsbury wrote: 'We can't always help things going to the devil, but we can make them go slowly, and sometimes turn them out of the diabolic way.'   With regard to the extension of the franchise, Balfour believed it inevitable; the walls had been breached; the flood tide would come in.   Apart from that, he held that the English electorate is by nature prone to Conservatism; he believed that 'the more you extend responsibility to the *whole* community [including women] the more Tory the result is likely to be'.   In general, it may seem that he has been right.

5

TOWARDS THE CABINET

1884–1887

In 1882, Balfour suffered his severest personal loss since the death of
May Lyttelton. His favourite brother, Frank, who at 32 had
already achieved eminence in science, was killed while pursuing his
favourite sport of mountaineering. Along with a well-known guide,
Petrus, he had attempted to climb the as yet unclimbed Aiguille Blanche
de Penteret on the Italian side of Mont Blanc.

Gerald Balfour at once went out to Switzerland and, in a series of
letters to Arthur, described how it took 16 men three days to recover
the body. Between Frank and Arthur there had been a special bond
of affection and interest, partly due to the fact that Frank shone in a
sphere which had long had a deep attraction for Arthur: the sphere of
scientific research.

Balfour as usual made no public parade of his grief; but the depression caused by his brother's death hangs over many of his personal
letters during 1882 and 1883. Cecil Balfour, who had gone to
Australia under a cloud, had been killed in the previous year; and
Balfour had a profound sense of the contraction within his family circle.

By contrast, his circle of friends expanded, and friendships deepened.
Alfred Lyttelton—the younger brother of Spencer—became an intim-
ate, and through him Balfour met the two Tennant girls, Laura and
Margot, daughters of the millionaire Scottish landowner, Charles
Tennant. Both girls appeared in London Society about 1882, when
Margot, later Asquith's wife, was 18.

Laura Tennant was the most brilliant, exciting member of a family
of whom it was said, 'There was hardly a gift of God that was not possessed by one or other of them.' She was witty, unconventional,

passionate, yet *spirituelle*. People wrote of her as 'a living flame . . .
a vision that had come and gone in a moment's glory'. This vivid
creature made a deep impression on all she met, not least on Arthur
Balfour whom she admired.

Here again there were those who thought Balfour and she would
make an ideal match. But Balfour's younger brother, Gerald, was
deeply in love with her, and Arthur would not compete. Laura,
however, was not in love with Gerald—to his great pain and grief—and
ultimately she married Alfred Lyttelton, upon which Mary Gladstone
wrote to Balfour: 'I should have liked it to be you instead of him,
because I often feel she is the one person who might have come nearest
to what May was.' Though Mary Gladstone knew by now that
Balfour would never propose to her, her love was such that his interests
were never far from her thoughts.

The marriage of Laura and Alfred Lyttelton lasted, however, less
than a year, for in 1886, at the age of 23, she died in childbirth. The
shock of her death passed through the whole circle of friends and
beyond. Even 30 years later, when Alfred Lyttelton himself died,
tributes were paid to the 'little lady who enthralled and bewitched the
world'.

Laura's will contains these references to Balfour:

'I leave Arthur Balfour—Alfred's and my dear, deeply loved friend,
who has given me so many happy hours since I married, and whose
sympathy, understanding and companionship in the deepest sense of
the word has never been withheld from me when I sought it, which has
not been seldom this year of my blessed Vita Nuova—I leave him my
Johnson. He taught me to love that wisest of men—and I have much
to be grateful for in this. I leave him, too, my little ugly Shelley—
much read, but not in any way beautiful; if he marries I should like
him to give his wife my little red enamel harp—I shall never see her if
I die now, but I have so often created her in the Islands of my imagination—and as a Queen she has reigned there, so that I feel in the spirit
we are in some measure related by some mystic tie.' Laura Lyttelton,
too, had come under the Balfour spell.

Margot Tennant, Laura's younger sister, remained among Balfour's
intimates. She, too, was clearly more than half in love with him;
but she was not one to whom Balfour could open his heart. She was
always somewhat of an eccentric, with a penchant for creating embarrassing situations; and later on Balfour tried to keep her at arm's
length, which no doubt explains her puzzled reference to him in her
autobiography: 'He was difficult to understand because I was never
sure he needed me, and difficult to know intimately because of his
formidable detachment.'

She spoke, indeed, of his 'charm and wit . . . his social distinction', and already in these years, when he was still in his early thirties, Balfour was emerging from the ruck of rich, elegant Society men. People observed the cool grace into which his earlier slight superciliousness had agreeably developed; they noted his ability to listen as well as to talk; he already delighted the all-powerful matriarchs of Society.

Of course, by a natural consequence, the daughters of the matriarchs were, at first, less impressed. Lady Betty Montgomery wrote: 'Our mothers, in the 1880's considered him such a wonderfully clever young man that one was slightly oppressed by the sense of admiration due, when one saw him standing there, looking serenely at us through his glasses, so that some of us dubbed him mockingly "The Adored Gazelle", while another favourite tag of mimicry was to declare that his reply to any question was "Theoretically: YES. . . . Practically: NO." '

Yet Lady Montgomery, like almost everyone else, eventually succumbed to the combination of charm with intelligence—and something else: 'His great amusingness . . . not wit in which of course he abounded . . . nor "Humour". . . . No, what I mean is real "funniness", which made one laugh oh! so heartily, when it came on one so suddenly, from the serene voice and grave, gentle gaze.'

One of the many upon whom these charms proved, ultimately, irresistible was Mary Wyndham whom Balfour had met with her mother at Lord Leighton's studio. This, the third Mary in Balfour's life, was the daughter of Percy Wyndham of Clouds, Wiltshire, and quite early in their acquaintance, in 1883 when she was 22, she married Hugo Charteris, Viscount Elcho, heir to the Earl of Wemyss. Balfour's first extant letter to her accompanies his wedding present—the first of several hundred letters she kept and carefully preserved. Her reply breathes, among other matters, the very air of serious aristocratic Victorianism: 'I went with Lady Wemyss to Clerkenwell where she reads to a Mothers' Meeting. She introduced me as her daughter-in-law to be who was to marry her son next Thursday!'

Her marriage, far from interrupting their friendship, stimulated it. Indeed, 13 years later, when their *affaire* had long since run into deep waters, she repined to him: 'If only you had married me in '81!' But in 1884, within a year of her marriage, Balfour was a frequent visitor to the Elcho establishment at Stanway, Gloucestershire, and Laura Tennant (later Lyttelton) recorded:

'It's such fun here—we all quarrel about everything—we talk up to the top of our bent—we grow hyper-sentimental and blow blue bubbles into the stars and Hugo Lord Elcho comes down upon them with jeers and in pumps and smoking suit. We play games and the piano—we none of us open a book or write a letter—we scribble and scrawl and invent words and language and reasonless rhymes. Alfred (Lyttelton) left yesterday and the salt of our talk is gone. He was the salt, Hugo the pepper, Arthur the mustard, St. John Brodrick the bread, Lord Vernon the butter.'

From this one gets an impression of the sheer *douceur de vie* for these young people at that time in history: they were gay, they were bright, they were flirtatious, and they were a good deal less inhibited than the majority of their contemporaries.   On the other hand, they were not crude nor merely fleshly.   They did not belong to the hard-drinking, hard-riding set, nor to the Dilke or Randolph Churchill sections of high Society whose pleasures tended to be carnal and undiscriminating. They were nearer to the upper professional classes of our time, except that they added a grace that came mainly perhaps from their utter freedom from sordid cares and mundane preoccupations with money.

Moreover, as far as Balfour was concerned, this was not the whole of life.   There was politics, too: and beyond that, there were meetings with philosophers, articles to be written (Balfour wrote about Cobden in 1881), and music.   Always there was music.   Mary Gladstone in 1883 records a rehearsal of the Handel Society at No. 4 Carlton Gardens: 'The heat, noise and dust indescribable, the orchestra being also present, discordantly rehearsing their parts.'

The séances continued at Carlton Gardens; and in 1882 came the foundation of the Society for Psychical Research.   Balfour's brother-in-law, Henry Sidgwick, was instituted as first president, and his Cambridge tutor, F. W. H. Myers, became secretary.   In the next decade, Balfour himself was elected president, and through the Society he became friendly with Sir Oliver Lodge and Sir Arthur Conan Doyle. William James, Roden Noel and Nicholas Murray Butler were others he met in this way.

Other new acquaintances swam into Balfour's circle in these years: George Wyndham, Mary's brother, for instance—a vivid, brilliant personality who loved literature equally with horse-riding, a man full of ideas and enthusiasms.   Opposite in temperament to Balfour, he attracted him by his swift understanding and his zest for living.   Eventually, they were to be in a close political relationship which came to an unfortunate ending; but their friendship scarcely faltered, before Wyndham's early death.

Harry Cust—Henry John Cockayne Cust, son of Lord Brownlow— was another friend of Balfour at this time, though 13 years younger than him.   Cust was a bright young man, later an M.P. and editor of the *Pall Mall Gazette*.   He was also rather too fond of the opposite sex. We meet him first of all in Mary Gladstone's diary in 1884: 'Protracted and ardent flirtation with Harry Cust, a nice boy in the cynical stage.'

But it is to Mary Elcho, *née* Wyndham, to whom one returns if one seeks the dominating female figure in Balfour's life during these years. Not that she can be said to have dominated a man who, after the experience of May Lyttelton, carefully spread his emotional interests over a wide field.   Certainly, however, she gave his private life a sort of centre.   Mary Elcho had neither the startling impact upon her contemporaries, nor the intellectual bravura, of May Lyttelton or Laura Tennant.   On the other hand, she did not nourish a hopeless love with the painful assiduity of Mary Gladstone.

She was not a classical beauty; and she was a tolerant, even gullible person, full of not always well-directed energies.   She had leanings towards the arts and politics, though without great sensibility or knowledge.   As a married woman, she became immensely hospitable— and fabulously unpunctual.   She was, as her daughter, later Lady Cynthia Asquith, wrote, a 'good conductor of conversation', possessing 'easily ignited enthusiasm' combined with 'open-mindedness'.   She was natural, spontaneous and tended a general conversation, 'like one zealously tending a newly-lit fire'.   Her vagueness was proverbial but engaging; she had a lively curiosity and a genuine unforced sympathy.

Her husband, Lord Elcho, was her opposite in almost all things. He hated house-parties and would withdraw, sometimes for days together, into the blackest silences, though his daughter, Lady Cynthia, loyally records that he had a sense of humour which sometimes burst out like a flash of lightning from a storm cloud.   She remarks that he mellowed with the years, perhaps because he developed deafness. This may have been just as well, for by 1885 tongues were already wagging, at any rate within the family circles.

There is, for example, a letter from Laura Lyttelton dated only '9 Oct', but which, since she died in 1886, can scarcely be later than 1885.   It is addressed to Frances Balfour, one of her close friends. Lady Frances Balfour, whose father was the eighth Duke of Argyll, had married Balfour's youngest brother, Eustace, in 1879 and, as Balfour's niece and biographer, Mrs. Blanche Dugdale says, had 'thrown herself with zest into the life of her new family'.   She came from one of the great Whig families, was deeply interested in political matters and could draw out Balfour when his own relations, who saw political affairs much from his own point of view, could not.   Laura Lyttelton is replying to a letter from Frances, who had urged her to some course of action (Frances's letter is not extant) with regard to Mary Elcho.   Laura writes:

'I never allow for a minute when I am with Mary that she is in love with A, for nothing so firmly convinces a wavering mind. . . .   Were I to say to M. "You are in love" she would believe me and poking the fire is productive of flame—and at present I think the conflagration is chiefly smoke.   Secondly I do constantly warn Mary of her friendship —not on the grounds of its being a too engrossing one, but on the grounds of the eye-sight of the world which is always foresighted and sees things in embryo. . . . I think that Arthur should be warned. Whatever he says, and of course, he will say a great deal and all to the point though not to the base, will not convince me that he is behaving well.

'I am sure M. is good and I know her very well, but I am sure she deceives herself and the truth is not in her about her own affections. I don't think M. is subtle enough to think out for herself what you say about the desire everyone has to get at Arthur *per se*. She likes him— he fascinates her—her attitude is that of looking up in wonder—not of standing on the same ground with him and piercing him with her understanding. Her weapons are weaponless worship. I don't mean in its full sense of adoration. . . . She reverences him and thinks him good and wonders continually why he likes her—and is, above all, grateful always. Then she feels she *must* not disappoint him—she is at the top of her bent with him: she tries to look at her best with him. She listens to him and he is not strong enough to withstand the easy delights of constantly pleasing and never annoying, jarring or disappointing her.

'If he did what I should say was un-Arthurian, *she* would say since *he* did it that it *was* Arthurian and her affection for Hugo is strangely mixed up with her affection for the man she knows can, will and does help Hugo more than anyone else does. Were I or you in her position we would cancel our engrossment. As it is she is not able to do so and is the most "*à jour*" woman I ever met.

'What Arthur should do is very easy to see. He should deny himself the gratification of the luxury—but few men make extra commandments for themselves, feeling I presume that their duty is done if they obey the Decalogue. I hope I am not hard on Arthur. I think with you that from the generosity of his nature, of his fine nature, it will be heeded.'

We see in this letter through the eyes of a woman, herself not totally unsusceptible to Balfour's charm, the immense personal prestige—or prestige of personality—he already had in his own intimate circle, combined already with doubts as to his complete sincerity: is he in love with Mary Elcho? Not at any rate in the way she is with him. Is she not just a luxury he is allowing himself (Margot referred to him 'as a self-indulgent man of simple tastes')—a luxury he ought to deny himself, but probably won't? Nor did he.

Of his own views on this matter we have somewhat naturally no direct record—he kept no diary. But that he must have seen the anomaly of his position cannot be doubted. He was, as Laura Lyttelton remarks, 'helping' the husband—mainly in politics, for Lord Elcho was at this time an M.P.—and at the same time helping himself to Elcho's wife, though we cannot doubt from the tone of her letters that it was she who pressed the liaison.

Of course, it was easy *not* to see matters in such a crude way: house-party life, with its formalities, the glitter of its personalities, the discussions of literature and politics, its croquet parties was not intimate in the way that living in a flat is intimate. Large houses allow privacies scarcely known today; the grinding of one personality upon another, produced by close, inescapable propinquity, did not often occur, and when individuals met, at lunch or supper, they could enjoy each other without being already bored with each other by constant meetings during the day. Indeed, at house-parties, particularly at Stanway, Balfour had sufficient intervals of privacy to write part of his philosophical work, prepare his political speeches and write to his friends.

II

At the beginning of 1885, the destruction of the Liberal Government—more from internal dissension than external pressure—seemed imminent. As Salisbury wrote to Balfour in 1881: 'It is the old story —Gladstone is master of the country but cannot manage the House of Commons. His greatest quality is eloquent indistinctness of expression.'

Even the latter seemed unlikely to save him early in 1885: not only was there mounting disaster in Ireland, the rising power of Germany and, shortly, the Gordon fiasco in the Sudan, but there was the threatening figure of Gladstone's own President of the Board of Trade, Joseph Chamberlain. This Birmingham demagogue, who was the mouthpiece of the Radical wing of the Liberals, was already disaffected from the Liberal leader, mainly but not entirely on Irish policy.

Yet, ripe as this fruit was for shaking from the tree, the Conservative leadership hesitated, and we find Balfour writing not with ill-suppressed jubilation, as might have been expected, but morosely to Lady Elcho in March, 1885: 'Politics show a uniform shade of gloom whose depth I have never seen equalled. Even the qualified satisfaction which an Opposition may be expected to feel in the misfortunes brought on the country by the incompetences of the Government is denied to us—for of all the things we fear, the one we fear most is having to take office. . . .'

One reason for this strange lack of appetite for office was a practical one: if the Liberals were turned out before the new constituencies were brought into being as a result of the franchise reform and redistribution, it would probably mean that the Conservatives would be in office only for a few months before a new election had to take place. By that time, the electorate might well have forgotten the reasons for the Liberal fall and, being in part a new electorate enfranchised by the Liberals, might return them to power.

But there were deeper causes for Conservative hesitancy about taking power, and the most important of them—as far as Balfour and his uncle were concerned—centred upon the figure of Lord Randolph Churchill. As we saw, the Conservative leadership was left vacant upon Beaconsfield's death—or rather put in the hands of a duumvirate of Salisbury in the Lords, Northcote in the Commons. Salisbury was content to leave it at that and remained loyal, at least in public, to Northcote, but his nephew had left him in no doubt of the general opinion of the younger end of the party about their Leader in the Commons.

Lord Randolph, however, was far from ready to let the matter remain in abeyance. He was virulently anti-Northcote, first, apparently, on Salisbury's behalf, and then frankly on his own. In this latter, he was greatly helped by his growing popularity in the country where some younger voters felt that, with his 'democratic' ideas, he was in the true tradition of Disraeli.

Meanwhile, as late as 1884, there were some older Conservatives who still distrusted Salisbury on account of his early unorthodoxy and stubbornness; worse still, he was thought to be an intellectual. Lady Frances Balfour notes in her diary for April 7, 1884: 'Salisbury has not got the confidence of the Conservatives at large, and outside Parliament they hang back from his lead.'

Churchill, on the other hand, had control of the newly-founded Primrose League, and had eyes on the National Union of Conservative Associations. Balfour frequently warned his uncle whither these moves were tending. At the same time, Northcote could by no means be ignored, and it seemed clear to Balfour that both the public support for Churchill and considerations of political tactics alike made it necessary to keep Churchill on the Salisbury side, at least until Northcote was rendered politically impotent.

Thus, when on April 2, 1883, Churchill wrote a letter to *The Times* newspaper attacking Northcote, Balfour's first reaction was one of fury. Lady Frances Balfour recorded: 'We all went to Carlton Gardens and found Arthur there, furious with Randolph Churchill for his attack on Northcote's leadership in his letter to *The Times*. I have never seen him so cross and agitated before.' Why, since he too was anti-Northcote, was he so angry? The reason was that he was already a better judge of political cause-and-effect than Churchill. He knew that such a brash letter would arouse sympathy for the old Conservative leader; and so it did, for when Northcote rose to answer a question in the Commons next day, he was greeted by an ovation, while successive speakers castigated Churchill.

When, a week later from the midst of his unpopularity, Churchill wrote an even more brash letter to *The Times*, Balfour was not angry at all. For this letter, although on the surface, pro-Salisbury, was in fact no less than a claim that Churchill himself was in the running for the Leadership of the Conservative party. Balfour saw that this—and its more polished successor in the May issue of the *Fortnightly Review*—was so blatant a piece of ambitious pleading that it could do no harm to Salisbury, but would inevitably rebound on Churchill himself, as far as solid Conservative opinion was concerned. His statement about 'Tory Democracy', and its effect one day when put into action 'by the man, whoever he be, upon whom the mantle of Elijah has descended', was found more alarming still, except in the Midlands and the north where 'Radical' Conservatism had its supporters.

But Churchill did not allow the grass to grow beneath his feet. Not only did he sweep into a round of speeches ridiculing Gladstone, but he also sought to use the National Union of Conservative Associations—an advisory body representing the constituencies—to further his ambition. He was elected chairman of it in October, 1883, and then demanded a share for the National Union in the executive power wielded by the Central Committee. Nevertheless, Balfour's view in January, 1884, was that it would be better to let matters ride: 'We should avoid, as far as possible, all "rows" until R. puts himself entirely and flagrantly in the wrong by some act of party disloyalty which everyone can understand, and nobody can deny.'

Balfour was learning the arts of politics, and learning fast. This was wise counsel, for in the end Churchill could be relied upon to hoist himself with his own petard; and Salisbury was by no means alone in thinking, as he put it: 'Randolph and the Mahdi have occupied my thoughts about equally. The Mahdi pretends to be half mad but is very sane in reality; Randolph occupies exactly the converse position.'

By May, 1884, it was borne in upon the public at large that Churchill was challenging not only Northcote but Salisbury too, and when the annual conference of the National Union delegates met at Sheffield on July 23, 1884, the battle was on. On that very same day Churchill to all appearances became the winner. The delegates voted in some 22 out of the 30 candidates he had proposed as well, of course, as himself. Some notes sent by Salisbury to Balfour immediately afterwards reflect his view that 'Sheffield was a mistake essentially'. He continues:

'I do not, as at present advised, believe in any intention to submit; or to yield any essential matter; but people are very much excited about the political conflict now approaching its crisis, and are very impatient of any thing that interferes with their chances.' (The crisis had arisen over the Sudan campaign; it was widely thought the Liberals would dissolve.) 'A temporary retreat on account of the peculiar circumstances of the moment would be wisest,' Salisbury thought, adding: 'It need involve no admission of defeat; nor compromise any future action.'

HJB

What actually happened was surprising for, a few days after his 'victory', Churchill agreed to a reconciliation with Salisbury. Why he should have done this has never been clear, and none of the reasons adduced is entirely satisfactory, particularly since the National Union, for which he had been so enthusiastic, was as a result, in his son's words, 'laid peacefully to rest in an obscurity' seldom broken since.

All the same, the Churchill-Salisbury 'union' did not mean peace. It meant, indeed, the end of Northcote's hopes of the Leadership and a future premiership; it meant that when the time came the Conservative party moved into battle with its ranks reasonably closed; but it also meant that a struggle had merely been postponed not simply between 'Tory Democracy' and genuine Conservatism, but between the stable and the unstable.

Balfour had played a considerable part in bringing the armistice about, and there are many letters during this period from his uncle to him containing such expressions as 'I rely on you to see that a definite plan' be made on this or that manœuvre. Balfour, however, was perfectly aware that Churchill was always capable of renouncing an agreement, that he commanded great support in parts of the country, and that the ultimate decision on the Leadership had yet to be taken. He also, however, knew that his uncle's tactful handling of the affair had earned him golden opinions among those Conservatives who understood the value of party unity; and that his uncle understood, and was grateful for, the help and advice Balfour had given.

His gloom, therefore, in March, 1885, mentioned in his letter to Lady Wemyss, was perhaps partly due to his reluctance to put matters to the test. Yet, so shaky was the Government, that the test could obviously not long be delayed. Had Balfour come to some sort of personal decision about this when once more, after the lengthy break in relations, he invited Churchill and the rest of 'The Fourth Party', along with Hicks-Beach and Cecil Raikes, to lunch at Carlton Gardens on June 8, 1885?

At any rate, it was as a result, though unexpected, of that lunch that the same night the Liberal Government was defeated and Gladstone resigned. For at Carlton Gardens, 'The Fourth Party' team decided that an Amendment to the Budget should be drafted and moved by Hicks-Beach. He did so, rather feebly, in a House made the more desultory by the summer heat. The Liberals suddenly decided to make the question one of 'life or death'; and when a division was taken Hicks-Beach's Amendment was carried by 264 votes against 252.

Pandemonium broke loose and Churchill leaped on to his seat waving his handkerchief in triumph. The victory was partly due to Parnell's taking 39 of his supporters into the Conservative lobby, partly to 76 Liberals abstaining from the vote. And beneath it all was the despondency of Government supporters who knew of the dissensions in the Cabinet between Chamberlain, Dilke and Gladstone, and who equally knew that two policies for the future of Ireland were in the balance—and liked neither.

'In this way', records J. L. Garvin in his *Life of Joseph Chamberlain*, 'disappeared at last the great and ill-starred Ministry of all the Talents and all the discords. It was the end, after somewhat more than fifty years, of the epoch of politics opened in 1832.' It was at the same time the beginning of Conservative ascendancy which was to continue almost unbroken for 20 years. But it is unlikely that a single member of the Conservative party or its leaders foresaw that at the moment of 'triumph'.

Who, first of all, would be called to form the new Government? At a meeting of Conservative leaders, the majority decided that they would take office if pressed by the Queen, but would prefer not to; Northcote was for accepting in any case. On June 10, the die was cast quietly and unobtrusively when General Sir H. F. Ponsonby, the Queen's secretary, approached Salisbury privately to inquire whether he would be prepared to form a government. The formation was still in doubt—but it *was* Salisbury who had been approached, not Northcote or Churchill. Numerous manœuvres were still to take place, but the Queen's choice was ultimately accepted, 'not only with unanimity but as a matter of course'.

In such casual ways are new eras heralded. But the struggle for power was by no means finished. Churchill clearly would have to be accommodated with reasonably senior office in the Cabinet; but at first he bluntly refused to serve at all if Northcote remained in the Commons as Leader of the House.

Northcote, for his part, though deeply wounded, agreed to go to the Lords as Colonial Secretary, and then refused when he heard that Churchill was to be his senior at the India Office. Balfour, acting as his uncle's emissary, persuaded Churchill out of his intransigence. He then found himself acting as emollient to Northcote's sudden determination not to participate in the Cabinet at all. Salisbury now wrote to Northcote (though the draft is in Balfour's handwriting): 'If you think the Colonial Office irksome—take the Presidency of the Council; or let us try some other combination. But do not leave us altogether. You place me in the wretched dilemma of either abandoning the Queen in the situation created for her by our action in the Commons; or of seeming to have abandoned or betrayed you—an offence of which my conscience is quite clear.'

In due course, Northcote went to the Lords, as the Earl of Iddesleigh, and became First Lord of the Treasury. The new Leader of the House and Chancellor of the Exchequer was Sir Michael Hicks-Beach. So

Churchill had got his way, though, as his latest biographer says, his actions were 'foolish and ill-considered', and had not further recommended him to Salisbury or to Balfour as evidence either of his balance or his decency.   Their attitude to him is well expressed in a letter Balfour wrote to his uncle during the crisis of cabinet-making:

'Of course the line I took tonight with R.C. and the line I suggested for tomorrow are based on the supposition that it was better to have him with us than against us.   This is, I think, certainly true if we consider only the period up to the end of the next General Election; if we look beyond it, it may well seem doubtful.'

The old Parliament had six months still to run before there could be any hope of dislodging Churchill; and even then the chances did not seem bright.

As for Balfour himself, his uncle at first proposed to make him his Under-Secretary at the Foreign Office, a post he held as well as the Premiership.   Eventually, however, Balfour's services were better recognised by his appointment to the Presidency of the Local Government Board.   The work—now carried out by a number of Ministries —was however choc-a-bloc with technical data and highly involved legislation; Balfour could not be expected to master all this in the six month's lease of life of what afterwards came to be known as the 'Caretaker' Government.   Naturally his record as President—a position without a Cabinet seat—was not inspiring.   Moreover he was still too fond of trailing his coat in the House and as yet too inept in pulling it from under his opponents' feet when they stamped on it.   When for instance he piloted a Medical Relief Disqualification Bill through the House, he managed to arouse Chamberlain—who scored heavily off him.

Churchill meanwhile was soon earning golden opinions in the India Office by his capacity for hard work, though he annoyed Salisbury greatly by being difficult over Royal wishes in connection with the control of the Indian Army.   For his more erratic actions, his health now began to be suggested as being responsible.   But when he annexed Upper Burma, more or less against Salisbury's wishes, he gained great favour with the imperialist voters of Victorian England, even if not with his Cabinet colleagues.

Balfour watched his progress with a certain natural jealousy.   He realised that, should Churchill's national popularity grow unchecked, Salisbury *en dépit de lui-même* might be forced into a closer alliance with him and one that might become permanent.   As it happened, the intimacy of Balfour's own relations with Salisbury suffered at this period, partly because of his uncle's immersion in foreign affairs, partly because he seems to have hinted to his nephew through Cranborne, his heir and Balfour's cousin, that he was not entirely satisfied with his nephew's parliamentary performances.

It is, indeed, about this time that according to Asquith, Balfour told John Morley, now a leading Liberal M.P. and shortly to become Chief Secretary for Ireland, that 'he had quite come to the conclusion that he had no aptitude for politics and that as a public man he was a failure'. In these days Balfour was easily discouraged; perhaps now that 'The Fourth Party' had finally disbanded—all of them except Wolff had posts in the Government—he felt himself, as it were, marooned.

At any rate throughout the 'Caretakers' administration he was ill at ease and uncertain; and when later on advancement was offered to him he even doubted whether it was seriously meant. But he did not cease plying his uncle with the latest gossip from the Commons, the trends visible in the Lobby and in the dining-rooms of the politically-conscious upper classes.

As for the new Prime Minister his problem, having come into power and managed to form a government, was how long could he expect to stay there? A General Election would have to take place in November: could he win it? Not, it seemed, without the support of the Irish whose goodwill (stimulated and cultivated by Churchill) had just brought him in. Salisbury therefore hastened to redeem his promise that the policy of coercion should cease, and he also brought into being, or partly into being, Parnell's plan for the peasants to acquire land by means of a State-aided purchase scheme; this was known as Lord Ashbourne's Act, his Lordship then being Chancellor of Ireland.

At this point, other ideas about Ireland began to be discussed behind the closed official doors of the Cabinet room. The new Viceroy of Ireland was Lord Carnarvon. He had been successful in passing the act federating Canada, and had sought federation for Ireland. He believed in the efficacy of federation in colonial affairs. He now suggested that it might serve well in Ireland; indeed he proposed that Ireland should be given a form of 'Home Rule' similar to that of the Canadian provinces, but that Ulster should not be included.

This may sound revolutionary for we have come to connect Conservatism in the nineteenth century with strongly anti-Home Rule policies; but at this time policies were not yet cut-and-dried. Almost anything seemed worth trying if there was any chance at all of pacifying that country. So Salisbury, far from rejecting Carnarvon's ideas out of hand, began to consider them seriously. But, because later Salisbury did not wish it to be thought that he had even toyed with such ideas, the episodes now to be related were long wrapped in mystery; they are clarified considerably in the Balfour papers.

Carnarvon had a secret discussion with Parnell on August 3, 1885, on the possibilities of a federated form of Home Rule for Ireland to be brought in by the Conservatives. This interview was afterwards stated to have been unauthorised by the Cabinet. Balfour certainly thought it was; even some eight years afterwards in a speech on July 1, 1893, he claimed that the interview was on Carnarvon's initiative alone and that he had acted without the knowledge of a single one of his colleagues. But at that time Balfour was still unaware of what had occurred.

There is, however, now in the Balfour papers—it is not known when it came there—a document signed 'S' in which Salisbury categorically states that Carnarvon did speak to him beforehand about the meeting with Parnell, that he (Salisbury) did not forbid it, though warning him to be careful of misrepresentation, and that no third party was present. The document in Salisbury's regular, flowing handwriting continues: 'In a letter written shortly before his death, he [Carnarvon] told me that the matter had been communicated to *three* of his colleagues. One no doubt was Ashbourne, who the other two were I do not know— probably R. Churchill and Beach' (then Chief Secretary for Ireland).

This episode is not merely of historical interest. For it was rumours of the meeting referred to, with its implicit suggestion that Salisbury was favourable to the idea of some sort of Home Rule for Ireland, that now led to overtures from Gladstone to Salisbury. It appears that Gladstone believed he could carry through the Home Rule policies, to which he had recently converted himself, only by means of a Coalition. An extra advantage of that would be to put Chamberlain in balk; it would, of course, also split the Conservative Party from top to bottom. Gladstone was presumably counting on raising the same fervour in Salisbury's heart as now raged in his own.

As yet, of course, neither the public nor his party knew of his change of heart; but Gladstone had come to believe, quite genuinely, that Home Rule and the creation of a sovereign Irish Parliament was for the good of the commonweal, and considered that some non-party arrangement, which had worked so well with the redistribution question, might be the best solution.

At least two overtures were made. One was through Canon Malcolm MacColl, who had acted as go-between in the redistribution affair. MacColl saw Salisbury and reported to Gladstone that Salisbury was 'prepared to go as far possibly as yourself on the question of Home Rule; but he seemed hopeless as to the prospects of carrying his Party with him'. MacColl later wrote to Salisbury saying that Gladstone thought it best for Salisbury to carry through the change with Gladstone's support as Leader of the Opposition. Here, of course, was the rub, and Gladstone can scarcely have expected the canny Salisbury to agree to what would be the dissolution of his party.

The second overture was made through Balfour himself. In December, 1885, while Balfour was at the Duke of Westminster's house-party at Eaton Hall, Gladstone, 'dropped in' (Hawarden was not very far away) and talked to him informally about his proposition, namely that the two parties should act together over Home Rule. He even suggested, Balfour later wrote, that there was a power behind Parnell which, 'if not shortly satisfied by some substantial concession to the demands of the Irish Parliamentary Party would take the matter into its own hands, and resort to violence and outrage in England for the purpose of enforcing his demands'.

Balfour goes on: ' "In other words", I said to Mr. Gladstone, "we are to be blown up and stabbed if we do not grant Home Rule by the end of next session." "I understand", answered Mr. Gladstone, "that the time is shorter than that." '

Gladstone, as we have seen, had reason for supposing that Salisbury would be sympathetic to the idea. Yet when Balfour put it to him, Salisbury decisively rejected it. Why had Salisbury's opinion hardened?

Many years later Balfour gave an explanation, but it is only partly correct. On October 9, 1905, Balfour wrote to Winston Churchill asking that he should suppress a passage in the life of his father dealing with 1885. Balfour continued:

'Mr. Gladstone at the end of 1885 was under the fixed impression that Lord Salisbury agreed with Lord Carnarvon and would have been glad to have carried through the measure for Ireland, upon more or less Gladstonian lines with Mr. Gladstone's assistance in the House of Commons. Lord Salisbury was to play the part of Peel in 1846, while Mr. Gladstone occupied the more agreeable rôle of Lord John Russell. Holding these views as to Lord Salisbury's opinions, Mr. Gladstone was naturally disappointed at the result of the mission to my uncle, with which, when we met at Eaton Hall, he entrusted me. He consequently put down the failure of that mission to the ambassador, and not to the policy. But in truth Lord Salisbury profoundly disagreed with Mr. Gladstone's views, and never for an instant entertained the thought of co-operating with him. I forget in what form I conveyed this fact to Mr. Gladstone, but as the subject did not permit in Lord Salisbury's opinion of any argument, I have no doubt the form was concise, or, as Mr. Gladstone describes it, "curt".'

It was, however, untrue that Salisbury had never 'for a moment' entertained the idea of a Home Rule policy. It was, certainly, referred to as 'autonomy' or a 'New Departure', but it amounted to much the same thing, and was referred to in Cabinet several times in the autumn of 1885, as becomes clear from Harding's *Life of Carnarvon* and Viscount Gladstone's *After Thirty Years*. It was also untrue that Salisbury had never thought of co-operating. What *was* true was that Salisbury was totally disinclined for 'the rôle of Peel', which meant splitting his Party. This was a fixed, irreversible standpoint from which he had never budged, and which had guided him always, not least in his actions over Northcote and Churchill earlier.   Yet even as late as December, 1885, Gladstone still cherished hopes of getting Salisbury to agree to a joint policy, and he insisted to his colleagues that the Conservative Government should be helped and encouraged to act, 'as far as we legitimately can'.

But by this time Salisbury had begun to understand that far from being a negative situation in the political game, there might be a positive advantage to be gained.   If he held firm it was not the Conservatives who would be split but rather the Liberals; it had become obvious to him that Gladstone on this matter of Ireland had been seized with a crusader's enthusiasm; and enthusiasm makes even the slipperiest politician reckless.   Balfour put this much more favourable picture to Salisbury in a letter on December 23, 1885; he referred to various sources from which he gathered that Gladstone would get 'no support from any *important* member of his late Cabinet except Spencer' (former Irish Viceroy), '. . . Hartington has publicly declared himself . . . Goschen is also firm . . . Morley is a Home-Ruler by conviction; Chamberlain and Dilke are anti-Parnellite, partly by calculation and partly by temper.   Without Hartington, Goschen, Chamberlain or Dilke, it is manifest that even the GOM cannot frame a Government— and I understand that the calculation is that we shall be forced to go on whether we like it or not.'

As far as immediate matters were concerned, however, Balfour thought 'we *must* get out of office, and at once'.   They might probably have to return because there was simply no one to take their places; in that case 'it is all important that that fact should be driven well into the minds of the public'.

This letter followed the General Election of November, 1885, which, while it kept Salisbury in power, made him no longer a free man, for in that election 86 more Liberals than Conservatives were returned. But Parnell's party had swept Ireland and his members comprised exactly 86.   Thus Salisbury was in power by favour of Parnell—a situation which realised Parnell's aim with fantastic precision.

This Salisbury could neither tolerate nor even see in it any future advantage.   Therefore, a few days after the Queen's Speech, notice was given of an Irish coercion Bill.   This established the Conservatives in their permanent rôle of defenders of the Union against moonlighters and cattle-maimers; it also automatically threw Gladstone into the posture of defender, since his Home Rule policy was now public knowledge—partly owing to his son's indiscretion the previous month.

The Conservative Cabinet, Balfour tells us, would like to have fallen in defence of the Union,—Churchill had just coined the phrase 'Ulster will fight and Ulster will be right'—but Gladstone's tactical skill did not even now desert him, and defeat when it came was on an English agrarian amendment to the Queen's speech proposed, significantly enough, by Chamberlain's supporter Jesse Collings. In the division, on January 26, 1886, 18 Liberals led by Lord Hartington voted with the Government, and 76 other Liberals abstained. Salisbury was, nevertheless, defeated by 79, and resigned next day.

Gladstone formed his third Cabinet on February 3, 1886, without any member of the Whig aristocracy, and with Chamberlain, somewhat hesitantly, as President of the Local Government Board. It was now that Chamberlain took not only the centre of the stage but a leading part in the wings, too. While it was possible for Gladstone to ignore the estrangement of the Hartington Whigs, he could not disregard the hundreds of thousands of Radicals who would follow Chamberlain at the polls, and Chamberlain—like his colleague Dilke who was, however, now out of politics because of the famous divorce case—was utterly opposed to giving Ireland a Parliament, however near his own plan for 'devolution' might ultimately have approached that.

But Gladstone *did* disregard Chamberlain, so deep was his feeling for Home Rule, and it was this that brought defeat to his Government a few months later on June 8, 1886. Three months earlier Chamberlain had resigned from the Cabinet as soon as Gladstone brought the Home Rule Bill before it.

Almost before this had occurred, a new relationship had been cemented between the Radicals and the Conservatives. On the face of it, such a relationship was most unlikely. Chamberlain, the Radical leader, the self-made man who had retired after 20 years' work making screws to devote himself to politics, was almost a Republican. As Mayor of Birmingham it had been doubted whether he would condescend to drive in the carriage which received the Prince of Wales on a visit. He had attacked the Church, aristocracy, House of Lords and the vested interests. Little more than six months before his rapprochement with the Conservatives began, he delivered a series of election speeches demanding social and agrarian reforms which horrified the Queen and caused Lord Iddesleigh to call him a new Jack Cade, and Balfour to describe him as 'the most vindictive of men' in a letter to Salisbury dated December 23, 1885.

Yet in the early months of 1886, at private dinner parties with Balfour and other Conservatives, Chamberlain was planning the change of sides which was to earn him the undying hatred of the Irish, and the name of Judas the Turncoat from the Liberals. It was, however this change of sides that was to keep the Conservatives in power for 20 years.

Balfour recorded some of these discussions. They turned largely on tactics. Chamberlain would point out that there must be no appearance of Tory-Radical manœuvre ('the mere suspicion that a Radical is going to get Tory support would of itself ensure his defeat'); yet 'the Tories are in a minority in the country and it is only by the help of the Radicals that anything material can be done'.

Then he would make a straightforward appeal: 'Now Balfour', he said at one dinner party, 'let us make a joint attack on the Whigs. The Tory policy I understand with regard to Ireland, and the Radical policy I understand. The Tories go in for coercion. I believe that if that could be carried out consistently for five years it would succeed. The Radicals go in for very large measures of reform and local government. They are ready to allow the Irish to manage and mismanage their affairs as they please, up to a certain point, with a determination of coming down and crushing them as soon as they go beyond that point—just as the North left the South alone year after year, but finally imposed their will by force. But the Whigs are too frightened of the Radicals to support the Tories, and too frightened of the Tories to support the Radicals. It is no particular secret now that what destroyed the last Liberal Government was not the Budget, but the proposal of a National Council for Ireland. The Whigs in the Cabinet would not accept it, and now we see them in the shape of Spencer and Granville, going in for Home Rule!'

Chamberlain was right. The Tories could not win an election on their own. The idea of winning it with Irish support was distasteful. The Radicals and the Whig dissentionists were their only hope. Balfour thought that Chamberlain would certainly be 'a very different kind of ally from the lukewarm and slippery Whig [Hartington] whom it is so difficult to differ from and so impossible to act with'. But Balfour could not conjecture what the impending reconstruction of parties as a result of the Radical move would involve. In politics, he said, quoting Chamberlain, 'There is no use looking beyond the next fortnight.'

Salisbury took what the gods had unexpectedly deposited in his lap. Gladstone was defeated in June, 1886, and resigned. Salisbury took office and dissolved; in the general election campaign that followed Salisbury pledged his word that 'so far as his influence and that of a Central organisation could prevail, no man who rose against (the Irish Home Rule Bill, 1886) should be opposed by a Conservative at the ensuing election.'

His intention was, of course, to protect Chamberlain and the Whig Liberals who had broken with their Party on this issue. There were obviously difficulties in implementing this pledge; but, on July 20, 1886, at the General Election, 316 Conservatives were returned against 191 Liberals. The Liberals were supported by 85 Irish Nationalists. On the other hand, 78 Liberals supported the Conservatives. Led by

Chamberlain and Hartington, these 'Liberal Unionists' supported the Tory Government steadily.

But not until 1892 did they become officially part of the Conservative Unionist Party; and this, for Balfour, had the advantage of not bringing the powerful Chamberlain into the highest councils of Conservatism until Balfour himself was established beyond question. It gave him the chance to further consolidate his position; he took the chance with alacrity and exploited it with skill and force.

III

At this election of 1886, Balfour was again returned for East Manchester—a constituency once reputed (mainly by Liberals) to be in the gift of the liquor trade. When Cabinet-making began, Salisbury promptly offered to serve under Hartington, leader of the dissident Whigs, in a Liberal-Unionist coalition. But Hartington refused; he pointed out that by including himself and his group in the new Government, Chamberlain and his Radicals would be left so isolated that they might be forced back into the Gladstonian fold. So Salisbury was reluctantly compelled to form a purely Conservative administration.

But though Chamberlain was no rival to Balfour, Churchill undoubtedly was. He was at the height of his power and popularity, having been a tower of strength in the electioneering against Home Rule. Compared with that, Balfour's own part had been modest, little more than a liaison officer to Salisbury, for his speech-making lacked the punch and bravura of Churchill's. What could he expect in the way of office? He put his chances low and, typically, he lost heart and began to shrink back so that if nothing came his way he would not at least be left looking high, dry and mortified.

Even during the manœuvring period before Gladstone's fall, Balfour had felt the weakness of his position. There is a certain air of forlornness, of doubt of his status in his letter to his uncle on March 24, 1886: 'I know', he wrote, 'that Jim [Cranborne] writes to you every day and Randolph occasionally.' Assured as Balfour was in Society, once politics had gripped him his calmness was easily assailed.

After the election his sense of failure began to obsess him. On the day Salisbury kissed hands, July 25, Balfour had his 38th birthday; he spent it alone in a hotel room at Great Malvern. His correspondence scarcely mentions politics at all. He writes about golf, walking by moonlight, writing an article on Handel, and about the 'Balfour Lectures' he had recently instituted at Glasgow University. It is as though he were purposely avoiding his true thoughts; and perhaps saying, in effect, that whatever happens to his political career, these interests at least will remain to him.

However many letters he writes not one will be to his uncle now; that would look too much like place-hunting.   But he does write to his sister-in-law, Lady Frances Balfour:

'I hear that Uncle R. goes to Osborne to-morrow.   I want you, *if you can*, to find out whether you think it desirable, having regard to all the circumstances, that I should come back to London at once.   *Unless I can be of use* I do not wish to be mixed up in the formation of the new Government.   One man has already written to me asking me to get him a place!   Ludicrous as it is, seeing that I do not know that *my* services will be required in the new Administration; still no doubt his example will be followed.'

Balfour then adds: 'I feel no natural vocation for being a Great Man's Great Man, still less for being thought to be so; therefore there are obvious motives for not leaving these solitudes; but, of course, they would not for a moment stand in the way of my coming up if I thought I could be of the slightest use to Uncle R.'

Shortly after writing this letter, an offer arrived from Salisbury of the Secretaryship for Scotland, a new post first instituted only in the previous year.   But even then, Balfour's virulent self-doubt persisted, and he wrote to his cousin Cranborne a letter, which has disappeared, asking whether Salisbury really wanted him to accept, or was it a sop thrown to a nephew?

Cranborne's reply was to the effect that he had been chosen for the post because 'there is every reason to suppose that you will be a good appointment'.   There was another reason: 'It was evidently necessary that you should have an office with which you would be readily put into the Cabinet, where Papa, I know, considers you would be most useful to himself and the country.   Papa knows quite well what he is doing—there is, I feel sure, no misapprehension.'

Papa knew, indeed, that he would need near him all the friends he could muster.   Cross, now Viscount Cross, had replaced Churchill at the India Office; Hicks-Beach, declining to lead the House again in view of Churchill's superiority in 'eloquence, ability and influence', had become Irish Chief Secretary; and Churchill himself was installed, triumphant, as Chancellor of the Exchequer.

Balfour was still cast for the part of 'Great Man's Great Man', and as a counterpoise to Churchill.   What irony, then, to learn that at this very moment Churchill was urging that Balfour be admitted to the Cabinet, and that Salisbury refused it because of his 'reluctance to give to a near kinsman an advancement to which others might think they had a greater claim'.   But, in November, crisis threatened the stability of the Government and Balfour was brought in.   Scarcely a month later, Churchill resigned office, as he had done several times before, but this resignation was accepted and put an end to his Ministerial career.

The events leading up to this have often been related. They are not to be ascribed either to the enmity of Salisbury or of Balfour. Balfour, indeed, had written to his uncle that his promotion to the Cabinet would perhaps be useful 'as a counterpoise even though a feeble one to Randolph. But this I say, not as rating myself high (Heaven knows!) but as rating the rest of my colleagues, from this point of view, low.'

Churchill, however, successfully encompassed his own ruin without any outside assistance—by intriguing against Cabinet policy with the German ambassador, Count Hatzfeldt, by causing general friction, and in particular by trying to cut the Army and Navy estimates at a time when, as Salisbury told him, 'The chances are in favour of war at an early date; and, when war has once broken out, we cannot be secure from the danger of being involved in it.'

Balfour, politically ebullient once more, shrewdly put the case in a nutshell in a letter to Salisbury on December 21, 1886: 'What we should keep in view is in the first place to secure that if R.C. leaves us, he does so on some point with regard to which he does not carry with him the sympathy of any considerable section of the party, urban or county; in the second place, that he deserts us in obvious alliance with Joe (Chamberlain); in the third place, that we regain, equally obviously, the alliance of Hartington and Goschen.'

This ideal solution—ideal as much for the Cabinet as for Balfour's personal ambition and the removal of rivals—did in fact come about. On the same day that Salisbury accepted the last of the many Churchill resignations (thus taking him by surprise), Balfour wrote to Salisbury that Churchill could not have left the Cabinet 'on any question, or at any time, more convenient to us. He has not resigned as Leader of the "Tory Democrats". He has resigned as a thwarted Chancellor of the Exchequer—and not only that, but as Ch. of the Ex. thwarted on a point on which he will, I believe, carry with him none of the party.'

The political turbulence and tergiversation of three most extraordinary years in British politics were nearly over. On the Conservative side, a single acknowledged leader was firmly in the saddle and stability was in prospect. From Balfour's point of view, rivals had been eliminated and the sun of his uncle's approval seemed to be shining on him again—particularly after his successful handling, as Scottish Secretary, of a tricky situation arising from the Scottish Land League's 'no rents' campaign. Certainly, the road ahead would be hard-going, but it would have fewer twists and hairpin bends to be negotiated.

There were, indeed, some immediate difficulties. The Liberal Unionist, G. J. Goschen, former Liberal Minister and financier, had been brought into the Government to replace Churchill as Chancellor. Goschen, who was 'crotchety and suspicious' (as Balfour warned Salisbury), began by demanding the resignation of Iddesleigh from the

Foreign Office—with every justification, for the old man was by general consent 'hopelessly inefficient', as Esher put it. Unfortunately, Iddesleigh died while taking leave of Salisbury, who had just dismissed him. To this embarrassment were added two others: Goschen who, according to the rule then obtaining, had to submit to re-election on elevation to the Cabinet was defeated and had to be found a safe Conservative seat. Shortly afterwards Hicks-Beach, who had become apparently indispensable, resigned from the Irish Secretaryship, as a result of bad eyesight, and also because of differences of opinion with Salisbury.

The Government, so recently elected, seemed suddenly to be on the verge of breaking up. As Balfour wrote to W. H. Smith, then War Minister, in a letter from Whittingehame a few days before Christmas, 1886: 'I take a very dark view of our future. I think we *must* break up.' But at this point Salisbury's gift for swift, bulwarking action made itself felt. He appointed Smith to lead the House, himself took over the Foreign Office once more, and put Edward Stanhope into Smith's shoes at the War Office.

This was in January, 1887. On March 5, Salisbury took an even more momentous step, though, it appeared at the time to be a rash one. With Ireland half aflame through planned resistance, and the forces of law, at any rate in Kerry and Clare, almost impotent, Salisbury announced to the nation that the new Chief Secretary to Ireland, the most thankless and dangerous post in the Cabinet, was to be his nephew, Arthur Balfour.

The first public reaction was astonishment, the second disbelief. Balfour had been learning 'the political game' with some success, but it had been largely back-stage. For all his not unskilful interventions in debate and his minor offices, it is probably true, as Sir Henry Lucy said, that: 'Up to the day when all the world wondered to hear that Mr. Balfour had been appointed Chief Secretary for Ireland, he was a person of no consequence. His rising evoked no interest in the House, and his name would not have drawn a full audience in St. James's Hall.'

His appearance was no doubt against him. In that parliamentary age when M.P.s, like all men of importance, tended to be big and bulky, and Irish M.P.s in particular were often as tough and rough as costermongers (and with the same powers of vituperation), Balfour's slim figure sinuously weaving its way through the Lobby often gave the impression of the elegant colt rather than of the strong shire-horse.

Sir Henry Lucy refers to him as 'the dilettante stripling', and mentions his boyish smile and his disposition to 'discover how nearly he can sit on his shoulder-blades' in the House. He was 'the very flower of graceful demeanour'. True, 'he was always a pretty speaker, with a neat turn for saying nasty things'. But his soft complexion and his idle sprawl on the 'bench below the gangway' had convinced most observers that he was 'at best no more than a Parliamentary *flaneur*, a trifler with debate . . .'

This is why a positive hail of criticism broke out when the announcement was made. Almost every paper in the country attacked his appointment. The *Pall Mall Gazette*, for example said: 'Mr. Balfour is, the very antithesis of a pachyderm. . . . To offer him the Irish Office is like the presentation of a silken bowstring to the doomed victim of the Caliph.' An Irish paper remarked that he was 'a silk-skinned sybarite whose rest a crumpled rose-leaf would disturb'. As for the Irish M.P.s, after a moment of utter disbelief, they chortled with glee: 'We have killed Forster, we have blinded Beach. What shall we do to Balfour?'

Only *The Times* spoke of his 'fresh, clear and alert intelligence'. Surprisingly few papers, however, suggested that he had got the job through nepotism; it was, after all, scarcely the sort of job a nepotist would want, though the young barrister, Henry Asquith, who had entered Parliament in 1886, wrote a few years later that Balfour as Scottish Minister was supposed to owe his office to family partiality. He had the reputation of being 'an idler, a philosopher and a dilettante, deeply imbued with cynicism and with a distinct flavour of effeminacy. . . . He was conceived as a charming, but rather spineless, trifler, drifting with lazy grace in a metaphysical cloud land. . . . People smiled when he was made Irish Secretary.'

To some extent doubts about his capacity for such a job were shared by Balfour himself. His doubts of himself as 'a political animal' at all were not yet entirely stilled: was he not meant really to be a quiet philosopher living on his estates? But then there was also the tug of social life, of being—though in the least vulgar way possible—someone in Society. There was, too, the question of his health. He had, after all, been 'delicate'; there was tuberculosis in the family—his father had died of it.

He decided to make a test of his health stand as a test for all. 'The history of Irish Secretaries', he wrote, 'since Mr. Gladstone came into office in 1880, was not wholly encouraging. Mr. Forster had never concealed the fact that if he had known what the office involved he would never have taken it. His successor (Cavendish) was murdered. Sir George Trevelyan, who followed, temporarily broke down under the strain. Putting all personal considerations aside, it would surely be very inexpedient if yet another Chief Secretary should be driven from office by the combined effect of tireless obstruction, bitter invective, and administrative perplexities.

'From my youth up I had never been robust. It, therefore, seemed wise before undertaking new and onerous duties to show myself to Sir

William Jenner.' (A leading physician, grandson of 'vaccination' Jenner.) 'Fortunately, after careful examination he "passed" me, and without further delay I crossed St. George's Channel, and was duly sworn in by Lord Londonderry, Lord-Lieutenant of Ireland, long my friend and once my fag at Eton.'

In fact the medical 'all clear', combined with an appointment that placed him constantly in the public eye, seems to have released in him a fount of unquenchable energy. He had made up his mind that politics was to be his main career; and before the year, 1887, was out he had become the most outstanding Minister in Salisbury's Cabinet, making his mark not only in a disrupted, angry Ireland but triumphing in the teeth of unresting opposition led by such giants as Gladstone and Parnell.

Despite the whirlwinds he reaped in the House of Commons, and the physical dangers he ran in Ireland, his nerve remained steady: always somewhere within him lay an untroubled pool of calm, a 'still centre', into which he could withdraw at will. 'I never think about politics in bed,' he once remarked.

Politics, finally, became his career; but it was never the whole of his intellectual life. 'When I am at work on politics, I long to be in literature,' he once told John Morley, 'and *vice versa*.' Far from being schizophrenic, this was an advantage: when the one became tiresome, he entered into the other. It is also probably relevant that, during his four years as Irish Secretary, his affair with Lady Wemyss entered into its physical phase.

6

'THE MOST POPULAR MINISTER'

1887–1891

Lord George Hamilton, First Lord of the Admiralty in Salisbury's Cabinet, wrote in his memoirs: 'The history of the House of Commons for the next four years' (i.e. from 1887) 'is really a record of Balfour's marvellous Parliamentary performances.' Sir Henry W. Lucy dedicated his *A Diary of the Salisbury Parliament, 1886–1892* to 'The Right Hon. A. J. Balfour, the principal product of the Salisbury Parliament.' Where Ireland had broken a number of other Chief Secretaries—and other Cabinets—it made Balfour, and kept what was never a strong Ministerial team in power for five years.

The reasons were both personal and political. If politics had *not* been Ireland, in Salisbury's famous phrase, Balfour would have knocked on the door of fame in vain, whatever his performances in the House of Commons. But the opportunity was there and he was the man for it.

In the House he was cool and infuriating. Irish M.P.s in the heat of debate sometimes even went so far as to shake their fists in his face; he ignored them and did not so much as allow a muscular twitch to be seen. When O'Brien or Sexton delivered a tremendous philippic, he would simply laugh at their heroics, and his reply would be a playful prodding in the ribs rather than a serious attempt to answer.

He refused to treat Parnell and his associates as true representatives of Ireland; and often, instead of answering himself, would show his disdain by simply sending in his Parliamentary Secretary, Colonel King-Harman (M.P. for Thanet) to read out a statement. Sometimes he would be dangerously playful or stingingly deferential; at other times he would be coldly noncommittal; at other times again, he would stab.

IjB

John Morley wrote that Balfour's 'favourite weapon was the rapier, with no button on, without prejudice to a strong broadsword when it was wanted'. Morley continued:

'His eye for the construction of dilemmas was incomparable, and the adversary was rapidly transfixed by the necessity of extricating himself from two equally discreditable scrapes. To expose an inch of unguarded surface was to provoke a dose of polished raillery that was new, effective and unpleasant. He revelled in carrying logic all its length, and was not always above urging a weak point as if it were a strong one. Though polished and high-bred in air, he unceremoniously applied Dr. Johnson's cogent principle that to treat your adversary with respect is to give him an advantage to which he is not entitled. Of intellectual satire he was a master—when he took the trouble; for the moral irony that leaves a wound he happily had no taste, any more than he had a taste for that extremity in temper and language which was rather the fashion of leading men at that time.'

Balfour, in fact, enjoyed the battle; it had a cathartic effect upon him, cleansing as it were of aggression a man whose normal manners were truly polite and occasionally excessively suave. He never lost his temper—though he once confessed that his nerves sometimes got on edge and it 'takes time to cool'—because, in the end, the debates in the House of Commons were to him a game. Business was done in an office, and there, as Morley said, 'Every word showed a hard grip of the matter in hand. . . . In business, he is absolutely without atmosphere.'

The business Balfour was concerned with in 1887, when he first entered the somewhat ramshackle Irish Office in Queen Anne Street, was simply the pacification of Ireland. Here he was luckier than his immediate predecessors. Policy was already cut-and-dried. While still in opposition, on May 15, 1886, Salisbury had for ever laid the ghost of Conservative flirtation with Home Rule—'autonomy', 'New Departure' or whatever periphrasis had been employed—when at St. James's Hall in London he had laid down his policy:

'Parliament should enable the Government of England to govern Ireland. Apply that recipe honestly, continuously and resiliently for twenty years, and at the end of that time you will find that Ireland will be fit to accept any gifts in the way of local government or repeal of coercion laws that you may wish to give her. What she wants is Government—Government that she cannot hope to be done by agitation at Westminster; Government that does not alter in its resolution or its temperature by the Party changes which take place at Westminster.'

Within days of his appointment, Balfour was echoing this—though foreshortening the process of amelioration: 'Cromwell failed because he relied solely on repressive measures. This mistake I shall not imitate. I shall be as relentless as Cromwell in enforcing obedience to the law, but at the same time I shall be as radical as any reformer in redressing grievances and especially in removing every cause of complaint in regard to the land.'

It was a stick-and-carrot policy—coercion followed by relief—but it was clear enough, and Balfour went to Ireland determined to carry it through. He did not allow himself to be sidetracked by notions of 'nationalism'. He was accused of not recognising the Irish nation; but he was right in replying that there was no nation to recognise. Pacification was a *sine qua non*, and he attacked the problem of achieving it entirely without sentimentality. Years later he said that 'what made Irish Government so difficult was English sentimentality'.

From the Irish point of view, in the words of the Irish historian, P. S. O'Hegarty, it was Balfour's coercion-cum-kindness, that killed Irish nationalism. Nor was it only 'official' kindness; apart from his constructive and forward-looking measures, he himself raised a famine fund when the potato crop failed in 1889, and during a tour of Ireland with his sister, Alice Balfour, in 1890, provided money from his own pocket to complete a bridge.

Balfour's first visit to Ireland as Chief Secretary was paid within a few days of his appointment in March, 1887. Dublin Castle, the centre of the 'English Ascendancy' and official home of the Viceroy, was a gloomy place, guarded by field-guns and great numbers of troops; and the route between it and the Chief Secretary's Lodge in Phoenix Park was patrolled. In these grim and almost warlike surroundings, Balfour met his staff, headed by the Permanent Under-Secretary, Sir Redvers Buller, and returned to London within the week with a clear picture of the problem on the ground. He then laid before the Cabinet his general views of what ought to be done in the immediate future.

His first objective was to apply counter-measures to the so-called 'Plan of Campaign'. This had been concocted by the Irish M.P. Timothy Harrington, and was launched by two other Irish M.P.s, William O'Brien and John Dillon, on October 23, 1886. Parnell knew little of it, and what he knew made him critical of its practical wisdom. In these years, however, Parnell was a sick man, and much preoccupied by his adulterous affair with Kitty O'Shea.

The plan called on tenants to treat with their landlords as a united body; if their offers of a reasonable rent were not accepted, they were to pay money into a fund to help those evicted as a result of the campaign. Any tenant who refused to co-operate in the plan was terrorised, either physically or by other intimidation.

The plan was effective on only about 84 estates, and on 60 of them voluntary reductions in rent were agreed. On 24 estates, the landlords refused reduction. Evictions followed, and created widespread tur-moil. It was the operation of this plan that had made Salisbury abandon hope of governing by the ordinary processes of law.

The first step therefore, was to draft a new and drastic crimes Bill, and to pass it through Parliament into law as soon as possible. To do this, it had been necessary to amend the rules of the Commons to allow the closure to be carried by a bare majority on the motion of any Member provided the Speaker consented and at least 200 Members voted for it; and this had been done in January, 1887, while Hicks-Beach was still Chief Secretary. But to get the Bill through Com-mittee, the Government had further to restrict debate by means of a 'guillotine' resolution—not opposed by Gladstone—fixing a time-limit beyond which clauses were to be put without amendment or dis-cussion.

'Criminal Law Amendment (Ireland) Bill', piloted by Balfour him-self at the end of March, gave power to the Lord-Lieutenant of Ireland to 'proclaim' (i.e. to proscribe) any association as dangerous and to suppress it. Conspiracy and intimidation were made punishable on summary conviction without a jury. Witnesses could be compelled to give evidence. A whole district could be 'proclaimed', so that trials could be held elsewhere than in the district concerned and with a special jury with a property qualification (i.e. on the whole, the landlord class).

The severity of the Act, which became law in July, 1887, made the Liberal-Unionists uneasy; a letter from Joseph Chamberlain to Balfour on March 30, 1887, criticised Balfour's draft of the Bill as too favourable to the landlords. Next day he wrote again saying that the Liberal-Unionists desired, however, that no tenant should be evicted because he could not pay an unjust rent. Balfour annotated this letter: 'This seems to me to be in a much lower key.' Churchill was equally doubtful, although he kept silent in public. But he wrote to Hicks-Beach: 'Arthur Balfour fills your place very badly. He made a terrible fiasco in introducing the Bill. Want of knowledge, the most elementary want of tact coupled with an excited manner and raised voice. Of course the Irish interrupted brutally and he was quite unable to cope with them.' Asquith, too, thought that Balfour's speech introducing the bill 'in matter and style one of the worst I ever heard'.

Conservatives, on the other hand, were heartened by his handling, and by his obvious knowledge of detail. They enjoyed the shrewd thrusts he gave against both the Irish Nationalists and the Liberals, for instance when he said: 'There are those who talk as if Irishmen were justified in disobeying the law because the law comes to them in foreign garb. I see no reason why any local colour should be given to the Ten Commandments.'

Shortly afterwards in the Land Bill, the bias, of which Chamberlain complained was in favour of landlords, was corrected; the Bill provided for a revision of rents on a sliding scale operating for three years instead of with the 15 years security which Gladstone had given them. It also gave tenants the right to appeal to County Court Judges; this, it was believed, would put a stop to oppressive evictions such as those carried out on Colonel O'Callaghan's property in County Clare. This estate was notoriously rack-rented, and the evictions of defaulting tenants had involved 36 families. The whole countryside was up against the police whom the Colonel called in to turn the people out of their houses. But Colonel O'Callaghan was within his rights, and Balfour sent the constabulary to assist him. At the same time Balfour made no attempt to conceal his disgust at the Colonel's heartlessness. The new Land Bill, he hoped, would prevent such further proceedings, for it embodied the concessions to tenants advised by Lord Cowper's Commission, set up in 1886 to inquire into rents and land-purchase.

Balfour also determined to 'proclaim' the Irish National League, an organisation which had been developed from the Land League in 1882 at a conference called by Parnell, Davitt, Dillon, Brennan, Sexton, Healy and Arthur O'Connor. Its moving force was nationalism, and it sought not just reform of the land law, but national self-govern-ment, local self-government and extension of the parliamentary and municipal franchises. Balfour's colleagues were doubtful of the wisdom of this 'proclamation', but Balfour insisted on carrying it through in a violently demonstrative House of Commons in August, 1887.

The first considerable 'action' consequent upon Balfour's war against crime was not long delayed. A day or two before the Land Bill became law, evictions were due to take place of some of the Countess of Kingston's tenants at Mitchelstown, County Cork. In view of the forthcoming legislation, the evictions were postponed. William O'Brien, however, one of the instigators of the 'Plan of Campaign', visited the estate and at a public meeting incited the people to resistance.

A summons was, therefore, served upon him to appear before the new Court set up under the Act and convened at Mitchelstown for September 9. O'Brien himself stayed in Dublin, but the two Irish M.P.s, John Dillon and John Mandeville, went to Mitchelstown to attend a mass-meeting in the Market Square during the hours when it was supposed that the trial would be taking place. A riot developed and the police fired on the crowd. Three rioters were killed and 54 police were injured.

A coroner's jury found wilful murder against the County Police Inspector and five constables, but none was brought to trial, and five months later the Queen's Bench in Dublin quashed the charges on technical grounds. The police had been stoned by the rioters, and indeed ridden down by tenants on horseback. As Balfour asked in the House: 'When an attack of that kind is made, are the police, who are men, to be said to have exceeded their duty when they resort to what should be resorted to only in the last necessity, but which, when the last necessity occurs, no officer should shrink from using?'

The Opposition ranted and raved, and it was Gladstone who first uttered the words: 'Remember Mitchelstown', which became the battle-cry of the Liberals and Parnellites against Balfour's policy in Ireland.

O'Brien was, of course, arrested. One of the results of this was to bring Irish disorder to the doorsteps of Londoners. On November 13, 1887, a meeting of the Social Democratic Federation was called in Trafalgar Square to protest against Mitchelstown. Although prohibited by the police, it nevertheless took place, led by such Socialists as R. Cunninghame-Graham, M.P., and John Burns. Although no shot was fired, the footguards and the lifeguards were called out, and there were horse and baton charges. There were over 100 casualties and two of the crowd afterwards died of injuries; the police also suffered severely, and the two Socialist leaders were sent to prison for six weeks. Thus ended what came to be known as 'Bloody Sunday'.

Balfour's swift defence of his police and officials at Mitchelstown, and his defence of the action of Captain Plunkett, the divisional magistrate for Cork District, had a profoundly heartening effect upon those whose duty it was to carry out the policy of pacification in Ireland. Present at the Mitchelstown affair was Edward Carson, a Dublin barrister prosecuting for the Crown. He praised the way that Balfour never 'boggled' over the aftermath of his policy: 'He simply backs his own people up. After that there wasn't an official in Ireland who didn't worship the ground he walked on. . . . It was Mitchelstown that made us certain we had a man at last.'

Balfour spent the three months from October, 1887, until Parliament met again in the following February, at Chief Secretary's Lodge, and there first met Carson. A lifelong, though not always smooth, friendship began. Years later Carson said: 'I was only a provincial lawyer and until I saw A.J.B. I had never guessed that such an animal existed. I have never seen anybody like him—nobody in Dublin had.' His warm feelings were reciprocated. Balfour later said: 'I made Carson and he made me. Carson had nerve. . . .' Balfour would have liked Carson as Solicitor-General, but other claims were too strong. Nevertheless, he later used his influence to help get Carson elected as M.P. in 1892.

Balfour took with him to Dublin as his Private Secretary, George Wyndham; they 'spoke the same language', and Wyndham helped reconcile him to his grim 'exile'. It was also a positively dangerous

exile, for the Irish had a long record of assassinations.   Balfour himself
had truly remarked in a letter to a friend on his appointment that:
'I shall have to lose either life or reputation.'

Yet, although he got no sort of thrill out of taking personal risks, he
was quite unconcerned for his own safety.   He wrote to a secretary at
the Home Office that, as far as police protection was concerned, it was
'entirely a matter for Scotland Yard to decide.   I ask no questions and
I take no precautions.'   Scotland Yard desired him to carry a revolver
which, when he remembered, he did.

But he travelled all over turbulent Ireland without mishap—except
once when in Dublin his brougham was run into from behind by the
escorting detectives' jaunting car!   His courage was of the absent-
minded variety.   A story is told of his visiting a distant part of Ireland
and chancing one day to enter a humble Irish cottage to ask for a drink
of milk.   'In the little room stood a piano.   While waiting, Mr.
Balfour with whom music was a passion, ran his fingers over the key-
board, and then losing all consciousness of Dublin Castle and his
milk, became absorbed in a sonata, to the great delight of villagers who
speedily congregated round the door.'

It was difficult for anyone, even an Irish peasant, to nourish personal
hatred towards the willowy figure with his pince-nez and smile.   Yet
as Chief Secretary he was hated as perhaps no English official in Ireland
was ever hated before.   He became known after Mitchelstown as
'bloody Balfour'; he was threatened with shooting and knifing and
physical tortures.   Violent cartoons of him proliferated, and he
received quantities of blood-curdling anonymous letters.   One is still
among his papers.   Posted in Liverpool on January 31, 1888, it had
red borders and the following, not excessively literate text:

'Bloody Balfour.   I write to inform you that your days are numbered.
You bloody ruffian.   How dare you arrest our beloved priests.   Are
you not content with arresting our Leaders. . . .?   If no one will shoot
you I will.   I will send you down to hell.   Remember you bloody curr,
your long legs will be shot off you.   Blood for Blood.   Signed W.L.F.B.'

'Do the Irish', Balfour is reported as having asked the well-known
priest Father Healey, 'really hate me as much as their papers say they
do?'   'My dear Sir,' said the priest, 'if they only hated the devil half
as much as they hate you, my occupation would be gone entirely.'

Friends in England, indeed, feared for his safety; and to some he
became a hero.   Lady Elcho for example, commenting on the Irish
wanting to send him to hell, said, 'But if you go to hell, remember you
are to take me with you as your Francesca.'   Balfour himself, however,
recognised, as he said in a letter to Margot Tennant on Christmas
Eve, 1889, 'that personal abuse has made my political fortune', both
inside and outside the House of Commons.

Balfour's firm policy in Ireland sometimes led to personally embarrassing moments and even comic episodes. In October, 1887, the eccentric writer, Mohammedan-by-adoption, and horse fancier, Wilfrid S. Blunt spoke at a meeting against Lord Clanricarde, the most notorious of Irish landlords, who owned 56,000 acres in County Galway and lived in Albany. The meeting was 'proclaimed'. Blunt was pulled off the platform and arrested by the police. Blunt, however, happened to be the cousin of George Wyndham and Lady Elcho.

Balfour wrote to Lady Elcho on October 27, 1887: 'We are trying to put your cousin in gaol. I have not heard whether we have succeeded. I hope so, for I am sure Blunt would be himself disappointed at any other consummation, though I should be sorry for Lady Anne who may not hold the same views about political martyrdom as her husband. He is a goodish poet and a goodish lawn tennis player and a goodish fellow—how bored he must be with the Harringtons and the Henleys! George asked my advice as to whether he should write a sympathetic letter to Lady Anne. I advised him not. There are some condolences to which it is difficult not to give an air of sarcasm! But it must be admitted that there is a certain awkwardness in George's position.'

The awkwardness arose in particular because in the previous month there had been a family party at Clouds, the Wyndhams' home near Salisbury, which had been attended by Balfour, Henry James the novelist, George Wyndham and Blunt himself.

Blunt was duly sentenced to two months' imprisonment and shut up in Galway gaol—'there', it was said, 'he wrote sonnets and picked oakum'. Salisbury wrote to Balfour; 'I was delighted to see you had run Wilfrid Blunt in.'

The story had a typically Balfourian sequel. Wyndham invited him and Balfour to dinner. He said to Balfour: 'I want you to be very forgiving and come and dine with me to meet Wilfrid Blunt.' Balfour whose absent-mindedness was now developing into a protective trademark, replied: 'My dear George, I don't know that I am very forgiving, but I do know I am very forgetting, and, not having the least idea to what you refer, I can only say that I shall be delighted to dine with you to meet Wilfrid Blunt.'

Wyndham himself was to become Chief Secretary under Balfour's Premiership at the beginning of the next century and, as a politician, then came to grief. In 1887, like Balfour, he was the object of the most scurrilous attacks. The *Star*, for example, wrote: 'Mr. Wyndham is Mr. Balfour's devil in Ireland. He writes his most insolent letters, concocts his most unreliable statistics, and generally outdoes his chief for the impudence and vulgarity which Mr. Balfour mistakes for strength and wisdom.'

Wyndham was, as his friend Charles Gatty later said: 'An artist by nature and a politician by accident . . . much of his political life was to him a *via dolorosa*.' He was a friend of Henley, Kipling, Whibley, and Yeats, and as such a close contact for Balfour with the contemporary literary world.

Gradually Balfour's periods of residence in Dublin grew less uncongenial. He could write to Lady Elcho: 'In this abominable place there is always something that must be done, or something that must be seen, and down I have to come to this gloomy place where the Nationalist Fancy paints me forging chains for the enslavement of their country. But where in truth I am merely doing my best to prevent them picking each other's pockets and cutting each other's throats!'

But there were golf and tennis and informal dinners and, from time to time, the Chief Secretary's ball. 'I am taking much care of myself,' he wrote to Lady Frances Balfour in February 1888, 'golf or real tennis 12–2, castle 2–7. The work that does not get done in the five hours remains undone; for I positively decline to take anything home.'

For some of his immediate subordinates he had a high regard, and among them was Sir Redvers Buller, the Permanent Under-Secretary for Ireland. But Buller resigned a few months after Balfour took over. He resigned, Balfour later said, 'because he was a soldier. It is pathetic to look back upon now—for of course he had no idea what a bad soldier he was going to turn out to be. I did my best to keep him in Ireland. But there was a crisis in Army affairs. . . . Buller insisted on leaving me to go back for Army reforms. Buller was a fine brain in a way—he drank too much though. I don't mean that he got drunk, but he would sit on all night like they did in Ireland in those days. He got through an enormous quantity of drink.'

Throughout his years in Ireland, Balfour had the invaluable support of Salisbury, and they were in constant touch by letters. Salisbury's longer experience of both life and politics enabled him to give his nephew the caution which he sometimes lacked. For instance, at the end of 1887 Balfour tried the experiment of imposing penalties on shopkeepers who, after due warning, still sold newspapers which supported 'proclaimed' meetings. This aroused considerable antagonism in responsible quarters in England as an interference with the liberty of the press. Salisbury saw the danger of unnecessarily arousing English prejudices: 'If you resolve to change your practice or tactics', he told Balfour on December 24, 1887, 'do it as unobtrusively as possible,—simply abstaining from that or this prosecution without giving any reason. Do not avow a change of Policy—even to your pillow: for pillows chatter in Ireland.'

Though Salisbury was shrewd and cautious, in major matters he supported Balfour to the hilt. There was, for instance, the case of the Donegal evictions. Defaulting tenants had fortified and defended their houses and crowds had assembled to applaud them while the local police went to and fro between them and the magistrates suggesting terms. These unedifying scenes often went on for hours because the military force was there only to overawe the crowds. The police, on the other hand, had no equipment for storming fortified buildings.

Balfour, therefore, ordered the resident magistrates in Donegal 'that if resistance involves serious danger to your men your duty will at once require you to use military force on the spot'. A day or two later, Balfour reported that 'the threat of firing and the threat of firing alone caused the surrender of the more fortified houses. This is a new departure and one of our best officials got literally white with terror when he was shown the text of the document. I think it possible, though not probable, that one day or another they will be firing at one of the Plan of Campaign evictions.' Balfour went on to suggest that a suitable battering ram or possibly a fire-engine might be supplied to the police.

Despite the inherent danger in using this sort of threat of force, Salisbury at once replied: 'I quite concur in your views. The necessity of firing would be lamentable; but not so lamentable as the leaving of the police to be mutilated.'

Balfour's aims in Ireland were considerably hampered by the religious question. Many Roman Catholic clergy were deeply involved in breaking the law. One recalls the agonies of the Jesuit poet, Gerard Manley Hopkins, who in these years was Professor of Classics at University College, Dublin. Realising that his Order, the Jesuits, was deeply involved in the Irish plots against England, he wrote in his notebooks: 'Against my will my pains, laborious and distasteful like prisoners made to serve the enemy's gunners, go to help on this cause.'

On the other hand was the fact that Gladstone was in constant touch with the Pope. It was felt that Salisbury's Government, too, ought to have some contact with the Vatican, although it was not officially possible since relations between the Foreign Office and the Vatican were not at this period tolerated. However, influential English Roman Catholics asked that the Pope should send over a representative to Ireland to inquire into the situation of priests involved in treasonable circumstances. Monsignor Persico, a Commissary Apostolic, arrived in Ireland in the summer of 1887 and stayed for some months.

An Irish Protestant Unionist, Professor S. H. Butcher, who met him at this time, described his impressions in a letter: 'I gathered, more from his private secretary than from himself, that he is horrified at the political part played by priests. . . . He observed with much emphasis: "One thing I see and know better than I ever did before—that there is no country in the world where the Catholic Church had such freedom as in Ireland. This must be said for English Statesmanship." '

As a consequence, in April, 1888, the Pope officially condemned the boycotting as 'against the principle of justice and charity', and the Plan of Campaign as unlawful. The Irish Bishops were directed to teach these precepts to their people 'prudently but efficiently'.

The reaction in Ireland was astonishment: 'The Pope', it was said, 'has turned Protestant.' Thus, the useful effects were not great: between 1887 and 1890 there were 23 prosecutions of priests under the Crimes Act, 15 of them taking place after the date of the Pope's declarations.

It required a catlike tread to negotiate the religious problems in Ireland and not least because of the Protestantism of Ulster. Balfour was a Protestant by upbringing and conviction, and distrusted the Vatican. Nevertheless he came to the conclusion that it was right, as well as expedient, for the State to provide the Roman Catholic majority with proper opportunities for university training. The conditions in the existing Irish universities were unsatisfactory. He proposed that a Roman Catholic college should be built and maintained by the State.

In August, 1889, he outlined his proposals in the House of Commons. Parnell pursued his usual course of approving anything he thought good for Ireland, but most of his followers foamed at the mouth at the mere thought of what one of them called 'Mr. Balfour's bribing university.' There was, too, a storm of protest from Ulster and from Protestant associations all over the country. The demands of the Roman Catholic authorities themselves were also intransigent, and the scheme had to be dropped, although Balfour never entirely lost hope of establishing Roman Catholic university education in Ireland.

II

By the autumn of 1889 Balfour's determined policy had taken considerable effect. Lawlessness had been curbed throughout the country and, in many places, order was entirely restored. The public in general was beginning to tire of the antics of people like William O'Brien and becoming reluctant to condone the repeated breaches of the peace which their conduct provoked. O'Brien himself sensed this and, while out of prison on bail, suddenly decamped to France and thence to America.

On October 31, 1889, Balfour wrote to Salisbury: 'I think we may safely *unproclaim* the greater part of Ireland. I am investigating the pros and cons from the Irish point of view.'

Yet, almost at the same time, events were combining to bring the popularity of the Government's Irish policy down to a nadir. In the House of Commons, although Balfour had remained the master of his matter and in general of his opponents, he was less at ease with some of his so-called colleagues.   Salisbury had written to him on October 26, 1887: 'The only unfavourable symptom in the present situation to my eyes is that Randolph is supporting us so zealously.   The arch-fiend is getting light-headed.'   This support was suddenly withdrawn in April 1888.   An Irish Private Member's Bill dealing with Irish local government had been amended, with the agreement of the Government, by a Conservative backbencher.   This amendment stated that any major constitutional change at that time was inexpedient.   Gladstone condemned the amendment and Balfour replied in a flippant manner, implying that the Irish people were not yet ready for any extension of local government.

This, as it happened, was in flat contradiction to Churchill's pledge in his first speech as Leader of the House in August, 1886, and Gladstone pointed this out.   At this, Churchill himself rose and, after declining to refer to Balfour as 'my honourable friend', emphatically declared that this was so.   The effect on the Government side was like a bombshell—and, as one observer said, 'even the graceful head of Mr. Balfour drooped'.   What made it worse was that Churchill had spoken after agreement with Chamberlain.   Very plainly, the breath of dissension passed through the formerly so stoutly-supported Irish policy of the Cabinet—and without such unanimity, so stringent a policy would be hard to continue.

In July, 1889, Churchill, in a speech at Birmingham, returned to the attack on Balfour's repressive policy.   He compared Balfour, in scarcely veiled terms, to Mr. Podsnap—'a person in easy circumstances who was very content with himself and was extremely surprised that all the world was not equally contented like him'.   The anger and contempt were obvious.

Balfour also suspected that Churchill might be trying to make common cause with Hicks-Beach, his predecessor as Irish Secretary. Salisbury certainly would have preferred Hicks-Beach to have Cabinet office, and there were even suggestions that he should again be offered the Irish Secretaryship.   Balfour naturally disagreed with this and pointed out, somewhat tartly, to W. H. Smith that 'I do not think Beach's presence will render Cabinets more agreeable *socially*; nor his absence materially increase the danger of the government in the House'.   But to save any suggestion of what Salisbury, in a letter to the Queen, called a 'cave' occupied by Churchill and Hicks-Beach, Hicks-Beach was offered and accepted the Presidency of the Board of Trade.

Moreover, by-elections were tending to go against the Government; and then came damage more deviously and obliquely inflicted.   In March and April, 1887, *The Times* newspaper had published a series of articles called 'Parnellism and Crime', in one of which appeared the facsimile of a letter dated May 18, 1882, alleged to have been signed by Parnell. In this Parnell seemingly apologised for having publicly condemned the murder of Lord Frederick Cavendish, then Chief Secretary, and the Under-Secretary, Burke, in Phoenix Park, Dublin, in 1882.

This was welcome grist to Parnell's enemies. Parnell promptly in the Commons declared the letter to be a forgery, but he did not go to law. This was taken by some as a sign of guilt. However, another Irish M.P., O'Donnell, believing himself to be implicated in the articles, sued *The Times* for libel. Counsel for *The Times* defence then produced further incriminating letters which Parnell was said to have written. Parnell now asked to have the authenticity of the letters inquired into by a select committee of Commons. This the Government refused, but brought in a Bill setting up a special Commission of three judges to investigate the whole of *The Times* charges.

The Commission started its hearings, and some five months later in February, 1889, an Irish journalist called Richard Pigott—red-faced, white-whiskered and foolishly smiling—came into the witness-box and admitted that he had forged the letters with his own hand. He absconded abroad, posted a full confession to *The Times*, and, when the British police tracked him to Madrid with a warrant for his arrest on a charge of perjury, blew his brains out.

Pigott, it was then revealed, had been a tool of Edward Houston's pro-Government 'Irish Loyal and Patriotic Union', which had been formed to fight Home Rule and the National League. It was said that Pigott was paid £1,500 by Houston, but in fact Houston's money came, not out of his Union's funds, but was advanced by friends. His friends were repaid after *The Times* had paid him, and *The Times* was said to have paid him £30,000.

The Commission itself went on to substantiate other charges made in the articles against Parnell and other Members of Parliament on the grounds of conspiracy, organising intimidation and circulating newspapers which preached sedition. But the discovery of forgeries obscured the larger indictments.

Balfour denied being influenced by the allegations on August 7, 1888: 'I have never relied upon the accusations advanced by *The Times*; I have always found sufficient material for my political controversies in the contemporary facts of Irish history. I have never had to go back beyond the year 1885 to prove that the Irish Leaders desire to obtain what they thought the freedom of their country by illegal and archaic means.'

Nevertheless, the Government, some of whose supporters had made great play with Pigott's revelations, was smirched. Consequently, Parnell's stock rose soaringly while the Government's descended correspondingly low. Irrationally, the revelation of forgeries sapped confidence in the whole case against Home Rule. Balfour, while typically deploring the 'absurd demoralisation or rather discouragement of our own side in the House', wrote to Sir West Ridgeway—Buller's successor as Permanent Under-Secretary in Ireland—that 'My private impression is that the worst is past and past without permanent damage. . . . It is clear that the Opposition never misses an opportunity for trying to implicate the Government in *The Times* catastrophe, and every effort will be made to show that we have given *The Times* illegitimate assistance. As, however, our record is quite clean in this matter, my impression is that the more violent the attacks on us, and on the Attorney-General, the better for the cause.'

It is at this time that Sir Henry Lucy records that Balfour is 'less light-hearted'. Things were—or seemed to be—going wrong, and as the spirits of Irish Members were rising, those of the Government were failing. 'There is no sign of waning resolution in Mr. Balfour. He may be counted on to die with harness on his back. But he is graver in his manner, less cynical in his replies, more inclined to admit that the representations of Irish members must receive, if they do not deserve, some consideration.'

It was, in fact, now that Balfour's efforts began to save the day for the Government. For his Development programme for Ireland—the carrot after the stick—began to take shape. The creation of the Congested Districts Board and the construction of light railways serving the poorest and remotest parts of those districts of the West Coast gained him a real popularity. Carson once recalled how an old peasant woman had said at the time, 'Thanks be to Mary and all the Saints and to bloody Balfour, ould Ireland will be saved yet.'

On May 31, 1889—a few months after the Pigott episode—he introduced a Drainage Bill for the Bann, the Barrow, the Shannon and the Suck. He wanted all his Bills to be discussed together; but the Speaker upheld the objection of the Irish Member who intended to get the railway and to obstruct the passage of the other schemes. A Treasury Grant of £380,000 was provided for the drainage, and the management was to be in the hands of occupiers of the lands and not of landlords. The latter would exercise no control and gain no direct advantage, for rents were not allowed to be increased on account of the improved value of the drained land.

The Bills went through the Commons to the accompaniment of the usual sneers about bribery; but the Irish Nationalist, Crilly, the Member for North Mayo, spoke up and told the Commons that unsalted mackerel had gone to the United States the year before by means of the only existing light railway and this represented a gain of £17,000 for Irish fishermen and curers. Railways could only benefit Ireland.

Balfour also began to consider a Land Purchase Bill, and a plan for bringing permanent relief for the poverty in the West. His legislation of 1890 was interesting since it was based on the acceptance of the principle of State responsibility for poverty-stricken areas. But he freed these arrangements as far as possible from State interference. Nothing in the finance was controlled by the Treasury or by Parliament, except salaries and administrative expenses. His Congested Districts Board—'congestion' meant that the soil was incapable of supporting the people rooted upon it—survived the birth of the Irish Free State and was dissolved only in 1923. The Board, as well as drawing up a series of reports on life in the poorest agricultural parts, also started work on the scientific improvement of the livestock of the peasants and the methods of the fishermen. It made grants to private undertakings big enough to be classed as factories, and gave women training in home-weaving. Factories began to explore the possibilities of using their labour. Later in the century some employers opened new factories in those areas and produced 'Donegal carpet'.

The Congested Districts Bill was introduced in March, 1890, and in October of that year Balfour started on a week's tour of Mayo and Galway accompanied by his sister Alice Balfour, Sir West Ridgeway and George Wyndham. No detectives accompanied them—a sign of a change of times since 1887. The Land Purchase Bill was introduced on March 24, 1890—the result of months of personal hard work, for Balfour liked to draft his own Bills. This Bill was undoubtedly the first great step towards removing the truest of Irish grievances against the English. The process that turned the peasantry into the owners of the land was not, of course, concluded in the lifetime of one Parliament. Needless to say, Gladstone opposed the Bill and Parnell voted with him, though not wholeheartedly.

The tide was once more turning in the Government's favour, and about this time there occurred an event which was further to undermine the popularity gained by the Home Rulers as a result of the Pigott inquiry. This was the fall of Parnell, an event which decisively turned the political tide that had been flowing strongly in favour of Gladstone.

The details of Parnell's liaison with Mrs. O'Shea, the wife of Captain W. H. O'Shea, M.P. and ne'er-do-well former officer of the Hussars, are well known. Parnell had for long been living with Mrs. O'Shea and had had three children by her; but since O'Shea himself was receiving money through his wife's aunt, he had not felt impelled to divorce his faithless wife. The aunt died in 1889; no more money was forthcoming for O'Shea, and he began divorce proceedings.

But to his decision there may well have been political undertones. O'Shea was a Liberal and a friend and protégé of Chamberlain. When Chamberlain turned against Home Rule, O'Shea turned with him. He and Chamberlain had, therefore, excellent reasons for wishing to discredit Parnell, and Home Rule and to weaken Gladstone as a result. There is no proof that Chamberlain egged him on to file his divorce suit; there is evidence that O'Shea offered Balfour an opportunity of exploiting the private affairs of Parnell.

O'Shea wrote to Balfour on December 26, 1889, as he put it, 'explaining matters'. His tentative approach was politely rejected by Balfour who wrote next day: 'I sincerely trust that no aggravation of inevitable suffering may be brought about by the unwarrantable introduction of political and Party feeling into private affairs, from which, in my opinion, they should be wholly dissociated.'

'Unwarrantable' as it may have been, Parnell's affair brought immediate benefit to the Conservative Party and Government. For Gladstone, urged on by English Nonconformist opinion, indicated that unless the Irish Party changed its leader he would cease himself to lead the Liberals. He thus presented the Irish Party with a difficult choice: should they, at English bidding, depose their brilliant national leader or should they, by retaining him, sacrifice all chance of Home Rule?

Parnell was sacrificed—but the Irish Party was splintered. Thus no benefit accrued, except to the Conservatives. Balfour was enabled to carry through the rest of his policies in Ireland without the usual hindrances. It facilitated the passing of his Land Bill through Parliament in 1891, and this in turn encouraged him to announce in August of that year the next item of his constructive programme—no less than the measure for Irish Local Government over which he had quarrelled with Churchill.

III

In the middle of August, 1891, after a long Session, Balfour left London for Bayreuth, there to attend the Wagner Festival. He was now, as Lucy noted, 'the favourite Minister', and as such the subject of observation from all quarters. There were those who remarked that four years of Ireland had both aged and hardened his face—he had also recently suffered from influenza—and that he had become, at 43, quite grey and more regularly wore spectacles. This being so it was felt that to spend ten days listening to the music of Wagner—then commonly regarded as an awe-inspiringly 'advanced' composer—was a sign of unusual taste if not of unusual mental strength.

But, the gossip writers pointed out, Balfour also played golf, and, according to Lucy, 'Golf, like Wagner, is certainly growing in favour, but to the average person it is too much like Wagner to create a general wave of enthusiasm round any one of its votaries.' But, added Lucy, when golf and Wagner competed for his presence, it appears that 'the minstrel wins'.

9. A.J.B. Spy cartoon of the Chief Secretary for Ireland,
published in *Vanity Fair*, September 24, 1887

10. Lord Randolph Churchill. Cartoon published in *The Graphic*, September 25, 1886, with the title ' "Vice Versa"—The Old Chancellor of the Exchequer and the New'. (W. E. Gladstone, 'the old chancellor', is on the Opposition Front Bench)

Radio Times Hulton Picture Library

Balfour's holiday in Bayreuth marked the end of his Chief Secretaryship in Ireland, though he did not then know it. It may be of interest, therefore, at this point to consider his own, later views of his work in Ireland and of the 'Irish question'. Asked in 1928 after the Irish Free State had come into being, what was left of his Irish policy, he replied: 'What was the Ireland the Free State took over? It was the Ireland we made, though the Liberals went back on our policy. . . . They could have done nothing with Ireland but for our work.'

Balfour was referring no doubt to what Garvin called 'some of the best provisions of humane legislation ever put on a statute-book— the measures for relieving Irish poverty'. Yet all that Balfour had stood for, his immovable anti-Home Rulism, was eventually destroyed. What were his real views on Home Rule? How did he foresee the 'Irish problem' being ended? He answered these questions in a speech in 1913, not indeed at a time when the Irish question was quiescent, but when he at least was no longer ministerially involved.

This speech leaves us no doubt that Balfour's attitude to Home Rule was fundamental. He begins by considering all aspects of the Irish claims and shows with great force that none of these will be satisfied by Home Rule. If the subject, he says, is approached from the side of Irish nationality, it must be observed that Home Rule would impose limitations on a new Irish Parliament such as were never desired by England in the case of the American colonies before the War of Independence; nor 'would they ever be tolerated by anyone of the self-governing Dominions'. Such limitations would not long be tolerated by the Irish Nationalist Members, whatever they may now say.

As for constitutional equity and administrative convenience, Home Rule would not bring about a delegation of Parliamentary power to a subordinate Irish Assembly. Ireland would remain grossly over-represented in the Imperial Parliament and grossly under-represented as far as Imperial affairs are concerned.

Furthermore, Home Rule would raise an urgent problem in Ulster. 'If the Irish of the South and West have an inherent moral right to claim administrative separation from the United Kingdom, had not Ulster an equal right to claim administrative separation from the rest of Ireland?' There are in fact, Balfour concludes, only two possibilities. One is to maintain the Union and keep Ireland in full political communion with England and Scotland. Since specific irritations due to the worst systems of land tenure and grievances connected with religion and finance have been removed, it is surely only a matter of time, and not a long time either, before Irish patriotism will as easily combine with British patriotism as Scottish patriotism now combines.

KJB

It is, he points out, only about a quarter of a century since the problem presented by the congested districts began to receive special treatment; it is only about 15 years since local government on a popular basis was set up; it is only about five years since the land system was remodelled under the Wyndham Act. 'Measured by the standard of a nation's life such figures are insignificant. Give the remedial measures a chance, and do not in the meanwhile meddle with the Constitution of the United Kingdom for other than purely administrative reasons.'

The only alternative, Balfour says, is to give Ireland (with or without Ulster) complete autonomy, 'requiring her to manage her own finances, pay her own bills, borrow on her own credit, control her own rebels, settle her own constitution;—remaining, if she so desires, a self-governing colony within the limits of the Empire.' Only such a policy, however ruinous to Ireland, and however perilous to Britain, will satisfy the most extreme claims of Irish nationality. Home Rule will never do this.

What Balfour foresaw as the second alternative in fact came about, almost exactly as he foresaw it. What is interesting is that, already in 1913, Balfour would have been prepared for the eventuality of autonomy; but the Conservatives by then had been out of power for seven years and were not to return to power, and eventually to grant autonomy, for another nine years. In the meantime, Ireland continued to be ruined and blood continued to flow; and, as for being a peril to Britain, even in the Second World War Balfour's prophecy remained valid.

7

LEADER AND LOVER

1891–1895

In July, 1891, the German Emperor visited England, and Balfour was one of a distinguished party at Salisbury's house at Hatfield. He described the occasion amusingly in a letter to Lady Elcho:

'On Saturday I went to Hatfield where there was such a party as you never saw:—Royalties in such numbers that everyone of less exalted rank had to be billetted out in the Town. We sat down 78 to dinner on Sunday; the private secretaries turned grey with anxiety as to how we were all to be seated (we were arranged at small round tables), but so far as I could learn only one German official was mortally offended by the place assigned to him. . . . As for the Emperor himself, I had no serious conversation with him, feeble chaff about golf being his idea of the small talk appropriate to my peculiar tastes. I therefore could form no estimate of him myself, and utterly distrust anyone else's.

'But he certainly has extraordinary energy, self-confidence and interest in detail; all very good things in their way; while the fact that he firmly believes that he has a mission from Heaven, though this will very possibly send him and his country ultimately to Hell, may in the meanwhile make him do considerable deeds on the way there. One observation of his which he made to Gwenny Cecil has I think infinite humour—they were discussing English Parliamentary Government and after hearing an exhausting account of its benefits, he summed up his view of the situation thus: "Thank God I am a tyrant!" '

This visit had a somewhat awkward aftermath for Balfour himself in the October following when, as First Lord of the Treasury, he received a note from the Queen's Private Secretary, General H. F. Ponsonby pointing out that the German Emperor's visit had cost nearly £7,000 and asking whether the Treasury would reimburse the Queen for some

£5,000 of this since the visit had been 'partly of a political character'.

Before this tricky question had to be dealt with, however—there had been earlier, embarrassing Parliamentary rows on the same subject—Balfour found himself involved in even more ticklish Royal business. He returned from Bayreuth at the end of August; the Prime Minister was still away, and W. H. Smith, the First Lord, was ill. Thus it fell to Balfour to deal, *vice* his uncle, with the highly confidential matter of the proposed marriage of Prince Albert Victor, Duke of Clarence. He was the eldest son of the Prince of Wales, and thus heir-presumptive to the throne. Unhealthy, listless and emotionally unstable, he had in 1890 been refused the hand in marriage of Princess Alix of Hesse. Next year he fell in love simultaneously with Lady Sybil St. Clair-Erskine, second daughter of the Earl of Rosslyn, and with Princess Hélène, daughter of the Comte de Paris, pretender to the French throne. It was Hélène, he decided, whom he wished to marry. There were, however, some obvious problems. Her father's position as a pretender was awkward from the English Royal family's point of view, and he was also a Roman Catholic. The Queen seemed to be in favour of the marriage, and sent a memorandum to Salisbury to this effect. Balfour himself, his uncle being in France, was called to Balmoral to talk to the Queen. Writing to his uncle on or about August 28, 1891 (the letter is undated), he puts the situation clearly and even humorously:

'The Queen thinks that no one has been told of the projected marriage but herself. This may be true in point of fact: but that the Princess of Wales knows what is going on I have not the least doubt. She drove the young couple down here yesterday, and in answer, as I understand, to a mute reproval from the Queen, who has always been anxious that they should not be thrown too much together, she explained that as far as the Duke of Clarence was concerned it was by pure accident that he met the Parisian. . . .

'We shall have a great deal of trouble over it all, but it is impossible not to see the humorous side of the business. Will it be believed that neither the Queen, nor the young Prince, nor Princess Hélène see anything which is not romantic, interesting, touching and praiseworthy in the young lady giving up her religion *to which she still professes devoted attachment*, in order to marry the man on whom she has set her heart! They are moved, even to tears, by the magnitude of the sacrifice, without it apparently even occurring to them that, at the best, it is a sacrifice of religion for love; while at the worst, it is a sacrifice of religion for a throne:—a singular inversion of the ordinary views on martyrdom.

'The way matters stand here I take to be as follows. The Queen is much touched by the personal appeal to *herself*. With admirable dexterity (this surely cannot be the young man's idea), they came hand in hand straight to her, and implored her to smooth out not merely the political difficulties, but the family difficulties also. In making her their confidante, they have made her their ally. She would have been in a much less melting mood if the approaches had been conducted in due form through the parents. But the Sovereign had been touched through the Grandmother. These as sentimental considerations are much strengthened by her desire to see the young man married, and by the dearth of suitable Protestant Princesses. All the little German princesses are, according to her, totally ignorant of the world, and utterly unfit for the position. In Princess Hélène she thinks she sees a clever woman—healthy withal—who will be the making of her husband.

'She feels to a certain extent the political difficulties with France—but she thinks they can be got over by making it a condition of the marriage that the young lady should break with her relations! As regards England, she appears to hold that the combination of romance and conversion—the brand plucked from the burning—will make it not unpalatable to everybody but the R.C.s—and the wrath of the R.C.s she contemplates with something like satisfaction!

'On personal grounds she has been absolutely won over to the marriage; the political objections a little frighten her, but she is in process of persuading herself that they may be ignored. I believe the Princess of Wales is working for the marriage. She hates the idea of a German alliance. She likes Princess Hélène. She thinks she will be a good wife for her son, and she looks no further.

'I suspect the Comtesse de Paris, in the interests of deerstalking, to be favourable also. She is more certain that it is good to be Queen of England than she is that it is bad to marry a Protestant. The Comte de Paris, on the other hand, is said to be a strict Roman Catholic—"but not bigoted" says the Queen. I shall be surprised, however, if he is not bigoted enough to object to his daughter changing her creed for a crown.

'In my conversation with the Queen last night, I did not say much beyond pointing out the extremely awkward position everybody would be placed in if, after an abortive attempt on the French throne, the Duke d'Orléans were to take refuge at the Court of his sister, the Queen of England.'

To this letter from Balfour, Salisbury telegraphed a reply by return:

'If the Queen speaks to you about the marriage, urge the Comte de Paris should be immediately communicated with. Point out that marriage with a French woman will be very unpopular, still more with one who was a Roman Catholic and has changed her religion to obtain the English throne. Some people will not believe conversion to be sincere, and that she will still act in the Roman Catholic interests: all will despise her for it. F.O. objections, though in the second rank, are

serious.   It will produce great and general offence abroad.   Germans
will be angry because she is French; Republicans in France and because
of her Orléans family French Royalists on account of change of religion.
Prevent any Royal consent being given.   Time will enable Canterbury
to work on the Princess and I doubt perseverance of the young Prince—
Salisbury.'

After interminable tergiversations and discussions, the project was
dropped, partly at least because the Pope refused to allow Princess
Hélène to change her religion.   On December 3, 1891, the Prince
became engaged instead to Princess Mary of Teck; but he died scarcely
a month later on January 14, 1892, and Princess Mary married his
younger brother, who was to become George V.   (Extracts from these
Papers, which have not before been published, are given in Appendix I.)

This brief personal acquaintance with the problems of monarchy—
which became deeper and closer as the years went by—heralded a
further step, and a big one, in Balfour's ascent of the political ladder.
W. H. Smith, who somewhat unexpectedly had proved a first-class
Leader of the House and First Lord of the Treasury, had for some
time been in feeble health.   As early as 1888, Balfour had been quite
matter-of-fact in his approach to his uncle on the subject: 'If Smith
goes', he had written on November 23, 1888, 'there are as far as I can
see only two men now on the Bench who can possibly succeed him—
Goschen and myself.'

But, he continues, there are 'grave objections' to himself, the main
one being that Goschen would object on the grounds that Balfour was
not even an M.P. when he (Goschen) was first in the Cabinet.   Yet
Goschen is a Liberal Unionist; he could hardly lead the Conservative
Party 'unless he consented to call himself a Conservative and join the
Carlton'.

Even so, there are other objections to him: 'His fussiness drives Smith
mad. . . .   He cannot stay on the Bench, through mere fidgetiness, for
ten minutes consecutively; during those ten minutes his perpetual
comments on what is going on quite drown the text, so that when one
gets up to reply, it is Goschen one feels inclined to reply to, as he is the
only person one had heard!'   All the same he is able and loyal and
'obviously honest'.

Chamberlain on the other hand, Balfour believes, 'would not and
could not join'.   Hartington, again, is likely to be soon removed from
the Commons since his father (the Duke of Devonshire) is seriously ill.
(In fact, he died shortly after Smith.)   Balfour did not even mention
Churchill—he was quite, and forever, out of the running; while Hicks-
Beach at the Board of Trade had been the subject of several slighting
references in letters from Balfour to his uncle, though himself expressing
his belief that Balfour would be the best man for the post.

Salisbury no doubt weighed these points—and others—in his mind; but when the Leadership became vacant in October, 1891, Balfour had to be the man. The body of Conservative M.P.s were against Goschen, though he had so often deputised for Smith. Many of them were strongly in favour of Balfour. Aretas Akers-Douglas, the Conservative Chief Whip, sounded a number of them out, and received enthusiastic replies. Hicks-Beach himself told him that Balfour was 'the only man possible and he has every necessary quality and must be Leader'. Walter Long, a country squire and later a contender for the Leadership wrote:

'I cannot say how important it is that Arthur should be made Leader—we want not only a man with his ability, courage and determination, but also one who will inspire our Party all through the country with courage and awake their *sentiment*. All this and more Arthur can do—his only fault, if fault it can be called—is a sort of indolence and a strong contempt for popularity—but his sense of duty is strong enough to overcome this—and if he is now made Leader he will realise the necessity of doing his utmost and of rousing himself. If any man now living can lead us to victory and keep us together that man is Arthur. Surely the fact that he is Lord Salisbury's nephew will not be allowed to interfere? The idea seems preposterous and ridiculous.'

Salisbury, however, was by no means happy about the necessity: '(The selection) is embarrassing and painful. Arthur will take the reins under very unpromising circumstances and will be exposed to very jealous criticism . . . I confess it will be very painful to me if—as seems possible—I have to pass over Goschen.' Salisbury had earlier written to his wife: 'There is no help for it—Arthur must take it. Beach was possible: Goschen is not. But I think it bad for Arthur—and I do not feel certain how the experiment will end.'

Goschen took the decision very well; Balfour, according to Salisbury, accepted promotion with 'rather a wry face'. This may seem strange since Balfour had now a strong, and natural, desire to advance in politics, and since clearly this was a step—only five years after he had first entered the Cabinet—to the premiership. One must, of course, remember that Salisbury's remark was made to Hicks-Beach, and may therefore have somehow been intended to soften the blow. On the other hand, Balfour, in saying good-bye to Ireland, was saying good-bye to the most successful part of his career to date, and he expressed his regret clearly in a letter, which again may be slightly suspect for it is addressed to none other than Goschen:

'I don't like leaving Ireland. It is odd, but nevertheless true, that quite apart from the interest attaching to Irish administration, there had grown up ties with the grim old Castle and this beastly town which it is painful to sever . . .'

Then Balfour adds: 'I feel as if I had had a good time which has for ever come to an end; and the thought is not agreeable.' A 'good time' is not the expression one might have imagined he would apply to his four years of difficulty and danger in a country on the verge of civil war. Yet he was, in a sense, correct: it was the toughness of Ireland which had turned him from a dilettante into a strong man, and enabled him to emerge from nonentity into eminence. Of *course* it had been a 'good time'.

He sailed from Ireland at the end of October, 1891, and crossed St. George's Channel—which being a bad sailor, he used to refer to as 'not the least invincible of Irish difficulties'—almost for the last time. Was it perhaps on this occasion that on a sheet of 'Chief Secretary's Lodge' writing-paper he broke into verse:

'What know we of the sea?   Its amorous deeps
Follow the wandering moon with vain desires—
In many a fragrant tropic bay it sleeps—
It moans round many a Northern crag; nor tires
Though everlasting tempests scourge its waves
Past [the grim cliffs of] (illegible) melancholy Isle
When evermore the spring withholds its smile
And evermore the frozen foam is cast
High on the rocks by the pursuing blast.

Yet storm and calm are but a passing show
Born of the restless mood of wind or skies,
Still and untroubled in the depths below
The mighty waters wrapped in darkness lie.
The secret then, slow creeping from the Poles
O'er freezing ooze and bare unfruitful sand
Silent and chill the torpid current rolls
About the old foundation of the land,
No boisterous challenge from the gale it hears
And changes not with all the changing years.

One of the immediate problems when he returned to England was the question of his successor at the Irish Office. Eventually W. L. Jackson, recently made Postmaster-General, was appointed. It is interesting to note Balfour's views on Jackson, given in a letter to his uncle in August, 1891. Here emerges the patrician standpoint which, for all his ease of manner, was as natural to Balfour as to his uncle:

'Jackson has great tact and judgement—middle-class tact and judgement I admit, but good of their kind. He justly inspires great confidence in business men and he is that *rara avis*, a successful manufacturer who is fit for something besides manufacturing. A Cabinet of Jacksons would be rather a serious order no doubt; but one or even two would be a considerable addition to any Cabinet.'

The appointment of Balfour as Leader was generally accepted without qualms by most Conservatives; Churchill as might be expected, wrote to his wife on November 23, 1891:

'So Arthur Balfour is really Leader—and Tory Democracy, the genuine article is at an end. . . . After all, A.B. cannot beat my record; and it was I who first got him into the Government then into the Cabinet.' The two latter assertions were, as we have seen, not true. But as for 'Tory Democracy', formulated in the Deptford programme of 1886, it had not so much ended as scarcely begun. It was, in any case, as Rosebery observed, an 'imposture'—Radicalism in Tory sheep's clothing—which may ultimately have been the reason for Conservative rejection of Churchill. Radicalism already had its new, more powerful representative in politics in the person of David Lloyd George, elected to Parliament for Carnarvon Boroughs in 1890.

Balfour first appeared in the House in his new rôle in February, 1892. It was a rôle that clearly made him feel somewhat uncomfortable. Instead of the cool sparring matches in which he rejoiced as Chief Secretary, he now found himself in a position almost as official as the Speaker's. True, his main charge was to shepherd his Party flock, but the other side of the House had also to be considered in the matter of arranging business, and this had been W. H. Smith's strong point.

Balfour treated the whole thing perfunctorily. Often he did not enter until long after business had begun; often he retired before the cry of 'Who goes home?' He thus broke an unwritten rule; and his transgression was ill-received not only by the Opposition but by his own side, too. Balfour, as Lucy remarked, 'regards his duty from a different point of view, lounging in when questions are almost over, and then delegating to his colleagues the task of answering those personally addressed to him'.

Perhaps it did not matter much, for in 1892 the Parliament of 1886 was clearly on its last legs. Legislatively, the Conservative Party had done well. Apart from its Irish achievements, its Local Government Act of 1888 creating 62 County Councils, had helped stir the administrative activities of the countryside; the Education Act of 1891 had made elementary education free; the Factory Act of the same year had raised the minimum age for employing children in factories to 11, and had fixed the maximum hours of labour for women at 12, with 1½ hours for meals. Meanwhile, Goschen at the Exchequer had managed to defray the rising expenditure, not least on an increased Army and Navy estimate and a special naval building programme.

Abroad, Salisbury had successfully negotiated pacts with Germany, France and Portugal, defining spheres of influence in Africa. The dockers' victory in the strike of 1889, and the booming Trade Unionism were as yet clouds no bigger than a man's hand upon the political backcloth.   Socialism, however, was abroad and a new understanding of the gross conditions of the workers.   Balfour himself reflected this understanding when, at a Press Fund dinner in June, 1892, he referred to 'the desire for the amelioration of the lot of the great classes of community', and thought it would be an 'interesting question' how far the 'democratic constitution now firmly established in these islands is going to deal successfully with the social problems with which we are brought face to face'.

Balfour once expressed his lack of interest in newspapers and said he seldom read one.   This was immediately seized upon by journalists to limn their crude picture of Balfour—a 'gimmick' to add to his absent-mindedness, his love of music and his sylph-like figure.   In fact, he was always informed by his private secretary of what the papers said.   Incidentally, he was always ready to 'use' the newspapers.   In his 'Irish Letter Book' there is a letter of 1888 to G. E. Buckle, editor of *The Times*, asking him to insert a letter under a 'fictitious signature (say "News")' to counter 'Gladstone's persistent mendacity'.

The Parliament of 1886 was prorogued in July, 1892.   At the General Election next month, Balfour held his seat at East Manchester, though with a steep fall in his majoriy.   The Liberals were returned to power, though their small majority of 40 meant that once again they were at the mercy of the Irish party, still split into pro- and anti-Parnellite groupings.   The Election was again fought on the Home Rule issue.   The business, serious enough in itself, was now clearly beginning to be, as it were, the escape vent for passions altogether too strong for their overt subject.   Home Rule was the boil which in-dicated that the body politic was not in good health—a body worried by signs of 'democracy', murmurs of Socialism, fears of a declining economy.   But it was easier to take sides, to explode, about something definite and tangible, like Ireland, than about something vast and not easily formulated such as radical changes in the social and economic structure, or the industrial rise of Germany.

Even Balfour was bitten by the bug, though how conscious of it, how ultimately cynical about it he was, is not clear.   During the Election campaign itself, while speaking in Midlothian, he warned his audience that Gladstone's solution for Irish difficulties would only add one more, namely Ulster; and he said that the Protestant North would resist such a domination as was envisaged by the Liberal leader.   In fact, 'Ulster will fight, Ulster will be right'.

A year later Balfour went further still.   At a gigantic demonstration in Belfast, he said on April 5, 1893:

'You have had to fight for your liberties before.   I pray you may never have to fight for them again.   I do not believe you ever will have to fight for them.   I admit the tyranny of the majority may be as bad as the tyranny of kings; and that the stupidity of a majority may be even greater than that of kings; and I will not say, and I do not think that any rational or sober man will say, that what is justifiable against a tyrannical king may not under certain circumstances be justifiable against a tyrannical majority. I hope and believe that this is but the utterance of a mere abstract proposition, and that circumstances which would justify such a state of things may never arise in this country.'

The Ulster crowds roared their applause and cheered Balfour to the echo. A man, accidentally run over by Balfour's carriage wheel, said that he would willingly be run over again to shake Balfour's hand.

When the Conservatives found themselves in Opposition, they were no doubt glad of a pause in their labours. It was clear enough that the Liberal Government could not long survive either its dependence on the Irish, or its leader's obsession with installing Home Rule. There was, however, one slight doubt in some Conservative minds: what now would be Chamberlain's attitude?

Immediately after the Election, on July 26, 1892, Balfour wrote to his uncle: 'I had a long and interesting talk with Joe. He has always been very cordial and open with me.' (It is interesting to note the change from Balfour's 'Chamberlain—the most vindictive of men'. But it is also worth mentioning that in March, 1892, Balfour had told Lady Elcho: 'Joe, though we all love him, somehow does not absolutely and completely mix, does not form a chemical combination with us.')

The upshot of Balfour's exchanges with him were satisfactory: 'Chamberlain's anxiety to work with the Conservatives and his dislike of Gladstonians is as hearty and severe as ever,' he reported. Chamberlain, in other words, had no thought of returning to the Liberal fold. When opportunity arose, he could now be brought into a Conservative Government, but from Balfour's point of view, brought in on a lower level than his own. Balfour felt fairly sure that Chamberlain would be an excellent ally. He was right in his forecast.

Gladstone duly presented his second Home Rule Bill to the House; it was duly attacked, passed in the Commons, rejected by the Lords, which had an overwhelming Conservative majority. It was easy—too easy as the constitutional crisis of 1910–11 was to make clear. But for the moment all was well. Home Rule was dead.

On March 2, 1894, Balfour received a letter from Gladstone under a 'private and confidential' seal:

'Dear Mr. Balfour. You will probably have divined with others that the current speculations and announcements about me, though unauthorised and for the moment untrue, are not without meaning. That I should give them such a meaning until after tomorrow, when I expect to bring my responsible action to a virtual close, would be improper, and I must ask you kindly to bear this in mind. But I am anxious that you should know from myself that it is my intention after a

Council which will be held to-morrow to tender my formal resignation to Her Majesty. And I hope you will accept this letter as a personal acknowledgement from me, the only one in my power to offer, for the marked courtesy and kindness to me individually which has marked your conduct in Parliament as Leader of the Opposition. Believe me with many pleasant recollections, and with every good wish, sincerely yours W. E. Gladstone.'

'P.S. Forgive me if this note bears token anywhere of visual powers not so good as they once were. And pray do not consider this letter as one leading to an answer.'

The next day Gladstone resigned and an era in political history came to an end.

Politics had sharply divided Gladstone and Balfour; both had given and taken from each other some sharp knocks, most memorable of which from Balfour were his two remarks in the Commons:

'Mr. Gladstone was formerly as ready to blacken the Irish Members' characters as he is now ready to blacken their boots';

and,

'I am quite aware that the only way to make Mr. Gladstone retract a statement is to send him a lawyer's letter.'

Yet, once the Kilmainham speech of 1884 had ceased to rankle, Gladstone's personal liking for Balfour had returned. Margot Tennant, writing to Balfour in January, 1888, reported that Gladstone said of him that 'he had never loved a young man so much as you and that your quickness had delighted him and your astonishing grip of difficult subjects'.

Balfour replied to 'Miss Margot': 'I am very glad you like the Old Man: for my part I *love* him, and *if* he be (as *I* think he is) the most unfair of Parliamentary speakers and the most unscrupulous of party managers, so I dare say would the most virtuous of mankind be, if, with his peculiar mental and oratorical endowments, they were subjected for 55 years to the blessed influences of free government!'

Balfour became a frequent visitor to Hawarden during this period. The last time was in 1896 (Gladstone died in 1898) when he rode up from the station on his 'bike' to which he had long been devoted—golf and 'biking' probably accounted for his slim figure. The G.O.M. was, however, shocked. He thought it ill-befitted the First Lord of the Treasury to ride a bicycle in public.

With Gladstone's resignation, Lord Rosebery, who had been Foreign Minister, succeeded to the premiership and formed a new Liberal Cabinet. Balfour never cared for Rosebery, and the feeling was mutual. Yet their backgrounds—Scottish, aristocratic, literary— were not dissimilar. Sir Frederick Ponsonby, son of Queen Victoria's private secretary, and himself in the service of the Court, wrote: 'I was always surprised at the way he (Balfour) and Lord Rosebery disliked each other, when really they were so much alike and there seems little difference in the way they looked on the various questions of the day. They were both literary, both very cynical, and both lazy. . . . There was always a certain rivalry between them. Rosebery said that for an amateur politician Balfour was wonderful: while Balfour told me he always admired the glib way Rosebery spoke when he knew little or nothing of the subject on which he was speaking.'

During Rosebery's undistinguished Government, Balfour was not particularly active in the Commons. He had, indeed, to remain much in London, but he found himself able to get on with his second book of philosophy and to enjoy more often social life where he remained the cynosure of fair women and clever men.

II

By the time Balfour became Leader of the House, the pattern of his private life was already firmly established. His time was divided between London, Whittingehame, country houses such as Longleat, Wilton, Ashridge, Stanway and Clouds, and annual expeditions to Austria and France. At Whittingehame, there had been many changes. No longer was it a silent, rather cheerless house. Both his brothers, Eustace and Gerald, now had small children and for six months of the year the families stayed on the Balfour estate. A new generation occupied the nurseries. Several of the children have put it on record that the months they spent at Whittingehame were the best of their small lives, with the round of picnics, galloping ponies and visits to the seashore nearby. Their elders seldom interfered; but when 'Nunkie', as they called Balfour, was present, it was a red-letter day.

'He was', his niece Lady Eve Balfour has said, 'the most important person in our lives. . . . I remember when I was quite small taking it for granted that the hill behind Edinburgh was called Arthur's Seat after *my* Uncle Arthur.' The children were never oppressed in his presence; rather they made him their confidante, for he was always ready to listen to them and scarcely ever took them to task. He treated them, in fact, as grown-ups. He also took part in their games: 'Everything was fun', says Lady Eve, 'if he was in it.' He was ready to discuss any subject with them; only when he was utterly bored by nonsense or pretentiousness did he issue 'gentle deadly little blasts of sarcasm', as his niece Blanche wrote.

Yet he was never unkind: 'Even when he laughed at you,' says Lady Eve, 'you loved him for it, because, in the way in which he did it, you could always share the joke.' He genuinely enjoyed the talk of young people; all his life he felt that the new generation was superior to the old—a most unusual characteristic in the distinguished of elder generations—and he was delighted to receive letters from his nephews and nieces as they, in turn, went out into the world.

At Whittingehame, his routine was: breakfast in bed, dictation of letters in his bedroom, lunch *en famille*—or with visitors, with the children at a side-table.   Then bicycle rides or golf or later tennis in the afternoons and leisurely tea, again *en famille* in the library.   After this Balfour retired to his reading and writing in his own sitting-room which nobody invaded unless by invitation or request.   At dinner the family, except the very youngest, met again with a certain formality. Afterwards there might be a little bridge (which he played badly) or some music.   He read for an hour or two before retiring for the night.

Cycling became a major pleasure, mainly because it gave him complete independence in getting about.   During the time he was learning to ride, he once appeared on the Treasury Bench with his arm in a sling and his foot in a slipper.   By means of the bicycle, he said, he first became acquainted with his own county and he would discuss, some thought excessively, roads, gradients and maps.   Later he bought one of the earliest motor-cars—a De Dion—from which also he gained great pleasure, but not perhaps ever as much as from the pedal-cycle, and he never drove himself.

For golf he developed a real enthusiasm, and between 1891 and 1914 devoted a month of every holiday season to it, playing at the North Berwick course and staying at a hotel there, overlooking the 17th green and the first tee, 'framed in a landscape', he wrote 'embracing the little harbour, the Isle of May, and other islands which skirt the Firth of Forth, and the stately profile of the Bass Rock'.   He played two or more rounds a day, and in the evenings did his official work and his writing.   Each Friday he drove to Whittingehame and spent the weekend there with his family and guests.

What was the attraction of golf?   In 1890, he contributed an article called 'The Humours of Golf' to 'The Badminton Library of Sports and Pastimes' in which he demonstrates that from every point of view—age, circumstances, lack of boredom—golf is the game nonpareil, and he sums up in a memorable *bon mot*: 'Care may sit behind the horseman, she never presumes to walk with the caddie.'

He personally, he wrote elsewhere, belonged 'to that unhappy class of beings for ever pursued by remorse, who are conscious that they threw away in their youth opportunities that were open to them of beginning the game at a time of life when alone the muscles can be attuned and practised to the full perfection required by the most difficult game that perhaps exists!'

Tennis, indeed, had been Balfour's first love—he never had much time for hunting, shooting or cricket—and he played it into his seventies. But golf was at once more distractive of care, and yet permitted a certain gentle rumination not unsuitable to a philosopher. He even went so far as to have a miniature course built round Whittingehame House itself; but he had a hard tennis court as well.

Life at Whittingehame sounds ideal, a positive symphony in relaxation. But there was another side to it which neither Lady Eve Balfour, nor his other niece and later biographer, Mrs. Dugdale observed or, at any rate, recorded. There *was*, however, a recorder of the other side. One of the daughters of Lady Elcho, Lady Cynthia Asquith, was roughly contemporary with some of the Balfour nephews and nieces, and while her mother resided at Gosford House, Longniddry, a short drive from Whittingehame, Cynthia was a regular visitor, and joined the young Balfours' dancing classes, conducted by a visiting master with his fiddle tucked underneath his chin.

Cynthia Elcho observed all the exciting things of a Whittingehame childhood; she noted how the whole household 'revolved like the solar system round the sun, worshipping him with an unveiled idolatry of which he seemed to be sublimely unconscious'. Yet she thought that 'Arthur Balfour never shone quite so brightly in his own home as elsewhere'. This was partly because the household, ruled by Alice Balfour, was decidedly old-fashioned and somewhat eccentrically ordered. Clocks, for instance, were always kept an hour in advance of Greenwich time, presumably to ensure that trains were caught. Smoking was allowed nowhere except in the grim smoking-room. All games and communal activities were banned on Sunday. Alice Balfour also had a mania for checking the numbers of spoons, forks and other cutlery. 'My impression', Cynthia Elcho adds, 'was that in some ways Arthur Balfour lived like a guest in his own house.'

Balfour was no doubt aware of the undercurrents of dislikes and jealousies that went on within his family circle—Alice's quarrels with her sisters and her sister-in-law, Lady Frances, not the least; but on the whole they did not interfere with his calm mode of life—and, in any case, all were united in making the way smooth for him.

Besides this, Balfour had a very deep love for his native heath, the Scottish Lowlands and East Lothian in particular. There is a very striking and beautifully written passage in a letter to Lady Elcho dated September 10, 1892, shortly after he had finally sold his Highland estate at Strathconan. Balfour was certainly chary of penning the warmer sort of personal epistle; but he could safely let himself go over his homeland:

'Certainly I like the Lowlands better than the Highlands. It may be that as I am no longer a Highlander I have a personal motive for coming to this conclusion. But whether it be for this or for some other reason, certain it is that as I looked, *not* I admit without a momentary pang, at the heather, the burns, the ever changing aspect of the un-changing hills, I did so no longer as a lover, but as an artist, even as a critic.   I looked, I admired, and was ready to pass on.

'I am too old to think that I could find an abiding home in the midst of scenery which, however, splendid looks most splendid in a raging tempest or in the transient gleams between two hailstorms.   I would as soon marry a woman who was never interesting except when she was in a passion.

'But the Lowlands when you know them, you can take to your heart. You can live in them and die in them.   They are filled with the un-dying selves of sad old histories, and yet are of all Britain the part most full of vigorous modern life and energies.   They are now, as they always have been, the real Scotland: not the queer mixture of poverty-stricken crofters, luxurious shooting-lodges, sham chieftains, sham tartans and London-born Highlanders which constitute Scotland to the Southern imagination.'

The false-romantic attracted Balfour no more than did scenery empty of life.   He did not abhor industrial England or Scotland, for it spoke of energy and national greatness.   The genuine, the solid, the real—whether in the music of Handel or the study of science—were what interested and moved him.

There is another sentence in the passage on the Lowlands which catches one's attention: '*I would as soon marry a woman who was never interesting except when she was in a passion.*'   In his correspondence during the 1890s, there are several scattered generalisations about women and about marriage—usually with a somewhat denigratory tone.   The subject of marriage evidently bothered him.   He was now between 40 and 50.   If he were to marry at all, he was of a ripe enough age.   As we saw, he had had marriage in mind in the 1870s, and he had certainly shown little antagonism towards the state of matrimony at that time.

What concerned him particularly was the question of the inheritance. (After 1902, when his brother Gerald had a son, it was always under-stood that he would be the heir.)   Towards the end of the decade, when he was 50, he discussed this matter with his sister, Nora, and she encouraged him in the idea of marriage.   But, he asked her, 'What have I got to offer to anyone—nothing but ashes?'   Was he perhaps thinking he had loved once and never again?   Was he rather sheltering behind a slightly baffling phrase because he had no positive inclination for the married state?   Or was it his long affair with Lady Elcho which had reduced him to ashes?

Here at any rate, the biographer is on firmer ground, for the relation-ship with Lady Elcho is well documented, mainly in the stream of letters, somewhat carelessly or accidentally preserved among Balfour's

11. Robert, third Marquess of Salisbury (1830–1903): uncle of A.J.B.

12. A.J.B., aged about 37

Etching by Charles Laurie

13. The Countess of Wemyss, aged about 70, born Mary Wyndham, later Viscountess Elcho

By courtesy of Lady Violet Benson

14. 'The Man on the Raft'. A.J.B. adrift between Joseph Chamberlain and the Duke of Devonshire. Cartoon published in *The Westminster Gazette*, January 20, 1904

papers. (It is curious that several packages of papers dealing with the private affairs of his friend, Harry Cust, should have carried instructions, duly carried out, that they were to be burned after his death, while his own correspondence from Lady Elcho is to be found not only at Whittingehame but even among the papers at the British Museum.)

One of Lady Elcho's letters dates the beginning of their 'intimacy', as she calls it, from 1885. By the turn of the decade, the affair was beginning to be bruited in family circles, not least Lady Elcho's own. Her letters tell of trouble with her husband. She begins to take precautions about the servants. A letter from Clouds, her father's home, in January, 1890, says: 'I am writing to George (her brother, George Wyndham) and will send this little superhuman scrawl by him for the sake of the Butler's feelings, and George must think what he likes . . .' She refers to their plans for meeting, and their rationing of public encounters to avoid scandal. She reminds him of his afternoon visits at Stanway to her 'East Room' when it 'was the right paradise for both of us'.

One letter will suffice to show both the strength of her feelings and the agitations into which she was cast by the situation. Writing from an Austrian spa she was visiting for her health—the letter is undated but clearly about 1890—she says:

'When I come home you may find me quite another Being! So many occurrences, circs., thoughts and impressions are conspiring from all parts and in all ways to make me re-make my Bed and alter my course etc. Like voices without, within and all around, they insist, press on, on relentlessly and I should like to be deaf to them and yet I hope they may never grow silent—and the voices of the Children are the loudest and strongest of all—you have often spoken rightly of them but *not at all* in the way you mean.

'It is all so *sad*, so painful, so hopeless and bewildering. So *hard* sometimes, so inspiring [*sic*] and always so bitter. In cowardice one almost wishes that death would intervene, but I don't want to struggle on and on and I want to struggle the right way. Pain and separation are worse than death—and fires seem around one which ever way one turns, fires which one flinches from and yet I feel my heart must be burnt out before I can live and yet I feel I cannot live without a *certain love* and why should it be death to the soul? Hang my soul I say! But what I dread most is the bitter hopeless repentance at the end when the clear sight comes and when hundreds suffer by one's own fault and it is too late, too late. Better were it if one had never been born—This I hope *you* will soon burn.' (Over-written is: 'Excuse this nonsense'.)

The dilemma to which she refers is not clear, but it can only concern some decision to be taken that would bring their liaison before the public—either by way of divorce proceedings or legal action by Lord Elcho. The dilemma must, of course, have been made more

heartrending by the fact that in this decade of her regular intimacy—
at one time, she mentions, they met daily—Mary Elcho bore almost a
child a year. It is possibly to the obvious problems raised by this
situation that the following letter by Balfour refers. (It is preserved
among other of his letters at Stanway. These letters were listed by
Mary Elcho, then the Countess of Wemyss, in the early 1930s after
Balfour's death; some contain blacked-out sentences and some have
been presumably suppressed altogether.)

It is prefaced by a note in Mary Elcho's handwriting: 'Letter from
A.J.B. written 6th March 1887 before he went to Ireland as Chief
Secretary'. It reads:

'My dear Francis. Accidents have occurred to a Chief Secretary for
Ireland before and (though I think it improbable) they may occur
again. If the worst (as people euphemistically say!) should happen,
cut open with your penknife the accompanying parcel and read the
scrawl inside. It relates to a matter with which only you can deal:—
but leaves unsaid through want of time all the things I would have said
to you and all the other dear ones whom (in the highly improbable
event above alluded to) I should leave behind.

'I do not at all feel in the situation of a soldier going on a forlorn
hope; but one cannot be sure in this weary world of anything—not
even of the competence of the police force. Yrs. A.J.B.'

Though Balfour did return safely from Ireland, the 'accompanying
parcel' is no longer attached to the letter. The addressee, 'Francis', is
presumably, Francis, Earl of Wemyss, Mary Elcho's father-in-law;
the exact nature of 'the matter' with which only he could deal on
Balfour's death remains uncertain.

After the first few years of the affair, Balfour was evidently the pursued, not the pursuer, even though in the early stages he was glad to be
pursued. By 1890 he was less inclined to be upset when their plans for
private meetings were upset by circumstances. Mary Elcho writes:

'You are more patient—more reasonable (which very word I kick at!)
in all things than I am (of *course* it is because you care less! *feel* less!). . . .'

Elsewhere she speaks of his 'eternal, tiresome, chronic, constitutional
rightness which makes you offensive and arrogant. I love your rightness, but I don't love being despised, and really what with being perhaps a little morbid and with feeling that I was loathsome to you—
that you hated me because of what you offensively call my "condition",
I began to fear that I might lose my nerve with you and be "afraid of
you" as some of your own family are supposed to be—now that would
be *fatal*; I quite admit that we have had what you call rows, I mean that
I have had fits of discontent or temper or call it what you like, but we
have never had difficulties about *plans* before or whole days passing
without seeing each other. . . . You say that you hate wasting time

doing nothing (quite sound) and that you never know my state of strength. Of course there are little difficulties on each side but the way is for each person to say out *everything quickly* (ha! ha!). . . . I always tell you everything Hugo says, agreeable or the reverse so that you may know where you are. . . . I am naturally reckless and don't hear gossip and my family are peculiar in one direction while yours (Aunt S and co.) are peculiar in another.'

She tries to be reasonable and understanding, but her infatuation is not easily suppressed: ' "I am not going to say you are different from what you used to be, for that would be wicked, wanton and unwise, but the fact remains "that you love me as much as a man can love a woman he has loved for ten years". Now I believe you love me more than many men would do after that time and I would not have you different in any way.'

What did Mary Elcho hope for? Divorce and remarriage, in those days, held unspeakable terrors and certain miseries; indeed Balfour, in as delicate a manner as possible, made it clear that he had no thoughts of such eventualities. Writing in 1892 about the marriage of his old friend, Alfred Lyttelton, whose first wife, Laura, had died, he says that his sister-in-law, Frances, had set her mind on his marrying the lady of Lyttelton's choice—D. D. Balfour. 'In vain', he says, 'I tell her that, *quite apart from other reasons*, Miss D.D. is and has been for two years, in love with Alfred and not with me; that, whether I have time for *Love* or not, I certainly have no time for Matrimony. . . .'

There were undoubtedly occasions when Mary Elcho's demands, however insinuatingly conveyed, bored and irritated him. She was, after all, far less near his intellectual mark than many other women then in Society; and her affection and passion were the more exigent. There is a certain tartness—indeed more than a touch of that ungraceful Whittingehame *froideur*—about this letter he wrote in reply to one of hers, now lost, whose terms one can imagine:

'Your letter gave me a little pain;—but not very much for I understand the reasons which moved you to write it. Yet I do not repent that I said nothing in my last epistle of the kind which perhaps you wished. Such things are impossible to me; and they would if said *to* me give such exquisite pain that I could never bring myself to say them to others—even at their desire. Moreover, if I am to speak all my mind, the mention of topics of such kind with shooting invitations, bicycles, cures for obesity and current literature is to my mind (word illegible) repulsion—though I think that in this respect I may be singular, but enough of this. I return the letters. . . .'

But, contrary to what one might suppose, there was never a complete break in their friendship; passion shaded off gradually into mutual interest, but the mutual interest remained and flourished to the end of

Balfour's life. They continued to see each other frequently—though even in the 'nineties Balfour had other close feminine friends, such as Etty Desborough who occasioned jealous outbreaks in Mary—and their letters, at least on her side, remained regular, though Balfour did not always read them and was often remiss in answering them.

It is not easy to date the end of their physical intimacy. As late as 1898 she writes intimately—about, for instance, a self-induced abortion —and she cannot for long conceal her longing for him, particularly when, as in 1898, she was away from England taking the cure at Kissingen in Germany. Occasionally she becomes quite skittish about their relations. She described herself in the third person—'a girl more well behaved than any in the world but who from long association and constant intercourse with a certain man who is old enough to know better and to whom she came with all the admiration of a disciple' has become, as a result of the 'direct teaching of this man, *very* different to what she was; indeed I may say "no better than she should be!" Look to it, take it to heart, dissolute man.'

To Lady Elcho, Balfour was the 'Hero'; like his family, she saw her duty as being to make him happy and smooth his path. Few men can resist such treatment; few men do not soon find it cloying. But Balfour, at least, concealed it as well as he was able, and continued to treat her with indulgence.

From the letters between them, one may learn much of Balfour's social as well as political interests and attitudes. We hear in 1893, of Oscar Wilde's invitation to him to go and see his new play, *A Woman of No Importance*; of his 'absolute dis-aptitude' for cards; of his meeting at the Roseberys' in 1885 with Matthew Arnold ('He has only one subject of conversation, and that is himself, but he treats it amusingly.').

We also hear much of his reading. In 1895, he writes: 'I have rather enjoyed myself reading theology and electricity, struggling with an extraordinarily tiresome French novel and playing four games of (real) tennis.' He re-reads *Esmond* after 20 years and 'the reperusal did not make me like it better or at all reconcile me to its author who with all his talent writes himself down "Snob" in every paragraph, and whose greasy moralisings make me sick. . . .'

He reads physiology and geology, and re-reads—'just when every-body else has forgotten it,—Edward Fitzgerald's letters. His tastes— many of them at least—I sympathise with. He liked Handel and dis-liked Tennyson's poems (except the first volume). So do I. He dis-approved of matrimony and Mrs. Browning. So do I. But he saw no merit in Miss Austen and his favourite occupation was sailing in a fishing boat:—both damnable heresies! Talking of Mrs. Browning, I am glad Mr. Browning is dead. In these days neither old poets nor old politicians sufficiently recognise the virtues of silence.'

Lady Elcho had a remarkable way of passing without pause, without paragraph, from the sublime to the ridiculous. She observes, for instance, that *What Maisie Knew* is a work of genius (a view not then generally held, partly because Henry James had few readers), and passes on to remark that Lady Campbell-Bannerman—wife of the Liberal politician—had become a 'huge mountain of flesh'. She switches from the details of a self-induced miscarriage (brought about by bicycling), to her attitude to death. This evoked an interesting reply from Balfour on August 17, 1899:

'I do not think, so far as I can judge in the absence of actual experience, that I am at all afraid of dying. But I have a shrinking horror of the separations caused by the death of those I love. I thought of Alfred and Laura; of Gerald, and of others, of what has been and of what might be, and went to bed a most miserable man. What horrible capacities for pain we have; if only our other gifts were in proportion!'

Balfour tells her sometimes of his more curious visits:

'To the A. Sassoons, at Brighton. Found there Rosebery, Devonshire and H. Farquhar. We discovered to our deep indignation that we had been brought down under false pretences. The Prince had been opening a hospital in the morning and was staying at the Reuben Sassoons till Monday! We were dragged *both* nights to a long, hot and pompous dinner at the latter—peopled with endless Sassoon girls. . . . I believe the Hebrews were in an actual majority—and tho' I have no prejudices against the race (quite the contrary) I began to understand the point of view of those who object to alien immigration!'

Or again:

'Last night I met Mrs. Joe Chamberlain for the first time. She is supposed to be a "replica" of Lady Hilda (Brodrick); and really *is* rather like. In any case a nice woman, simple, natural and refined:— not the least shy nor overweighted with all the new responsibilities— Birmingham, London and half-a-dozen step-children—so suddenly thrust upon her. She professes the keenest interest in English Politics, and I gather that much of the correspondence that passed between her and Joe during their long engagement turned upon the arid subject:— very remote I should have thought from "Love's young dream".'

One of these letters is worth attention for its prophetic nature. In August, 1892, Balfour wrote to Mary about her brother, George Wyndham's, visit to the fortune teller. 'She appears to have told him "everything which he ever did", to have prophesied many good things, but to have incidentally announced that he was to die at 50!' And in 1913, Wyndham did die, aged 50.

There are scattered references also to Spiritualism in which Balfour remained always deeply interested, as was the whole of Society from Queen Victoria downwards. (She is said to have written many journals on the subject, which were destroyed after her death by her secretary and the Dean of Windsor.)   In the same letter Balfour notes: 'Professor Oliver Lodge, Ricket and F. Myers have got outstanding results of the funiture-moving type under the most stringent tests.   The experiments have taken place in a small island off the Riviera coast belonging to Ricket and thither Nora and H. Sidgwick have transferred in order to see with their own eyes what is being done. . . .'

Oliver Lodge, then Professor of Physics at University College, was a frequent guest at Stanway.   Cynthia Asquith gave us an amusing sketch in *Haply I May Remember* of Lodge, dignified, serious and quite humourless, lecturing with blackboard and easel on electrons, cyclons and wireless telegraphy with Balfour and Wyndham plying him with intelligent questions.

Indeed, Lady Cynthia's two books of reminiscence, delightful in themselves, are particularly revealing of Balfour as he was in her own family circle.   He was not, she wrote, 'aloof' as he has often been portrayed: 'I can never think of him as a "negative" man.   I too often heard him speak with enthusiasm; saw his eyes glow with it too.'   But she also suggested that, as a child, she sometimes felt an obscure discomfort in his presence, despite his charm and interest in young people.

Balfour would play the intellectual games her mother demanded with gusto and skill.   One of these games was 'Clumps'—'the father and mother of "Twenty Questions"', she called it.   In this game, ambitious players despised being given a concrete object to guess and would insist on something 'abstract', but this led to arguments as to what was concrete and what abstract.   But 'Arthur Balfour's despair of making certain players distinguish between the two categories finally obliged us to ban the question "Abstract or Concrete?"'

Balfour was not easily bored, nor easily deflected from a serenity of outlook which came to him quite early in life.   But stubborn ignorance was a *bête noire*, particularly when displayed by clerics.   These verses written after a dull sermon show how strongly he felt that religion should not be betrayed by fools:

> 'The worthy man we heard this morn
> By no intruding doubts seems torn
> But speaks in what he deems God's House
> The word of God—unheeding Strauss.
>
> Secure in pious ignorance
> He counts not Science's advance
> Seems of no proof the need to feel
> Why it is wrong to pick and steal,
> Nor doubts the World began to be
> About four thousand years B.C.
>
> 'Tis melancholy thus to find
> Our worthy parson lag behind

While all the world in eager race
Press on the philosophic pace
Content to find a pat solution
For all their doubts in Evolution.

Toll then the passing bell for Faith, which lies
Sick unto death. Around his dying couch
Philosophers prescribe, Divines look wise
And afar off, with heads bowed low, they crouch . . .'

(Here the verses break off.)

Balfour's regular visits to Stanway were to him as much a domestic occasion as a social one, but the house-party proper was the main relaxation of his life both from politics and philosophy. Here must be mentioned the much-publicised phenomenon of 'The Souls', of whom Balfour was said to be the leader. 'To me', he wrote, 'the name of the "souls" seemed always meaningless and slightly ludicrous. It seems to imply some kind of organisation and purpose, where no organisation or purpose was dreamed of. In so far as it has any existence, it was a spontaneous and natural growth, born of casual friendship and unpremeditated sympathy.'

'The Souls' were, in fact, a group of friends and acquaintances from the aristocracy, politics and the upper strata of the professional classes who chanced to meet in the ordinary course of upper-class social life and found that they had mutual interests. The name itself was mainly a joke, said to have been the inspiration of George Nathaniel Curzon, who wrote verses bringing in the names of 'members'.

Nevertheless, the phenomenon should not be underestimated, for it was the forerunner of a considerable and very real change in the structure of Society. As late as the 1880s, aristocratic Society tended —there were of course always exceptions—to be formal, dull and, as far as the men were concerned, sottish. After hard days of riding and shooting, the males often fell into slumber after a heavy dinner: frequently, the gentlemen never joined the ladies at all. On the one hand, there were those who, under the influence of the Prince of Wales preceded by the Prince Regent, confined themselves to the racecourse, the gaming tables and the less respectable forms of metropolitan life; on the other, were the landed gentry who followed the routine of country life which, on the whole, was dull. Conversation in either set cannot have been said to sparkle; it was not much less boorish than it had been in the eighteenth century.

But two separate impetuses were gradually bringing about a change. The leisured classes, who had no profession or actual work, were still large; but the sons of landed proprietors, partly as a result of the agricultural depression in mid-century, were no longer content to put in a few years in the Guards or sit perfunctorily in Parliament; they began to try and carve out careers for themselves, and in this they were joined by the sons of successful business men. Among the former one must number both Salisbury and Balfour, though there the example is modified by a long heritage of political exertion; more typical is the younger generation, for example, Curzon, Wyndham, Wolmer and the Lytteltons.

The other impetus was the invasion of Society by what Lord Midleton called 'The posse of young American brides who appeared in England in the seventies and eighties including brilliant women like the Duchess of Manchester, Lady Randolph Churchill, Mrs. White and others. They were impatient of the old system of shooting parties in feudal palaces where elderly guests were included in the party because they entertained in their turn, but who, following a heavy day's shooting, counted it no crime to fall asleep after dinner. The new order insisted upon being amused.'

It was from the change brought about in this way that 'The Souls' came into being. The ladies were as prime and important an element in these parties as the men; indeed there were those who suggested that one ought to ask 'What shall it profit a man if he gains the whole world and loses his own particular Soul?' The fact was that, although flirtations and *affaires* were common among the group of friends, so was a real interest in new ideas; each vied with the other in introducing some new star of the literary, legal or political firmaments—and bores were not invited a second time.

It was never, therefore, quite true, as the Duchess of Marlborough—the American heiress Consuelo Vanderbilt—implied in her book *The Glitter and the Gold* that 'The Souls' were 'A select group in which a high degree of intelligence was to be found happily allied to aristocratic birth.' H. G. Wells, later often invited by 'The Souls', was nearer the mark when he saw, from his own particular angle, that under their influence 'a number of people in society were taking notice of writing and were on the alert for any signs of literary freshness'.

Margot Asquith (*née* Tennant), a young member of the group, remarks that 'We did not play bridge and baccarat and our rather intellectual and literary after-dinner games were looked upon as pretentious.' She adds that Balfour was the most distinguished of 'The Souls', and 'It was considered an impertinence on our part to make him play pencil games or be our intellectual guide and critic.' The intellectual powers of, at any rate, the ladies among 'The Souls' ought not, however, to be exaggerated. Reginald Brett, Viscount Esher—that remarkable man behind-the-scenes and annotator of late Victorian and Edwardian life—wrote to his friend, the Duchess of Sutherland, that Balfour's book, *The Foundations of Belief* 'will give an infinity of trouble to many of his lady friends and admirers. . . . It is really hard when you are the apostle of a charming sect to trouble their minds with abstract speculations!'

Balfour was undoubtedly the centre of the group and idolised by the ladies; one cannot pretend that the idolatry was displeasing to him, though no doubt he did not seek it. He had no need to. Lady Betty Montgomery, an admirer already mentioned, is also quick to point out that there was no such society as 'The Souls'—'the appellation was given to us in heavy chaff by outsiders who rather envied the happy group of friends who met together so often in beautiful country houses and brilliant London ones'. But she adds a curious sidelight: she says that about the end of the 'eighties 'some of we women friends' started a class of ethics, taught by a former Girton student. Balfour teased her about this and she replied: 'But Mr. Balfour, nobody could be more humble than we are about it.' 'Humility', Balfour returned, 'is good but it is not sufficient for the study of ethics.'

Lady Desborough, then Etty Grenfell, of Taplow was one of the stalwarts of the group and her house was often its meeting-place. Commenting in a letter to *The Times* of January 21, 1929, on Haldane's references to 'The Souls' in his memoirs, she says the nickname was begun by Lord Charles Beresford at a dinner party at Lord and Lady Brownlow's house in the early summer of 1888: ' "You all sit and talk about each other's souls—I shall call you the Souls." ' She adds that they were no clique; most of them mingled in a number of the 'sets' of the day: 'Society was very inter-changeable; the members of all the various sets, including the racing world, were often to be met at the country houses singled out by Lord Haldane as those frequented by the "Souls"!'

Lady Desborough, referring to Haldane's criticism that 'The Souls' took themselves too seriously, says that the opposite criticism would be more pertinent: 'Lightness of touch was perhaps carried to its extreme limit.' As for 'exclusiveness or arrogance or sententiousness', these were 'abhorrent to them, for such moods of the mind were foreign to their whole outlook upon life'.

Though, as suggested in an earlier chapter, 'The Souls', particularly at the Balfour end of the scintillating spectrum, were in a sense precursors of the 'Bloomsbury' set, they were much more frivolous and much less self-conscious. They were not so rarefiedly 'highbrow'. In one other respect they were radically different. The American Duchess of Marlborough (quoted above), not entirely a sympathetic observer, noted that at the famous party Lord Cowper gave at Panshanger to celebrate Curzon's becoming Viceroy—Curzon being a late 'Soul'—she felt 'even then the prevalent spirit of patriotic dedication. It could be sensed in their optimism and in that joyous fraternity bred in public schools and universities which echoed in their speeches.'

The Empire interested and excited them.   The Bloomsburyites could never be accused of either patriotism or interest in the Empire.   'The Souls', many of them, were the parents of that golden generation who, as Lady Desborough puts it, 'were to bear the sharpest anguish of the war'; and she is probably right in saying that it was from parents such as these that many of them derived their 'tone', that mixture of 'courage and kindness and high sense of honour, the wit and gaiety and grace and gentleness', that speaks out from the letters and the memoirs of such youths as Hugo and Yvo Charteris, Julian Grenfell and many others of the children of 'The Souls'.

Wells, meeting 'The Souls' in the late nineties, felt that it was like going 'to a flower show and seeing what space and care can do with favoured strains of some familiar species'.   He gives this glimpse of Balfour.   He 'played the rôle', says Wells, 'of the receptive, inquiring intelligence.   "Tell me", was a sort of colloquial habit with him.   He rarely ventured opinions to be shot at.   He had the lazy man's habit of interrogative discussion.'

To this Margot Asquith adds: 'His wits gave him confidence in his improvisings and the power to sustain any opinion on any subject, whether he held the opinion or not, with equal brilliance, plausibility and success, according to his desire to dispose of you or the subject. He either finessed with the ethical basis of his intellect, or had none. This made him unintelligible to the average man, unforgiveable to the fanatic and a god to the blunderer. . . .'

Wells had a particular regard for Balfour; 'he', he wrote, 'at any rate was high above governess-made level. (Grey, Curzon, Tyrrell.) There was always an odour of intelligence about him that made his average Conservative associates uncomfortable.   He had a curious active mind, he had been attracted by my earlier books and, through him and through Cust, I came to know something of a group of people who centred round him and Lady Mary Elcho.'

Harry Cust, already mentioned, was a prominent member of 'The Souls', and a great friend of Balfour.   Tall and blond, he was heir to the Earl of Brownlow, an M.P., and in the 1890's was appointed editor of *The Pall Mall Magazine*, financed by the American, W. W. Astor. He called upon all his friends for help and one gets a curious glimpse of Balfour, First Lord of the Treasury, in his shirt-sleeves in the offices of the paper—on a site where the Garrick Theatre now stands—writing 'Occasional Notes'.

It was Cust's too close connection with a titled member of 'The Souls' which brought about his plea for Balfour's help.   The lady, whose husband had been on a mission abroad for 18 months, discovered she was with child by Cust.   Balfour was asked to advise, took Counsel's opinion, and in due course matters were smoothed over so that the child, a girl, was accepted as part of the noble and injured husband's family. Such *contretemps* were not uncommon among the group whose intercourse was by no means purely intellectual.

By the end of the 'nineties, we find Lady Elcho writing from Kissingen (undated, 1898?) that she had been talking to 'the old Prince Christian' on his one subject—'the well-worn and utterly wearisome and futile theme of the "Souls". . . . I hope he has never done *me* the injustice of considering me "intellectual".' By this time, indeed, their heyday was over, and many of the members were dispersed, or too deeply concerned in affairs, to have time for their former unfettered intercourse through long week-ends.

Moreover, their effect on Society had been achieved and passed by. They had, as we have seen, done something to leaven the lump—it was presumably to this Balfour referred when he told Margot Asquith that 'No history of our time will be complete unless the influence of the Souls upon society is dispassionately and accurately recorded.'

What, in brief, was that influence? Most important, perhaps, is the fact that 'The Souls' made literature, and art, and ideas (even scientific ones) fashionable in the highest, most influential quarters. Aristocracy of blood and aristocracy of intellect seldom come together: What young Wells has since been a familiar of a First Lord and future Prime Minister, Cabinet Ministers, Dukes, Earls and the most beautiful women in the land?

But from Balfour's point of view 'The Souls' were something much more. His niece and biographer wrote truly that: 'It was in the companionship of the men and women who were "The Souls" that the undercurrents of his real affections and feelings ran nearest to the surface of his social enjoyments.'

8

THE PHILOSOPHY OF FALLIBILITY

The Foundations of Belief, 1895

In November, 1892, Balfour wrote to his brother-in-law, Henry Sidgwick: 'Will you tell Nora that I have accepted the Presidency of the Society for Psychical Research and that I do not care a hang for my political reputation?' Balfour, as we have seen, had an almost lifelong interest in the investigation of psychical phenomena, but it was a considerable feather in the Society's cap to have persuaded the First Lord of the Treasury to become its president. Equally, it was something for a First Lord to be so persuaded. After the first flush of interest in psychical matters, particularly in the higher circles of Society, there had been several much-publicised cases of fake mediums which had confirmed the majority of scientists in their refusal to have anything to do with the subject. Against their imputation of credulity, only a few responsible people stood out, among them Professor W. F. Barrett, Professor Balfour Stewart, the Sidgwicks, F. W. H. Myers and, in America, Professor William James.

Balfour himself never became a 'believer'. But he was quite certain that, if psychical phenomena existed, they ought to be investigated, and with the same thoroughness and scrupulousness as had been devoted to light, heat and mechanics. In this he was surely right; and by giving the prestige of his name and his personal support to such inquiries, he may now properly be regarded as one of the pioneers who made it possible for the more recent experiments in extra-sensory perception to take place under scientific auspices and with results none the less interesting and valuable, even though yet incomplete. Balfour in politics was to become a master of the noncommittal;

yet on certain subjects—psychical research was not the most important
—he was always ready to take a firm line.

His presidential address to the Society—delivered at Westminster
Town Hall on January 26, 1894—sums up his attitudes lucidly; it is,
moreover, typical of his subtle approach and of his remarkable suasive
gifts. He begins by referring to Professor Hertz, a corresponding
member of the Society, who at the same time was an acknowledged
physicist of the first rank and the man who proved experimentally the
identity of light and certain electro-magnetic phenomena, first theoretically elaborated by Clerk Maxwell. Balfour then takes mesmerism
and hypnosis as exemplifying a small section of phenomena outside
the ordinary field of scientific investigation which, at first ignored, were
now accepted as right and proper subjects for science to study. Yet he
admits that scientists cannot altogether be blamed for their narrowness; only by narrowing down a field of inquiry is scientific success
likely to ensue. Moreover, much depends on the general scientific
drift of an age. That drift, however, Balfour asserts, is now towards
investigation of certain matters, previously felt to be outside the purview
of science proper.

There are difficulties. There is the possibility of fraud. There is
also the fact that, while in the physical sciences only the five senses—
'the only generally recognised inlets through which the truth of external
nature can penetrate into consciousness'—are concerned, psychical
research involves also 'some abnormal and half-completed sense'.
Psychical phenomena cannot be put into a 'retort and boiled over a
spirit lamp and always give the same results'. But he believes this
to be a 'very unphilosophic view', and he asks: 'Is there, after all, any
inherent *a priori* improbability in there being these half-formed and
imperfectly developed senses, or inlets of external information, occasionally and sporadically developed in certain members of the human race?
Surely not. I should myself be disposed to say that if the theory of
development be really sound, phenomena like these, however strange,
are exactly what we should have expected.' Quoting 'the theory of
natural selection', he suggests that such faculties may have withered
because they were unnecessary for the struggle for existence, but may
well be reviving now.

Some of the facts psychical investigators come across are 'odd' in the
sense that they are out of harmony with the accepted theories of the
material world. If the earth collided with a stellar body, that would be
extraordinary, but not disruptive of astronomical theory; if a man—
as has often been told him—can by exercise of will make another
at a short distance turn round and look at him, that would be
far more *scientifically* extraordinary. Yet 'there is a vast mass of
evidence in favour of what we now call telepathy'. But what is the

nature of the connection between the influenced and the one who influences?

Balfour points out that in his address he has confined himself to 'the somewhat unpicturesque phenomena of telepathy' because he wishes to enlist the 'best experimental and scientific ability'. He wants to bring to scientific notice the simple, definite experiments in telepathy which hint at conclusions beyond our 'habitual theories of things', so that 'all interested in science will be driven to help, as far as they can, to unravel the refractory class of problems which this Society is endeavouring to solve'.

It is, indeed, with telepathy and precognition, rather than apparitions and survival of death, that since Balfour's time real progress has been made. Telepathy, certainly, has now been established beyond all reasonable doubt, even though but a small corner of the sheet of mystery has yet been lifted. Without doubt, however, there is far less scientific and materialist dogma to be encountered than when Balfour gave his address 70 years ago. Both scientists and laity are more inclined to accept what Balfour hoped might be accepted—'that there is at least strong ground for supposing that outside the world, as we have, from the point of view of science, been in the habit of conceiving it, there does lie a region, not indeed open to experimental observation in the same way as the more familiar regions of the material world are open to it, but still with regard to which some experimental information may be laboriously gleaned; and even if we cannot entertain any confident hope of discovering what laws these half-seen phenomena obey, at all events it will be some gain to have shown, not as a matter of speculation or conjecture, but as a matter of ascertained fact, that there are more things in heaven and earth not hitherto dreamed of in our scientific philosophy.'

II

But here, indeed, is one of the main, recurring themes of Balfour as philosopher, as science's spokesman, as statesman, the point where the three overlap: it might be summed up in the words 'In God's name, admit you may be wrong.' Mill, Balfour noted, calmly accepted the doctrine of 'action at a distance' and was contemptuous of those who saw any difficulty in it—'Why seek to go behind experience in obedience to some *a priori* sentiment for which no argument can be adduced? So reasoned Mill.' Yet it was Faraday's obstinate *disbelief* in 'action at a distance' that provided some of the crucial discoveries on which the electrical industries and electrical theory of matter are founded. Very often, Balfour noted, scientific discovery does not result from a humble waiting on experience but from treating 'observation and experiment not as guides to be meekly followed, but as witnesses to be broken down in cross-examination'.

'Sense-experience', Balfour believed, was not necessarily the only source of rational conviction; one particular or fashionable mode of interpreting 'sense-experience' might well blind not merely the man in the street but also the scientist himself. The practical results of science —its technological aspect—would suffer by such narrowing, and to Balfour, the statesman, this was of the most serious import. From early in the 1890s and to the end of his life, he preached the necessity of science if Britain were to maintain her leading position in the world. He demanded more scientific education and sought to provide for it in his Education Act. But above all he stressed the need for scientists to keep an open mind about facts and stressed the vital importance of theory: 'It is perfectly impossible', he told Convocation of the Victoria University in Manchester on October 21, 1891, 'that any nation should really keep in the van of industrial progress if it ignores and neglects the teaching of theoretical science. . . . The speculations of the most abstract mathematics, of the highest chemistry, and of physics in all its branches, not only carry us into provinces which seem absolutely remote from human experience, as it is or ever can be, but they are also mixed up with dividends, with mills and manufactures, and with all the elements of the most material progress. . . .'

'Natural science', he told the British Association for the Advancement of Science, in his presidential address to them in August, 1904, 'must ever regard knowledge as the product of irrational conditions, for in the last resort it knows no others. It must always regard knowledge as rational, or else science itself disappears. In addition, therefore, to the difficulty of extracting from experience beliefs which experience contradicts, we are confronted with the difficulty of harmonising the pedigree of our beliefs with their title to authority. The more successful we are in explaining their origin, the more doubt we cast upon their validity. The more imposing seems the scheme of what we know, the more difficult it is to discover by what ultimate criteria we claim to know it.'

This develops, in a more assured manner, what Balfour had already stated in *A Defence of Philosophic Doubt*—that science, at its core, was irrational or at any rate inexplicable by ordinary logical processes. More importantly, it demonstrates the central enigma of science, an enigma that is still little nearer solution but of which the outlines are essential to have in mind for all those who work in the scientific mode. As he puts it in *A Defence of Philosophic Doubt*, 'The full complexity of any true belief about reality will necessarily transcend the comprehension of any finite intelligence. We know only in part, and therefore we know wrongly.'

Yet, to turn again from the mystery to the practical, we must go forward; we cannot go back. We discover the uses of steam; steam demands coal. But while it is steam that has put Britain in the forefront of the nations, steam is extravagantly wasteful. 'At the end of the century', Balfour said in the inaugural address of the Cambridge University Local Lectures, on August 2, 1900, 'we contemplate the unbroken course of its industrial triumphs. We have, in truth, been little better than brilliant spendthrifts. Every new invention seems to throw a new strain upon the vast, but not illimitable, resources of nature. We dissipate in an hour what it required a thousand years to accumulate.' What next? Old manufacturing countries, like Britain, are being swiftly drained of their natural wealth: 'Only by new inventions can the collateral evils of old inventions be mitigated.'

In such a way does Balfour's philosophical speculation at once feed upon, and feed, his knowledge of science, and so the two together combine to produce action in the statesman. Just how important and effective such action was is not easily ascertainable—whether in its effect upon his hearers or readers, its emergence in legislation, or through that less obvious, but perhaps even more powerful facility a Cabinet Minister possesses of easing and expediting the matters which seem to him of paramount importance. Here a nod is indeed as good as a wink and both are far superior to a memo.

Consider, however, one aspect. The *Oxford History of Technology*, volume 5, has this to say about the period before Balfour's influence was brought to bear on matters of technology and education:

'A large share of the responsibility for the relative decline of Britain at this time (1850–1900) must certainly be ascribed to those who failed to see the basic importance of education, and above all of technical education.'

After 1900, the general attitude to education changed fast; and some at least of the impetus behind must be put to Balfour's credit and to the Education Act of 1902 that he himself, in the teeth of obstruction, saw on to the Statute Book.

III

Early in 1895, Balfour wrote to R. B. Haldane, philosopher, politician and Liberal M.P. for Haddingtonshire: 'I am now wearily struggling with the dregs of my book, which is to be sent forth.' The book, which appeared in February, was *The Foundations of Belief, being Notes Introductory to the Study of Theology*. It is Balfour's second full-scale philosophical study and the most popular of his books. It quickly caught the public's attention partly, no doubt, because First Lords of the Treasury do not frequently write philosophical treatises; and it was several times reprinted, going into a second edition in the same year.

The book, in fact, is quite likely to recommend itself, at least in its earlier parts, even to those who dislike metaphysics, for it is entertainingly written, lively, amusing and even humorous in places; it is speculatively suggestive and its fine-spun threads of language are in themselves attractive. For its verbal illustrations it goes to bonnets and music-hall songs; and its side glances—at the nature of genius, the 'Naturalist Catechism', dancing and sexual selection—are agreeable. Clearly, Balfour has learned a great deal about the art of writing and presentation in the 15 years since his first book. *The Foundations*, as Balfour says in his 'Preliminary' is intended for the general reader; the general reader can still enjoy it.

But for all that, Balfour balks no philosophical issue and there is no question of writing down. *The Foundations* is indeed a model of what writing about philosophy should be; parts of it may without too gross exaggeration be compared with the prose (not, of course, the content) of Bishop Berkeley on whom Balfour wrote a brilliant essay and whose 'suave glittering' sentences (in W. B. Yeats's words) undoubtedly influenced him. Yet there is no luxuriating in, no toying with, words. There are certainly some passages where some aspect of his general *thèse* seizes him and immeasurably heightens his writing. As we noted above (Chapter 3), transience and mutability particularly move him, and a celebrated passage from *The Foundations* was quoted. There are others, notably that referring to the dubious 'immortality' of even the greatest artists:

'If they survive at all, it is but a shadowy life they live, moving on through the gradations of slow decay to distant but inevitable death. They can no longer, as heretofore, speak directly to the hearts of their fellow-men, evoking their tears or laughter, and all the pleasures, be they sad or merry, of which imagination holds the secret. Driven from the market-place, they become first the companions of the student, then the victims of the specialist. He who would still hold familiar intercourse with them must train himself to penetrate the veil which, in ever-thickening folds, conceals them from the ordinary gaze . . .'

The thought of the ice-age to come haunts him ('till the last inhabitant of a perishing world is frozen into unconsciousness'); the sense of the pitiful smallness of man in the universe awes him ('far as we seem to have travelled, yet, measured on the celestial scale, our intellectual progress is scarcely to be discerned, so minute is the parallax of Infinite Truth'). Yet there are also moments when faith and belief and beauty move him no less powerfully, though none of these abstractions have for him quite their ordinary meaning. Since knowledge is always imperfect and change and disagreement are everywhere in evidence, 'where and what are those immutable doctrines which, in the opinion

of most theologians ought to be handed on, a sacred trust, from generation to generation?' They do, however, exist, though they are seldom
explanations. They are more usually statements of fact (e.g. 'Caesar
is dead'); or ethical imperatives ('Stealing is wrong'), or great principles
(such as that 'God exists'):

'All these statements, even if accurate (as I assume, for the sake of the
argument, that they are), will, no doubt, as I have said, have a different
import for different persons and for different ages. But this is not only
consistent with their value as vehicles for the transmission of truth—it
is essential to it. If their meaning could be exhausted by one generation, they would be false for the next. It is because they can be
charged with a richer and richer content as our knowledge slowly
grows to a fuller harmony with the Infinite Reality, that they may be
counted among the most precious of our inalienable possessions.'

But here we verge on one of Balfour's main themes, 'Authority',
and it is better first to consider the main outline of the book as a whole.

IV

The late Professor Clement C. J. Webb, in his British Academy
memoir, said that Balfour's philosophical writings 'had all one theme:
the importance of attending not only to the rational grounds but to the
non-rational causes of belief'. This is too sweeping a generalisation.
Balfour's major works were certainly devoted to criticism of what he
lumped together as 'Naturalist' philosophy, and one recurrent critical
point was that mentioned by Webb. The first two of the four parts
into which *The Foundations of Belief* is divided deal in general with
'Naturalistic' attitudes already discussed in *A Defence of Philosophic
Doubt*—but they deal with them far more firmly and convincingly.
He begins by considering the character of the knowledge produced by
the natural sciences unaided; he dismisses, somewhat lightly (in a chapter set in smaller type and marked 'not for the general reader') the
Kantian Idealism only then being absorbed by English philosophers;
and he concludes the two first sections by asking what remedy remains
if Naturalism's affirmations leave us in 'the cold grasp of its negations'
and if Idealism 'has not as yet got us out of the difficulty'?

One answer—and it is no doubt accepted by thousands—is to leave
the two regions of knowledge (scientific and spiritual) to exist side by
side. There are, however, inconveniences, not least being the demand
for a scheme of knowledge which 'shall give rational unity to an
adequate creed'. Such an all-reconciling theory 'by which each
inevitable claim of our complex nature may be harmonised under the
supremacy of Reason' does not seem likely to be quickly discovered.
Balfour, therefore, proposes an approach at 'some lower speculative

level' and 'by the aid of some more comprehensive, or at least more manageable, principle'.

Balfour now introduces the important term 'Authority'. Here he speaks out clearly with the voice of Burke, though there does not appear in his writings to be any direct reference to the greatest of the English conservative philosophers. Balfour states that many, perhaps most, of our beliefs and actions are based not upon reason, nor yet upon direct spiritual insight, but upon ancient inbred knowledge, custom, social pressures and tradition in which reason plays little part. Of course, the Rationalists from the Encyclopaedists downwards have insisted that reason and reason alone 'can be safely permitted to mould the convictions of mankind'. Imagine, says Balfour, if it were so! If every positive act, moral precept, loyalty, convention were to be brought to the individual bar of reason each time, chaos would result. The individual has neither the time nor the necessary ratiocinative power to estimate 'with open minds the claims which charity, temperance and honesty, murder, theft and adultery respectively have upon the approval or disapproval of mankind'.

Such reasoning is, of course, impossible—and happily so: Authority plays an immense, inevitable and on the whole beneficent part in the production of belief. Prejudice, prescription, presumption—the Burkeian triad—remain mankind's truest guides, and we tamper with them at our peril. Certainly, change is necessary, and in such change 'the solvent action of criticism and discussion' has its part, though it is, Balfour suggests, 'probably a small one'. Such actions 'supply business to the practical politician, raw material to the theorist'. But in fact it is 'the multitude of incomparably more important processes by whose undesigned co-operation alone the life and growth of the State is rendered possible'. Not least among the powers of Authority is its ability to produce 'psychological climates'. Reasoning doubtless has much to do with this. 'Climates' produce 'beliefs', 'beliefs' produce 'climates'; but although reasoning plays a part are the results themselves rational: 'Do they follow, I mean, on reason *qua* reason? or are they, like a schoolboy's tears over a proposition of Euclid, consequences of reasoning, but not conclusions from it?'

In other words, Balfour recognises that for many beliefs due to Authority human beings like to adduce a reason; but the reason adduced may often be absurd. Those who felt they had to support Charles I and the Royalist cause adduced, or rather produced, the reason called the 'divine right of Kings', an abstraction of 'extraordinary absurdity'. In the same way, the modern democratic movement was 'nursed through its infant maladies' by such theories as the 'rights of man'. Such theories may be temporarily necessary, but they tend to build abstraction upon abstraction, and to lead logically to many ridiculous conclusions.   'Authority', Balfour repeats, 'is in all cases contrasted with Reason, and stands for that group of non-rational causes, moral, social and educational, which produces its results by psychic processes other than reasoning.'   But there is a temptation to turn causes into reasons, and hence 'Authority' into 'authorities'; it thus ceases to be the opposite of reason and becomes a species of reason—and as such must be judged as reasoning.   It may then be quite acceptable; but it can never be the '*foundation*' for a system of belief.   'An authority' or 'authorities' cannot be the logical foundations of a system, though they may support it.   In Authority there are no infallible guides.

Balfour sums up this section of his book (pp. 226-30) in a very re-markable passage where he suggests that it is from Authority that Reason itself draws its most important premises; and he points out again the small amount of influence reason has in reality upon our lives and the lives of communities.   This, he suggests, is a good thing; and he adds, in a paragraph that should be brought to the notice of every sort of 'planner':

'Not merely because we are ignorant of the data required for the solu-tion, even of very simple problems in organic and social life, are we called on to acquiesce in an arrangement which, to be sure, we have no power to disturb; nor yet because these data, did we possess them, are too complex to be dealt with by any rational calculus we possess or are ever likely to acquire; but because, in addition to these difficulties, reason-ing is a force most apt to divide and disintegrate; and though division and disintegration may often be the necessary preliminaries of social development, still more necessary are the forces that bind and stiffen, without which there would be no society to develop.'

Authority, of course, has perpetuated error and retarded progress. None of the influences, least of all reason, which have moulded the history of the race, have unfortunately been productive of unmixed good: 'The springs at which we quench our thirst are always turbid.' Yet religion, ethics and politics are supplied by Authority, as it supplies the essential elements in the premises of science.   It is in these respects —not our capacity for convincing and being convinced by the exercise of reasoning—that we truly excel the brute creation.

In this section on Authority Balfour sums up a great deal of what he has said in the earlier part of the book, and in *A Defence of Philosophic Doubt*.   But it is the first time he used the word 'Authority' as an omnibus expression.   Where did it come from?   It seems probable that he adopted it from the proceedings of the Metaphysical Society or, if he was not an attending member himself (he may possibly have been in its last year), from acquaintance with its members.   The Society frequently heard and discussed papers in which the term was used in something of the same way: 'Authority in Matters of Opinion' was a paper read on March 13, 1877, by James FitzJames Stephen which in itself referred to Sir George C. Lewis's *An Essay on the Influence of Authority in Matters of Opinion* (1849, republished 1875). But the word is certainly not used there in the very broad sense that Balfour gives it. It is used in something approaching that sense by Roman Catholic writers (though, from his own point of view, Balfour effectively disposes of such aspects of authority as 'Papal Infallibility' on pp. 223f.). The Roman Catholics, however, limit the scope of the word, whereas in Balfour it not only looks backward to Burke but forward to Bergson and to Jung.

It is possible, as Russell Kirk suggests, that Balfour would have done better to substitute for Authority Coleridge's term, Reason (though that would have added confusion even though avoiding the 'stormier tract of speculation'), or Newman's 'Illative Sense' (though there the theological undertones would have raised equal storm). Certainly the word has caused considerable misunderstanding; early reviewers professed to find in this section the forces of Tory reaction, and later commentators have felt that in opposing Authority to Reason Balfour did not always take care to avoid confusing reason with reasoning. In fact, as far as the political angle is concerned, there is only the implication not the statement. For that we have to turn to Balfour's lecture delivered to the Manchester Athenaeum and printed in the *National Review* of May, 1885, where he gives us the pure spring of Conservative doctrine based on Authority. For example:

'Society is becoming more and more sensitive to the evils that exist in its midst; more and more impatient of their continued existence. In itself this is wholly good; but, in order that good may come of it, it behoves us to walk warily. It is, no doubt, better for us to apply appropriate remedies to our diseases than to put our whole trust in the healing powers of nature. But it is better to put our trust in the healing powers of nature than to poison ourselves straight off by swallowing the contents of the first phial presented to us by any self-constituted physician. And such self-constituted physicians are about and in large numbers—gentlemen who think that they pay Providence a compliment by assuming that for every social ill there is a speedy and effectual specific lying to hand; who regard it as impious to believe that there may be chronic diseases of the body politic as well as of any other body.... Of two evils it is better, perhaps, that our ship shall go nowhere than that it shall go wrong, that it should stand still than that it should run upon the rocks.'

Balfour's strictly political thinking (or at any rate writing) was not extensive; it did not approach even the meagre two volumes collected from the contributions of his uncle, Lord Salisbury, to the *Quarterly Review*, but what there is of it has the same cautiousness allied with decisive realism.   For instance, Balfour's notes (some of which were used in his 'Fragment on Progress', delivered as the Lord Rector's address at Glasgow University on November 26, 1891) show the direction of his thoughts on democracy and aristocracy:

'There is no such thing as democracy in the ordinary sense of the word. Government is always of the few:—but in an Aristocracy the few are selected by law:—in a democracy by merit—or chance.   The people do not govern in either case: but in the second they have the right of choosing their governors.'

Again, if we are to decide whether a party was right in not passing a proposed measure at a certain time, we have to consider not merely whether it would have been beneficial but 'also whether the available political energy (always a strictly limited quantity) could at that time most advantageously have been utilised in passing it'.   The force available for political action, his notes continue, will 'equal the strength of public opinion minus the internal friction of the Governmental machine.   The friction of the governmental machine in England is due to (i) The strength of the Opposition; (ii) The effective (but the real) lukewarmness of the supporters of the Government (not the lukewarmness they feel but the lukewarmness they dare to show); (iii) Difficulties in using the forms of the constitution.'

Government action, he continues, does not necessarily mean that the majority of the members of the State are deliberately consenting parties to it.   The real checks to Government action do not come from the Opposition (which unless aided from the Government side can do nothing); they 'are unknown and unsuspected by the public.   They act by *anticipation*.   The Government is restrained from proposing measures by the expectation of difficulties.'

Balfour sees clearly, too, that 'a nation's political aptitudes are not determined by its powers of political reasoning but by the manner in which its political sentiments act on its organisation and surroundings. Loyalty (the strongest political emotion) is an element in the stability of party as well as constitution: and comes out on the whole for good in the species of veneration for the leaders of parties which is found strongly developed in the English character.'

These (though incorporated in some published essays) are really the thoughts and judgements of a man deeply involved in political life, and guides for his own future conduct, rather than political theory as such. But this, too, is typical of the central Conservative tradition: theory, abstraction are generally distrusted.   Particulars are preferred to lofty generalisations, though it may be necessary, as Burke found, to counter abstraction with abstraction, idea with idea—to counter but not to construct an opposing ideology.

It is only in recent years that the profundities of Conservatism have been fully appreciated and their sound heard. The airy and visionary optimism of liberalism, the noise of the planner's pick and the leveller's sapping, for long militated against it. In the last decade, however, such writers as Richard Law (Lord Coleraine), Michael Oakeshott, Peter Viereck and Russell Kirk have put philosophical Conservatism back on the political map, and Kirk in *The Conservative Mind* has studied aspects of Conservative thought in both English and American writers from Burke and John Adams through Coleridge and Randolph to Macaulay, Tocqueville, Henry Adams, Babbitt, Santayana and T. S. Eliot. Among this distinguished company he places Balfour, and his brief chapter on him is full of illumination.

V

The fourth and final section of *The Foundations of Belief* is entitled 'Suggestions Towards a Provisional Philosophy'. Balfour did not for a moment believe that 'the unification of all belief into an ordered whole compacted into one coherent structure under the stress of reason' was a possibility; but it was an ideal never to be abandoned and always to be striven towards. In fact, section four does little more than draw certain conclusions from the philosophical criticism that has preceded it and to postulate God as the necessary condition not merely of religious but of all belief. If, as he has demonstrated, an irrational process lies at the root of every rational one, and reason is a natural product and that the whole material upon which it works it neither creates nor controls, then 'We shall in mere self-defence be driven to hold that, behind these non-rational forces, and above them, guiding them by slow degrees, and, as it were, with difficulty, to a rational issue, stands that Supreme Reason in whom we must thus believe, if we are to believe in anything.'

Science itself drives us to this belief. But so for the same reasons does ethics, no less a natural product, no less planted in sources 'which have about them nothing which is ethical'. Science requires a rational God; ethics requires a moral God. Moreover, if a 'providential' origin is ascribed to science and ethics, there is no reason for denying it to such qualities as human capacity for sympathy, repentance and so on, and to beauty. This certainly has the advantage of countering the freezing touch of Naturalism: 'The most unlovely germ of instinct or of appetite to which we trace back the origin of all that is most noble and of good report, no longer throws discredit upon its developed off-shoots.' With regard to Beauty we are no longer precluded from 'supposing that in the thrill of some deep emotion we have for an instant caught a far-off reflection of Divine beauty'.

If, on the other hand, we look in the same way at theology, we inevitably transcend the common division between 'natural' and 'super-natural'.   At the same time, we must assert that every addition to knowledge, whether scientific, ethical or theological 'is due to a co-operation between the human soul which assimilates and the Divine power which inspires'.   Equally, on this supposition, we cannot deny inspiration to the ethico-religious teaching of the great Oriental reformers, and to many others: 'These things assuredly are of God and whatever be the terms in which we choose to express our faith, let us not give colour to the opinion that His assistance to mankind has been narrowed down to the sources, however unique, from which we immediately, and consciously, draw our own spiritual nourishment.'

Obviously a number of problems arise as a result of these proposi-tions, but many of them lead directly to the heart of theology and Balfour, therefore, does not deal with them.   But he was certainly aware of them and not least of the need for a satisfactory theory of inspiration, as he mentions in a letter to Mary Gladstone (Drew) in January, 1892.   He does, however, tackle the problem of whether his views would be more satisfactory if considered in a Christian setting rather than in a merely Theistic one, how, in fact, the Incarnation could be absorbed into the postulate.   But he believes that the very uniqueness of the doctrine puts it beyond the range of ordinary critic-ism, though this does not necessarily apply to the historical evidence for Christianity.   In the latter respect, he returns to ethics and, with bor-rowings from Kant, suggests that Providence having enabled man to create ethical ideas, may well be supposed to have provided some satisfaction for ethical needs, both in time and in eternity.

What then of our need for a personal God ('that shall appeal to men of flesh and blood, struggling with the temptations and discouragements which flesh and blood is heir to'); what of the problem of evil and pain, if God is omnipotent and loving?   The Incarnation alone, Balfour believes, provides the answers which are not philosophical but personal. The Christian worships no 'remote contriver of a universe to whose ills He is indifferent', but one who, though innocent, also suffered.

Esher, in that same letter from which we quoted in the previous chapter, remarks of his reading of *The Foundations of Belief* that:

'At Cambridge when all the "intellectual" set was agnostic, Arthur used to be looked upon as a curious relic of an older generation, with affectionate pity.   I could see his brothers' Frank and Gerald, brotherly patronage extended to him mentally when he used now and then to come down to Trinity on a visit.

'Arthur's opinions have not varied.   He was then a "Christian" of a queer undefined sort, and in that faith he has abided.   He has done more—for he has justified philosophically his faith—an operation not

common as you know. What is queer is that there is a strong resemblance between Arthur's argument and that by which Dr. Newman was
ultimately landed in the Roman Catholic Church!'

The nearness of some of the sentiments in the earlier book to the
credo quia impossibile has been pointed out. In *The Foundations*, Balfour
himself refers to the Latin tag and says that it may be a 'pious paradox';
what commends itself to him as an axiom is not 'I believe because it is
impossible' but 'I disbelieve because it is simple.' Balfour personally
found Roman Catholicism repugnant; philosophically he was more
aware than most men of the illimitable chasm between 'Authority' and
'the authorities', as his reference to Papal Infallibility shows.

But Esher's remarks about Balfour's continuing Christian-ness are
relevant in various ways. As was suggested in Chapter 3, Balfour very
slowly assimilated Christian doctrine to his thought; he has not really
done so in *The Foundations*—God comes in all too glibly at the end as a
reasonable way out from a mass of intolerable negatives, as Balfour
himself admitted (see letter quoted pp. 58-9). What, however, we realise
again is that, throughout his life, Balfour had an obstinate, almost
blind, personal faith in God—'a living God', as he wrote, 'to whom
men may pray'. Balfour's problem was how to fit this living, private
faith into the setting of a world, scientific, materialist, naturalist, which
he himself, scarcely less than its fiercest proponents, found impossible
to ignore. His philosophical works, indeed, are not so much a criticism
of these tempting ideas and outlooks as a desperate attempt to find some
corner among them for that simple but obstinate faith. The shrewd
knocks he gave to materialism and the 'naturalistic' philosophers are
really almost as much knocks to demand entry for the faith that sustained him in despite of his intellect.

Where would that faith fit? How could it cohere? Certainly it was
irrational, and much of the emphasis of this supremely reasoning man
upon irrationality was a reflection of the fact. Yet there is no real
paradox; Balfour nowhere (despite his critics) disposed altogether of
reasoning—indeed he often underlines its uses. But reasoning he felt
led to a mystery. Faith, too, was a mystery. Perhaps the two
mysteries were really one. He scarcely expected to come to a satisfactory synthesis between intellect and faith; and certainly never
claimed to do so. He hoped to 'delineate, and, if possible, to recommend a certain attitude of mind'. In fact—apart from its autobiographical interest—*The Foundations* does still make a reader re-examine
his common assumptions and think again about 'accepted' facts. He
would certainly claim to be a philosopher in the sense he indicates in a
footnote: 'To Philosophy I give an *epistemological* significance. I regard
it as the systematic exposition of our grounds of knowledge. Thus, the
philosophy of religion or the philosophy of science would mean the

theoretic justification of our theological or scientific beliefs.' But he did not claim to be a metaphysician. Metaphysical treatises, despite their reasoning, were, he thought, 'works of imagination at least as much as of reason. Metaphysicians are poets who deal with the abstract and the super-sensible instead of the concrete and the sensuous.' Spinoza's reasoning, for example, is excessively unconvincing; yet many still read him because he was endowed with a religious imagination, enabling him to find in 'notions the most remote from sense-experience the only abiding realities; and to convert a purely rational adhesion to the conclusions supposed to flow from the nature of an inactive, impersonal and unmoral substance, into something not quite inaptly termed the Love of God'.

This definition, though it strikes us as unusual, indicates clearly what Balfour himself found and cherished in such writers as Spinoza; it also perhaps indicates what he himself would like to have done but did only, and then partially, in the field of aesthetics. Perhaps this is what he is really getting at in a letter to Oliver Lodge, his physicist friend, shortly to become first principal of Birmingham University, written on April 15, 1899, some four years after *The Foundations* appeared: '*Philosophic Doubt*', he says, 'though now in certain respects rather antiquated, is perhaps more satisfactory because a more definite piece of work than *The Foundations of Belief*,—and this because precision in the work of destruction is always easier than in the work of construction—or (more accurately) because definite arguments can be and ought to be met with definite replies.'

As for 'the conflict between Science and Religion', he did not doubt, he said five years after *The Foundations*, that 'in some way or other future generations will, each in its own way, find a practical *modus vivendi* between the natural and the spiritual'. The further triumph of science, he thought, would only convince mankind that 'Spirit' must be invoked to explain the very fact that, in such developments, there was no room for Spirit. *How* 'the theoretic reconciliation' would be effected, he did not know—'for I mistrust the current philosophical theories upon the subject'.

VI

Meanwhile, the search for 'reconciliation' went on. Towards the end of 1895, a suggestion often made that the Metaphysical Society, or something like it, should be reconstituted, was taken up seriously by Wilfrid Ward, later editor of the *Dublin Review* and son of W. G. Ward the Roman Catholic logician. Wilfrid Ward wrote to ask Balfour for his views and whether he would be interested in a new society, to which Balfour replied on December 7, 1895: 'I cannot but think that a more useful, if less ambitious, organisation than the old Metaphysical Society may be the result of your labours.' On the following January 24, Balfour, Ward and two contributors to the liberalising Anglican compilation, *Lux Mundi*—Canon Gore (later Bishop of Birmingham) and Balfour's old friend Dr. Talbot (then of Keble College)—met in a private room at the Carlton Club, London, to determine the name and purpose of the projected new society.

It was decided that it ought to aim more definitely at 'construction' than had its predecessor, that therefore complete atheists should not be invited to join, and that it should be called the 'Synthetic' Society. It was intended to discuss and to try to find common ground within the generally theistic position. The first meeting did not, however, take place until two years later on February 28, 1898, in the Westminster Palace Hotel, and decided to meet on the last Friday of the months of January to May. After dinner, a paper of no more than half an hour was to be read and seven minutes were allowed each member for discussion afterwards. Its total membership was 54 and, as well as Balfour and Ward, included Lord Hugh Cecil, Lord Rayleigh, Baron von Hügel (the historian of mysticism), F. W. H. Myers (the spiritualist don), R. B. Haldane, Oliver Lodge, Pringle-Pattison, William Temple, G. Lowes-Dickinson, G. K. Chesterton and George Wyndham (who shared the duties of secretaryship with Ward). Seven former members of the Metaphysical joined, including Balfour himself, Sidgwick and R. H. Hutton.

The membership was overwhelmingly theist to start with and was thus, as Maisie Ward points out in her study of her father (*The Wilfrid Wards and the Transition*, 1921), in danger of suffering from 'a general diffused friendliness'. She records that her father once remarked to Balfour that the hotel waiters thought the Society was called 'the Sympathetic Society'. Yet some of the Hegelians disturbed the more orthodox Christians, and F. W. H. Myers became so intransigent in his spiritualism that Ward was doubtful whether he ought to have been allowed into the Society. Sidgwick was, as Gore put it, 'the life and soul' of the Society, mainly because, though still agnostic, he was veering gradually towards theism and was thus still unsettled and questing in his views, whereas many of the members had (to quote Gore again) 'lost any real hope of obtaining any strikingly new light on the deepest matters. It was quite otherwise with Sidgwick.' Further to prevent any suggestion of a mutual admiration society, one rule laid down 'that for the purposes of our debates no arguments should be based on the assumption of either a supernatural inspiration of the Bible or a supernatural authority residing in the Church'.

Of Balfour's part in the proceedings, there is no available record, although when the Society was wound up in 1908 Balfour himself had the papers bound together and presented each member with a copy. According to Maisie Ward's account, however, it seems as if, in the end, the Society discovered that some kind of faith that had been eliminated from discussion at the beginning constituted the essential core of Christianity for most of the members—which parallels the development in Balfour's own thought.

The Society is not greatly evident as a subject in Balfour's correspondence, but he had this to tell Lady Elcho about its first meeting: 'Fairly promising I think. Your brother George had taken a good deal of trouble about the arrangements—the Bishop of Rochester, W. Ward, Hutton of the *Spectator*, my brother Gerald, Bryce and last but not least Martineau aged 91. We elected some members, Alfred (Lyttelton) among the number, and Ward read a paper. Nothing much in it or in the discussion which followed, the point of chief (sentimental) interest being Martineau's contribution—clear, vigorous and in parts (when describing the defunct Metaphysical Society) amusing: though naturally not very profound or original. I have promised to read a paper at the next meeting—but the reading will end in speaking from notes, as I have no time to write.'

Of Balfour himself, escaping the House of Commons for a brief hour or two and slipping into the Westminster Palace Hotel for a Friday with the Synthetic, we catch a glimpse in the words of Professor Clement C. J. Webb, himself a member of the Society: 'It was a pleasure never to be forgotten to listen to his talk at table; and, when we turned to philosophical debate, to follow his acute criticisms of the paper before us or of others' comments upon it. The "toploftiness", which an Irish M.P. is said to have ascribed to him, was never in evidence at these meetings. My recollection is of the unfailing charm of his manner, of the unreserved frankness with which he threw himself into the discussions, of the courteous attention and quick appreciation with which he listened to every reader or speaker.'

The Synthetic Society was one of the forerunners of the British Academy of which Balfour was an original Fellow. But the days of high debate, between the intellectual leaders of the land, effectively died with the death of Queen Victoria. That fragmentation of learning, so often bemoaned in recent times, was even then beginning; for a divine and a physicist to argue on the deepest level was rapidly becoming impossible, partly because of terminology, more because the disciplines of learning grew further and further apart and more and more mutually incomprehensible. The time of C. P. Snow's split culture had dawned even before the Synthetic Society put up its shutters in 1908.

VII

Balfour, as before noted, said: 'When I'm at work on politics, I long to be in literature, and *vice versa*.' By literature he no doubt also meant the writing of philosophy; but even in the narrower sense, Balfour wrote considerably about literature and literary men, and for a man alleged to be lazy he did a remarkable amount of reading and writing for one so occupied in government.

Much of his purely literary writing was, it is true, done for a particular occasion; he spoke about Scott, Burns and Carlyle, for example, on anniversary days, or occasions of unveiling memorials; his writing about Berkeley was in the form of a long review of a volume of his life and letters; and his remarks on novels were part of a talk to the Sir Walter Scott Club. Nevertheless, though composed for an occasion, they were in no sense 'occasional'. There is no hint in Balfour's literary compositions of 'Gleanings in a Library' or 'pipe and slippers'. His taste and views were far too definite for that. Even when discoursing on such a whimsical-tending subject as 'The Pleasures of Reading', he hit hard at the pomposity of those who would make literature a chore or a religion. His writing, even now, is eminently readable, perhaps mainly because it is frankly revealing of its author's true tastes, though none of it possibly was quite so frank as his remark in a private letter to a niece on February 20, 1895 that '9/10 of "In Memoriam", 9/10 of the Idylls and more than 9/10 of some of the other volumes (of Tennyson) might be pitched into the sea with no great loss to anybody'.

Yet in public, too, he pursued his iconoclasm. Observing that the middle third of the nineteenth century appealed to him not at all, he continued:

'It reminds me too much of Landseer's pictures and the revival of Gothic; I feel no sentiment of allegiance towards any of the intellectual dynasties that then held sway; neither the thin lucidity of Mill nor the windy prophesyings of Carlyle, neither Comte nor yet Newman, were ever able to arouse in me the enthusiasm of a disciple; I turn with pleasure from the Corn Law squabbles to the great War [i.e. the Napoleonic Wars]; from Thackeray and Dickens to Scott and Miss Austen, even from Tennyson and Browning to Keats, Coleridge, Wordsworth, and Shelley.'

Balfour read widely all his life. No doubt he read Shaw (he certainly saw some of his plays), Kipling, Pater, Yeats and the rest who made up some of the 'nineties spirit; but he did not write about them. The whole 'hotted-up' atmosphere of that time can scarcely have appealed to him. He preferred the eighteenth century. Yet he was not a man living in times past. His mind roved constantly forward;

he was 'on the ball' in a way few statesmen have been, even in his late seventies.   Nor was it that he ever felt himself to be 'out of his time'; it was rather that his mind had that particularly Scottish gift of getting to the heart of the matter and treating the rest as 'epiphenomena'.   It was part of his distinction; it was also part of his Achilles's heel as a politician.   The heat and flurry of English life that began in the 'nineties and persisted until the outbreak of the Great War left him cold, even though tolerant.   He saw it as a spectacle, forgetting that heat, however, foolishly generated, has the power to melt, and that flurry, however apparently capricious or frivolous, can often sweep away no less effectively than a mighty rushing wind.

9

THE THIRD MAN

1895–1901

'What a pricked bubble the Rosebery is!' Chamberlain observed to Balfour in a letter of December 8, 1894. The last Gladstone administration, now headed by Lord Rosebery, was clearly limping to its close, defeat threatening it at every turn, a party without a real leader, a Government without a soul. Defeat when it came was almost fortuitous, and need not even have meant resignation. St. John Brodrick (later Lord Midleton), who had been Financial Secretary to the War Office in the preceding Conservative Government, had learned that the supply of small arms ammunition and of cordite (the new smokeless propellant explosive) were both exceedingly short. He saw this not only as a serious matter in itself but as one which might well help bring the Government down.

He sought the assistance of Balfour and Chamberlain. Balfour, St. John Brodrick later wrote, 'with fervid memory of old "Fourth Party" plots, positively bristled with delight. The military M.P.s on both sides of the House were quietly mobilised, though Balfour insisted on warning Campbell-Bannerman of the Opposition's views on the shortage of ammunition, to which the Liberal leader replied by letter that there was no case to be met'. Thus armed, and in a House where the Government Whips scented no danger at all, the Brodrick plan went into action, and the Government was defeated by seven votes. The Government chose to resign rather than to dissolve—or even to rescind the vote on the Report stage—and thus put the Conservatives immediately into power, with a General Election to follow later on. This manœuvre, repeated by Balfour ten years later, was intended to give the Government a tactical advantage; but neither then, nor at the General Election of 1906, did it do so.

The Rosebery Government was destroyed on Friday, June 21, 1895. On the Sunday following at Hatfield, Lord Salisbury received the Queen's Commission, and on Monday Chamberlain and the Duke of Devonshire, the Liberal Unionist leaders, met Salisbury and Balfour at Salisbury's house in Arlington Street. There the Liberal Unionists were told that they might have four Cabinet offices—Salisbury taking the Premiership and Foreign Secretaryship—and 'Arthur Balfour would, of course, be First Lord of the Treasury'. To the surprise of all, Chamberlain chose to be Colonial Secretary, a post comparatively new in itself and one that had previously been of little importance.

Chamberlain, indeed, offered to go to the War Office; he did not like Salisbury's proposal of the Home Office. Balfour then chimed in to say that if Chamberlain preferred the Chancellorship of the Exchequer 'there was no reason' why he should not have it. But Chamberlain stuck out for the Colonial Office, 'in the hope of furthering closer union between them (the Dominions and Colonies) and the United Kingdom'. He might perhaps have added also that the Exchequer, though a more distinguished post, was directly subordinate to the First Lord of the Treasury; what he did say was that he had told Goschen he would not claim it. So what was indeed to become the most important post in the Government was thus settled. For the rest, the Duke of Devonshire became President of the Council with titular responsibility for Education; Goschen chose the Admiralty rather than the Exchequer which Sir Michael Hicks-Beach was then offered and accepted. Lansdowne—Balfour's old friend 'Clan'—became Secretary for War, after successful periods as Viceroy in Canada and India, and Brodrick—Balfour's younger friend—was appointed his Under-Secretary.

It was a strong team, not least because of the adherence, and representation in the Cabinet, of the Liberal Unionists, an 'epoch making' event as Garvin rightly called it. Just how strong it was and how much it appealed to the Victorian voter was shown at the General Election when the Conservative-Unionists got 411 seats to the combined Liberal, Irish, Labour total of 259. It was, as R. H. Gretton calls it, 'a return to safe ground'; Liberalism had been put resoundingly in its place, and not only because of the intolerable divisions within it and its lack of leadership. In the mid-1890s the nation as a whole was uneasy at the radical change it sniffed in the air—an air, an atmosphere redolent in the arts of 'decadence' (the Wilde *affaire* called the new arts in doubt); in business of brash new millionaires enriched from the Rand and widespread money-making, gambling fever; in conduct of a wild search for pleasure, sport, and sensation. Socialism, not merely as a cloth-capped working-class movement, but allied to the arts and to intellect, was as alarming as the new popular sensational press and the blaring advertisements on the hoardings. For the middle classes, politically speaking, the alarm canalised itself in the way Chamberlain expressed it in a letter to Balfour on December 8, 1894:

'The intermediates—the men who hold the balance of elections—are disgusted and frightened . . . frightened at the projects of confiscation which are in the air and found expression at the Trade Union Congress the other day. If I am right, they want to be assured that the Unionists will take up the question of Social Reform in a Conservative spirit and meet the unreasonable and dangerous proposals of the extremists with practical proposals of their own.'

Social reform was certainly needed for, despite the appearances of prosperity, poverty and slumdom were everywhere evident. And was prosperity more than skin deep? The year 1895 itself saw depression and widespread unemployment. But there were more sinister signs still. Because of hostile tariffs, the export of manufactured articles had for some time been stationary. British steel production had fallen below that of America and Germany, and Britain was paying her way by increasing exports of machinery (which in due time would enable the exportees to do without British manufactured goods), of ships (which would enable them to do without her shipping) and of coal, an irreplaceable asset (as Balfour said in his address on 'The Nineteenth Century'). Agriculture was ruined, as Ensor puts it, a second time over; Britain's wheatfields were diminished by another half million acres between 1890 and 1900, and at the latter date covered only a little over the acreage of 1872.

The first fine flush of industrial expansion, with Britain years ahead of any foreign rival, was over. Both the United States and Germany were becoming massive industrial and productive competitors, hammering upon the doors of world trade and world markets—and very many of those potential markets were marked red upon the maps. However cursorily Britain had regarded her colonial possessions in the past, the envious eyes of others were already bringing a new awareness of their importance; and also of their possible value to the mother-country when trade and industry were no longer so expansive.

In all these were implicit not merely economic, but also diplomatic and political problems of the greatest magnitude; and, attached to these problems, whole chains of secondary circumstance. For example, the ultimate resort of diplomacy was war; therefore the military preparedness of the nation required overhauling. In the matter of Britain's industrial future, there was clearly a need for more and more skilled artisans and technological workers: was education sufficiently available? As for the Empire, what in fact was its relationship with Britain? Was that relationship capable of development?

N_JB

The Salisbury Government of 1895, though it became immersed in the disastrous and costly war in South Africa, was at least not unaware of these massive problems, and two of its leading members—Chamberlain and Balfour—had firm ideas how to deal with them.   We shall see how close their lines of thought were, yet how different in detail and in method of application.   Not that either of these Ministers had much time to spare for thinking about basic policies.   Though Balfour had no department to administer, he had the daily business of leading the House and, as he told Lady Elcho: 'I have nightly to send to the Queen a full account of our full proceedings, set forth in my best handwriting.' (This chore is now done by the Chief Whip.)   In addition, he had to answer for a Prime Minister who was not only in the Lords but increasingly a recluse (though active in his reclusion), and later a failing man.   Salisbury, indeed, sometimes did not recognise his own Ministers when he saw them (or so it was said); it was certainly true that late in the Boer War at an impromptu committee meeting with the King he picked up a signed photograph of that monarch and remarked pensively: 'Poor Buller, what a mess he made of it.'   So that inevitably Balfour tended to be a go-between, a stand-in on occasions when his uncle was absent (as increasingly often he was), and a mediator between Cabinet and Premier, or Premier and his followers.   Thus, much of Balfour's work was an oiling of the wheels of government, and as such is difficult to record; not least of its success, however, may be measured by the fact that he kept Chamberlain and Salisbury, men and politicians totally different in outlook as in background, working together smoothly.   Deep-lying rivalry there certainly was between Balfour and Chamberlain; but we may agree with Garvin that 'Balfour was the hinge of the Unionist combination. . . .   Between them (i.e. Salisbury, Chamberlain, Balfour) there was excellent colleagueship.'

Examples of Balfour's intermediaryship are numerous.   One not previously published is in reference to Chamberlain's plan (discussed with his American friends) to bring in the New World to redress the evils of the old; in other words, to involve the Americans directly in dealing with the power of Turkey, particularly in the question of the Armenian massacres.   Salisbury writes to Balfour on December 27, 1895:

'I read it (Chamberlain's letter) with perfect dismay.   Randolph at his wildest could not have made a madder suggestion.   I am afraid Mrs. J. is trying her hand at programme making.'   (Mrs. Chamberlain, the third, was American by birth.)

To this Balfour replies (December 29, 1895):

'I return Joe's letter.   The scheme does not seem very practicable. But the failure of Rosebery's policy and the victory of the Sultan over

Europe is so complete that I am not surprised at his looking rather far afield to find an issue from the existing impasse. He forgets, however, that in addition to other difficulties the U.S.A., even if willing to work with us, has no Treaty rights over Turkey; and that while they certainly will not work with us, their doing so might and *probably* would bring down the Turkish Empire with a rush.

'It is in some ways unfortunate that we cannot turn American sentiment on the Armenian question (if it exists) to some account, in as much as the U.S.A. having no shadow of interest in the Mediterranean are not regarded with the insane suspicion which stupefies Europe where England is concerned.'

Balfour was the smoothing agent, the manager, as it were, of the inmost Conservative counsels, although, as we shall see, he often inclined more to Chamberlain's viewpoints than to Salisbury's. He was also, to some extent, the *deus ex machina* of politics in a more particular sense. In this connection there is a curious, previously unpublished episode regarding Henry Asquith, the brilliant young barrister who had been Home Secretary in Gladstone's and Rosebery's Cabinets. After the fall of the Rosebery Government, the Liberals were in a disunited condition and ineffectual as an Opposition. Salisbury himself observed this, not as a debating point, but as a serious drawback to a healthy political situation. (English readers will recall a parallel situation in 1960.) Salisbury said that, the dual character of English parties being for the moment destroyed, there was a danger that Britain would fall 'into that condition of Parliamentary groups which is fatal to the constitutional existence of more than one Parliamentary system on the continent. It is bad for them (the Liberals), it is bad for us, and it is bad for the country.'

One problem was the Leadership of the Liberal Party. It seemed to most observers that Asquith alone had the requisite powers to pull the party together, though he was junior in the Party's hierarchy. But he was a poor man. He had, it is true, made a great deal of money from his practice at the Bar; but such a practice could not be combined with high office nor with important function in the Opposition. Asquith had, however, recently re-married and his second wife was Margot Tennant, one of Balfour's younger admirers. Her father was the Scottish millionaire, Charles Tennant.

She wrote to Balfour in the winter of 1898 asking if Balfour would use his influence with her father to persuade him to make Asquith independent of the Bar. Her husband, she said, was making between £5,000 and £6,000 a year at the Bar, but he would have to give up most, indeed all, of this work if he became Leader of the Party.

Balfour might well have rejected this plea as likely to be extremely embarrassing, but he did not. He wrote to Tennant at Christmas, 1898, saying that, as a great personal friend of Asquith, he rejoiced to

think that he was likely to get in the prime of life the great position
for which his capacities so eminently fitted him—though from the
official point of view he (Balfour) might well live to regret it since he
was the most formidable debater on his side of the House.   But for
these rosy prospects to be fulfilled one thing was absolutely necessary—
that he should be in a position at a moment's notice to leave his
practice at the Bar: 'No man can lead either the Opposition or the
House of Commons if he is tied by a profession.   A party may not
give much but it claims everything.'

Balfour steered delicately clear of actually suggesting that Tennant
should increase Margot's allowance, but he pointed out that Asquith
would obviously hesitate to go into politics full time if there was any
question of Margot's comfort being adversely affected.

Tennant's reply has a certain irony.   It was not a question of money
for him but a question of politics.   He was a Liberal and also a stickler
for precedence and seniority.   He believed that Henry Campbell-
Bannerman was entitled to the position of Leader, and he would do
nothing which might prevent that coming about.   (In fact Campbell-
Bannerman did become Leader and Asquith had to wait for another
decade.)

It may have been true, as Salisbury declared to Balfour in a letter
on July 31, 1895, that: 'I do not believe in managing a party on
principles of magnanimity.'   Both he and his nephew were, however,
capable of the greatest magnanimity both in personal and, in the widest
sense, political matters.   Balfour and Asquith long remained firm
friends; and the break, when it came 20 years later, was not the 'betrayal' Margot Asquith was later to call it.

Balfour was a more consistently good behind-the-scenes 'manager'
than he was a leader of the House.   He was still capable of flashing the
rapier; but, as we have seen, he took his duties as Leader somewhat
perfunctorily.   There were, records the backbench Conservative
M.P., A. S. T. Griffith-Boscawen, many complaints against his leadership—'lack of grip and want of knowledge of the feelings of the rank and
file'—quite early in the new administration's life.   Balfour did not
cultivate his followers, nor could he easily simulate interest in those
who did not, in fact, interest him among M.P.s—and they were many.
This did not to any great extent affect his personal popularity; even his
shortcomings delighted the political cartoonists and sketch writers.
Here is how one of them described him in the House at this time:

'Prayers and Private Bills have been disposed of; now our Minister is
being sniped at by Members on both sides, but Balfour is not there.
Presently, from behind the Speaker's chair emerges a tall, gaunt figure,
limp and lackadaisical, angular and artless is its owner.   It is Arthur,
sweet Arthur, who had dropped in to see that all is well within the

Chamber. He makes his way to his seat into which he flops weary. You wonder if he was born tired like the man who couldn't eat roast beef, so exhausted did it make him to reach for the mustard. The elongated body slides down until the neck, thin and delicate as a woman's, reaches the ridge of the Treasury Bench behind. Up go two square-toed, thick soled, spatteed feet on the table opposite. The legs are arched and suggest a switch-back railway. The soft brown meditative eyes, denoting the man of thought rather than the man of action, are now peering upwards through glasses into the amber glow of the fanlight in the ceiling. As he gazes, he yawns.'

II

No sooner had the new parliamentary session opened in the winter of 1895 than an epidemic of trouble broke out all over the world, and Lord Salisbury spent his days and nights at the Foreign Office. There were, for instance, the Armenian massacres resulting from the Sultan of Turkey's pan-Islamic policies, to which we have already referred. Salisbury, along with France and Russia, demanded reforms, but refused all pressure to declare war on Turkey.

Much more extraordinary was the sudden irruption of the United States into world affairs, an irruption which very nearly led to war with Britain. The Venezuelan incident was regarded at the time as being most mysterious in origin; at this distance, it is quite evident that the United States, buoyed up by the sudden realisation of her industrial and productive power, wanted to flex her diplomatic muscles, and what better way of doing so than by twisting the Lion's tail? In the United States a certain amount of Anglophobia still lingered, not least on the part of Irish-Americans; although rich American heiresses were already claiming titled English bridegrooms, Americans were still widely regarded by Britons as country cousins—an attitude that the Americans themselves were well aware of.

At any rate, at the end of 1895, President Grover Cleveland took it upon himself to interfere, on grounds of the Monroe Doctrine, in the long-standing boundary dispute between the Republic of Venezuela and British Guiana. The Venezuelans had recently seized British territory and fired on a British gun-boat. The President's legal grounds were shaky, but his words were big:

'It will in my opinion be the duty of the United States to resist by every means in its power, as a wilful aggression upon its rights and interests, the appropriation by Great Britain of any lands which after investigation we have determined of right to belong to Venezuela.'

This had to be taken as a public warning to prepare for war. Salisbury, however, stood firm. He was certainly not prepared to admit the principle that the United States should be allowed to meddle with

Britain's overseas territories. The crisis was ultimately resolved by a resort to arbitration—almost the first such resort in a major international dispute.

At the height of the crisis, it fell to Balfour to make a public speech, the first by a Cabinet Minister since the affair developed. Balfour had American friends—not least among the wives of such of his colleagues as St. John Brodrick and Joseph Chamberlain. 'The idea of war with the United States', he said in his speech at Manchester on January 15, 1896, 'carries with it some of the unnatural horror of a civil war. . . . The time will come, the time must come, when someone, some statesman of authority, more fortunate even than President Monroe, will lay down the doctrine that between English-speaking people war is impossible.'

This sentiment marks the beginning of Balfour's determination to promote Anglo-American understanding—to make the co-operation of America and Britain the most powerful plank in a new international balance of power. This sounds platitudinous today, but very few people in 1895 had the foresight to see how important it would become. Much of what it has, in fact, become is due to Balfour's work both during the First World War and afterwards. He himself, as we shall see, visualised an even closer tie than has come about, and discussed the matter in long private letters with President Theodore Roosevelt.

In the 'nineties, Balfour thought that one way of promoting Anglo-American co-operation was by propagating the bimetallist theory which had already gained many adherents in the United States. Balfour's first speech in the House of Commons in 1878, it will be remembered, dealt with currency questions and bimetallism. He believed that silver as well as gold should serve as standard value for currency. But when official envoys from the United States visited England in the hope of achieving an international bimetallist agreement, Balfour was unable to impress his Cabinet colleagues with his convictions of the importance of the double standard. Both Hicks-Beach, the Chancellor of the Exchequer, and City opinion were strongly mono-metallist; and eventually he allowed the idea to drop. But unwillingly, for he believed—at this time—that much of Britain's economic difficulties were due to the world shortage of gold which was the basis of trade. He wrote to Goschen on January 25, 1895:

'I personally am convinced—rightly or wrongly—that our difficulties with India and Lancashire, and the general depression of trade are very closely connected with our present ridiculous system of international currency.'

We may perhaps see in bimetallism Balfour's 'answer' to economic difficulties, as protection was Chamberlain's. But at this time Chamberlain's theory was still unformulated—and so was Balfour's reaction to it. Bimetallism is now merely dusty history, whereas protection (or rather its antithesis) is still current politics. One can only speculate on whether bimetallism, generally adopted, might not have eased those economic conditions which caused much of the acrimony and the political disruption occasioned by the later debates on tariff reform.

Much more ominous was the Jameson Raid, a disastrous prelude in 1895 to the disastrous war in South Africa of 1899. The immediate sources of trouble may be briefly recounted. The Republic of the Transvaal, in the north-west of Southern Africa, had become vastly rich owing to the discovery of gold mines. Its President, the tough Paul Kruger, though the foreign affairs of his Republic remained in British hands, had long refused to join in any South African Federation, and had already seen a vision of a Boer paramountcy. The immediate cause of trouble was that many of those who had exploited the mines were not Boers and Kruger consistently refused to allow them either a vote or a say in Transvaal affairs. Over against Kruger was Cecil Rhodes, the 'colossus' of politics and finance, who led the British as well as the Cape Dutch, and was Premier of the Cape Colony at Cape Town. Rhodes began organising a rebellion of the Transvaal non-Boers—called Uitlanders; and of this Chamberlain, the Colonial Secretary, was cognisant. At the same time Rhodes was planning an attack by some 470 police, led by his friend and medical adviser, Doctor Jameson, on Johannesburg. It was a bold plan, but an impossible one, and it failed.

But Jameson's force fought bravely, and for a time he became a hero in Britain. Balfour's first impression was one of admiration. Lady Frances Balfour reported that he remarked that 'he should probably have joined Jameson had he lived there . . . that Jameson's character was the only attractive feature in the matter, though he ought to be hung all the same.'

Then came a telegram from the German Emperor conveying his congratulations to Kruger on having maintained the independence of his country against 'armed force'. This put a more serious complexion on the matter. Rhodes resigned, and Jameson and the officers of his force were put on trial. The leaders of the rebels in Johannesburg were also put on trial and some were condemned to death, but saved by Chamberlain's interference. It was widely suggested that Chamberlain himself had a responsibility for the raid, but this has never been proved, and it is unlikely. (Doubts have continued to be voiced mainly because of the refusal to allow the full text of Chamberlain's letters to be seen; versions only of them were presented in J. L. Garvin's *Life of Chamberlain*.) What certainly appears from the Balfour Papers is that Chamberlain, though averse to an inquiry, believed that a House of Commons committee would not, as he put it, 'do any harm'. The joint committee of both Houses was duly formed and did much—but by no means everything—to clear him. (What Chamberlain often failed to do was to keep Salisbury and Balfour in touch with events. For example, there is a letter among Balfour's Papers in which Chamberlain apologises for not informing them of a dispatch he sent on February 4, 1896 to Sir Hercules Robinson, the High Commissioner in South Africa, printed in *The Times* of February 8. The letter opens with the word 'peccavi'.)

In the next few years, Kruger imported quantities of war material, built forts and allotted large sums for intelligence work. He increased his oppressive measures against English residents, and British subjects in the Rand petitioned the Queen.

The more deep-lying causes of South African problems do not concern us. It may, however, be worth remarking that, in attitude to the events leading to war, there was little difference of opinion in the triumvirate of the Cabinet. None was a 'Jingo', greedy of aggrandisement and shouting for blood. Of the three Salisbury was least an Empire man; but both Balfour and Chamberlain were convinced of the growing importance to Britain of Empire—they differed only in emphasis and in method of drawing the bonds tighter, as we shall see later in this chapter.

As for war, none of the three visualised it in 1895–6 as more than a remote possibility. Balfour was probably particularly influenced in his belief in a peaceful outcome by personal letters he received from his friend, George Wyndham, who visited South Africa shortly after the Jameson Raid. Wyndham noticed that even 'The Dutch of the (Cape) Colony are absolutely loyal to the British connection and, although with a little resentment still lingering against the raid, they are thinking more of pure politics, native questions and of railway and tariff competition against the Republic than of racial animosity and republican castles in the air. The English, on the other hand, are less annoyed with us and less jingoistic than I feared.'

Meanwhile, abroad, Kitchener slowly pushed forward towards the reconquest of the Sudan, and an Irish Land Bill, sponsored by Balfour's brother, Gerald, now Chief Secretary for Ireland, was passed into law—not without difficulty, as Balfour told Lady Elcho:

'The Irish Peers, consistent to the last, finished their unique performance by dividing in favour of a most absurd and indeed dishonest amendment of Lord McNaughten's. They were beaten by six votes:—and had not we of the Commons taken some of the "whipping" into our own hands, and brought up peers on our own account, we should have been in a minority again:—thus further prolonging the session and still further discrediting the House of Lords. It has been a baddish business and I fear *some* of the blame (to put it mildly) must rest in very high quarters.' (August 16, 1896.)

It was not only in 'very high quarters' (whoever they were) that the Irish continued to be a problem. Four of their dynamiters, who had been in prison for some years, were released at this time by Sir Matthew White Ridley, the Home Secretary; the result was an acrimonious debate in which the Home Secretary was defended by Balfour. Other Irish dynamiters were, however, still at large, and mainly financed from the United States. Secret Service methods had been adopted to counter their activities, not least the appointment in 1890 of Nicholas Gosselin as head of a small group of agents under the Home Secretary. Their work was the subject of a letter of praise from Balfour at the end of 1896. Gosselin's report on the round-up of a dynamiting conspiracy —mainly financed by a rich Irish-American called William Lyman— is still fascinating reading (see Appendix II), and forms a small chapter in the early history of the Secret Service.

III

Not even the most violent of his political enemies could ever accuse Balfour of militaristic tendencies. He probably shared the simple feelings of the Queen on the subject of war which he reported to Lady Elcho on November 2, 1895. The Queen, he wrote, 'has the utmost horror of war, on the simple but sufficient ground that you cannot have war without a great many people being killed'. Nor could anything be less likely than Ponsonby's suggestion in his *Recollections of Three Reigns* that 'Balfour always imagined that had fate decreed that he should be a soldier he would have been a great tactician. All that was necessary was to apply the principles of logic and you pulverise the enemy.' He did not, however, disguise his opinion that brains were necessary in generals, and that English generals tended to suffer for lack of them.

Nevertheless, quite early in the nineties, Balfour became aware that the era of peace was in all probability drawing to a close. Where, when and how war on a large scale might break out was not, of course, apparent to him; but, as we shall see, there were indications from Germany, from France and from the Far East that war was a possibility. Both in the privacy of his thoughts and the publicity of the House, Balfour began to develop what his friend, Brodrick (Under-Secretary to Lansdowne at the War Office) called 'his rising flair for military matters'. Balfour gave both encouragement and practical help in the Cabinet to both these colleagues and to Field-Marshal Lord Wolseley who now became the Secretary of State's principal adviser on all military questions, with general supervisory powers over the military departments of the War Office. Opposition was particularly strong to any increase in military power from the Chancellor of the Exchequer, not to mention the Liberal Opposition. Salisbury was lukewarm in all

military matters; Chamberlain seems not to have realised the significance, even for his own co-ordinating Empire policies, of the military
arm.   Yet in three years Lansdowne and Brodrick backed by Balfour,
managed to add ten battalions of Foot besides two Guards battalions
to the army; to raise the strength of all the Line battalions; and to
increase the Artillery by 15 batteries, thus securing the largest additions
to the army since 1871.   They secured £5,000,000 for military works,
carried out army manœuvres, and provided a large increase in stores.

It is undoubtedly true, as Brodrick claimed, that 'without these
achievements we should not have been able in 1900 to send 185,000
men to South Africa in the first six months of the War'.   The early
defeats of British troops in the Boer War were not so much due to
shortage of supply or shortage of men but to their deployment. The
Royal Commission's report on the South African War stated plainly
and briefly that 'no plan of campaign ever existed for operations in
South Africa'.

Planning!   Such a thing scarcely existed, much less co-ordination of
the defence arms, the Empire forces and the economic and political
aspects of war.   A Colonial Defence Committee had briefly existed,
the Carnarvon Commission had briefly sat on the question, and the
Hartington Commission of 1888 had proposed a permanent defence
committee, but nothing had been done.

Balfour, however, had thought deeply about the matter and had
engaged in conferences and correspondence with Sir Charles Dilke and
Henry Spenser Wilkinson whose book, *Imperial Defence*, had pleaded for
a radical reorganisation and a Defence Ministry.   As a result of
Balfour's impetus, a Defence Committee was at last constituted under
Hartington's leadership (he was now Duke of Devonshire).   It immediately resulted in the usual quarrel between the civilian and the
military man.   Moreover, Lord Salisbury, though 'he pooh-poohed . . .
a Defence Committee whose members were all professionals because
professionals were all narrow minded', infrequently attended the
Committee's meetings which themselves were of irregular occurrence.
Balfour's proposals that the Committee's agenda should be as elastic as
possible and should focus on problems common to the two Defence
Departments were accepted by the members.   But there was agreement neither on the membership of the Committee, nor on its rôle.

Balfour himself became deeply involved in his Leadership and did not
become a regular member of the group until after 1900.   But he sought
in the background to smooth its path from such antagonisms as those of
Goschen, the First Lord of the Admiralty, who no doubt encouraged
by his entourage, opposed any open discussion of the navy by plans in
case of a war with France in 1898.   Under Balfour's influence, Lansdowne was more co-operative, but the War Office was not anxious to

exchange information. Through constant disagreements among its members, the Defence Committee was ineffective during the Boer War.

But Balfour was never in any doubt of the supreme importance—at any rate potentially—of a Defence Committee which really worked. When he himself came to supreme power in 1902, the Committee was reconstituted and became the Committee of Imperial Defence with the Prime Minister as Chairman. This, as we shall see, was one of Balfour's lasting achievements. Throughout this earlier period from 1895 onwards, however, all he could do was to throw his weight in Cabinet and in the confidence of Lord Salisbury against the attempts of the Chancellor of the Exchequer, Hicks-Beach, to bear down all attempts to expand the fighting services.

Every kind of difficulty, logical and illogical, met the would-be reformer of Britain's national defence system in the 'nineties, from the inbred fear of politicians that a too-powerful army was a threat to the civil power to the time-consuming argument between those who believed a strong navy met every requirement (the 'blue water' school) and those who wondered what would happen if an enemy launched a 'bolt from the Blue' against Britain while the navy was elsewhere or dispersed by storm.

IV

If illogicality and stubborn prejudice bedevilled the defence question, sheer mania, of the religious variety, lay dragon-wise across the path of the educational reformer. Both defence and education were to Balfour the essential objectives for Britain if she were to remain a leading power in the world. Education was, indeed, a great many other things, too; but, in the immediately political sense, Balfour would not have disagreed with the Liberal, W. E. Forster who, for his reforms, used as his principal argument that: 'Upon the speedy provision of elementary education depends our national prosperity.' In the 'nineties Balfour stumbled and nearly fell over both his great object-ives. In the 1900s, as Prime Minister, he returned to them with powerful tenacity and went a very long way to achieving what he had set out to do.

The Education Bill of 1896, which had been promised in the Queen's Speech, was not in the first instance Balfour's affair. It was presented by Sir John Gorst (Balfour's erstwhile colleague of 'Fourth Party' days); but he intervened in its early stages and the Bill ultimately substituted for it was entirely his brain child. The Forster Act had set up Board Schools paid for and managed by the local ratepayers to fill in the ever-increasing educational gaps left by the Voluntary Schools managed by the Church of England and other denominations. In the 'nineties, the

Voluntary Schools, for various reasons, became very short of money. If primary education was to continue to exist at all, these schools needed aid and State aid was the only possibility. This the Bill of 1896 proposed to give. At the same time, an Education Committee was to be set up by each County Council to control all National Schools, both Board and Voluntary.

The Nonconformists at once objected to the fact that rates were to be given to the support of Church of England Schools; and the Church of England also objected to being controlled by non-Church authorities in the form of Education Committees. Within the Cabinet there was also dissension, not least from the Nonconformist Chamberlain who wrote to the Duke of Devonshire, nominally in charge of education: 'They are the very maddest proposals I have seen in the course of my life. They would absolutely break down, in the interests of the Church and the Roman Catholics, the so-called compromise of 1870. . . .'

Balfour's views of sectarianism have already been shown in *The Foundations of Belief.* Ironically enough, all his political life was to be harassed by it. Worse for him, perhaps, was the fact that, disregarding it himself, he never really understood the strength of it. The Bill of 1896 was common sense; only gradually and with the greatest difficulty did Balfour come to realise that in politics common sense is not enough and, indeed, except at odd moments, is often too much.

At first it seemed as though the Bill would get through; at its second reading it was heavily supported by the Irish Members (acting under orders from the Roman Catholic bishops) to the fury of the English Nonconformists, also largely Liberals, who in revenge declared that Home Rule was dead! But in the Committee stage opposition really began, and it took five nights to pass two lines with 1,200 amendments yet to be moved. During one of these amendments, Balfour intervened and threw over Sir John Gorst, who was piloting the Bill. Balfour then called a meeting of the Party at the Carlton Club and propounded a plan of campaign to which the Members agreed, though in fact it was an impossible one. He proposed to adjourn, not prorogue, Parliament in August until early in January, that the Bill should be hung up meanwhile and then concluded, and that Parliament should be prorogued in time to begin a new session in March. Clearly, however, the Opposition could prolong discussion on the Bill until the exigencies of Supply compelled the Government to drop it and begin a new session— and Balfour had already announced that the Bill would not be closured by compartments.

Another week of Committee stage passed with endless amendments being moved and discussed; finally, Balfour had to bow to the inevitable and announce the abandonment of the measure. Sir William Harcourt, then Leader of the Liberal Party, sounded a long note of triumph; Balfour's reputation as Leader was at its nadir. It was a question now of *sauve qui peut*. Both the Queen and Salisbury were angered at so ignominious an ending to the Bill, and Balfour set about preparing a substitute. He wrote to Lady Elcho on November 28, 1896:

'I am oppressed at this moment with many cares—the lightest of them being the total impossibility of devising a generally acceptable Education Bill. I have expended treasures of ingenuity on this most thankless task.'

Even this Bill—presented by Balfour himself—which was merely directed to relieving 'intolerable strain' by giving an aid grant of 5s. a child in the Voluntary Schools, came up against stern opposition. Yet it was important to get it through to enable the schools to get relief in the current year. Balfour resorted to ruthless tactics. He proceeded to take up all the time of the House and then to refuse to accept any amendment at all in Committee, thus avoiding the Report stage. The House found itself a mere voting machine. The Bill passed third reading on March 25.

Although the method was somewhat dubious, the Government's confidence in Balfour's leadership was restored. But only because he had a strong Cabinet behind him was it possible; not least because Chamberlain abstained from debate and in his Nonconformist stronghold of Birmingham actually pleaded that, since Voluntary Schools could not be abolished, they ought not to be starved. No wonder that Balfour wrote to him: 'I can assure you that I had rather do business with you even on subjects where there may be some difference of opinion between us than with some of my colleagues in matters where there is perfect agreement. Can I say more?'

Religious matters did not end with the Education Bill. Much fuss and flurry went on in the 'nineties about the issues of Ritualism and anti-Ritualism in the Church of England. In the House, Balfour got himself a reputation for tolerance in these matters; but in private he called much more strongly 'a plague on both your houses'. Perhaps he realised that such matters were a sign of the Church being on the defensive. Despite *The Foundations of Belief*, the Synthetic Society and all the thousands of defences of the Christian faith against the barbs of the rationalists, the Church felt itself to have been punctured at the heart; quibbles over points of doctrine took the place of faith and works. As Balfour told an audience at Haddington celebrating the union of the Free and United Presbyterian Churches of Scotland, on January 15, 1901:

'Do not suppose I am an advocate for that colourless thing known as an undenominational creed. . . . What I plead for is that Christian men should understand there is a permission to differ without these differences carrying with them into ecclesiastical life, into political life, or into private life, any other difference which should make common work for a common object impossible.   After all, let us remember that whatever else the Church is, it is, among other things, a practical organisation to carry out a great practical work.   It is something more than an organisation to produce a body of school divinity.'

More frankly still, he wrote to his old friend, Edward Talbot, now Bishop of Rochester, on February 6, 1903:

'I confess to entertaining the gloomiest apprehensions as to the future of the Church of England.   I can hardly think of anything else.   A so-called "Protestant" faction, ignorant, fanatical, reckless, but everyday organising themselves politically with increased efficiency.   A ritualistic Party, as ignorant, as fanatical and as reckless, the sincerity of whose attachment to historic Anglicanism I find it quite impossible to believe. A High Church Party, determined to support men of whose practices they heartily disapprove.'

Certainly, historically speaking, the Ritualists seemed bent on giving away all that their forefathers had held dear, and without doubt they precipitated a split from which the Church of England has not yet recovered.   Balfour, brought up in Evangelicalism, had considerable distaste for ritualistic practices.   He preferred the long-established forms of Protestantism.   There is an amusing side-light on this in a letter Balfour wrote to W. T. Stead, editor of the *Westminster Gazette*, on December 30, 1895.   Referring to a new Church hymn-book with new tunes, he wrote: 'In my opinion the editor of a hymn-book who deliberately divorces old words from their accustomed setting is an iconoclast of the worst order.'

V

'Boredom was writ large over the whole place,' wrote one M.P. about the House of Commons at the close of the session of 1897; and this dull listlessness prevailed up to the outbreak of the South African War.   It was partly due to the fact that little domestic legislation was likely, the Government having tried the patience of some of their supporters over Chamberlain's Workmen's Compensation Act; and partly, also, to the paralysis of the Opposition due to the lack of a generally recognised leader, when Harcourt resigned.

But there was another reason.   During this period, however flaccid the House was, the diplomatic activity behind the scenes was intense, and it occupied the leading Ministers almost to the exclusion of anything else.   Much of this activity revolved round the question of Germany.   Was an alliance possible?   Was it necessary?   What would the cost be? It was Chamberlain particularly who pressed the view that 'splendid isolation' was no longer possible, and that, of the possible alliances, one with Germany would be the most advantageous and, in the long run, the least dangerous. There were supporting reasons for so thinking. France, for example, had compensated for defeat by the Prussians by becoming bombastic, and in 1898 there occurred the Fashoda affair when Kitchener, fresh from his victory at Omdurman, hoisted the Egyptian flag at Fashoda, Upper Nile, at practically the same moment as Major Marchand hoisted the French flag. For six weeks war with France seemed imminent, though in the same year the arrival at the French Foreign Office of M. Delcassé began a new era in Anglo-French relations.

Salisbury was by no means ill-disposed towards an understanding with Germany, though he had rejected Bismarck's offer in the previous decade; with the Germans as a race he believed Britain ought to be friendly. But he had considerable—and by no means misplaced—distrust of the German Emperor, Wilhelm II, grandson of Queen Victoria, and of his emissary in Britain, Count Hatzfeldt, the friend of Churchill. It was true that during his lifetime Salisbury had little conception of the grandiose schemes of world conquest the Kaiser was nourishing; but his instinct determined him to caution. Not so Chamberlain. He believed that 'isolation' must be broken by alliance with Germany, and from 1897 he engaged, with Salisbury's knowledge if not his whole-hearted agreement, in discussions with Hatzfeldt, and that strange, tall member of the German Embassy, Baron Eckardstein who, with his English wife, wanders with somewhat deceptive joviality through the London Society of the 'nineties.

At this point Balfour comes into the picture of negotiations. At the end of March and the beginning of April, 1898, Salisbury was away in France recovering from illness, and Balfour was acting as Foreign Secretary. On March 24, Sir Nathan Rothschild, the famous financier and a strong pro-German, invited Hatzfeldt to meet Balfour and Chamberlain at his house, an invitation interpreted by Hatzfeldt as being an approach to an attempt at rapprochement between Britain and Germany. But on the 24th came the news that Russia had seized Port Arthur in China, and the British Cabinet registered its strong disapproval of this move which it regarded as preliminary to 'the dismemberment of China'.

This Far Eastern grab had begun when Germany leased the harbour of Kiao-Chau in Shantung. Balfour formally requested a meeting with Hatzfeldt, having already decided to reverse Salisbury's earlier refusal of a lease of Wei-hai-wei, a port on the Gulf of Pechili, and to keep the balance of power. From this, little emerged except the German sense of aggrievedness; but from the Wei-hai-wei decision (from which Chamberlain had dissented) arose a great shout of complaint in the country and in the House, it being felt that Britain had lost the day.

Balfour in the House countered this in a powerful speech, and telegraphed to the Queen a message containing the key words: 'It was not worth while to promote a war with Russia in order to keep her out of Port Arthur.' Nor was it—but, as Chamberlain's biographer, Garvin, admits, Chamberlain himself (this was why he dissented from the Cabinet decision) believed that Russia should have been turned out of Port Arthur by force, which would almost certainly have precipitated war.

Meanwhile, Chamberlain's talks with Hatzfeldt and Eckardstein continued, with Chamberlain aiming to push things ahead quickly and the Germans bedevilled in motive, not least by the varying voices of their own side. Chamberlain kept Balfour reasonably well acquainted with the course of discussion and Balfour, in turn, sent resumés by post to Salisbury at Beaulieu. At the same time, the posts were bearing to-and-fro from Berlin to London commentaries from and to Hatzfeldt and the German Chancellor. From all this correspondence, it begins to appear that, as Balfour put it to Salisbury, 'Chamberlain went far in the expression of his own personal leaning towards a German alliance', but that on the whole the Germans preferred, in Hatzfeldt's words, Balfour's 'practical common sense' to what the Kaiser called Chamberlain's 'theoretical and vague fantasies' and found him 'more to be trusted'.

Balfour himself, as he told Salisbury on April 14, 1898, was 'inclined to favour an Anglo-German agreement' but thought that 'it must, if possible, be made at the worst on equal terms. Of this loving couple I should wish to be the one that lent the cheek, not that imprinted the kiss.' Salisbury was more cautious still: 'The one object of the Emperor', he wrote to Balfour on April 9, 1898, 'since he has been on the throne has been to get us into a war with France. I never can make up my mind whether this is part of Chamberlain's object or not. The indications differ from month to month.' Balfour agreed that 'Joe is very impulsive'; and Hatzfeldt himself reported that Balfour had told him that 'Mr. Chamberlain sometimes wished to advance too quickly'. This, adds Hatzfeldt to the German Chancellor, 'gave me the impression that this *personal* ill-success of Mr. Chamberlain in this matter was not altogether unwelcome to him' (Balfour).

Later in April, Eckardstein went to Homburg and there discussed matters with the Emperor himself. The Emperor told him to go ahead with Chamberlain; yet the very next day the Emperor instructed his Foreign Office that an Anglo-German alliance was then undesirable. At this, Salisbury having heard of Chamberlain's further talks set down his view in a letter to Balfour on April 26, 1898:

'My dear Arthur. I think it would be desirable that if possible you should see Eckardstein' (or, as Salisbury prefers it, Eckerstein) 'which I understand you have not hitherto had an opportunity of doing, and ascertain from him precisely what passed at Homburg.' (Balfour apparently did not see him, perhaps because Eckardstein shortly left again for Germany.) 'Especially we wish to know what it is the Emperor wants. He knows all the difficulties we have in concluding a secret agreement; and I gather that an open agreement would not suit his purpose. Though he is a dangerous friend in some respects, he is on the whole the least unreliable of our three suitors. France and Russia seem to look upon a negotiation as merely a contrivance for enabling them to seize the territory under discussion while the negotiation is going on. Germany, no doubt, would do the same if she had a chance, but not having territorial access to any place in which both of us are interested, she is compelled to resort to other and less effective plans for compassing her ends. The only circumstance in her friendship which I greatly distrust is her constant desire to push us into a war with France: a policy in which she may get assistance from friends in our camp. But I agree we must face this danger as we can: we cannot safely draw back now from the advances to which Eckardstein has committed us. But it becomes a matter of some importance to know what these advances are; not only because without that knowledge it will be difficult for us to act; but also, because, as long as he is only telling third persons, it may be that he is returning answers to the Emperor which imply that he has made proposals to us much larger than have really reached us: and a new quarrel with the Emperor will be the ultimate result.

'Though we are driven to move much nearer to him, I am much puzzled to guess how we can give him any comfort. I imagine that what really preoccupies German statesmen is not the cutting up of China but the cutting up of Austria; and how can we help him there?'

In the end it did not matter what 'the advances' had been, for negotiations stopped when it was learned that all that had so far passed had been revealed by the Emperor to the Czar. Chamberlain, indeed, continued to seek new ways of rapprochement, even it appears as late as November 4, 1898, telling Eckardstein that Balfour himself no longer agreed with Salisbury's 'peace at any price' policy and realising that Britain had to show that she could also act. In less than a year, Britain was certainly compelled to act, and it was not a show to bring the House down. But Balfour courted war no more than Salisbury did: Chamberlain was ready to run such risks, as Salisbury knew and as we have seen over the Wei-hai-wei affair.

As late as 1902, Chamberlain still believed that an alliance with Germany was a possibility. Such an alliance, it has been represented, would have saved the worst consequences of the World War of 1914, though war there probably would have been. It is equally possible to argue that had Chamberlain not wasted so much time and effort—and the time and effort of his leading colleagues—in nugatory discussions with Germany, it might have become clear earlier that the Emperor's visions excluded Britain as an ally and saw her as the great stumbling-block to world dominion.   It might also have been possible to make common cause with France at an earlier stage, and thus to present a front which would have at least delayed the Emperor's military plans.

Neither Balfour nor Salisbury, of course, lacking the benefit of our hindsight, saw this; but they were cautious by instinct, avoiding both war with France and war with Russia.   Chamberlain, on the other hand, had psychological need of an 'enemy'; when the breach with Germany finally came, none was more implacably anti-German than he.   The breach came mainly because it was clear that Germany was demanding Britain's adherence not merely to Germany but—and without real tit-for-tat—to the Triple Alliance, in other words to the dangerously liquescent Habsburg Empire.   'The cutting up of Austria' —Balfour to whom Salisbury had addressed these words must have recalled them many times as the new century developed.   As for war itself, the hostilities in South Africa gave pause to all who incautiously saw it as Britain's ultimate policy sanction.

Before this final breach, Balfour himself was involved in negotiations with Germany on, however, something much less than an alliance. After skilfully handling a potentially dangerous situation arising out of the United States's war with Spain, Balfour again took over the Foreign Office during Salisbury's absence in the August of 1898. During this period, Balfour negotiated a very difficult and delicate agreement with Germany over the control of Delagoa Bay, a Portuguese African possession through which the Transvaal had its access to the sea and over which Britain already had a right of pre-emption. Portugal had approached the British Government for a loan, offering her African colonies, including Delagoa Bay, as security.   Germany was determined that in the event of a loan the lien on these possessions should not be Britain's sole monopoly, and Salisbury though unwillingly had agreed to begin negotiations for a secret convention over territorial partitions in Africa.   Balfour took over the negotiations on August 10, 1898.   He found the Germans intransigent, but he managed to produce a convention which was signed on August 30 which did not give way too much to Germany and yet did not offend Portuguese susceptibilities.

What the agreement basically laid down was that, in the event of Portugal wishing to dispose of her colonies—to, as it was put, 'a third power'—Britain and Germany should agree on their disposal and administration.   This part was, of course, secret and, as Salisbury wrote: 'I only hope that it will not come into use for a long time.'   In fact it did not, for Portugal improved her finances in another way.

And, though Germany had agreed to renounce her interests in the Transvaal, it did not prevent her interfering in the South African War nor from extorting further blackmail in the shape of a bargain abandoning British rights in Samoa.

VI

The war with the Boers broke out in October, 1899. Its causes and its justification do not here concern us; certainly the Cabinet as a whole (including Chamberlain) were reluctant to go to war, but the chain of events was too powerful for them. What is much more important is that few of them really believed that war would take place. Balfour, for example, as late as August 27, 1899, told Lady Elcho: 'You ask me about South Africa. I somehow think that war will be avoided— though,' he added somewhat strangely, 'whether this will in the long run be for the good of mankind is another question.' He was still surprised at the end of the year. Had Milner, the High Commissioner who had certainly lost patience with Kruger, expected war, he asked Chamberlain?

Chamberlain replied on January 7, 1900: 'It is difficult to answer. He did and he did not. His opinion, like that of everyone else, varied. He hoped for peace and feared war. Until the ultimatum was actually delivered, no one could be certain of the real intentions of the Boers, and there is some reason to suppose that they themselves were divided and that Kruger wavered. . . . It is clear that war was inevitable *at some time or another*, unless we were prepared to give up all we were contending for; but I believe there were times during the negotiations when the Boers were ready to patch up a peace and wait for a more favourable opportunity.'

The unexpectedness of the war, even more the unexpectedly effective opposition from the Boers, is important to remember. The Salisbury Government, both then and even today, is fiercely attacked for its unpreparedness. In fact, as we saw above, Lansdowne and Brodrick, backed by Balfour, had done much to make new forces available. What they had not done was to make co-ordination effective through the Defence Committee; nor had they seen to it that the army system of promotion brought the best men to the top. But they had, after all, other and apparently (or, indeed, in reality) much vaster problems to cope with; and they had a populace and an Opposition who, after decades of piping peace, were hard to convince of war's possibility, much less of the need to unlock the Treasury chest to the extent that the upshot proved necessary.

In the early weeks of the war, Balfour was once again standing in for his uncle, whose wife had recently died, and, as acting Prime Minister, had to bear the brunt of the consistently bad news.   Soon after it began, indeed, Balfour had his doubts.   He wrote to his sister Alice in November from Balmoral:

'The Queen was most anxious that I should stay.   She is, naturally enough depressed and worried, and she seems to find some comfort in having a Minister at hand to whom she can put questions; even though the answers may not be very consoling.   I do not think the position very satisfactory.   I have no doubt we were wrong to occupy Dundee and Glencoe in the first instance; I am equally sure that the selection of Ladysmith for the important stand was unfortunate.   For this purpose Colenso was the proper place.   It is, however, now too late to change, as a retreat from Ladysmith *with all the stores* would be a hazardous operation.   This is not wisdom after the event: it represents Wolseley's views expressed to me weeks ago.   But we were clearly right, having selected our General, not to hamper his discretion by orders from home —though whether the right General was selected in the person of White is quite another matter.   Meanwhile Buller feels himself obliged to abandon his original idea of leaving Kimberley and Ladysmith to look after themselves and delivering a heavy attack on Bloemfontein. He has come to the conclusion (doubtless on sufficient grounds) that something of a *direct* character must be done to relieve these places.   I am very sorry:—partly because if practicable the first plan was strategic-ally the soundest—partly because its abandonment seems to me to indicate that he regards Ladysmith (at least) as much less defensible than I think it ought to be.   I cannot understand how so large a garrison as we have there, amply supplied as I believe they are with ammunition and food can be in any danger.   Perhaps, however, Buller is thinking as much of a counter-attacking raid on Pietermaritz-burg (which is indefensible) and Durban as of preserving Ladysmith. On the whole, however, I am dissatisfied.'

He had good cause for dissatisfation.   The English forces in South Africa were in a parlous situation.   Sir George White, commanding the Natal field force, soon found himself hemmed in at Ladysmith, while Kimberley with its large civil population (including Rhodes himself) and Mafeking were also under siege.   Sir Redvers Buller—Balfour's colleague of earlier days in Ireland—led the main British army and sought to relieve Ladysmith by an attack on Colenso.   This was a fatal move and it was repulsed.   Buller staggered back and clearly had no idea what to do next.   Shortly after this had been learned in London, it was also reported that Buller had actually signalled White telling him to surrender Ladysmith; although White refused to do so, even on the order of the C.-in-C., he made little attempt to break out.

At this point, Balfour took a hand.   The news reached London on Saturday and Balfour was the only Cabinet Minister in town.   Lans-downe and he had already discussed Buller's future and Lord Roberts had been mentioned as his successor.   But Salisbury had been doubtful on account of Roberts's age—he was 67. Now, however, without further consultation, Balfour telegraphed Buller in the name of the Government: 'If you cannot relieve Ladysmith, hand your command over to Sir Francis Clery and return home.' Balfour set about convincing his uncle that Roberts, despite his age, was the man, and in due course Roberts, who had already pleaded with Lansdowne for the job, was sent out. At the same time as Lansdowne told him of his decision, he had also to tell Roberts that his only son had been killed in the Colenso action. Balfour wrote to Salisbury on December 18, 1899: ' "I have" ', (he quoted Roberts) ' "for years been leading the most active and abstemious life, waiting for this day." There is something surely rather fine in the simplicity of the utterance, and, coming from the mouth of a man who knew his only son to be dying, it is pathetic as well.' As for Buller, he added, 'For ten years he has allowed himself to go downhill.' (Years earlier, as we saw, Balfour commented on his addiction to the bottle.)

Roberts justified the expectations of Balfour and Lansdowne, and succeeded in turning the tide. But Salisbury had insisted that he must go out with an associate who was a younger man, and suggested Kitchener, the hero of Omdurman. So Kitchener went out as Roberts's Chief of Staff and took over towards the end of 1900 when Roberts left South Africa believing the war to be practically won, an impression which, as it turned out, was erroneous.

Even at this time Balfour's attitude to Kitchener was not entirely uncritical—perhaps he had a premonition of the later troubles involving Kitchener which were to harass him during his Premiership. Balfour met him first in 1898 when he and Kitchener were staying together at Balmoral where, Ponsonby tells us, Balfour was 'wonderful in drawing out Kitchener'. It is also recorded that Balfour helped Kitchener to write his Guildhall speech when he received the acclamations of the nation on his victory. Kitchener, however, rejected Balfour's draft as being in much too 'beautiful language'.

During the meeting at Balmoral, Balfour wrote to Lady Elcho: 'I do not find it easy to form any very confident estimate of his capacity. He possesses, without doubt, boundless courage and resolution; how far he could adapt himself to wholly different and perhaps larger problems than those with which he has been dealing, I do not feel confident. He seems to have a profound contempt for every soldier except himself; which, though not an amiable trait, does not make me think less of his brains'. Generals, indeed, were very vulnerable in the South African War. Buller was not the only one to be removed; there was also the case of Sir Henry Colvile. Throughout, Balfour, as we shall shortly see, was critical of the military leadership.

He was equally critical of the Admiralty in a letter to Salisbury dated January 1, 1899 (though this is almost certainly an error for 1900). Referring to the arrangements for collecting information on the shipments of contraband of war by German vessels through Delagoa Bay, he writes: 'I am extremely indignant with the Admiralty for their want of foresight in connection with the detention of neutral vessels. It appears that they have now for the first time discovered that there is some ambiguity in the authorised Admiralty instruction as to the kind of evidence which justifies detention. . . . In short, if a search at sea is impossible and a search in port is illegal, we may as well apologise to the Germans and withdraw our cruisers altogether from the neighbour-hood of Delagoa Bay. . . . I cannot suppress my amazement that the Admiralty should never have raised the question until they had actually got a German mailpacket on their hands.' Ironically enough, he adds in a postscript that arrangements have been concluded for purchasing guns from French firms and 'inquiries are now going to be made of the German firms'.

Balfour himself was under pressure from time to time from Chamber-lain on the subject of arms and supplies. We find Balfour writing to Chamberlain in January, 1900, that 'It is quite true that the reserve of guns of field artillery is dangerously low. But orders have been given for more. As regards guns of position, we are purchasing every gun which can be obtained at short notice either at home or abroad.'

There was considerable trouble at this time owing to the fact that the decisions about Buller, Roberts and Kitchener were not conveyed to the Queen, mainly no doubt, due to the absence of Salisbury. Lord Wolseley, the Commander-in-Chief, had also not been informed. Balfour told Salisbury in a letter of December 19, 1899 that, when he had arrived at Windsor the day before, he had found the private secretary, A. J. Bigge (later Lord Stamfordham) full of grievances on these matters. Balfour, however, would not admit that the Queen should have been told of the telegram ordering Buller to relieve Lady-smith—'this', he said, 'represented a theory of constitutional govern-ment which I could not accept. The Queen's advisers must be permitted to issue important military orders without her previous sanc-tion.' (We shall note in the next chapter how a similar problem arose between Balfour and Edward VII.) She certainly should have been told of Robert's appointment, but he felt that was the duty of Lans-downe, Secretary for War. When he met the Queen herself, he found her much less complaining. Balfour was, indeed, according to Ponsonby, 'a great success with Victoria, although to me he never seemed to treat her seriously. His philosophical outlook and his cynical view that nothing mattered made it difficult for anyone to dis-agree with him. All the same, the Queen admired him and thought his speeches brilliant.' It was during one of his meetings with the Queen at this time that Balfour, who had referred to his depression over the military disasters, was cut short with the famous words: 'Please understand that there is no one depressed in *this* house; we are not interested in the possibilities of defeat; they do not exist.'

It was shortly after this visit that Balfour made his three speeches at Manchester on the subject of the war and roused violent indignation—not merely in the Opposition newspapers. He attempted to defend the Government on the grounds that the nation were not behind them in taking rapid action in providing vast supplementary estimates for the war. He admitted that the military efficiency of the Boers had been underestimated, but said he still thought the force of 25,000 sent out was sufficient had it not been for what Balfour infelicitously referred to 'as the unhappy entanglement of Ladysmith'. Parts of his speeches suggested an acquiescence in mishaps and reverses; and he did not provide for public licking of lips any sort of scapegoat. He was the last person to join in the newspaper chorus of complaint against Lansdowne. He did not believe that War Office maladministration was at the root of the defeats and he did not propose to say they were. Nor would he admit blunders.

This is probably where he went wrong. His speeches were realistic; he told the nation that 'we still have to go through a period of great darkness and difficulty before the light of success shines assuredly before our eyes'. Whatever it was the public wished to hear, it was not this. It had been astonished, depressed and then infuriated to see the British Lion being cast in the dust by unkempt, untrained Boer farmers. It would have been well to have gone at any rate a little further and admit frankly what Balfour certainly admitted privately in a letter to Sidgwick on January 15, 1900: 'It is true that there is one fact, or set of facts, which I did not state, and which I am unwilling to be driven to state, namely, the mistakes that have occurred are entirely due to the advice of experts respecting matters on which experts alone have the right to form an authoritative opinion.' He did not disguise from him his view that the Generals had been supplied with everything but brains.

In another letter on January 24, he added: 'I not only think blunders have been committed, but I think they have been of the most serious kind, imperilling the whole progress of the war. . . . The chief blunders have been made, in my private opinion, by our Generals in the field, but I do not of course think it desirable to make any such statement public. . . . I have said in these speeches not all that I thought, but nothing I did not think. I cannot give my full opinions without blaming gallant men whom I do not wish to blame; but I entirely decline to make a scapegoat of people who I do *not* think deserve any such fate. Far rather would I leave public life for ever. . . .'

In the same letter he rebuts allegations that he himself had treated matters flippantly, and a certain note of petulance shows through: 'This war has never been out of my thoughts for one moment for the last two months.   I know that I sacrificed my whole holiday to assisting to the best of my ability those colleagues of mine in whose special department the conduct of the war rests, and that the time of anxiety I have been going through is far greater than anything of which I have had experience, even in the worst periods of our Irish troubles.'

The sacrifice of a holiday when Britain's fortunes were at their lowest ebb and casualties in South Africa were phenomenal may not strike one as an enormous forfeit for an acting Prime Minister, particularly when the note of being sorry for oneself is distantly sounded.   But Balfour undoubtedly did work hard, and some of his remarkable equanimity (always an invaluable asset in government) was due to the fact that he played hard, also.   By July of that same year he is recounting to Lady Elcho how very 'busy and very frivolous' he has been, at the Eton and Harrow match, at Panshanger with the D'Abernons, Chesterfields, 'Jenny Churchill and her young man', Lady Windsor, the de Vescis, etc.   'His mind', he once told his sister, Lady Rayleigh, 'did not naturally turn to politics.   He never thought about them in bed, which was the test.   He regarded them with calm interest, but as for getting excited over them as some people did, he could not do it. There was Goschen; he got quite worried if things went wrong, and as for Chamberlain, he thought of nothing else.'

His composure was not quite as imperturbable as he liked to suggest, but it was certainly remarkable.   He never, for instance, allowed the prospect of political defeat to disturb him; indeed he sometimes welcomed it. He was, at any rate, always quite cool in assessing its possibility.   He wrote to George Wyndham in December, 1899: 'Dear Gerry.   What the result of the next General Election may be no one can, of course, foretell.   My own personal view is that we shall be defeated—probably not by a very large majority, and that the next administration will be a short-lived one.'

VII

It was decided to go to the country in October, 1900, and the 'Khaki' election, as it was called, quickly disproved Balfour's forecast. The Conservatives were returned with a slightly enlarged majority despite their unpopularity of a few months before.   The Liberals, however, had remained deeply divided, not least by their 'Pro-Boer', 'Anti-Boer' factions.   Moreover Chamberlain had fought the election of his life, though subject to every kind of personal and political slander. The fact was that, of the two major parties, only the Conservatives were wholehearted in desiring to pursue the war to the bitter end—but it was that bitter end that the populace now demanded with unmistakable voice. That end, though it seemed to be approaching, was not yet quite achieved; Kruger at any rate was gone, on a Dutch man-of-war bound for Marseilles, but the Boer leaders in the field—Botha, de Wet, Smuts, Hertzog—still fought on.

The new Cabinet-making was not easy. The public was demanding strength; Balfour knew that his uncle was weakening and showing signs of both age and infirmity. Salisbury himself would scarcely admit it, and there was the Queen who would be horrified to think that he was to depart from the scene. But Balfour was certain that Salisbury should at least relinquish the Foreign Office. On October 18, 1900, he wrote to Aretas Akers-Douglas, former Chief Whip and now Commissioner of Works, who was in Balmoral, asking him to show the following to the Queen and to Bigge:

'I do very earnestly hope that the Queen will not insist on Lord Salisbury keeping *both* offices. It requires no doctor to convince his family that the work, whenever it gets really serious, is too much for him. I have twice had to take the F.O. and three times, if I remember rightly, he has been obliged to go abroad at rather critical moments in our national affairs. He is over 70 and not a specially strong man. If the Queen desires (as I am sure she does) to keep him as P.M., I feel sure she would be well advised not to insist on his being also Foreign Minister.

'Lord James may be right in thinking that public opinion on the Continent would view with dismay Lord Salisbury's retirement from office: but this is only because they fear that the control of our foreign policy would thereby fall into the hands of Chamberlain, whom, for some reason or another, they have chosen to erect into a political bogey. I do not believe they would be the least alarmed at an arrangement which left Lord Salisbury P.M. and put the conduct of F.O. details into the hands of Lord Lansdowne.'

So it was arranged. Chamberlain by his own choice remained Colonial Secretary, apparently acquiescing in Lansdowne's preferment. Thus, the situation at the top remained unchanged with Balfour still being next in succession. Balfour was grateful, though he did not say so in so many words. After all Chamberlain had long been the outstanding, or perhaps 'notorious' would be the better word, member of the Government. The gratefulness was expressed in another way. When the new Parliament met, Chamberlain was savagely attacked and accused of profiting, via Birmingham companies, in the war. He could and did well defend himself; but it was Balfour with his most scathing banter who put his accusers to flight: 'Wanted', he said, 'a man to serve Her Majesty, with no money, no relations.' Again some 18 months later, when the City of London presented Chamberlain with an address in recognition of 'his patriotic statesmanship and his work in consolidating the Empire', it was Balfour who spoke with unexpected warmth of Chamberlain. Julian Amery, biographer of this part of Chamberlain's career, notes that 'We must mark these words in view of what the relative positions of Balfour and Chamberlain were then and were afterwards to become.' Chamberlain and his family long remembered Balfour's words: they 'would count in times of strain not yet foreseen'.

Other changes were small. Lansdowne was succeeded at the War Office by St. John Brodrick. Somewhat sarcastically, Balfour reported to his uncle on October 23, 1900, that C. T. Ritchie, the President of the Board of Trade, 'is the only member of the Cabinet so far who has put forward a personal claim! I agree that he must have the Home Office.' Ritchie's place was filled at the Board of Trade by Balfour's brother, Gerald, who had been since 1895 Chief Secretary for Ireland. The new Chief Secretary was George Wyndham, not in the Cabinet since the Irish Viceroy, Lord Cadogan, retained his seat. Earlier in 1900, in a letter to Wyndham's sister, Lady Elcho, Balfour had made a most unprescient remark, saying that George's 'Parliamentary position is now assured and as far as I can see beyond the reach of fate' (March 16, 1900). Four years later Wyndham was out of politics for good—not without damage to Balfour and his Government.

During the Cabinet-making Balfour pointed out to his uncle—as it was later pointed out by the Opposition—that in the new Cabinet there were no less than four Cecil relations: Salisbury himself, the two Balfours and Salisbury's son-in-law the Earl of Selborne (who had become First Lord of the Admiralty). Salisbury replied that there had been exactly the same number of relations in the Government in July, 1895, minus Salisbury's eldest son, Lord Cranborne, now Under-Secretary for Foreign Affairs. The arrangement had been before the country during two General Elections, and had not provoked any adverse comment. Relations, he said, 'cannot be treated as a class apart who can be employed but not promoted'. Nevertheless the 'Hôtel Cecil', as the Liberals called it, remained a small but useful stick with which to beat the Government.

Scarcely had the new Cabinet settled in than the Queen, who had reigned longer almost than the longest memory, died. An old age was out; time to begin a new. Yet many looked back knowing that they had seen the last of an epoch when Britain reigned unchallenged, that things would never be quite the same again. History seldom rounds off a century with the death of a sovereign; more seldom still do the two coincide in rounding off what even the most precise historian could not but regard as the end of an era. In his memorial speech in the House, Balfour, however, looked forward and saw the importance of the

Crown as bound to increase 'with the development of those free, self-governing communities, those new commonwealths beyond the sea, who are constitutionally linked to us through the person of the Sovereign, the living symbol of Imperial unity'.

There was more in this than mere rhetoric. He added in a letter to Lady Elcho on February 10, 1901: 'The King will take up a good deal more of his ministers' time than did the Queen:—I think he is in the right.' This, in itself, was ironical presage of his own not always easy relationship with the new sovereign. But his belief that the sovereign must become 'the living symbol of Imperial Unity' was far wider in significance. Chamberlain, at the Imperial conference of 1897 and again in 1902, tried to make the Empire cohere by putting it into a sort of Prussian strait-jacket. The Empire refused; it refused his Council of Empire, his appeals for contributions to defence, his trade negotiations. Only on reciprocal preference did the Empire leaders show any eagerness; and it was for this that Chamberlain now began to battle, knowing, however, that it could not come without a fiscal revolution at home. This battle brought division and strife in the Conservative party for many years, and victory did not come for 30 years. In the meantime, the Empire might well have splintered and vanished, if indeed reciprocal preference was the be-all and end-all that Chamberlain believed.

Balfour was no less convinced of the importance of Empire; but he put his trust rather in the silken bonds of sentiment—vague and idealistic as they might seem—than in the strait-jacket, in a fluidity of connection rather than in a rigorous constitution. Salisbury phrased the difference beautifully—and with it the true milk of conservatism—in one of his speeches on May 7, 1902:

'There are very important men, men of great interest and authority, who think that the moment has come for some legislative action on our part which should federate the Colonies. I exhort them before they do so, carefully to consider what steps they are going to take and what results they may expect from them. We have no power by legislation to affect the flow of opinion and of affection which has so largely risen between the mother country and her daughter states. . . . The tendency of human beings, and of statesman—who are human beings—is to anticipate all such matters, and to think that because their own wretched lives are confined to some sixty or seventy years, therefore it is open to them to force an anticipation of the results which the national play of forces and of affections and the alteration of the judgments and the mutual feelings of various peoples in the world will bring before us.'

Balfour sought to get the Empire to think of itself as one great family —a sentimental conception which, however, remains even today the only cohesive element, and which Balfour was to put into words, even into a sort of formula, at the Commonwealth discussions in 1926. His conception was already clear when on February 6, 1901, he wrote to

King Edward VII urging him to allow the Duke and Duchess of Cornwall—later King George V and Queen Mary—to go out to Australia for the opening of Australia's Commonwealth Parliament. ('Commonwealth' here used, of course, in the narrower sense of the Federated Australian State Parliament.) The King had been against the Duke and Duchess going. Balfour wrote:

'Mr. Balfour cannot help feeling that there are on the other side reasons to be urged which touch the deepest interests of the Monarchy. The King is no longer merely the King of Great Britain and Ireland and of a few Dependencies whose sole value consisted in ministering to the wealth and security of Great Britain and Ireland. He is now the greatest constitutional bond uniting together in a single Empire communities of free men separated by half the circumference of the globe. All the patriotic sentiment which makes such an Empire possible centres in him or centres chiefly in him; and everything which emphasizes his personality to our kinsmen across the sea must be a gain to the Monarchy and the Empire.

'Now the present opportunity of furthering the policy thus suggested is unique. It can in the nature of things never be repeated. A great Commonwealth is to be brought into existence after infinite trouble and with the greatest prospect of success. Its citizens know little and care little for British Ministries and British Party politics. But they know and care for, the Empire of which they are members and for the Sovereign who rules it. Surely it is in the highest interests of the State that he should visually, and so to speak corporally associate his family with the final act which brings a new community into being; so that in the eyes of all who see it the Chief actor in the ceremony, its central figure, should be the King's Heir, and that in the history of this great event the Monarchy of Britain and the Commonwealth of Australia should be inseparably united.'

The Duke and Duchess of Cornwall left for their tour in the Spring of 1901, vising Australia, New Zealand, South Africa and Canada.

VIII

At the turn of the century Balfour was 53. He had made new friends, or at any rate acquaintances (for his friendships were few and old), and he had met future adversaries such as Lloyd George, the fiery Radical with whom he had crossed swords as early as 1894—and who in the end was to become the closest of colleagues. He had come across Winston Churchill, remarkable son of a remarkable father, who already in 1899 (July 11) was writing Balfour to thank him for his words 'in so encouraging a tone after I have lost the Government a couple of seats'. There was Carson, his protégé of Irish days. Carson had crossed swords with his former chief over the question of a Roman Catholic university for Ireland. This did not prevent Balfour offering him the post of Solicitor-General in 1900. But as Balfour explained in a letter to his sister-in-law, Betty, on April 27, 1900: 'Unfortunately Carson has behaved badly both to Gerald and myself:—to myself chiefly on account of a bad liver and irritable nerves: to Gerald largely through a misconception that ought never to have been entertained.'

There were, too, the inevitable partings of life. He was deeply saddened by the death in August, 1900, of Henry Sidgwick, the philosopher and his brother-in-law, to whom intellectually he owed a great deal and of whom he wrote to Lady Elcho: 'Though I never was a disciple of his, I do believe that he had something valuable to say which he has left unsaid.' So to a greater parting still, the death of Lord Salisbury on August 22, 1903. 'He had ever treated me as one of his own children,' Balfour told Lady Elcho; and to the King he wrote:

'Mr. Balfour never had any secrets from him; his kindness and affection were unchanging and unchangeable and though it would be too much perhaps to say that through an official connection which lasted from 1876 to 1902 there never was any difference of opinion between them on public affairs, it is assuredly true that such rare and occasional differences as may have occurred did not for an instant disturb, or tend to disturb, the love and confidence which existed between them. That this was so is Mr. Balfour's greatest consolation at the present moment.'

If Salisbury's influence on his age was imponderable—so that on his death men referred to 'the Nestor of his generation'—his influence upon his nephew and successor was profound. They were in many ways alike. Both had been 'delicate' as boys; both had been interested in science and both, though they read 'Strauss and Renan, Comte and Thomas Huxley, continued to worship Christ'. Neither cared for the hunting and shooting of their class; both were Tory by birth and conviction, though no more to be associated with the 'backwoodsmen' of the party than with the business men who were soon to control it. Brodrick, serving in successive Governments under Salisbury and Balfour, noted the 'remarkable' alikeness in outlook: 'Passion and prejudice had no effect on either. Both, if strongly moved, took refuge in gibes.' They were in maturity brilliant in debate and repartee but, said Brodrick: 'I doubt if anyone could remember a set speech delivered by either of them which showed their full powers.'

In one respect they differed vastly: Salisbury had a facile pen while Balfour composed with much difficulty and with many erasures. Yet both preferred an *ad hoc*, almost unprepared, speech to one carefully composed beforehand. Both had a curious failing. In Balfour's case it was a total amnesia for facts and figures—'he would substitute counties for provinces, squadrons for regiments, and the like', says Brodrick—while Salisbury had a similar blind spot for faces.

As the years went on the similarities grew—naturally, since Balfour studied his uncle's political methods and adopted as many of them as changing circumstances would allow.   The result was an achieved unity of outlook and action that, since one was Leader in the Commons, and the other Premier from the Lords, had a unique influence on the destinies of Britain for more than a quarter of a century.   Just how close their minds came we may judge from a comparison between an election speech by Salisbury in 1885, and a speech by Balfour made nearly 40 years later at Peebles.   Salisbury said: 'The Conservative points the working man forward to obtain wealth which is as yet uncreated: the Radical, on the contrary, does not tell him to create new sources of wealth, but says that the wealth that has already been obtained is badly divided . . . and that the real remedy is to look back and fight among yourselves for the wealth that has already been obtained.' Forty years later Balfour said that no greater mistake could be made than in thinking that by confiscating capital and appropriating wealth for the State the number of poor men would be diminished: 'It is perfectly easy to equalise down; the problem of the statesman is to do what he can to equalise up. . . .   Output and production of wealth is that on which we live, quite irrespective of how it is distributed.'

Neither was a Tory absolutist, nor, on the other hand, a Tory 'democrat' in Churchill's rather vague sense.   Balfour would certainly have subscribed to his uncle's remark in the *Quarterly* in 1883 that 'The object of our party is not, and ought not to be, simply to keep things as they are.   In the first place, the enterprise is impossible.   In the next place, there is much in our present mode of thought and action which it is highly undesirable to conserve.'   To both, politics was the art of the possible.   Being the art of the possible, Balfour—though deploring with Salisbury the 'placing of a great empire under the absolute control of the poorest classes'—would be more inclined to acquiesce in doing so, inevitably since he was compelled, as Lord Birkenhead wrote, to be more susceptible to 'the democratic conditions which the age imposed'.

Perhaps this was what Balfour meant by his reply to a question the pertinacious Margot Asquith (Tennant) put to him one day.   She tells in her autobiography how sometime near the end of the century she said to Balfour that Lord Salisbury 'does not care fanatically about literature or culture; he is not a scholar; he does not care for Plato, Virgil, Homer or any of the great classics.   He has a wonderful sense of humour and is a beautiful writer of a fine style, but he is' (she thought) 'above all a man of science and a Churchman.'   All this, she added, could equally well be said of Balfour.   To which Balfour replied: 'There is a difference.   My uncle is a Tory . . . and I am a Liberal.'

Thinking as one on the future of Empire and on Pan-Anglo-Saxonism—though not on defence—it was left to Balfour to carry forward the

precepts of Salisbury and ancient Conservatism into a new age that
would have appalled Salisbury, and in which, as Russell Kirk has said,
'The taste for organic change had become itself almost institutional.'
How would he fare?   What would he save from the wreckage?   What
would be his final place in history?   The first decade of the new century
would supply the answers.   Earlier in this chapter ¡we saw Balfour
'limp and angular', feet up, yawning in the Commons.   Now, as he is
about to enter into the greatest office Britain has to offer, it may be well
to remind oneself of that other Balfour—a little older, a little more fine-
drawn, yet in essence unchanged—who still seemed unique to his
friends and acquaintance in Society.   'He became', wrote Consuelo
Vanderbilt, Duchess of Marlborough, 'one of my truest friends, a
friendship I remember, with humility and gratitude for there has, I
believe, never been anyone quite like him.   He resembled some fine
and disembodied spirit.   The opinions he expressed and the doctrines
he held seemed to me the products of pure logic.   Invariably he sensed
the heart of the matter and freed it of sordid encumbrance, and when
he spoke in philosophic vein it was like listening to Bach.   His way of
holding his head gave him the appearance of searching the heavens
and his blue eyes were absent, and yet intent, as if busy in some abstract
world.   Both mentally and physically he gave the impression of
immense distinction and of a transcendent spirituality.'

10

PRIME MINISTER

The Uneasy Chair, 1902–1905

Just 13 months before he died, Salisbury retired from the Premiership and Balfour slid into the vacant chair with the maximum of grace and the minimum of fuss. The King's action in calling Balfour on July 12, 1902, two days after Salisbury's resignation, was accepted 'not only with unanimity but as a matter of course'; and at a joint party meeting on July 14, Conservative Members of both Houses unanimously elected him Leader of the Party. Liberal Unionist support was pledged by the Duke of Devonshire, and Austen Chamberlain offered a message of loyalty from his father, then recovering from a serious cab accident.

'It has all happened', Esher wrote, 'as we thought. He (Balfour) has taken the lead without question from anybody. Although a great influence is withdrawn by the retirement of Lord Salisbury, still in great measure this is mitigated by the supreme energy of Arthur.' Chamberlain, adds Esher, had been touched by Balfour's loyalty to him during the difficult times of the South African War and determined that he should succeed Salisbury and that he would serve under him. Indeed, earlier in the same year, in February, he had let it be known, via Balfour's private secretary, J. S. Sandars, that he was not a candidate for the Premiership and that he would be willing to serve under Balfour, 'but mark,' he added, 'I would not serve under anyone'. Nevertheless, Balfour did not accept the King's commission without first visiting Chamberlain on his sick-bed.

The next step was Cabinet-making, and here Balfour made his first mistake. Hicks-Beach, the Terror in the Treasury, was determined to leave office; Balfour, although in imperfect sympathy with him, was loth to let him go since, as he said, Hicks-Beach 'had justly earned a greater financial reputation than any Chancellor since Mr. Gladstone'. But Hicks-Beach insisted; and Balfour in his turn ought to have insisted also—that Chamberlain should become Chancellor of the Exchequer. The post was, indeed, urged on Chamberlain by various friends; but he wished to remain Colonial Secretary. If he had gone to the Exchequer, it is possible that Balfour would have been not only a successful states-man but a successful politician too, for, had Chamberlain's fiscal ideas been promulgated from within the Cabinet rather than from without, they might have been so tempered that the imbroglio of the next year would have been avoided.

Balfour had to look elsewhere for his Chancellor; and good men, as he told Chamberlain in a letter of July 25, 1902, were hard to find. He was no less convinced than was Chamberlain that the Cabinet ought to be given a fresh look, not least to revive interest in a régime already eight and (with the two-year Rosebery break) almost 15 years old. But 'What men are there,' he asked Chamberlain, 'who, if introduced into the Cabinet, would add to its distinction and efficiency?' Two only he could see—Austen Chamberlain and George Wyndham, and they now entered the Cabinet as Postmaster-General and as Irish Secretary, a post which Wyndham had previously but without a seat in the Cabinet.

No new names, however, occurred to Chamberlain either; and in due course C. T. Ritchie, Home Secretary in the previous administration, was chosen as Chancellor of the Exchequer. He had not lost his habit of pressing claims to his preferment; he was also, Sandars recorded, given to 'heavy and affected pleasantry. . . . His abilities were of the second class, but he was a hard-working minister of pedestrian methods.' He was certainly not the man to seize the public imagination, and he did not prove to be exactly the man Balfour needed for the key position of Chancellor. His place at the Home Office was taken by Akers-Douglas, previously at the Office of Works. Devonshire remained Lord President, the Marquess of Londonderry took over the presidency of the Board of Education, with the Warden of All Souls, Sir William Anson, as his Parliamentary Secretary. Lansdowne and Brodrick retained their offices, with Selborne succeeding Goschen at the Admir-alty. Walter Long retained minor office; Andrew Bonar Law, a Glasgow ironmaster, became Parliamentary Under-Secretary to the Board of Trade. Sir Alexander Acland-Hood followed Sir William Waldron as Chief Whip.

It was not an inspiring team; nor, we can see now with the advantage of hindsight, was it one likely to hold together for any length of time in the new conditions of the new century. But it would serve, Balfour thought, as a viable Government in the background while he pushed through the really important things in the field of education, defence, a reorientated foreign policy. As for the future, Balfour was realistic enough to admit to himself that, untoward incident apart, the Government he headed was unlikely to have a long life: the pendulum had had a good rest on the Right, it was bound to swing before long; politically speaking, his policy must be *carpere diem*.

Two other significant personalities come into the *mise en scène* of Balfour as Prime Minister: one was a secretary, the other the King. It is not usual for a private secretary to be considered in the same context as a Prime Minister's colleagues in the Cabinet; yet sometimes, though not always, he may be of nearly equal importance, a man without power but with immense influence. Such was John Satterfield Sandars, a man five years younger than his master, formerly a barrister, and later private secretary to Sir Henry Matthews, Home Secretary in the 1886 Government. Sandars was the Home Office's liaison with the Irish Office and thus came in touch with Balfour.

It was this man—volatile, energetic, an easy conversationalist—who became Balfour's eyes and ears in political circles, somewhat in the same fashion as Balfour himself had been for Salisbury in the early 1880s. We find Sandars, in letter after letter, summarising situations and relaying gossip, and even suggesting courses of action. During Balfour's absences from London, he sometimes even took a great deal upon himself in matters affecting Ministers and the Cabinet. But his actual power should not be exaggerated. He did not, as Petrie has suggested, make up Balfour's mind for him; to believe so is totally to misunderstand the power and penetration of that remarkable mind. Sandars certainly smoothed the path for his master the better to allow Balfour to concentrate on what he considered, and with justice, to be fundamentals. To imagine that Sandars did work that Balfour was too lazy to do is to be mistaken.

Balfour's ease of manner was deceptive. Certainly he was intelligent enough to conserve his energy by transacting much of his business in bed whence he rarely rose before lunch. But, as Sir Winston Churchill tells us: 'No Minister in charge of a Bill ever worked harder, or was more thoroughly conversant with all the essentials of the legislation he was proposing. He minutely and patiently studied every aspect and possible pitfall of any measure for the conduct of which he was responsible.' And Sir Winston underlines part of what Sandars did for Balfour when he writes that Balfour 'was more effective upon large general issues, than upon the definite administrative decisions required from high executive officers in a continuous stream during periods of disturbance'.

If a Prime Minister's private secretary is important, no less so are his relations with his Sovereign who, however shorn today of real power,

may yet be a potent influence.   With Queen Victoria, Balfour, as we
have seen, got on well, partly perhaps because, as Dilke observed,
Queen Victoria had 'real brainpower', and Balfour appreciated intellect.   Moreover, the Queen was incredibly well informed.   She spent
her days in tireless application to official papers.   Balfour, called to the
Isle of Wight when she died, observed with some astonishment the large
number of boxes of State papers in her room.   Her son, Edward, on
the other hand, did not care for reading of any sort, except possibly
French novels, and his occasional indiscretions had made his mother
reluctant to allow him access to confidential papers.   Socially, he
mixed in circles whose horsey, raffish pursuits bored Balfour to extinction, although inevitably they met and from time to time, dined together
at the same houses and even, it is recorded, played cards together.
Although Balfour's manners, even with those who bored him, were
always perfect, the King must have perceived something of his real
feelings, for he remarked on one occasion to Ponsonby that he often
got the impression that Balfour was condescending towards him.

Balfour had crossed swords with him as early as 1899 when he
objected to his proposed contribution to a newspaper.   As he pointed
out, 'The world of letters is a democracy and rather a rough democracy.
A person in the Prince's position, however otherwise competent, enters
such a world at a disadvantage. His slightest utterance will be critically
and perhaps indignantly scrutinised.   He may be attacked unfairly;
yet he can hardly defend himself for if he did every scribbler would at
once endeavour to provoke him into further controversy for the glory
(and profit) of breaking a literary lance with his future Sovereign.'
Balfour's warning was, no doubt, given also with politics in mind; the
Prince of Wales was known to be an intimate of such Liberals as
Campbell-Bannerman.

In 1902, there was a further tiff.   Lord Lansdowne had promised
that the Shah of Persia should receive the Garter after certain matters,
involving Christians and non-Christians in Persia, were cleared up.
The King did not like the Shah and refused to give him the Garter.
A letter was sent by his direction to Balfour containing such criticisms
that, as Lord Newton says in his Life of Lord Lansdowne, it was clear
that if Lord Lansdowne ever saw it he would be compelled to resign.
Thereupon Balfour consulted the Duke of Devonshire, the Lord
President, who agreed that Lansdowne must not leave the Cabinet.
Without further discussion Balfour wrote strongly to the King, who
grudgingly yielded.   The Shah got his Garter.

There were also differences of opinion on the grant of peerages; there
was trouble over the Anglo-French entente; there was the King's wish to
visit the Pope to which Balfour strongly objected, although eventually
giving way; and, more important, there was Balfour's determination

that the King was not to see confidential Cabinet papers, '*as of right*'. He had, he believed, a perfect right to see Cabinet decisions and the reasons for them, but the policies being matured in Cabinet were none of his business. 'It is impossible for us to yield in a matter of this kind,' Balfour adds. The King was much dissatisfied by this ruling, particularly as it affected the deliberations of the Committee of Imperial Defence. Indeed, under Balfour, the Crown's direct influence on policy continued to diminish, a somewhat ironical corollary to Balfour's memorial speech in the Commons on the death of the Queen when he said: 'In my judgement the importance of the Crown in our Constitution is not a diminishing, but an increasing factor.'

Antipathetic is too strong an adjective to describe the relations between the King and his Prime Minister. Compliments sometimes passed, and Balfour often guarded the Crown from criticism. The King, as he wrote to Balfour on December 5, 1902, 'much admired the skill, temper and patience which, if he may be allowed to say so, you have shown in steering such a difficult and very controversial Bill [Education] through the House.' Balfour, on his side, strove, as he told the King, on February 3, 1905, to avoid debates on the Civil List expenditure (the King had proposed repairs at Windsor and Buckingham Palace) because they are 'disagreeable and injurious to the highest interests of the monarchy'.

Nevertheless, it can be said that a certain lack of mutual understanding did exist. As we shall see, the King's part in such affairs as that of Curzon and Kitchener was not wholly happy. Later on, Balfour resented the glib talk which ascribed to the King most of the kudos resulting from the Anglo-French *entente*. He afterwards wrote to Lord Lansdowne: 'So far as I can remember, during the years which you and I were his Ministers, he never made an important suggestion of any sort on large questions of policy.'

On the giving of peerages and honours, a chore that always irritated Balfour greatly, two letters of his to the King are of interest. One letter, in which he tells the King that he does not believe in peerages for Civil Servants, also throws out the idea that to get over the difficulty of giving hereditary peerages to those persons 'who neither by social standing, or wealth, or birth, would seem specially fitted recipients of such distinction', we 'ought to have a system of life peerages, instituted with proper limitations'. Balfour returned to this idea during the constitutional crisis later in the decade.

The other letter (of June 5, 1905, actually addressed to Knollys, the King's Secretary) shows Balfour at his most scathing. The King wanted to give the O.M. instituted in 1902, to Sir George White, who acquitted himself less than gloriously in the Boer War. Balfour comments:

'I have little to say about this most excellent officer, except that nobody has ever supposed that he is a man of great abilities, military or otherwise. So far as courage and character are concerned he has, and can have, no superior; but though the O.M. would add to his reputation, I do not think he would add to the reputation of the O.M.' (Sir George got it, all the same.)

Balfour's refusal to enlarge the King's authority in matters political has been called 'Whiggish'. The expression is meaningless; the decline in the monarch's political powers had begun during the reign of Victoria, and Balfour saw no reason to try to halt the inevitable. Balfour had a far wider conception of kingship, as we saw. This was symbolically recognised by the addition to the King's title 'of United Kingdom of Great Britain and Ireland' of the words 'and of the British Dominions beyond the Seas'. (By 'Dominions' was then meant everything beneath the British flag, not merely Dominion status.)

II

Although Balfour agreed with Salisbury's dictum that politics is the art of the possible, he knew that any self-respecting politician sometimes has to attempt the impossible. We saw earlier that the reform of the educational system was, to his mind, imperative if Britain was to continue to be a first-class power. Defeated in the 'nineties, he became determined after the turn of the century to try again; and the Education Act for which he was personally responsible, began its progress through a stormy House before he succeeded his uncle; by the time it finally passed into law he had become Prime Minister.

Nothing demonstrates better Balfour's tenacity nor his willingness to risk all than his Education Bill. Salisbury had been against it; so was Chamberlain who again and again warned him that the Government would be brought down if he persisted. But persist he did against every sort of odds; rightly, for upon the 1902 Act all subsequent development in Britain's educational system is based. The aim of the Bill was little different from the failed Bill of 1896; the opposition to it came from the same quarters as before. But, from the intellectual side, more support had come, notably from Sidney Webb, the Fabian chairman of the London County Council, and from Robert Morant, one of the most remarkable Civil Servants of the time.

The general drift of the Bill was to bring education in England up to the standard long since achieved in most German states, where already by 1885 there were two and a half times more students, proportionate to the population, than there were in England. Balfour's chief objectives were to unify and improve secondary and elementary education, to level up the schools which lagged behind, and to do so by providing more money from the rates (though there were early suggestions that the money should come from the State or that there should be 'local option'.) Until this time secondary education was controlled partly by County Councils and County Borough Councils, and partly by the School Boards whose main concern was, however, elementary education. The Bill sought to abolish these Boards throughout the country and to put both secondary and elementary education under the Councils. Voluntary Schools were also to be brought under these new authorities, though the managers of the Voluntary Schools, in return for providing the buildings, were to retain the right to appoint teachers; the current expenses of their schools were to be defrayed, like those of the non-voluntary schools, out of the local rates. Thus, public money was to be made available for the first time to ensure properly paid teachers and a standardised level of efficiency for all children alike.

To advance the story somewhat, it is now generally agreed that the Act resulted in a boom in education, in increased numbers at grant-aided secondary schools, and the growth of new universities—Manchester, Liverpool and Leeds received their Charters in 1903 and 1904, followed by Sheffield in 1905. The Act, in fact, was the first essential move towards remedying the dearth of higher-educated personnel, not least in science and technology.

For all its obvious usefulness, however, it almost brought Balfour's Government down, and it was certainly one of the factors contributing to the electoral disaster of 1906. This is one of those ironies that are poor advertisement for the British system of government. The main trouble, as in the 'nineties, came from the Nonconformists, who generally supported the Liberal Party. They claimed that the result of the Bill would be to subsidise Church of England schools out of the rates; their slogan, 'The Church on the rates', swept through the country, was bandied on platforms, and flourished in newspapers. An amendment to the Bill, placing religious instruction under the authority of the whole body of the managers of a school, did not appease them. It put an end to what had often been the dominance in these matters of the parson: but this, in turn, caused a storm among the Church Party, until then strong supporters of the Bill.

Balfour, who hated religious controversy, once again found himself in the House, and on platforms outside the House, immersed in religious controversy of a particularly arid and, to the intellectual mind, of a singularly unimportant kind. H. G. Wells had still at this time a great, though slightly waning, admiration for Balfour, and in his novel *The New Machiavelli* attempted what he called a 'sort of caricature-portrait of him' under the name of 'Evesham'. He describes Evesham-Balfour during the wearisome period of steering the Education Bill through the sectarian rapids:

'Have I not seen him in the House, persistent, persuasive, indefatigable, and by all my standards wickedly perverse, leaning over the table with those insistent movements of his hand upon it, or swaying forward with a grip upon his coat lapels, fighting with a diabolical skill to preserve what are in effect religious tests, tests he must have known would outrage and humiliate and injure the consciences of a quarter—and that perhaps the best quarter—of the young teachers who come to the work of elementary education?

'In playing for points in the game of Party advantage, Evesham displayed at times a quite wicked unscrupulousness in the use of his subtle mind. I would sit on the Liberal Bench and watch him, and listen to his urbane voice, fascinated by him. Did he really care? Did anything matter to him? And if it really mattered nothing, why did he trouble to serve the narrowness and passion of his side? Or did he see far beyond my scope, so that this petty inequity was justified by greater, remoter ends of which I had no intimation?'

Certainly there were 'greater ends' beyond politics. For Chamberlain, who, as his biographer admits, 'cared nothing for the issues at stake', politics alone counted. On August 4, 1902, he wrote to Balfour:

'The Education Bill has brought all the fighting Nonconformists into the field and made of them active not passive opponents. Their representations and appeals to old war cries have impressed large numbers of the lower, middle and upper working classes who have hitherto supported the Unionist Party without joining the Conservative organisation. The transfer of their votes will undoubtedly have immense importance at a general election and I do not think that any seat where there is a strong Nonconformist electorate can be considered absolutely safe.

'I hear that Middleton considers that the Corn Tax was an important factor at Leeds.' (A by-election had gone against Conservatives.) 'In my opinion it was only a convenient instrument used by the Nonconformist Party to support their own grievance.'

Balfour refused to panic; he would not relent. On September 3, 1902, he told Chamberlain:

'I am further provoked by the extraordinary campaign of lies which has been set on foot against it (the Education Bill), and by the total indifference to the interests of education which seems to be shown by the contending parties. But I have to admit that these considerations are relevant, if it be true that we cannot pass the Bill in its present shape, or if it be true that, when passed, it would be made to work with such an amount of local friction as to render it a curse instead of a blessing. On the other hand, unfortunate as a defeat on it would be, and reluctant as I am that the Government should go out before you have been able to settle South Africa, and before we have done one or two other legislative matters which require to be dealt with, anything

would be better than the kind of concession which permanently con-
ciliates no opponent but does permanently endanger all confidence
among friends.'

Strong words indeed!   But when Balfour was determined, it was impossible to deflect him; and he only became determined when he had
come to a conclusion by means of the subtle dialectic of which he was
master, and which subjected every proposal to as close and deep a
scrutiny as he gave to the philosophy of Mill or Spencer.   He never
lacked support in the Cabinet, not least from the old ex-Liberal Duke
of Devonshire (much to the ex-Liberal Chamberlain's disgust); but the
real intellectual support came from another quarter, from that Robert
Morant mentioned above.

Morant, then an official in the Education Office, was introduced to
Balfour by Bishop Talbot and was thus enabled to put his views
privately, not through any intermediary.   Balfour at once conceived
a liking for the tall, gaunt man who had spent much time in Spain
before entering the Civil Service.   Their minds were attuned.   Both
approached any problem with the same intellectual attitude.   In
these years Morant and Balfour were frequently together, both in
London and at Whittingehame, and their collaboration not merely
produced a unique Education Bill but also forced it through the House
and the country against the most fearful odds.   Morant had both
vision and the ability to work hard; the latter he also demanded of his
subordinates, and this earned the enmity of those who regarded the
Civil Service as a comfortable cushion against the hard world outside.
No doubt he was ruthless, and he could be brusque; but British education owes as much to him as it does to Balfour.   In due course, he
became Permanent Secretary of the Board of Education; his subsequent
career was chequered.   But for Balfour, as for none other, he had
unbounded admiration and respect, both of which Balfour reciprocated.
'Balfour', wrote his niece and biographer, 'never inspired a deeper
devotion in a subordinate and the zeal of another never had more
influence on himself.'

It was partly Morant's arguments that finally brought Chamberlain
to see that the Education Bill was one of the most important pieces of
legislation ever proposed, and in due time he joined Balfour in fighting
the opposition.   Apart from the political forum, Balfour also wrote a
pamphlet, 'Letter on the Criticisms of an Opponent', a scathing attack
on Dr. John Clifford, the militant minister of a London Baptist Chapel,
who led 'passive resistance' to the Education Bill.   Eventually, moderate opinion on both sides moved steadily in the Bill's favour, and it
became law in December, 1902.

The aftermath of the Bill's becoming law was, however, protracted
and unhappy.   Balfour could plead (as he did for instance in a speech

in Manchester) that 'I tell you that there are at stake issues greater than the fortunes of any political party; there is at stake the education of your children for a generation'. But no less than 7,000 summonses had to be issued against persons who 'passively' resisted payment of the education rate in England, and distraint sales of their goods took place in over 300 cases: to such rank stupidity had they been brought by sectarian passion. In Nonconformist Wales, the County Councils themselves were the passive resisters. Lloyd George set out to wreck the working of the Act which protected the Church schools, no doubt partly with the disestablishment of the Welsh Church in view, certainly not to the benefit of those working-class voters he was supposed to represent.

Yet, even at this time, Balfour was curiously attracted by the little Welshman. In the final debate on the Bill in December, 1902, Balfour said: 'There is the Hon. Member for Caernarvon boroughs' (i.e. Lloyd George) 'who, through these debates, has played in my judgement a most distinguished part, though, I confess, I wish he had left unsaid, even from his own point of view, a great many things which he sometimes said . . . the Hon. Gentleman has shown himself to be an eminent Parliamentarian.' Not long afterwards Lloyd George was writing to his brother, William: 'Balfour tried to smile pleasantly at me today. He doesn't want to quarrel with me. As one man on our side said, "you are so obviously one of his favourites—he was very upset by your speech yesterday, but still he didn't hit you hard".'

It is here perhaps worth mentioning that, while during the grand debate on the Education Bill Balfour's main critics were Radicals, Nonconformists and Liberals, subsequent criticism has come from Conservative quarters. The Act has been dubbed 'State socialism' (whatever that means), and a dereliction of basic Conservative principles of 'astute delay and amelioration'. The Act has been declared to be out of keeping with the rest of Balfour's political career; and he himself is supposed to have said later that 'I did not realise that this Act would have as its consequence more expense and more bureaucracy.' (The remark itself I have been unable to check either in Balfour's speeches, letters or authentically reported conversation. It is quoted in Amery's *Life of Chamberlain* and there used to beat Balfour for 'socialism'; the source is there given as Elie Halèvy, *A History of the English People*, but Halèvy himself, contrary to his custom, gives no source for it.)

Surely, however, Conservatives are not to be barred altogether from legislating on important matters; and the matter of education was of the greatest importance to the future of Britain. It is possible that education for a minority was not improved by the Act; but the whole point of it was to give education to greater numbers. Legislation cannot be forever delayed or left to the Opposition. In this Act, says Halèvy, 'triumphed the disinterested Machiavellianism which constituted the essence of Fabianism. . . .' (A reference to Sidney Webb's part in the educational agitation.) This is dogma run mad. The essence of Toryism, one might add, is anti-dogmatism. Balfour was the truer Tory for acting out of character. Why should the devil always have the best tunes? Why should Conservatives not carry through reforms that are evidently essential and, in this case of education, much too long delayed?

As a pendant to Balfour's emphasis on education, it is worthy of note that, throughout the years of his Premiership, however harassed he was, Balfour remained deeply interested in the newest developments in science. His interest was by no means dilettante. Science had fascinated him, as we have seen, from the beginning. Partly through his brother-in-law, Lord Rayleigh, the discoverer of the gas argon, he was in close touch throughout these years with leading scientific men, such as J. J. Thomson, Ernest Rutherford, John Larmor, and Oliver Lodge, whom he also knew socially. Balfour's correspondence in these years contains many letters on what would then have been considered as abstruse scientific subjects. Lodge replies to a letter from him on July 19, 1904: 'You have been probing into some of the deepest parts of present-day physics.' The subject was atomic radiation.

In 1904, Balfour gave the Presidential Address to the British Association for the Advancement of Science—as his uncle, Salisbury, had done before him—and Lodge vetted his manuscript, urging him not to 'strengthen the popular superstition which calls Darwin "the Newton of Biology". I urge that he was the Copernicus. . . . The Newtonian era in Biology, when it comes will give a theory of life and, incidentally of death.' After his address, Rutherford wrote to him praising its scope, and Balfour replied on September 13, 1904, expressing 'the very great pleasure with which I received your letter of September 1st. Your own name will for all time be associated with the growth in our conceptions of the physical universe, and it is with the utmost satisfaction that I learn of your approval of my attempt to deal from the outside with the problems to whose solution you have so greatly contributed.' Professor A. S. Eve, Rutherford's official biographer, adds that 'it is noteworthy that this philosopher quickly understood the importance of the work of the physicist'.

Balfour had Salisbury's gift for putting the concepts of science into concise, almost epigrammatic form. Salisbury, for instance, once described the ether to the British Association as being 'the nominative case of the verb to undulate'. Whether Balfour at this time grasped the destructive and military implications of Rutherford's work on nuclear physics it is not possible to say; but it is very possible that he had heard and pondered Rutherford's 'joke' to the effect that 'some fool in a laboratory might blow up the universe unawares'. This 'joke', it is surprising to recall, was first cracked in 1904.

III

For more than half his Premiership, Balfour lived on borrowed time. From the beginning of 1903 to his resignation at the end of 1905, there was scarcely a month when his Cabinet did not threaten to dissolve. Balfour was determined that should not happen until his main aims were accomplished; and he succeeded. Education had caused dissension in the Cabinet, but what caused it to split in 1903—as it caused a split in the country also—was a controversy over the merits of free trade and the merits of Protectionism. It was not a new controversy, but it had been in abeyance, for all practical purposes, for the previous 60 years. Its reappearance at this time was a result of those same factors which, as we have seen, were combining to change the economic status of Britain *vis-à-vis* foreign nations.

In essence, the situation was simple. When a nation is industrially and economically so far in advance of any rivals as Britain was in the middle of the nineteenth century, it has no need to try to control the import of its neighbours' produce and products by putting prohibitive taxes on them to prevent their entry or to price them out of the home market. When, on the other hand, their volume increases and their prices fall below those of home products—perhaps, because the working and social conditions of their producers allow the costs of production to be so much smaller—then there may well seem to be a case for imposing 'protectionist' taxes so that home-produced goods are not priced off the home market.

This had certainly begun to happen by the beginning of the twentieth century; but how far had it gone? At the turn of the century, as it happened, trade had for a time recovered, and British exports rose to £291 million. It dropped later; but all the same remained at a high level until 1905. The increase, however, was mainly due to one industry—coal; this was sufficient to mask stagnation in textiles and decline in iron and steel in which fields German and American industries were replacing imports from Britain. In agriculture, the crisis deepened with continually falling prices.

Some sections of British production would benefit from protection; others would not; but all would be affected by, for instance, a tax on imported wheat. It was the overall effect that had to be weighed; a decision was not lightly to be taken since the short-term effects of protection could easily mean starvation for the poorer classes. If, for example, a foreign country was flooding Britain with cheap corn, it was being bought because millions of people had need of bread at the cheapest possible price. If the price was increased by taxes, many of them would not be able to afford bread. There would, at the very least, be a time-lag before home produce would be as cheap as foreign; in any case, could home agriculture ever supply sufficient corn for the rapidly expanding population? Protection, on the whole, was likely to be more beneficial to the industrialists than to the public generally, at any rate, than to the lower-paid members of it. They might later expect to share in its beneficial effects, although probably not without a fight for their share; and the main spear-heads of the fight, the trade unions, were not then very effective.

It is not without significance that it was the former Birmingham industrial magnate, Joseph Chamberlain, who first raised the 'protectionist' banner, though his original aims were merely to unify the Commonwealth by allowing their goods into Britain while keeping out those of foreigners. This, as we have seen, was as far as the Dominions would move in meeting Chamberlain's plea for closer relations with the mother country. But as opposition developed, more sweeping demands were made.

Balfour's attitude to 'protection' was purely empirical, never doctrinaire. He was not yet certain that the economic situation was so grave as to warrant such a serious step with so many dangerous ramifications. Intellectually, he was as scornful of the extreme 'Cobdenite' doctrine of free trade as he was of the rabid Protectionism of the industrialists. Yet he was always willing to compromise, and to seek to judge each specific case on its own merits, not merely because this would help in his prime aim of keeping his Cabinet together, but also because this represented his true attitude to the matter. Let it, however, be said that Balfour disliked all matters of finance, not least in his own private affairs which is perhaps why, when he died, they were in a considerable tangle!

The controversy arose directly out of the Colonial conference of August, 1902, though it was then scarcely controversial at all. Many of the Colonial representatives had asked for preferential treatment for their imports to Britain, particularly imports of corn. Chamberlain, no less concerned for imperial unity than Balfour, though more rigid in his ideas of encompassing it, became immediately convinced that this was the key. As he was sailing shortly to South Africa, he asked for a Cabinet decision on the matter. A so-called 'registration' duty on corn—it was, in fact, a tax—had been imposed by Hicks-Beach in the last years of Salisbury's Government. The Balfour Cabinet now decided on November 19, 1902—some days before Chamberlain departed—that, in the words of Balfour's official letter to the King, 'as at present advised, they would maintain the corn-tax, but that a preferential remission of it should be made in favour of the British Empire'. This is as definite a decision as could well be, and it is, therefore, surprising that Ensor states that 'no decision was taken for the time being'. It is true that no official note of the decision was conveyed to the Canadians; it also appears that several members of the Cabinet were under the impression that the question was still open although there may have been a vote. But, as at this time no minutes of Cabinet meetings were made, the exact form the discussions took is not recorded.

Chamberlain, at any rate, was aware of the decision. This is why he was so astonished to find, when he returned to England in March, 1903, that Ritchie, Chancellor of the Exchequer, was proposing in his Budget not only to prevent the use of the corn-duty for preferential purposes but to repeal the duty itself. Balfour, according to Mrs. Dugdale, always maintained that Chamberlain had good grounds for complaint on this matter. In fact, Chamberlain had had some intimation of Ritchie's proposal while still on the high seas for, when Ritchie informed Balfour of his Budget scheme, Balfour asked Chamberlain's son, Austen, to inform his father immediately. To oppose Ritchie at this late stage before the Budget would have probably meant his resignation; and Balfour did not feel he could afford another change at the Exchequer so soon after the departure of Hicks-Beach.

These arguments must certainly have weighed with Chamberlain himself for ultimately he acquiesced in the necessity of submitting to Ritchie. But Chamberlain felt himself free to make his own position clear. He had, according to Amery, thought out the general principles in talk with Milner in South Africa, and he elaborated them in a speech at Birmingham in May, 1903, on his return. He further defined his views in the Commons later in the same month. What exactly were those views? Imperial preference was one thing, out-and-out protection was another. Now the hue-and cry began, and Balfour was besieged by clamour for a statement of the Government attitude. Winston Churchill, for example, was up in arms and wrote to Balfour on May 25, 1903:

'At Birmingham he [Chamberlain] advocated preferential tariffs with the Colonies; in his letter of Monday to Mr. Lovesay, he revealed plain protectionist intentions; and in the House on Friday last he showed himself prepared to use old-age pensions as a lever to attain these ends. Now I see it stated by Mr. Bonar Law that you are agreed with him in all this.

'I honestly hope that is not true, that you have not taken an inevitable decision. . . . I am utterly opposed to anything which will alter the free trade character of this country; and I consider such an issue superior in importance to any other now before us. Preferential tariffs, even in respect of articles which we are bound to tax for revenue purposes, are dangerous and objectionable.   But of course it is quite impossible to stop these, and I am persuaded, once this policy has begun, it must lead to the establishment of a complete protective system involving commercial disaster and the Americanisation of English politics. . . .   I submit these two points: 1. From a national point of view, there is no case for a fiscal revolution: not in the trade returns, nor income tax receipts, nor in a colonial demand, nor in a popular move-ment.   2. From a party point of view: the Government is probably less unpopular than any which has ruled eight years in England.   Their record—army and expenditure apart—will make a fine page in history. They have no reason to dread an appeal to the constituencies; and even if a general election should result in a transfer of power, the Conservative Party would be in a strong minority quite able to protect those causes and institutions which they cherish.'

Balfour's reply to Winston Churchill on May 26, 1903, suggests that, at this stage, he was not sure of the extent of Chamberlain's self-commitment to protectionist policies: 'I have never understood that Chamberlain advocated protection, though, no doubt, he is ready— and indeed anxious—for a duty on food stuffs, which may incidentally be protective in its character, but whose main object is to provide an instrument for fiscal union with the Colonies, a very different thing. These are evidently quite different things from protection both in theory and practice.   But undoubtedly the matter is one of extreme difficulty, and requires the most wary walking.'

Churchill's objections to protection were equally strongly held by some members of the Cabinet, including the Duke of Devonshire, Ritchie, Lord Balfour of Burleigh, Scottish Secretary, and Lord George Hamilton, Secretary of State for India.   A Cabinet crisis was clearly at hand; and the Budget debate on April 23, 1903, when Ritchie had proposed repealing the corn-tax and gone out of his way to show his free trade intransigence, made it inevitable.   Those Conservatives, who were already convinced protectionists, protested bitterly against Ritchie in the House of Commons.   To ease the situation, Balfour got the Cabinet to agree that he should tell a deputation of protection-ist Conservatives that there would be a possibility of reviving the tax, 'if it were associated with some great change in our fiscal system.   Such an announcement may cause some disquiet in certain circles: but in view of possible eventualities, such as the necessity of retaliating on foreign countries, or the expediency of a closer fiscal union with our Colonies, it seems desirable to make it.'   Balfour had already started on his course of trimming.

Cabinet discussions continued in June, 1903.   On the 9th of that month Balfour wrote to the King:

'The whole time of the Cabinet was occupied by a discussion of the present position created for the Government by Mr. Chamberlain's and

Mr. Balfour's recent utterances on the subject of retaliation on the Colonial preferences.' ('Retaliation', by which was meant the use of tariffs as a method of reprisal against those countries who applied them to Britain's exports, had been suggested by Salisbury as a means of getting other countries to reduce their tariffs with particular reference to the United States who had adopted the rigorous MacKinley system of protection in 1890.) 'On these subjects, as Your Majesty knows, the Cabinet is not agreed. And though they do not involve immediate action, in as much as no one suggests any variation from our traditional fiscal policy till the country has had an opportunity of expressing its opinion, still the fact of division is among us, greatly weakens our position and gives the Opposition a new and unexpected advantage in the Parliamentary game.

'Mr. Balfour has used and is using, every effort to avert any rupture among his colleagues; and he is very loyally supported by all the other Members of the Cabinet. He hopes that it may be found possible to avert, or if not to avert, at least to defer, any crisis which may threaten the existence of the Government.'

Chamberlain himself sought a *modus vivendi* with his Cabinet col-leagues—none of whom was an ardent supporter of his theories. Meanwhile, however, he had attracted supporters outside the Cabinet, who were more vocal and more pugnacious. The young L. S. Amery, for example, felt that Chamberlain's Birmingham speech 'was a challenge to free thought as direct and provocative as the theses which Luther nailed to the church door at Wittenberg'. He at once set about founding a Tariff Reform League. On the other side, Hicks-Beach from his retirement made a fighting speech which delighted the free-trade Unionists; he began to organise a 'Free Food League' in which he was joined by 54 Unionists, including Lord Hugh Cecil, and Churchill. The country as a whole began to take sides, not, it may be remarked, over a specific question of policy, but over an abstract, not to say highly technical, economic theory. Indeed no real principle was involved. Looking deeper, however, one may see in it a reflection of a real division in aim between the old Conservatives and the new. For many it was a means of letting off steam, of purging bad blood, of having a high old time, such as democracies seem to require when neither war nor disaster is imminent. It might well be compared with the eternal 'Irish question', at that time quiescent.

Balfour continued to keep on an even keel. In his Commons speech on the Finance Bill on June 10, 1903, he recognised that times had vastly changed since Peel made Britain a free-trade country. He was himself, he said, by no means committed for ever to a doctrine of 1845. But it would be folly to interfere with a 'great system' without the subject being thoroughly examined and all the aspects thoroughly understood—always assuming, too, that differences of opinion 'shall not go beyond the question on which we differ, shall not strike at the root of party unity or party loyalty'.   Already Balfour envisaged the very thing happening that had happened to Peel—a split party.   Balfour always thought of this as the ultimate catastrophe.

In the course of the same speech, he admitted—indeed defended as correct—that on the general subject of fiscal reform he had no 'settled conviction'.   Already the heat engendered was such that his honesty was regarded as mere shuffling.   Sir Wilfrid Lawson, a Liberal M.P., wrote and circulated the following doggerel about him:

> 'I'm not for Free Trade, and I'm not for Protection.
> I approve of them both, and to both have objection.
> In going through life I continually find
> It's a terrible business to make up one's mind.
> So in spite of all comments, reproach and predictions,
> I firmly adhere to Unsettled Convictions.'

Intellectually, 'unsettled convictions' are excellent; but they do not make—when openly admitted—for good government.   By August, 1903, matters had gone far beyond the point where reason could prevail—or where the King's suggestion that it might be possible 'to refer the whole matter to a Royal Commission' was even conceivable. During his golfing holiday at North Berwick, Balfour considered the possibility of a serious split in the Cabinet; he writes to Lady Elcho that he thinks he will lose Devonshire and 'with him, of course, all the waverers'.   In a letter to the King five days later, he does not entertain 'any confident hope that he will retain the co-operation of all his colleagues for the scheme which he himself favours'.

This scheme, incidentally, was embodied in a Cabinet memorandum he had circulated under the title of 'Notes on Insular Free Trade'. In this—as in the celebrated Sheffield speech in October—he pleaded for liberty in fiscal negotiations.   This meant that in dealing with foreign Governments, the Cabinet should be able to threaten, and if need be to employ, 'retaliation'.   As far as the Colonies were concerned, he felt that only preference could be offered since 'it is hard to see how any bargain could be contrived which the Colonies would accept, and which would not involve some taxation of food in this country'.   There were ways, he told the King, by which such taxation might be imposed which would in no degree add to the cost of living of the working classes.   (Esher had reported that the King had told Ritchie he would not consent to food taxes.)   But he did not believe that, in the present state of public feeling, any such plan would get a fair hearing, and if he made it part of the Government programme it would probably break up the party.

He had, therefore, decided to say that though Colonial preference was eminently desirable both to British commerce and Imperial unity,

15. A.J.B., when Prime Minister, aged 55
Radio Times Hulton Picture Library

16. Joseph Chamberlain (1836–1914) when Secretary of State for the Colonies

Elliott and Fry Ltd

17. George Nathaniel Curzon (1859–1925) when Viceroy of India

Radio Times Hulton Picture Library

18. Frederick Edwin Smith (1872–1930). First Earl of Birkenhead

Radio Times Hulton Picture Library

it had not yet come within the sphere of practical politics. He thought that most people in the Unionist Party would accept it, but there would in all probability be several resignations from the Cabinet 'because it goes too far, or because it does not go far enough'.

Whatever happened, however, he told the King, Mr. Balfour 'will do his best to steer between the opposite dangers of making proposals so far reaching in their character that the people in this country could not be expected to acquiesce in them—and, on the other hand, of ignoring in a spirit of blind optimism the danger signals which indicate approaching perils to our foreign and to our Colonial trade'.

So the month of September, 1903, opened ominously. It seems clear that Balfour had already decided that the extreme free-trade Ministers in his Cabinet—Ritchie, Hamilton and Balfour of Burleigh —would have to go. Balfour's decision that he would ask them, rather than Chamberlain, for their resignations was taken for several reasons: in the first place, he inclined himself towards a modified version of Chamberlain's views, and in the second place the 'Cobdenite' (i.e. free trade) Ministers had shown their antagonism openly, had stirred the Party against him, had even caballed for a new administration and a new Prime Minister.

On the other hand, Balfour was aware that he had gone by no means far enough to satisfy Chamberlain; he was prepared for a resignation there, too. Chamberlain, in fact, wrote asking to be allowed to resign on September 9. To this Balfour did not reply, knowing that he would see Chamberlain before the Cabinet meeting of the 14th. During those conversations, the resignation seems to have been left in the air, though it was clear that it might in the end have to be accepted.

The Duke of Devonshire, however, Balfour sought to retain; he was a trusted, solid figure such as all Prime Ministers like to have about them. His free-trade views were somewhat less rigid than those of his colleagues, but he had made it clear that he opposed any changes which, while they might improve the conditions of certain of the higher classes of labour, might also for millions 'reduce the margin between poverty and absolute want'. If the suggested closer ties with the Colonies were only to be purchased at the expense of privation and hardship on the part of our own people, then there was 'no policy more certain to hasten the dissolution of the Empire'. It was for just such humanitarian views, completely without self-interest, that he was so highly regarded among Unionists and the country at large. To him Balfour suggested that the dogmas of free trade had been useful but ought to be modified, and he added: 'Just as I am not a Socialist, so I am not a Protectionist.'

The plan was, therefore, to keep the Duke of Devonshire as a point of stability, but to lop off the extremes at each end of the Cabinet.

Q JB

The sequence of events now becomes of first importance since, as a result of a misreading of what followed, Balfour's honesty and straight-forwardness have been called in doubt. Here we have no Royal letters to help us—presumably Balfour reported events verbally to the King—and such accounts as those contained, for example, in Spender and Asquith's *Life of Oxford and Asquith* are misleading and ill-informed.

When the Cabinet met on September 14, 1903, Balfour knew that both the 'Cobdenite' Ministers and Chamberlain might resign. It has been suggested that he concealed the fact that Chamberlain *was* resigning from the Cabinet, and that if this had been known to them the 'Cobdenite' Ministers would have remained. But the fact is that Chamberlain's final decision to resign had not been taken; it *was* taken during that Cabinet meeting; *and Chamberlain said so in so many words*. For this we have the authority of his son, Austen, who was present, and who writes: 'I heard him announce that intention (i.e. to resign) at Cabinet'. Austen Chamberlain, then Postmaster-General, adds that, 'I drove back with him to Prince's Gardens when the Cabinet was over, and re-proached him with having taken this decision without a word to me, but added that as he was resigning, I should certainly do the same.' It must (incidentally) have been at this point that Chamberlain told his son that an hour or so before the Cabinet he had agreed with Balfour's suggestion that he should use his influence with his son to induce him to remain a member of the Government, and Balfour had revealed his intention of recommending him, if need be, as successor to Ritchie as Chancellor of the Exchequer. From Balfour's point of view, this continued co-operation in the Government of the son who entirely shared his father's fiscal creed was a public sign that there was no real cleavage betwen Balfour and Chamberlain.

Nevertheless, returning to the Cabinet itself, there can be no doubt that some Ministers, having themselves resigned, left the Cabinet room without the slightest idea that Chamberlain had also resigned or, at any rate, that his resignation had been accepted. (Ritchie however, did hear Chamberlain's words of resignation, as he admitted in the House of Commons on March 7, 1904.) How could this be since Austen Chamberlain had heard it perfectly clearly? Churchill's explanation is probably nearest the mark. He writes: 'It often happens that when a certain amount of conversation is going on between gentlemen, every-one present does not derive the same impression from it. Especially is this so when some are naturally preoccupied about their own posi-tion.'

But then there is the question of the Duke of Devonshire. He had not resigned with his 'Cobdenite' friends, though it appears that they assumed that he was acting with them. The Duke, it seems, had had the impression that Chamberlain had offered to resign, but that his offer had been refused. The Duke himself, however, being still a member of the Cabinet, ought to have received the usual note from the Prime Minister of what had happened in Cabinet, as was the practice. Had Balfour, in fact, intended to deceive him in order to keep him? Here again Churchill gives us the answer. The fact was that Balfour *had* written the note, *had* despatched it in the usual red Cabinet box, the Duke *had* received it—but had not read it because, dining out of London, he had left his Cabinet key behind. The box remained unopened, and was returned to London; next morning the Duke had forgotten all about it.

Meantime, he had sent his written resignation to Balfour on the grounds that he could not remain in the same Cabinet as Chamberlain! On being told by Lord Derby at Devonshire House that Chamberlain had in fact resigned, the Duke 'jumped as if he had been shot and said "I know nothing about it" '. He then at once withdrew his resignation. Thus most of what Balfour had desired to achieve had come about, not by underhand means, even though partly by accident.

The Duke's remaining, of course, at once involved him in the accusation from his former 'Cobdenite' colleagues that he had made a separate peace for himself. From one of them, Ritchie, he received an abusive letter accusing him of breach of faith and dishonesty. This put him in acute distress. Though his behaviour had been entirely honourable, it had led to gross misunderstanding.

When, therefore, Balfour proclaimed his fiscal policy—which became the policy of the Party—at Sheffield on October 1, 1904, the Duke was glad to find some expressions in the speech on which he could base his resignation. This time it was final. For once Balfour was furious and showed it. He wrote to the Duke: 'Till 1 o'clock this afternoon, I had I confess, counted you not as an opponent, but as a colleague— a colleague in spirit as well as name. . . . Had you resigned on the 15th or had you not resigned at all, the healing effect' (of the new declaration of policy) 'would have suffered no interruption. To resign now and to resign on the speech, is to make yet harder the hard task of peacemaker. . . . (The administration's) fortunes are at their lowest and its perplexities at their greatest.' (Esher commented to his wife: 'Poor Arthur very peevish and petulant'.) But almost immediately Balfour sent a second letter regretting any strong expressions in the first. Nor did Balfour's admiration for Devonshire waver. Years later he recognised that the Duke had been in a 'muddle': 'He got himself into such a position that he had to behave badly to somebody— and there it was! But it never made the slightest difference to my love for him.' (There is a curious wheels-within-wheels addendum to this sorry tale. According to Derby, it was the Duchess of Devonshire who got Ritchie to write the abusive letter. She believed that the Duke would then resign afresh, Balfour would fall, and the Duke be sent for to form a Government!)

The position, therefore, after the Cabinet changes, was that Balfour had lopped off his intransigent free-trade Ministers, but in place of the protectionist Chamberlain he had brought in his protectionist son Austen Chamberlain as Chancellor *vice* Ritchie, and the man who took Chamberlain's place as Colonial Minister, Alfred Lyttelton, was also a protectionist. Balfour had pressed Milner to succeed Chamberlain at the Colonial Office, but Milner preferred to see things through in South Africa. He would also have liked Brodrick, whose popularity had reached its nadir, to leave the War Office in favour of Akers-Douglas. In the end, however, H. O. Arnold-Forster—another bad choice—took Brodrick's place and Brodrick became Secretary for India *vice* Hamilton, resigned. Londonderry took over the Lord Presidency from Devonshire, and Salisbury (until 1903 Lord Selborne) became Lord Privy Seal.

The appointment of Austen Chamberlain was Balfour's attempt to remain in alliance with Chamberlain, still a commanding figure in the country. At the same time, he wanted to see whether, under the influence of Chamberlain's speeches up and down the country, Con-servatives as a body would swing towards Protection. There was, it must be remembered, no sign of such a massive swing at this time. That is why the Prime Minister's own fiscal statements were so cautious.

His intention was now clearly to temporise, not because of any inability to make up his own mind on policy itself, but because he had begun to realise more strongly than ever that it was not the question of policy but of something very like public hysteria. In his Sheffield speech, he hoped to provide a moderate position for the bulk of the Party to adhere to if they wished. They did not wish; they wanted a fight. Meanwhile the Opposition rejoiced. Although a body of opinion rallied to him, Balfour would scarcely have had the appetite to steer through the morass of the next two years had not his eye been firmly fixed on those more important, overriding aims to which we have referred.

It was, therefore, a question of holding on, and at the same time of holding the Party together. That was why he allowed no formal, personal break with Chamberlain; it was also why we find in his cor-respondence of this time such letters as that to Hicks-Beach on October 14, 1903, where he seems to suggest to the 'Cobdenite' and organiser of the Free Food League that: 'If I am not mistaken, the chief physical difference between us is that I am much more drawn towards a Colonial arrangement than you are. I feel real and deep anxiety about the Protective policy of our Colonies both in its commercial and its Imperial aspects: and if I thought practicable, which (as at present advised) I do not, I should not shrink from some sacrifices for the purpose of keeping important channels of trade permanently free and open to British commerce.   I gather that you have so little hope of this, or rate the value of it so low, that you hardly think the matter worth serious thought.'

In Parliament, matters became increasingly difficult.   When the House met in February, 1904, Balfour was down with influenza, and an Opposition attack was feebly met by Cabinet Members.   The result was that some 25 Unionists went into the Opposition lobby while seven others abstained from voting.   Sandars wrote to Balfour on February 21, 1904, about this dismaying development that: 'The issue, therefore, is this.   If we avoid either frightening or irritating these 25 Unionists we shall carry on.   If, on the other hand, we alarm or annoy them on the fiscal question, they can turn us out at a moment's notice.   The large majority of them I do not believe want to have us out; but they might yield again to temptation if the circumstances provoked them. . . . His (the old Duke's) advice to them last week to vote against the Government determined many of them: and the dramatic way it was given at the meeting was engineered by Winston.'

A week or two earlier, Churchill, whose free-trade affirmations we have noted, wrote asking Balfour whether he was responsible for a statement in the *Daily Telegraph* that Churchill and other Unionist M.P.s were no longer to receive the Government Whip.   Balfour replied in an amusing letter on February 1, 1904.   He said that it appeared that a mistake had been made by 'the authorities responsible for the issue of Circular Letters'.   However, he continued, the mistake was not 'without some plausible justification.   A hasty reading, for example, of such a phrase as "Thank God, we have an Opposition" which occurs, I think, in one of your speeches, is apt to lead to misunderstanding. It was rashly interpreted by some as meaning that the policy of the country would be safer in the hands of the Opposition rather than in the Government's, a meaning clearly inconsistent with Party loyalty. Obviously, it is equally capable of a quite innocent construction.   It might, for example, be a pious recognition of the fact that our heaviest trials are sometimes for our good.   Or, again, it might mean that a world in which everybody was agreed would be an exceedingly tedious one; or, that an effective Opposition made the Party loyalty burn more brightly.

'There are, in short, countless interpretations, quite consistent with the position I understand to be yours, namely that of a loyal though independent supporter of the present administration.

'Exegesis is a harder task to perform in explaining, or explaining away, a letter which you seem to have written to the electors of Ludlow, apparently advising them to vote against the Unionist Candidate.'

After this splendid piece of tail-tweaking, Balfour informs Churchill that he will continue to get the daily Whip.

Meanwhile, Austen Chamberlain reviewed the financial situation. 'It is most unsatisfactory', Balfour told the King. 'The expenditure is greater and the revenue less than was expected, and the prospects for next financial year are by no means reassuring.' In March, 1904, affairs for the Government began to go into a dizzy spin. In the very days that the Committee of Imperial Defence was being made part of the Constitution, vital questions of army reform being decided and Lord Lansdowne and Cambon were entering on the final stage of the negotiations for the Anglo-French Entente, Balfour was faced in the House by the revolt of over 100 Protectionist 'whole hoggers'. They compelled him at the last moment to withdraw an amendment which, though tabled in the name of a private Member, was known to have been drafted in the Whips' office. Observers such as Lord Esher and St. John Brodrick both had the impression that Balfour was no longer in control of his Cabinet. This was never quite true.

After Balfour's speech in Edinburgh in October, 1904—a speech which in essence reiterated the policy of the Sheffield speech a year before—the Opposition tried to pulverise him with a number of resolutions specifically condemning Chamberlain's programme as well as Balfour's. The Whips reported that they could not hold the Party against all these resolutions. Balfour announced his determination to walk out before the first division was taken and to ask his followers to do likewise. On several occasions at the end of 1904 and the beginning of 1905, this tactic was adopted. Sir Henry Lucy describes him as, under the indignant protests of the Opposition Leader, Sir Henry Campbell-Bannerman, 'with smiling countenance, langorous grace and lingering steps, he fared forth, followed in single file by his colleagues on the Treasury Bench'. It would scarcely have been possible for a Leader out of control to have carried his colleagues with him in this unusual manœuvre.

Throughout these 'nightmare' months, as Brodrick called them, Austen Chamberlain never ceased to support to the hilt Balfour's leadership. The tacit theory that Balfour was holding the House while Joseph Chamberlain attempted to 'educate the country' on the matter of tariffs held in a remarkable and indeed an unlikely way. But in February, 1905, Chamberlain wrote asking for a meeting with Balfour for fear they were drifting 'insensibly apart'. Six days later on February 18, 1905, Balfour wrote to Chamberlain: 'The prejudice against a small tax on food is not the fad of a few imperfectly informed theorists: it is a deep-rooted prejudice affecting a large mass of voters, especially the poorest class, which it will be a matter of extreme difficulty to overcome. I confess that it seemed to me last night that you underrated this difficulty. . . .' He refers to Chamberlain's Protectionist views, 'which I am quite unable to share'.

Chamberlain replying on February 24, 1905, reiterated his belief that prejudice against food taxes could be overcome and 'has already largely disappeared among the artisan population and even in agricultural districts I am sure that where proper house-to-house education has been undertaken the labourers are open to conversion'. He added an obvious *riposte*: 'I also want very much to know how you propose to carry out your own policy of Retaliation. At present I do not see how it can be worked in bits. I do not sufficiently understand your scheme at present to speak with sufficient knowledge upon it.' Chamberlain also tried to alarm Balfour by quoting from a letter he had received from Robert L. Borden, Canadian Conservative Opposition Leader, to the effect that much more was involved in the trade programme with the Empire than economics: 'The continuance of Canada as a dependency of the Empire may be and probably is in question.' Balfour was not alarmed.

He did, however, take up this latter point with his new Colonial Minister, Alfred Lyttelton, to whom on May 27, 1905, he wrote: 'If by "Colonial Preference" is meant (as I suppose it is) closer commercial union with the colonies (as per half sheet of notepaper), and if by "first item in my programme" is meant (as I suppose it is) that I regard it as the most important part (though the most difficult) of fiscal reform, and fiscal reform itself as the most important part of the Unionist policy, why should I not give the assurance asked for?—and why should any colleagues resign?'

Balfour was here referring to his celebrated remark that the differences within the Conservative Party on the question of tariffs could all be boiled down to a statement which would not require more than a half sheet of notepaper for its full expression. The very tortuousness of the sentences in the letter quoted, however, are some indication of the state of mind to which Balfour had been reduced in this last year of his Government—despite the fact that he still found time to discuss philosophical matters with his old friend Professor Pringle-Pattison. The rest of his letter is explained by Lyttelton writing to Austen Chamberlain on May 28, 1905:

'The P.M. is ready to announce on Tuesday in the House of Commons that Colonial Preference, i.e. the adoption of closer commercial union with our Colonies in order to bring about freer trade between them and the mother country is the most important, though the most difficult, part of fiscal reform and fiscal reform itself the most important part of the Unionist policy.

'He is willing to make Colonial Preference the first item in his programme subject, of course, to the proviso that it is not necessarily to be carried out because it is no doubt a problem of great intricacy affecting very widely separated countries while retaliation may be at any rate in isolated cases very speedily applied.'

From his own personal standpoint, Balfour here made a considerable concession; he did not *really* think that the most important part of Unionist policy was fiscal reform.   Even so it scarcely satisfied Chamberlain: moreover, as Balfour told Lady Elcho on June 5, 1905, referring to a speech he had made in similar terms at the Albert Hall, Chamberlain 'put an interpretation on my utterances which has driven the free-fooders wild'.   It is not easy, without much practice, to walk a tightrope.

For a time Balfour was the object of a tug-of-war between Free-Traders and Protectionists.   This position, however unenviable it may sound, at least kept the Government in some sort of equilibrium.   It was sometimes quite overlooked that Balfour, too, had a policy: retaliation.   But, as the more thoughtful observed at the time, how could there be retaliation against those who penalised Britain in their markets or dumped in Britain below cost price *without* a general tariff? How was Colonial Preference to be granted without putting duties on corn and meat?   It was food taxes that Balfour believed would bring terrible defeat on the Government.   In any case he had no great election hopes.   It was time alone he strove to win.

11

PRIME MINISTER

Successful Statesman, 1902–1905

APrime Minister whose Cabinet breaks up under him can
scarcely be called a successful leader, even though his failure
is extenuated by circumstances. Yet he can still be a great
Prime Minister. Leadership is not everything: a subaltern may be a
brilliant leader, and lack either intellect or vision. Balfour was not a
manager of men, but as Lord Birkenhead said, his was 'the finest brain
that has been applied to politics in our time'. Balfour's achievements
as Prime Minister—and they are great achievements—were the product
of intellect, of vision and of personal determination.

Nowhere is this more evident than in the sphere of defence; nowhere
do his qualities of prescience, and his great grasp of what needed to be
done appear more strongly. Problems of defence planning had long
preoccupied him. In 1902, as Prime Minister, he at last saw a chance
of getting something done. One result was the Committee of Imperial
Defence; and 'No one', as Hankey has said, 'has ever seriously con-
tested that Balfour was the founder of the Committee of Imperial
Defence.' The organisation called the Defence Committee, consti-
tured in 1895, had scarcely functioned. The South African War, with
its series of humiliating defeats, had shown the need for overhauling the
whole defence conception; and the Elgin Commission of Inquiry was
very critical of things as they were. Lord Esher, who sat on the
Commission, was even more critical in his private journals, not only of
the lack of liaison between military leaders and the Cabinet but of
Cabinet inactivity. There was another reason for re-thinking defence:
'Radical technological advances in naval vessels, and rapid-firing guns,

combined with the emergence of such highly disciplined and efficiently led armies as that of Germany, were creating new strategic theories which necessitated the use of the land and sea forces as two elements of the same team.'

During Balfour's Premiership there were three notable advances in the field of defence planning, in the following order: first, came the revival of the Defence Committee and its reorganisation into the Committee of Imperial Defence—its first session was on December 18, 1902; second, the War Office (Reconstitution) Committee, set up under Esher in November, 1903, which put its first report into the Prime Minister's hands in January, 1904; and, third, the official minuting of the Committee of Imperial Defence, with certain important changes, on May 4, 1904.

The first step was taken by Balfour after representations made to him by Brodrick, the War Minister, and Selborne, First Lord of the Admiralty, that an active co-ordinating body should be set up to survey the Empire's military needs, to ensure the co-operation of their two departments, and to deal with the most 'important problems of all, viz.: those which were neither purely naval, nor purely military, nor purely naval and military combined, but which may be described as naval, military and political'. This merely confirmed Balfour's own sharp awareness of the urgency of defence needs. From the first, Balfour emphasised that the Prime Minister must be chairman (though, curiously enough, Devonshire took the chair in the first year). He also insisted that the Committee could call whom it wished to its counsels, but that it had no executive authority, and that it remained subordinate to Cabinet decision. He did not want a committee purely of service members; the presence of Cabinet Ministers was essential to give the deliberations authority. The Treasury, the ogre of war preparations, would not be represented; thus it would not be committed in any way before proposals reached the Cabinet. A drastic innovation was the presence of serving military officers and political Ministers on a basis of equality. Another innovation was the appointment of a clerk to keep minutes of the meetings; this was later to develop into a Secretary and a secretariat.

Balfour attended every meeting, which took place weekly, of this 'transitional' Committee of Imperial Defence. Its first task was to consider home defence and the possibility of invasion. At the end of 1903, in order to bring imperial matters more into focus, Balfour invited the Canadian War Minister, Frederick Borden, to attend meetings *as a member*. Balfour told the King that the Committee had the potentiality to become an 'Imperial Council'. He added that 'Unfortunately it appears that this particular gentleman is of rather inferior quality—but we shall be careful what we say before him! And the compliment remains the same. A new precedent of great imperial significance will thus have been set. . . .'

The final constitution of 1904 was, to some extent, affected by the findings of the War Office (Reconstitution) Committee set up by Balfour in November, 1903. It was not set up without difficulty. There were, Balfour told the King on October 23, 1903, hitches partly owing to the difficulty of finding a military member not identified with a clique nor with the existing War Office administration. Sir Henry Bracken-bury, formerly Director-General of Ordnance, would not do, since the naval member, Admiral Sir John Fisher, C.-in-C., Portsmouth, would not serve with him. Eventually Sir George Sydenham Clarke, who had been secretary to the Colonial Defence Committee and to the Hartington Committee, was appointed. He had been an intelligence officer and later Governor of Victoria. In due course, Esher's committee proposed an Army Council of officers and Civil Servants, on the lines of the Board of Admiralty and a general staff system on German lines.

Fisher, one of the most extraordinary naval officers who ever served, was bitterly critical of the army; even then—and more so later—he believed that the navy was Britain's most important defence arm, not least because it would attack. Shortly afterwards, when Fisher became First Sea Lord, he pushed forward those reforms which enabled Churchill so effectively to mobilise great naval strength in the summer of 1914.

As far as the Committee of Imperial Defence was concerned, the War Office Committee backed up everything that Balfour had done; it also strongly recommended a permanent secretariat charged with collating military information for the Prime Minister's use as head, not only of the C.I.D., but of all the nation's defensive preparations. Decisions could properly be taken only after the assimilation of masses of technical and non-military information: this the permanent secretariat was to provide. The secretariat, though completely subordinate to the Prime Minister, was also to 'anticipate' his needs. Furthermore its information would be continuous so that whoever the Prime Minister might be the material would be at hand. This secretariat was embodied in Balfour's treasury minute already mentioned above, and set up its H.Q. in Disraeli's old house in Whitehall Gardens.

The C.I.D. in its new phase concentrated upon the reliance on sea-power for imperial defence, defence against invasion and the defence of India. All these were closely linked, as we shall see, with immediate political events. A sub-committee on over-seas expeditions was set up; and many wider strategic matters were explored and reported on.

It is perhaps necessary to add that the conceptions and plan of the Committee was Balfour's. Even the idea of a permanent secretariat he had mentioned to Dilke in 1893: 'I have *always* been in favour of a Defence Committee of the Cabinet' (rather than a Ministry of Defence) 'with expert advisers and permanent records carrying on the work from Government to Government.' Sandars writing to W. M. Short, Balfour's personal secretary, on January 17, 1913, pointed out that Balfour had launched the Committee before the appointment of the Esher Committee. It owed nothing in its inception either to General Sir John Colomb—M.P. and military expert—or to Sir George Clarke, though later on Clarke (who became the C.I.D.'s first permanent Secretary) did concern himself with some features which were introduced into it. (Clarke—who was dismissed in 1907—thought his contribution had been much greater than was recognised.) Sandars also reveals that at one time Balfour had doubts about having a permanent Secretary because he did not 'wish to stereotype the new body on the lines of a Government Department'.

Esher, the Chairman of the War Office (Reconstitution) Committee, was himself, however, to play a curious and important rôle in Balfour's further plans for the Committee of Imperial Defence. Reginald Brett, Viscount Esher, was an unusual person. He constantly refused offers of office—he refused to become War Minister when Balfour offered him the post in 1903. Yet he had a great desire to influence public affairs, more, however, as a puppet-master behind the scenes than as a principal actor in the glare of the footlights. He was a close personal friend of King Edward to whom he was sycophantic and over-demonstrative: from time to time, as he tells us in his journals, he would, even in private, kiss the King's hand. But he was never self-seeking. One may hold it against him that he expunged large parts of Queen Victoria's letters before they were published. On the other hand, his backstairs influence was normally for good rather than ill. That is not, however, to deny that his actions as unofficial adviser to the Crown could be embarrassing and even personally damaging to some; Brodrick believed that it was Esher's enmity that forced his resignation in 1903.

Esher and Balfour got on well together. Both were determined to set defence matters on such a footing that even the Liberals could not upset them. That they might do so was Balfour's constant fear. It was not unjustified, for when Sir Henry Campbell-Bannerman's Liberal Government came into power in 1906, there was a period when it seemed quite likely that the Committee of Imperial Defence would be abolished or, at any rate, allowed to decay. It was Haldane who prevented that. To forestall whatever might occur Balfour, who in this matter trusted Esher implicitly, had him appointed as a permanent member of the Defence Committee at the end of 1905, just before he left office. As Esher reminded Balfour in a letter of December 31,

1909: 'I always remember that you put me on the Committee to "hold the fort for you" '.

Balfour himself was so convinced of the fundamental importance of the Committee of Imperial Defence that he personally compiled long reports on meeting an invasion of Britain, on Indian defence, and on the army. After his Government fell in December, 1905, he completed another report on the possibility of a raid by a hostile force on the British coast. But the nub of his achievement was that he had evolved the office of the Prime Minister to the point where supreme responsibility for co-ordinating the defence of the Empire was vested in one man and in a department under his immediate direction. It was as a result of this that the Crown granted special precedence for the Crown's First Minister, and this was acknowledged by the creation of the title 'Prime Minister', which came into effect on the change of government in 1906.

It may be added that until the appointment of Esher as Permanent Member, Balfour had strongly set his face against having anyone except the Prime Minister on the Committee as of right. The King was dubious on this point. Knollys, the King's Private Secretary, wrote to Sandars on February 15, 1904, that the King had 'understood that certain officials were *always* to attend meetings of the Defence Committee . . . otherwise it would be open to an unscrupulous P.M. to "pack" the Committee on any particular occasion'. It was also in connection with the Defence Committee deliberations that Balfour decided that the King could not be allowed to see confidential Cabinet papers before decisions of the Cabinet were taken on them.

What lay behind the foundation of the Defence Committee was of course, not so much the question of defending small, threatened parts of the Empire, as the fear of a general war. The ultimate cause of such a war was the fact that Britain's power was being overtaken by rising nations, and the *Pax Britannica* was unlikely to hold much longer: she had rivals now to her once unchallengeable supremacy. Hence the decline of the policy of isolationism, and the new understandings sought abroad. In these new circumstances, it was Balfour who pondered and prepared. As Austen Chamberlain wrote:

'It is impossible to over-rate the service thus rendered by Balfour to the Country and Empire. Without this Committee and the work done by it under him and his successors, the outbreak of the Great War would have found us wholly unprepared for the problems with which it at once confronted the Government, and, humanly speaking, victory would have been impossible. It may be added that apart from the service he rendered by creating such an organ, it would be difficult to overstate Balfour's personal contribution to its earliest inquiries.'

For instance, Chamberlain notes that the strategical principles Balfour laid down on Indian defence were found to be still sound 25 years later.

Who would be the first aggressor? Balfour's own report on the problem of invasion envisaged France as the invader, as did most of the secret planning until the signing of the Anglo-French *Entente*. This did not necessarily nullify the planning: even if the invader was another nation, invasion might still come through the Channel ports, as it almost did in 1940. Some also of the military intelligence agencies were still working on the principle that France was the enemy, with Russia as the *éminence grise*. Yet reports came in of the large number of German tourists, waiters and hairdressers who frequented Britain's south-eastern coasts, and the military and naval centres. German plans for a railway line across the plains and deserts of Asia Minor to Baghdad, and the Persian Gulf, could possibly bear contradictory interpretations: but the increase in the German navy was obviously alarming, clearly a danger signal to the world's greatest maritime power.

There is little evidence that Balfour, *while still Prime Minister*, was certain that there would be a large-scale conflict with Germany: that it existed in his mind as a possibility cannot be doubted since his military *confidante*, Esher, as early as September 9, 1904, was saying: 'The low countries were the battlefields of Europe for centuries and will be again. It is vital to Germany to absorb Holland. Kiel is insufficient for a power that desires naval supremacy and colonial empire. That Germany is always contemplating the absorption of Holland into the *Empire* is certain. So that there must come a day when France and England will have to fight Germany in order to *neutralise* the Dutch Kingdom, and this day may not be very far off.'

Three years later Balfour was almost certainly convinced. Esher— no doubt strengthened in his view by the German interference in Morocco—was already prophesying, with remarkable accuracy, the course of events. In a letter dated September 4, 1906, he says: 'The years 1793-1815 will be repeated, only Germany, not France, will be trying for European domination. She has 70 million of people and is determined to have commercial pre-eminence. To do this, England has got to be crippled and the low countries added to the German Empire. France contains 40 million of people, England about the same. So even combined, the struggle is by no means a certainty.' And a day or two later he writes: '*L'Allemagne c'est l'ennemi*—and there is no doubt on the subject. They mean to have a powerful fleet, and commercially to beat us out of the field, before ten years are over our heads.'

Balfour probably shared Esher's views. It was not, however, till July, 1907, that he wrote to the Permanent Secretary of the

Committee of Imperial Defence, suggesting the need for reconsidering the plans to counter invasion if invasion from Germany was now in view.

Whoever the attacker, Balfour knew that attack would come. Having provided an embryonic organisation to co-ordinate the direction of a future war, he turned to the more detailed reorganisation of the war departments. He put the position as he saw it to the King in his Cabinet report on December 14, 1903:

'What are, in Mr. Balfour's opinion, the objects to be aimed at may be roughly summarised as follows: we want an army which shall give us sufficient force for at least any immediate needs of Indian defence; and, in conjunction with the auxiliary forces, for Home defence, which shall be capable of expansion in times of national emergency—which shall if possible be less dependent on men in civil employment (i.e. the Reservists) for filling up the ranks on mobilisation—and which shall throw a smaller burden on the taxpayer. This last is of peculiar importance, not merely because of the present conditions of our finances, but because the demands of the navy are so great and so inevitable that the total cost of imperial defence threatens to become prohibitive.'

As far as the War Office was concerned, there were difficulties of every kind, not the least being the raging unpopularity of Balfour's friend Brodrick, the Secretary of State. This was partly due to the publication of the Elgin Commission's reports revealing the inefficiency and, it was said, even corruption which had obtained while Brodrick had been first Under-Secretary, and then War Minister, during the South African War. The personal accusations were doubtless unfair; but the public and Opposition were in full hue and cry, and an Argyllshire by-election seemed to underline the fact by yielding the Opposition a sensational victory. The situation was the more troublesome to Balfour because of his close personal relations with Brodrick. He wrote on February, 1903, to Lady Elcho:

'St. John. Never before has his stock been quoted so low. I really do not think it is his fault; but, whether his fault or not, his unpopularity now is the most serious menace to the Government. He was the subject of a vote of censure on Monday and Tuesday; and though everything was done that oratory (i.e. *my* oratory) and "whipping" could do, if the Irish had not abstained (not because we asked or desired it, but because they thought, rightly enough, that with the Government, George's Land Bill would go too) our majority would have been a small one. Many good observers think the feeling against St. John so violent that we shall never get through Army estimates without a fall! He is naturally depressed, poor old boy; and my thoughts continually referred to 1900, and the sleepless nights which Hilda (Brodrick's wife) and Muriel Marjoribanks endured through their fears that St. John would not be made Secretary of State for War! N.B. *never* wish for anything overmuch.'

It was inevitable that Brodrick should resign, and this he did during the Cabinet reshuffle of the autumn of 1903. He was then 'promoted' to the India Office, upon which an M.P. of his own party, not unnaturally, complained: 'Either he had failed at the War Office or he had not. If he had not, why was he removed from it; if he had, why was he promoted to the India Office?' It was perhaps as a result of this clamour that when two other of his personal friends were driven to resignation, Balfour did not offer them other office.

Esher was offered the post, but replied: 'I really do not think I can bring myself to sacrifice all independence, my "intime" life, for a position which adds nothing to that which I now occupy', and he proposed instead Akers-Douglas. In the end, H. O. Arnold-Forster, then Secretary to the Admiralty, was appointed. It was not the happiest choice. Arnold-Forster—he was the orphan son of Matthew Arnold's brother and had been adopted by the Forsters—was an intense, hard-working man, rather too cocksure. It was said that in his belief in his own infallibility he could give His Holiness the Pope 'two stones and a licking'. He swiftly crossed swords with the King on the subject of bringing Sir Ian Hamilton back from his military mission to Japan, and when the King suggested that Haig, then Inspector-General of Cavalry in India, should go to the War Office, he coolly replied that there was no vacancy. Knollys, the King's Secretary, intimated that the King felt that Arnold-Forster was 'not quite a gentleman'. Towards the end of the Government, Sandars reported to Balfour (October, 1905):

'A.-F. claims to be an infallible oracle. He said with glee that the militia was going from bad to worse, that is of course because he has not taken the slightest trouble to improve them, which was the basis of your memorandum. The Volunteers again are a blot on his administration, that is because you will not allow him to reduce their numbers and to irritate every officer and man in the Force; and the third point is that he is not allowed to sack Neville [Lyttelton] and put someone whose name he would not give me in his place. I suppose it is Nicholson.'

But even had Arnold-Forster been a less abrasive character, he could scarcely have found his position easy. For one thing, there was the King demanding that he should be consulted about all questions of army policy; and notably about appointments. His interest, though valuable in some cases, particularly in connection with the army medical department, could be embarrassing where personalities were involved, and almost comic when it led, for instance, to him ordering the Guards to be equipped with new greatcoats and caps—without, incidentally, informing the War Minister. A more serious challenge to Arnold-Forster's authority was presented by the fact that he was not

19. George Wyndham
(1863–1913)

Radio Times Hulton Picture Library

20. Alfred Lyttelton (1857–1913)

Radio Times Hulton Picture Library

21. Admiral of the Fleet, Sir John Fisher, First Sea Lord 1904–10 and 1914–15

The National Portrait Gallery

22. A.J.B. and Sir Edward Carson leaving the War Cabinet

Radio Times Hulton Picture Library

given a seat on the War Office (Reconstitution) Committee. Balfour believed, no doubt correctly, that a Minister occupied with the day-to-day work of a department could not give it sufficient time.

It was, however, Arnold-Forster who had to bear the brunt of the results of the Commission's report. The Army Council, mentioned above—and which Brodrick himself claimed to have established before he left the War Office!—was to be presided over by the Minister, and was to have supreme power; to ensure this, it was proposed to abolish the post of the Commander-in-Chief. There was instead to be a new post of Inspector-General whose function would be simply to inspect and to report, not to be a Commander entrusted with powers to give orders, to be the equal not the superior of officers commanding Army Corps. In addition, there was to be a 'selection' board outside the administrative system of the War Office to advise on higher military appointments.

All these proposals at once raised opposition, of which Arnold-Forster found himself the unwilling butt. The King, for example, insisted on the precedence of the military over the civilian members of the new Army Council, and he did not see that there was any objection, as one or two members of the Cabinet had suggested, to the Inspector-General presiding over the selection board. But he was overruled. Lord Roberts, who had at first been quite happy to occupy the new post of Inspector-General, was influenced by the King, and eventually refused it. Roberts left the War Office 'for good in a devil of a temper'. This did not end the Cabinet's troubles with him. He proceeded to tramp the country propagandising for a vague scheme of 'universal military training'. Balfour did not think that the country would accept it for a moment. He wrote to the King's Secretary, Knollys: 'I am bound to say that I do not think it would be right for H.M. to give the prestige of his name to a movement which in its present shape is almost certain to fail.'

Dissension accumulated; the upper reaches of the army fought each other with a will. The Army Council was eventually formed: it found the greatest difficulty in agreeing on anything or achieving anything. Arnold-Forster strove, ineffectually, to prune expenditure and to provide for a 'short term' army. Shortly before the end of the Government, Balfour was driven, as he told the King on February 2, 1905, to form a sub-committee of the Defence Committee to try and find out why Arnold-Forster's army scheme was not being carried out! Not surprisingly, he asked the King to keep the matter very secret.

Towards the end of 1905, it appears that Balfour was succumbing to the idea of removing Arnold-Forster: Knollys complains of the delay in Sandars's plan for getting rid of him. Esher was again thought of as substitute.

R<small>JB</small>

It was enough to make any Prime Minister want to resign.   But Balfour hung on.   Something was emerging from the chaos; somehow the basis of a modern army was being established.   Moreover, there was one other military matter nearing fruition: a new gun.   Perhaps nowhere else were Balfour's foresight and mastery of detail so well displayed as in his dealing with the 18-pounder gun.   It had been decided to re-arm the artillery with quick-firing guns.   The special committee concerned with the matter were on the point of recommending the making of two types—a 13-pounder for the Horse Artillery and an 18-pounder for the Field Artillery.   But, as the smaller gun was giving better results in trials, it was suggested that both arms of the artillery should be given the 13-pounder.

Balfour determined to go into the technical aspects of the question himself.   He soon saw clearly the advantages of the 18-pounder.   He gave an order for complete re-armament with this gun at the end of December, 1904—'this is a great weight off my mind', wrote Balfour to the King.   But there were technical troubles, and it was not until the middle of 1905 that the gun was put into full and successful production. It was this gun that was first fired in earnest in Flanders in August, 1914.

This gun was the final reason why Balfour, political chaos around him, still delayed his resignation.   Until its production was in full swing, he would not be satisfied.   He afterwards told Mrs. Dugdale (though it is not recorded in her biography) that this reason for delaying his resignation was 'far more important than the others and one of which none of my colleagues was aware. . . .   The re-arming of the Field Artillery I considered vital for the safety of the Empire and worth risking a débâcle in the Unionist Party and I was determined not to go out of office until we were so far committed to the expenditure that no Liberal Government could have withdrawn from the position.'

Balfour's fears of what a future Liberal Government might do to the defence measures he had initiated were proved to the hilt over his naval reforms.   Balfour's problems here were less complex in a way because he had two excellent First Lords—Selborne and the Earl of Cawdor— and a First Sea Lord of genius—however bluff and egotistic—in the person of Fisher.   Fisher, being a professional and technical man, saw that the German Admiral Tirpitz's fleet was built with only one end in view—to fight the British.   Against every sort of opposition, from the public, from his colleagues, and even from within the Government, Fisher grabbed semi-obsolete ships, redistributed the fighting navy in three fleets, built the *Dreadnought*—a battleship which made all others then in the world inferior—and planned for more, economised in crews, and established a Navy War Council. Navy estimates, of course, rocketted—from £27 million in 1900 to £36 million in 1904, though these were reduced by £3½ million in the last year of the Government.

Throughout, Balfour backed him to the hilt. When later in 1912 Winston Churchill gave Asquith's First Lord, Reginald McKenna, the credit for naval reform, Fisher wrote to Esher (April 2, 1912): 'He (Winston) ought to have gone further back than McKenna for the credit. *It was Balfour!* He saw me through—no one else would allow 160 ships to be scrapped, etc., etc., etc.' The Campbell-Bannerman Government, which followed Balfour's, abandoned the programme, threw away most of the lead which the genius of Fisher had secured, and encouraged Germany to try to draw level again.

II

War was often round the corner in the first years of the century. In the Far East, Russia's advances in Manchuria and China threatened one of the most valuable of Britain's commercial markets, and seemed aimed at the newly-rising state of Japan, a country which had scarcely been discovered 50 years earlier. Before Balfour became Prime Minster, Britain had signed with Japan a limited alliance for five years. This was in 1902. Balfour seems to have had his doubts, over this definite gesture of farewell to 'splendid isolation'. In a memorandum, he argues the case against it on the ground that it might involve us in 'fighting for existence in every part of the globe against Russia and France, because Russia has joined forces with her ally over some obscure Russian-Japanese quarrel in Korea.' But he soon came to see its value, particularly as its final terms provided for neutrality if one of the parties was attacked by another single power; only an attack by two powers bound the other party to come to the help of its ally. In 1905 he determined to seek a renewal and strengthening of this alliance before his Government left office.

Towards the end of 1903, the tension between Russia and Japan heightened. There was an odd corollary of this, involving the British Cabinet and the King. Chile (of all countries) had two warships for sale. The Japanese made an offer for them, but were outbidden by the Russians. Since apparently the Japanese were either unwilling or unable to raise their bid, the British Cabinet felt that steps should be taken to prevent Russia obtaining the ships. The only means to do so was, it was thought, a further bid from Britain herself. But it was not clear where the money was to come from. Balfour approached the King. The King's reply was contained in a most urgent cipher telegram on November 28, 1903: 'I have received your letter and quite comprehend the gravity of the situation. We *must* have those two ships at any cost; if the Japanese will not buy I strongly advise asking Sir E. Cassell to lend the money, being sure he will if you mention my name.

We must show the Russians a firm hand as there is no doubt they mean mischief by trying to outbid the Japanese.   Let me urgently beg of you to bring my proposal before the Cabinet.   Edward R.'

The suggested approach to Cassell, the financier and intimate of the King, was apparently not made.   Balfour ciphered the King on November 13, 1903 to the effect that a Cabinet Committee 'after lengthy sitting and consultation' had authorised a commercial agent to make a firm offer to the Chilean President of £1,650,000 'with absolute guarantee of payment'.   To prevent the Chileans using this offer as a lever to induce the Russians to increase their offer, the Chilean Government were to be asked to say what sum they would accept if this was thought to be insufficient.   The King at this stage 'hopes it may end by nobody buying the ships'.   But Britain bought the ships on the next day.   The King's Secretary then wrote saying that he would 'be interested to hear how it is proposed to deal with the money part of the affair'.   What the Cabinet's answer was seems to have been lost to history.

The King, however, though in no doubt about his attitude to Russian expansion, was extremely worried about the possibility of Britain being involved in a Russo-Japanese war.   He wrote privately to Balfour: 'That we should be engaged in another war so soon after the South African war has been brought to a close would be most disastrous, and I cannot disguise from you that I am in abject horror at the mere thought of it, as it would inevitably cripple our resources most seriously; I have reason to believe that Russia does not want to fight Japan.   She can gain nothing by it, and would probably be a loser, but she holds the latter (i.e. Japan) in supreme contempt, which Japan probably knows and it makes her doubly angry.'

To this Balfour replied in a most revealing document.   He says that his views are only provisional, but there is no reason to suppose that, if challenged, he would have abated an iota of their realism.   He wrote:

'The interest of this country is now and always—peace.   But a war between Japan and Russia, in which we were not actively concerned and in which Japan did not suffer serious defeat would not be an unmixed curse.   Russia, even if successful, would be greatly weakened. She would have created for herself in the Far East an implacable and unsleeping enemy.   She would be under the permanent obligation of keeping in those regions an Army and a Fleet which would be most burdensome to her finances; and Mr. Balfour concludes from all this she would be much easier to deal with, both in Asia and in Europe, than she is at present.   For these reasons Mr. Balfour would do everything to maintain peace, *short* of wounding the susceptibilities of the Japanese people.'

Japan, in short, was to act as a decoy, to draw off Russian strength in the Far East, and at the same time as a policeman for British interests there.   So it turned out.   In the bitter war with Russia that began in

February, 1904, Japan was surprisingly successful. Russia took her rebuff in the Far East as definitive—and paradoxically made her desire an understanding with Britain. When the Great War came, Japan and Russia were both on the British side. There were, of course, disadvantages since the Anglo-Japanese Agreement excited hostility in China and suspicion in North America. Moreover, the alliance was carried on beyond its point of usefulness; for, in due course, Japan became the strongest power in the Far East and herself a threat to British interests there.

But that was in the unforeseeable future. For the present Balfour's concern was to see that, while Russia and Japan fought, Britain was not physically involved. This is why he behaved so—to all appearances—tamely over the Dogger Bank incident. On the night of October 21–22, 1904, the Russian Baltic Fleet, under Admiral Rodjesvensky, was sailing through the North Sea on a journey to attempt to reverse Japanese naval supremacy in the Pacific. Owing to the poor Russian navigation, the fleet sailed some 30 miles off course and into the middle of some Hull trawlers engaged in night fishing. The Russians, knowing that France was about to aid them along their course, immediately concluded that the British were doing the same for Japan and that the fishing trawlers were really disguised Japanese torpedo-boats. They opened fire, destroying one of the trawlers and killing two fishermen. In England, where the remarkable Japanese successes had been enthusiastically applauded, and where the Russians were hated as tyrants, there was widespread anger. When it was later learned that the Russian Admiral had attempted to justify the action, and that an international commission of inquiry, so far from punishing, was to hear both sides without prejudice, popular anger flared up. Balfour, though all his instincts were towards restraint, found it wise to let the nation know that provisional naval orders had been given for the Home, Channel and Mediterranean Fleets to prepare for action. Admiral Fisher wrote to his wife on November 1, 1904: 'I have been with the P.M. all day. It has nearly been war again. *Very near indeed*, but the Russians have climbed down. Balfour is a splendid man to work with. Only he, I, Lansdowne and Selborne did the whole thing.' The Russians moderated their attitude; by December the worst was over.

Shortly before the Russo-Japanese war was ended by the Peace of Portsmouth on August 23, 1905, the new treaty had been signed with Japan. Britain now bound herself to go to the aid of Japan, not merely if attacked by two enemies but if attacked only by one. There was also a rather curious clause to the effect that, if Britain were to become involved in war in defence of her interests on the Indian Frontier, Japan was to come to her assistance. Balfour himself was doubtful

about this clause.   He wrote to the King on June 19, 1905: 'There is a
real danger, that if a radical Government came into power, it would
reduce our Army below the limits of safety; and this danger will be
greatly augmented if they think they can rely on an unlimited supply
of men from Japan.   In the opinion of Your Majesty's present advisers
it is not consistent either with the security or the dignity of the Empire
that the defence of any part of it should depend mainly upon a foreign
power, however friendly and however powerful.'   But the treaty, as a
whole, was generally accepted; even Chamberlain wrote to Balfour on
October 18, 1905: 'I congratulate you on the Anglo-Japanese treaty
which was indeed a great stroke of work.'

How large a hand did Balfour have in the management of foreign
affairs?   It seems to have been very considerable, particularly in the
events leading up to the Anglo-Japanese Treaty.   Austen Chamberlain,
then Chancellor of the Exchequer, wrote later that 'No Prime Minister
ever took a closer interest or . . . more active part in the conduct of
foreign policy. . . .   It is safe to say that Lansdowne took no important
step and sent no important despatch without first consulting him.   It
does not detract from Lansdowne's services as Foreign Secretary to say
that his chief accomplishments would never have been achieved but
for the constructive mind of Balfour and the constant support he gave
him, not only in executing his foreign policy, but in conceiving and
shaping it.'   Equally, Austen Chamberlain was sure that the alliances
with Japan and France were 'decisive for our own fate and it may well
be for the world's when the day of Armageddon came'.

III

The alliance with Japan greatly altered the complexion of the Indian
problem which was one that harassed Balfour until the signing of the
new treaty.   The draft of a memorandum on this subject in Balfour's
own handwriting is extant—no doubt it was the basis for the C.I.D.
paper which Austen Chamberlain found so useful a quarter of a century
later.   In it he discusses to what extent a Russian attack on India
would be facilitated if Russia got a free hand in Persia; and to what
extent, and how, Britain could frustrate such designs by making
'Persia the theatre not merely of operations strictly defensive in character, but also of an aggressive movement upon the Russian Line of
Communications'.   It might, in this respect, be necessary to maintain
the integrity 'of that portion of Turkish territory in Asia which adjoins
the Russian and Persian frontiers'.

Balfour continues: 'The most formidable aspect of an Anglo-Russian
war is admittedly the difficulty of hitting Russia herself.'   He thought
an attack on the Caucasus important; Fisher had told him that such

a blow could be struck in the Black Sea without serious risk to the navy even if Turkey was hostile. If a similar blow could be struck on the southern land side of the Caucasus, Russia's power of attack in Central Asia would be seriously crippled.

A Russian attack on India would be mainly along the northern Afghan frontier, supported by two main lines of railway, both secure from possible interruption by Britain. Russia was also contemplating construction of a railway through northern Persia. Attack on the Caucasus might be possible by Britain constructing two railway lines in Turkey and west Persia, which would enable large forces to be thrown into Azerbaijan.

Such was the background to the 'Indian problem' during Balfour's Premiership; it was not until 1907, and an Anglo-Russian understanding, that it went into abeyance. But for Balfour the 'Indian problem' had another, far more difficult aspect—namely the presence there as Viceroy of George Nathaniel Curzon, eldest son of the fourth Baron Scarsdale of Kedleston in Derbyshire. Curzon was the clever, pushing young man whom we noted as one of the ornaments of 'The Souls'; he was also a member of Wilfrid Blunt's 'Crabbet Club'. He had become a Conservative M.P., then Under-Secretary to the Foreign Office in Salisbury's 1895 Government, and subsequently in 1898 Viceroy with an Irish Viscountcy, although he was still under 40. Balfour knew him well, though he was not quite so sure of Curzon's super-brilliance as Curzon was. When Curzon went out to India, he already knew a great deal about the East which he had visited and about which he wrote a number of books. At first his zeal for reform had a salutary influence on every branch of Indian government. Before long, however, the immense power and panoply of rule that surrounded a viceroy went to his head. His health had never been good and he became tetchy and resentful of advice or check from any quarter.

He began to assert for the Indian Government that dominance which, as Balfour remarked a little later, 'would raise India to the position of an independent and not always friendly power'. Serious difficulty began at the time of the Delhi Durbar in 1903. Curzon wanted to mark the occasion by a remission of taxes as a gesture from the King Emperor in connection with his accession. The Cabinet unanimously rejected the proposal on the grounds that, if the King got the credit of reducing taxation he would be saddled with the odium of increasing that taxation when it became necessary.

From a letter from Knollys to Sandars on January 6, 1903, it appears that Curzon had aired his views on the subject to journalists. Knollys writes: 'I wish Curzon had not gone to the Press camp. It was not very dignified, certainly not necessary, and it looks as if he wished to be written up, which perhaps he does!'

A few months later Curzon asked for permission to spend four months leave in England in the next year, 1904. The King thought he should be allowed to remain no more than two months at the most, but Balfour approved Curzon's request, 'in spite', he added to Knollys, 'of Curzon's extraordinary behaviour and still more extraordinary letters'. This referred to Curzon's letters, now imperious, now excessively friendly, with which he showered all the members of the Cabinet who were his intimate friends from Balfour to Wyndham and Brodrick.

But before this visit occurred, other unfortunate events took place. Curzon, always obsessed by fear of a Russian penetration of Central Asia, attempted to 'tighten up' relations with Afghanistan. This country, though independent, had for long received a British subsidy and British protection. Grievances obviously arose from time to time, especially with India, and it was these that Curzon proposed to have redressed before any further supply or subsidy was granted. The Cabinet insisted on carrying its point of view rather than Curzon's —a decision justified by the loyal conduct of the ruler of Afghanistan during the next 20 years. Curzon submitted, but with an ill-grace, and with the usual outpouring of ill-considered complaints.

A still more difficult situation arose when Curzon in the same year decided to call Tibet to account. About this time, Russia was actively intriguing in Tibet and there were hostile acts by Tibetans on their frontier with India. The Government, however, was not anxious to exacerbate relations with Russia, and refused to allow Curzon to send an armed expedition into the country. After pressure by Curzon, the Cabinet agreed, however, to allow Colonel Sir Francis Younghusband to go to Tibet as a negotiator, accompanied by an armed force, to discuss questions only of trade, frontier and grazing rights. This was as far as they would go. As Balfour told the King on November 6, 1903: 'The Cabinet are apprehensive that the Viceroy entertains schemes of territorial expansion, or at least of extending responsibilities which would be equally detrimental to Indian interests and to international relations of the Empire.' When the expedition arrived at Lhasa in July, 1904, all these orders were disobeyed. Colonel Younghusband used drastic threats over trade, the razing of all fortified positions between Lhasa and the frontier, the establishment of an Agent at Gyantse to receive communications from the British Government, and the payment of an indemnity.

The Cabinet at once vetoed the establishment of an Agent, and reduced the period of the indemnity. This Curzon took as an open rebuff to his policy and, as Brodrick says, his dissent was so forceful and the effect on him so deep-seated that strong representations were made to the Prime Minister, in view of this and other differences of opinion, that it would be unwise for Curzon to be re-appointed to the Government of India after his leave expired. (It subsequently appeared that Younghusband had not received all the official instructions before he signed his agreement with the Tibetans. Balfour expressed his anger with Younghusband for exceeding his brief in a letter to Knollys, October 6, 1904. But the King admired Younghusband who a little later was awarded the K.C.I.E.)

But what eventually brought matters to a head was Curzon's ridiculous contest with Kitchener, a more tortuous—but much more popular —character than Curzon. At Curzon's own insistence and much against the advice both of his officials in India and of Brodrick at home, Kitchener had been sent out to India to take over the position of Commander-in-Chief of the Indian Army, a post which Curzon himself had held and which he found to be both onerous and distasteful not least because of his unconcealed contempt for the military. Obviously such determined, not to say pig-headed, characters were bound to clash.

Kitchener knew nothing of Indian history or conditions. On the other hand, he knew a great deal about the organisation of armies wherever they were. From the first he strongly objected to the system by which the executive control of the army in India was vested in the Commander-in-Chief, with the administrative control left in the hands of the Government of India itself, acting through the Military Member, then Major-General Sir Edmund Elles, who like the C.-in-C. had a seat on the Council. His objection was partly due to his own autocratic nature, but partly also because it led to a ridiculous and wasteful bureaucracy. For example, the military department and the Commander-in-Chief's department sat in the same building—and wrote each other some 10,000 letters a year. Again, Kitchener had demanded that a reserve of 500 rounds of ammunition per man should be maintained for troops designated as a striking force: this was discussed between the two departments for 15 months. For a time Curzon attempted to keep the peace, but after he had been, quite properly, thwarted in his policies in Afghanistan and Tibet, his patience grew thin. So did Kitchener's.

It was actually while Curzon was on leave in England in the summer of 1904 that Kitchener, who had long been writing by the 'back-door' to his friends in the Home Government, sent a memorandum to the Committee of Imperial Defence condemning the system of military administration in India, and urging that a great part of the functions of the Military Member should be transferred to the Commander-in-Chief. According to Lord Ronaldshay, Curzon had been invited to a meeting of the Defence Committee where this memorandum was circulated. He at once objected to it as being *ultra vires* because it concerned not Indian defence but the controversial question of Indian administration.

Balfour withdrew the memorandum. Kitchener then promptly resigned and, in order to get him to withdraw his resignation, the Cabinet proposed to Curzon—now back in India—that a committee should be sent out to settle the whole question of military control, in conference between him and Kitchener. To this proposal Curzon did not reply.

Meanwhile, with Kitchener's serious charges against the military department's lack of preparedness before him, Curzon clashed head on with Kitchener in Council. At this stage, a Cabinet committee was set up to consider the situation which was becoming intolerable. It was unanimously decided that the dispute be settled by making the Commander-in-Chief master in his own house with full control of purely military questions and confining the Military Member to supply.

This was embodied in the form of a despatch to the Government of India dated May 31. It came as a thunderbolt to Curzon, but even now he sought to struggle against the inevitable. He attempted to exceed his powers in appointing General Sir Edmund Barrow—a noted enemy of Kitchener—to a new military post in the Council over the heads of the Cabinet at home, but the Cabinet refused to be dragooned. He even attempted to enlist Kitchener in the struggle for Indian autonomy against the Cabinet. He telegraphed to London saying that Kitchener was in agreement with him; Kitchener himself, however, stated that so far from agreeing to anything, he had left the room because the Viceroy was in a state of collapse.

Apart from the increasing wildness of Curzon's communications to the Cabinet, he made several speeches showing his disloyalty to the Home Government. Some of these are reported by his biographer, Lord Ronaldshay. On one of them, Balfour commented to the King on July 19, 1905, that it was 'deplorable in taste and temper; and that no such public exhibition of disloyalty to the Home Government has ever yet been made by an Indian Viceroy. Mr. Balfour looks forward to the development of the incident with the gravest anxiety. Sir Herbert Fowler' (Secretary for India in Rosebery's Cabinet) 'is understood to be so indignant with the Viceroy's conduct that he means to press the attack to the utmost; and how the Government are effectively to defend against an unanswerable charge one who has left no means unused, legitimate or illegitimate, to defeat their policy, it is difficult to see. On personal, even more than on public grounds, Mr. Balfour is deeply grieved.'

A few days later Balfour complains to the King that Curzon's and Kitchener's accounts of Indian military reform are totally at variance:

'Neither of these eminent men can be said to emerge from the controversy with any credit whatever. But as they have come to a working agreement and as this agreement leaves untouched the essence of the proposals which, largely in consequence of Lord Kitchener's views, the Government have pressed on the Viceroy, it seemed to the Cabinet that "least said soonest mended" and they therefore resolved not to make more bad blood even by the most legitimate condemnation of the tone which the Viceroy has thought fit to adopt in his recent utterances.'

Even at this late stage Balfour, believing mistakenly that the breach had been healed, was evidently anxious to avoid a final rupture. But on August 10, 1905, Knollys informed Balfour that 'as regards Curzon, he (the King) is afraid he is beginning to think he had better resign. It is evident that he will now never get on with the Home Government and the attempt to appoint Sir E. Barrow shows and accentuates his position towards Brodrick'.

A few days later Curzon resigned, and his resignation was accepted. In the letter previously quoted, the King had suggested that Lord Ampthill, the Governor of Madras, who had been acting Viceroy during Curzon's leave in England, should be appointed as his successor. The Cabinet disagreed and would have preferred Milner who refused. They then appointed Lord Minto recently returned from being Governor-General of Canada. This refusal of his nominee led to unpleasantness between the King and his Prime Minister, as, so one gathers from Esher's letter to Knollys, did the Government's publication of the correspondence between Curzon and Brodrick on the appointment of Barrow in the form of a White Paper. This was done in self-defence, since both Kitchener and Curzon were busy issuing statements to the press.

Esher felt that Balfour and his Cabinet had been extremely remiss in not keeping His Majesty informed and in not seeking the King's authority before action was taken. This is reflected in a letter from the King's Secretary to Sandars on September 9, 1905. He points out that 'the Government condoned Curzon's shortcomings respecting Tibet and Afghanistan by sending him back to India, and on the other points by declining to accept his resignation in June (I think) and that they knew before he returned that they and he disagreed on the question of the Military Member of the Council. . . . I confess I cannot admit that he was, as you say, "practically dismissed". Surely if there had been any question of that, Brodrick would not have telegraphed to him on August 13, that he had received his telegram of resignation with the "deepest regret". . . . As regards your reference to Minto and him, one really cannot put the two men in any way on the same level. It would be like coupling Pitt with Perceval.'

Balfour himself was still mystified, and certainly saddened, in

October for he wrote to Sandars on October 20, 1905: 'It is a wretched world and I really cannot get to the bottom of the Kitchener-Curzon squabble.   K. distinctly declares that G.C. is a liar: G.C. with very little circumlocution indicates that his opinion of K. may be similarly expressed.   Barrow's evidence certainly goes to show that K. did not behave straightforwardly about the appointment of the new Military Member, and G.C. writes to me in the most positive manner that in no single particular has he misrepresented K.!   I do not easily think ill of mankind but, upon my word, these two old friends of mine are gradually compelling me to take a very dark view of our poor fallen nature.'

Nor did Balfour's personal troubles with Curzon end with Curzon's resignation.   Balfour received a telegram from Knollys on September 1, 1905, saying: 'The King desires me to inform you that he thinks Viceroy of India should be offered an Earldom and at once.   He hopes that considering Viceroy of India's character such an offer made immediately might soothe his feelings.'   Knollys returned to the charge a few days later pointing out that Curzon must be given an honour since he is regarded as a demi-god by the natives; otherwise it would look as if Kitchener had turned him out.

Balfour replied to Knollys on October 7, 1905, that Curzon certainly deserves an honour and his differences with the Government did not cancel his claim.   But: 'It would never do so to time this public recognition of his services as to suggest that it was in the remotest degree connected with his action in the Curzon-Kitchener dispute.   In that dispute he was (as I think) in the wrong.   It would be absurd to take a step which would be universally interpreted as meaning that I believed him to be in the right.   Such a course would moreover be extremely unfair both to Brodrick and Kitchener, whose feelings I am bound to consider as well as Curzon's or my own.'   He suggested that decision should be postponed till January or February.   For, he asked, what would happen if, as seemed likely, Curzon publicly pursued the controversy on his return from India?   If Balfour offered Curzon a peerage, it would then appear as though he had attempted to close his mouth.

The King understood Balfour's points, and (Knollys told Balfour) sent the following message to Curzon: 'I cannot but hope that on your return you may consider it advisable in the interests of the British Empire at large, and especially as regards India, not to enter into any further controversy regarding the different issues with my Government which compelled you to resign, as the effect would be very serious. It is always inadvisable to wash one's dirty linen in public.'   According to a letter from Knollys to Balfour on February 24, 1906, he did not return a very satisfactory answer to the King's letter.   Certainly 'all the private letters that reach this country show that he was, right up to the moment of departure from India, bitterly hostile to the India Office and its late Chief'.

Nevertheless, Curzon took the King's advice and kept silent after his return to England. By this time Balfour and his Government were out of office, and when Balfour approached his successor, Sir Henry Campbell-Bannerman, on the question of a peerage for Curzon, the Liberal Pime Minister declined to submit his name.

These, then, were the real reasons why Balfour did not put Curzon's name forward for an honour—reasons accepted as valid by the King. The letters quoted show that Lord Ronaldshay was incorrect in suggesting that Balfour refrained from offering a peerage because he knew that Curzon would refuse any honour on his recommendation. There was no 'deliberate silence' from Balfour, as Ronaldshay suggests, when the King desired to confer a peerage on Curzon. Curzon who, on being appointed Viceroy, had accepted an Irish peerage with a view eventually to returning to the Commons, was in 1907 elected as an Irish Representative Peer to the House of Lords.

For Balfour the affair was one of unalloyed misery, and its culmination came at a time when his Government itself was hanging by a thread. In one way he blamed himself for the final events. He told Brodrick once, with others present, that the greatest mistake of his political life was to allow Curzon to return to India after his home leave in 1904. For Curzon, during that leave and deeply afflicted by his wife's grave illness, was clearly at breaking-point. Yet how difficult, politically and personally, such a decision would have been! Certainly the matter weighed in Balfour's mind for years; late in his life, when it seemed unlikely that he would complete his autobiography, he asked Brodrick to set down the facts. Brodrick did so in his *Records and Reactions, 1856 to 1939*, and, though himself the most abused member of the Cabinet, he does so fairly.

Kitchener was a devious, unpleasant man; Curzon was grievously unstable. But it was not, as we have seen, just the affair with Kitchener that caused Curzon's downfall. The fact that Curzon had personal friends in the Cabinet merely exacerbated the unpleasantness; whatever Kitchener's influence through his friendship with Lady Salisbury, it can scarcely be said to have been greater than Curzon's with the Cabinet. 'Favouritism', if it had existed, would have helped Curzon more than Kitchener. John Morley, who succeeded Brodrick at the India Office in the administration that followed Balfour's, had publicly lamented the 'surrender to Kitchener' two months before. But in January, 1906, he told Brodrick: 'I have read all your papers and I told the Cabinet today that I would not have stood from Curzon for two months what you have stood for two years.'

But, for Balfour, it was not the last of Curzon.   A yet unhappier incident occurred 20 years later.

IV

Balfour has frequently been accused of dropping friends from Government office when they came under public rebuke; it has been offered as a further example of his 'coldness'.   There was an incident in 1903 when W. Hayes Fisher, formerly Balfour's Parliamentary Private Secretary and then Financial Secretary to the Treasury, resigned after a firm of which he was a director was condemned in court by Mr. Justice Buckley.   Fisher was certainly innocent of any dishonourable action: but he asked for Balfour's advice and Balfour suggested that he had better resign.

Much more criticism of Balfour arose out of the Wyndham affair. Wyndham had taken over the Irish Secretaryship in the Cabinet reshuffle of 1900 when the previous occupant, Gerald Balfour, became President of the Board of Trade.   Under Balfour's influence, he had pushed ahead with a Land Purchase Act which, by means of a large contribution from the State, bridged the gap between what tenants could pay and landlords could afford to accept.   Incidentally, the scheme, which became law in 1903, worked perfectly down to as late as 1932.

Shortly before the Bill was formulated, however, the then Under-Secretary in Ireland—that is, the permanent head of the Irish administration—resigned, and Wyndham believed that the only person who could take his place and work out this most intricate piece of legislation was a distinguished Indian Civil Servant, who also happened to be an Irishman, Sir Anthony MacDonnell.   But MacDonnell was a Roman Catholic and known to be a convinced Home Ruler.   Balfour warned Wyndham that the appointment 'would excite the most violent suspicion among your friends; that everything you did against the Orange extremists would be put down to his advice; while even the most rigorous action you might take against the Nationalists, would, on his account, he regarded as mere tinkering and compromise'.   Similar advice came also from Lansdowne, himself an Irish landlord.

MacDonnell's work on the Bill gave the greatest satisfaction.   Then the troubles began.   An Irish Peer, Lord Dunraven, who had assembled a conference of landowners and chiefs of the Nationalist Party as a prelude to the Bill, now formed a non-party association to promote 'devolution', under which some measure of control over finance and legislation would pass from Westminster to Dublin.   Although the scheme lacked Government approval, MacDonnell provided much information for the purposes of what was called the 'Irish Reform

Association', and even drafted part of the scheme himself—on Dublin Castle notepaper. The Northern Ireland Unionists heard of the scheme and at once made their alarm known. It subsequently turned out that MacDonnell had in fact twice written to Wyndham mentioning his co-operation with Lord Dunraven, but he had inserted these references towards the end of long letters full of administrative detail. Wyndham, then greatly overworked, had not apparently read to the end.

At the same time, it is now known that MacDonnell earlier than this had been dissatisfied with Wyndham's attitude and had written over his head to Knollys, with the intention of bringing it to the eye of the King. On March 16, 1904, for example, MacDonnell wrote to Knollys mentioning that there was deep dissatisfaction with the Government over the university question and saying that Wyndham's statement in the House of Commons was felt to close the door completely to the 'reasonable satisfaction' of Roman Catholics. Significantly, Knollys sent this letter to Sandars suggesting that it was *not* shown to Wyndham.

Again in November, 1904, during the Unionist agitation against him, MacDonnell wrote to Knollys who quite properly passed this letter on to Balfour. Sandars replied: 'I don't know that Sir Anthony's conduct in writing to you—no doubt for the King's information—is held by Mr. Balfour to be in accordance with the best tradition of the Civil Service. He should have been content to put his case in Mr. Wyndham's hand.'

Rumours now began to fly that the Government was seriously considering something not far from Home Rule. Conservative Members were outraged. Sandars wrote to Balfour on September 16, 1904, asking him for a public announcement on the subject of Home Rule, 'for what with the irritation caused by MacDonnell, and now this devolution scheme of Dunraven's, there has sprung up a sense of uneasiness among our own men.'

It was Wyndham who rose in the Commons on February 16, 1905, to repudiate MacDonnell's action in supporting the Irish Reform Association. MacDonnell then disassociated himself from the proceedings of the Association, but could not be persuaded to leave his post and return to India. Ulster men, some Conservatives and the Irish Nationalists combined to raise a hue and cry. They demanded—and continued to demand for the next 18 months—the publication of Wyndham's letters to MacDonnell, and this Balfour steadily refused, though as Wyndham said there was nothing damaging in them, except the appointment itself.

In March, 1905, Wyndham's nerve began to give out and he asked Balfour to accept his resignation. This was not the first time. On

January 28, 1905, he had written saying that he knew he had 'become an element of weakness in the Government' and offering resignation. In March, however, Balfour accepted, because, it has been said, he had not the courage to stand by one of his Ministers who had got into trouble, however little the trouble was of his own making. This is untrue. Winston Churchill wrote in his study of Balfour in *Great Contemporaries* in 1937 that 'those nearest and dearest to George Wyndham declared that the Prime Minister backed him with the whole of his strength, that he refused time after time to allow him to resign, and that it was only when, in the end, Wyndham's health and nerves completely broke down under the varied stresses, and at the entreaty of his wife and family, heavily backed by the doctors, that Balfour finally accepted his resignation'. Austen Chamberlain, then Balfour's right-hand man, said 'I know what it cost him to part with Hayes-Fisher and Wyndham.'

It was said at the time—and has been repeated parrot-fashion by certain 'historians'—that Balfour was as responsible as Wyndham and ought also to have resigned. But there is a letter, previously unpublished, among the Balfour Papers from Wyndham to Balfour dated September 1, 1906 in which Wyndham writes: 'It is more to the point that both you and Lansdowne warned me that the appointment might get me into trouble. That I offered, to both of you, to "stand the racket".' Against this specific undertaking on Wyndham's part, there can be no possible slur on Balfour; and it is typical of Balfour that, despite the gossip and calumny spread against this incident by his opponents, he never for a moment thought of publishing this letter.

The clamour followed him into Opposition. Wyndham himself gives the reason for it in a letter dated September 15, 1906: 'This clamour originates with Irish Unionists, and their sympathizers in England, chiefly in London. They want two things. First to attack and misrepresent all that was *good* in my Irish policy, and second they want to damage you.'

The letters between Wyndham and MacDonnell were published after Balfour's death (*Quarterly Review*, January, 1932) and proved his point. Balfour himself regarded the whole business as typical of the lunatic fringe of politics. He wrote to Wyndham on September 5, 1906: 'I do not deny that I am greatly bored at this foolish revival of a foolish controversy (over MacDonnell). I am afraid it will do some harm and, contemptible as I think the charges against Members of the late Cabinet in connection with MacDonnell's appointment and the Dunraven Scheme, I would gladly bring them to an end if I saw a way to doing so.... I think we are all very ill-used at having to deal with this silly and sordid controversy when we are not being paid £5,000 a year for our labours.'

A month later the MacDonnell 'mystery', so-called, was reopened by what Sandars in a letter dated October 7, 1906, referred to as 'a malevolent cabal', led by Wyndham's successor as Irish Secretary, 'honest and simple' Walter Long as Sandars sneeringly refers to him. This was one of the first hints of a movement against Balfour's leadership which was to lead to his resignation from the leadership of the Party five years later.

For Wyndham, this was the end of his political career. But he remained Balfour's devoted friend until the end of his life, which as we have seen came prematurely as the fortune-teller had foretold. Neither his sister, Lady Wemyss, nor his mother Mrs. Percy Wyndham, ever harboured a sense of reproach against Balfour.

Before turning to the rapidly tangling affairs at home and not least within the Cabinet, the signing of the Anglo-French Convention in 1904 must be recorded. It was one of the shining achievements of Balfour's Government. Balfour as always took the major decisions, but more than usual of the discussions were left to Lansdowne. As we have seen, Balfour resented the suggestion that King Edward had been the moving spirit in the agreement. But to the King's real part in cementing the *entente*, Balfour paid powerful tribute in his speech on the death of the King in the Commons in 1910. It would be, he said, to belittle the King to 'suppose he took upon himself duties commonly left to his servants'. Balfour continued: 'We must not think of him as a dexterous diplomatist—he was a great Monarch; and it was because he was able naturally, simply through the incommunicable gift of personality, to make all feel, to embody for all men, the friendly policy of this country, that he was able to do a work in the bringing together of nations which has fallen to the lot of few men, be they Kings, or be they subjects, to accomplish. He did what no Minister, no Cabinet, no Ambassadors, neither treaty, nor protocols, nor understandings, no debates, no banquets, and no speeches were able to perform. He by his personality, and by his personality alone, brought home to the minds of millions on the Continent, as nothing he could have done would have brought home to them, the friendly feeling of the country over which King Edward ruled.'

The *entente* with France, along with Britain's new alliance with Japan, firmly and finally ended the long policy of isolation. Britain now had serious commitments in Europe. Though, as we have seen, military talks were begun during Balfour's Premiership, the convention by no means implied a military alliance. Indeed, there were in 1905 good reasons to think that such an alliance would be of little use. In March that year the German Emperor personally intervened in Morocco, and caused fear and trembling in France. France's military deficiencies were revealed with startling frankness in a debate in the

French Chamber.   One result was that Delcassé, the French Foreign
Minister and the builder of the *entente*, was forced out of office.
Balfour wrote to the King on June 8, 1905: 'Mr. Balfour pointed out
(in Cabinet) that M. Delcassé's dismissal or resignation under pressure
from the German Government displayed a weakness on the part of
France which indicated that she could not at present be counted on as
an effective force in international politics.   She could no longer be
trusted not to yield to threats at the critical moment of negotiation.
If, therefore, Germany is really desirous of obtaining a port on the coast
of Morocco, and if such a proceeding be a menace to our interests, it
must be to other means than French assistance that we must look for
our protection.'

Balfour did not doubt the necessity for the reorientation of British
policy.   Yet he sometimes felt the need of discussing the ramifications
of such major change.   Lansdowne was too deeply involved to see
matters afresh, and Balfour would often discuss the deeper issues with
Salisbury, the fourth Marquess, President of the Board of Trade in
Balfour's Cabinet.   Salisbury was not entirely convinced that the
trend of events was happy.   In a letter to Balfour on November 9,
1905, he referred to a recent speech in which Lansdowne had declared
that Britain had abandoned the policy of isolation not only in Asia but
also in Europe, and that the Japanese and the French agreements
had carried this change of policy into effect.   Salisbury writes: 'Circumstances no doubt have driven us in respect to France further than we
intended. . . .   I recognise that in certain eventualities our diplomatic
understanding with France might develop into a military alliance, but
that I should regret and should avoid it as long as possible. . . .'   Salisbury thought it would be a pity to estrange Germany; but he saw clearly
that the French agreement 'was in its inception not a departure from
our previous foreign policy, but strictly in accordance with it'.   This
was, indeed, from one point of view strictly true since the alliance with
France re-established the equilibrium of Europe, which had been disturbed when Russia was defeated in the war with Japan.   She was
thus no longer of value to her ally, France, who as a result lay at the
mercy of Germany.   That a Salisbury should see that the equilibrium
in Europe so long held by a Salisbury was being restored by the French
alliance may well have given added assurance to Balfour.

V

Austen Chamberlain listed three major achievements of Balfour's
Premiership which he carried through 'by his own force of will' and
which stood the test of time: Committee of Imperial Defence, Education
Act, and—somewhat surprisingly—the Licensing Law reform of 1904.

This reform was a case, says Ensor, of 'grasping the nettle', just as the Education Act had been; it is also a fine example of Balfour's gift for drafting durable legislation. Again in this case, he drafted it himself; as Austen Chamberlain says: 'That the Bill was wholly his work I can testify, for I was a member of the Cabinet Committee appointed to draft a Bill, and the draft which the Committee produced bore no resemblance to Balfour's scheme which replaced it.'

Throughout the nineteenth century there had been constant agitation to prevent the undoubted evils that alcohol can bring by closing public houses—a mistaken judgement on cause and effect, as the United States experiment showed. But it was generally agreed that in some places—particularly those whence there had been great movements of population consequent upon industrial development—there were too many licensed premises. But if some of these licenses were withdrawn, ought not compensation to be paid? This was the point on which there was no agreement, the proposal to compensate from public funds being fiercely attacked. A deadlock had arisen. Balfour saw that compensation was just, since hard cash had in the first place being paid for the properties; but to avoid controversy on using public funds for compensation, he proposed that it should come from a fund levied on the trade itself, on the theory that the closing of particular public houses in an area meant that those remaining increased in value by getting the trade which formerly went to those abolished. For all that, Balfour's Bill was attacked as endowing the trade and being a 'brewers' bill'. Nothing could have been less true. The public houses that escaped closure would not necessarily attract the surplus trade; in any case one object of the Bill was to bring about less drinking. Nevertheless, the brewers accepted the situation, and the Bill worked well for over 30 years.

To Opposition attacks, Balfour replied effectively that the Temperance Reformers did not help their cause by coupling it with injustice. Lloyd George suggested that Balfour had brought in the Bill for the special benefit of a corrupt section of his supporters in East Manchester, his chairman of committee there being a leading representative of the liquor trade. It was a silly suggestion; even the most dogmatic Radical knew that Balfour was not merely incorruptible but a man whom no one would ever remotely dream of attempting to corrupt. As Ensor, by no means a pro-Conservative historian remarks, Balfour was 'one of the purest characters in front bench politics': the breath of scandal, unjustly no doubt, fell upon Joseph Chamberlain and upon Law, and not least upon Lloyd George himself but never upon Balfour. It is one of the many advantages of hereditary wealth that it makes its possessors in public life impervious to corruption as to dubious 'pressure' groups—a fact overlooked by those Radicals and levellers who seek to impose swingeing death duties.

VI

During the autumn and winter of 1904–5, Balfour suffered much from a series of feverish colds, and once from an attack of phlebitis. (Donald Tovey, said by Joachim to be the most learned man in music who ever lived, beguiled Balfour's convalescence by playing Bach and Beethoven to him.)   Balfour was 56, though he seems to have had no particular consciousness of growing older (except, as we saw, in the sense that he no longer felt it incumbent upon him to marry); he was still spare and upright, the moustache somewhat fuller and tinged, like his hair with silver grey, the side-boards now less long, the eyes still the most remarkable feature: that curious, indrawn melancholy more evident than ever, at least in repose.   His physical life was healthy; there was golf and cycling in the recesses, although motoring—he never drove himself—attracted him a great deal; he had a gift for calm, unaided sleep, and the ability to turn his mind to philosophical speculation and reading in his hours of freedom: 'Though exceptionally hard-worked in the region of public affairs,' he writes to Pringle-Pattison during one of his heavy colds, 'my close confinement has given me enough leisure to look more or less perfunctorily, through Dewey's book' (presumably John Dewey's *Studies on Logical Theory*, published in 1903) 'some of Schiller's Essays, and the articles in this quarter's *Mind*. . . .'

But undoubtedly politics were beginning to pall.   This does not alter the truth of Chamberlain's observation that, whatever the impression Balfour sometimes gave and subsequent commentators have sometimes accepted, 'from the time when he became Chief Secretary for Ireland, politics became his ruling passion to which, in the measure which their pursuit made necessary, he was prepared to, and in fact did, subordinate all others'.   Nevertheless, Balfour was a man who might have a surfeit even of a 'ruling passion'; and he did not fear being out of office—there was much he meant to do that could only be done when he was freed of government.   Thus he wrote to Joseph Chamberlain on November 2, 1905:

'I do not mean to have another session like the last one.   In the middle of August I thought my weariness of office might be attributed to mere physical fatigue.   But it is not so.   I have had my holiday; am perfectly well and cheerful; but I find that ten years of leading the House of Commons has given me an unutterable desire for change, and I never go upstairs to bed without thanking Heaven that, in a very brief period, I shall have left my official residence and gone back to the comfort and repose of my own house.'

There was evidently little doubt in his mind that the Conservatives would not be returned to power.   His Cabinet limped and would not long hold together; Balfour, as Austen Chamberlain said, *was* the Cabinet in its last 18 months.   The country was no longer behind him, nor was it particularly interested in the Government's fortunes.   Nevertheless, though his main achievements had been satisfactorily settled into law, he did not mean to go down without a fight.   Sandars told him that the forecast of the next Budget was not a 'rosy one', and added that 'it provides no inducement for struggling to remain in office'.   That did not mean, however, that he would softly pad away—not least because as a statesman, rather than as a politician, he feared the advent of the Liberals to power.

On the other hand, he did not mean to compromise what might be called his own compromise on the matter still bedevilling his own party: the question of tariff reform.   He writes to Sir Joseph Lawrence, a Conservative M.P. and tariff reformer, on October 26, 1905: 'Now, as ever, a considerable section of the Party are protectionist in the true sense of the word.   On this point, the Party have not agreed for 60 years.   Personally, I am not a protectionist, and it would be neither right, nor fair, to pretend that I was.'

He wanted to avoid any imputation that he was bringing in protection by the back door.   He writes to his brother, Gerald (who had followed Long at the Local Government Board when Long succeeded Wyndham as Irish Secretary) on November 10, 1905:

'Not only am I reluctant to put forward on the platform detailed plans of fiscal change, but I view with some apprehension any pledge to put a general import duty upon manufactured goods.   It is quite true that, if revenue had to be raised, such a duty would be quite consistent with my economic views.   But, surely, if we were to announce it when the necessity for additional revenue is not demonstrated, the universal inference would be that the tax was put on, not to raise revenue, but because it would afford some protection to manufacturers; while if I were to supplement the proposed declaration of policy, as I should have to do, with a statement that such injury to the agricultural consumer as this import duty might inflict would be made good to him by using the proceeds of the tax to relieve his rates, should I not go near to Joe's methods of bribing each class of the country in turn?'

Chamberlain, equally, stuck to his point, and complained to Balfour that members of the Government attacked him, thus sowing dissension. 'I wish', he wrote to Balfour on November 4, 1905, 'that members of the Government who are most opposed to me, Londonderry, Stanley, (Postmaster-General, later Earl of Derby) and Brodrick, could be induced to leave me out of their speeches.   They might state their own views without forcing me into personal conflict' (struck out) 'controversy.'

Gerald Balfour had his own problems at this time.   There had been serious unemployment in 1904 and there was a recurrence in the

autumn of 1905.   Gerald Balfour's Unemployed Workmen Act had
been passed in August, 1905, giving his Local Government Board
authority to establish unemployment committees in any locality
where needed.   These new bodies were to keep a register of unemployed and could, at the cost of the rates, establish Labour Exchanges,
assist emigration or removal, and even, in some places, acquire land for
farm-colonies.   But they might not spend anything by way of wages or
maintenance unless the cost was defrayed by voluntary generosity.

In October, 1905, Sandars reported to Balfour that petitions were
already being sent to the King on account of distress among the unemployed.   Sandars continues: 'The Home Office tell me that while
there is no more distress than last year—on the contrary employment is
a *little* better—there is to be much more activity among the agitators.
The Social Democratic organisation is busy—their aims are political—
they see a general election in sight, and they mean to demonstrate their
power.   The Metropolitan Police expect some trouble this winter with
the organised forces.'

An appeal for funds was issued to the public in November, headed by
Queen Alexandra, who wished to take an active part in the matter.
Gerald Balfour wrote to his brother on November 18, 1905: 'I hope you
may be able to say something to dissuade the Queen from trying to
interfere with the delicate machinery of administration.   So far as I
can judge, her only idea of assistance to the unemployed is by way of
doles.'

The newly awakening working classes, incidentally, provided apt
material for a pre-election stunt by the Liberals.   This arose out of the
fact that Milner, British High Commissioner in South Africa, had in
1903 asked the Cabinet to agree to the employment of cheap Chinese
labour in the Rand gold mines in Transvaal.   After some heart-search-
ing the Cabinet agreed that indentured Chinese coolies should be
brought into South Africa on a three-year contract.   These contracts
were entered upon voluntarily.   But, owing to local objections, the
Chinese were to live throughout their period of service in large com-
pounds with no society but their own.   The Opposition at once raised
the cry of 'slavery'.

The matter was then allowed to drop until about the middle of the
year 1905 when effective use of it was made in by-elections.   Liberal
speakers appealed to the British working classes by suggesting that here
was an example of the Conservative Government regarding labour
purely as a commodity—a point upon which Socialists felt strongly.
Milner further added to the flames by an injudicious statement—a
'bad business' Balfour dubbed it, writing to Lyttelton—for which,
however, Milner wished to take full responsibility. Sir Henry
Campbell-Bannerman pledged himself that, if he took office after the

elections, he would stop the 'slavery'. (He swiftly discovered reasons for not doing so and even repudiated the use of the word 'slavery' in this connection.) But, as was intended, the damage had been done to the Conservative Government.

Long before the end of 1905, Balfour had conferred with his colleagues about the need for departing, about which few of them had any doubts, and also about the manner of their departure, on which there were divided opinions. Balfour was for resigning rather than dissolving because the first course would involve the Liberals in taking over and producing a policy before going to the polls. Balfour explained his point of view to Chamberlain on 2 November 1905:

'Controversy begins in connection with the proposal to resign, or to dissolve, in this autumn. For my own part I should have liked this course (i.e. resignation), not merely because on personal grounds, I am very anxious to get out of office, but because the chapter of accidents is always *against* a Government and while some untoward event might cause us fresh embarrassment, it is beyond the ordinary range of possibility that any event, either at home or abroad, would add to our strength.

'It would be perfectly constitutional for me to say on the first Amendment to the Address on which I receive inadequate support that I did not think that I could under these circumstances, with advantage, attempt dealing with so large a problem as Redistribution, the principal measure of the Session. I should in that event resign; C.B. would form his Government, announce his programme, and dissolve. I may say (of course in the strictest confidence) that the King, who would, I think, greatly dislike an unmotived resignation or dissolution, is quite prepared for this course.

'There is no suggestion here of "riding for a fall'. I am confident that a sufficient *approach* to a fall will come without any riding at all. . . .

'You may perhaps think I exaggerate the advantage of resignation, and I quite agree that the broad result of an election is not likely to be profoundly modified by any difficulties the other side may have in framing either a Government or a policy. But these difficulties are real and great, and they are increased by personal differences and jealousies, which will make the next Cabinet an eminently unfriendly collection of friends. I should infinitely prefer getting them "into the open" before the fight begins.'

Balfour knew that defeat was coming; it might still be possible to start the victors off on the wrong foot. With this idea of tactics Chamberlain disagreed, and so a little later in the month, on November 26, 1905, and from another angle, did the King who wrote that he could not 'help regretting that Mr. Balfour should not have abandoned his idea of resignation, and that he should not have instead decided on meeting Parliament'. He added that, of course, as 'a Constitutional Sovereign' it was not for him to advise. As late as December 2, 1905, Balfour reported to the King that the Cabinet was still not unanimous on the question of resignation or dissolution.

In the end, Balfour's view prevailed. He resigned on December 4, 1905, and Campbell-Bannerman—despite his followers' advice to refuse office—became Prime Minister and formed a Cabinet. Nor did the fact that Campbell-Bannerman went to the polls next month in January, 1906, without a policy at all affect the issue in the least. This election, which ended almost 20 years of Conservative domination, was the greatest cataclysm in the Party's history. A Government that had begun life in 1900 with a majority of some 130 now found itself in Opposition with only 157 seats all told.

On the eve of the poll, Balfour wrote from the Queen's Hotel, Manchester, to Lady Elcho: 'I doubt my getting in tomorrow.' His doubts were justified. He was defeated by 2,000 votes. His brother Gerald and his friend, Alfred Lyttelton, were among others defeated. Birmingham alone, still dominated by the magic of Chamberlain, held firm and in fact increased its Unionist strength, though the surrounding areas defected. Cheshire, a Conservative county, returned not a single Unionist member. In the whole of Wales, not one Conservative was returned. Conservatives, although many of them had expected defeat, were appalled by the extent of it. 'The most sober and careful electioneers on our side have been completely out,' Balfour wryly remarked to Salisbury on January 20, 1906; but he himself had forecast an 'unfavourable result' to Akers-Douglas.

The lasting achievements of Balfour's Premiership would not produce their true beneficial effects until years later; some of them by their very nature—the Committee of Imperial Defence for example—were not viable material for the hustings, while the Education Act was still a bone of contention, however irrelevant contention. That solid achievement, indeed, was a contributory factor in the defeat.

To the more positive causes of defeat—fiscal vacillations, the Labour vote, Chinese 'slavery' and the general dislike which all governments long in power accumulate—ought to be added one more: the decay of the Conservative Party organisation. This, of course, is a regular Conservative reproach after each electoral defeat; it is, just as regularly, justified. Between 1886 and about 1901, the National Union and the Conservative Central Office were linked together by Captain Middleton and he brought them up to be a model of technical efficiency, even though the National Union itself was hardly any longer a channel of communication between the Party leaders and their supporters in the country. Middleton lost interest in his organisations some years before he resigned in 1903; under his successor they began to deteriorate rapidly. As a writer in *The Times* put it some years later, 'the dissensions in the Unionist Party on policy before 1906 synchronized with a disintegration of the organisation'.

One of the most significant causes of defeat was the Labour vote. There had always been a good deal of working-class support for the Conservative Party, but this was lost at the election, as Salisbury observed to Balfour, partly because of the cry of 'food taxes', a piece of ammunition Chamberlain had gratuitously given the Opposition. But the rise of the Labour Party itself was an unpredicted factor. In the General Election of January, 1906, no less than 53 Labour Members were returned to the House of Commons; 24 of them were ordinary 'Lib-Labs', but 29 were returned under the Labour Representation Committee to sit as an Independent Party. Balfour wrote to Salisbury's wife, Alice—who had sent him a brief note, 'Damn. Damn. Damn.'—that: 'What has occurred has nothing whatever to do with any of the things we have been squabbling over the last few years. Campbell-Bannerman is a mere cork, dancing on a torrent which he cannot control, and what is going on here is a faint echo of the same movement which has produced massacres in St. Petersburg, riots in Vienna, and Socialist processions in Berlin.' To Austen Chamberlain he wrote, more prophetically still, that: 'I am profoundly interested in this new development, which will end, I think, in the break-up of the Liberal Party.' A day or two later he wrote to Knollys that, because of the appearance of this 'Fourth Party' (the Irish Nationalists being the Third Party), 'the election of 1906 inaugurates a new era'. Balfour, far from being dismayed, told Knollys that if this development had not occurred he would not have much minded leaving politics for good: 'but I am so profoundly interested in what is *now* going on' that he was glad to remain.

VII

It was while Balfour was sitting in his suite at the Queen's Hotel in Manchester during the pre-election days of January, 1906, that a momentous meeting took place. It had little or nothing to do with the electioneering then in progress; but Balfour, though he made some excellent speeches as the rain pelted down through the Manchester grime, had a remarkable gifts for withdrawing himself and turning his active, inquiring mind to some unconnected matter. This time it was to a subject that had long puzzled him, namely, the extraordinary coolness with which the Jewish Zionists, then persecuted in many parts of the world, particularly in Russia, had greeted the offer Chamberlain had made, and he had supported three years previously, for a Jewish settlement in Uganda, East Africa, under the British flag.

'Why', he said to his Chairman of Election Committee as he relaxed in his hotel, 'did not the Jews leap at such a chance?' The Chairman was himself a Jew, Dr. Charles Dreyfus, the head of a chemical dye works, and he now offered to bring before Balfour a man who could throw light on the matter. This was Chaim Weizmann, a Jewish refugee from Russia, at that time demonstrator in organic chemistry at Manchester University. Balfour, in fact, had met him for the first time almost exactly a year before, also in Manchester, after a mass-meeting. At that time, Weizmann, already a leading Zionist, wrote to his colleague, M. M. Ussishkin: 'We couldn't talk much, but he (Balfour) invited me to see him in London.' Dreyfus, he added, is 'pro-Palestine, and we could submit to Balfour and others a memorandum on our trade purposes . . . so we could *eo ipso* paralyse Greenberg and Co.' Greenberg and others thought that the East African offer ought not to have been rejected out of hand; Weizmann and his group believed that nothing less than Palestine would do for the home of Zionism.

No memorandum had been sent, and there was no meeting between Balfour and Weizmann in London. But on January 9, 1906, the two did meet and had a long conversation. In a letter to his wife later that day, Weizmann wrote: 'Balfour said he saw no political difficulty about obtaining Palestine, only economic ones. We also talked about territorialism—I tried to show him how impossible it is and promised to send him a memorandum.' It was, in fact, quite clear that Weizmann convinced Balfour that it was vain to seek a home for the Jewish people anywhere else but in Palestine. As Balfour told his niece shortly before his death: 'It was from that talk with Weizmann that I saw that the Jewish form of patriotism was unique. Their love of their country refused to be satisfied by the Uganda scheme. It was Weizmann's absolute refusal even to look at it that impressed me.'

Here was the embryo from which, 11 years later, the Balfour Declaration emerged. We shall trace the course of birth in a later chapter. There is, however, more to this meeting in the Queen's Hotel, Manchester, on January 9, 1906, than politics. It is clear from subsequent events and from the account given by Mrs. Dugdale, who herself knew Weizmann well, that as far as Balfour was personally concerned, the conversation was something more than just another of the endless interviews a Prime Minister has in the course of an election campaign. Dreyfus may have had in the back of his mind the thought that the meeting might be of immediate political value because in the next-door Manchester constituency, Winston Churchill, now a Liberal, was standing as a candidate and seeking to get support from the considerable number of Jewish electors. Not so Balfour. At this meeting some sort of immediate chemical fusion occurred; 'an unusual sympathy', as Mrs. Dugdale puts it, 'sprang up almost at first sight between . . . these two singularly magnetic personalities . . . widely separated by every material circumstance of life and tradition.'

It was not a purely personal matter: in that respect Balfour was singularly impervious to 'magnetism'. It was, as almost always with Balfour, an idea that sparked off his deepest feelings. Brought up on the Old Testament—by Evangelicals no less studied than the New—and believing that both the Christian religion and the civilised world owed great debts (in science as well as in philosophy) to the Jews, Balfour thought the debt had been 'shamefully ill-repaid'. Their unique position in the world and its history fascinated him. One of the daughters of Sir Anthony de Rothschild, Lady Battersea, who stayed at Whittingehame in 1895, recalled Balfour's inquiries about Claude Montefiore, 'about the Jews, alien immigration, synagogues'. Zionism, he later told Weizmann, 'is a great cause, and I understand it'.

For Balfour, however, Zionism represented more than an idea. His emotions also became deeply involved, a rare thing for him, and, as we shall see in a later chapter, his attitude to the whole Jewish question provides an insight into his very deepest psychological processes. It is made the more revealing by the fact that he was no idoliser of the Jews: his letter (p. 139) may be recalled when he humorously complained that he found it difficult to stomach a Jewish dinner party. He had even told Weizmann that he had once had a long talk with Cosima Wagner at Bayreuth and 'shared many of her anti-Semitic postulates'. (To which Weizmann replied: 'I pointed out that we, too . . . had drawn attention to the fact that Germans of the Mosaic persuasion were an undesirable and demoralising phenomenon, but said that we wholly disagreed with Wagner and [Houston Stewart] Chamberlain both as to diagnosis and prognosis.') He was certainly aware of the difficulties—and the violent antagonism towards a national home—of Jews assimilated into various nations, not least those in England, such as the Rothschilds whom he knew.

Moreover in 1904-5, he himself, as Prime Minister, had taken a very strong line on the question of alien immigration and had explained why he considered that the influx of Jews into Britain must be checked: 'A state of things could easily be imagined', he said in the Commons, 'in which it would not be to the advantage of this country that there should be an immense body of persons who, however patriotic, able and industrious, however much they threw themselves into the national life, remained a people apart, and not merely held a religion differing from the vast majority of their fellow-countrymen, but only intermarried among themselves'.

Balfour denounced anti-Semitism; but it was under his Premiership that the Aliens Bill restricting immigration passed into law in 1905 following the report of the Royal Commission on Alien Immigration set up in 1902. Thus, his attitude to the Jews was by no means un-complicated; it might even be called ambivalent. As Leonard Stein puts it, 'Seeing in the Jews a highly gifted race and believing that the qualities he admired in them, given a chance to express themselves, would contribute to the enrichment of civilisation, he was anxious that they should somehow be enabled to maintain their separate identity; yet because they possessed in a marked degree distinctive characteristics which in themselves commanded his respect, he was for that very reason uncertain and uncomfortable about their place in a Gentile society.' Yet, Stein adds, 'Of all the British statesmen responsible for the Declaration, none had so sensitive a grasp of the problem, none had probed into it so deeply, or had given it such anxious thought.'

For Balfour, the Jewish question was neither just another political problem nor even a special interest: it was a facet of his character.

12

IN OPPOSITION

Down but not Out, 1906–1909

When Conservative Members re-assembled in the House of Commons after the election in January, 1906, Balfour was not present: he had no seat. Furthermore his much-reduced party was both disconsolate and deeply divided. But Balfour returned from defeat with renewed zest, typically as ever a zest arising from his intellectual interest in the situation created by the Labour successes. He was determined from the outset and, as far as lay in his power, to heal the breach in the Conservative party and to start off the new session in a fighting spirit. Even before a seat had been found for him in the City of London by the withdrawal of the elected member, Alban Gibbs, and a by-election giving him a majority of over 11,000, Balfour had been having talks with Chamberlain.

Chamberlain wanted a meeting of the Conservative Party to discuss the future; to this Salisbury recommended Balfour not to agree in a letter on January 28, 1906. He said that: 'No attempt should be made to unite the Party by a formula designed to conceal their differences. I am afraid that policy has only led the electors to distrust us. They are stupid enough to suspect even verbal refinements. . . . I should announce the definite line in Parliament for the Party to take it or leave it.'

Balfour was a more skilful tactician. He agreed to Chamberlain's suggestion of a Party meeting, though, he explained, with reluctance. It would mean, he wrote, that 'all our differences would be dealt with in a manner which is certain to be published and will probably be irritating'. Moreover, what procedure was to be adopted? 'There is no case in history, so far as I am aware, in which a Party meeting has been summoned except to give emphasis and authority to a decision at which the Party have informally already arrived; still less is there an example to be found of a vote being taken at such a meeting. How then are we to proceed on the present occasion? Are you and I to agree upon some question on which the meeting can vote Aye or No? If so, what is this question to be and how is it to be formulated?' (As Robert MacKenzie has pointed out, Conservative Party Meetings were infrequently held and were no more than perfunctory: Party policy was always decided by a small coterie of leaders.)

Chamberlain replied that he thought the Party as a whole should be asked to express their opinion freely as to the best policy for the future, and if he and Balfour could come no nearer to agreement beforehand, they ought to be able to devise some means of putting their programmes before the meeting in a manner which would not be personal. Then Chamberlain, rather confusedly, adds: 'It will be clearly understood that the decision is not binding on the Leaders, or any of them, but is merely taken for information. . . . A vote after discussion in a thoroughly representative meeting would furnish all of us with a really valuable indication of what is practicable, as well as what is desirable.'

Balfour replied: 'It is clear that the members of the Party must have an opportunity of "blowing off steam" on any subject they like, and the two subjects which they would most like are certain to be fiscal reform and party organisation.' He then puts his finger on the crux of the matter: 'But is your idea of requiring them to choose between the Glasgow speech or the "Half sheet of notepaper" really practicable? If they choose the Glasgow speech, how can you refuse to become their Leader? If they reject the "Half sheet of Notepaper", how can I continue to lead them? There is something amounting to absurdity in asking a Party to give an opinion on an important question of policy, and, when it has given that opinion, perhaps against its titular leader, asking that leader to be good enough to continue his work on their behalf. This difficulty will not arise if the meeting occupies itself merely in hearing and expressing various opinions, if the difference between the Glasgow speech and the "Half Sheet of notepaper", is left an open question. But if, on the other hand, we take the course you propose, it seems to me that should the vote go against you, *your* position will not be made easier; should it go against me, *mine* will become impossible, and you will have to reconsider your decision to "refuse the Leadership under all circumstances".' (Chamberlain had already stated that there would be no question as to the leadership.)

Chamberlain took the point. Could they not, then, see whether their policies could not be closer aligned? In a letter to Balfour on February 10, 1906, he reminded him of his often-expressed conviction 'that after all the differences which appear to exist were only insignificant and academic. If that be true, we ought to be able to find a thoroughly satisfactory *modus vivendi*.'

There was no personal question between them; they are both ready to make sacrifices. 'Is it not possible now, in opposition, to remove this suspicion of dual aims and to give the Party a lead which will certainly be accepted by the great majority as an official policy while it will not exclude anyone who is not really irreconcilable?' Where he differed from Balfour, he said, was in what Balfour omitted to say rather than what he said. 'But above all—and this is serious—I object to the interpretations of what you have said by those who are, I think, more Balfour than Balfour himself.' Surely it would be possible to produce 'some kind of joint programme or declaration to which both of us can agree'. Such a declaration would be carried at any meeting of the Party 'by an immense majority'.

Balfour at this point began to feel that the discussion was going round in circles. Suggesting that a decision as to the exact course to be pursued at the Party meeting should be deferred until 'you have seen what I say tomorrow in the City', he adds:

'What that will be I do not myself yet know, in the sense of having prepared a speech, but it will be my first important utterance after the adverse decision of the constituencies.'

This must have reminded Chamberlain of the little girl who asked how was she to know what she was going to say until she had said it. Balfour's City speech turned out to be the old plea for not confounding expediency with principle. It moved hardly at all towards Chamberlain's position.

However, the Party meeting was arranged, and on its eve Austen Chamberlain drafted a letter to which Sandars made some additions. It was accepted by both Balfour and Chamberlain and published on February 14, 1906. Another letter was added by Chamberlain and the two together came to be known as the 'Valentine Letters', because of their day of publication. The letter which Balfour signed runs as follows:

'The controversy aroused by the fiscal question has produced, not unnaturally, an impression which I have constantly combatted, that the practical differences between fiscal reformers are much deeper than is in fact the case. The exchange of views which has recently taken place between us leads me to hope that this misconception may be removed and with it much friction which has proved injurious to the Party.

'My own opinion, which I believe is shared by the great majority of the Unionist Party, may be briefly summarised as follows: I hold that fiscal reform is, and must remain, the first constructive work of the Unionist Party. That the objects of such reform are to secure more equal terms of competition for British trade, and closer commercial union with the Colonies. That, while it is at present unnecessary to prescribe the exact methods by which these objects are to be attained and inexpedient to permit differences of opinion as to those methods which divide the Party, though other means may be possible, the establishment of a moderate general tariff on manufactured goods, not imposed for the purpose of raising prices or giving artificial protection against legitimate competition, and the imposition of a small duty on foreign corn, are not in principle objectionable, and should be adopted if shown to be necessary for the attainment of the ends in view or for purposes of revenue.'

There was enough here for Chamberlain to latch on to, and something like a concordat was arranged between the two leaders. This meant that there was now no need to ask the Party meeting to choose between the respective policies; as Balfour had always intended, it became simply an 'opportunity for blowing off steam'. The meeting was attended by some 650 Peers, M.P.s and—on Chamberlain's insistence—the defeated Conservative candidates. Balfour presided, and appealed for a 'united constructive policy'. The Duke of Devonshire complained that the Valentine Letters only achieved a compromise, and stated that he and his friends (i.e. the Free-Traders) would continue to act independently. At the end, a vote of confidence in Balfour's leadership was carried unanimously. Balfour may have been no great leader of men; but he was a master of tactics.

For the time being, the Party was quiescent. It was heartened also by the fact that Balfour went into the fight against the Liberal Education Act, which was meant to repeal most of his measures, 'like a warhorse'. During these spring days of 1906 'his manner and delivery were his very best, and his own men warmed behind him'. By the end of the year, however, the Whips and the party managers were again reporting dissatisfaction among Conservatives inside and outside the House of Commons. Milner, for example, although putting the dissatisfaction mildly, told Sandars that what Balfour wanted 'is a lieutenant such as Lord Salisbury had in Randolph and Lord Derby in Dizzy. He can't suggest a lieutenant to do the swashbuckling, but one is necessary. He thought Bonar Law would do—if (and it is a big if) he would be loyal.' He might have suggested the brilliant F. E. Smith, a newcomer to the House whose speeches—insulting, clever, vitriolic—impressed all hearers.

A few days later Sandars went more deeply into matters. The tariff reform movement is very active and is gaining financial strength. He tells Balfour that it has been guaranteed £10,000 a year for five years: '*On dit* that several Radical manufacturers have subscribed, being afraid of predatory Socialism and being keen on the possible advantages of a tariff.' Moreover, he says, 'with the exception of the *Daily Telegraph*, we have not a single organ of the London Press which would support the orthodox Party and its leader'. There has, he thinks, 'been a general weakening of your authority throughout the country. To this weakening, Austen and Long and Bonar Law, Maxse and Amery and others have contributed and are contributing. . . . George Curzon has designs of some kind—he is manœuvring for a seat in the House of Commons—but Hood cannot yet fix him with any responsibility beyond opposition to yourself.' Sandars is certain that tariff reform will capture the National Union in which Henry Chaplin, a former President of the Local Government Board, and others were active agents. He goes on:

'It is pointed out by the more ardent section that, since your letter of February 14 last year, nothing has been said, no public speeches have been made by you in furtherance of this—the first constructive test of the Unionist Party. They do not argue that you wish to go back on your words; they do say that the policy of fiscal reform does not fill your heart and mind; they argue that in a case where you are really and profoundly moved, as in the matter of education, you will fight, and fight hard, and spend the last ounce of your strength over it. And they contrast the matter in which you are interested with that which does not earn a speech, or part of a speech.'

(Here, certainly, Sandars was right.)

Sandars warned him, further, that for lack of such a speech, it was likely that the moderate men would drift away. For the moment Hood (Chief Conservative Whip) thinks that the 'mass of the Party are loyal to you and want to be loyal to you. (Of course, in this statement he does not include Maxse, Long and the minor mandarins.) They thoroughly appreciate your great services to the Party, your ripe experience and the extraordinary skill you exhibit in leading the Party in Parliament. But, says Hood, they are not proof against the blandishments of those who promise that they can sweep the country with a fiscal policy which will be of enormous national benefit, and they cannot be made to see that their chance will come sooner if only they will concentrate on the iniquities of the most vulnerable Government of modern times.' Hood, indeed, believes that the fortunes of the Party depend on Balfour's speaking on the fiscal question. Otherwise it may happen that our 'army' will by degrees melt away 'until anarchy is succeeded by a new authority'.

To this plain speaking, Balfour replied on January 24, 1907, that he has no intention of giving the Party a 'constructive policy' while in opposition. This merely sets up for their opponents the targets they require; he still believes that the real business of an Opposition is to oppose. It may well become necessary to point out that 'if the Party is to be destroyed—which can easily be done by either wing—the disloyal Tariff Reformers have at least as much to lose as anybody else. This is a policy only to be adopted in the last resort.'

TJB

In his speech a few days later at Hull, he developed his reasons for refusing to offer 'programmes while in Opposition', recalling that Gladstone's programme of social reform announced in 1891 was subsequently a source of great embarrassment to his Party.   He raised the polemical fiscal question on to a higher plane by pointing out that Britain depended entirely upon its manufactures and hence its relations to its trade rivals, world markets and 'the markets which are to be'.

Such fundamental conceptions were not likely to penetrate the fume and sweat of controversy raised by Tariff Reformers and Free-Fooders. It certainly did not still the slowly-rising insurrection.   In this same month Esher reports Balfour as being 'depressed at the dead set made against him in his Party'.   Again in October, 1907, Austen Chamberlain in a letter asks once more for a new pronouncement on tariff policy.   He also asks for a 'programme', for example a Conservative old-age pensions scheme to put up against the Liberal proposals on housing, and their land policy of purchase and ownership.

Three weeks later at the annual meeting of the National Union, Balfour specifically mentioned Chamberlain's points as being things to be worked for.   He put a little extra emphasis on preference, attacking the Government for throwing away opportunities recklessly at the Colonial conference.   His speech had its effect; the resolution that had been put down declaring war on the free-traders was not even formally discussed.   This meeting, at least, took to heart Balfour's plea for unity.   At this same meeting, incidentally, Balfour paid tribute to Joseph Chamberlain: he had recently had a stroke.   For all effective purposes he now moved off the political stage, though he kept his interest in politics and was occasionally to be heard advising from the wings.

Dissatisfactions against Balfour continued to seethe for the next four years, but they were to come to a head only after, and only partly as a result of, a series of events which were to overshadow tariff squabbles, as a great tree overshadows the squirrel in its branches, and which were to shake the foundations of the British Constitution.   The friction between Lords and Commons, which culminated in the Parliament Act of 1911, was no new thing.   There had been rumblings of discontent from the time when the first Reform Bill had been passed only under threat that the Crown would create enough new Peers to swamp the Conservative majority.   The difficulty arose because the Conservative Party had for long had a large majority in the Lords which could and did during Liberal Governments amend or veto bills of a radical nature that had been passed in the Commons by the Liberal majority.

A headlong clash was an ever-present possibility, though neither party wanted such a thing.   In April, 1906, Balfour wrote to Lansdowne, the Conservative Leader in the Lords, suggesting a tactful

procedure: 'I incline to advise that we should fight all points of difference very stiffly in the Commons, and should make the House of Lords
the theatre of compromise.   It is evident that *you* can never fight for a
position which *we* have surrendered; while, on the other hand, the fact
that we have strenuously fought for the position and been severely
beaten may afford adequate grounds for your making a graceful concession to the representative Chamber.'   This tact was duly exercised
by the Lords in accepting the Trades Disputes Bill, which relaxed the law
of conspiracy in respect of peaceful picketing and exempted trade union
funds from liability in Court actions for damages.   Neither Lansdowne nor Balfour were particularly happy about this Bill, but Balfour
in a speech on the third reading in November, 1906, asserted his belief
in the capacity of Englishmen to use exceptional powers with moderation.
He was more doubtful of the provision which extended the exemptions to
employers' associations.   He thought that combinations of employers
might prove as dangerous in the future as combinations of workmen.

The Education Bill was a different matter.   This was clearly an
attempt to overthrow his constructive legislation and upon quite
specious grounds.   Its object was to withdraw rate aid from denomina-
tional teaching: behind this was the Nonconformist desire to humiliate
the Church of England.   (The victorious Liberal majority of 1906
included no less than 200 Nonconformists.)   Balfour decided to fight;
his speeches on the Bill in the Commons were in his very best vein.   The
Bill passed, however, and went to the Lords, the Government having
begun to closure the debates by guillotine in the middle of June.
Balfour, of course, knew his subject inside out which was more than
could be said for anyone on the Liberal side.   How then to use
the Lords?   He decided on a memorandum to the Conservative Party in
the Lords suggesting drastic, but cleverly worded, amendments.   The
Lords transformed the Bill, and returned it to the Commons in December.   The Government refused to consider the amendments in
detail and asked the Commons to reject them as a whole which they
did by 416 votes to 107.   The Lords reaffirmed the amendments, and
the Prime Minister, Campbell-Bannerman, thereupon decided to drop
the Bill.   Perhaps he preferred not to fight on a matter with which the
Opposition (in the person of Balfour) were a good deal better acquainted than he was.

Balfour knew in his heart that conflict had only been postponed.
Nor did he believe that the ultimate challenge would be evaded by any
sort of reform of the Lords.   A section of Conservatives had instigated
a Bill to remedy the obvious weaknesses in the constitution of the House
of Lords: this had been referred to a select Committee which sat
throughout 1907.   Its report suggested various changes, including a
modification of the hereditary principle.

This seemed to Balfour to carry particular dangers. In a speech in Manchester in October, 1907, he said that power was vested in the House of Lords, not to prevent the people of this country having the laws they wished to have, but to see that the laws were not the hasty and ill-considered offspring of one passionate election. He pointed out, too, that any attempt to substitute for the House of Lords something like the American Senate would increase, not diminish, the power of the Second Chamber—and increase it at the expense of the House of Commons. An elected Chamber in which the hereditary principle played no part would 'insist naturally, rightly and properly, on having their voice in the Constitution or support of the Government, their voice in the general consideration of financial administration'.

In a letter to Lansdowne on February 22, 1908, Balfour more clearly expressed that essential Conservatism which he was later to define as no more than common sense. He said that the House of Lords was justifiable partly on historical and partly on practical grounds, and it had worked well: 'It is only bad political theory which asks for anything more.' He himself had always been in favour of Life Peers. Since that reform could not be carried out without making the House unwieldy in size, the number of hereditary Peers permitted to take part in proceedings would have to be curtailed; probably the only way to do that would be to enable the Peers themselves to elect the requisite number from their own body:

'I believe that in practice this would give you almost the same House of Lords that you would get by more elaborate methods of selection. It would almost certainly exclude the idlest and most incompetent and the least reputable, but it would avoid all the fancy franchises, and the fatal admission that the ancient ground of hereditary qualification was insufficient to qualify for the upper House. If it is not a sufficient qualification, it is no qualification at all, and your reform' (i.e. that proposed by the Select Committee) 'based upon the hybrid principle would, in my opinion, only be a half-way house to its abolition.

'It may seem paradoxical to say that the so-called "accident of birth" is more easily defended on what some people would call its naked absurdity than birth plus acknowledged services. Nevertheless I think it a fact; and if it be desirable to find a place for acknowledged service in the second Chamber, I would do it by the addition of Life Peers, not by any inquiry into the personal claims of hereditary Peers.'

During this period the Peers, i.e. their Conservative majority, saw fit to reject a number of other Bills, including, in 1906, the plural voting Bill, and later two bills dealing with land-owning in Scotland. Encouraged, perhaps, by a series of Conservative successes at by-elections, the Peers in 1908 also rejected the Licensing Bill, which the Liberals sought to substitute for the Act passed during Balfour's premiership.

No doubt under the influence of the Nonconformists, the Liberal Licensing Bill proposed to cut down the number of public houses in a rigid ratio to the population and to provide limited compensation and that spread over 14 years. Balfour saw the Bill as a direct attack on the rights of property. There was in his view every reason to get it defeated. The Peers dealt with it in an even more uncompromising way than they had dealt with the Education Bill.

The Liberals were enraged; this was the last straw, and their supporters throughout the country were working up to a fine frenzy of indignation. Violent threats to the Lords were heard; politics were becoming bitter and uncompromising. Campbell-Bannerman had already threatened 'that a way must be found, and a way will be found, by which the will of the people, expressed through their elected representatives, will be made to prevail'. In June, 1907, a resolution was carried through the Commons declaring that 'the power of the other House to alter or reject bills must be so restricted by Law as to secure that within the limits of a single Parliament the final decisions of the Commons shall prevail'. The Government considered an appeal to the electorate, though action was not taken. It was at this time that Lloyd George made his famous remark that the House of Lords was not 'the watchdog of the Constitution, but Mr. Balfour's poodle'.

In 1908, the Prime Minister, Campbell-Bannerman, died and was succeeded by Asquith. Campbell-Bannerman had always disliked Balfour, mainly because of Balfour's habit of making rings round him in Commons debate. Asquith, as we have seen, was a personal friend on whose account Balfour had not hesitated to write to his father-in-law ten years before when it seemed that Asquith might have got the Leadership over the head of Campbell-Bannerman. This personal friendship between the new Prime Minister and the Leader of the Opposition was to have important results, even though eight years later it was to terminate in unhappy circumstances. It did not, however, prevent the final crisis in the Lords *versus* the Commons struggle, which was precipitated by Lloyd George's Budget in 1909.

II

Balfour fought the Liberals tooth and nail in these years. Yet simultaneously he was deeply involved in some of the Liberal Government's most secret proceedings. Never, surely, has the leader of an Opposition played quite such an odd rôle. The situation arose because of Balfour's unchallenged authority in matters of defence. Under Radical pressure, the naval programme instituted under his leadership had been greatly cut down and Campbell-Bannerman pleaded for a disarmament conference, though knowing that the German Emperor would not for a moment consider it.   Some, however, of the Liberal leaders were more aware, and more concerned about, the overhanging threat of war. Not least among these was R. B. Haldane, the Liberal War Minister. Sandars reported to Balfour on March 7, 1906: 'Haldane made a long and good speech on army estimates.   He has not sat at your feet in vain, for it is a speech founded on your defence pronouncement.   It was very moderate in tone, pleased our boys, but was sulkily received by his own side.'

Thus encouraged, Balfour wrote on July 20, 1907, to Sir George Clarke, then just about to leave his post as Permanent Secretary of the Committee of Imperial Defence, having quarelled with Admiral Fisher. He asked whether the situation of Germany made a less sanguine view of invasion necessary.   Balfour, had stated in 1905 that he did not believe that the invasion of Britain was a serious possibility.   Various new developments now made him ponder the question again.   Later in the year he received a letter from Field-Marshal Lord Roberts which decided him to take some positive action.   Roberts pointed to the great developments, not merely in German naval potentiality but in her mercantile marine, and port accommodation.   He thought that if the British Fleet in home waters were ever reduced to the position of the Russian Far Eastern Squadron in 1904, then invasion might be attempted.   Roberts's inquiries had shown that the time required from the date of the order to the shipping to leave port to the time of dis-embarkation, if there were no naval interference, would be no more than 94 hours.   He added: 'Any foreign power which could gain and maintain for a few months the command of the sea will now have these islands completely at his mercy.'

Balfour noted in his private papers that Roberts's view was that Germany would have to strike first because if Britain had the initiative she might never be able to strike at all.   'The Germans are, I under-stand in possession of our plans for capturing their maritime trade, and they know that this maritime trade will be destroyed, and their mer-chants ruined without any compensating gain, if we are allowed to strike first.'   Roberts, thought, however, that if an Anglo-German war broke out but once and the Germans were beaten, the war would almost unfallibly be the first of a long series.   This was because British naval forces could not touch German factories.   (There was then, of course, no air arm; but nobody apparently foresaw its inevitability).   Roberts reported also that there were said to be some 80,000 Germans in the United Kingdom, almost all of them trained soldiers.   They worked in many of the large hotels at the chief railway stations and, he thought, if a force was got into England it would have the advantage of such immediate intelligent help and reinforcement as no other army upon foreign soil had ever enjoyed.

Roberts was, therefore, convinced that compulsory training was indispensable to the security of Britain and the Empire. With this latter, Balfour disagreed. Nevertheless, he sent Roberts's letter forward to Campbell-Bannerman. A sub-committee on invasion was set up in the autumn of 1907—it was in effect a full committee of the normal members of the C.I.D.—and began to hear expert evidence, which included such alarming revelations as that Britain had 'nothing in the way of a secret intelligence agent there (Germany), but we are in process of getting one', that the Firth of Forth was undefended, and that even the meetings of the C.I.D. were insecure, the German Emperor having recently stated that he could obtain any printed paper of its deliberations at will.

When Campbell-Bannerman died in April, 1908, his successor, Asquith, called Balfour into the counsels of the C.I.D. This was, indeed, an extraordinary step—'an event quite unique', as Esher told the King 'in the history of political development'. He knew of no case where the Leader of the Opposition had been brought into counsel with the heads of the Government upon the most vital questions of national policy and defence. Esher thought it a novel departure full of good omen.

The particular matters under discussion were the reports of the sub-committee on 'invasion' that had been appointed at Balfour's request and had recently produced its report. Asquith, Grey (the Liberal Foreign Secretary), Haldane, Lloyd George as well as Roberts, Lord Lovett and Colonel A'Court Repington were present. They listened, Esher says, apparently 'dumbfounded' at Balfour's closely-reasoned exposition of a subject which he clearly grasped in every detail. They did not even ask a question. This somewhat dismayed Balfour and he was glad to receive a letter from Esher speaking of their appreciation. This he said, in a reply to Esher, 'relieved a certain anxiety which I could not help entertaining as to the effect of what I had said; for, when one is asked to come before a Committee and be examined, and, after one's statement, not a soul puts any question, one is left in an uncomfortable ignorance as to what effect has been produced. On this point, you have reassured me.'

Consultations apparently continued between Balfour and the Committee throughout the year. Nor were they entirely confined to purely military matters. As we gather from this letter from Balfour to Asquith in November, 1908, Balfour found himself in the curious position of giving semi-political advice to his Opponents. He writes:

'This is just to recapitulate what I told you last night of my conversation with Lord Roberts, Colonel Repington, Lovett and S. Scott.

'I told them that, in my judgement, any statement on national defence on the broad lines adopted in 1905, could not be made *now* without bringing the military and naval relations of Germany and Great Britain into prominence; that I was convinced the Government would think this highly inexpedient at the present moment; and that personally I was entirely of their opinion. I think they all agreed.

'I gathered that what they really want is not so much a general survey of the recent aspects of the problem of defence, as a statement of the last decision come to by the C.I.D. as to the number of foreign troops with which our home army must be prepared to deal before we could regard ourselves as absolutely secure from attack. They told me they had some reason to think that this number was 70,000; but whatever it was, they wished to have it made public.

'I told them that, so far as I was concerned, I saw no objection to this course; and that, in any case, they need not think that my feelings would be hurt by their emphasising any difference between the findings of the C.I.D. in 1908 and their findings when I was Chairman of that body. I had always recognised that there must be constant revision of every great decision arrived at; and that circumstances have so manifestly altered in the last few years, that it would be strange indeed if some consequent modification had not to be made in the practical conclusions of earlier years.

'They did not, of course, conceal their intention of using any facts and figures which the Government might think fit to make public for purposes of their own propaganda.

'I strongly urged Lord Roberts before making his speech to see Lord Crewe' (then Colonial Secretary) 'and said that, if it were possible to see you at the same time, I thought very great advantage would result.' (A copy of this letter was sent also to Lord Roberts.)

A little while later in December, 1908, Esher tells us that he was asked by Asquith and Haldane to see Balfour about the defence schemes. They had offered to him all the papers, which he had declined to see, but said he would gladly hear an explanation of what was intended. Esher, who had been a Permanent Member of the C.I.D. since 1905, was delegated to give the explanation and spent four hours with Balfour in his room at the House of Commons. He tells us that Balfour 'took the most profound interest in General Sir Archibald Murray's paper'—Murray was Director of Military Training—'which we went through carefully with maps. We then discussed the whole strategical position, and I showed him my marked chart of the North Sea. His love of these questions is profound. His superiority to his contemporaries in grasp and courageous thinking is also marked.'

Many a politician placed in this curiously invidious, yet important, position would have felt himself drawn embarrassingly in two directions simultaneously. Matters however, in Balfour's opinion, were much too serious for any political capital to be made from his special knowledge. It is true that he opposed certain of the army reform schemes —including the preparation of an expeditionary force—that Haldane proposed in the House of Commons. But he knew full well what pressures Asquith's Government was under from its Radical wing in the matter of retrenchment in army and navy expenditure. This was why, of course, the Asquith Government had to play down in public their own convictions about the German danger.

But what becomes indisputably clear from Balfour's letter of November 6, 1908, to Lansdowne, is that the Asquith Cabinet was fully aware of the German danger. This letter also shows that Balfour and the Unionist leaders were prepared to give exactly the same patriotic assurance of support six years before the war began as, in fact, they tendered in 1914:

'Asquith asked me to speak to him last night after the House rose. He was evidently extremely perturbed about the European situation, which, in his view, was the gravest of which he had any experience since 1870. He said that incredible as it might seem, the Government could form no theory of the German policy which fitted all the known facts except that they wanted war, and war at the present time clearly much more than it did in 1870, would certainly involve Russia, Austria, and the near East—to say nothing of ourselves. I observed that the almost incredible frivolity of the excuse for hostilities which the Germans had devised would shock the civilised world beyond expression, and that it was difficult to see what Germany expected to gain by a war in which she must lose so much morally and was by no means certain to gain anything materially. Asquith's only answer to this objection was that the internal conditions of Germany were so unsatisfactory that they might be driven to the wildest adventures in order to divert national sentiment into a new channel. I said that, quite apart from the Entente, we should, as I understood it, be involved under treaty obligations if Germany violated Belgian territory. Asquith assented, and said that (as we all know) the Franco-German frontier is now so strong that the temptation to invade Belgium might prove irresistible. He gave me no information and I believe had no information which is not in the newspapers, but I was very much struck by the pessimistic tone with which he spoke of the position. I told him he might count upon the Opposition in case of national difficulty—an attitude of which, I am confident, you and all my colleagues will approve.'

In one respect, however—the naval side of defence—Asquith and Balfour found themselves, publicly at any rate, deeply divided. Balfour's view was, as he put it in a private letter: 'If we fail in maintaining our sea power, it does not matter in the least where we succeed: tariff reform, social reform, all reforms are perfectly useless. As a nation we shall have ceased to count.'

Earlier, in 1906, Balfour had been prepared to wait and see what the Liberal Government would do with regard to the navy because at that time he was informed that our naval strength was a good deal above the 'two-power standard' and that if there had then been war with Germany, Germany would have been totally outclassed. It would, therefore, from the national point of view, have been foolish to raise the question in the House with the consequent publicity and the revelation to all and sundry of our overwhelming superiority.

But that superiority could not last, not only because of German rivalry, but because there were elements in the Cabinet—and not the Radicals alone—who believed that there were more important uses for money at home than in the building of large warships. Their advisers, it must be admitted, were equally divided, the old 'bolt from the blue' *versus* the 'blue water' schools still being no nearer agreement. Lord Roberts thought that it would be possible to land large numbers of men on the English coast without the Admiralty having sufficient warning of the attempt to prevent it. Admiral Sir John Fisher, the First Sea Lord, on the other hand, believed that the embarkation of large numbers of men for invasion would take weeks to organise and carry out and could not come as a surprise. Obviously any estimate of naval requirements would depend on which view was taken. The situation was further bedevilled by the fact that Admiral Lord Charles Beresford, who had taken charge of the Home and Channel fleets in 1907, was thoroughly opposed to the ideas of Fisher.

The situation came to a head when Fisher convinced Reginald McKenna, the First Lord of the Admiralty, that there should be immediate provision in the estimate for six new Dreadnoughts. Lloyd George and Winston Churchill—Chancellor of the Exchequer and President of the Board of Trade respectively—held out for four. According to the published programme of the Germans however, they were to have ten battleships completed by spring of 1911; and that, it seemed obvious, was an intentional underestimate. Even Asquith believed that they would have 13 or perhaps even 17. This, Balfour thought, might soon be a serious under-estimate. (Subsequent inquiries seem to cast doubt on whether the German naval building was accelerated). There was then some evidence that contracts for the German 1909–10 programme had been given out in the autumn of 1908, and that material for the projected ships had been collected in advance. This information came from secret sources and could not be used publicly. But Fisher passed it on to Balfour.

Balfour, therefore, demanded that eight ships should be laid down at once. So serious did he consider the matter that he began a series of speeches intended to rouse the country to the dangers; his friend, George Wyndham, in a speech at Wigan in 1909, first produced that invaluable rhyming expression which summed up the campaign: 'We want eight, and we won't wait.' This was a crusade in which Balfour could wholeheartedly take part, since it was one lying nearest to his own strongest convictions.

It had, of course, also political advantages. For one thing it diverted attention from the nugatory tariff reform controversy. It also seriously incommoded the Government, and the Conservatives played it up for all it was worth in the campaign preceding the first election of 1910. Asquith insisted that there was no need for panic and that the building programme would remain at four battleships. He asked, however, that he should have authorisation to lay down four, what he called, 'contingent' ships later that year if this was necessary. In July, in fact, it was announced that the four contingent ships would be built. Conservative propaganda had succeeded; and the Liberals suffered a resounding defeat in a by-election at Croydon. As it turned out, by 1911, the Germans had in fact only six battleships, despite the forecasts of Asquith and Balfour.

The Conservatives were greatly assisted in their pursuit of the naval question by a Liverpool-Irish journalist called James Garvin, who had been appointed editor of the *Observer* by Northcliffe. From 1905 onwards he was fed by Admiral Fisher with inside information (even from within the Cabinet); Fisher's purposes were served, so were Garvin's who rode to celebrity on the reputation of omniscience thus created. Later, he was made considerable use of by Balfour—largely through Sandars—in the pre-election campaigns of 1910.

In December, 1909, Balfour, intent on electoral preparations, sent Garvin an encouraging letter after a powerful article on German naval rivalry. In this letter Balfour wrote:

'Has it occurred to you that there may be some little game on between our Government and the Germans . . . ?

'It is of immense importance to Germany that the present Government should remain in office. They are perfectly capable of trying to help them by some "shop window" arrangements with regard to armaments,—it may be with regard to other matters also. Even if it served no other purpose, such an arrangement, however illusory, might be dexterously used to undermine our criticisms on Naval policy.

'I have no proofs—only suspicions.'

'By this deft stroke', the biographer of the *Observer* remarks, 'the Navy issue, which had first appeared in the *Observer* primarily for electioneering purposes, was removed from that plane.'

Meanwhile, owing to the constant criticisms of Admiral Lord Charles Beresford, the Government had decided upon an inquiry into the Admiralty, which was, in effect, an inquiry into Fisher's policies. Later in the year Fisher resigned, not without some slight pique that Balfour had given a boost to Beresford in a speech at Glasgow on October 19, 1910, when he spoke of him as 'the ablest sailor who has command of a modern battleship'. On this occasion Fisher wrote to Arnold White: 'Balfour has reinflated the Beresford gas-bag by lauding him as a great sailor! And how he could quote Beresford as to trade protection being in danger is incomprehensible when he, Balfour, *knows* of Sir Arthur Wilson's evidence before the Beresford committee refuting it in *toto*. But be sure *you* never breathe a word of this and burn this letter. Such is politics! And a very strange thing of all is Balfour has written me an affectionate letter since his Glasgow speech! (We have a common bond in the submarine and the big gun!)' However this pique did not last for Fisher had a deep admiration for Balfour and for Balfour's understanding of what he had attempted to do with the navy. It is an ironic corollary to all this that no one was to discover more intimately than Balfour how far Fisher's preparations fell short of reality; only once was there to be a genuine line-of-battle contest such as Fisher envisaged—it was at Jutland when Balfour was first Lord of the Admiralty. Many Dreadnoughts never fired a shot in war. It was not to be that kind of war. For the blockade war which came, Fisher had not prepared; he had starved the navy of convoying overseas for the sake of the Dreadnought; happily for him, and for Britain, Germany had almost equally lacked prevision.

III

What makes Balfour one of the most fascinating of politicians to study is his ability, at almost any moment, to stand back from the hurly-burly and take a bird's eye view. He did this twice in the year 1908. On January 25, he delivered at Newnham College, Cambridge, the Henry Sidgwick Memorial Lecture. He chose as his subject 'Decadence'. Whatever the philosophical train of thought which led him to this subject, there can be little doubt that the choice also reflected his deeper and darker thoughts of his country's present and future, of her decline from undisputed economic and industrial mastery, of her less independent position in international politics.

On the face of it, however, his lecture is far from being about decadence in the everyday sense of the word. He is not, he tells us, referring to the artistic and literary developments of the last decade of the previous century, often described as decadent. What he wished to discuss was 'the decadence which attacks, or is alleged to attack, great communities and historic civilisations: which is to societies of men what senility is to man, and is often like senility, the precursor and the cause of final dissolution'. He believes that there are causes of decadence beyond those commonly adduced, such as civil dissensions, military disasters, pestilences, famines, tyrants, tax-gatherers, waning wealth, depopulation or slavery. He considers the example of Rome, and points out that, although all these so-called causes existed in the Roman empire, they were adequately counterpoised by a rapid advance in humanitarian ideals, a decline in intolerance, great esteem for education, physical culture, even for research. Obviously one must search for 'causes more general and more remote'.

It is more possible to regard decadence as a process of social degeneration which occurs 'when, through an ancient and still powerful state, there spreads a mood of deep discouragement, when the reaction to recurring ills grows feebler, and the ship rises less buoyantly to each succeeding wave, when learning languishes, enterprise slackens, and vigour ebbs away'. This certainly, he thinks, adequately describes what happened to the Roman Empire. Yet its decline into the 'thick darkness' of the Middle Ages was but a prelude to the 'unveiling the variety and rich promise of the modern world'.

But, he insists, when some wave of civilisation has apparently spent its force, we should not as of right expect it to be the prelude to a new advance. Progress from Roman times—and, of course, earlier—was from east to west. If, however, the energy of the development in the western-most communities 'is some day to be exhausted, who can believe that there remains any external source from which it can be renewed? Where are the untried races competent to construct out of the ruined fragments of our civilisation a new and better habitation for the spirit of man? They do not exist; and if the world is again to be buried under a barbaric flood, it will not be like that which fertilised, though it first destroyed, the western provinces of Rome, but like that which in Asia submerged forever the last traces of Hellenic culture.'

Can we, on the other hand, hope to escape the fate to which other races have had to submit? Balfour does not pretend that to this question there are any very satisfactory or convincing answers to be found. Yet there *are* new and powerful forces at work which may possibly affect the situation favourably. One of these forces—and here Balfour returns to a favourite theme—is 'the modern alliance between science and industry'. This force—and not politicians or political institutions—has altered the whole material setting of civilised life in the last 100 years. It is, he emphasises, science rather than industry which is the great 'instrument of social change, all the greater because its object is not change but knowledge; and its silent appropriation of this dominant function, amid the din of political and religious strife, is the most vital of all the revolutions which have marked the development of modern civilisation'. Science, he believes, is a force comparable to that exercised by religion or patriotism or politics by which men have been relieved 'from the benumbing fetters of merely personal pre-occupations'. Pure science, however, like philosophy, cannot directly touch the mass of men: to do that philosophy needs religion, and science needs practical applications.

It may, he supposes, seem fanciful to compare the appeal of religion to the 'higher side of ordinary characters' with the influence of science.

But, he insists, 'if it be remembered that this process brings vast sections of every industrial community into admiring relation with the highest intellectual achievement, and the most disinterested search for truth; that those who live by ministering to the common wants of average humanity lean for support on those who search among the deepest Mysteries of Nature; that their dependence is rewarded by growing success; that success gives in its turn an incentive to individual effort in no wise to be measured by personal expectation of gaining; that the energies thus aroused may affect the whole character of the community, spreading the beneficent contagion of hope and high endeavour through channels scarcely known, workers in fields the most remote; if all this be borne in mind it may perhaps seem not unworthy of the place I have assigned to it'.

One may here feel that Balfour is being merely fanciful in his tracing of the process by which science affects society, but as he himself points out he raises the matter rather as 'an aid to optimism, not a reply to pessimism'. At the same time, many would agree that the really new factor at work in the civilised communities is science and that science is a ground for hope that the West may escape decadence. It is true that Balfour did not foresee that science might bid fair also to threaten the existence not merely of the West but of the whole world. At the same time, his final claim in this essay is modest enough to remain acceptable even now: 'Whatever be the perils in front of us,' he said, in the last paragraph of his lecture, 'there are, so far, no symptoms either of pause or of regression in the onward movement which for more than a thousand years has been characteristic of western civilisation.'

The lecture on decadence may perhaps be described as an essay in para-politics. But two of its sub-sections have a more directly political bearing. One was his reference to 'democracy'. He pointed out that over large and 'relatively civilised portions of the world popular Government is profoundly unpopular, in the sense that it is no natural or spontaneous social growth'. Moreover, while democracy was 'an excellent thing' and 'quite consistent to its progress', it was not in itself 'progressive'. It had a regulative not a dynamic value; if it meant, though it never did, substantial uniformity instead of legal equality, 'we should become fossilized at once'. He emphasised that 'movement may be controlled or checked by the many; it is initiated and made effective by the few'. That is why it was a good thing that societies were not composed of men of roughly equal mental capacity, but 'of a majority slightly below the average and a minority much above it'. Such a society 'might go wrong, but it would go'.

His second political reference is to the problem of empire. He saw, in considering the decline of the Roman empire, that though it had brought civilisation, commerce and security to the West, it 'must surely have lacked some elements which are needed to foster among Teutons, Celts and Iberians the qualities, whatever these may be, on which sustained progress depends'. This lack became more evident when the power of Rome began to be withdrawn. When a superior civilisation, however beneficent, began to withdraw, the inferior civilisation was not likely to be self-supporting 'unless the character of the civilisation be in harmony both with the acquired temperament and the innate capacities of those who have been induced to accept'.

Balfour's lecture was published later in the year 1908. One of its readers was the President of the United States, Theodore Roosevelt. This may seem unlikely reading for a man who has gone down into history as a blend of Boy Scout and cowboy. But more recent studies— such as Howard K. Beales's *Theodore Roosevelt and the Rise of America to World Power*—show that the President was a deep, knowledgeable thinker and policy-maker on a world scale. At this time, he had not met Balfour, but no doubt he remembered that it was Balfour's decisive action which prevented British intervention in the American war with Spain over Cuba in which Roosevelt had become a national hero. Roosevelt's policies were, on the whole, progressive; he had departed from the Monroe Doctrine by intervening in Asiatic affairs between Russia and Japan, and in European affairs at the Algeciras Conference.

Whether Balfour sent Roosevelt his lecture on 'Decadence' or whether Roosevelt had read it on his own volition is not recorded. But he discusses the lecture in a letter to Balfour from the White House, dated March 5, 1908. He agrees with Balfour in having 'ugly doubts as to what may befall our modern civilisation'. He adds that 'it is a rather irritating delusion—the delusion that somehow or other we are all necessarily going to move forward. . . . I have a very firm faith in this general forward movement. . . . But there is nothing inevitable or necessary about the movement.'

In this same letter, however, he refers to a more specifically political question, arising no doubt from Balfour's references in the lecture to the alien and barbaric immigrants who became a source of weakness and peril to the Roman empire in its latter days. Roosevelt says: 'It is equally to the interest of the British empire and of the United States that there should be no immigration in mass from Asia to Australia or North America. It can be prevented, and an entirely friendly feeling between Japan and the English speaking people preserved, if we act with sufficient courtesy and at the same time with sufficient resolution.'

It was, perhaps, this letter that decided Balfour early in 1909 to put some of his most cherished and far-seeing ideas on the future before the President. Among the Royal papers there is a very remarkable document headed 'The Possibility of an Anglo-Saxon Confederation'. It is preceded by an 'Introduction' with the remark in brackets, 'Not sent to Roosevelt'. This suggests that the rest of the document *was* sent to Roosevelt, though there seems to be no reply to it among the Balfour papers. This may be explained by the fact that Balfour and Roosevelt met later in the year. In March, 1909, Roosevelt handed over his Presidency to Taft and left America for a 15-month trip, hunting in Africa and touring Europe. Of this meeting there appears to be no record: only this document remains as a copy on flimsy sheets. It is not clear why it should be among the Royal papers, nor to whom the introduction and copy of the document to Roosevelt was sent. Most probably it was to the Ambassador in Washington.

In the introduction Balfour begins by remarking that an Anglo-Saxon Federation is a far cry and probably cannot be realised for years: 'not, in fact, until some other power rises in the world which makes a rapprochement of England and the U.S.A. a matter of importance from the point of view of defence'. It is, however, 'all important' that the United States should be well disposed towards England during the forthcoming decade. 'Unless America is friendly towards England now, the Confederation of the Empire and still more of the Anglo-Saxon race may never be possible. One of Germany's main objects in building up her fleet (by 1916, she will have 38 Dreadnoughts and 20 Indomitables in the North Sea) is to be in a position (at any rate if she can get support from outside) to say to Britain: "No, I will not allow Imperial preference. I will fight if I don't get most favoured nation treatment myself and I will arouse the world against you." '

Balfour goes on to say that Imperial preference was certain to make Britain extremely unpopular in Europe, at any rate for a time. 'The fear of this unpopularity, especially if Germany had a powerful fleet on our shores, might make it impossible to "put through" an Imperial preferential tariff, with disastrous results to the Empire. If America were actively ranged against the proposal, it might turn the scale.'

Balfour refers to Roosevelt's imminent departure for Europe, and continues: 'It is as well to impress him before he starts with the possibility of an Anglo-Saxon Federation. He will then, if he does not already, fully appreciate the situation, view European affairs through glasses tinted with this point of view instead of some other, such as a German-American alliance. An ex-president has a difficult part to play if he is not to retire into private life. He can hardly return to Party politics. The rôle of a great world statesman might easily suit and keep him out of conflict with American politicians. Roosevelt might easily be inspired to lay the foundation of an Anglo-American understanding. In any case, a sympathetic attitude towards Britain on his part might be of incalculable value in the next few years.

Balfour, as we have seen, had long been devoted to the idea of a closer bond with America. But he had apparently been stimulated in this matter in recent years by talks with Admiral Fisher. According to a letter from Sandars to Fisher, both were anxious for a complete *entente* with the United States. Sandars adds: 'He (Balfour) has always been "an American" . . . he never allows the expression "foreigner" or "foreign State" to be used in speaking of America or Americans.' In what follows—that is the part of the document sent to Roosevelt—a great deal of the scope, subtlety and vision of Balfour's political outlook becomes startlingly clear.

He begins by saying that disarmament is still a dream and that, moreover, four or five of the great nations are ambitious of world conquest. 'The tendency at present', he writes, 'is strongly in the direction of the development of a few world powers. Universal peace will come only when these powers have divided the world between them—more or less in proportion to their strength—or, if one nation becomes overwhelmingly superior to the rest.' Balfour goes on—with an eye to Roosevelt's possible international ambitions—to suggest that world politics were beginning to dominate the international situation and that 'people who can look forward and grasp the essential factors which will govern the future grouping of the nations may be able to exert a profound influence on the political future of the world.'

Among the important factors working to change the future were the increased speed of locomotion and the transmission of news, both of which do away with the importance of natural geographical features. This was producing a community of race and to some extent of language; it was also assisting the growth of nationalism, for example 'pan-germanism, pan-slavism, British imperialism'. In addition, there was the spread of education and the increasing power of the press: 'It is not likely, for instance, that the Balkan States or the small South American Republics will be able to continue an independent existence for many years longer.'

It was, however, already possible to forecast the general development of the nation states of the world. 'The Russian empire will extend from the North Pacific and Vladivostok in the East to the confines of Pan-Germany in the West. It will try to absorb Norway and Sweden to get an outlet to the North Sea. Whether it will succeed in assimilating them depends mainly on the character of civilisation and the system of representative government, which Russia will develop for itself, and the racial persistence of the Norwegians and Swedes. If no racial sympathy develops, the other great powers will probably conspire to maintain the Norwegian Peninsula as an independent neutral state to weaken the strength of Russia.'

Balfour thought that Russia would try to absorb the Slav and Serb portions of Hungary and the Balkan states in order to get to the Mediterranean: 'It is extremely improbable that, once Russia has established a constitutional government in her own territories, she could absorb the people of Turkey, Persia and Arabia. Their racial, political and religious ideas are probably too divergent ever to admit that they are forming part of a Russian democracy.

'Whether Russia reaches the Atlantic. the Mediterranean and the Indian Ocean by absorbing the peoples which now stand in her way or not, she will be enormously powerful. She will be one of the chief powers of the world and quite invulnerable. But in any case she will be an entirely land power'—since she would have no oversea possessions. 'Except in so far as she wishes to gain an outlet to the three seas already mentioned, she will be essentially pacific. A Russian Empire will be a "natural" division of the earth's surface, though its actual power in the counsels of the world will largely depend on whether it is allowed to get possession of the states which at present bar its exit to the sea.'

After this essentially realistic—and not entirely unprophetic—analysis of the situation and aims of a new Russia (Balfour, of course, did not foresee that the new Russia would be no less authoritarian than the old), he turns to the future of Germany. He thought that Germany would try to absorb the German part of Switzerland, Denmark, and Holland. 'Local patriotism and the opposition of the great European powers is the only real obstacle to these countries joining the German empire.' Germany would, of course, have central Europe in her power; the German oversea possessions, he thought, were unimportant, though Germany was extremely anxious to extend them in order to provide for her increasing population and to avoid losing them to another power.

In the *festung* Europe that Hitler made during the last war, this situation, in general, obtained, though German Switzerland escaped. Balfour's prophetic powers, at this point, gave out. He wrote of the probability of a 'Latin empire—a loose federation for trade and defence—looming up in the future as a counterpoise to an all-powerful Germany'. This federation would probably include Spain, Portugal, France, Italy with Belgium, French Switzerland, and Greece; and it 'would be pacific'. Despite the various groupings and trade arrangements in recent times, there has been no sign of a Latin empire. Far from it. Italy remained, until the downfall of Mussolini, the odd man out; Balfour did not foresee Mussolini.

He then turns to the Far East: 'It is absolutely certain that no European people can absorb the Asiatic peoples. They must develop for themselves, however they may be exploited for commercial purposes in the meantime. The rise of Japan and the reform movement in China point to the possibility of an Asiatic empire in the future. If there is any real vitality in the Asiatic peoples, that empire will probably embrace India. The British policy in both India and Egypt provides for the development of self-government by a gradual process which will involve no dislocation of the trade connection between England and India and Egypt, even when autonomy is practically complete. When the East does awake, it will find its most pressing need is territorial expansion.' He thought that the growth of the Turkish empire would be problematical and, if the young Turk movement had any vitality, it would probably move eastwards. It might even absorb Egypt; and an 'empire formed mainly at the expense of Russian ambition would be supported by the other great powers'.

Balfour also thought that Africa could never be the home of the white race, for it was already in the possession of 'many millions of an inferior black race with whom white men cannot live and work on equal terms and the climate is not suitable for hard manual labour'. In his view, Africa north of the Zambesi must be regarded as a sphere in which the progressive races could develop commerce or construct naval bases but nothing else: 'It will be given over to the negro and, in the North East, to the Mohammedans.'

From this broad survey, Balfour drew various conclusions. He thought that the world was probably dividing itself into great racial states representing the Slav, the German, the Latin, the Asiatic, the Turko-Mohammedan and the South American people: 'It is doing so without the necessary intervention of any catastrophe such as a big European war.'

Thus, the new boundaries would be natural boundaries: 'There will be no obvious anomalies on the map of the world. The days of conquest, when whole populations were massacred or bodily removed, are gone forever. Even the long-dreaded conflict between East and West, between Christendom and what was known as Heathendom, for the possession of Europe, is now recognised as a figment of the imagination. A civilised nation will now never be overrun or dispossessed of its territories.' This latter remark was in curious contradiction to what he had said in the introduction—the part that was not sent to Roosevelt —though it may be that he had in mind merely the over-running of a civilised by an uncivilised nation.

But there were certain underpopulated areas such as Australia and South Africa which were sought after by Japan, and Germany respectively: 'Not until these countries are more thickly populated than they are today can their future as Anglo-Saxon states be assured, unless they are protected by a power invincible at sea.' Here we glimpse a vision of Balfour's real thoughts about the further development of the Empire. The future for a rapidly overpopulating Britain, equally rapidly becoming completely unself-supporting, lay in closer integration with the Empire. But what Balfour's recent immersion in naval matters had shown him clearly was that the naval might of Britain alone in the future would be insufficient to protect the all-important extremities of Empire from greedy hands.

Now he gets down to bed-rock.   He believes that the United States and Britain should federate to 'be a more than equal counterpoise to the other great nations of the future and also partly in order to secure to them the undisputed possession and development of the still thinly populated areas of the world'.   Balfour takes the argument a step further.   He says that the British Empire and America must work together—or go into opposition.   'The British Empire is just beginning to try to consolidate itself.   At the Colonial Conference of 1911, it is just possible, at that of 1915 it is almost certain, that some form of imperial preference will come.'   This is bound to cause German hostility: 'Whether or no England will be able to carry through an effective measure of imperial preference will depend mainly on the strength of her Navy.   If she fails, her Empire will probably drop to pieces in the course of the next century and Australia and South Africa might become internationalised with a patriotism of their own.   Or Australia might be flooded with Japanese and Chinese because it had not the strength to protect itself.   South Africa might become predominantly German through immigration. . . .'

As the new countries filled up, the British Empire could become enormously strong, for it would possess the undoubted command of the sea and naval bases at strategic points in every part of the world. 'But there is no question that at present the issue is still in doubt, especially if America throws in her lot against Britain.'   He here referred to tentative bids by Germany for American friendship.   Balfour continues:

'If America elects to pursue its own destiny alone, it must either make up its mind to be content with its present boundaries, and have no real say in the politics of the world (because a Navy without bases thousands of miles from Europe, Australia or the greatest part of Asia, is almost useless), or it must embark on a career of conquest.'

But, Balfour continues, America has already decided not to remain in isolation, and he points to the case of the Philippines, Cuba, the Panama Canal and her naval estimates.   'She is', he states, 'already beginning to feel the need of territorial expansion.   She has large sums of money invested abroad, millions of pounds worth at sea.   She cannot afford not to be a world power.'

Now Balfour comes very near the bone indeed: 'To put it bluntly, America can only expand at the expense of Britain.   England already possesses all the thinly populated areas on the earth fit for white settlement.   She already holds practically all the strategic points.   The Panama Canal will be completed by 1915 or thereabouts.   England today can command the entry to it from her West Indian possessions,

Unless England and America begin to come together, the Canal is certain to be a fertile source of friction between the two races. Have England and America anything to gain by refusing to pursue their destinies together and electing to be in opposition? Nothing that anybody judging from a broad standpoint—that of posterity—can see. On the contrary, they have everything—race, language, political ideals and history—to bring them together. In a loose federation neither will sacrifice its own individuality. There will simply be super-imposed on English, American, Canadian, South African and Australian national sentiment a common anglo-saxon patriotism.'

On one point, Balfour was quite definite: 'If England and America do not federate, the history of the world will continue to be one of warfare, for a number of world powers will be competing for the supremacy. . . . If they unite against the rest of the world they will be beyond attack. . . .' An Anglo-American federation would be a sea empire with no land borders to defend. It could expand gradually since it would possess the thinly-peopled spaces and the seas would be in its hands.

Balfour then discusses specific details. He says that a sea empire would overcome the great practical difficulty of securing a uniform system of government: 'No such thing would be necessary. Each state would manage its own affairs exactly as it liked. It would even fix its own tariff, subject only to the members of the confederation being granted a uniform percentage preference. The Federal Council would only deal with the question of preference and the question of defence. For these purposes no permanent government would necessarily be required and the meetings of the Federal Council would not have to take place oftener than about once a year. A joint Foreign Office and Admiralty might be instituted, but its importance would be greatly diminished if an Anglo-Saxon confederation were in existence. For such a confederation would be practically unassailable and would dominate the world. . . . It would practically dictate peace by sea to the rest of the world. The burden of armaments would thus be greatly reduced. The balance of power, which is the subject matter of foreign politics today, would be permanently upset.'

Balfour does not imagine that public opinion is ready for such a scheme at present but he thinks that the way might be paved and people become accustomed to the idea. And he concludes, in a note that presumably was not sent to Roosevelt, that 'It would be a fitting combination to Roosevelt's career that he should go down to history as the prime author of the greatest confederation the world has ever seen'. He believes that probably no one could do anything to start the ball rolling but Roosevelt.

It was a bold and visionary scheme, but not 'the baseless fabric' of merely an idealistic dream. It was in fact a development of the *pax Romana* in which peace was (in his own word) to be 'legated' to the rest of the world—a world government, however, enforced, not by tramping legions, but by sea.

If it had been originated by a German, one might regard it as a typically grandiose scheme of world power. In fact, of course, as far as Britain was concerned, it meant in some sense—as Balfour would certainly be aware—a diminution of power, which in those still palmy, proud days of the Empire idea, must have raised storms of English indignation. For America was then still regarded by most Britons as 'the country cousin', and the idea of giving up no matter how small a part of sovereignty to what still appeared to be so minor a power would have been violently resented. Very few could then foresee that America would, almost within the lifetime of Balfour himself, become the most powerful nation in the world. If there had then been more people to foresee such an eventuality, there might well have been more to see virtue in the idea of an Anglo-Saxon confederation. If an effective confederation had then been brought about—that is, before 1914—it is likely that both of the two World Wars would have been avoided. No doubt Balfour thought that British diplomatic skill and the genius for (occasionally devious) compromise would prevent her being submerged by such confederation, and indeed, against the still largely untested American diplomacy, would enable her to be the effective leader.

Balfour's scheme never, of course, got further than paper and speculation. But it is extraordinarily revealing of his deepest political thinking. Moreover, Balfour's attitude to America had important practical results, not least in his highly successful mission to the United States in 1917.

In the revelation of Balfour's world-thinking which the above document provides, two outstanding factors are omitted: the development of air power, and the development of militant socialism (or Communism) as a world force. Yet in July, 1909, Blériot had made the first aeroplane crossing of the Channel: and on May 12, 1911, Balfour himself with MacKenna and others was taken up for a flight at Hendon under the auspices of the Parliamentary Aerial Defence Committee. As for Socialism, we have already seen that Balfour had pointed to the appearance of a large body of Labour members as the most significant development in English political history resulting from the election of 1906. But it required the dark imagination of a Wells to see in the flimsy machine of Blériot a precursor of 'war in the air', and the dogmatic fanaticism of a Marx to be certain of an armed Communist nation.

13

IN OPPOSITION

Losing Battles, 1910–1911

Those who have written about England in the years immediately preceding the Great War have sometimes indulged themselves— or perhaps their nostalgia—with halcyon memories of perpetual sunshine, of a nation in the full bloom of prosperity, of an era of peace rudely shattered by the thunderbolt of war. These are mirages. There was, indeed, a widespread determination to enjoy life to the full, but there was a kind of desperation about it, a sense of enjoying a last fling, almost a touch of the last days of Pompeii. It was, after all, a decade of war—in which England was not involved only by the grace of God and the wisdom of Balfour and the Marquess of Lansdowne. War, indeed, was yet no nearer than the Pacific and minor brushes in the nearer East. Yet there were such threatening occurrences as the affair at Agadir, there was Lord Roberts with all his renown stamping the country demanding conscription, there was the naval rearmament programme in Britain and in Germany.

These factors—and there were probably other more obscure ones— combined to introduce an element almost of hysteria into the political scene. Respected and level-headed political leaders lost their judgement and followed courses both fatuous and perilous. Members of the Privy Council and former Ministers of the Crown openly encouraged sedition in a part of His Majesty's Forces stationed in Northern Ireland; milder ones supported the militant sufragettes; Ministers in the Liberal Government allowed themselves to become involved in the dubious affair of the Marconi shares and, though cleared of the charges of serious corruption, were seen by all to have acted with crass stupidity. Political life took on a bitter tinge and personal friends suddenly realised that they were political opponents and avoided each other's company.

Even Balfour, constitutionally incapable of pursuing political vendettas into private life, began increasingly to feel a sense of exasperation. It was, indeed, exasperation more with his own Party than with his opponents and this in turn, though it cannot be said to have affected his innate political judgement, certainly in due course inhibited his political energies. It was not so much that his appreciation of the dangerous constitutional situation that arose as a result of the Lords rejecting Lloyd George's Budget of 1909 was incorrect, as that he did not put it with sufficient force and persuasive power to the rest of his Party; though, as we shall see, there were practical reasons that made that extremely difficult to do.

It was on April 20, 1909, that Lloyd George, the Liberal Chancellor of the Exchequer, introduced one of the most revolutionary budgets of modern times. He had a prospective deficit of £16,000,000, mainly owing to increased expenditure on the Navy and on old-age pensions. He also had two other factors in his mind: the first was that his Government was losing support in the country—its by-election record during 1908 had been of almost unmitigated failure. Secondly, he knew that his only chance of getting controversial measures past the Lords and into law was by tacking them on to measures of finance, which, it had long been accepted, the House of Lords were not in the last resort able to reject. At this stage, it seems clear, the Budget was not an attempt to precipitate the struggle between the Liberal Party and the Lords, but rather to circumvent raising the question of the Lords' veto.

In his Budget, Lloyd George dealt with these points in the following ways: he imposed new taxes on income and supertax, heavier death duties, larger imposts on alcohol and tobacco, taxation of the motorist (though this was to be used for a road fund and not to meet the general expenditure), and there was to be a reduction of £3 million in the sinking fund payment. Many of these taxes, of course, appealed to the Radical and Labour supporters of his Party since most of them were directed at mulcting the rich. Lloyd George rubbed in this point by referring to his proposals as a 'war budget—for raising money to wage implacable warfare against poverty and squalidness'.

What, however, most enraged the Conservatives—though the rage took some days to gather momentum—was the fact that, inserted inside the Finance Bill, was a Land Valuation Bill skilfully tied in with the imposition of new taxes on land. It was this that gave some justification to the Peers' ultimate rejection of the Bill; it also went like a dagger to the heart of the old Conservatism. The Land Valuation clauses were a death blow to the landed gentry, and through them to the whole system of rural life which had been England's strength down the ages.

Of course, self-interest was here involved; it is significant that the last remnant of the old Whig landed gentry in the Liberal Party also complained to Asquith about this Land Bill. But the Bill did more than damage the pockets and possessions of a handful of land-owners; it marked the virtual end of Old England. It also underlined the shift of power in the Conservative Party itself; the landed gentry were gradually giving way to the 'new men' with the industrial money-bags.

Balfour was himself a landowner; but a comparatively small one. That did not detract from the strength of his opposition. He wrote to his niece, Eve Balfour, on July 6, 1909:

'The motive of the Government in putting them' (i.e. the Land Taxes) 'on was to please the "mass" of the voters, or, as your friend puts it, "the poor". This is precisely the crime that lies at their door. They have chosen a particular section of the community, and a particular kind of property which they think, both unpopular and helpless, and have proceeded to mulct it—demagogism in its worst aspect. As you and I own but little of it, *this* part of the Budget will not make much difference to us. But this only increases my indignation.'

The Budget had to be fought. The Conservative Party, properly pursuing its own interests, demanded it. It is foolish to speak, as do Liberal historians, of the Party falling into a trap prepared by Lloyd George; they could do no other than fight. Balfour saw this; and he also saw that for once he could unite his Party in opposition for, though the free-traders were not as utterly opposed to the Budget as were the tariff reformers, few of them doubted the need for resistance. In the Commons, the Conservatives fought it line by line from the beginning of May to the beginning of November. They divided against everything that could be divided against; and, whenever the House sat late, they made certain as far as possible that the time so gained was devoted not to the Bill but to discussing whether or not the debate ought to continue at that hour.

It must have reminded Balfour of old Fourth Party days. At 1 a.m. Balfour or Austen Chamberlain would move to report progress. This would be debated at length, usually until the closure was moved from the Government Front Bench. This would be divided against by the Opposition who, when it was carried, would force the Government into the lobby again to defeat the motion to adjourn the debate. At three o'clock, and probably again at five o'clock if the House was still sitting, Balfour or one of his lieutenants would move the same motion again and the same tedious procedure would be gone through.

But the point Balfour hammered hardest at was the illegality of inserting a Valuation Bill into a Bill for raising revenue: 'I defy any constitutional lawyer in this House,' Balfour would say, 'to claim it is legitimate for the House of Commons to introduce into its Finance Bill grave measures of Valuation and compulsory registration. How dare you describe it as a Finance Bill? By your own admission it is a compulsory registration Bill.' Outside Parliament the debates were no less acrimonious.

On November 4, the Lloyd George Budget passed the House of Commons. Now for Balfour came the question of destiny: should the Lords reject it or should they not? Even before the Budget passed the Commons, Sir Edward Grey, the Liberal Foreign Secretary, had said: 'Mr. Balfour and Lord Lansdowne are keeping two doors open. They are debating whether they should pass the Budget or not. We know their wishes, not the extent of their nerve.' It was perfectly within the power of the Lords to reject. Conservative Peers had heavily outnumbered Liberals since the last quarter of the nineteenth century. But the Conservative majority had used its powers with great circumspectness, not to say timidity, until the return of a Liberal—and strongly Radical—Government in 1906. During the course of that Government, as we have seen, it became much bolder. We have also seen that Balfour had agreed with Lansdowne that points of difference should be fought 'very stiffly' in the Commons, but that the House of Lords should be the 'theatre of compromise'. Nevertheless, neither he nor Lansdowne had compromised over the Education Bill. He was perfectly aware of the powers placed in the hands of the Conservative Opposition by the Conservative dominance in the Lords; he was equally perfectly prepared, as has been noted, for a reform of the House of Lords—even a radical reform; but while the inequality existed, he was in certain cases prepared to make political use of it—up to, but not beyond, a certain point.

That great Conservative thinker, George Saintsbury, probably put Balfour's point of view better than anyone else. On a point of Radical change, he said, 'Fight for principles as long as you possibly can consistently with saving as much of it as you possibly can; but stave off the fighting by gradual and insignificant concessions where possible. We cannot always help things going to the devil, but we can make them go slowly, and sometimes turn them out of the diabolic way.'

Certainly there was a question of principle involved in the Finance Bill, as there had been in the Education Bill. It was worth trying to see what could be saved, or at least ameliorated, by means which history and the Constitution had—however inequitably—provided. The danger, of course, was that the Government would then be forced by its more determined members to ask the King to create sufficient new Liberal Peers to alter the balance of power in the Lords, as had happened in 1832; and this would inevitably mean bringing the King into, or near, the arena of politics. It, therefore, contained a danger for the Constitution. There was, however, no certainty that Asquith *would* proceed to that point; nor was there any sound basis for assuming that, as Balfour pointed out in a preface he wrote to Bagehot's *English Constitution* in 1928, 'the creation of Peers by the Crown was the "remedy" provided by the Constitution for a deadlock between Lords and Commons'. He further pointed out that 'Cases might easily be imagined in which one or two applications of this "constitutional remedy" under modern conditions would practically destroy the historic Constitution so far as the Second Chamber is concerned'. But even if it were to come to that point, Balfour no doubt felt in 1909 that a deft withdrawal could be made at the last moment. If so, he had not considered the degree of passion in his followers and in the country at large.

There was one other person deeply concerned in this affair: the King himself. He had heard rumours of the Peers' decision to reject and, after consultation with Asquith, he summoned Balfour and Lansdowne. News of this summons soon spread and Sandars told Knollys in a letter on October 8, 1909—four days before the consultation—that 'the air here is charged with political gossip. Reporters watch Carlton Gardens and Lansdowne House.' The King at the talks expressed his desire to avoid collision between the two Houses and suggested that some *via media* should be found if possible. Balfour and Lansdowne informed the King that no definite decision had been taken since there had been no meeting of the Conservative Peers; but they could, of course, give him no assurance that the Peers would not reject the Budget.

One thing, indeed, might have made the Conservative leaders hesitate, even at this late moment; this was if there had been the possibility of the country's finance being paralysed as a result of a rejection of the Budget. But Mrs. Dugdale reveals that anxiety on this score had been removed by a disclosure 'which Mr. Lloyd George made—by chance or otherwise—in private conversation with a friend of Balfour's before the Finance Bill left the Commons. The Government, so the Chancellor of the Exchequer confided, had been engaged for some time in drafting a "stop-gap Budget". This showed that chaos would not follow upon rejection.' The situation was met early in March of the next year by a Treasury Borrowings Act.

The actual moment when Balfour decided to use the Lords to throw out the Bill was not known when Mrs. Dugdale wrote her biography. It can now be pinpointed almost exactly: it was three months before the Bill reached the Lords. Garvin, Editor of the *Observer*, appealed in his paper on August 8 for Balfour to go to Birmingham and reply to a speech to be made there in September by Asquith: 'Let Mr. Balfour himself go to Birmingham and there declare the triple policy of Tariff

Reform, Social Reform and Naval Security.'   Two days later Balfour wrote to Garvin:

'Your letter has much gratified me.   The *Observer* and the *Telegraph* were admirable.   Many men have spoken to me about the articles, and they have produced the happiest effect.

'I have promised to go to Birmingham the week after Asquith, if they can secure the Bingley Hall, so that your advice on this point has not been thrown away.'

Here Balfour implicitly accepts the Tariff Reform viewpoint—*and that viewpoint demanded that the Lords should reject the Budget on the basis of Tariff Reform*.   Garvin himself wrote later in an autobiographical fragment: 'From the beginning of August, Mr. Balfour's mind was made up. . . . After the Limehouse speech' (of Lloyd George on July 30, 1909) 'Mr. Balfour's decision and dexterity were the master influences upon the situation from first to last.'   Esher, too, after lunching with Balfour in November, 1909, wrote: 'Certainly from the day of Lloyd George's speech at Limehouse (July 30) the fate of the Budget was sealed.'

From August onwards, Garvin was in close touch with Balfour— or more frequently, with Sandars, whom he met, or corresponded with, almost daily for months.   Before the end of August, the *Observer* had gained for Balfour the support of most of the Tariff Reformers. On September 22 there appeared Garvin's article headed: 'Mr. Balfour, a Man of Action.'   Buckle, editor of the *Times*, also a Northcliffe paper was, however, violently opposed to the rejection and called on Balfour in September to tell him so, without result.

There were, too, those in his own Party who counselled caution. Hicks-Beach—now Lord St. Aldwyn—wrote to Balfour on September 20, 1909, that, though he disliked the Budget, he did not want the Lords to throw it out: 'Let people suffer a bit by Radical legislation; then they will soon put an end to it.'   Lord James, Lord Balfour of Burleigh and Lord Lytton were equally opposed to action by the Lords.   So, at this time though not later, was F. E. Smith.   As his son and biographer, Lord Birkenhead, says: 'He (Smith) was convinced that the Lords should pass the Budget, so that when its brutalities were exposed and the Unionists returned to power, its terms could be altered and softened, its more violent clauses repealed.'

Balfour's speech at Birmingham, however, sealed the decision already made; the Budget *would* be rejected by the Lords.   Moreover, the fight had now become Tariff Reform versus Socialist finance.   To this, no Conservative free-trader could reasonably object; if it came to the point, they were more Conservative than Free-Traders, less horrified by Tariff Reform than by a whiff of Socialism.   For the extremists, Balfour had still not gone far enough towards protection—'I wish he could have been a little more definite on the question of the food taxes', wrote Amery to Garvin, but added, 'On the whole he is doing thundering well.' The election now looming could be faced with, at least, equanimity; it might possibly even be won.

On the same day that the Finance Bill passed to the Lords, November 16, 1909, Lansdowne proposed a motion 'that this House is not justified in giving its assent to the Bill until it has been submitted to the judgement of the country'. This followed a precedent set by Lord Salisbury in the early years of his Parliamentary career. The motion itself was very carefully drafted, mainly by Balfour himself. He was supported in his attitude by the advice of the constitutional lawyers, Anson and Dicey, who declared that rejection would be perfectly proper. The debate in the Lords began on November 23 and continued for a week during which most of the well-known Peers spoke.

Lansdowne made a brilliant opening speech, arguing on the weakest point of the Government case—namely, that they had no right to tack on to a Finance Bill serious matters which were unconcerned with finance. This, he said, fully justified the Lords in reviving the right to reject even a money Bill, a right which had been conceded in the Commons argument of 1689. He believed that the Lords would do themselves less harm by fighting than by abandoning for all time the right to interfere with the financial policy of a Radical government. He was supported with some violence by the 86-year-old Earl of Halsbury—later to play a decisive part in Balfour's own political fortunes—and by Curzon. Of the Unionist Peers, Lord Balfour of Burleigh and Lord James argued the case for passing the Bill.

By now, however, the result was inevitable. On November 30, by 350 votes to 75, the Lords rejected the Finance Bill. By this time Lloyd George, at any rate, was spoiling for a fight, and the rejection delighted him. Knollys, no doubt in this matter speaking the mind of the King, told the Clerk to the Privy Council 'very gravely and emphatically that he thought the Lords mad'. Asquith promptly moved a resolution in the Commons 'that the action of the House of Lords in refusing to pass into law the financial provisions made by this House for the service of the year is a breach of the Constitution and a usurpation of the rights of the Commons'. Since the legislature had refused Supply, a dissolution was inevitable and it was announced that the writs for an election would be issued in January.

Meantime, in secret Asquith had asked the King for guarantees that, if the occasion arose, he would make a creation of Peers sufficient to pass the Bill as had been done in 1832. But the King had notified Asquith on December 15, 1909, that he would not create new Peers until after a *second* General Election; and this, if anything could, justified in part Asquith's statement in the Commons in the February following that he had received no guarantee nor even asked for one.

In December, 1909, Balfour was suffering from pulmonary catarrh, and was prevented from playing a full part in the election campaign. He spoke, however, to his constituents in the City, pointing out that the attack on the House of Lords was only the culmination of a long-drawn-out conspiracy to secure a single Chamber legislature. He spoke also on tariff reform, on the navy, and the war clouds hanging over Europe. Indeed Balfour made the question of tariff reform the principal subject of his last-minute message to the electors on the eve of the poll, and joined with Joseph Chamberlain, retired in Highbury, in signing a denial that protection would affect the working-class cost of living.

It has been said that the election was fought mainly on the merits of the Budget; but the more knowledgeable voter understood quite well that what was really at stake was the question whether the House of Lords was to retain its ancient power of veto. The results of the election underlined this fact. The Conservatives regained 100 seats lost at the election of 1906, the figures for the new Parliament being: Conservatives, 273; Liberals, 275. Thus the Liberal majority was reduced to the point where Asquith could carry on his Government only by depending on Labour and Irish Nationalist support. In the new Parliament, there were 40 Labour members and 82 Irish Nationalists.

The Irish saw their chance of getting Home Rule at last. Their leader, John Redmond, promptly demanded that the only bar to this aim—the Lords' veto—should be abolished in that very year. He insisted that no question of the Lords' reform was to be allowed to confuse the issue and that the British Budget must wait upon the introduction of a Parliament Bill abolishing the veto. Asquith was not prepared to go so far or so fast. The Irish then threatened to vote against the Budget, and thus turn out the Government.

At this point, the King, no doubt instigated by the Liberal leaders, made an informal approach to Balfour to see whether, in event of the Irish deciding to vote against the Budget, the Conservatives would support its passage. Balfour replied on February 15, 1910, that, although it would be embarrassing to all parties were the Government to be immediately defeated, 'it would be vain to ask the Unionist Party on tactical grounds to vote black where they had before voted white'. He prophesised, however, that the Irish threats would *not* be carried out and that the Government would re-present the Finance Bill, that it *would* pass and the Government would nevertheless survive.

What then was the position of the Conservative party? Only a resounding victory at the polls would have justified the rejection of a money Bill by the Lords. Now they were left high and dry without a policy, or at any rate without a stirring call to put to the electors. The election result, indeed, had been deadlock. All sorts of schemes were propounded, ranging from referendum to Imperial Federation, and Sandars busily sought ideas and advice from Garvin and others as to the next step. He, indeed, helped Garvin's deputy, Gerard Fiennes, to prepare articles for the *Observer* suggesting an inter-party conference on the reform of the House of Lords. Garvin went so far as to discuss with Balfour the idea that the Conservatives should approach the Irish Nationalists to get their support. Balfour replied that such a move would be 'eating dirt'.

Without doubt, the Budget had now to be passed, and, as Balfour had prophesied, when it was reintroduced it was passed by the Commons and next day by the Lords. On April 29 it received the Royal assent. Lloyd George had won—and, having won, he and the Liberals were determined to press home their advantage. Asquith immediately announced that the Government intended to modify the veto power of the Lords. A series of resolutions was tabled depriving the Lords of any veto over money bills, giving them a suspensory veto of two years over other bills and reducing the duration of Parliament from seven to five years. A Bill based on these resolutions was drafted and sent to the King, and Asquith made it clear that he would ask for the creation of sufficient Peers to overwhelm the Conservative majority in the Lords to force the Bill through. From the point of view of King and Constitution this posed a yet more serious danger. On April 29, 1910, Balfour attended a meeting at Lambeth Palace, called by the Archbishop of Canterbury (no doubt at the instigation of the King) with Esher and Knollys present. What emerged is not known in detail; but it appears—its significance will become clear later—that 'Mr. Balfour made it clear that he would be prepared to form a Government to prevent the King being put in the position contemplated by the demand for the creation of peers'. But this offer was not brought to the attention of the King nor to that of his successor. Had it been, the dangerous events ensuing in 1910–11 might have been avoided.

It is necessary at this stage to look closer at the Parliament Bill. It proposed that money Bills in future should under certain conditions become law without the consent of the Lords; it was to be left to the Speaker of the Commons to decide whether a particular Bill complied with the definition. Other Bills, if passed by the Commons in three successive sessions and rejected each time by the Lords, should nevertheless become law, provided two years had elapsed between the Bill's first introduction to the Commons and its final reading there. A third proposal was that five years should be substituted for seven as a maximum duration of Parliament. It was these proposals that Asquith determined to force through; and if the Lords did not accept them, would ask for guarantees of the creation of a sufficient number of Peers to pass the Bill.

Meanwhile, in the debate on the Royal Address which had mentioned the resolutions on the Lords, Lansdowne had, though scarcely enthusiastically, accepted the principle that there should be some reform of the Lords.   He was not prepared to renounce the hereditary principle, but he thought that a certain non-hereditary element might be secured by life peerages—a proposal, as we have seen, that Balfour had made earlier—and by Government nominations to the Lords for a substantial term.   Halsbury, of course, was totally opposed to all change.   It was, however, decided to go into committee on the matter.

What made the Conservatives more amenable to the proposition for reform was, no doubt, the probability that a reformed House of Lords would forestall any large-scale creation of Peers to pass a specific Bill.   At a meeting at Lansdowne House, Balfour—who knew that there was a growing distaste for the hereditary principle in the country —suggested that the only way to fight against government by a single Chamber was to admit an elective element into the Lords, and he added: 'Although at first I thought the elective and non-elective elements would at once clash, and the remaining hereditary element be thrust out, I have come to the conclusion on reflexion that this danger is not as great as I at first thought, and that such a House as we were discussing might stand at any rate for fifty years.'

In April, 1910, political circles were agog with rumour.   Balfour began to prepare for a new election in June or July.   Meanwhile, in secret there had been Liberal attempts to get the Prince of Wales to bring influence to bear on his father in an attempt to solve the deadlock over the Constitution.   The Master of Elibank, Liberal Chief Whip, was the moving spirit and he believed that the Prince regarded the intervention of his father as an agreeable possibility.   It seems likely that King Edward, too, was informed of the proposal; but no action was taken because, quite suddenly, on May 6, 1910, the King died.   Both parties then called a truce and for a time discussion was stilled.

From this armistice grew the idea of a conference between the party leaders.   Garvin fanned it and acted as go-between for those liberals (Haldane, Lord Loreburn, Lloyd George) who supported it and Balfour, who was doubtful of its succeeding.   It might, at any rate, calm the political passions of the electorate at large.   It might also, however, be a Liberal trick to postpone settlement until a time more politically convenient to themselves.   Was the new King, George V, to be brought in?   If he were, it would surely be unfair at the beginning of his reign and because of his inexperience.   (Balfour did not, of course, know that, as Prince of Wales, the King, according to the wife of the Liberal Minister, C. F. G. Masterman, had been present at all the inner Liberal discussions on the Lords for over a year.)

It has been said that it was King George himself who finally suggested a conference between the Party leaders on both sides as a means of solving the pressing problems. It is true that, at an early private audience with the King, Asquith had 'said he would endeavour to come to some understanding with the Opposition to prevent a General Election and that he would not pay attention to what Redmond said'.

But the proposal when it came was the result of a decision taken at a heated Cabinet meeting (Churchill being against it), and was contained in Asquith's letter to Balfour, dated June 9, 1910:

'The lamented demise of the Crown, while it does not affect the essence of the constitutional controversy, has, in the opinion of my colleagues and myself, brought about an unforeseen but undeniable change in atmosphere and perspective.

'We believe that reasonable men of all parties share the view that, if it be possible to find by agreement a way of approach towards a solution of the problems which have to be confronted, it would not only jar upon the national feeling, but be a serious blot upon our national credit for good sense, that the early months of the new reign should be absorbed and distracted by an embittered constitutional conflict.

'If, as I do not doubt, you are to this extent of the same mind, I would venture to suggest that a meeting between us, that is yourself and myself, might possibly be a useful preliminary to further discussions.

'Of course the kind of meeting I have in view would be private, informal. It might perhaps take place in London next week.'

To this, Balfour, at once agreed. Presumably some personal talks between the two leaders then did take place privately. The conference itself, however, when it opened on June 16, 1910, comprised eight members—this may have been the result of pressure upon Asquith from the Labour supporters of his Party, who were suspicious of such a conference, and from a number of advanced Liberals, led by Josiah Wedgwood. The members on the Liberal side were Asquith, Lloyd George, Crewe, and Birrell; for the Conservatives were Balfour, Lansdowne, Austen Chamberlain and Cawdor. The proceedings were entirely confidential, and the Press were informed only of the dates when meetings were held. They continued at intervals until November.

According to Asquith's biographers, the general scheme of discussion was to cover the relations of the Houses in regard to finance; provision of some means of dealing with persistent disagreement between the two Houses whether by limiting the veto, joint sitting, referendum or otherwise; and the possibility of some changes in the composition and numbers of the Lords. In the first week, some progress seems to have been made: Asquith spoke in the House of Commons before the end of July to the effect 'that our discussions have made such progress, although we have not so far reached an agreement, as to render it in the opinion of all of us not only desirable but necessary that they should continue'. Nicholas Murray Butler, President of Columbia University, and others were called in to advise on constitutions. But by the end of October, hope of agreement had faded.

No complete record of the discussions at this conference was made, or at any rate has been made available. There is a good deal of conflict in the papers and biographies of those present at the conference as to what occurred; and as to what caused the breakdown. There is even contradiction in Balfour's own papers. For example, on October 20, 1910—a fortnight before it was announced that the conference had failed—Balfour wrote to Alfred Lyttleton that:

'The precise crisis on which we separated last Friday related to *every* form of constitutional change. We contended that constitutional change as such should be distinct both from ordinary and financial legislation, and that the proper method of dealing with it if the two Houses differed in two successive sessions was not to refer it to a giant sitting but to a plebiscite. This, it seemed to me then, and seems to me still, is in itself both logical and expedient; and it has the merit of giving to the other side a remedy against deadlocks, and to ask for security against rash innovation by a new and reckless House of Commons.

'On the question of "devolution or "provincialism" or "Home Rule" all round (or by whatever name it is to be known) I say nothing at this moment. I doubt whether most of those who talk about it have thought it out; certainly I am not prepared to dogmatise upon the subject. It never came up in any practical shape at the conference, and the rumour to the contrary is a pure invention of the Times correspondent.'

On the other hand, in a memorandum which Balfour circulated to the conference when all hope of agreement had been given up, he fixes the point of failure as arising when the proposed changes in the relations of the two Houses were discussed in connection with a definite question—Home Rule. This memorandum shows that the Conservatives would have compromised about safeguards against hasty legislation, provided that the safeguards were made permanent instead of temporary. 'We could not', Balfour says, 'make ourselves responsible for a scheme which seemed to imply that, since the people had on three separate occasions expressed their hostility to Home Rule, it was high time to withdraw the subject from their cognisance and to hand it over to the unfettered discretion of the House of Commons and the Joint Sitting.'

At these conferences, there was no intransigeance on either side. There are no villains in this particular piece. The difficulty was that it was not a question of two men, or even eight men, trying to agree among themselves: behind each man was pressure from the diversity of two parties, neither of them in any sense all firmly of the same mind on this or on any other subject. Balfour himself was ready to go a very long way in meeting the Liberal points of view and saving a situation which he now saw could become a serious threat to the British system of Government.

The failure of the Conference depressed him a good deal. On the morning it ended, Asquith saw him and wrote later to his wife: 'We all agree that AJB is head and shoulders above his colleagues. I had a rather intimate talk with him before the conference this morning. He is very pessimistic about the future, and evidently sees nothing for himself but chagrin and a possible private life.' Was there here a hint of that mood of exasperation that compelled him to resign his leadership of the Party less than a year later?

The contributory factor to his despondency may have been a lingering regret at a decision which he had been obliged to take—and which many years later he said he would still have taken in the circumstances—on a surprising proposal put before him in great secrecy by Lloyd George early in the previous month, October, 1910. This was nothing less than a suggestion for a Coalition Government. It was a bold scheme and in the memorandum dated August 17, which Lloyd George had submitted to Asquith and some other members of the Cabinet, he urged 'that a truce should be declared between the Parties for the purpose of securing the co-operation of the leading Party statesmen in a settlement of our national problems—second Chamber, Home Rule, the development of our agricultural resources, national training for defence, the remedying of social evils and a fair and judicial inquiry into the working of our fiscal system'. He emphasised that there were a number of problems urgently demanding solution, not least being the rise of foreign competitors. None of these problems, he thought, could be effectively dealt with 'without incurring temporary unpopularity'. No Party could afford this, and so the true interests of the country suffered. He further added that neither Party had the services of more than 'half a dozen first-rate men'. Coalition, a National Government, would repair this deficiency.

Asquith's reaction, though lukewarm, seems to have been that anything was worth trying at this stage. He and the other senior Ministers agreed that the proposal should be put before Balfour. Possibly Churchill and F. E. Smith, both enthusiasts for Coalition, were the intermediaries, but it also seems clear that Balfour and Lloyd George themselves met and discussed the matter. Balfour at first was inclined to be favourable towards the idea. It seemed to offer a chance of further discussion towards a solution of the immediate constitutional problems; moreover Lloyd George's memorandum proposed, among other things, that there should be a great extension of technical instruction, that national defence should come under close scrutiny, and that some system of compulsory selective military service on the Swiss model should be investigated: all these matters, as we have seen, were central to Balfour's deeper political thinking and obviously could best be considered on a non-Party basis.   He discussed the matter with some of his colleagues and found them, too, inclined towards the idea.

But by October 22, when he replied to an appeal by Garvin to support the Coalition proposal, he had decided against it. In his reply to Garvin's letter, he agreed that the country had reached a stage—'long since foreseen by statesmen of all shades of opinion'—when the equality of the two major parties gave undue parliamentary power to Radical extremists and Irish Nationalists: 'This is a position full of peril because it means, while the Unionists cannot hold office at all, the Liberals can only hold office on terms extremely distasteful to the more moderate of them, and very dangerous to the country and the Empire.'

How this situation was to be avoided he did not know; but he doubted whether any form of Home Rule was going to settle the question: 'Is it not in the nature of things that in such cases incomplete concessions (and provisional powers are necessarily incomplete) only increase the appetites they are intended to satisfy, while they provide new instruments for extorting more?'   As for Federalism, this would surely be a retrograde step in the United Kingdom.   In America, Canada and elsewhere it was a stage in the progress from separation to unification; in the United Kingdom it would be a step from unification towards separation.   Moreover, would it mean that there was to be an English as well as a British Parliament at Westminster, an English as well as a British Executive at Whitehall?

The Coalition proposal had been reduced, in effect, to a bargain over Home Rule.   Balfour's views on Ireland were determined; they were also utterly realistic.   As we saw earlier (pp. 119 ff.) he knew there was no half-way house between rule from London and complete independence.   But this was not the main reason why he came down against the Lloyd George proposal.   Nor certainly was it, as Ensor suggests in mysterious terms, the result of pressure from 'strong semi-occult forces lower down in the Conservative Party'.   Certainly, he was influenced in his decision by the advice of Akers-Douglas.   Akers-Douglas told him—what was certainly true—that the rank and file of the Conservative Party would be amazed and disillusioned by such a volte-face and the suggestion that they should work with those they had so recently and so bitterly opposed.   Obviously this was a most serious consideration; Balfour had often said, and he said it again now to Lloyd George, that 'I cannot become another Robert Peel in my Party.'   That is, he would not run the risk of dividing the Conservative Party into two opposed sections.   But over and above this, Balfour realised that the whole system of British Government depended on thesis and antithesis, on the interplay between two powerful Parties, and that to form a Coalition, except in the national emergency of war, was a far more serious threat to the Constitution than even the *ad hoc* creation of Peers. This aspect of Balfour's reasoning has been insufficiently brought out by all those who have written on this subject. Many years later, in conversation with Mrs. Dugdale, Balfour expanded on what he called Peel's 'unforgivable sin'—the giving away a principle on which he had come into power—and he further criticised some of Lloyd George's proposals in detail. But it was upon the hard rock of the Party system that he stuck.

Perhaps, too, he had no great hopes of a Coalition being a practical possibility: if the two Parties had failed to agree in the narrower field of the constitutional question, why should it be supposed that they would more easily agree in the wider, indeed all-inclusive, sphere of domestic and foreign politics? Yet he appreciated the scope and magnitude of the proposal; and he savoured to the full Lloyd George's advocacy of it at secret meetings they had. Perhaps it was this that made him the more tenacious of Coalition, with Lloyd George as Premier, a decade later.

Lloyd George later commented that had Balfour's decision been otherwise and the Coalition been formed, Germany 'might have hesitated before plunging the world into the disaster of the Great War'. This is pure speculation, and furthermore it ignores the complexities which crystallised into the outbreak of war. It is possible that had the Constitutional Conference reached a settlement, he might have supported the Government until parliamentary developments made combination inevitable; but the conference failed.

On balance, it seems to me, Balfour's judgement was right. It was certainly supported by a meeting of the 'shadow' Cabinet on November 6. But for a politician to be right is no guarantee of his success: whatever the constituencies thought of the matter, there were some leading members of the Party who differed from Balfour in his decision, among them F. E. Smith. So that the decision added a little more to the growing dissatisfaction in the Party with Balfour's leadership of it.

III

With the rejection of this proposal and the breakdown of the constitutional conference, party strife was renewed. Asquith decided that the best thing to do was to dissolve Parliament and to hold an election before Christmas. The position now reverted to what it had been before King Edward's death. That is to say, the Parliament Bill had had its first reading in the Commons; it now passed to the Lords who, on second reading, postponed consideration of it.

Preparations for the election began, and Balfour decided that the only way to recover the seats lost, largely in the north in 1906, was to play down the Tariff Reform question. He thus declared himself at the Albert Hall on November 29, 1910, as having 'not the least objection to submitting the principles of Tariff Reform to a referendum'. The referendum idea was largely supported by Bonar Law, himself a Tariff Reformer; but this did not prevent the two Chamberlains being deeply hurt and, rightly, seeing that it was the end of Tariff Reform and Imperial Preference as a measure of practical politics. Yet, for Balfour himself, it represented no change in his essential middle-of-the-road attitude to tariffs, promulgated years before.

The results of the General Election of December, 1910, showed little change: Liberals and Conservatives both had 272 seats, while Labour had 42 and the Irish 84. Yet there *was* change. For Balfour personally, a small group of obstinate Tariff Reformers—Goulding, Milner, Ridley—now conceived a lasting antipathy; for the nation, there had vanished the last hope of altering the balance of parties and thus solving the constitutional problem by normal means. It was this fact that concerned Balfour much more than his personal position. On December 15, 1910, Sandars wrote on his behalf to Garvin pointing out that the 'dead heat' election led to an impossible situation:

'No doubt Asquith will ask the King to ensure that the Parliament Bill passes the House of Lords. If the King refuses the creation of sufficient peers, Asquith will resign, the King will send for Balfour who will say:

' "I am very sorry, sir, to say that with every desire to help Your Majesty in the difficult circumstances in which you are placed, I see no prospect of my being able to serve you. I could, doubtless, form a government; but that government would be beaten in the House of Commons within 24 hours of meeting Parliament. I could not, in decency, ask Your Majesty for a dissolution. The Country would not tolerate another Election at this moment.

' "What *am* I to do", then says the distracted Monarch: "Can you recommend any other person to whom I may apply?" "No, I cannot", replies Mr. Balfour, "I would gladly serve, of course, under or with anyone. . . . No personal feelings would stand in the way. . . . But honestly I know of no statesman who can command a sufficient Parliamentary following; and in short I have no alternative to suggest but that Your Majesty should again summon Mr. Asquith".

'Reluctantly the King sends for Asquith—Asquith repeats his demands: the King is faced with the necessity of promising the creation of a battalion of emergency noblemen.'

To save the King and the country, 'this grave humiliation', Sandars continues, Balfour sees no alternative to letting the Bill pass the Lords. 'hateful as it is'. He adds:

'(Balfour) does not disguise from himself that there will be many who will say that it is better that the Government should be involved in the laughter and ridicule which would accompany the appearance of this vast mass of puppets, summoned to register the decrees of their task-masters, than that the Lords should strike their flag without firing a shot. But, as at present advised, he thinks there is less real public mischief attending the latter course. He has not, of course, yet made up his mind.'

But the point really is that if Balfour had known in December, 1910, what he was not to discover until the following July, this *impasse* would probably never have arisen: what he was ignorant of was the crucial fact that in November, 1910, *before the election*, Asquith had gone to King George and obtained from him a pledge that, in the King's words, 'in the event of the Government' (i.e. Liberal Government) 'being re-turned with a majority at the General Election I should use my pre-rogative to make peers if asked for.' Asquith's methods of forcing this pledge have been described by Jenkins as 'not over-delicate'. That is an understatement. When the King asked Asquith what he would do if the pledges were refused, he replied: 'I should immediately resign, and at the next election should make the cry "The King and the Peers against the People".' Even the King's request to see Balfour and Lansdowne was refused. He then said: 'I have been forced into this, and I should like the country to know it.' This, too, was forbidden him. As the King later said, they 'behaved disgracefully to me'. Asquith afterwards described the events as 'the most important political occasion in my life'.

But what could Balfour have done, even if he had known of the pledge? As we saw, before the second election at the meeting on April 29, 1910, with Esher, Knollys and the Archbishop of Canterbury, Balfour had said 'he would be prepared to form a government to prevent the King being put in the position contemplated by the de-mand for the creation of Peers'. But he would not have held out much hope of this Government lasting. 'I have never denied', he wrote to Stamfordham on August 9, 1911, 'that if 9 months ago I had been asked to take office and go to the country *on the bare question of the Parliament Bill* I should certainly have done so, but with the greatest doubts as to the results of the Election. But please observe that, had I been consulted in November, I might have been able to alter that question into quite a different one, namely, does the country think it right that the King should be driven to promise, many months before the event, that the prerogative should be used, not to get the Parliament Bill through but to get the Parliament Bill through *in the exact form desired by Mr. Redmond*? On this issue an election, taken under the new register, might have produced, and would have produced very different results from those which actually followed from the election taken under the old.'

Balfour felt, with every justification, that he and the Conservative Party had been unfairly kept in the dark, and hence deprived of the chance of deciding their own line of action and, so, possibly winning the election. The Government had outmanœuvred them by making the King a pawn in the political game.

Knollys, as we saw, played a dubious part in all these extraordinary convolutions. Balfour's statement at the meeting on April 29, 1910, did not reach the King until Knollys retired. When he saw the memorandum, the King dictated and initialled the following minute: 'It was not until late in the year 1913 that the foregoing letters and memoranda came into my possession. The knowledge of their contents would undoubtedly have had an important bearing and influence with regard to Mr. Asquith's request for guarantees on November 16, 1910.'

As well as suppressing this memorandum, Knollys also gave the decisive advice to the King to give the pledge for which Asquith asked on November 16—despite incidentally, equally strong advice against doing so from the King's other Private Secretary, Stamfordham (Bigge). Yet it was Knollys who was in the strongest position, having been at the Archbishop of Canterbury's conference, to know that Balfour would have agreed to form a Government.

Knollys played one more devious rôle *vis-à-vis* Balfour. In a letter to Stamfordham of August 9, 1911, Balfour explains this final straw which led up to his quarrel with Knollys: 'I dined with Lord Knollys (by H.M.'s command)'—these words are erased—'*after* the Election' (in December, 1910) 'and just before I left for the Continent. Shortly before the company separated I learned to my surprise that the dinner had been held with the knowledge and approval of the Prime Minister and that presumably, therefore, everything I said in the freedom of friendly conversation was to be repeated to him. I told Lord Knollys at the time that if these were to be regarded as the only conditions under which H.M.'s Private Secretary could see politicians outside the circle of his Ministers, H.M. would be parting with a valuable right which all his predecessors had enjoyed. This, however, by the way.

'A more important point is this—do you think it fair that I should be asked to discuss public affairs, under circumstances which imply freedom and confidence with an ambassador by whom I was deliberately kept in ignorance of the most essential features of the situation? Both Lord Knollys and the Prime Minister were, from the very nature of the case, intimately acquainted with all that had taken place with regard to the pledges in November. *I* had not an inkling that in

November anything of importance on this subject had been arranged between the King and his Ministers. Lord Knollys seems, therefore, to have endeavoured to extract from me general statements of policy to be used as the occasion arose, whilst studiously concealing the most important elements and the actual concrete problem that had to be solved. He did this *after* the event, when nothing that I said could possibly aid the King, though it might possibly embarrass me. He could only have done it in order to extract in the course of an "un-buttoned" conversation *obiter dicta* to be used when the occasion arose. It seems to me, looking back on this transaction with the full knowledge which I now possess, to have been one of the most singular examples of domestic diplomacy of which I have ever heard.'

Balfour continues that, in his opinion, no ill consequences have, as it happens, ensued, and nothing that he said on the occasion of the dinner (at the Marlborough Club) seems to run counter in the smallest degree to his previously expressed views. He adds, however, that Stamfordham's versions of his observations to Knollys do not quite tally with the version written down on the same night by Esher. This version makes it clear that Balfour thought the point of difference in November between the King and his Ministers was on the propriety of dissolving Parliament at that time. Balfour says that he never sus-pected that dissolution was in fact not the point of controversy at all:

'What it comes to is this—had I been consulted in November, 1910 or could I have made the issue before the country the propriety of creating Peers to enable Home Rule to be carried in *this* Parliament without the deliberate approval of the constituencies, I should have taken office and dissolved early in 1911.' (This point is clearly re-iterated in a letter from Sandars to Derby, August 3, 1911.) '*After* the December Election clearly no fresh dissolution was possible till after the Coronation. The country was sick of elections; and would not have tolerated three in 13 or 14 months. The Government was, therefore, at that moment, complete master of the situation. Whether a change of Government and a dissolution was practicable after the Coronation was another question. *I* at least was preparing for such a possibility, when I first learned that the November pledge made the Crown, the House of Lords and the Opposition all equally powerless. This is the whole story so far as I am concerned. I cannot tell you how greatly I feel for H.M. in the circumstances of quite unparalleled difficulty in which, through no fault of his own, he has found himself involved.'

What Esher's note makes abundantly clear is that Balfour had said that he would take office, but that he thought it imprudent, *if it was simply a question of to dissolve or not*, for the King to dismiss his Ministers and summon the Leader of the Opposition. If he could have gone to the country in December, 1910, on the clear issue of a mass creation of peers, he believed, in other words, that his chances of winning would have been greater.

To round off this unhappy incident with Knollys it should be recorded that, as Balfour no doubt intended, Stamfordham showed Knollys his letter. The next day, August 10, 1911, Knollys rushed up to see Sandars, and, Sandars writes to Balfour that, 'in language of unrestrained violence he complained bitterly. He said that your letter amounted to an accusation of "gross treachery and dishonourable conduct". I asked what purpose was served by telling Asquith that he was meeting you at dinner, obviously for a political discussion, if Asquith was to learn nothing of what passed at it. Knollys could not answer this. He only persisted in saying that the King, and not Asquith, was informed of the terms of the conversation. . . . His irritation and nervous disturbance . . . but I think he has been much affected by the unpopularity he has suffered in the course of recent months. He told me that the Tories, as he calls them, treated him with studied coldness and he pointed out that he was suffering from the unfounded charge of influencing Peers who voted for the Government.'

In letters of August 18, 1911, and August 20, Knollys writes to Sandars complaining of 'false and calumnious accusation which he (Balfour) had brought against me'. He also complains that Balfour has not answered his complaints. In fact it was not until three weeks later, on September 7, 1911 that Balfour wrote to Knollys denying that he had charged him with 'gross treachery', and reiterating that: 'Conversations between H.M.'s Private Secretaries and Members of the Opposition which the latter conceived to be informal and confidential have, in fact, been reported to the P.M.—this will, I suppose, not be denied.'

Next day, September 8, 1911, Knollys replied: 'The King was so unhappy (that is the only word I can use) at the idea that he might have acted differently; that he might have adopted the alternative course of sending for you to form a Government; that I determined to ascertain from you whether you could have done so for H.M.'s information only.' Knollys says that the Tories have accused him of canvassing Peers which he denies, though 'I certainly was most anxious that the Parliament Bill should not be rejected by the House of Lords.' He adds: 'We shall for the future have to meet as strangers.'

Balfour replied to Knollys on September 10, 1911 that he had not suggested that Knollys repeated *his* private conversations. He was not making an attempt to injure Knollys. 'What injury *could* I do you even if I wished? Am I the sort of person who wishes to do people injuries even those who are not my friends? . . . I hate rows;—and with you of all people! If, however, you take a different view, will you let me have a word at Balmoral *before* we meet; so as to make matters as little awkward as possible?' (A note on this letter in Mrs. Dugdale's hand states that Lord Knollys was at pains to avoid seeing Balfour during the visit to Balmoral.)

Next day Knollys wrote somewhat ungraciously that he was 'willing to drop the matter'. On November 9, 1911, Balfour's personal secretary, W. M. Short, rounds off the episode in a letter to Alice Balfour: 'Mr. Balfour yesterday received a visit from Lord Knollys; and I gather that a reconciliation took place.' The reconciliation was somewhat superficial. On being asked a little later by Lady Desborough whom he would and would not like to meet at her house-party, he replied: 'My dear Ettie, I should enjoy meeting any man in England, except Lord Knollys: him I will not meet.'

We have moved ahead of history here, not merely to show Balfour in the unusual rôle of party to a quarrel, but to give some indication of the sort of temper in which high politics during this period were being conducted.

Returning to December 1910, Balfour—still with no idea of the King's promise to Asquith—reiterated his view that the King was in 'a most difficult position' in a letter to Lansdowne. Any demand for pledges to the King would be unconstitutional: 'The creation of 500 Peers is a revolution. It is so because no action on the part of the Sovereign can be part of the accepted machinery of the Constitution unless it is capable of repetition. Even those who think it proper to convert an assembly of 600 into one of 1,100 would hardly think the same of a subsequent scheme for turning one of 1,100 into one of 1,900. . . . [In any case] a sovereign may be asked *to act*; it is no part of his duty to *promise*.'

This letter was in reply to a request from Lansdowne whose advice had been sought, through an intermediary, by the King. The King's state of mind, knowing what he had done, on receipt of this reply may be imagined.

The Parliament Bill reached the House of Lords on May 23, 1911. It was there debated, and a long series of amendments made in the Committee stage which lasted until July 6, 1911, the Peers' policy being not to reject but to send the Bill back to the Commons transformed. It was delaying action; for the Commons, as everyone knew, would not accept the changes.

In the first week of July, 1911, Balfour was informed privately, and for the first time, of the pledges the King had given. He was officially told of the position by Lloyd George on July 18. His first reaction was that it was 'a shocking scandal' that the Government had exacted such pledges about the Peers *before* the last election. He then called together the Conservative 'Shadow' Cabinet which met on July 7, at his house in Carlton Gardens. There for the first time the question of surrender by the House of Lords was discussed as practical politics. But what exactly was the position? Had the King promised to make an *unlimited* number of Peers or had he confined himself to a specific number? This, too, would have very important bearings on the actions of the Opposition. Salisbury was therefore asked to sound the King on this subject on July 22. Six days later, Stamfordham wrote to Salisbury:

'I am told that a statement is going the rounds of the Unionist Party that the King will *not* make an unlimited number of Peers, and that your authority and my own is quoted in support of this theory.

'But I understood that when you saw the King the question you submitted to H.M. was: "Is it the case that Your Majesty has undertaken to create an unlimited number of Peers and so swamp the House of Lords with a permanent Liberal majority?' The King replied: "Certainly not—I have only promised to make sufficient to pass the Parliament Bill; not one more nor less."—and this I understand to be the case. Of course, if, unfortunately, the Opposition elect to oppose the Bill and bring all their forces into line, while H.M. would still only create sufficient Peers to pass the Bill, their minimum number might assume proportions which would not be unworthy of the name "unlimited". But then H.M. has assumed that the Opposition were as anxious as the Government to avoid the creation of one single Peer. Of course, I quite see that it may be argued that the King is pledged to make what might appear to be *"unlimited"* Peers, but this could only be if the Opposition forced him to do so. But we must remember that the bill will have to pass.'

Balfour now took up the correspondence and wrote to Stamfordham on August 1, 1911; 'I hear that you have expressed the opinion that the King would under no circumstances consent to create more than 120 Peers in order to pass the Parliament Bill. This statement, coming from you, carries, of course, absolute conviction to all who hear it. Yet it seems to me wholly inconsistent both with Lord Knolly's verbal statements to me, made on behalf of H.M., and with the letter which H.M. authorised the P.M. to write to Lord Lansdowne and myself. Is it true? Or is not true? If it is true, I find myself in the position of having given public advice to my Party, based on a total misconception of H.M.'s intention and the nature of his pledges to the P.M.

'For my advice was founded on the belief (justified, I thought by the King's actual words to myself) that his pledge rendered the House of Lords powerless. Your version of the pledge carries with it no such consequences; the House of Lords could easily outvote the creation of 120 Peers brought into existence to pass Home Rule and in my opinion they not only could but would. You will thus see the immediate urgency of letting me know authoritatively whether your views, or

what I understand are your views, of the scope of H.M.'s declaration
to the P.M. are to be accepted as representing the facts of the case.
My whole treatment of the crisis must evidently depend on your
answer.'

The 'public advice to his Party' which Balfour refers to had been
given in a letter in *The Times* on July 25, 1911. This mentioned the
fact that Lord Lansdowne had now come down on the side of surrender,
and said that the Unionists in the Lords ought to follow their trusted
leader: 'But if this be impossible, if differ we must, if there be Peers who
(on this occasion) are resolved to abandon Lord Lansdowne, if there be
politicians outside who feel constrained to applaud them, let us all at
least remember that the campaign for the restoration of constitutional
liberty is but just begun, that this is but an episode in it, and that unless
the forces conducting it possess unity and discipline, ultimate victory is
impossible. It would in my opinion be a misfortune if the present
crisis left the House of Lords weaker than the Parliament Bill by itself
would make it, but it would be an irreparable tragedy if it left us a
divided Party.'

Stamfordham replied to Balfour's letter in two letters, both dated
August 1, 1911. In the first he denies saying that there were to be no
more than 120 Peers created: 'All I *have* stated and I repeat again is
that the King never undertook to create an unlimited number of Peers
with a view to establishing a permanent Government majority in the
House of Lords.'

To this Balfour replied that Stamfordham's reply seemed quite clear:
'It means, does it not, that whatever number of Peers were required to
pass the Bill, that number would be created, even though the creation
had the effect of flooding the House with 400 new members?'

Stamfordham's second letter shows signs of failing temper: 'There
seem to me times for plain speaking. You say in reply to my letter that
you *think* it is clear.—Let me tell you that this whole question was raised
by Lord Salisbury asking to see the King which he did on July 22 in
order to ask whether it was the case that H.M. had consented to make
an *unlimited* number of Peers with a view of, as I said in my letter of
7.30 this evening, swamping the House of Lords. The King's reply
was to my mind perfectly clear: "Certainly not. I have agreed with
the P.M. to make only what is necessary to give the Government a
majority to pass the Bill!"'

'But evidently there has been a good deal of gerrymandering with the
King's words. If Salisbury had said "Have you limited the number of
Peers you will make to X Y Z?" the King would I feel certain have
replied equally: "Certainly not and etc."'

'Of course if, thanks to the Halsburyites and Salisburyites, the
Government find they cannot be sure of passing their Bill, the King to

his great chagrin, will have to make Peers sufficient to leave no chance
of defeat to the Government, but, as I said before, H.M., like your
humble servant, thought that Government and Opposition wanted to
avoid the creation of *one* Peer; and therefore hoped that none would be
asked for.

'P.S. *Certainly* if the King is told by the P.M. that he requires X
number of Peers in order to guarantee passing the Bill, X Peers must
be made, even if it exceeds the mystic number 120, which I am supposed to have named.'

Next day Stamfordham wrote again, though it cannot be said that this
letter of August 2, 1911 clarified the position in any way: 'But please
make no mistake—while the King did say he had made no promise to
create an unlimited number of Peers, but only sufficient to pass the Bill
—that Bill has to pass and if by the action of the Opposition the Government found they required 400 Peers that number would have to be
made.'

As Balfour saw the matter a few months later, on October 18, 1911,
'the real difficulty, of course', (he wrote to Salisbury), 'was that neither
the King nor his entourage knew enough about politics to be able to
anticipate contingencies. If they had, they would never have acquiesced in November, but, having acquiesced, and the pledge having
been given, and apparently interpreted by both parties to it as a promise to get the Parliament Bill through in any form approved by the
House of Commons, neither the King nor Stamfordham, nor perhaps,
anybody else could say for certain how many Peers this would involve.
It is certain the King would have desired to have as few as he could;
but how many that few would have been if the Bill had been thrown out
and the new Session begun, must always be a matter of speculation.'

The King himself, as is known from Nicolson's *Life of George V*, was
resentful of the way he had been treated by the Liberals, and believed
he had not been accorded the confidence or the consideration to which
he was entitled. More particularly, he resented the fact that the
pledge had been kept secret, not merely before, but also during the
December election of 1910.

Could Balfour have done anything to strengthen the King's position?
There is a curious letter from Salisbury to Balfour dated December 14,
1910, in which he says: 'The King is, I think, evidently anxious to save
this situation if he possibly can, but he is almost hopeless. You know
however the man—how he talks . . . can anything be done to hearten
him up?' Salisbury goes on to assume that he has not given any
guarantees and that after the election was over Asquith might ask for a
categorical Yes or No with the threat of immediate resignation. 'Do
you not think', Salisbury asked Balfour, 'that the moment has arrived
when you ought to intimate to him that, in that event, he will not be

left in the lurch?   I am not so sure that I am as despairing as he is of
a central Government, but he ought to be made aware—if he has not
been made aware already—that either you or someone else *will* form a
government.'

The keeping of the secret of the pledge until July, however, precluded all such possibilities.   On July 14 the Cabinet called for the
King's pledge to be put into operation; a few days later they informed
the Opposition that the King had agreed and that the intention was to
proceed to a creation of Peers even before the Lords had an opportunity of reconsidering the Bill subsequently to the rejection of their
amendments by the Commons.   To Balfour's mind the dilemma was
now perfectly clear and the decision that ought to be taken equally
obvious: the Lords had to chose between having a permanent Liberal
majority in their House as a result of a large creation of Peers, or
accepting the Parliament Bill.   There was, Balfour believed, no
alternative but to accept the Bill.

Unfortunately many of his leading colleagues disagreed with him.
On the morning of July 21, 1911, the Conservative 'Shadow' Cabinet
met again at No. 4 Carlton Gardens.   Balfour, Lansdowne, Curzon
and a majority of the members were for surrender; but Selborne,
Halsbury, Salisbury, Austen Chamberlain, Edward Carson, F. E. Smith
and George Wyndham were for resistance to the end.   The same
afternoon there was a meeting of some 200 Conservative Peers at
Lansdowne's house.   Instead of pressing on them the virtues of his
own decision to surrender, and intimating that he would resign if his
advice were not followed, Lansdowne appeared merely, according to
his biographer, Lord Newton, 'to invite expressions of opinion, and the
opportunity was at once seized by Lord Halsbury, Lord Selborne, Lord
Salisbury, the Duke of Norfolk and Lord Willoughby de Broke to raise
the standard of revolt'.

Thus, the party began to divide into the 'die-hards' and the non-
resisters.   The latter were led by Curzon who saw clearly that further
resistance could achieve nothing and would damage the Lords, the
Conservative Party and the Monarchy; but, unlike Balfour, he believed
he could convince others that his views were correct.   He, therefore,
set up a small committee to contact those Peers who rarely came to
Westminster, but who were essential for the critical vote, and to get
Balfour to give a clear lead to the Party.

IV

By this time Balfour had had enough.   He refused to call a full party
meeting and he cancelled the meeting he was due to address in the City
in the following week.   He wrote, however, a memorandum to the

'Shadow' Cabinet but it was never sent, perhaps because it demon-strated too clearly Balfour's contempt for the 'last ditchers'.   Of them he said:

'I regard the policy which its advocates call "fighting to the last" as essentially theatrical, though not on that account necessarily wrong. It does nothing, it can do nothing; it is not even intended to do anything, except advertise the situation.   The object of those who advocate it is to make people realise what (it is assumed) they will not realise other-wise, namely, the fact that we are the victims of a revolution.

'Their policy may be a wise one, but there is nothing heroic about it; old military metaphors which liken the action of the "fighting" peers to Leonidas at Thermopylae seem to me purely for music-hall con-sumption.

'I grant that the music-hall attitude of mind is too wide-spread to be negligible.   By all means play up to it, if the performance is not too expensive.   If the creation of X peers pleases the multitude and con-veys the impression that the Lords are "game to the end", I raise no objection to it, *provided it does not swamp the House of Lords*.   All my criticism yesterday was directed against a policy so profoundly modify-ing the constitution of the second Chamber that it would become, with regard to some important measures, a mere annexe to the present House of Commons.   From this point of view the creation of 50 or 100 new peers is a matter of indifference.   I regard the importance attached to the particular shape in which the House of Lords are to display their impotence in the face of the King's declaration, as a misfortune.   The attention of the country should be directed not to these empty man-œuvres, but to the absolute necessity of stemming the revolutionary tide, by making such use of ministerial power impossible in the future.'

Balfour suppressed this memorandum; it showed too clearly his opinion that both sides of his party were behaving with foolishness and hysteria.   However, on July 24, he published a letter of support for Curzon, then anxiously propagandising against the die-hards.   This in effect was merely a plea for loyalty to the leader, Lansdowne; but it upset Austen Chamberlain who wrote to him: 'Nothing that you have said on any of these occasions has prepared me for the line you have now taken up or given me a hint of your intention to treat this as a question of confidence in the Leadership of either yourself or Lansdowne.   On the contrary, you have repeatedly stated that this was a question which must be decided by each individual for himself.   The crisis at which we have now arrived has been visible for a year past.   We have frequently discussed it. Yet till this morning you had given no lead.'

Balfour replied that no question of disloyalty to himself had arisen. He also pointed out with some asperity that, although he had de-nounced the resisters rather than answered their arguments, so had Chamberlain.   There is no doubt that by this time even so equably-natured a character as Balfour was beginning to feel frustrated and impotent.   Others had felt it much earlier.   Asquith and Balfour had both been attacked in a letter to *The Times* from a 'Peer' (probably either Rosebery or Selborne) for attending a political ball given in June, 1911, by Winterton and F. E. Smith.   The writer spoke of the levity with which they were treating the great constitutional crisis and how unthinkable it was that any of the great political antagonists of the past should have met under similar circumstances!   One of the sons of Lady Elcho later heard Balfour, in reply to this attack, say that 'If he had known he was going to be attacked for going to a fancy-dress ball in plain clothes and leaving at 10.30 p.m., he would have gone as a harlequin and stayed till four o'clock in the morning.'

By the end of July, Balfour was wearied by the foolishness of some of the Conservatives.   The wilder ones among them, according to Wilfrid Blunt, even spoke of armed resistance.   Others pretended to believe that, when it came to the point, no Peers would in fact be created and that it was only a question of calling Asquith's bluff. After an evening of violent speeches at the so-called Halsbury banquet on July 24, 1911, some of the diners wished to draw the 86-year-old leader of the die-hards in triumph in his coach.   Gradually the violence crystallised into open criticism of the leadership of Balfour and Lansdowne.   In some cases, this was due to personal grievances.   In the Coronation Honours List, for example, Asquith had proposed that F. E. Smith should be elevated to the Privy Council, but Balfour wrote to him saying that he thought Hayes Fisher, formerly his Private Secretary, should be preferred.   At this stage, there was no criticism in public of Balfour by his own party; in private, much dissatisfaction was being expressed.   As early as January, 1911, the Left-wing news-paper *Reynolds's* had remarked hopefully: 'The young sparks of the Tory Party are united and decided—they want a new leader for the Party.   They cannot understand Prince Arthur, as he is called. The Right Hon. Gentleman as he stands languidly at the table in the House of Commons, resembles a faded flower of Cambridge culture, and he is described by the ladies as "sweet".'   In August, Garvin wrote to Waldorf Astor that, 'so serious is the situation that I myself question whether any power on earth can hold up A.J.B. for long'.

On August 7, 1911, the Conservatives tabled votes of censure in both Houses, and in the Commons Balfour moved 'that the advice given to His Majesty by His Majesty's Ministers whereby they obtained from His Majesty a pledge that a sufficient number of peers would be created to pass the Parliament Bill in the shape in which it left this House is a gross violation of constitutional liberty, whereby, among many other evil consequences, the people will be precluded from again pronounc-ing upon the policy of Home Rule.'   Balfour was careful to avoid any hint of criticism of the Sovereign himself—indeed to such an extent

that a Conservative remarked that 'Asquith has sacrificed the King to
to his Party, and Balfour has sacrificed his Party to the King'. Next
day, however, one of the die-hards, Lord Hugh Cecil, openly dis-
approved of the Sovereign's behaviour—a speech as we now know
which disturbed the King himself a good deal, especially as he had
been receiving a number of unfriendly anonymous letters.

Some time before this, however, the public had grown tired of the
controversy. The Coronation, and the 'battle of Sidney Street', were
far more attractive. Moreover, the summer of 1911 was one of the
hottest on record: there were more cooling things to do than to listen
to the hot air of the dying constitutional debates. As the day of the
crucial vote drew nearer in the House of Lords, it became clear that
Curzon's efforts were beginning to take effect. On the afternoon of
August 10, the thermometer rose to 100 degrees: the speechmakers were
flaccid; and when the division came, 37 Conservatives (plus 13 bishops)
supported the Liberals. The Government had got its way by 17 votes,
the die-hards were defeated, the dubious creation prevented. 'I am
indeed grateful', the King remarked, 'for what they have done and
saved me from a humiliation which I should never have survived. If
the creation had taken place, I should have never been the same again.'
It was Balfour who had won the day for the King and moderation;
and for true Conservatism: in matters of principle, delay the evil day
but if necessary give way before the violent clash. The one person
who had not been saved was Balfour himself.

He did not wait for the Bill to go through the House of Lords. He
left England for the spa of Bad Gastein in Austria the day before. His
action may be interpreted either as resulting from pique or as a mark of
his contempt for the party which he led. We have seen that there had
been growing discontent in the party with his leadership, and it was not
entirely confined to those who vehemently opposed his policy of
surrender to the Liberals. No public criticism of him had as yet been
made, but there were enthusiastic meetings in honour of Lord Halsbury,
the leader of the die-hards, and there were other signs that at last
Balfour had come up against a situation in the party which he could not
manipulate.

Not unnaturally he felt strongly on the subject. He wrote a few days
later to Lady Wemyss: 'Politics have been to me quite unusually odious.
I am not going into the subject, but I have, as a matter of fact, felt the
situation more acutely than any in my public life—I mean from the
personal point of view. As you know I am very easy-going, and not
given to brooding over my wrongs. But last Friday and Saturday I
could think of nothing else: a thing which had not happened to me since
I was unjustly "complained of" at Eton more than 40 years ago.
On Saturday the cloud lifted; yet it *has not* and perhaps *will* not disappear

till recent events are things barely remembered.' Balfour added
that he was trying to forget politics amid the cataracts and the pines
and that he was writing an article on his philosophy.

Balfour's private secretary, Sandars, left a note on events of this
time and from it we gather something of what rankled most in Balfour's
mind as he took the Bad Gastein cure. Balfour, he said, felt that
Chamberlain had split the Party in 1903, committed it to a false step
in 1909, and split it once more in 1911. His own efforts in this direction had been to strain every nerve to prevent disunion in the Party
and he felt that a fair-minded man would admit that he had saved the
Party from breaking up and that it went into the General Election of
1910 united. Despite this, however, in the matter of the Lords, a
minority of the 'Shadow' Cabinet had declined to accept his advice
and had gone out into the world and embarked upon a policy of active
resistance to him. Sandars quotes Balfour as saying in private: 'I
confess to feeling I have been badly treated. I have no wish to
lead a Party under these humiliating conditions. It is no gratification
to me to be their leader.'

V

Balfour had clearly thought of resigning the leadership before he left
London. During his stay at Bad Gastein he definitely decided upon it.
From the point of view of power and from the point of view of his
career, it was a serious decision to take since, at the age of 63, it seemed
unlikely that he would find any future in politics, at least in the Lower
House. At any rate, he returned to London in September, 1911,
with his mind made up. As it happened it was in the September
number of the *National Review*, that its editor, Leo Maxse, wrote the
article in which, in the course of demonstrating that the Conservative
Party needed a new leader, he invented the slogan 'Balfour must go'.
On the September 8, Balfour wrote to Lady Elcho saying that he was
sorry to resign, the dominating factor being 'that I have been continuously in difficult office, or leading the Party in the House of
Commons and the country for 25 years without a single break. I
don't believe our parliamentary history has any parallel to it in point of
mere duration; and political work is far more exacting now than at any
period in our history.' At the same time he called Balcarres, successor
to Hood as Conservative Chief Whip, and Steel-Maitland, Chairman
of the Party, up to Whittingehame and broached to them the idea of his
resignation. They agreed that there was dissatisfaction within the Party,
but they were reluctant to consider a change in the leadership. There
was certainly no evidence as yet that anyone would be so bold as to try
and evict him. The state of mind of most of the Party, except the

extremist minority, was probably well expressed by Austen Chamberlain who wrote on August 20, 1911 'I confess that Balfour's leadership at times makes me despair of the fortunes of a Party so led. He has no comprehension of the habits of thought of his countrymen and no idea of how things strike them. . . .   But I am too much attached to him ever to join any combination against him or his leadership.'   Much the same thing was being said by Lord Derby, a supporter through thick and thin.

Balcarres and Steel-Maitland asked who might succeed him. Balfour suggested that Austen Chamberlain should lead in the Commons and Curzon in the Lords. (This assumed, of course, that Lansdowne would retire from the Lords as Leader; in fact, he did not do so.)   The other contestant for the leadership was Walter Long; curiously enough the day after this meeting at Whittingehame where Balfour had stated his preference for Chamberlain rather than Long he received a letter from Long inviting him to retire.   Meanwhile the Halsbury Club was formed—on October 7—and whatever variety of views its members had, they all combined in feeling that a new leader ought to be found, Selborne, Winterton, Amery and Carson being the most vocal.

On October 30, Balfour informed Akers-Douglas that his mind was made up, and Law knew by November 4.   On November 7, Balfour informed the King of his intentions, giving as his reasons matters, as he also told Derby, 'mainly concerned with health'—a somewhat conventional way of putting it.   The actual public announcement he made at a meeting of the City of London Conservative Association on the afternoon of Wednesday, November 8.   Again, he dwelled on his health and the need to resign before he became 'petrified and inelastic'. He also referred to 'a certain feeling of unrest in the Party'.   Austen Chamberlain, in a letter on the same day to his father, said 'I think the restlessness in the Party, particularly outside the House, has affected him, as requiring more labour than he can give to deal with it satisfactorily and as indicating demands on the leader's strength and time to which he no longer feels equal.'

His resignation came, despite the preliminary rumblings, as a surprise to many inside, as well as outside, the Party.   Joseph Chamberlain, for example, on hearing of Balfour's intention on the morning of the resignation, wrote to him saying that the whole Party in the House of Commons would regard his retirement as a grave misfortune, 'perhaps even a disaster'.   He even said that when the Halsbury Club met again he would make it clear that there was no wish for Balfour's resignation. Asquith, expressing surprise in a speech on the following day, said that 'by universal consent Balfour was the most distinguished member of the greatest deliberative assembly in the world'.   Asquith's wife, Margot, put matters much more strongly when she wrote privately to Asquith on November 9, 1911: 'It serves them darned right—now if they don't all perceive it the whole world will—the vast gap that separates Arthur from all his colleagues in everything—prestige, intellect, charm, brilliance.'

But there were those among the shrewdest observers of the political scene who felt that with Balfour's departure it was more than a merely personal era that was over. Balfour himself in his resignation speech had referred to the fact that the demand made upon legislators and administrators for work which was 'neither administration nor legislation, is becoming so heavy that both legislation and administration are likely to suffer'. He felt it would become more and more difficult to get men of adequate leisure and position who were prepared to undergo the great toils attaching to political life in the future. He spoke with distrust of the possibility that affairs of State would devolve into the hands of those who were prepared 'to be politicians and nothing but politicians, to work the political machine as professional politicians'.

Some, however, saw that his resignation symbolised an even deeper break. Alfred Lyttelton had written to Balfour earlier: 'It is with a sense of oppression and misgiving that I foresee in action the intolerance and crude slap-dash of Birmingham unchecked by the great intellectual forces which your presence and control guaranteed, and upon which the best moderate opinion relied.' (It was Glasgow not Birmingham in the end.) H. G. Wells, who as we have seen at one time came under the Balfour charm, wrote many years later on the subject of his resignation that: 'When his essential liberalism came face to face with this new baseness of commercialised imperialism, with all its push and energy, he made a very poor fight for it. He allowed himself to be hustled into the background of affairs by men with narrower views and nearer objectives. He could not control these new people but he hampered them and so they turned upon him.' Wells was indicating roughly the spirit that divided the Conservative Party of the nineteenth century from that of the Party of post-World War I. The division, that is to say, between the Party led by the landed gentry and the Party led by business men.

The point was underlined by the Party's choice of successor: in the end it was neither Austen Chamberlain nor Walter Long, but the Glasgow ironmaster, Andrew Bonar Law who had previously held no office more important than that of Parliamentary Secretary to the Board of Trade. The tactical reasons for this choice we need not discuss. But after Balfour had made his resignation speech he retired to Whittingehame and two days later, Sandars, keeping him posted on developments, wrote: 'I have just heard that it has been settled that

Bonar Law will be elected leader of the Party in the House of Commons. Much intrigue has been at work. Walter (Long) up to some few hours ago, appeared to be winning. Austen was so satisfied that Party detriment would result that he wrote a considered letter to Walter, pointing out that he, Austen, would withdraw, and that he and Walter together ought to concentrate upon the unanimous selection of Bonar Law. It was rather a clever move on Austen's part, because he forced Walter's hand. Walter's party had decided in any case that if they could not command a sufficient number of votes for Walter, they would transfer these votes to Bonar Law rather than have Austen. Austen therefore, as you see, has turned this movement into another channel by forcing Walter into joint action with himself to secure the election of Bonar Law.'

Short, Balfour's personal secretary, expanded the details in an informative letter to Balfour's sister Alice. Writing on November 11, 1911, he said: 'Bonar Law's methods are open to much criticism. In this struggle he has been run by Max Aitken, the little Canadian adventurer who sits for Ashton-under-Lyne, introduced into the seat by him. Aitken practically owns the *Daily Express* and the *Daily Express* has run Bonar Law for the last two days for all it is worth. B.L. has been inflexible throughout in his intention to stand, no matter what the harm of Party division might be. The real B.L. appears to be a man of boundless ambition, untempered by any nice feeling; it is a revelation to me. He found Goulding had committed himself to a hearty support of Austen. He went to Goulding and, reviving ancient memories and rash promises, he ordered his support, and this support and influence was then transferred by Goulding from Austen to B.L.'

Balfour had said to Sandars a few months earlier: 'Some people do not like the qualifications in my speeches. They are not expressed to save myself, but to protect my Party in the future when the statements of leaders are recalled to injure the Party.' Law never qualified, partly because unlike Balfour he was unable to see any other side of a given case except his own—and, as Jenkins puts it, 'only the more salient features of his own'. Unlike Balfour, Law was not troubled by misgivings; it was this that the commercial wing of the Conservative Party wanted.

In the choice of Law, Jenkins finds a sign of the bitterness and frustration of the Conservative Party, enraged by its defeat over the Parliament Bill; from this time it began to move ever faster towards extreme courses and fits of violence. Certainly extreme courses were shortly to be pursued and, while the onus for this cannot be laid upon Law personally, it is difficult not to believe that had Balfour still been Leader, his moderating—or if one prefers it, his equivocating—counsels might have avoided the dangers about to beset the Party.

Balfour himself had foreseen in his resignation speech that 'revolutionary suggestions' would be brought forward—on Home Rule, on disestablishment and on universal suffrage, and he spoke of a steadily growing disgust among the better classes of the population with the Liberal régime. He felt that it was better to resign in mid-session, before these matters came to the fore, in order to give his successor time to get into the saddle. Nor did he draw his attack on the Government mild; he spoke of it floating helplessly down the revolutionary stream, attacking the Crown, the second Chamber and binding the representative Chamber hand and foot, and 'having finished their bribes, they are now lapsing into the old Radical practice of destroying churches, passing what they conceive to be judicious reform Bills from the gerrymandering point of view'.

14

BACCARAT, BEAUTY AND GOD

Criticism and Beauty, 1909;
Theism and Humanism, 1914

'Let me say at once, explicitly, categorically, dogmatically that I prefer baccarat to Bridge,' Balfour writes to Lady Elcho. 'Why? (one) because it requires no brains or attention and yet stirs your interest; (two) because, if you are unfortunate, you do not involve a partner; (three) because it requires no organisation, no selection of players, no discussion about the stakes; (four) because you begin when you like, you go on while you like, you stop as soon as you like; (five) because if you are wise, you don't win from your friends; and if you lose, your friends don't lose with you!'

In fact, neither baccarat nor bridge held much attraction for Balfour. The letter is quoted not to suggest that between 1911 and 1914 Balfour turned from politics to frivolity—the opposite was true—but rather as an example of his lively curiosity about Society, and his life-long habit of commenting upon it. He was interested in people and their habits; he would have made, at a later date, an excellent social anthropologist—or a writer of *causeries*. The list of people he met, dined with, or invited to Whittingehame is almost an intellectual history of his times. We have noticed his acquaintance with Wells, Henry James, and a whole gamut of scientists and philosophers. In this matter he had no political prejudices. The Webbs, for example, were among his friends in these years and he attended some of the meetings of their Co-efficients Club which between 1906 and 1908 discussed informally social and municipal questions. He writes to Lady Elcho on November 12, 1909: 'The Sydney Webbs and Professor and Mrs.

Lodge were here for the week-end—indeed the Webbs stayed till Tuesday. The talk was abundant but strenuous: Mr. and Mrs. W. being little moved by the more frivolous side of life! But they were extraordinarily pleasant and interesting.'

He was much taken by Bernard Shaw's play, *John Bull's Other Island*— perhaps partly for its reflections upon Socialism—and he went to it no less than five times in 1907, one occasion inviting Campbell-Bannerman to accompany him, and on another taking Asquith. His interest in psychical research continued and we hear on July 30, 1911 that 'Mrs. Besant came to dinner at Carlton Gardens to talk occultism with Gerald and me.' (This was at the height of the constitutional crisis.) He attended concerts, as he did throughout his life, and when asked his opinion about the question of the Order of Merit he stated that in his opinion Elgar was undoubtedly the 'greatest living English composer', but, he added, to give him the O.M. would cause pain to Parry and Stanford.

On the proposal to give the O.M. to Augustine Birrell, who was a well-known essayist in addition to being a Liberal Minister, he delivered himself of the typical observation: 'I am rather afraid that people will say that had Birrell not distinguished himself in the field of politics, nobody would have thought of giving him the O.M. for his labours in the field of literature. Morley has escaped the charge but only just.'

Balfour judged people as people and with considerable acuity; in view of later suggestions that somehow or other he was sold on the question of Jews, it is worth observing that he had for them no indiscriminate love. He writes to Lady Elcho on August 23, 1911 referring to his meeting Berenson and Wildstein and remarks: 'Their eager interest in all things of the mind instead of attracting half repels. It all seems so much on the surface.' On the other hand Weizmann, as we have already seen, and Bergson whom he met in London in 1911, attracted him considerably for their intellectual powers.

He writes to his friend Professor Pringle-Pattison at Edinburgh on November 21, 1911: 'I did have some talk with Bergson when he was in London. He seems very pleasant and unassuming. . . . He is, I think, quite conscious that he will have to modify or at least develop the theological aspect of his philosophic scheme. His general view of philosophy is, as I gather, that it must be built up like science, gradually and bit by bit. . . . He told me that he had begun life as a mathematician and a follower of Herbert Spencer! It was the mathematical treatment of time, and the fact that all the "time" equations found a spatial application which drove him by reaction into his characteristic theory of "duration". I'm not sure that I fully understand his point.'

Philosophy was one preoccupation of his leisure in the three years

preceding the outbreak of war.   But so were friendships old and new—
and the termination of old friendships by death, as happened in the
case of Alfred Lyttelton, who died in 1913: 'I am afraid', he wrote to
Lady Wemyss after the funeral, 'I utterly lost my self-control.'   Death
of old and loved friends often affected him in this ungovernable way;
we may recall his break-down on hearing of the death of May Lyttelton, Alfred's sister, and we shall come across this again on occasions
during the war.

He entertained more frequently at Whittingehame in these years,
partly because he was not held so tightly in London, and partly also
because the children of his brothers and sisters were now growing up
and were frequent visitors.   He liked children and had a way with
them, entirely without ostentation or obvious exercise of his charm: they
returned his affection with unquestioning adoration.   All the old
personal friends—Lady Wemyss, the Desboroughs, the Brownlows—
came and went and Balfour's house-partying habits suffered no diminution.   It was perhaps Balfour's delight in the society of women—a
delight most of them reciprocated—that made him, unlike most of the
members of his Party, inclined to women's suffrage.   His brother
Gerald's wife, Lady Betty Balfour, a strong supporter of the suffragist
movement, wrote frequently to Balfour on the subject and he replied
in such letters as the following: 'I am and have always been, a steady,
though not vehement, supporter of the movement; and I do not think
my opinions have undergone any very substantial change during the
years in which the subject has been before the country and the House.
I have never pretended to think that it was a question of abstract right.
I do not think that sex constitutes either a claim or a disability: neither
do I believe that any very important change, political or social, would
follow on the reform if it were granted.   But if it is really desired by
women (as in spite of assertions to the contrary I am inclined to think
it is) in my judgement the request should be conceded.   Of course I
have always been aware that opinions like these are very unpalatable to
a large number of my own anti-suffrage colleagues and supporters; and
are pitched in too low a key to please the ardent supporters of suffrage.
This I cannot help.   But what I do rather complain of is that I should
be expected to act as if I took the same view of the importance of this
subject as those who think that it is a vital question.'

In another letter to Lady Betty, he tells of her 'little Manchester
suffrage friend' visiting him and giving him a flower wrapped in paper
as a token of her regard: 'I was deeply and even painfully moved because I am sure that she thought that my sympathetic attention to her
fervent pleading, meant not merely the will, but the power greatly to
further her objects.'

In these years Balfour continued to enjoy golf and tennis—and continued to have no interest whatsoever in hunting, shooting or fishing. As a golfer and tennis-player, he was no mean performer. He writes to his sister Alice from Cannes in February, 1912 that he has been playing golf for Cannes against Nice; and that he has won two prizes at lawn tennis—'both of course under handicaps', he adds with some pride. Both these interests no doubt added to the equableness and equilibrium of his life, and certainly went far to preserve the lithe figure that he retained until his eighties.

Nevertheless he was not entirely free in these years of personal worries: money began at last to enter into his thoughts. We have seen that he inherited most of his grandfather's—the Nabob's—fortune not merely intact but added to by the skilful husbandry of his father. His investments, left in the hands of his advisers, were sound and wise, although in the way of landowners in that period he found himself from time to time needing to make retrenchments and adjustments in the running of his estate. But he writes to Lady Elcho in March, 1913, that: 'I am uneasy about my affairs.' This uneasiness had a special cause. Some time in the first decade of the twentieth century, Balfour and his brother Gerald became interested in a series of inventions for the artificial drying of peat to be used as a fuel. They put a large sum of money into a company, known as 'Wet Carbonising' formed to commercialise these inventions. This company went bankrupt a few years before the outbreak of the war and, no doubt, accounted for Balfour's 'uneasiness'.

But neither Balfour nor his brother were content to leave matters there. They developed what, with little exaggeration, one might call a mania on the subject of peat—and mania is a most un-Balfourian trait. Having lost a large sum of money, they proceeded over the coming years to lose some more by financing a company called 'Peco' which also went bankrupt—though this is to jump forward into the 1920s. Their total loss appears to have been something like a quarter of a million pounds. Balfour and his brother believed, and continued to believe, despite their unhappy experiences, that powdered peat as a fuel could be of immense service to mankind and might well have greatly helped the industrial development of some countries which have no other natural fuel. The Peco process is apparently still used in certain countries with some measure of success and it is a possible fuel for gas turbines since all other dried powdered fuels are too abrasive.

But how they could continue to pour large sums of money into such an obviously uncommercial scheme is a minor mystery. It seems to have become to both of them almost a crusade and 'while both were normally extremely tolerant men, they were very touchy about any criticism of their investment in Peco', the present Lord Balfour notes. Perhaps here again we may see the typical Balfourian process of initial indecision and distaste for making up, and therefore closing, his mind, followed by utter ruthlessness in pursuit of a decision once it was taken: in other words, he had been convinced, intellectually-speaking, by the possibilities of the peat process and, so high was his regard for his own intellect, that he was quite certain of his rightness.   Added to this was perhaps a certain touch of almost feminine wilfulness—or, one might call it, terrier-like refusal to let go.   But it will be noticed that, on the whole, this characteristic only emerged strongly in what might be called the less important pursuits of his life: he could be ruthless as a politician but without any limpet-like clinging to an *idée fixe*.   Balfour pursued Peco in the same way, though without the exclusiveness or intensity, that other men pursue gambling, women or drink; it was his form of the self-destructive urge; but it never brought him within sight or even hailing distance of ruin.

II

When Balfour required escape from politics or from Society, he turned, as always, to philosophical speculation.   Sailing on strange seas of thought alone was for him at once distraction and a refuge. When he had removed himself so contemptuously from the displeasing political scene in the summer of 1911, he told his sister Alice that 'I am, or was, very angry about politics.   I am still angry when I think of them; but then I think of them very little.'   He was thinking instead of an article for the *Hibbert Journal* on the subject of Bergson's philosophy and the article duly appeared two months later in October, 1911. Balfour found much in Bergson to attract him without necessarily convincing him.   Bergson's *Evolution Créatrice*, he says, 'is not merely a philosophical treatise, it has all the charms and all the audacities of a work of art', and the same could be said of Balfour's essay about him. Indeed, Balfour reveals more of himself when dealing with the subtler perceptions of sense than when he considers more formal philosophy. Speaking about Bergson on the subject of instinct, Balfour writes that, for Bergson, man 'in rare moments of tension, when his whole being is wound up for action, when memory seems fused with will and desire into a single impulse to *do,—then* he knows freedom, *then* he touches reality, *then* he consciously sweeps along with the advancing wave of Time, which, as it moves, creates'.   Balfour comments: 'However obscure to the reflective sort such mystic utterances may seem, many will read them with a secret sympathy.'   There was always in Balfour this 'secret sympathy' for insight above reason.   That does not prevent his continuing to ask, for example, how it is in Bergson's philosophy 'that if instinct be the appropriate organ for apprehending free reality, bees and ants, whose range of freedom is so small, should have so much of it?   How comes it that man, the freest animal of them all, should specially delight himself in the exercise of reason, the faculty brought into existence to deal with matter and necessity?' His conclusion about Bergson, for whom he has great sympathy, is also revealing of himself. He says:

'I suggest with great respect, that in so far as M. Bergson has devised his imposing scheme of metaphysics in order to avoid the impotent conclusion to Naturalism, he has done well. As the reader knows, I most earnestly insist that no philosophy can at present be other than provisional; and that, in framing a provisional philosophy, "values" may be, and must be, taken into account. My complaint, if I have one, is not that M. Bergson goes too far in this direction but that he does not go far enough. He somewhat mars his scheme by what is, from *this* point of view, too hesitating and uncertain a treatment.'

The subject of aesthetics had long interested Balfour and on November 24, 1909, he had delivered the Romanes Lecture in the Sheldonian at Oxford on 'Questionings on Criticism and Beauty'. It is one of his most attractive philosophical studies. He read a good deal in preparation for it. He told Lady Elcho that he had studied an able book on the metaphysics of aesthetics 'by an Italian professor named Croce', then scarcely heard of in England. He agreed with most of Croce's rejections 'including his rejection of any merit in Ruskin (from the point of view of theory)'. But Balfour complains that Croce's mode of thought is too transcendental and his terminology too difficult, as well as his opinions being too alien, to be of much use to him. 'Damn the lecture', Balfour concludes. The result was that he wrote nothing of the lecture beforehand. It was delivered from notes amounting to no more than about 100 words. Hugh Redwood, a newspaper reporter, tells us that newspaper men had a deep admiration for Balfour for he was always able, although speaking from a few notes, to tell them to the minute exactly for how long he was going to speak. Redwood continues:

'When Balfour delivered the Romanes Lecture at Oxford, we were asked to arrange for a verbatim note to be taken, with a view to publication. We sent our best man, who wrote flawless shorthand at the highest speed . . . but Balfour called for more than stenography. Much of his charm lay in his conversational manner and it was part of his conversational manner to leave many of his sentences unfinished. Transcribing a verbatim note of him was no easy matter at the best of times, when one knew what he was talking about. Transcribing the note of a metaphysical discourse, out of one's depths from the very beginning, was a sheer impossibility, as our man very quickly discovered. He was greatly worried: what on earth would happen if he failed to produce a transcript as ordered?

'Unable to think of any other way out of the difficulty, he went to

Balfour and asked if he might borrow his manuscript in order to check his notes. "I haven't a manuscript," was the reply. "You are welcome to my notes if you can make anything of them, but I don't think they will help you much." All the notes for the Romanes Lecture, perhaps 100 words in all, had been written on the inside of an old envelope, split open.

'Balfour was much amused at his caller's discomfiture, but he did a wonderfully gracious thing. He went through the whole lecture with him, correcting, explaining and revising until it was perfect. When they had finished, a much-relieved scribe felt emboldened to make a request: Might he keep the envelope? And he brought it back to the office, in memory of a treasured experience.'

Balfour, *pace* Redwood and his reporter, was very dissatisfied with the account: 'The lecture, as reported, gave most imperfect expression to my views;—was, indeed, sometimes barely intelligible.' So a few months later he recomposed his lecture; it also was printed, so that there are now two versions extant. In this lecture, as always, Balfour was at his best when dealing with works of art to which he reacted both strongly and finely. He begins by stating that the attempt to lay down laws of beauty and to fix criteria of excellence has failed. At present, attempts to find formulae for the creation of 'new works of beauty by taking old works of beauty to pieces and noting how they were made seem to be futile'. Another sort of criticism has taken its place and it is, he believes, an admirable sort of criticism:

'The modern commentator is concerned rather to point out beauties than to theorise about them. He does not measure merit by rule, nor crowd his pages with judgements based on precedents. He takes his reader, as it were, by the hand, wanders with him through some chosen field of literature or art, guides him to its fairest scenes, dwells on what he believes to be its beauties, indicates its defects, and invites him to share his pleasures. His commentary on art is often itself a work of art; he deals with literature in what is in itself literature.'

Balfour thinks that we cannot have too much of this sort of criticism. In fact, certainly by the 1920s it was already felt that we had had too much and this style of criticism had descended to what Balfour himself goes on to refer to as the style of 'lo, here! lo, there! This is good! What subtle charm in this stanza!' etc. Yet, as he points out, we cannot get over the fact that 'the same work of art which moves one man to admiration, moves another to disgust; what rouses the enthusiasm of one generation, leaves another hostile or indifferent'. It is, therefore, natural for men to speculate in what beauty consists. More particularly, men are driven to try and discover a scale of values for the arts, not based on ethical or quantitative bases, but 'merely on the aesthetic emotions actually experienced'.

Balfour's conclusion, in one sense at least, is 'negative', as he himselı admits.   He cannot see that we can go much beyond the statements embodying personal valuations, or that we can define the dogmas of aesthetic orthodoxy.   'We can appeal neither to reason, nor experience, nor authority.   Ideals of beauty change from generation to generation. Those who have produced works of art disagree; those who comment on works of art disagree; while the multitude, anxious to admire where they "ought", and pathetically reluctant to admire where they "ought not", disagree like their teachers.'

But he then, as it were through the back door, brings in value criteria from the sphere of ethics.   Love for instance—love of 'God, oı country, of family, of friends'—and admiration have, he believes, an inherent value apart from their practical effects, and we cannot measure their worth solely by their external consequences.   Similarly with beauty.

Love is governed by no abstract principles, it obeys no universal rules and it is obstinately recalcitrant to logic; but because we cannot give any account of the characteristics common to all that is lovable why should we be impatient?   The same thing applies to beauty. 'That is for every man most lovable which he most dearly loves. That is for every man most beautiful which he most deeply admires. Nor is this merely a reiteration of the old adage that there is no dis- puting about taste.   It goes far deeper; for it implies that, in the most important cases of all, a dispute about either love or beauty would not merely be useless; it would be wholly unmeaning.'

Balfour himself sees that this point of view—it is no substitute for a theory of aesthetics—is not tolerable unless there be added to it 'some mystical reference to first and final causes'.   A failure to establish the 'objective' reality of beauty, after all, finds a parallel in other realms of speculation and that even so we do not doubt that is one of the best and greatest possessions we have it in our power to enjoy.

What is most attractive about the Romanes Lecture is not, however, so much the philosophical aspect which, as Balfour himself admitted, is mainly observations preliminary to aesthetics, as *The Foundations of Belief* was 'introductory' to theology.   It is rather the air of sophistica- tion which plays round the whole essay, and is characteristic of Bal- four's approach to art.   Writing, for example, about the great Gothic buildings of the Middle Ages, he observes that every style is there mixed and each generation added according to its own views.   But 'I am convinced that nothing but considerations of time or money—very solemn considerations in the Middle Ages as now—nothing but these considerations prevented the old work being pulled down and the whole fabric being built up according to the views of the architects of the day.   I believe that the architect who lived during the time, let us say, of the Middle Pointed or Later Decorated would as soon have built in the earlier school of Gothic architecture as any self-respecting woman of the present day would consent to appear in a crinoline, which was the universal female attire when I was a young man.'

Or again: 'I am certain that there are many persons living who will never be taken in by a forgery—but who have no very great power of enjoying an original.'   Or of ancient Greek music: 'Titian limited to a lead pencil.'

It is in such remarks as these that the free spirit in Balfour shows up most clearly; he was in all things a sensitive, subtle observer, totally unswayed by fashion, totally unimpressed by generally accepted attitudes.   In politics, those who knew him well detected the same spirit; they called it cynicism.   It was, in fact, something much less common: a fresh, bright mind.

III

All his life, Balfour was accustomed to make speeches from a few notes jotted down on the back of a long envelope.   He followed the habit even when he came to deliver the first of ten of the 20 Gifford Lectures at the University of Glasgow in the winter of 1914.   To deliver an hour of closely argued philosophy with no more than a dozen half-finished sentences actually written down is an astonishing feat.   It was, however done in no bravura spirit.   Balfour, as we noted elsewhere, found the process of prose composition laborious.   He preferred to work out his theme in his mind and to *ad lib.* as far as illustrations went; in such *ad libbing* he often found inspiration; he also avoided the boredom of simply reading out a lecture, and the lecture itself gained in interest as his audience watched a mind actually in the process of thinking.

Balfour once explained his method to Lord Riddell, the newspaper proprietor and liaison officer between the British delegation at the Paris peace talks in 1918 and the press.   'I am incapable', Balfour told him, 'of preparing the language of a speech, and at best can do no more than get a line of argument clearly in my mind.'   He went on, however, to explain that what was thus produced was not suitable for reproduction in print: 'I do not believe that finished excellence can be obtained either in speaking or in anything else without some use of the file.'   Thus, the Gifford Lectures, as we have them now, are considerably re-written, though the argument itself and its order are substantially the same.   They were discussed beforehand with relatives, not least with his brother, Gerald, and also with such friends as Sir Oliver Lodge; and their preparation occupied his leisure in 1912 and the autumn of 1913.

The lectureship had been founded by the Scottish judge, Lord Gifford and, though the subject had to be natural theology, the angle of approach was left to the lecturer's free choice. Balfour decided to consider his theme from the point of view of the ordinary, intelligent man who, whether or not he knew anything of the historic schools of philosophy, never considered it in any vital relation to the beliefs and disbeliefs which represented his 'working theories of life and death'. To such men 'so much metaphysical debate is not, or does not appear to be, addressed to the problems of which they feel the pinch. On the contrary, it confuses what to them seems plain; it raises doubts about what to them seems obvious; and, of the doubts which they *do* entertain, it provides no simple or convincing solution.'

From this point of view, Balfour hoped that the effect of his argument would be 'to link up a belief in God with all that is, or seems, most assured in knowledge, all that is, or seems, most beautiful in art or nature, and all that is, or seems, most noble in morality'. It was, he said, 'the God according to religion, and not the God according to metaphysics' to whom he referred. While the attribution of personality to God was inadequate, he certainly meant

'. . . something other than an Identity wherein all differences vanish, or a Unity which includes but does not transcend the differences which it somehow holds in solution. I mean a God whom men can love, a God to whom men can pray, who takes sides, who has purposes and preferences, whose attributes, however conceived, leave unimpaired the possibility of a personal relation between Himself and those whom He has created.'

The inquiry with which his lectures are concerned, he states, is 'whether, among the beliefs which together constitute our general view of the universe, we should, or should not, include a belief in God'. His method, therefore, will take account of facts as they are: 'A creed of some kind, religious or irreligious, is a vital necessity for all, not a speculative luxury for the few.'

What, in fact, Balfour does in these lectures is 'to show that all we think best in human culture, whether associated with beauty, goodness or knowledge, requires God for its support, that Humanism without Theism loses more than half its value'. He claims that:

'Beauty must be more than an accident. The source of morality must be moral. The source of knowledge must be rational. If this be granted, you rule out Mechanism, you rule out Naturalism, you rule out Agnosticism; and a lofty form of Theism becomes, as I think, inevitable.'

His argument, indeed, is an inversion of Descartes: 'Descartes rests the belief in science on a belief in God. I rest the belief in God on a belief in science.' What applies to science applies also to other parts of 'human culture'.

Y_{JB}

It will be seen that Balfour's underlying thought here differs little from what he demonstrated in his earlier books; and that, for instance, his passage on aesthetics here is all of piece with those in his Romanes Lecture.   His exposition is firmer, his illustrations are new, and possibly the subtleties of his thinking more convincing.   Philosophically, he is non-materialist but equally non-idealist which had become the usual reaction to nineteenth-century 'naturalism'.   It is an in-between position which is unlikely to appeal to many minds, certainly not as a permanent basis for thought.   Balfour, however, never ceased to explain that he laid no such claims; all speculation was of a temporary nature, likely to be carried away on a sort of Bergsonian 'flux'.   It could do no more than suggest doubts about philosophical dogma, and cleanse the channels for others to fill with fresh water.   But by 1914 others were already filling those channels: Balfour was to some extent already fighting battles long ago lost by his naturalist opponents.   Much of what he had to say adequately countered such Humanists as G. E. Moore: but it could well be argued that the most significant English thinker in 1914 was F. H. Bradley, one of whose later works, *Essays on Truth and Reality*, appeared in that very year.   Balfour merely lumped Bradley with the neo-Hegelians; he refused to be drawn into references either to him or to what he called 'the Pragmatists, the new Realists'. This is a real measure of the inadequacy of his approach in 1914 even to the narrow and qualified objectives he set himself.

IV

This does not mean that *Theism and Humanism* is a dated work in that we now see no difficulty where Balfour found 'problems'; it simply means that the philosophical tide has flowed into different channels. Nor does it mean that the book is 'dusty' and boring.   Far from it. It is full of stimulus as it is of beautifully-phrased subtleties.   It remains true even today that, for example, 'We now know too much about matter to be materialists.'   It is equally true for us that 'Sensibility belongs to the world of consciousness, not to the world of matter.   It is a new creation, of which physical equations can give no account; nay rather, which falsifies such equations.'   Even now, with electrical equipment for illuminating brain-actions, is there an accepted answer to the problem Balfour puts thus:

'In a strictly determined physical system, depending on the laws of matter and energy alone, no room *has* been found, and no room *can* be found, for psychical states at all.   They are novelties, whose intrusion into the material world cannot be denied, but whose presence and behaviour cannot be explained by the laws which the world obeys'?

Balfour's argument—that 'our beliefs about beauty and virtue must have some more congruous source than the blind transformation of physical energy'—may provide no acceptable answers; but it is still worth being reminded, so vividly, that no answer has yet been found.

That argument we need not pursue in any detail; but some of his more striking ideas are worth recalling. He suggests, for instance, that the main interest of history—and the cause of its being written—is in its aesthetic appeal. This depends largely, not on the way history is told, but on its accuracy, or supposed accuracy. Fact, indeed, in itself, he observes, has 'contemplative or aesthetic' interest: 'A tale which would be inexpressibly tedious if we thought it was (in the "law court" sense) false may become of absorbing interest if we think it true.'

Balfour is equally thought-provoking on altruism, on probability and on 'atomism'. He points out that as far back as Democritus it was confidently asserted that the world consists of atoms, and 'that its infinite variety is due to the motions and positions of immutable and imperceptible units. . . .' Through successive centuries the theory never died: Bacon, Gassendi, Hobbes and Newton accepted it. In the hands of Dalton it started a new epoch in chemistry. Today it lies at the root of all modern theories of physics. None of those who believe in the atomic theory had, at least until modern times, any experimental warrant for their convictions. But, then, 'If experience did not establish the belief, whence came it? If it represents nothing better than an individual guess, why did it appeal so persistently to leaders of scientific thought, and by what strange hazard does it turn out to be true?'

There are, he says, many other examples of the same kinds of belief which 'anticipate evidence, guide research, and in some shape or other turn out to be true'. They are assumptions made by generation after generation of scientists and thinkers, for which, until perhaps a thousand years later, there is found no demonstrable proof. In other words, scientists set out to prove what they already believe—a process strictly contrary to accepted scientific method. What, Balfour asks ironically, can we do 'but criticise their credulity and wonder at their luck? unless, indeed, their luck be a form of inspiration'. But can we imagine what some positivist philosopher might have said about 1842 if, for example, the conservation of energy had been a theological dogma instead of a scientific guess? He would, Balfour suggests:

'. . . have used Joule's first investigations on Work and Heat to upset the very dogma they were intended to establish. "Here" (he would have said) "you have a believer in these metaphysico-theological methods of discovering the laws of nature and mark what happens. In true medieval fashion he begins with some fanciful deductions from the way in which he thinks God must have made the world. Fortunately, however, though his principles are medieval, his methods are modern. Not only is he a most brilliant experimenter, but he has the courage to put his own speculations to an experimental test. He takes the minutest precautions, he chooses the most favourable conditions, and what happens? Does he prove his case? Do his results square with his theories? Does he find a fixed relation between work and heat? Does he justify his views of God? Not at all. Between his lowest determination of the mechanical equivalent of heat, and his highest, there is an immense and lamentable gap. What does he do? He takes their mean value:—a very proper method if he *knew* there *was* a mechanical equivalent of heat; a very improper method if the reality of such an equivalent was the thing to be proved. Clearly, if he had not put his theological opinions into his scientific premises when he began his experiment, he never would have got them out again as scientific conclusions when he had reached the end.'

This is, however, not to suggest that ' "If you want to reach truth, follow your unreasoned inclination." ' They are beliefs, not unlike scientific hypotheses—'guesses directed, not by the immediate suggestion of particular experiences (which indeed they sometimes contradict), but by general tendencies which are enduring though sometimes feeble. Those who make them do not attempt the interrogation of Nature wholly free from certain forms of bias.' The 'secular movements' of science, he observes, are not unlike Bergson's *élan vital* forcing its way along different paths of organic evolution: 'There is in both a striving towards some imperfectly foreshadowed end.' It is clear, at any rate, that scientific discovery cannot be wholly due to reasoning and experience: 'We seem forced to assume something in the nature of a directing influence. . . . And if "a Power that makes for truth" be required to justify our scientific faith, we must surely ·count ourselves as theists.'

Such was the first half of Balfour's Gifford Lectures. The second half was due to be delivered in the winter of 1914. For obvious reasons, it was postponed. With the fees paid for the lectures already given, Balfour had constructed a pair of high wrought-iron gates which were erected in the garden wall at Whittingehame. There they still stand with the date, '1914', interwoven with the scroll-work. Sometimes during the war, his niece tells us, he would look at the gates and wonder whether posterity would be puzzled as to why he had chosen that year for this particular form of commemoration.

15

ON THE BRINK

1912–1914

Although Balfour was able to devote more of his time in the three years between his resignation of the Conservative Leadership and the outbreak of war to philosophy, he was very far from being 'out of politics'. There were those who had felt that he would gradually retire towards the wings and, in due course, to the political twilight of the Upper House. But those contemporary observers were unaware how deeply and, at what level, Balfour remained at the centre of the political web. They probably did not know, for instance, that Balfour was invited by Haldane to become a regular member (rather than, as previously, an occasional adviser) of the Committee of Imperial Defence in 1912; they were certainly completely unaware that Balfour proposed himself as Prime Minister in a letter to the King in 1913 in reply to the King's request for advice.

Both these facts are surprising, and indeed abnormal. But then the whole period of English politics preceding the outbreak of the Great War was abnormal. Matters which had been boiling up at least from the time Asquith became Prime Minister, now came to explosion point. There were railway strikes, constant lock-outs, dock disputes, and stoppages in the coal-fields involving, in Wales, rioting and even looting. From July, 1912, the suffragist movement passed from hunger strikes to a campaign of crime, with arson as its favourite method. The smell of corruption—which had not tainted British public life for many years—floated even into the precincts of the mother of Parliaments. It was rumoured that certain Ministers had corruptly influenced the Government's decision to accept the tender of the Marconi Company for the proposed 'imperial wireless chain'. The Ministers—Lloyd George,

Sir Rufus Isaacs and the Master of Elibank—were cleared of the implication of having used their powers to make money out of the Marconi shares, though two of them admitted an error in judgement in having purchased shares in a parallel company formed for the United States; and they expressed their regrets to the House of Commons.

The affair was badly handled not only by the Government—thus leaving the public doubtful about the honesty of Ministers—but also by Law, Leader of the Conservative Opposition.   As Margot Asquith wrote to Balfour on June 20, 1913, referring to Law's violence over the matter, 'Bonar Law was very pitiful—a small attorney at the Old Bailey (*I* know you can't have *everything* as a Leader but *must* you have this?)'   It may have been just—but it certainly didn't appear to be just—when Asquith shortly afterwards made Isaacs the Lord Chief Justice of England.   Kipling circulated a bitter satire on this subject.

Against such a background, the events stemming from the Government's introduction of the third Home Rule Bill for Ireland in April, 1912—events which included the instigation of civil war by leading members of His Majesty's Opposition—may appear less incredible than they otherwise might; but that they could be taking place within two years of the outbreak of the greatest war in history to date gives their incredibility a touch of lunacy.

It is here relevant to consider the state of mind of both Government and Opposition leaders at this time.   Asquith himself was tired and was already reduced to murmuring 'wait and see' which became his nickname. As early as April, 1912, Sandars in a private letter refers to Asquith's 'nerve and virility being atrophied and gone'.   In another letter of May 25, 1912 he tells Balfour of a *tête à tête* dinner he has had with W. G. Tyrrell, Edward Grey's private secretary, Grey being still Foreign Minister.   Tyrrell, he writes: 'in confidence assured me that they (i.e. the Liberal Cabinet) were really anxious to find an occasion for resignation.   They were tired and stale—he said—they were worn with repeated crises and they were plagued with internal differences.   A defeat in Committee on their big Bills, or a series of very bad divisions, would suffice for the purpose.   Tyrell said "I am speaking for Cabinet Ministers and not their supporters."   This new strike following other labour troubles was disquieting them very much; and Edward Grey felt far more anxious about these domestic troubles than he did about the clouds on the foreign horizon.'   Tyrrell also told Sandars that Lloyd George no longer counted in the Cabinet and that 'his nerves are more shaken than people generally know—he has neurasthenia'. On the grounds of the wish being father to the thought, we may discount some of Sandars's observations; but by no means all.

On the other hand, the Opposition was, though for different reasons, in no better shape.   Here Balfour comes back into the picture.   He

had returned to the House of Commons—to a royal welcome from the
Conservatives—on March 19, 1912, and had thrown himself vigorously
into support of the supplanting leader, Law. At Law's request, he
threw his weight wherever and whenever it was wanted, in or out of the
House of Commons. He supported him loyally and, indeed, told
Derby, during a minor crisis, that 'if Bonar Law goes the Party, as far
as I can see, is doomed'.

But the fact remained that he was no longer the director of the
Opposition's operations. This showed up very clearly in the Opposition's attitude, under Law's leadership, to Lloyd George's National
Insurance Bill, introduced in 1912. The Conservatives themselves
were divided about the Bill; some of them wanted not to crush it out of
existence, but to make it an even better Bill than it was. Law said no,
and his latest biographer, Robert Blake, has this tribute to pay to
Balfour: Law, he says, 'personally believed that, for the Conservatives
social reform was not on the whole a profitable line to pursue. If the
country wanted more and better social reform, it would not vote
Conservative. But a public declaration to that effect was unwise, and
Bonar Law's inexperience and bluntness had led him into a trap which
Balfour would probably have avoided.'

Balfour, in fact, had entered into discussions with Lloyd George on
the question of the National Insurance proposals at a time when it was
hoped to work the Bill in co-operation with the Conservatives. Balfour,
we are told by W. J. Braithwaite, took a very quiet part in the discussions, but was very friendly to everybody: 'His eyes have got a
questioning, honest look.' But Balfour told Lloyd George at intervals
during the discussions that 'he was not quite sure about the finance of
the scheme'. Lloyd George, Braithwaite continues, was anxious to
placate Balfour, and he observes that 'there was always (in spite of, or
perhaps in consequence of, the education fight in 1902), an underlying
friendship between these two men'. In view, however, of Law's
attitude, the discussion could scarcely be more than unproductive.

In the greater matters issuing from the Home Rule Bill, Law's biographer believes that the worst extravagances might have been avoided
if Balfour had still been Conservative Leader. Lord Midleton—
formerly as St. John Brodrick one of Balfour's Cabinet Ministers—
believed, contrarily, that both Law and Balfour together 'must, from
their indecision at this period both as to the Parliament Act and Ireland,
bear a considerable responsibility for the chaos into which the country
was plunged and remained up to the great war'. The truth probably
lies somewhere in between. Since Balfour was no longer Leader he
can scarcely be yoked with Law as responsible for chaos; on the other
hand, had he been Leader, the efforts he made to avoid extreme courses
might well have had more success. But it seems improbable that any

one man could have stemmed the swell and momentum of events
which were as much psychological as political.

We have already seen what Balfour's considered views on Home
Rule were. From his non-partisan point of view, Asquith's Third
Home Rule Bill, which was of a federalist nature, had an added drawback: it brought into a Home-Ruling Ireland the large British-
descended colony in north-east Ulster and it sought to bring this
Protestant minority under the rule of Ireland's Roman Catholic
majority. Apart from this Ulster itself wanted to remain under the
Westminster Parliament. These feelings in Ulster may, *sub specie
aeternitatis*, have been inconsequential; but they were of ancient origin
and they were strongly held. This Balfour—who had more direct
experience of Ireland than anyone on either side of the House of
Commons—knew, and he urged Asquith before proceeding to the
coercion of Ulster to get a mandate for his action from the country.

But Asquith, in Irish matters, was as sublimely confident as he was
sublimely ignorant. He had no comprehension of Ulster's outraged
distaste for the prospect of being subject to the government of an alien
people with an alien religion. He believed that he could 'manage' the
House of Commons. Yet it is clear that at the same time he knew in
his heart that he could never coerce Ulster. On that point, Churchill,
Lloyd George, and Grey agreed with him: yet when a Liberal backbencher moved an amendment to exclude the Ulster counties from the
federal proposals, Asquith refused to accept it.

There were various attempts to extricate the Government from this
impasse. There was no lack of advice from both sides of the political
fence. Law and Asquith talked secretly at Max Aitken's house at
Leatherhead, and Law sent an account of the conversations to Lansdowne and Balfour. Curzon intervened, and the King himself held
discussions with leaders of both Parties. Meanwhile, Carson assumed
the leadership of the Ulster Conservatives and organised mass meetings
at which Conservative leaders, including Law, spoke in violent terms
and with threats of civil resistance—more bluntly, civil war—in the
spirit of Randolph Churchill, who years before said 'Ulster will fight,
and Ulster will be right.' Subjected to Carson's rabble-rousing
speeches, it was clear enough that in the last resort Ulster would, indeed,
fight. Law may have seen the horrifying dangers into which this could
lead the whole country, but the virulence of his speeches hardly suggests it. Many Conservatives thought that, to avoid such eventuality,
the Government should dissolve and go to the country. But Asquith
believed that, even though his Government were successful at such an
election, it would not reconcile Ulster; whereas a defeat would not be
accepted as a verdict against Home Rule.

In such dangerous circumstances, Balfour suggested an admittedly dangerous alternative: that the King should order a dissolution in the same manner as William IV had done when Melbourne was Prime Minister. Balfour was aware that, in that case, the dissolution rebounded upon the King himself for the ensuing General Election did not give Melbourne's opponent, Peel, the necessary majority and he was soon forced to resign, the King being obliged to send again for Melbourne. Balfour, therefore, made the following proposal in the form of a memorandum which (contrary to Mrs. Dugdale's statement) was sent both to the King and to Law. In it, he considers what the King might do if the Government remained intransigent and risked civil war:

'Is he (i.e. the King) or is he not, to become, however unwillingly the accomplice of a policy whose consequences may shake the Empire and shatter the discipline of the armed forces of the Crown?

'The decision will be a very difficult one, but if the King came to the conclusion that, except in obedience to a clear mandate from the country, he ought not to allow Ulster to be coerced, his best course, as it seems to me, would be to force a dissolution.

'How is this to be done? Not, I think, by refusing his assent to the Home Rule Bill, but by changing his advisers.

'The first of these courses might be represented as unconstitutional. Not so the second. This at least is my view, which I shall be prepared to argue on the proper occasion. The question arises—whom shall he send for? If he sends for Lansdowne or Bonar Law, he will, however unjustly, be accused of favouring one particular Party in the State. What then is he to do?

'Were I in his place, I should be disposed to consider the propriety of sending for Rosebery or myself, not to form a Government in the ordinary sense, but to dissolve and act as his advisers until the new Parliament was returned, but no longer. There would be no difficulty in carrying on the routine work for the Offices during these few weeks without any paraphernalia of Parliamentary Secretaries and Under-Secretaries.

'There are, of course, endless objections to this plan; but its advantages are manifest. Neither of the two Ministers suggested could be accused of straining the Constitution in their own personal interest, for by hypothesis, neither of them is to retain office after the new elections. No Party programme would, or could, be issued by them under such circumstances, and the exceptional character of the crisis would be emphasised by the exceptional character of the temporary Ministry. They would, by speech or address, make only one appeal to the country, the appeal, namely, that the country should take upon itself the full responsibility for all the consequences which Home Rule must bring with it.

'I'm not sure that it would not be better for Rosebery, if he would consent, to act alone, for I'm still closely identified with the Party of which I was once a Leader, and this cannot be said of R. His "lonely furrow" would, after all, enable him to play an important rôle in public affairs. But I do not know whether he would look upon the matter in exactly the same light. If he refused to act, either alone or with me, I should not hesitate, in the circumstances I have indicated, to become sole Minister.'

The effect of Balfour's memorandum was overtaken and dissipated by a memorandum put before the King by Law and Lansdowne, making roughly the same point about the need for dissolution, but not containing the typically Balfourian finesse of a caretaker Ministry. The King was extremely anxious not to be again involved in the sort of constitutional difficulty which occurred over the Parliament Act. Balfour engaged in some correspondence with Stamfordham in which he made the point—which Stamfordham found 'difficult to answer'— that the creation of some hundreds of Peers in order to carry the Parliament Bill, which would have been inevitable had the die-hards won in 1911, was equally as exceptional a case as dissolving Parliament in order that the Sovereign might change his Ministers. By this time Stamfordham had hopes that both Parties might come to agreement on some means of excluding Ulster from the Bill while giving Home Rule to the rest of Ireland. 'What other basis', Stamfordham asked Balfour, 'can be found? If none, we shall drift on into civil war!'

On the problem of the King's prerogative, Balfour replied to Stamfordham on October 9, 1913: 'There are two separate cases to be considered: One—where there is a difference in respect of policy between the King and his Ministers—two—where there is no such difference, but where the King thinks that the ministerial policy— whether good or bad—should be referred to the people.

'In the first of these cases, it is accurate to say that the people are called in to decide between the policy of the Ministers and the policy of the King. And assuredly this should never be done unless the King is "sure to win". The second case is different from this. The King need have no opinion, and certainly need express none, upon the merit of the ministerial proposals. All he insists on is that his people should share the responsibility of carrying them into effect.'

But any proposal, however diplomatically conceived, to use the Royal prerogative was foiled by advice from other counsellors on both sides of the political fence. Nor did the King's numerous talks with various political leaders result in any viable plan or any possibility of compromise. The lust for action, for treading the dangerous tight-rope of civil war, was too strong.

By this time Carson and F. E. Smith, along with other enthusiasts, had made it clear that Ulster would reject the terms of the Home Rule Bill, if necessary, by violence. Volunteers were organised and arms began to be imported. Carson was to head the provisional government in Ulster. A Covenant, on the lines of the old Scottish Covenant, was drawn up, and signatures obtained not only in Ulster, but in many large towns in England and Scotland. The violent speeches of Carson and Smith were paralleled in the House of Commons. The name of 'traitor' was flung at Asquith and something heavier still at Churchill—a bound copy of the Orders. Law stated that Ulster would prefer foreign to nationalist rule, a remark immediately translated by Churchill as a threat that Ulster would secede to Germany. Even Balfour prophesied that if Yorkshiremen were put in the position of Ulstermen they would spend their days in drilling and their nights in importing arms, and he drew an analogy between Ulster in 1913 and the American colonies in Washington's time.

It was one thing to make debating points, even threats of violence, in the House of Commons; it was quite another to become involved, as did the Conservative Leader, Law, and others in attempting to amend the army annual bill to prevent the use of the army by the Government to impose Home Rule on Ulster. Law wrote to ask Balfour's opinion on this matter. Balfour, then delivering the Gifford Lectures at Glasgow University, wrote back at once pointing out that one effect of the proposed amendment would also be to preclude the army from protecting the Roman Catholics of Belfast against 'Orange' bigotry. Moreover, it would set a very dangerous precedent in the event of Labour unrest. There was a good deal of opposition also from the rank-and-file of the Conservative Party, and in due course Law dropped the idea.

But events now followed which made any such idea completely unnecessary. The agile brain of Lloyd George, assisted by Asquith, conceived a plan of offering to defer the workings of the Home Rule Bill for some six years. This was immediately rejected by the Conservatives; Carson remarked: 'We do not want sentence of death with a stay of execution for six years.' At this point, both sides showed signs of panic and confusion: the Government, it appears, believed that Carson was on his way to Ireland to take some irrevocable, military action; Carson, on his side, believed that the Government intended to use the army to seize tactically important points in Ulster in order to impose the terms of the Bill immediately. There were rumours of naval movements and of decisions to arrest the Ulster leaders, including Carson.

Asquith denied the intention of using the armed forces to crush political opposition to the Home Rule Bill. But at the same time, army officers in Ulster were officially offered the alternative of being posted from Ulster, if they had Ulster connections, or of being immediately dismissed from the army if from conscientious motives they were not prepared to carry out their duties when ordered in Ulster. A number of them, in fact, elected to be dismissed and this gave rise to what has become known as 'the Curragh mutiny' though, as is obvious, there was no question of mutiny since they had merely accepted an alternative offered them.

All the details of what occurred are still not known. Some military leaders, it is clear, were delightedly playing politics, and there was outcry in the House of Commons and in the country. Suggestions were made that the Government had attempted to precipitate the crisis in Ulster—indeed Balfour himself accused Asquith in the House of having planned to coerce Ulster and then of not having had the nerve to go through with it. The Liberal War Minister, J. E. B. Seely, resigned, but the tide of allegations against the Government went on. There were rumours of large-scale mutinies and of a head-on conflict between the army and the Government.

Law made haste to exploit the situation. He was supported strongly in the Commons by Balfour. Outside the House—in fact in Hyde Park—there was a mass-meeting of Peers, M.P.s, members of Conservative clubs, contingents from the City and thousands of working men and women. Brass bands played patriotic tunes and speakers headed by Carson protested 'against the use of the army and the navy to drive out by force of arms our fellow subjects in Ireland from their full heritage in the Parliament of the United Kingdom'.

Among this motley crew was the unexpected figure of Balfour. He, too, was wearing the little red, white, and blue badge inscribed 'support loyal Ulster'—a badge which is preserved still among his personal papers. When he appeared and mounted the lorry which did duty as a platform, he was greeted with great delight by the crowd who began to sing 'For he's a jolly good fellow'. He explained that he was making his first, and probably his last, speech in Hyde Park.

Meanwhile, it was learned that on the night of April 24, 1914, a ship had landed a cargo of 35,000 rifles and 3,000,000 cartridges at Larne for the Ulster volunteers; the arms had been bought at Hamburg. The authorities had been completely outwitted and the weapons quickly distributed throughout Ulster. Carson had not informed Law beforehand of this illegal act, but, on learning of it, Law at once associated himself with it and took full responsibility for what had been done. Field-Marshal Lord Roberts was equally delighted and congratulated Carson on a 'piece of organisation that any Army in Europe might be proud of'.

Asquith, in his heart, must now have realised that the Home Rule Bill in the form proposed had no chance of becoming law. But this did not prevent Churchill, widely regarded as being implicated in a plot to stir up trouble in Ulster so that forceful action could be taken, from continuing to make violent speeches, and Balfour in the House accused him of outbursts of 'demagogic rhetoric'.   Balfour went on to make the following statement: 'The Right Hon. Gentleman (Churchill) appears to hold the view which, so far as I know, has never been held by a responsible British statesman—at any rate not for centuries—that there are no circumstances in which it is justifiable for a population to resist the Government.   They must be most rare.   Such circumstances in any reasonable community must be of a type which could only occur once in two or three centuries without shattering the whole fabric of society.   But they *may* occur; they *have* occurred; and there has never been any question with regard to some of us on this side of the House that the coercion of Ulster, in the sense of compelling Ulster to leave a free government under which she is happy, and put her under a government which she detests, is one of those cases.'

This is the clearest—and perhaps the only—statement in which Balfour allied himself with what after all would have been a mutiny. He was not involved in the organisation of resistance in Ulster, which had been primarily the concern of Carson, seconded by Law and F. E. Smith.   Yet he had supported them in the House of Commons and elsewhere.   Possibly Balfour, in his own fashion, had responded to the fever that passed through even the calmest political veins in 1913 and 1914.   On the other hand, as A. P. Ryan, the historian of what he calls 'Mutiny at the Curragh', says, the question of whether Carson and Law are considered mutineers 'depends on the importance attached to Balfour's arguments that there are circumstances in which it is justifiable for a population to resist a Government'.   Was this in fact such a situation?   Certainly Asquith and the Liberal Party generally had made no attempt even to face the fundamental issue which Balfour had put very clearly in his speech in 1913, namely that, if the Irish Nationalists wished to secede from the United Kingdom, the Ulstermen no less strongly wished to remain within the United Kingdom: 'why should the wider patriotism of Ulster consent to the sacrifice?'   It was all very well to speak of safeguards for Ulster, but if Britain withdrew from Ireland how could such safeguards be implemented?   Such a proceeding would, he considered, 'from the point of view of ethics, be profoundly immoral'.

It must further be remembered that, however tolerant Balfour was, he had no doubt of the strength of intolerance at the heart of Roman Catholicism—he had been brought up to understand Papism and to distrust it.   He had understood, too, that in fact there were only two possible alternatives: to continue to rule Ireland progressively and to keep her within the United Kingdom, or to give her complete autonomy with

the exclusion of Ulster.   This he stated in 1913, and this substantially
came about nine years later.   He was already aware that there could
be no resistance since there was nothing to resist; the army was effectively out of the political situation and Asquith knew that the game
was up.

Asquith now sought ways out of his impasse.   He proposed that the
Home Rule Bill having passed to the Lords and being, therefore,
bound to become law within a short period, he should bring in an
amending Bill.   He did not say what sort of amending Bill and the
Conservative leaders were in a quandary as to how to dispose their
forces.   Balfour suggested to Law that the amending Bill should be
passed with one amendment only—that it must be followed by an
immediate General Election.

There were manœuvrings and counter-manœuvrings, and shortly
Asquith began to make overtures to Law for a compromise.   He
proposed that there should be a conference presided over by the King
and, though Law was doubtful of its success, the conference in fact
opened with the King in the chair on July 21, 1914.   The conference
broke down; then the gun-running spread from Ulster to Dublin.
British troops came into conflict with the Dublin crowd and three
people were killed.   The amending Bill was delayed and, in fact,
never came before the House.   For on July 30, 1914—five days only
before the outbreak of the Great War—Law and Carson told Asquith
that to advertise domestic strife would weaken the Government at a
critical moment, and suggested that the Bill should be indefinitely
postponed.   Asquith gratefully agreed.

II

During the Home Rule crises, much of Balfour's political energy
and intellect were involved elsewhere, namely with the war now looming, and the preparation of Britain.   This was not, for him, a political
matter at all.   Many Conservatives, during the ragings of the Ulster
question, decided that social relations with Home Rulers had become
impossible.   Balfour, on the contrary, though behind the scenes, was
already working closely with the Government, although more official
Conservative offers of co-operation on defence were rejected—specifically by Haldane in the House of Lords in February, 1913.   Balfour
showed himself once again as the statesman only half hidden beneath
the cloak of the politician.   A comparison with the Leader of the
Conservative Party is apt though unflattering.   Law, says his biographer, 'does not on the whole, appear to have taken much interest in
foreign policy before the war. . . .   He displayed no particular prescience with regard to the impending disaster.   Until the last week in

July, for him as for most Unionists, the Irish problem filled the horizon to the exclusion of almost everything else.'

Many Britons knew in their hearts that Germany was going to make war; very few of them could believe that war would in fact come about. This is a paradox; yet it adequately describes the state of mind of the rulers as well as of the ruled in Britain. As usual, those who openly declared that Germany was bent on war were extremists, for example, H. M. Hyndman who was turned out of the International Socialist Bureau in 1910 for saying so; and, at the other extreme, Field-Marshal Lord Roberts who pointed out the German danger in speech after speech. Asquith envisaged war some years before; yet when Colonel House, President Wilson's confidential agent, returned from Berlin in May, 1914, and told Asquith, Grey and Lloyd George, that the German military oligarchy was determined on war, he found that 'the difficulty was that none of these men apprehended an immediate war. They had the utmost confidence in Prince Lichnowsky, the German Ambassador in London, and von Bethmann-Hollweg, the German Chancellor.' Like many of their Conservative opponents, they were too involved in the buzz and fuss of the Irish imbroglio to have a clear head for the more distant, but infinitely more threatening, grey shape of German militarism.

There were exceptions. There was Haldane who was at the War Office until June, 1912, when he became Lord Chancellor. It was Haldane, as we have seen, who ensured that the underlying principles of Balfour's defence policy were carried on after he ceased to be Prime Minister. It was Haldane who early in January, 1912, asked Balfour to join the Committee of Imperial Defence. Balfour had not—as Blake states—been a member of the Committee since 1906: he had, as we have seen, been called before it and had participated in some of its work. Even in 1912, he did not accept Haldane's proposal. There were good reasons against his doing so, as Sandars had put in a letter on January 11, 1912: 'Your contention was', Sandars reminds him, 'that the responsibility for the acts of the Committee must rest exclusively on the Government of the day. Again there is the point that membership of the Committee has been held to be a bar to any criticism of Government business.' (Sandars also asked Balfour whether he would reciprocate were he Prime Minister, and gave as his own opinion that no member of the present administration was worthy of being invited.) The other difficulty, of course, was the fact that Balfour was no longer Leader of the Opposition. To become a member of the Committee was in some sense to go behind Law's back and that Balfour would not do, for, as Law's biographer puts it, 'Balfour's relations with Bonar Law continued to be marked, as they always had been, by an impersonal, but impeccable correctitude.'

Nevertheless Balfour did sit, at Asquith's request, as a member of a sub-committee of the Committee of Imperial Defence which between January, 1913, and May, 1914, reviewed once more the subject of the possible invasion of Britain—a matter which, as we have seen, had for long exercised Balfour's mind.   Among the subjects discussed were the provision of local forces to meet raids with a central force to deal decisively with invasion; the compilation of the War Book; the development of a territorial force; the use of aircraft to assist warships.   The conclusions were that two regular divisions of troops must be retained in Britain after the departure of an expeditionary force.   The War Office did not agree to this.   In the end, when war broke out, two divisions were kept in Britain temporarily and the navy undertook to defend all the United Kingdom when the whole six regular divisions finally departed.   The Germans, in fact, never attempted invasion and, apparently, never seriously considered it.   Nevertheless there could be no certainty of this in pre-war years.   The Government were right to take precautions.

Hankey gives a sidelight on Balfour's part in this sub-committee's work.   The sub-committee was meeting to draft its report under the Prime Minister's chairmanship in his room at the House of Commons. Balfour was not present: it was assumed that, owing to the extreme political tension over the Irish Home Rule Bill, he had deliberately absented himself.   In fact, with Carson, he was addressing a meeting in the City in opposition to the Bill.   Hankey continues:

'There were two points on which the sub-committee could not reach agreement.   I myself and various members of the Committee tried our hands at drafting, but we could not bring everyone into line, and the Committee was on the verge of complete deadlock.   Suddenly the door opened, and Balfour's tall, loose-limbed figure sauntered into the room and sat down by the Prime Minister.   Almost immediately he grasped the points at issue, and there and then, with inimitable skill, he drafted paragraphs which brought the whole sub-committee together.   As he strolled back with me after the meeting he made this remark: "I spent the first part of the afternoon in abusing the Government in the City, and the second part in solving their difficulties at the House of Commons!" '

There was another member of Asquith's Cabinet with whom Balfour, in the two years immediately before the war, discussed defence matters: this was Winston Churchill, who had become First Lord of the Admiralty in October, 1911.   There is a good deal of correspondence between the two men, whose relations had once been rather prickly, on such subjects as submarines.   Balfour writes to Churchill on January 9, 1912: 'I entirely agree that submarines modify the whole question of home defence.   The old naval theory which rejected *in toto* the policy of separate flotillas for the purpose of defending our shores (in the shape of gun-boats, etc.) was doubtless right at the time; but I do not believe that we can, or ought, now to avoid *some* differentiation in the type of ships allocated respectively to independent operations on the high seas, and those tied closely to a base. The Germans at one time built even their battle fleet to fight us in the North Sea, and were able thereby to use some of their displacement for carrying armaments instead of coal. I do not know whether they still continue a policy which, on the whole, seems of very doubtful wisdom, but which certainly gave them some advantage at the moment.' A year and a half later he wrote to Fisher that he was 'more than ever convinced that the days of the dreadnought are numbered.'

On February 14, 1912, Churchill circulated not only the Cabinet but also Balfour with a copy of the new German Navy Law which showed the extraordinary increase in the striking force of ships of all classes. In the next month he invited Balfour, along with Asquith and the King, to see the fleet exercises off Portland Bill. In March Churchill showed him documents which Balfour read 'with the deepest misgiving'. In a letter thanking him for the documents, Balfour shows how even the most realistic politicians could scarcely believe the evidence of their eyes: 'A war entered upon for no other object than to restore the Germanic Empire of Charlemagne in a modern form appears to me at once so wicked and so stupid as to be almost incredible. And yet it is almost impossible to make sense of modern German policy without crediting them with this intention. I am told that many good observers in France regard a war in May as inevitable. Personally, I am more disposed to think that, if war comes, it will come when the disparity between our naval forces is less than it is at present. On the other hand, I suppose the Russian Army is likely to be more formidable a year or two hence than it is at present. But imagine it being possible to talk about war as inevitable when there is no quarrel and nothing to fight for. We live in strange times.'

In June, Churchill asked him to put on paper for Grey's benefit some views on Anglo-French relations which Balfour had expressed in conversation. Balfour pointed out that the *entente* with France which had been negotiated during his Premiership had come to have a wider scope than the strict letter of the agreement contemplated. But it was now clear that it would be impossible for either France or Britain to remain indifferent to any serious attack upon the other. He thought that it would be better to conclude a firm alliance with France so that the general staffs would know accurately the amount of assistance upon which they could rely and 'no longer feel themselves at the mercy of political moods and fancies'. An alliance, being stronger than a treaty or an understanding, would, he thought, relieve international strain rather than aggravate it. On the other hand: 'There are many people

ZJB

in this country (I am one of them) who would do everything in their power to save France from destruction but have no mind to be dragged at her heels into a war for the recovery of Alsace and Lorraine. Such persons want to be assured that the France for which they are asked to fight is France defending her own independence, and the independence of Europe, not the France of Louis XIV, of Napoleon or even of the Second Empire.'

Balfour thought that the answer to this problem was to require a power who calls on its ally for assistance to express his readiness to submit the points in dispute to arbitration. But these proposals, although certainly they would have cleared all doubt about Britain's commitment to France in August, 1914, were not accepted by the Asquith Cabinet. In fact, as we now know, the military conversations between the general staffs had already developed in the direction of an alliance and it was at this time that the Cabinet discovered the fact and became, as Lloyd George put it 'aghast; hostility barely represents the strength of the sentiment which this revelation aroused'. Churchill in a private letter to Balfour on June 18, 1912, said: 'Asquith and Grey think that there are so many quarrels about which no one will go to the Hague. But after all there is nearly always the *pretext* as well as the *cause* of war: and if the pretext can be dissipated by being arbitrated upon, the big national antagonism simmers down again, and how often passes away altogether!'

Churchill, indeed, came in these years to rely strongly upon the wisdom and experience of Balfour, and this was shown on the outbreak of war. Churchill was quite obviously much more in sympathy with Balfour's viewpoint than with the changing viewpoints of the Cabinet of which he was a member. It seems that the question of their close relationship was raised in Cabinet quarters, for on July 13, 1912, Churchill writes to Balfour: 'The P.M. quite approves of my keeping you informed and I'm sure it is in the public interest that you should be so.' He then goes on to tell Balfour—three days before he told the Cabinet—that he thinks it much better 'unless the Canadians will give us three ships, which is not at all impossible, to contain the Mediterranean for the next few years with a cruiser force. Certain I am that it will be thought very provocative for the *British* Government to build three extra ships without any new fact having come to light, such as further Austrian building, to justify it.' The proposal about the cruiser force was in fact accepted by the Cabinet on July 16, 1912.

Balfour, on his side, had sources of information and passed on ideas and observations he thought important. He writes to Churchill on July 13, 1912: 'I had a good deal of talk on Sunday with Major O'Gorman. I gathered from him that the Germans are doing a great deal more as regards "dirigibles" than McKenna seemed to suppose when

he talked to me last year upon the subject.   I'm afraid also that they
are doing it with success.   Verb. sap.'

War was coming.   Balfour, like everyone else, hoped against hope
that it would be averted.   Its causes were many and various.   One
was obvious: the aggressive German naval policy alone would render it,
from the British point of view, ultimately inevitable.   Balfour placed
his finger on this in a long letter he wrote to Professor Ludwig Stein for
publication in the German periodical, *Nord und Süd*, in June, 1912:
'There are two ways in which a hostile country can be crushed.   It can
be conquered, or it can be starved.   If Germany were master in our
home waters, she could apply both methods to Britain.   Were Britain
ten times masters in the North Sea, she could apply neither method to
Germany.   Without a superior fleet, Britain would no longer count as
a power.   Without any fleet at all, Germany would remain the greatest
power in Europe.'

There were other causes of war, quite apart from deep-lying ones.
One was certainly the ineptitude of the Government, not least in allowing the Germans to imagine that Britain was concerned, to the exclusion of all other considerations, with the affairs of Ireland.   (A month
after the war broke out, Asquith was still fussing about the Home Rule
Bill.)   The Cabinet by early 1914 was rather less cohesive than Balfour's Cabinet in 1905, even though Lloyd George was certainly
exaggerating when he told his brother in 1933 that Grey, whom he
terms a 'charlatan', was 'a calamitous Foreign Secretary both before
and during the war.   I think he could have averted the war and I am
quite convinced he could have saved the Balkans for us and thus short-
ened the war by two years.   By 1916 he was in a blue funk, thoroughly
paralysed by the jeopardy into which he had plunged us.'

Balfour's last doubts about the eventuality of war had vanished by
the beginning of 1914.   His niece notes incidents that clearly indicate
the nature of his thoughts—his reaction, for instance, to the sound of
firing practice from ships in the Firth of Forth.   In May of the same
year he and Lady Wemyss (formerly Elcho) visited her son Hugo ('Ego')
then in camp at Bulford on Salisbury Plain: 'He was in a sweet sleep in
his little tent bed when I found him.   He gave us tea and we were very
happy.'   Towards the end of July, Balfour remained at his house in
Carlton Gardens against his normal habit.   He was in constant touch
with affairs, mainly through his friendship with Churchill who showed
him the latest telegrams from abroad and afterwards spoke of him as
being a 'veritable rock in times like these'.   On July 29, 1914, he met
by chance in a London street Admiral Lord Fisher who told him that
Churchill had ordered the fleet up the Channel—this he learned indeed
before the Cabinet.   Balfour later said: 'I was quite sure after my talk
with Fisher that day that we should have war, and I remember walking

home from Park Crescent and looking at all the people in the street going along happily, and saying to myself that I knew that war was coming upon them.' Lady Wemyss lunched with Balfour on the day the British ultimatum to Germany was given. She writes: 'I saw already written on his face how much he had been through. He told me of our ultimatum, which expired at midnight. . . . He had written very strongly to Haldane advising that the Expeditionary Force be *sent at once*, "mobilised and embarked". The Government, of course, had great difficulties and had nearly fallen to pieces three days before.'

16

THE WAR

Two Sorts of Power, 1914–1916

The story of how the first Great War broke upon Britain has been exhaustively examined from every conceivable angle. It was the end of the old world, the end of a way of life; it was a crusade—usually conceived of as a brief one—entered into joyously by dewy-eyed young men. Or, alternatively, and retrospectively, it was all part of a monstrous plot by the armament manufacturers or by the rich, fearful of the increasingly militant poor, or it was the beginning of the end, by mutual extinction, of the capitalist world. From the beginning, however, there were those who suspected that its causes were a good deal more complex than any 'plot', and that both in its course and its results far more serious, and quite unlike, a crusade. There were even one or two people whose knowledge took them beyond this suspicion of these facts into certainty, and one of these undoubtedly was Balfour.

He was aware not only of the complexities of the issues but of the overall military situation both at home and abroad; he had not for nothing sat in on the Committee of Imperial Defence, and he had moreover, as we have seen, a remarkable, indeed unique, gift for what one might call the wider strategic speculation. But in this he was almost alone among the leaders of either Party. Asquith, it is now fairly clear, had no intention—mainly no doubt due to his knowledge of his divided Cabinet—of going to war with Germany unless Belgium was invaded. The Conservative leaders, on the other hand, were in general convinced that Britain should fight Germany in support of France. Unfortunately, Law, the official Conservative Leader, did not make this completely clear to Grey, the Foreign Minister, when he spoke to him a few days before the war began. Law's latest biographer quotes him as telling Grey: 'That it was not easy to be sure what the opinion of the whole of his Party was. He doubted whether it would be unanimous or overwhelmingly in favour of war unless Belgian neutrality were invaded.'

But, after meetings with Balfour and Lansdowne on August 1, Balfour's view prevailed and an official message was sent to Asquith, signed by Law, to the effect that the Conservative leaders believed 'it would be fatal to the honour and security of the United Kingdom to hesitate in supporting France and Russia at the present juncture: and we offer our unhesitating support to the Government in any measures they may consider necessary for that object'. This seems to have been largely as a result of Balfour's pressure for, according to Austen Chamberlain, Lloyd George, who was present at the meetings, had the impression that, although Balfour understood the gravity of the situation, neither Lansdowne nor Law seemed to do so.

In fact Balfour, before this meeting, and on his own initiative, had gone so far as to proffer Conservative support and indeed had stated to Churchill that the Unionist leaders would be quite prepared to join a Coalition Government, although he felt that such a necessity would be a very great misfortune. The suggestion of a coalition, as we now know, was far from Law's mind, and far enough from Asquith's. The Prime Minister made no official response to the coalition proposal and indeed, a month after war broke out, was still exacerbating Conservation opinion by pressing to put the Irish Home Rule Bill on the Statute Book, though with a clause postponing its operation until the end of the war.

On the question of war or no war, Asquith did reply, making it clear that Britain would not intervene unless Belgium were invaded. But events overtook him for Belgium was invaded on August 4. But if from the beginning the Liberal Government had been able to heal its divisions and to decide to make it clear that Britain would go to war in defence of France, matters might have gone very differently—or at least Balfour thought so. He stated later:

'I think if I had been Foreign Minister I should have talked to Lichnowsky (the German Ambassador in London in 1914). I should have said, "I speak for myself alone, but I speak with a full sense of my own responsibility. Take it from me that if Germany attacks France, England will come in." I should not have said to him that she would have come in at once but I should have made perfectly clear my conviction that sooner or later she would do so. I think that would have been the action that a strong Foreign Minister would have taken. I think it might have had an effect on Germany. But Grey did not attempt it.'

Not that Balfour had a low opinion of Grey, unlike Lloyd George as we have seen. Indeed he stated very much later that he believed Grey to be a great Foreign Secretary, and in time of peace that thesis could be sustained. But when the diplomats washed their hands of the method of diplomacy and gave way to the Generals, Grey gave way with them.

On August 4, 'the lights', in Grey's famous remark, 'went out all over Europe', and Britain was at war with Germany. It was not, unfortunately, the end of Government hesitations. Churchill had indeed mobilised the fleet, but there had been no decision taken about the next vital step, the despatch of troops to the Continent. Balfour, with Lansdowne, now devoted himself to pressing this necessity upon the Cabinet. He wrote on August 4, to Haldane—who was temporarily in charge of the War Office—urging that as many troops as possible should be sent at once to north-eastern France. Haldane replied, inviting him to visit him for a talk which he did at eleven o'clock on the same day. Thus, as Balfour's niece remarked, 'the hour that saw us at war with the greatest military power in the world was the hour when two metaphysicians discussed in no metaphysical spirit the destination of England's Army'.

Balfour made a memorandum of this talk next day in which he said that he had gathered that the Government was still hesitating on military not on political grounds. They believed that if the force that was available for sending abroad was kept at present at home, it would form the nucleus of a much more formidable army; if that force were sent at once it would form a trifling addition to the troops at the disposal of the French, and if it were destroyed would render Britain weaker in the most decisive moment of the war. Haldane also argued that if Britain were deprived of regular troops, the free action of the Fleet might be hampered: 'As regards this argument' (Balfour notes), 'I was disappointed to hear him use it. He repeated it more than once, and at each time I reminded him that the sub-committee of Imperial Defence was of opinion that a mobile column consisting of two really effective divisions of regular troops, in addition to all the other regulars and irregulars in the country, would be sufficient to secure us from raids.' And Balfour adds: 'On the whole I was rather depressed by a certain woolliness of thought and indecision of purpose, which seemed to mark his conversation.'

The same day, August 5, Balfour was called by Asquith into a 'council of war' with the P.M., Lloyd George, Grey, Churchill and Fisher. The following day the Cabinet sanctioned the immediate despatch of an Expeditionary Force, four divisions and the cavalry division. Haldane at once informed Balfour of this step, adding that the troops should be on the transports by August 9. Privately Balfour thought that the decision might well have been taken earlier and that

after August 3 'every hour's delay seems to me to have been an unnecessary waste of priceless time'.   It was, Balfour believed, Kitchener
who had forced the decision and, however much he later criticised
Kitchener, he always held this to be a great point in his favour.

Thus the forces were despatched, the battle soon to be joined—and
appalling shortcomings to be shown up in the blackness of the casualty
list.   But for the time being the mood of the country was all heroism,
except among a minority of Socialists and old Radicals, represented by
John Burns and John Morley both of whom had resigned from the
Cabinet on the outbreak of war.   The White Feather had not yet made
its appearance, but the ugly sight of the old or middle-aged forcing the
young into the trenches was already common.   Balfour writes to Lady
Wemyss on August 29, 1914, that he is strongly against employers
offering their employees the choice of getting the sack or joining Kitchener's New Army.

Balfour himself had no sons to worry about, but many of his friends
had, and many of his family had.   There was, for instance, one of his
nephews, Oswald, who had recently passed out of Sandhurst.   On
August 11, Balfour drove down to say good-bye to him in camp before
he left for France.   His niece records that 'as we drove off after saying
good-bye, Balfour leaned forward till his nephew could no longer be
seen, and then threw himself back and gave way to an uncontrollable
burst of tears'.   Tears are not what we would normally associate with
Balfour, but at moments of extreme emotion—the death of May
Lyttelton and later of Alfred Lyttelton—they gushed forth.   As we
shall see, however, his personal contact with members of his family who
were in the fighting line had a more than emotional effect on Balfour's
mind; for it influenced opinions which he gave in the councils of war.

For, of course, a man of Balfour's experience and commanding
position could not long remain unmobilised.   Towards the end of
August, by the King's wish, Asquith asked Balfour to head the administrative committee of a fund raised by the Prince of Wales for the relief
of distress due to the dislocation caused by mobilisation and war.   In
October, 1914, he was asked to supervise a scheme for the civil population in case of invasion; this involved evacuation, removal of valuables
and destruction of food, and, with Hankey, he was occupied in instruct-
ing Lords Lieutenant and Mayors on the organisation of the civilian
population of the south and east coasts of England in case of invasion.
By early 1915 the scheme was complete.   We hear in a letter to Lady
Wemyss that he is also writing a defence of the blockade for the Foreign
Office to soothe American feelings.   He attends a conference of Trade
Unionists convened by Lloyd George.   He writes a memorandum for
Churchill on the subject of cordite.   He was still receiving from
Churchill all the naval news and undertook some investigations for him

during November when he met Admiral David Beatty in the Firth of
Forth. He even found himself involved in a committee set up to consider the nationalisation of the drink industry!

For Churchill, Balfour alone of the Conservative leaders retained
great respect. As Blake says: 'Churchill was an object of distaste to
almost every Unionist—except Balfour—and for different reasons, to
very many Liberals too.' However greatly Sandars may have influenced his master, in this respect at least he was impotent. For Sandars
had an anti-Churchill mania, and it eventually caused his final split
with Balfour. Sandars tells him, with glee, on October 2, 1914, for
instance, that Gwynne has had an interview with Churchill on using
Kitchener's New Army to keep the field divisions and brigades up to
strength: 'But Churchill would not listen, and Gwynne had no sooner
advanced his proposal than he began to dance about the room, and in
a loud voice to declare his hostility to this scheme, and to protest that he
would have a million armed men on the Continent in the fighting line
by April next. Upon this Gwynne observed, "How do you propose to
keep this enormous force of new troops re-inforced?" And this en-
quiry brought Churchill to a pause and he said, "That, no doubt, is
a matter for anxious consideration." ' Sandars goes on to observe that
Churchill was 'almost unbalanced . . . in his present mood unmanage-
able and really dangerous'. A little later in the month (October 29)
Sandars observes that: 'The tired officers and men (of destroyers) hear
of valuable ratings dead in the trenches at Antwerp or else interned in
Holland' (as a result of Churchill's scheme for naval divisions taking
part in infantry fighting). Sandars even suggests that the services of
Prince Louis of Battenberg had been dispensed with not on the grounds
of his nationality but in order to get someone else as First Sea Lord 'who
will withstand Churchill's insane adventures'. Prince Louis's nickname, Sandars says is 'quite concur'.

To such gossip and opinion, Balfour remained impervious. He was
certainly aware of Churchill's impetuosity, not to say hot-headedness.
In a letter on September 8, 1914, to his sister, Alice, he refers to
Churchill after a comment on the lack of liaison in the early fighting
with the French: 'The French fighting on the left flank has been bad,
and in consequence of its badness the brunt of the battle has been on
us, with all the consequent losses. The two French Generals on the
right during the retreat have been arrested. In spite of the grumblings
of *The Times*, it is very fortunate in my opinion, that there were no
correspondents at the front. It would have been almost impossible to
prevent a great outburst of British feeling, which would have greatly
damaged the effective co-operation of the allies. As it was, it required
Kitchener's personal intervention to smooth things down.' Balfour
then continues:

'Winston in his most characteristic mood talks airily of a British army of a million men, and tells me he is making siege mortars at Woolwich as big as, or bigger than, the German ones, in order to crush the Rhine fortresses!

'I have been begging him to do all he can to diminish the strain on the *personnel* of the Navy. It is what the Germans are counting on. No doubt he is right in saying that if *we* suffer by keeping the sea, the Germans probably *also* suffer by staying in port. It is not good either for the efficiency or the morale of the Fleet to be bottled up as they appear to be at this moment.'

Important as his close liaison with Churchill was, both in its immediate and its ultimate results, it was overshadowed at the beginning of October by Asquith's invitation to him to become a full member of the Committee of Imperial Defence. His swift acceptance meant that he moved from indirect to direct influence on the course of the war: it meant also that he was in fact functioning as a member of the War Council, as it came to be known, in November of that year. Already by October 28, 1914, Asquith is thanking Balfour for his memorandum on 'Overseas attack' and says that 'some of your suggestions have already been adopted, and all shall be most carefully considered'. Balfour was actually far deeper in the innermost councils of the Cabinet than even his membership of the Defence Committee would suggest. There is, for example, a letter to him from Asquith on November 24, 1914, which says 'the existing situation both military and naval, is critical. I propose to have at noon tomorrow a consultation at 10, Downing Street . . . to take a full survey of all its aspects. I shall be greatly obliged if you could make it convenient to attend it. The only Ministers summoned are E. Grey, Lord K., Winston and Lloyd George. They may bring with them one or two experts. Naturally I don't wish this to be known. Yours always, H.H.A.'

Balfour translates this a day or two later (November 27) for Sandars to whom he writes: 'You realise, do you not, that Asquith is anxious that the character and composition of this and future similar meetings of the sub-committee should be kept private, because he fears that if they become known more of his colleagues will express a wish to attend.' ('Sub-committee' is an odd way of referring to what was clearly the prime executive group of a nation at war.) In the same letter Balfour reports that: 'Kitchener has entirely altered his views about invasion . . . now he finally declares invasion to be impossible. I, who have never thought it likely, am not perhaps prepared to go this extreme length.'

In December Balfour was asked to prepare a memorandum on how far Britain dare run down industry in favour of recruiting; this was before the great debate on conscription.

Meanwhile a great agitation had arisen in the press and the House of Commons about alleged shortages of armaments. G.H.Q. in France were not entirely guiltless in causing the fuss—it drew fire away from their far from successful conduct of the war in France. The Government tried officially to play this down; Balfour, however, knew that it was no scare. He had had dozens of letters from Captain William Balfour of Balbirnie, then in the trenches and a member of the original branch of the Balfour family who had married Lady Ruth Balfour, a niece of the Whittingehame branch. A typical letter reads: 'They must have shells; the 8,000 we lost the first day unavailingly should be written on Asquith's tombstone for saying we had plenty of ammunition, and the losses and suffering round here the past week have simply been due to the German guns and we not having anything to answer them with.'

Thus, when the agitation over shortages of ammunition grew into a demand for the appointment of a parliamentary committee of inquiry, there was, as Lord Beaverbrook says: 'One potent voice raised in favour of the appointment of the shell committee. Balfour expressed grave discontent with the failure of the Government to carry into effect the opinion of the meeting which he had attended in the third week of March, and on April 8 the shell committee was finally constituted and announced in the House of Commons on April 15.' Balfour himself served on the committee along with Lloyd George.

The stumbling block was found to be Kitchener, who had been brought up in an atmosphere of severe military economy, and the committee, whose job it was to mobilise industry and secure Government control over all armament factories and workers, was constantly hampered in its work by his refusal at the War Office to give it proper co-operation.

Of course, as Balfour was quite aware, neither Kitchener nor the Government generally was entirely responsible for the series of military defeats. Balfour, in company with Asquith and others, visited France on July 5, 1915 for the first Calais conference with the French. Balfour's impressions of his visit are contained in an uninhibited letter to his brother, Gerald, on May 31, 1915:

'I have never been able to see why French' (i.e. Sir John French, later Lord Ypres, first Commander-in-Chief of the British Expeditionary Force), 'was so confident of being able to break the German line. . . . When I was at the front I argued this question with Sir John and I confess that, while I was ready to yield to his authority, I thought his arguments unconvincing. . . . You must remember that French has been given a great deal more than the number of troops for which he asked, and that he knew exactly what shells he had at his disposal. When I was with him about April 20, he told me he would be ready for a general advance as soon as he had 1,000 rounds per gun, and that he would have that before May 1. It is perfectly true that the proportion of high explosives is much too small; but of this he was well aware. It is a curious thing that the advance was actually made in the week when the supply of high explosive shells was at its absolute minimum!

'Nothing, in my opinion, will excuse the want of foresight and imagination which has put us in this difficulty about munitions of war; but Billy [Captain William Balfour] is entirely wrong when he puts this down to civilian Ministers, and suggests that they are indifferent to the interests of the Army, and have their own axes to grind. I certainly hold no brief for the civilian members of the late Government [a coalition was formed in May, 1915] who are open to severe criticism from many points of view. But the deficiency of the munitions of war is due entirely to the War Office; and if the civilians committed any fault in the matter (which perhaps they did) it is that of having trusted too much to the soldiers. Things are going better now but they are still unsatisfactory . . . there is dissatisfaction with the management of the Army in Flanders. I hope this is not more than the natural result of heavy losses and comparative failure. But I am a little uneasy.'

This letter is less than fair to French, as we know from Churchill's account. French was under all sorts of pressures, not least from his Gallic allies, and was removed from his command later in the year. Nevertheless, Balfour was certainly correct in believing—and thus early agreeing with Lloyd George—that all the blame could not be put on the civilians back home; the staff was at least as much to blame and so was the War Office. Indeed no truer word was said about this early part of the war than was later written by Lloyd George in his war memoirs: 'The blunders of Germany saved us from the consequence of our own.'

II

One of the blunders was certainly the Dardanelles expedition, and in this affair, whose consequences reached far beyond military or strategic consideration, Balfour was closely concerned. He was concerned in the project at first indirectly, through his close relationship with Churchill, the First Lord of the Admiralty, in whose fertile brain the plan to open the Dardanelles and force the Bosphorus was first conceived. Later—in January, 1915—Balfour was on the subcommittee of the C.I.D. with Kitchener, Lloyd George and Churchill to consider the scheme of a diversion of war to the Balkans area. It is sufficient to say that it was one of the many plans put forward as a result of the stalemate in the Western theatre of operations.

Certainly, as a plan, it had obvious attractions. Turkey had come into the war on the side of the Germans while Russia, after some early successes, had suffered defeats. If by an attack on the Dardanelles, Constantinople could be taken and the Straits opened, Russia would at once be relieved, for she could be aided in the Black Sea by munitions, supplies and sea power which could not otherwise reach her owing to the German blockade. At the same time Rumania, which tottered on the edge of throwing in her lot with the Germans, and the Greeks would be compelled to join the Allies.

The reactions of Churchill's colleagues to the idea were lukewarm or at best acquiescent from the beginning. But Churchill himself, with his usual *brio*, was determined to put the plan into operation. Fisher, the First Sea Lord, who Churchill had brought back into office in 1914 at the age of 74 and against some protest, was, it now appears, strongly against the expedition. Yet, as Churchill himself has written: 'He agreed with that chief' (i.e. W.S.C.), 'with the full approval of the War Council, to carry out the operations against the Dardanelles. For three months or more he signed and sent every order to the Fleet attacking the Dardanelles. He added important vessels to it upon his personal initiative. When after the fall of the Outer Forts success seemed possible, and even probable, he offered to go out and take command himself of the decisive effort that must be made to force the passage.'

After a preliminary bombardment of the Dardanelles forts in November, 1914, by British cruisers—a foolish business since it forewarned the Turks of our intentions—the expedition was finally decided upon in January, 1915. But already in that month Fisher, without informing his chief, wrote to Asquith warning him against any sort of naval bombardment of fortified coastal defences—in other words, against an operation against the Dardanelles. Even worse, Fisher disclosed these matters to Law who thus discovered that behind the apparent unanimity of the Admiralty—for Churchill and Fisher had worked previously in great harmony—there lay hidden a probably dangerous conflict. Law quickly spread the news of the disagreement throughout the Opposition. It confirmed all the Conservative doubts about Churchill's judgement, and it hardened the opinions of Law and his colleagues against the Dardanelles expedition. Before long, it became one of the precipitating causes of the first Coalition Government.

But what of the position of Balfour? It seems clear that, in the beginning, he shared Churchill's optimism about naval operations against the Dardanelles. But he was extremely dubious about the question of landing military forces. The bombardment from the sea in November, 1914, had been followed by another at the end of February, and there had been an attempt to force the Straits by warships alone in the third week of March. It had failed. It was then decided that a landing should be effected with troops. On April 8, 1915

Balfour wrote a warning letter to Churchill. He begins by pointing out that the hoped-for shortage of water in the Turkish garrison of Gallipoli had no basis of fact, at least according to Intelligence reports he had seen. He then goes on:

'As you know, I cannot help being very anxious about the fate of any military attempt upon the Peninsula. Nobody was so keen as myself upon forcing the Straits as long as there seemed a reasonable prospect of doing it by means of the Fleet alone;—even though the operation might cost us a few antiquated battleships. But a military attack upon a position so inherently difficult and so carefully prepared, is a different proposition: and if it fails we shall not only have to suffer considerably in men but still more in prestige, but we may upset our whole diplomacy in the Near East, which at the present moment, seems to promise most favourably. If you can get your subs. through, we shall evidently be able to blockade the 70,000 Turks now massed in the Peninsula. They will not be able to get supplies by sea: and the only road can be absolutely denied them by ships in the Gulf of Xeros. If and when an arrangement could be come to with Bulgaria, quite a small force would lock up the whole of the Turkish garrison until they surrender from starvation or panic; and in the meanwhile, without at all abandoning our scheme, it would I should have thought be worth considering whether we should not delay its completion till we have destroyed the Turkish army in Syria. Compare Napoleon in 1805!'

Balfour's position was closer to Fisher's than Fisher suspected. He was mistaken in writing to Law that 'I regret to say your A.J.B. has been backing W.C. *all through* and I have refused to have anything to do with him (A.J.B.) in consequence!' Nor indeed was Churchill himself quite so certain of the matter as Fisher supposed. For on receiving Balfour's letter he replied on the same day, April 8, 1915, saying that he had in mind the possibility of a postponement of a few days if the question of decision in the Italian campaign against the Austro-Hungarians was likely. But at the same time he reminded Balfour of the approaching 'fatal danger of German submarines', and told him that he should not be 'unduly apprehensive' about the military operation: 'The soldiers think they can do it, and it was their influence that persuaded the Admiral to delay the renewal of his attack till their preparations were completed. The military attack is in addition to, and not in substitution for, or derogation from, the naval attack. Both attacks mutually aid each other; and either, by succeeding, would be decisive.' He thought that with naval artillery to support it, the army would advance 'comfortably' as far as the line of the Suandere river. This in turn would greatly aid the naval attack upon the Narrows. Churchill then says:

'No other operation in this part of the world could ever cloak the defeat of abandoning the effort against the Dardanelles. I think there is nothing for it but to go through with the business, and I do not at all regret that this should be so. No one can count with certainty upon the issue of a battle. But here we have the chances in our favour, and play for vital gains with non-vital stakes.'

Whether Balfour was persuaded by these arguments or not, he had no power to prevent the landings, which took place in April at the toe of the Peninsula and at Anzac. The troops held on but did not advance. At this time, Churchill afterwards complained, Fisher 'set himself to stint the campaign and put obstacles in the path of action. He resisted the despatch of the most necessary supplies, apparatus and reinforcements. By this time an army had been landed and 20,000 men killed or wounded. The army was clinging on to the dearly won positions by tooth and nail. He had advocated the sending of this army.'

The Fisher-Churchill debate continues even now. It concerns us only because, when the storm broke and Fisher resigned and Churchill was removed from his office, it was Balfour who took over his post as First Lord of the Admiralty, and thus had the Dardanelles operations on his hands. It was under his direction, therefore, that in August further landings were attempted and came nearer to success, though failing in the long run. Balfour wrote to his sister, Alice, on August 28, 1915: 'The failure at Gallipoli, due, as far as we can make out, entirely to the weakness of the General in command of the left wing, is certainly the worst thing that has happened to us since the retreat from Mons. We were *very* near a great success . . . I cannot conceive what Willie Selborne meant by saying that we had the submarine situation "well in hand". He didn't get that from me.'

Wherever the fault lay, it was under Balfour's tenure of the Admiralty that the evacuation of Galipoli took place—an evacuation carried out with almost no loss largely owing to the arrangements made by General (later Field-Marshal) Birdwood. By the end of the year the army General Staff, though aware that success in opening the Dardanelles and the Bosphorous 'would undoubtedly have a great, and a more or less immediate effect, both direct and indirect, in the main theatre of war and on the Arab and Mohametan worlds', were strongly against any further offensive efforts there, and the scheme was dropped.

The war outlook was, indeed, bleak. A General Staff paper on the Future Conduct of the War, dated December 16, 1915, could see scarcely any point where the Allies had sufficient forces to apply new pressures, and indeed passed the buck back to 'Diplomacy' by suggesting that Turkey should be detached from the Central Powers and set against Bulgaria. They insisted (*pace* Hankey) that this was 'one of the penalties for general lack of preparation against an enemy who was fully prepared'. The future seemed dark, indeed, to the General Staff. A policy of playing for 'stalemate'—a long drawn-out defensive operation—would be useless: 'It would be wiser to make peace now than to play for stalemate.' All that was left was a new, vast offensive on the present front; if the Allies 'cannot win victory by those means they are at least far less likely to win it by any other means'.

Discouraging as all this was, it was facing facts. The Allies lacked means, not least in terms of transport, to try diversions; a war of attrition was imposed, not by stupid generals, but by the context of the times, industrially and scientifically. Only developments in speed could alter warfare; only new military and more industrial power would turn the tide.

III

A few months before, in May, 1915, a political crisis had blown up. It arose as a result of Fisher's sudden resignation, his departure to Scotland and his refusal to return to office despite requests by Lloyd George, Asquith and McKenna. His resignation finally decided Law. He told Lloyd George that, if Fisher resigned and Churchill remained, he would not restrain the Conservatives from demanding a public debate upon the issues that had provoked the crisis. The Opposition would deliver an attack upon the Government whatever the consequences might be.

Churchill had himself proffered his resignation to Asquith who refused to accept it, but when Asquith heard of Law's threat he realised that he could not save Churchill from the wrath of the Conservatives. He and Lloyd George then saw Law and it was decided that a Coalition Cabinet should be formed. Law now consulted Lansdowne and Chamberlain —not Balfour—and Asquith offered to form a Coalition administration in which the Conservatives would be fully represented.

Balfour's position in these affairs and in the subsequent Cabinet-making was obviously delicate. He had early in the year discussed with Law his difficulty in supporting the Government without the power of criticising or influencing its conduct of the war; and, as early as December 1, 1914, wrote to Lord Durham: 'I, who have no official position at all, have been trying to help the Government carry out a policy which has been essentially changed more than once, and with which *in its first form* I had nothing whatever to do.'

But, although Churchill had informed him of Fisher's resignation, Balfour's opinion on the formation of a Coalition Government was not asked, nor was it offered. Indeed, if Law had had more say than Asquith in the composition of the First Coalition Cabinet, Balfour might well have been omitted from it altogether, or given some minor post. Law did not demand much for the Conservatives. The key ministries—Prime Minister, Exchequer, Foreign Secretary and Minister of Munitions—remained in the hands of Liberals. But as a result of an unlikely set of circumstances, instead of being given a small post, Balfour in fact was the only Conservative to get a key post—First Lord of the Admiralty.

This came about in a strange way. When Churchill had told Balfour of Fisher's resignation, Balfour had undertaken to prepare his Conservative colleagues for the news and 'steady their opinion'. Churchill wrote later, 'nothing could exceed the kindness and firmness of his attitude'. Balfour, however, was unable to engage the sympathies of the Conservatives in favour of a man most of them distrusted and detested. On May 17, 1915, Churchill went to Asquith's room in the House of Commons with a list of his proposed changes at the Board of the Admiralty resulting from Fisher's resignation. Asquith told him that he had decided to form a National Government by a coalition with the Unionists; and it was shortly borne in upon Churchill that the consequent reconstruction involved his own resignation. He was then asked his advice about his successor and answered at once that Balfour was the only person to succeed with the least break in continuity.

Asquith accepted this suggestion with alacrity. Others were not so keen on the appointment. Lloyd George, indeed, told Asquith that the work of the Admiralty in wartime was no place for a man of 67 and, moreover, a man who would have difficulty in adapting himself to the constant pressure of work at a desk. Hankey, Balfour's friend and Secretary of the Defence Committee, made similar representations to Asquith, who however refused to change his mind: 'He is tougher than you think,' he told Hankey. Asquith's reasons for wishing to have Balfour at the Admiralty are obvious: not only was Balfour completely *au fait* with the overriding strategic issues from his work in the Committee of Imperial Defence, but in the Admiralty's present state of disruption, a Minister of great political weight and equanimity was required. Law did not possess such qualifications. Nor did anyone else among the Conservative Opposition.

Balfour's own feelings were expressed in a letter to Asquith on May, 19, 1915: '*A propos* of our conversation yesterday evening, I hope you understand that if, as Bonar Law tells me, my accepting office in any Coalition Government is in his view desirable, and even necessary, I am quite indifferent as to what office I take, except that I do not think I could usefully be responsible for any heavy administrative office, except the Admiralty. On the other hand, I am perfectly ready to join the Government without portfolio, or to accept any office (Chancellor of the Duchy, etc.) which would carry with it no heavy office

A1ᴊʙ

work. Indeed personally I should prefer it.' It was, in the end, Churchill who became Chancellor of the Duchy.

It has been said that, though it is difficult to criticise Asquith's choice, it is impossible to maintain that it proved unquestionably right. It is probably true that Balfour did not shine in this office—possibly no one other than Churchill could have done so at that time—whereas by contrast he did shine in his subsequent office as Foreign Minister. But two points should be borne in mind before any harsh criticism is made of Balfour's performance as First Lord of the Admiralty: one is that he went into that office without the benefit of a First Sea Lord and in conditions of considerable disruption within the Admiralty itself; secondly, most of the very important decisions affecting his office were not in fact taken by him alone but by what was now termed 'The Dardanelles Committee' which was an inner Cabinet concerned with war strategy and so named because, it was felt, the most important problem it had to consider was that arising from the Dardanelles expedition. The membership consisted, as well as Balfour, of the Prime Minister, of Kitchener, the War Minister, of Lloyd George, Law, Carson, Churchill, Crewe, Curzon, Selborne and Lansdowne. As Blake points out, 'as an instrument of policy it had from the first grave defects'. It could not take decisions that bound the rest of the Cabinet and it contained too many powerful personages for there to be much unanimity. (In addition many of the Conservatives—but not Balfour —had a deep distrust of the Prime Minister.) It is, therefore, quite beside the point for Beaverbrook—who is in any case *parti pris* on Law's side—to remark that Balfour as First Lord was 'unsuitable. His erudition and his powers of reasoning did not equip him for the post of political head of the Admiralty at the height of a naval war.'

Balfour's first task was obviously the appointment of a First Sea Lord. Prince Louis of Battenburg was, as we have seen, barred by his German birth from returning to the post he had filled at the opening of the war; Sir Arthur Wilson, who was holding the office in the interim, declined to serve under anyone but Churchill, nor had Balfour much confidence in him, fearing his 'rashness'. The transfer of Sir John Jellicoe, then in command of the Grand Fleet, does not seem to have been considered. It was probably on the advice of Hankey and other members of the staff that Sir Henry Jackson was appointed. Jackson was a scientific officer who had worked with Marconi in the early days of wireless telegraphy, and he had a good technical knowledge of ships and gunnery. This was all to the good; for Balfour, apart from his scientific leanings, had an insatiable interest in technical information. This did not mean that the two always saw eye to eye. Sir Henry Oliver, later Admiral of the Fleet, then at the Admiralty, says that he and the Principal Private Secretary had a plan to deal with Balfour and

Jackson when they differed in opinion: 'We used to give them time to cool down and then Graham-Greene' (the Private Secretary) 'went and talked to Balfour and I talked to Jackson and we always managed to get them to make it up.'

Co-operation between the two became closer as a consequence of one of the most important acts of Balfour while Lord of the Admiralty. Under an order in Council of July 28, 1915, he set up a department of Invention and Research dealing with matters very dear to Jackson's heart. The department later became—in 1919—the Committee for Scientific and Industrial Research. 'This', Sir George Thomson writes to me, 'was one of the first examples of Government science. I don't know that it had any influence on the war, and my father' (J. J. Thomson) 'complained that the work they did on the detection of submarines was ignored until there was sudden panic, when it was too late to develop it properly. However, I think it probable that the existence of this body helped in making science known to the governing classes, and led indirectly to the foundation of the Department of Scientific and Industrial Research much as radar and the atomic bomb led in the last war to increased expenditure on science.'

Interestingly enough, Balfour appointed Weizmann—their meeting has already been recounted—to a position in the Admiralty laboratories where he invented a new bacterial process for producing acetone (an important constituent of explosive) from horse-chestnuts. A year later, on December 10, 1916, Edison, then head of the American Naval Consulting Board, could say that both sides had failed to take advantage of modern science: but it is to Balfour's credit that he had initiated a step in the right direction. As President of the department of Invention and Research, Fisher was appointed and several subsections were set up. On the one that dealt with submarines, mines and searchlights there served such men as W. H. Bragg, Glazebrook, Merz and Rutherford. Balfour must have been intensely interested by the experiments of Rutherford and of Sir Richard Paget who went out in boats on the Firth of Forth and listened to the sounds made by submarines. Sound-ranging in France also came within the Board's purview and, by means of this work, enemy guns were located with remarkable precision and then quickly attacked by Allied batteries.

A constant stream of ideas and instruments began to flow from the department's work and were sent to the Sea Research Stations at Hawkcraig, Aberdour and Parkeston Quay to be tested on trawlers and submarines. A viable listening instrument was produced and Balfour at once gave rush orders for 1,000 of them. The experimental station at Parkeston Quay was set up under Balfour's direct orders after discussion with Jellicoe and Bragg; Balfour visited it on several occasions. This development under his auspices at the Admiralty was to become, in the decade after the war, one of his deepest interests.

But it was the more urgent, day-to-day activities of the Admiralty that were all-important in 1915 and 1916. There was, first of all, a decision to be taken on whether or not to evacuate Gallipoli following the failure at Suvla Bay. The decision was complicated by the fact that the French suddenly offered four divisions under the command of General Sarrail for service at Gallipoli. This put a more favourable light upon the position in the Dardanelles. But again a complication occurred. Bulgaria had thrown in her lot with Germany and there was evidence to show that there was to be a combined German and Bulgarian offensive against Serbia early in October, 1915. The only power capable of helping Serbia in the time was Greece. It was, therefore, thought that the Allies must procure the entry of Greece into the war. The only means of doing so appeared to be to send a substantial Allied force to Salonika.

Was it Salonika or Gallipoli that was to be the *point d'appui*? The decision caused great differences of opinion, accompanied by threats of resignation, in the Cabinet. At first, Balfour, with Asquith and Churchill, were against evacuation of Gallipoli; but by November, 1915, following advice from Kitchener who was on the spot, Balfour changed his mind. Consequently, the army was withdrawn from Anzac and Suvla Bay on December 19, and so ended the Churchillian hang-over into Balfour's ministry.

It did not, however, end the dissension in the Cabinet which now began to centre on Kitchener, the War Minister, who was showing himself increasingly obdurate and unimaginative in his unaccustomed office. Balfour's view was expressed in a conversation with his niece in 1915. In this he remarked that Kitchener 'knows nothing—he does nothing right . . . he is not a great organiser—he is not a great administrator—nor a great soldier—what is more, he knows it. He is not vain. He is only great when he has little things to accomplish. . . . *I must call his greatness personality*. He has that in the highest sense.' Balfour believed that the War Office needed a civilian—someone perhaps like Runciman—who would not override his experts and his colleagues on technical points.

We now turn to the major naval action at sea during Balfour's time at the Admiralty. On May 30, the Admiralty became convinced that the German High Seas Fleet was putting out at last in full strength, and orders were given to the British battlefleet to leave their bases and meet the enemy. Neither Balfour nor Sir Henry Jackson—nor Sir Henry Oliver, the Chief of the Naval Staff—had been particularly anxious to force forward the day of a decisive fleet action. Balfour believed rather in a policy of attrition and a constant tightening of the blockade. Admiral Jellicoe was equally cautious. Both believed that the German policy was to tempt the British into the southern portion of the North Sea, which was crowded with mines and haunted by submarines, by holding out hopes of a general action.

As Balfour put it in a report to the Cabinet in October, 1916: 'The general action would be refused but in the meanwhile some very unpleasant accidents might happen to our fighting ships.' He believed that the proper way of dealing with the situation was to retain the Grand Fleet in the north unless the Germans 'have so far committed themselves to a forward movement that they can't retire without trying conclusions with the British. . . . What the enemy would like to see would be a series of small and inconclusive operations in which by a timely retirement their own battlefleet would avoid disaster, while by mines and submarines we should lose a ship here and a ship there, till the cumulative effect became serious.'

Whether Balfour was right or wrong in supporting this view is a matter of controversy still; that he was supported by his principal advisers at the Admiralty is not in doubt. It was certainly true that Jellicoe was 'the only man who could have lost us the war in an afternoon', and to urge him into a position where he might to do so would have been folly.

The anxiety, therefore, when news of the battle at Jutland on June 1 became known at the Admiralty may be imagined. Hankey writes of Balfour being at the Admiralty in 'a state of very great excitement' on May 31. Although no messages came from Jellicoe until Friday, June 2, disabled ships had already begun to reach port. How much should the nation be told? Balfour believed that nothing should be said until a message came; the message duly came and Balfour issued a completely unvarnished statement of the facts as far as he knew them at that time. The facts, as it happened, were not as bad as at first reported, but the communiqué that Balfour issued came to many as a catalogue of 'appalling disaster'. Alarm and despondency spread through the nation, only to turn into anger, when better news came, against Balfour for having, so it seemed, exaggerated the losses.

Balfour might, perhaps, have waited for more information before issuing the communiqué, but when this was pointed out to him he reminded his naval advisers that the pressure on Jellicoe must at that moment be inordinate; and the suggestion that he should add some reassuring note he rejected. A week later he defended himself in a speech: 'If my candour, if my desire immediately to let the people know the best and the worst that I knew, was in any way responsible for that result (i.e. creating despondency), I can only express my regret. But confidence in the desire of the Admiralty to deal straightly and fairly with the British public will be increased by what has occurred, and if that be so there is nothing to regret.'

It has been said that Balfour misjudged the mentality of the man in the street by facing him with what, at that time, seemed to be the unpalatable truth. Was this so? If the facts had been accurate, it was Balfour's plain duty to state them; the weakness of the argument in his favour is that the full facts were not, or at least not entirely, known. There was at least one obvious gain: for when at last the Germans admitted their losses, which they had formerly concealed, confidence in British war reports became overwhelmingly unshakeable both at home and abroad.

In Balfour's view Jutland was a missed opportunity. Yet in overall strategy it was an incomparable gain. Never again did the much-battered German High Seas Fleet put to sea to fight. Jellicoe remained in undisputed possession of the North Sea, and the east coast towns ceased to be bombarded. 'From the point of view of the grand strategy,' says Hankey, 'Jutland was as sweeping a success as Trafalgar.'

The menace of submarines, however, remained and grew. This increasingly occupied Balfour's mind. We have seen that he set up a department to concentrate on counter-measures; however, towards the end of 1916, both Asquith and Grey were hinting that larger measures still were necessary, not only in view of the devastating facts, but in view of the effect of those facts upon the public. Both suggested that there might well be changes in the Admiralty itself and Asquith was in favour of replacing Sir Henry Jackson by Jellicoe. Balfour himself would have preferred to bring Jellicoe to the Admiralty but to keep Jackson as well. This did not recommend itself to Jellicoe and, before the end of December, 1916, Asquith had his way: Jellicoe became First Sea Lord and the chief command at sea passed to Admiral Beatty. Meanwhile, however, Balfour himself had ceased to be First Lord.

Whatever the public view of his tenure of this office may have been, those who worked with him at the Admiralty were regretful to see him go: their memories of the acrimonious pre-Balfourian days were still strong. Sir Henry Oliver, the Chief of Naval Operations, spoke of Balfour always with the highest regard, and it was after all Oliver who remained under Balfour, as under Churchill, in the supreme command of the whole maritime war.

IV

Throughout Balfour's time as First Lord of the Admiralty, a further political crisis had been brewing. The basic reasons for this were, of course, the lack of progress in winning the war, the enormous casualty lists and the growing shortages caused by the success of the German submarine campaign. But there were other reasons of a more personal kind. There was, on the one hand, a genuine feeling that Asquith was not prosecuting the war with sufficient energy; and there was the frustration of a number of politicians, such as Lloyd George and Law, who felt that they themselves should have a larger hand in the conduct of the war. All these matters combined to produce the machinations that resulted in the fall of Asquith in December, 1916.

In the early part of these political convolutions, Balfour again played little part, though in a sense he was a storm-centre; but in the latter part he was the crucial figure. As early as August 18, 1915, he had been warned by Margot Asquith that Northcliffe (proprietor of *The Times* and the *Daily Mail*) 'has backed himself to break this Cabinet and he will do it. Henry never takes any interest in papers that attack him but our Allies do.'

A month or two later in October, 1915, according to a note by Sandars, Balfour was already reserving for himself the right to act in whatever way he thought proper should there be a Cabinet crisis. 'Lord Stamfordham', Sandars records, 'called to see Mr. Balfour on Monday the 18th of October. In the course of the conversation, Mr. Balfour said that he was quite prepared to continue a member of the present Government so long as his services were required, but that he reserved to himself full liberty of action should there be a serious split in the Cabinet with consequent resignations. He was not disposed to remain a member of any "rump" Cabinet.'

This is a significant statement since, after the collapse of the Asquith Premiership, he was to be accused by Margot Asquith of disloyalty. Some three years afterwards, she wrote not without bitterness (February 10, 1919): 'I wonder what the world would think if they knew that Lloyd George's *first* quarrel with my Henry was about you—Lloyd George wished to get rid of you as you know. Henry insisted on saving you from this Lloyd George-Northcliffe plot. . . . You don't love anyone as much as I love Henry and you are always detached and happy in your own way.'

Whatever Lloyd George thought of Balfour, Balfour himself was becoming convinced that Lloyd George was the only possible war leader, and in his view the speedy winning of the war and the cessation of the slaughter took precedence over individual likes and dislikes. Balfour, however, was not among those who discussed the future of the Government, and in particular the office of War Minister, vacant as a result of the death by drowning of Kitchener. The jockeyings for this office have been detailed—not entirely uncontroversially—by Beaverbrook and by Law's biographer, Blake. Asquith, it appears, had thought of one or two candidates for the office but not of Lloyd George. It was Law, after a private agreement with Lloyd George, who suggested him to Asquith, and the suggestion was adopted. But the affair was perhaps even more tortuous than Beaverbrook and Blake describe it.   There is, for example, a letter from Balfour to Salisbury dated June 17, 1916 which reads: 'I have kept out of the business altogether, but one piece of information (of, I think, a very unpleasant kind) has come to my knowledge.   It is most confidential, and you must not repeat it to a soul.   It is that Asquith was thinking of putting Austen (Chamberlain) at the War Office, and that Bonar Law intervened on the ground that this would be a slight upon himself!   This procedure seems to be so inconsistent with the idea that I had formed of Bonar Law's character that I had the utmost difficulty in believing it. But I am afraid it is hardly open to doubt.'

Yet, as the autumn of 1916 grew on and the gloom of the war news deepened, it was clear that a change in one Ministry would not suffice— nor did it satisfy the ambitions of the new Minister.   What Lloyd George wanted was a new War Council, headed by himself and assisted by Law and Carson, from which the Prime Minister was to be excluded.   Lloyd George actually handed a memorandum to this effect to Asquith at the very beginning of December, 1916.   Asquith rejected it and Lloyd George turned for support to Law and the Conservative Ministers.   He also inspired a newspaper article suggesting that unless his demands were accepted he would resign and then appeal to public opinion against the Government for its alleged incompetence in managing the war.

At this stage the Conservative Ministers met.   (Balfour was not present—he was lying ill in bed with influenza.)   Though they were very far from wishing to see Lloyd George in supreme power, they were agreed that the Government ought to resign, and Law informed Asquith of their opinion.   Asquith now decided to compromise and agreed to the formation of a small War Council with Lloyd George as active Chairman and himself as President.   He disagreed, however, on the other personnel of the War Council and ultimately promised only to see and seek terms with Lloyd George.   We may now leave Balfour to take up the tale for, though still ill in his room, he wrote a memorandum describing the events of the political crisis, because, as he says, he 'realised that the dispute about personnel really centred round me; Lloyd George wanted a change at the Admiralty, which was being resisted by the Prime Minister.   I thereupon wrote the following letter explaining my views, and offering my resignation.'   (Balfour is exaggerating when he says that the crisis centred round him; at this stage the leading figure in the crisis was, of course, Asquith himself.)

Balfour's letter to Asquith, dated December 5, 1916, reads: 'I have been mostly in bed since the political crisis became acute, and can collect no very complete idea of what has been going on.   But one thing seems clear: that there is to be a new War Council of which Lloyd George is to be the working Chairman, and that, according to his ideas, this Council would work more satisfactorily if the Admiralty were not represented by me. In these circumstances I cannot consent to retain my office, and must ask you to accept my resignation. I am well aware that you do not personally share Lloyd George's views in this connection. But I am quite clear that the new system should have a trial under the most favourable possible circumstances; and the mere fact that the new Chairman of the War Council *did* prefer, and, so far as I know, *still* prefers, a different arrangement is, to my mind, quite conclusive, and leaves me no doubt as to the manner in which I can best assist the Government which I desire to support. The fact that the first days of the reconstructed administration finds me more than half an invalid, is an additional reason (if additional reason were required) for adopting the course on which, after much consideration, I have determined.'

Balfour's memorandum containing the text of this letter goes on to state that Asquith replied by sending him a copy of his letter of the previous day to Lloyd George in which he explains that he has the King's authority to accept the resignation of all his colleagues and form a new Government 'on such lines as I should submit to him'. The letter says that Asquith has decided that it is not possible to have a new War Committee without the Prime Minister as its Chairman. He does not believe that Balfour should be removed from his post at the Admiralty and thinks that he must be a member of any War Committee. Nor does he believe that Carson, who has been suggested as a member of the new War Committee, is 'the man best qualified among my colleagues past and present'. He agrees only that the War Committee ought to be reduced in number so that it can sit more frequently.

Balfour received Asquith's reply on December 5, 1916, and sent off an answer at 4 p.m. on the same day. When he wrote it, as he points out in his memorandum, he did not know that Lloyd George had already resigned and that the Prime Minister's own resignation was to follow. His letter to Asquith reads:

'I am very grateful for your note and its enclosure. I very highly value your appreciation. I do not, however, feel much inclined to change my views. I still think (*a*) that the break-up of the Government by the retirement of Lloyd George would be a misfortune; (*b*) that the experiment of giving him a free hand with the day-to-day work of the War Committee is still worth trying, and (*c*) that there is no use trying it except on terms which enable him to work under conditions which, in his own opinion, promise the best results. We cannot, I think, go on in the old way. An open breach with Lloyd George will not improve matters, and attempts to compel co-operation between him and fellow workers with whom he is in but imperfect sympathy will only produce fresh trouble. I am, therefore, still of opinion that my resignation should be accepted, and that a fair trial should be given to War Council à la George.'

This letter makes it clear that Balfour desired to resign not, as Blake supposes, in order to spike Lloyd George's guns but, on the contrary, in order to allow Lloyd George to take supreme control of the war. This should have been equally clear to Asquith, and his expressions of hurt surprise when Balfour later joined with Lloyd George are to say the least exaggerated.

The result of these moves was that, on December 6, Law and Lloyd George both visited Balfour who was still in bed and various alternatives were discussed. It was agreed that it would be best to form a government of which Lloyd George would be Chairman of the War Committee and in which Asquith should be included. Balfour's memorandum comments: 'To me it seemed clear that, if such a Government were possible, it was only possible with Bonar Law as Prime Minister, and it was in the highest degree improbable that Asquith would consent to serve under Lloyd George. Bonar Law explained that he had been sent for by the King, and had suggested a meeting at Buckingham Palace, at which both he and Lloyd George were very anxious that I should be present.'

The reason why they wanted Balfour at these deliberations is clear. Although they were not then aware either of his views expressed in his letters to Asquith nor of his offer of resignation, they knew that his adherence to any alternative government to Asquith's was desirable in order to give it an appearance of sound respectability. Balfour's credit stood firm and it had no rivals: Law could not guarantee the Conservative support needed for a new government—Balfour could. Somewhat naturally, Lloyd George was shy about seeking his aid since, as he correctly imagined, Balfour knew of his opposition to him as First Lord of the Admiralty. But, Lloyd George writes, 'I underrated the passionate attachment to his country which burned under that calm, indifferent and apparently frigid exterior.'

By 'passionate attachment to his country', Lloyd George presumably meant Balfour's backing for him as Prime Minister, but Balfour had not yet gone quite so far as that. His plan was still that Asquith should remain Prime Minister but should go to the Lords and that Lloyd George should become First Lord of the Treasury and Chairman of the War Committee. Meanwhile three other Conservative leaders— Curzon, Lord Robert Cecil and Austen Chamberlain—put their oar in and informed Asquith that they would not remain in the Government if Law and Lloyd George both resigned. Law had already elicited that Asquith would serve neither under himself, under Lloyd George nor even under Balfour—though we are told that Asquith gave 'a moment's consideration' to this latter proposal. Balfour himself, however, refused to head any government in which Asquith was not included.

Matters were at this complicated—and not very elevating—stage when the Buckingham Palace meeting, called by the King, took place on December 6. Those invited were Balfour, Law, Lloyd George, Asquith and Arthur Henderson, representing Labour. Balfour himself was asked by the King to come half an hour earlier, and his memorandum of their private conversation says: 'I explained my view of the situation to the best of my ability, insisting that as far as my opinion was worth anything, it was quite impossible for the same man effectively to carry out the ordinary duties of a Prime Minister and Leader of the House of Commons, in addition to those of Chairman of the War Committee. The King asked me to be ready to start the discussion at the meeting after he had bid the members welcome. Accordingly I said a few words upon the double necessity of altering our accustomed machinery, and of maintaining, if possible, a National or Coalition Government. A general conversation ensued, very moderate in form, but, so far as Asquith and L.G. were concerned, with a sub-acid flavour. Asquith insisted that he could give more effective support to the Government outside it than if he were a member. He claimed that his hold over his Party in the House of Commons and in the country was undiminished, and that he would, therefore, be able to prevent anything in the nature of either factious or pacifist intrigue.

'Henderson, for his part, dwelt upon the difficulty he anticipated in inducing organised labour to associate itself with any government of which Asquith were not a member. Asquith denounced the action of the press, which he said had played a most pernicious part both before and during the crisis, and which ought to be controlled in Britain as it was controlled in France. There seemed to be a general consensus of opinion on the part of the three members principally concerned that a return to the Sunday arrangement was now impracticable. [On the Sunday it had seemed possible that Asquith and Lloyd George might agree.]

'When the King, at the end, asked me my opinion, I observed that there were only three persons from whom a Prime Minister could be chosen, and they were all present at the table, but that I gathered that if either B.L. or L.G. were selected to fill the place, A. would refuse to serve under them, while H. believed that organised Labour would stand aloof. Both these gentlemen thereupon interrupted me and said that they had not gone quite so far as I seemed to suppose. A. in particular said that he must consult his friends before offering a final opinion.

'Shortly afterwards the King brought the meeting to a conclusion, it being understood that B.L. was to form a Government, which should, if possible, include A., and A. was to consider whether such inclusion was practicable or not from the point of view of his immediate friends.'

This completes Balfour's own account of the actual meeting at Buckingham Palace. From other accounts—principally that of Lord Stamfordham—it seems clear that on Balfour's proposal it was agreed not merely that Law should form a government and that Asquith should serve under him; but also that, if Asquith would not so serve, then Lloyd George should make the attempt.

After the meeting Balfour and Law had a discussion at Carlton Gardens. Law explained that he was reluctant to be the head of a new government because, 'by whatever name it might be described, L.G. would undoubtedly be its most powerful member, and he (B.L.) would much prefer that the forms of power and its substance should go together.' 'I told him', Balfour wrote, 'that while I agreed with him in thinking that L.G. ought to be the dominant spirit on the War Committee, his (i.e. Law's) functions as Leader of the House and Prime Minister were of such vital importance to the success of the administration that it was a waste of time to define as to whether the head of the War Committee or the head of the Government was its real leader. I did not convince him, and he then asked me whether, if A. showed any readiness to serve under him, it was wise to push him a little further, and try to get him to serve under L.G. I replied in the negative.'

In the event, Asquith refused to serve under anyone and thus, as arranged at the Palace meeting, Lloyd George became Prime Minister. Asquith went into Opposition and took with him the majority of his Liberal ex-Ministers, which meant that Lloyd George had to fill the main offices in his Cabinet from the Conservative Party. In his Cabinet-making he worked closely with Law, and of course the question arose as to Balfour's willingness to be a member of the new administration. For Lloyd George it was important that he should, for the reasons of prestige and respectability we have already mentioned. It seems that casually after the Buckingham Palace meeting, Law had proposed that Balfour should become Foreign Minister; and at 9.30 that evening, he again visited Balfour and 'brought me a formal request that I should undertake the position of Minister for Foreign Affairs. If I consented, it would in the view of L.G. and himself, greatly help with the rest of our Unionist colleagues. I agreed to the proposal.' This account does not accord particularly well with those given by Beaverbrook and Law in which there are certain journalistic touches such as Balfour saying that the offer was 'putting a pistol at my head'. There is, however, little doubt that Balfour's acquiescence made the second Coalition Government possible, as Law saw clearly when he wrote to Beaverbrook: 'Under all the circumstances I think that the part played by him (Balfour) was the biggest part played by anyone in the whole crisis. It was quite plain to me that he would have given anything, apart from the sense of duty, to be free from the responsibility of being a member of the Government. He knew that Lloyd George had been trying to have him removed from the Admiralty, and at that time it was at least doubtful whether Lloyd George could form a strong Government. Yet he took his decision without a moment's hesitation, and he did it, as he explained to me afterwards, for this reason—that unless the new Government succeeded, then the only alternative was to return to the old situation with the conditions, if possible, even worse than before.'

There could scarcely have been a better reason, or a more honourable one; though there are those, like R. Churchill in *Derby*, who cannot conceive of a decision being taken on patriotic or commonsense grounds. Such criticism requires us to ask: Was Balfour merely a necessary pawn in Lloyd George's game? Many years later, in fact after Balfour's death, his niece put the question to Lloyd George himself and received the reply that he believed that Balfour was 'wasted' at the Admiralty: 'It was never the right place for him. I was determined to use that vast sagacity of his on the things he could do best. And was I not justified? Think of him in America! Think of him in Paris!' It has to be remembered that at the time Lloyd George demanded Balfour's removal from the Admiralty, the Foreign Office was not, in fact, vacant; even so, in any reconstruction it clearly would become vacant. Moreover, as already observed, these two politicians had had considerable personal regard for each other long before; as a Balfour family letter put it, they 'fell in love with one another at the Buckingham Palace conference'.

Was Balfour disloyal to his friend and Prime Minister, Asquith? As we have seen, Asquith had chosen to ignore the clear statement in Balfour's letter to the effect that he believed Lloyd George should have a free hand; but that did not prevent him feeling aggrieved by Balfour's action in joining the man he regarded as 'the enemy'. Many years later Margot Asquith in a letter to Mrs. Dugdale said that her husband 'would never have resigned but he felt certain that A.J.B. would never desert him and would refuse absolutely ever to serve under a man who had *never* stopped intriguing with Northcliffe to get rid of him. . . . That Lloyd George (a Welshman!) should betray him he dimly, if rather late, did understand, but that Arthur should join his enemy (L.G.) and helped to ruin him (Henry), he never understood.' This very lack of comprehension in itself suggests that control of a vast war machine might well have been beyond Asquith by 1916.

Asquith's cup of bitterness was indeed overflowing. For apparently Curzon—who now became a member of Lloyd George's inner War Cabinet—had gone to him and told him that 'I would rather die than serve under Lloyd George'.   When Curzon's adherence to Lloyd George was announced, Asquith is said to have remarked: 'It is an almost unbelievable story.'

There were other sensational appointments in Lloyd George's Cabinet.   Lord Milner went into the inner War Cabinet, while Lord Derby became War Minister.   Carson took Balfour's place at the Admiralty.   Balfour himself as Foreign Minister, though not in the inner War Cabinet, had a right which he regularly exercised to attend its meetings when matters concerning his own department were being discussed.

But perhaps the most sensational fact of all was that in this Government under a Liberal with strongly Radical tendencies all the key offices were held by Conservatives.   As Blake puts it: 'The change of Government was the death knell of the old Liberal Party.'

17

THE WAR

Foreign Minister 1916–1919

As Balfour ascended in the lift and walked across the strip of scarlet drugget towards the room of the Secretary of State for Foreign Affairs on December 6, 1916, a sense of the past, of his own past, must have filled his mind. He himself, now white-haired though slim as ever, had known the room well in his early days in the House when his uncle occupied it, and some picture of his younger self, lean, languorous and with long, brown side-boards may have returned to him. The room itself—with its three curtained windows looking northwards across Horse Guards Parade and its three windows looking westwards across St. James's Park—had, indeed, altered little since the days of Lord Salisbury. In front of the fireplace was the gay fireguard presented to Salisbury by Li Hung Chang; the warm leather sofas and armchairs, the mahogany map-racks, and the yellow standing-desk in the corner—all were the same. Upon the ceiling was the same Etrusco-Byzantine stencilling and upon the desk the same brass and glass inkstand to which some three years later Balfour's successor as Secretary of State, Lord Curzon, was to take such strong objection.

On that dark December morning in 1916, however, Balfour's first act was to hand over the guidance of affairs for the time being to his cousin, Lord Robert Cecil, who had doubled his former office of Minister of Blockade in the second Coalition Government with the Under-Secretaryship for Foreign Affairs. Balfour had arranged this temporary absence with Lloyd George's agreement in order to allow himself to recuperate from a severe attack of influenza, an infection to which he had long been prone. During the next two years the lanky, angular Cecil was frequently to act as Balfour's deputy, not on account of illness, but because of Balfour's absences abroad; and a greater proportion of the Foreign Office's routine work was to be left during Balfour's term of office in the hands of the permanent Civil Servants there.   Balfour was right to depute as much work as he could: there were plenty of matters that he could not depute and which required the most serious deliberation—matters, in fact, that were major preoccupations of the Government itself.   It is sometimes said that on the outbreak of war diplomacy confides the achievement of its aims to the hands of the military.   This is true; but nevertheless the Foreign Office itself becomes more rather than less important, though its functions go, as it were, into reverse.   Instead of seeking to keep the peace, the Foreign Office in wartime often finds itself the spearhead in the provoking of war, as it had certainly been under Balfour's predecessor, Edward Grey.   It is not hard to see why.   Britain was not merely fighting the war herself, she was also assisting, both with money and munitions, her Allies to fight it.   The burden was heavy and it had not by the end of 1916 been lightened by even the smell of success.   Thus, the more the burden could be shared by securing the attachment of new allies from among the neutral nations, the more bearable it would become and the more likelihood of ultimate victory there would be.

In procuring new fighting allies, Grey had not been unsuccessful. After enormous and devious diplomatic activity, Italy and Rumania had been brought to the point of declaring war on the side of the Allies on August 27, 1916.   A price, of course, had to be paid in terms of the post-war distribution of some of the territories it was hoped to win. The terms were agreed at the Treaty of London.   They were secret and they caused heartburning and misgiving among all the contracting powers, except naturally Italy herself.   Other secret arrangements concerned Russia and the future of the Near East.   Here there were seeds of conflicts amongst the Allies themselves, because of the traditional Russo-British rivalry—and the equally traditional Franco-British rivalry—in the eastern Mediterranean and in Asia Minor. These secret treaties, although negotiated before Balfour became Foreign Minister, were to concern him considerably both in America in 1917 and at the peace-making at Versailles.   Not surprisingly, they smacked of barter, bribery and underhandedness, and, in the long run, they were a nuisance: so is any loan that has to be repaid.   But in the short run, they or something like them, were absolutely essential to Britain's prosecution of the war.   Grey, though he failed to bring Bulgaria in on the side of the Allies, secured aid from Portugal, attracted the Liberal element in the confused Greek situation, firmly handled the matter of contraband, thus keeping the United States if not sweet at least complacent, and prevented Sweden from joining Germany as appeared likely to happen early in the war.

But at the end of 1916 when Balfour became Foreign Minister, it was abundantly clear that the ultimate key to a victory was in the hands of the most powerful of the still unattached nations—the United States. The global military situation at that time looked black for the Allies, though in retrospect it was not so black as it seemed. For Rumania had already collapsed, Bucharest had fallen, and the Rumanian army was henceforth confined to Moldavia. There was grave news from inside Russia. The Western Front looked as grim as ever, although Germany had failed at Verdun and suffered defeats on the Somme. Austria-Hungary had, indeed, been routed on the Russian front, but the defection of Rumania meant that her vast resources in Wallachia of corn and oil now fell entirely into German hands and undoubtedly helped them to prolong the war. On January 8, 1917, Germany declared for unrestricted submarine warfare. Undoubtedly the United States ambassador in Britain, Walter H. Page, was right when he wrote to President Woodrow Wilson after his country's entry into the war: 'We came in in the nick of time for them—in very truth. If we hadn't, their exchange would have gone down soon and they know it. I shall never forget the afternoon I spent with Mr. Balfour and Mr. Bonar Law on that subject. They saw blue ruin without our financial help.'

But when Balfour returned from his recuperation in Brighton in January, 1917, the United States was still technically a neutral; and how to bring them into the war was the prime problem, particularly since President Wilson, far from appearing warlike, was directing his energies to bringing about peace. Almost a year earlier, in February 1916, Colonel E. M House, the President's Special Representative, had hinted during meetings with members of the War Cabinet that the President might propose a conference with the aim of bringing the war to an end. House added that he did not believe that American public opinion would be behind the United States Government entering into the war at that stage; Grey replied that if the United States did not enter the war 'public opinion would not support the President in taking a strong line with regard to conditions of peace or intervention subsequently'. Grey then went on to state that, as long as Britain's allies 'were ready to continue the war and believed that they could expel Germany from their territory and defeat her, we must support them with every resource we had; if, on the other hand, Russia or France, or both, were to come to us and say that they could no longer continue the war and that they must make peace on the best terms they could get, my own personal feeling would be that we should then suggest to them that, if this was really the case, we had better all propose the mediation of the United States. But there was no symptom as yet of their being inclined to give way or of their lacking confidence; and for us to suggest mediation to them would confirm the suspicions that Germany was always trying to create in their minds, that we were going to throw them over.'

Ten months later, on December 4, 1916—two days before the second Coalition Government fell—Grey had again circulated some reflections on the situation to his colleagues and had referred to the earlier meeting with Colonel House. He reiterated the point that nothing but the defeat of Germany could make a satisfactory end to this war or secure a future peace; but he believed that, in stating such determination, Britain ought 'to make it clear that our object is not to force but to support our Allies. Increasing mischief is being made between us and our Allies by German propaganda. This propaganda represents the war as one of rivalry between Great Britain and Germany: it insinuates that France, Russia and Belgium could have satisfactory terms of peace now, and that they are continuing the war in the interest of Great Britain to effect the ruin of Germany which is not necessary for the safety of the Allies, but which alone will satisfy Great Britain. It is just possible that this insidious misrepresentation, false though it be, may create in Russia, France, Italy or Belgium a dangerous peace movement. What I fear most is that one of the great Allies, when told, as they ought to be told now, that our support in shipping or finance, one or both, has to be curtailed in a few months, will abandon hope of ultimate victory and demand that the war be wound up on the best terms available. If either France or Russia came to this decision, it is probable that the other would follow suit, Italy would drop out, and we should be left with the option of entering peace negotiations or continuing the war alone.' Certainly, however, it is for those of the Allies who have been occupied by the enemy to decide when it is opportune to speak of peace, and in case they should, Grey believes that President Wilson should be asked to intervene—'his influence would be exercised whole-heartedly on behalf of Belgium at any rate, a point on which we cannot yield without sacrifice not only of interest but of honour'.

Very soon after Balfour took over the Foreign Ministry—Lord Robert Cecil was still deputising for him—the next move came. Walter H. Page, the United States ambassador in London, presented Cecil with a German Note containing what it called an 'offer of peace'. The Note, however, contained no specific proposals. Swift on its heels came a Note from President Wilson addressed to all the belligerent and neutral powers. It began with the ill-conceived statement that the war aims of both sides were 'virtually the same, as stated in general terms to their own peoples and to the world'. This caused immediate indignation in the public, but the Foreign Office took great pains to see that newspaper comment did not go so far in criticising it as to imperil relations between the two countries. Northcliffe, however, told Page in private that 'everybody is as angry as hell'. King George V was so dismayed that Wilson should think that Englishmen were fighting the war for the same reasons as the Germans that he is said to have broken down at luncheon.

Lord Robert Cecil expressed his attitude forcibly in private to Page who cabled the results to President Wilson. Page reports Cecil as saying: 'There is nothing that the American Government or any other human power can do to bring this war to a close before the Allies have spent their utmost force to secure a victory. A failure to secure such a victory would leave the world at the mercy of the most arrogant and the bloodiest tyranny that has ever been organized. It is far better to die in an effort to defeat that tyranny than to perish under its success. . . . I had hoped that the United States understood what is at stake.'

Lord Robert could scarcely have been expected to have said less than he did; yet, however hurtful it was to pride, it was clearly danger-ous to do anything which might alienate the United States. There was after all a group of Americans associated with English pacifists whose intention it was to bring about peace on almost any terms, and indeed, to compel Britain to accept the German terms for ending the war. This group, and there were others, even threatened that they would influence the American Government to place an embargo on the shipments of foodstuffs and munitions to the Allies unless the German terms were accepted: without such shipments it is doubtful whether Britain could have long survived.

At this stage Balfour returned to the Foreign Office and drafted a reply in precise terms to the President's note. Unlike Cecil and most of his countrymen, Balfour did not dispute the President's right to point out the similarity of the aims of the belligerents—'as expounded by themselves'. But if those aims were interpreted in the light of recent history the similarity disappeared. He agreed with the President that unless the war secured a permanent peace it would have been fought in vain, and he suggested that there were two means by which this could be secured apart from the limitation of armaments: the first was to see that the distribution of territories after the war harmonised more closely with the wishes of the European races concerned; the second, to contrive some international machinery by which war would be rendered, if not impossible, at least more difficult. No arrangement could be deemed satisfactory which did not restore Belgium and Serbia to independence and prosperity and fulfil the wishes of the inhabitants of Alsace, of the Transylvanian-Rumanians, of Poland and perhaps of Bohemia. Would the United States Government have the will and the power to give armed support to the decision of a League of Nations?

According to Sir Cecil Spring Rice, British ambassador in Washing-ton, Balfour's note had a remarkable effect 'on the minds of those whom you would regard as of your make'; but upon President Wilson himself it made little impression, for on January 22 he delivered a speech to the Senate again appealing to the belligerents for what he called a 'peace without victory'. Page, who had read the speech before it was delivered, had urged the President to omit that phrase, but he did not do so. Page observed in his diary that this showed that 'the President does not know the Germans; and he is unconsciously under their influence in his thought. His speech plays into their hands.' At this moment of frustration, Balfour might well have reflected with some bitterness and regret on a letter he had received the year before from the former President of the United States, his friend Theodore Roosevelt, which said: 'You do not need to be told that if I had had control of the Government we would have acted in decisive fashion long ago.'

It was, however, that darkest moment that comes before the dawn. For there now occurred what one might call the Pearl Harbor of the First World War. On January 16, 1917, Admiral (Sir) Reginald Hall, Director of Naval Intelligence, placed upon Balfour's desk a message intercepted from the German foreign Under-Secretary, E. Zimmermann, to the German Minister in Mexico. This communication, decoded with great skill by Admiral Hall's staff, proposed a German-Mexican alliance aiming at the reconquest of Mexico's 'lost territory in Texas, in New Mexico and California'; and it suggested that Mexico should secure Japan's secession from the Allies and her participation in this venture. Zimmermann sent this message on the eve of Germany's declaration of unrestricted submarine warfare; its object was to avert America's consequent entry in the war by opening— or rather reinvigorating, for General Pershing was already in pursuit of the rebel Villa—a second front on the North American continent.

Balfour was delighted. This at any rate should make clear, even to President Wilson, the nature of Germany's aims and the fact that even United States soil was not excluded from them. But Hall intervened to point out that it would be impossible to prove the telegram's authenticity without letting the Germans know that the Admiralty was reading their secret codes—and without proof of authenticity the Americans might well regard it as a 'find' too convenient to be true. So Balfour had to wait almost a month before the telegram was received from less compromising sources. Meanwhile he sounded out the Japanese ambassador on his country's relations with Mexico—for if Japan were really to join the enemy, the Russians would probably make a separate peace.

Then on February 24, 1917, in what Balfour himself called 'as dramatic a moment as I remember in all my life', he handed over to Page, the American ambassador, the sheet of paper containing the decoded message. Balfour did the business with full protocol in order to show that the British Government was pledging itself that the communication was authentic. A few days later the German Foreign Office admitted the message to be genuine.

A recent student of the episode believes the telegram was of capital importance in bringing America into the war. It certainly helped. But already the President, on receipt of the news that Germany was to use unrestricted submarine warfare, had dismissed her ambassador from Washington. The American public itself was clamouring for action, and the sinking without warning of the American merchant ship, *Algonquin*, on March 15, 1917, finally precipitated America's declaration of war on April 2.

When the news came, Page hastened to the Foreign Office. Balfour rose, shook him by the hand, and said: 'It is a great day for the world.' The afternoon was spent with Balfour, Lord Robert Cecil and Page in consultation about ways in which the United States could help the Allied war effort. Balfour reiterated that American credits in the United States big enough to keep up the British rate of exchange were the *sine qua non*, even more important than ships or food or munitions.

It may well have been on the same afternoon that Balfour asked Page 'why the British were so unpopular in the United States'. Page says: 'Among other reasons, I told him that our official people on both sides steadfastly refused to visit one another and to become acquainted. Neither he nor Lord Grey nor Mr. Asquith nor Mr. Lloyd George had ever been to the United States, nor any other important British statesman in recent times, and not a single member of the administration was personally known to a single member of the British Government. "I'll go", said he, "if you are perfectly sure my going would be agreeable to the President." '

Page welcomed the idea enthusiastically and the British Cabinet confirmed the proposal. Balfour, Page wrote, 'is chosen for this mission not only because he is Secretary of State for Foreign Affairs, but because he is personally the most distinguished member of the Government.' Later he wrote: 'Mr. Balfour accurately represents British character, British opinion, and the British attitude. . . . I know his whole tribe, his home life, his family connections, his friends.'

On April 9, 1917, the President cabled to London with an advance welcome for Balfour, and suggested that the mission should be announced as diplomatic rather than military. In private he told Colonel House that he visualised certain dangers and feared that some Americans might suspect 'an attempt in some degree to take charge of us as an assistant of Great Britain'.

Balfour was delighted at the opportunity: 'From the tone of his voice', his niece and biographer remarks, 'one might have judged him setting off for the golf links for some eagerly anticipated match, and I

recall none of the customary groans that preceded the embarkation on a
boat of any kind.' The mission itself was composed of some 33 members from the Foreign Office, army, navy, and economists and other
experts in various war sciences. They included Lord Cunliffe,
Governor of the Bank of England, General T. Bridges, Eric Drummond
and Francis Dormer. It was essentially a technical mission, but for
success it required the creation of an atmosphere which probably
Balfour alone could achieve.

The mission started from Euston Station, London, on April 10 in the
deepest secrecy. Its first move was by train to Dumfries where it had to
wait for 24 hours owing to the activities of the German submarines off
the north coast of Ireland. Balfour and his party stayed at the Station
Hotel and there the leader of this so far secret mission rather thoughtlessly
broke the security regulations. He tells the story himself in a fragment
of his autobiography: 'I regret to say that my share in this operation
(i.e. the secret move) was of a sort which was bound to destroy my
whole prestige as a master of secret diplomacy in the eyes of my staff.
We were stopped without notice at Dumfries under the Admiralty
orders, and the utmost avoidance of publicity was enjoined upon us all.
With what contemptuous indignation, therefore, did my companions
discover that I had destroyed all hope of preserving the incognito
upon which our safety was supposed to depend, by supplying a specimen of my signature in response to a civil request made by the liftboy
at the Station Hotel. I had no excuse to offer when reproached with
this singular indiscretion and my authority received a shock from
which it never recovered.'

After 'this disgraceful episode', as he calls it, he and his party
embarked at Greenock. Further delays occurred, not least as a result
of a storm, during which Balfour remarked that he would rather drown
in his nightshirt than in the life-preserver he had been offered. The less
boisterous moments of the voyage have been described by Sir Ian
Malcolm, then Balfour's personal private secretary, but Balfour himself
only remembered receiving by wireless the dire news that the German
submarine campaign was succeeding. 'I could not help thinking that
we were facing the defeat of Great Britain,' he later told Admiral Sims.

The ship berthed in Halifax harbour on April 20, 1917, and the
mission reached Washington two days later. At New York, Colonel
House boarded the train. The party was met by motor-cars, and a
cavalry escort, and its members passed through cheering crowds and
streets fluttering with the Stars and Stripes and the Union Jack to a house
in 16th Street which had been put at Balfour's disposal by its owner,
Wayne McVeagh. The party were guests of the United States Government throughout their visit. Balfour remembered one small incident
connected with his stay at the house that gave him, he said, 'abiding

pleasure'. Each morning he found 'two charming children waving the Union Jack when I left the doorstep for the business of the day. I felt that their welcoming smile supplied the one thing that our luxurious dwelling lacked.'

Next day, April 23, Balfour called on President Woodrow Wilson at the White House. Whatever his private views of the President may have been—and certainly they were modified by later experience at the Versailles conferences—Balfour was a superb diplomatist and moveover able to appreciate the many gifts of culture which the President had. The President, on his side, had been primed by his ambassador in London, Page, who wrote to him with enthusiasm and insight about Balfour:

'He is one of the most interesting men that I have ever had the honour to know intimately—he and Lord Grey. Mr. Balfour is a Tory, of course; and in general I don't like Tories, yet Liberal he surely is—a sort of high-toned Scotch democrat. I have studied him with increasing charm and interest. Not infrequently when I am in his office just before luncheon he says, "Come, walk over and we'll have lunch with the family." He is a bachelor. One sister lives with him. Another (Lady Rayleigh, the wife of the great chemist and Chancellor of Cambridge University) frequently visits him. Either of these ladies could rule his empire. Then there are nieces and cousins always about—people of rare cultivation, everyone of them.'

And Page cleverly added something designed to appeal to Wilson's 'culture': 'I went with him to a college in London one afternoon where he delivered a lecture on Dryden, to prove that poetry can carry a certain cargo of argument but that argument cannot raise the smallest flight of poetry. Dry as it sounds, it was as good a literary performance as I recall I ever heard.'

Balfour himself spoke of the completely frank discussions he had with the President and with his old friend Colonel House: 'We were all absorbed in the problem of successful co-operation, and as this necessarily involved ranging over the immense field of our common interests, a singular unanimity brooded over our friendly discussions.' He adds that 'there were no secrets between us then or afterwards on any of the many subjects that came up for discussion'.

One difficult matter that Balfour had to convey to the President was the existence of the various secret treaties into which Britain had been compelled to enter in order to ensure victory. There was the Treaty of London (already mentioned) and the agreement of St. Jean de Maurienne then being negotiated, both concerning the Italians. There was also the 'Sykes-Picot agreement' between the British and the French. These may well have been distasteful to the President, but they caused no discord in the discussions, and indeed he was never called upon to endorse them; they were snags of the future more than of the present. Both House and Frank L. Polk (a Councillor in the State Department) wrote afterwards saying that Balfour and the President 'got along marvellously well' and 'got on tremendously'.

Such cordiality paved the way for easiness of mutual understanding when the mission got down to serious business. Balfour in one of his earliest talks discussed what he considered to be the critical point, namely finance. He spoke on this subject to McAdoo, Secretary of the United States Treasury. Apart from the generally desperate condition of British and Allied finances, the matter then chiefly pressing was the fact that the British balances in the New York banks were in a serious condition. By April 6, 1917, for example, Britain had overdrawn her account with J. P. Morgan to the extent of 400 million dollars and had no cash available with which to meet this overdraft. The obligation had been incurred in the purchase of supplies both for Britain and for the Allied Governments. Securities, largely British-owned stocks and bonds, had been deposited to protect the bankers. This money was now coming due. After some difficult discussions, it was at length arranged that the American Government should pay this overdraft out of the proceeds of the First Liberty Loan. This act, there is no doubt, saved the credit of the Allied countries. It was only the beginning of America's financial support, but it was an important beginning and one of the most important results of the Balfour mission.

In the course of the talks, Balfour was asked when he thought the war was likely to end. After discussions with his naval and military advisers, he replied that war could not be ended until the summer or autumn of 1919. The same question had been put to the French and Italian missions then in America and precisely the same answer obtained.

Scarcely less important than finance was the question of meeting the submarine menace. Before that could even be approached, however, the misunderstandings and resentments caused by the British blockade, the blacklists and the seizure of goods in prize courts, had to be cleared up. Balfour himself discussed these matters with Polk, under whose jurisdiction they were. As one of these conferences was approaching its end, writes Burton J. Hendrick in his *Life and Letters of Walter H. Page*, 'Mr. Balfour coughed slightly, uttered an "er", and gave other indications that he was about to touch upon a ticklish question. "Before I go", he said, "there—er—is one subject I would—er—like to say something about." Mr. Polk at once grasped what was coming. "I know what you have in mind," said Mr. Polk in his characteristically quick way. "You want us to apply your blacklist to neutrals." [In other words, the British hoped that the United States, now that it was in the war, would adopt against South America and other offenders those same discriminations which this country had so fiercely objected to when it was itself a neutral.] The British statesman gave Mr. Polk one of his most winning smiles and nodded. "Mr. Balfour", said Mr. Polk, "it took Britain three years to reach a point where it was prepared to violate all the laws of blockade. You will find that it will take us only two months to become as great criminals as you are!"

'Mr. Balfour is usually not expressive in his manifestations of mirth, but his laughter in reply to this statement was almost uproarious. And the State Department was as good as its word. It immediately forgot all the elaborate "notes" and "protests" which it had been addressing to Britain. It became more inexorable than Britain had ever been in keeping foodstuffs out of neutral countries that were contiguous to Germany. Up to the time the United States entered the war, Germany, in spite of the watchful British Fleet, had been obtaining large supplies from the United States through Holland, Denmark and the Scandinavian Peninsula. But the United States now immediately closed these leaks. . . . Possibly, therefore, Mr. Balfour's mirth was not merely sympathetic or humorous; it perhaps echoed his discovery that our position for three years had really been nothing but a sham; that the State Department had been forcing points in which it did not really believe, or in which it did not believe when American interests were involved.'

Balfour's success with the President—success, however, that had its gaps as we shall see—was paralleled and indeed overtopped by his success in public. Congress, after some hesitation, asked him to address them and the President himself sat in his box and listened to his speech.

Vast banquets and enthusiastic meetings took place in aid of the British Red Cross and the Liberty Loan. British singers, such as Dora Gibson, sang patriotic songs like 'To Victory' in order to spur on the American people to buy bonds and more bonds. Occasionally Balfour managed to get in some tennis and had intimate talks with his old friend, Joseph Choate, formerly the American ambassador in London. He visited Virginia and along with Viviani, head of the French mission, made an expedition to George Washington's tomb.

At the end of Balfour's visit, the British ambassador in Washington, Sir Cecil Spring Rice, summed up the effects of the mission: 'It is quite impossible to exaggerate the importance of the work done here, and an enumeration of the details would give a very poor impression of what has actually been done. It is more in the nature of a new light and a new atmosphere. It is rather rain and sunshine than seed, although good seed had been sown.' Apart from Balfour's great qualities of intelligence, tact and genuine interest in other human beings, some of his particular success in the United States was probably due to the fact that the ordinary American, who had been brought up to gibe at the

airs and graces of English gentlemen, suddenly discovered the fascination and the human sympathies of such a gentleman, a 'real aristocrat'
at last seen in the flesh. Balfour's visit also emphasised the kinship
in blood and ideals between England and the old-established American
families.

After Balfour's visit Page records in a private letter to his son that
Americans previously had 'actually been coming to believe ourselves
that we were part German and Slovene, Pole and what not, instead of
essentially being Scotch and English. . . . Our national life should
proceed on its natural historic lines, with its proper historic outlook
and background.' During Balfour's visit, it is worth noticing, even the
Irish members of Congress had welcomed his appearance before them,
and though Wilson himself had raised with Balfour the question of
Ireland, he had easily agreed that it should be left in abeyance until the
end of the war.

Balfour reached Liverpool on June 9, 1917. During that summer the
tale of military woe increased, and the problem was whether American
aid was going to arrive in time, whether indeed it might be 'too little
and too late'. Both Page and the American naval liaison chief, Admiral
William S. Sims, sought to speed up naval aid from America. Referring to the submarine situation, Admiral Sims said plainly that 'the
Allies are losing the war'. It produced very little effect on President
Wilson. It seemed clear that the President regarded Page and Sims as
both having sold out to the British and their reports were treated with
suspicion. The State Department apparently thought that the British
were using, or attempting to use, American warships in European
waters to protect British commerce while British warships were being
kept safely in harbour.

Page in despair turned to Balfour: 'Whatever else they think of the
British in Washington', he remarked, 'they know one thing—and that
is that a British statesmen like Mr. Balfour will not lie.' Balfour gladly
consented to write giving the true facts of the naval position. He asked
Admiral Jellicoe to draft the despatch in consultation with Edward
Carson, the First Lord of the Admiralty, but Balfour himself gave the
document its final shape and he signed it. It put the situation precisely
and bluntly; it asked for armed small craft of any kind from the only
Allied country able to supply them in order to augment the patrolling
system. The letter had some effect for the President himself discussed
with the British adviser in the United States, Sir William Wiseman,
the balance between capital ships and light craft in the United States
shipbuilding programme.

In the matter of finance, the United States acted with similar
dilatoriness. A few weeks after Balfour returned home he sent a telegram to House which House described as panicky, but which, in fact,

scarcely exaggerated the situation: 'We seem to be on the verge of a financial disaster that would be worse than defeat in the field,' Balfour cabled. 'If we cannot keep up exchange, neither we nor our allies can pay our dollar debts. We would be driven off the gold basis, purchases from U.S.A. would immediately cease, and the allies' credit would be shattered. A consequence which would be of incalculable gravity may be upon us Monday next if nothing effective is done in the meantime.' House made representations to the President and a little later Balfour could cable again that he was most grateful to House for his intervention: 'the results are already apparent'.

These borrowing arrangements, however, were some years later to cause controversy in which Balfour himself was involved. In August, 1922, he wrote a note in reply to the United States demand for repayment of war debts. In this he pointed out that although Britain was owed more than she owed, she was unlikely to be repaid by many of the debtors and he felt that it could not be right that one partner in the common enterprise should recover all that she had lent while another, recovering nothing, should be required to pay all that she has borrowed. The Allied war debts were to become a bitter memorial to the extravagant expenditures of the First World War.

Balfour returned to the subject of Anglo-American co-operation, which as we have seen was the subject of his widest speculation, when he addressed the Pilgrims Dinner in London on July 4, 1917. He spoke neither as flatterer nor *ad hoc* propagandist when he said that the United States and Britain were not working in the war for narrow or merely selfish objects but in the freedom of great hopes and great ideals: 'We have not learned freedom from you, nor you from us. We both spring from the same root. . . . Are we not bound together forever? Will not our descendants, when they come to look back upon this unique episode in the history of the world, say that among the incalculable circumstances which it produced, the most beneficent and the most permanent is, perhaps, that we are brought together and united for one common purpose in one common understanding—the two great branches of the English-speaking race? . . . This is a theme which absorbs my thoughts day and night. It is a theme which moves me more, I think, than anything connected with public affairs in all my long experience.'

This grander strategy was no doubt in his mind when in December, 1917, he suggested to Colonel House not merely that there should be a temporary naval agreement for warlike purposes between the two countries, but that the United States should join with Britain, France, Italy, Russia and Japan in a defence maritime pact 'for a period of four years after the conclusion of the present war'. He told the Cabinet in a memorandum that 'I confess for reasons of high policy, there is nothing

I should like more than a defence alliance with America, even for four years, that would be capable of extension and development should circumstances prove auspicious.' He realised that the difficulty would be, first, Britain's alliance with Japan and secondly, of course, America's long-standing refusal to be involved in European affairs. So it turned out. President Wilson rejected the treaty of mutual assistance on those very grounds. But Balfour, as long as he retained his position as Foreign Minister, devoted himself to preserving the understanding between the two great powers in fresh and healthy form.

Page himself, the ambassador with whom Balfour had achieved such close understanding and whom he admired as one of the best friends of Britain in her darkest hours, left England broken in health at the beginning of 1918. Balfour with Lord Robert Cecil and other Ministers saw him off at his departure from Waterloo Station. A few weeks later Page was dead. Balfour often spoke of this parting scene with his friend and always with emotion: 'I loved that man,' he told an American, 'I almost wept when he left England.'

II

Balfour in his later days was accustomed to say that, looking back on his life in politics, he felt that what he had been able to do for the Jews was the thing most worth while. It certainly remains true that when his name is mentioned today in non-specialist company it is the 'Balfour Declaration' which springs to mind first of all. Yet the Declaration issued on November 2, 1917, and stating that His Majesty's Government viewed with favour the establishment in Palestine of a national home for the Jewish people, was in fact issued by a majority decision of the British Cabinet. Balfour signed it officially as Foreign Minister. It would certainly not have been signed or issued had it not fitted in with the Cabinet's conception of future political realignments consequent upon the vast rearrangements of frontiers caused by the upheaval of the war.

Nevertheless, the cause of the Jews was dear to Balfour's heart. It is essential to an understanding of Balfour himself to ask why. Balfour, after all, was not given to idealising either persons or races, although he could embrace ideas, usually practical ideas, with conviction and pursue them with tenacity, as he did with the idea of improving education and of setting Britain's defence house in order; and in a sense it was an idea, a conception, that first interested him in the Jews.

It is true, as we have seen, that he had been very much impressed by Chaim Weizmann when he met him first in 1906, and since then Weizmann had earned Government thanks for his acetone invention, but any suggestion, such as was made by Lloyd George in his war memoirs, that British policy towards the Jews was a kind of *quid pro quo* for Weizmann's work in chemistry is quite fantastic. Equally so is Viscount Samuel's statement in his memoirs that the Jewish National Home was 'partly a *douceur* given instead of a knighthood to a Jewish inventor for timely discovery in the production of explosives'.

Primarily what had first interested Balfour in the Jewish race was what interested Lloyd George—an intimate acquaintance with the Old Testament. Balfour's mother, as we have seen, was an Evangelical and the Bible was for her, and thus for her children, the prime guide, philosopher and friend. Like Lloyd George, Balfour knew where Dan was and where Beersheba. But it was perhaps the uniqueness of the Jews and their position in the world and in world history that intrigued him most. The Jews alone remained, from the periods of the great migrations, a wandering race spread through the world and without a geographical land of their own. 'There is no parallel to it,' Balfour said in a speech in the House of Lords on June 21, 1922, 'there is nothing approaching a parallel to it, in any other branch of human history. Here you have a small race originally inhabiting a small country of about the size of Wales or Belgium [he might have added Scotland], at no time in its history wielding anything that can be described as material power, sometimes crushed in between great Oriental monarchies, its inhabitants deported, then scattered, then driven out of the country altogether into every part of the world, and yet maintaining their continuity of religious and racial traditions to which we have no parallel elsewhere.'

It was the paradoxes that surrounded the history of the Jews that fascinated him—not least the paradox that the founder of Christendom was a Jew who had been rejected by his own race. He felt, too, that the continuity of religious and racial tradition which had been preserved by the Jews, despite their tribulations and their scattering across the globe, was in itself astonishing; and he appreciated that the return of the Jews to the cradle of their race would be an historical occurrence that in the long run would put even the wars of the twentieth century in the shade. Moreover, as a man interested in science, he could not overlook the Jewish contribution, to philosophy, music and the arts of civilisation in general. He felt that Christendom owed the Jews a debt which Christians had made little attempt to requite. Indeed, the opposite was true for they had been constantly persecuted, not least in his own time, when the series of Russian pogroms started in the 1880s. He did not blind himself to the fact that the Jews themselves had on occasions been the cause of their own miseries; but he felt that this was hardly surprising in view of their agelong sufferings.

All this goes a long way to explaining Balfour's interest in the Jewish question; yet it does not fully satisfy us, for Balfour had many interests in life but few he pursued with such a determination and indeed passion. As the historian, L. B. Namier—himself a Jew—remarked in his book *Conflicts*: 'Balfour, generally so aloof, so sceptical, so detached, had been converted to a surprisingly passionate belief in Weizmann's enterprise.' To press for an explanation is to involve oneself in psychological speculation. But one might hazard a guess that the passion devoted to the subject by Balfour was the psychological redress paid by a rich and, on the whole, happy man, protected by his birth and ancestry from most of the 'slings and arrows of outrageous fortune', to the poverty and suffering of the world as a whole. He himself may not have had this poverty pushed daily down his throat, but he was too intelligent a man not to know it existed and too scrupulous a man to be able to ignore it entirely. He might have taken up good works, as his mother had done, or in a wider field as the nineteenth-century Lord Shaftesbury had done. But this would have been at once too ostentatious and too much out of character. The Jews—at least the Jews he was mainly concerned with—were at a distance, in fact at all four points of the compass. May we not here see an attempt to assuage guilt, according to a theory of what Balfour himself referred to 'as the new psychology' whose author, as Balfour himself pointed out, was a Jew? It is perhaps significant in this context that the Jews who opposed most bitterly the idea of a home for the Jews in Palestine were wealthy men.

Before the war and the Turkish entry into it, the idea of a Jewish national home in Palestine was a mere will-o'-the-wisp. Palestine, like the other Arab regions of the Near East, had long been under Turkish suzerainty. But the war made it clear that the sick man of Europe was now at last breaking up; his demise would not only leave a dangerous vacuum for power rivalry, but would put a Jewish home just within the bounds of possibility. For hundreds of years many Jews had hoped for a return to Palestine, but it was not until 1897 that Theodor Herzel founded a Zionist Organisation and adopted a programme 'to create for the Jewish people a home in Palestine secured by public law'. Failing to obtain a charter from the Turkish Sultan for a large settlement in Palestine, Herzel turned to the British Government which in 1903 made an offer of an autonomous settlement in British East Africa (Uganda) under a Jewish Government. This was declined by the Zionist Congress as being incompatible with Jewish history. These moves had occurred during Balfour's Premiership. He was at that time puzzled as to the reasons behind the Jewish rejection of Uganda and when he first met Weizmann he was concerned to seek the reasons. It was Weizmann who first broadened his idea from the simple conception of relieving the misery of the Jews to a comprehension of the spiritual side of Zionism.

Not long after war broke out, Weizmann along with two Continental Zionist leaders, Sokolow and Tschlenow, were introduced to Lloyd George by C. P. Scott, editor of the *Manchester Guardian*. Lloyd George's imagination was said to have been kindled by this meeting although Asquith, then the Prime Minister, remarked that his Chancellor of the Exchequer 'does not care a damn for the Jews or their past or their future, but thinks it will be an outrage to let the Holy places pass into the possession or under the protection of "agnostic and atheistic" . . .' Weizmann was then reintroduced to Balfour by the Jewish philosopher, Professor S. Alexander, and the two met again at Carlton Gardens on December 12, 1914. Weizmann found that the conversation he had had with Balfour eight years back was still fresh in Balfour's mind and they went on with it. It was not, said Weizmann afterwards, 'a practical conversation. It developed about abstract ideas and principles.' (This underlines again the point that Balfour's interest was always most easily aroused by ideas.) Towards the end of the talk, Balfour told Weizmann: 'You may get your things done much more quickly after the war. . . .' He listened to what Weizmann had to say of the German Jews and, Weizmann told his friend Ahad Ha'am: 'He was, I assure you, most deeply moved—to the point of tears.'

Weizmann observed that the crux of the present Jewish tragedy lay in the fact that the Jews who were giving their energy and brains to Germany were doing it as Germans and not as Jews. They were enriching Germany not Jewry. The Zionists could not accept them as Jews, yet the Germans did not recognise them as Germans. Thus the Jews had become the most exploited and most misunderstood of peoples.

Balfour had apparently not been aware of this situation for, as Weizmann later said, 'a leading British statesman like Mr. Balfour had only the most naïve and rudimentary notion of the Zionist movement'. During the same conversation Weizmann spoke against Russia, and Balfour, 'wondered how a friend of England could be so anti-Russian when Russia was doing to much so help England win the war'. Weizmann mentioned a pogrom which had occurred when the Russians were advancing despite the fact that there were thousands of Jews in the Russian army. 'It was news to Balfour.' Balfour asked Weizmann in what way he could help him. Weizmann replied, 'not while the guns are roaring. When the military situation becomes clearer I will come again.' 'Mind you come again,' said Balfour. 'It is not a dream. It is a great cause you are working for; and I understand it. I would like you to come again and again.'

During 1915 and 1916, Weizmann and his fellow-Zionists devoted most of their energy to trying to form a united front in all the Allied countries and not least in the United States. Through Herbert

Samuel, who was in the Liberal Government, they discovered Grey's personal attitude.   He was in sympathy with the Zionist ideal but afraid lest mention of a British protectorate over Palestine might offend the French.   The French and also the Italians had made it clear that they would seek control over both Syria and Palestine once the Turkish yoke was removed.   Indeed the French claim had been admitted by the secret Sykes-Picot agreement which foresaw a division of Palestine leaving Tiberias and part of Galilee in French hands.   Nevertheless, the British Government did not really wish to see Palestine in the hands of any other great power.   Weizmann pressed at this tender spot: 'If Britain does not wish anybody else to have Palestine, this means it will have to watch it and stop any penetration of another power.   Such a course involves as much responsibility as would be involved by a British Protectorate over Palestine, with the sole difference that watching is a much less efficient preventive than an actual protectorate.   I therefore thought that the middle course could be adopted: viz. the Jews take over the country; the whole burden of organisation falls on them, but for the next ten or fifteen years they work under a temporary British protectorate.'

In Autumn, 1916, Weizmann was again in touch with Balfour, then still First Lord of the Admiralty.   There now began to loom large the antipathy of some Jews to the idea of a Jewish home in Palestine. Weizmann explained that, to an Eastern Jew who had preserved the tradition, Palestine was hope and an article of faith, but for many Western Jews the meaning had been lost.   This Balfour could understand: 'But why should they oppose it?' he asked.   'Why can I afford to be a Zionist and not they?'   'There are,' he told Weizmann, 'two men who are riddles to me.   Why isn't Claude Montefiore a Zionist and why is Mond a Zionist?'   (Montefiore was a theologian and a scholar, Mond was an industrialist.)   Weizmann explained that many Jews, assimilated to the countries where they lived, preferred to conceal, or at least not to emphasise, the fact of their Jewishness for anti-Semitism lurked everywhere, even in England.

Balfour also pointed out that were England to assume responsibility for Palestine, she would be suspected of seeking territorial aggrandisement.   He thought the United States ought to undertake the task, or at the very least England and the United States jointly.   'He strongly objected', Weizmann writes, 'to strategic or other opportunist considerations being brought forward as an argument for assuming the responsibility for Palestine. . . .   He made me often ashamed of my niggling mind.'

Towards the end of 1916, the Foreign Office observed that there were hints in the German press of the possibility of a Jewish state being set up in Palestine after the war, under, of course, Turkish supremacy.   At this stage the Zionists submitted their first formal programme to the Foreign Office still under Grey. Shortly after Balfour took over, serious conversations with the Zionists started. Balfour convened a meeting on February 2, 1917, at which, as well as the Zionist leaders there was present Sir Mark Sykes, unrivalled in his knowledge of the Middle East and recently a convert to the Zionist idea. It was he who first brought into the negotiations the hard possibility that there might be Arab opposition to a Jewish national home in their midst and suggested that the Jews should attempt to look at matters through Arab glasses. In March, 1917, Balfour warned Weizmann that there might well be difficulties arising from the French and Italian claims in Palestine and he suggested that, failing an agreement with France, it might be best for the Zionists to aim at a joint Anglo-American protectorate. Meanwhile the Zionists were having success in their meetings with the French Foreign Office and, in April, the French agreed that after an Allied victory in the Middle East they would recognise Zionism. In America, too, the Zionists had success for their leader was an American-born Jew, a judge of the Supreme Court, Mr. Justice Brandeis, with whom Balfour had two talks during his visit to America. It seems, says Balfour's biographer, Mrs. Dugdale, from such notes of these conversations as survive that Balfour pledged his own personal support for Zionism to Brandeis. These notes are no longer to be found among Balfour's papers, but if he gave such a pledge it was a serious step indeed, for by that time he was Foreign Minister. Brandeis, however, was not sanguine of official American support and believed that Zionist policy must be to keep to the simple demands for a British Protectorate. Balfour, however, himself continued to hope that the United States would be associated with a Protectorate should it be secured. It was for this reason that Balfour suggested that Weizmann should go as British representative on an American commission which was seeking to detach Turkey from the central powers. The commission, however, ended in failure.

At the end of June, 1917, Weizmann, accompanied by Lord Rothschild—an exception to the rule that wealthy Jews were on the whole anti-Zionist—called upon Balfour at the Foreign Office and suggested that the time for a definite declaration of support and encouragement had come. Balfour asked them for a draft to put before the War Cabinet. This was prepared by the Zionist political committee under Sokolow and handed to Balfour by Rothschild on July 18, 1917. Meanwhile, however, the anti-Zionist Jews were making their opposition felt. On May 24, 1917, David L. Alexander, President of the Board of British Jews, and Claude Montefiore, President of the Anglo-Jewish Association, violently repudiated the Zionist position in a letter to *The Times*. They had a powerful ally within the Cabinet itself in the person of

C1JB

Edwin Montagu, a Jew, then Secretary of State for India. It was he who, in the absence of Balfour and Lloyd George from the Cabinet, struck the draft Declaration from the agenda. Lord Rothschild remarked: 'As soon as I saw the announcement in the paper of Montagu's appointment, I was afraid we were done.'

They were not done, however. Montagu put in a memorandum to the Cabinet of passionate protest and for a moment swayed it against the Zionists. Balfour was not present, but he told Weizmann that 'his sympathies had not been changed by the attitude of Montagu'. In the meantime, however, the difficulties with France had been cleared up and the Foreign Office was anxious to reap all the advantage there might be in a Declaration. It was for some reason expected to have a direct result on the Russian Revolution, then passing out of its Menshevik phase. Lenin and Trotsky, in fact, took power in the same week of November, 1917, that the Balfour Declaration was finally issued. There was also the propagandist value not least among some sections of Allied Jews, apathetic towards the war. Nevertheless Montagu's opposition was responsible for the compromise formula which the War Cabinet finally agreed upon and published as the Balfour Declaration on November 2, 1917. The document was in the form of a letter to Lord Rothschild and read: 'His Majesty's Government view with favour the establishment in Palestine of a national home for the Jewish people, and will use their best endeavours to facilitate the achievement of this object, it being clearly understood that nothing shall be done which may prejudice the civil and religious rights of the existing Jewish communities in Palestine or the rights and political status enjoyed by Jews in any other country.' Weizmann would have preferred the bolder wording of his draft: 'Palestine as the national home of the Jews.' No matter, the Declaration caused demonstrations of vast enthusiasm among Jewish masses in Allied countries and particularly in the United States.

Balfour in Cabinet added that by 'national home' he understood was meant 'some form of British, American or other protectorate, under which full facilities would be given to the Jews to work out their own salvation, and to build up, by means of agriculture, education and industry, a real centre of national culture and focus of national life'. He emphasised that it 'did not necessarily involve the early establishment of an independent Jewish State, which was a matter for gradual development in accordance with the ordinary laws of political evolution'.

Before the end of the year 1917, the Declaration was altered from a gesture to a statement of intention when General E. H. H. Allenby, commanding the Egyptian Expeditionary Force, occupied Palestine and dismounted from his horse outside the Damascus Gate of Jerusalem to enter the Holy City on foot. Palestine remained under military rule until, in 1920, the Supreme Council of the Peace Conference resolved that the Balfour Declaration should be incorporated in the treaty of peace with Turkey, and that the Mandate—a new idea developing out of the peace talks—should be handed over to Britain. The civil administration of Palestine was established in the same year under the First High Commissioner, Sir Herbert Samuel, a Jew and a former member of the Cabinet. Balfour himself remained influential in all these matters, and as late as 1928 he, Churchill, Weizmann and L. S. Amery—who had had a hand in drafting the Declaration—lunched together and heard Weizmann's proposal for a Palestine loan from the League of Nations. (The Foreign Office and the Treasury were against this.) Balfour himself spoke at a vast demonstration in the Albert Hall in 1920 organised by the English Zionist Federation to thank the British Government, and in particular Balfour, for the decision to incorporate the Declaration in the treaty of peace with Turkey.

In 1925 Balfour accompanied by Weizmann, then President of the Zionist Organisation, went at the invitation of the Jews to attend the opening of the Hebrew University on Mount Scopus, outside the walls of Jerusalem. He was met by a vast concourse of Jews at Alexandria and wherever he went in the Jewish settlements he was met as the great Gentile saviour of the Jews. On the other hand, the Arabs, by this time, were no longer acquiescent, and their newspapers appeared with mourning borders on the day of his arrival. In Jerusalem Balfour was much delighted to hear a performance of his favourite, Handel's *Belshazzar* sung in Hebrew—the same oratorio, a performance of which as a young man he had financed at the Albert Hall. At the opening of the University itself upon the hill from which the Roman destroyers of Jerusalem had conducted their siege of the city, Balfour addressed a crowd of 10,000 people. He himself wore the scarlet robes of Chancellor of Cambridge University (which he became in 1919) and when he rose to speak it seemed, we are told, as if the cheering of the multitudes would never cease. It is noteworthy that the Balfour family interest in the Jews, which began with him, has continued down to the present day. His niece and biographer, Mrs. Dugdale, and the present Earl of Balfour have all visited the country at the invitation of the Zionist Organisation and later at the invitation of the Government of Israel.

The Balfour Declaration has, from the moment of its inception, come in for a good deal of criticism. As we have seen there were those Jews who believed that it was a better policy for the Jewish race as a whole to become assimilated in the countries in which they found themselves, and that to call attention to themselves by becoming a nation was to risk outbreaks of anti-Semitism, exacerbated by nationalist feeling. But after the Nazi extirpation of Jews—and of even half and quarter

Jews—'assimilated' for hundreds of years there must be few of the race who today would support this view. Ever since the middle 1930s, the idea that there was a land where Jews were not persecuted and where they largely governed themselves must have been the only hope for millions of their race in Europe.

Politically speaking, however, it must be confessed that Balfour's optimism about the future of the Jews in Palestine was ill-judged. It was, as he said, true that Jewish Palestine was only a 'small notch' in the Arab territories; but it was exactly the sort of notch which Arab rulers or Arab dissidents could conveniently raise to a rallying-point whenever internal politics demanded some distraction. There is also the point that Jerusalem is the third holy city of Islam, the Dome of the Rock being the place whence Mohamed is traditionally supposed to have ascended to Heaven. Nor can we suppose that in early days— or even later—all the English officials under the Mandate entirely submerged the traditional pro-Arabism that received a fillip from the war successes and the books of T. E. Lawrence and others. Again and again, Balfour appealed to Jews and Arabs to work together and to remember, as Balfour put it in his speech at the opening of the Hebrew University, 'that in the darkest days of the darkest ages, when Western civilisation appeared almost extinct, smothered under barbaric influences, it was the Jews and Arabs in combination, working together, who greatly aided the first sparks which illuminated that gloomy period'. In the light of the continuing bitterness between Arabs and Jews at the present time, these hopes appear merely naïve. That does not mean that Balfour and those who thought like him were wrong in establishing the Jews in Palestine: it is in essence a criticism of the nationalist mania and of those who play upon it.

III

Affairs in the Cabinet in 1917 were largely dominated by a quarrel between the Prime Minister and the Chief of the Imperial General Staff, Sir William Robertson, and his Commander-in-Chief of the British Expeditionary Force in France, Sir Douglas Haig. In this quarrel Balfour himself played a minor but influential rôle. Though not a member of the War Cabinet, he was given the right to attend whenever he thought fit and did in fact: out of the 500 Cabinet meetings held under the second Coalition Government he was present at more than 300, despite in this year, as we have seen, spending some of his time away from the centre of affairs in the United States.

The trouble arose partly out of a clash of personalities: even at a dinner party Lloyd George would have been unlikely to have got on with either Haig or Robertson on whose 'inexhaustible vanity' and 'stubborn and narrow-minded egotism' he often expatiated. But it was certainly more than a personal matter which divided them. As we have seen, as early as December 16, 1915, the military men had insisted that the only way to win the war was to go on battering at the main doors of the enemy on the Western front. They were utterly opposed to opening up fronts in other parts of the world and, when taxed with rigidity of idea, they pointed to Gallipoli.

The General Staff produced chapter and verse in support of their view. But the fact remained that the war was not being won and the casualty lists were enormous and consequently damaging to morale at home. By the beginning of 1917, Lloyd George was restive but dare not take the step of removing the men in whom he had no confidence— he was after all presiding over a Coalition Government without the support of a parliamentary majority party. Instead he attempted to get Haig subordinated to the French Commander-in-Chief, General Nivelle, but in this he failed. So however did Nivelle's offensive. By no means deterred, Haig and Robertson now laid before the Cabinet proposals for a new offensive in Flanders to be undertaken by the British Army. Lloyd George was more than dubious; the soldiers, he pointed out, were always optimistic and always without warrant. He would prefer to try a new theatre of war, to reinforce the Italian armies and to break through the Austrian defences. But he was overborne and finally agreed—supported by Balfour—to yet another attack in France. This led to the 'Passchendaele' campaign, perhaps the most bloody, deadly and useless campaign ever permitted by a British Cabinet.

In the face of this appalling blunder, Lloyd George, under the influence of General Sir Henry Wilson, conceived the idea of a Supreme War Council with France, Britain, Italy and America as members, sitting at Versailles. The real point of this organisation, as far as Lloyd George was concerned, was that it provided a substitute for the policies of the responsible military advisers of the British Government. It was a plan dubious in origin and dangerous in effect for it put the British contingent at Versailles in an obviously invidious position. The essence of it was that the British military representative at Versailles should be 'wholly independent of his War Office', a course adopted by none of the other Allies. Ultimately, it led to disunity between the French and British armies under the pressure of the German offensive in March of the next year. Lord Robert Cecil wrote to Balfour on November 18, 1917, asking him to tell Lloyd George of his opposition to the Supreme War Council as it was an attempt to override the C.I.G.S. and other advocates of the Western Front. Balfour agreed, as he told Lord Robert, that 'as regards the new Paris machinery, he would be a rash man who would say it was going to succeed. It certainly will not succeed if the personages concerned—military and political—try not to make it work.' He added however: 'But I cannot believe the present system is satisfactory; and the only other alternative . . . is the one towards which the French are evidently going to press us—namely a single Commander-in-Chief of *all* the armies, and that a Frenchman. Of such a solution I confess myself profoundly distrustful.' In fact it was exactly this solution which occurred next year and it occurred at the instance of Haig himself, the French general, Foch, becoming the Supreme Commander.

As the extract from his letter to Lord Robert shows, Balfour was by no means 100 per cent. for Lloyd George's idea. But at this point, Lloyd George seeking, Lord Beaverbrook says, 'a way of capturing Balfour's full support for his cause', asked him to use his personal persuasion on General Robertson either to accept the post of British military representative on the Supreme War Council as successor to Sir Henry Wilson or to retain his post of Chief of the Imperial General Staff with somewhat reduced powers. Neither course, naturally, recommended itself to Robertson, the latter for obvious reasons and the former because he realised that it was basically a manœuvre of Lloyd George. Balfour visited him on February 14, 1918, and made a note of their discussion. He pointed out to Robertson that he himself had nothing to do with 'the contrivance of the Versailles plan', but thought that with a little goodwill it could be made to work smoothly and efficiently, 'and, that, if this were so, I thought he should consider it his duty to work the plan'. They discussed the matter for half an hour with, Balfour adds 'I regret to say, no result at all'. Lord Beaverbrook comments on this meeting that Balfour 'failed to persuade the soldier, but he convinced himself'.

This is not entirely true. Balfour, no doubt, continued to have the doubts that he had expressed to Lord Robert Cecil. But—and this is a crucial point for an understanding of his attitude at this time—he believed that Lloyd George was the irreplaceable war leader and that, as such, he must be supported. This did not by any means involve blind following of a leader. Balfour believed that it was easier to stem the more extravagant expressions of the Prime Minister's genius through personal contact and persuasion than by blunt opposition. In fact, Lloyd George was almost always open to the softening advice of Balfour whose altruistic detachment he recognised.

For the same reason, Balfour did not resent, as others might have done and as Curzon was later to do, Lloyd George's setting up of a private secretariat working in huts erected in the garden of No. 10 Downing Street and supplying him with information and advice, particularly on foreign affairs. There did not seem to Balfour any reason why the Prime Minister should not have as many sources of advice as could be made available, and in wartime, even more than in peace-time, the Foreign Minister is after all subject to the Prime Minister. However much rope Balfour himself as Prime Minister had allowed his Foreign Minister, Lansdowne, the ultimate decision in matters of moment had remained his. It may have been true that there were occasions when Lloyd George failed to consult Balfour on matters of foreign policy; but it would be untrue to say, as Vansittart says, that Balfour 'did not mind'. 'We all', Balfour remarked on one occasion, 'unfortunately suffer from the P.M.'s method—or lack of method—of doing business and must keep our tempers as best we can.'

Moreover the risks of lack of liaison between the Prime Minister and his Foreign Minister were lessened by the fact that Balfour's old friend and colleague, Sir Maurice Hankey, was then Secretary to the War Cabinet and saw both these Ministers daily. He was the link in the chain of vital communications. It was for this reason—and for others—that in later years Balfour exclaimed: 'I tell you that without Hankey we should not have won the war!'

Conveniently for us, Balfour summed up his views on Lloyd George pretty frankly in a letter written to Lord Robert Cecil in this year, 1917. He wrote on September 12:

'He is impulsive; he had never given a thought before the war to military matters; he does not perhaps adequately gauge the depths of his own ignorance; and he has certain peculiarities which no doubt make him, now and then, difficult to work with. But I am clearly of opinion that military matters are much better managed now than they were in the time of his predecessor. . . .

'Is there any one of his colleagues in the present War Cabinet you would like to see in his place? Is there any member of the late Government you would like to see in his place? Do you believe there is in the House of Commons any genius on the back benches fit for the place? Do you think there is somewhere in the undistinguished mass of the general public some unknown genius to whom if we could but find him, we might entrust the most difficult, and the most important task with which British statesmanship has ever been confronted?

'For myself I am inclined to answer all these questions in the negative, and that being so, the most patriotic course appears to me to provide the man whom we do not wish to replace with all the guidance and help in our power.'

It should not be supposed from the foregoing that Balfour was inactive or impotent in his office. True, he was served by high Civil Servants of great gifts and intelligence—Lord Hardinge, Sir Eric Drummond, Sir Eyre Crowe—and to them he did leave a good deal of routine work. Hardinge's position, incidentally, led to the curious situation of Balfour's defending him—a Peer—in the House of Commons.

Hardinge had been Viceroy of India when the Mesopotamian expedition was equipped and had then returned to England as permanent head of the Foreign Office. A report on the mismanagement of that expedition implicated him—and incidentally Sir Austen Chamberlain who had been Secretary of State for India—and Hardinge wished to resign. Balfour refused his request and Parliament demanded a debate. Balfour had encouraged Hardinge to defend his actions in the House of Lords, and he now asserted in the Commons debate that this was entirely correct since the subject of discussion did not concern Hardinge's present post at the Foreign Office. Many persons, he claimed, and perhaps the whole Cabinet, were as responsible as Hardinge for the Mesopotamian disaster: 'and it makes my blood boil to think that only one man whom you suppose you can attack with impunity, should be sacrificed, when, if he was guilty, multitudes are no less guilty than he'. Hardinge was saved and, as one Civil Servant wrote to him, the whole Civil Service 'ought to be grateful to you for the gallant stand you made'. Balfour at this time also showed that the teeth of the panther, once so dangerous in debates, had not been drawn. The General Staff had rashly proffered criticism of British diplomatic action in, of all places, Mexico: 'Let them remember', he wrote in a stinging memorandum, 'that while diplomatic failures may hamper the Army, military failures make the Foreign Office helpless.'

It is in this period of his life that the amusing stories of Balfour's alleged indecisiveness, his philosophical quandaries upon political affairs, begin. Many of them are apocryphal. But some are illuminating such as the one told by Harold Nicolson, then a junior official in the Foreign Office. He wrote in *People and Things*:

'It must be admitted that Mr. Balfour was not a man from whom it was easy to extract a decision. On one occasion I remember it was essential to obtain his decision between two weighty alternatives. After several attempts to extract from him something more than a brilliant academic thesis, it was decided to face him with the end of a pistol. A short minute was sent up to him as follows: "Mr. Balfour. There are only two alternative courses open. Alternative A would necessitate (here followed the suggested course of action). Alternative B would necessitate (ditto). Which of these two courses do you wish us to adopt?" "Yes", wrote Mr. Balfour in reply to this question and he initialled it A.J.B. We then had recourse to Sir Ian Malcolm (Balfour's personal private secretary) who explained to the Chief that the single word "Yes" was not a very helpful answer. "But", protested Mr. Balfour, "when I wrote the word Yes I only meant that I agreed that there were two courses open. I still agree with the proposition." And then suddenly something would happen and Mr. Balfour would be seized with galvanic energy and decision.'

At the beginning of the autumn of 1917, matters requiring Foreign Office decisions began to pour in. Once more, peace feelers began to be put out by Bulgaria, Turkey and Austria. More importantly, Von Kühlmann, the Austrian Foreign Minister, had indicated a desire for conversations with the British Government. Balfour believed that this proposal, though it had come via the Spanish Government, must not be ignored. He believed that Baron von Kühlmann might be 'genuinely anxious to find a basis for settlement'. On the other hand, he might wish to have secret talks with the British Government which he could later divulge in order to create mischief among the Allied powers. To forestall this, Balfour suggested that the Allied ambassadors should be called together and informed that Germany had indicated her desire of entering into conversations and that we would at once communicate to the Allies any proposals that might be made. Balfour thought that the Germans would not agree to this and 'if I am to speak my whole mind, I am by no means sure that a refusal on their part to proceed further in the matter—and on such a ground—would not, *at the moment*, be the best thing that could happen to us'. Lloyd George talked the matter over with the French and discovered that they, too, suspected a trap.

Eventually, Balfour's plan of talking to the Allied ambassadors was adopted and on October 8, 1917, he telegraphed to Madrid the British willingness to receive any communications that the German Government might wish to make and 'to discuss it with their allies'. No reply ever came. Indeed, the conference between the central powers and the Bolsheviks at Brest-Litovsk was soon to show that Germany was nowhere near ready for negotiations on terms that the Allies would accept. It was a tricky situation as Balfour recognised in a memorandum sent to the War Cabinet on September 20, 1917: 'From the Foreign Office point of view we have now reached a most critical and difficult stage of the war, the middle stage, when fighting has lost none of its violence, when all the natural channels of diplomacy are still choked, but when nevertheless, some at least of the belligerents are endeavouring to start informal conversations about terms of peace.'

No one in their right mind would wish to turn down any genuine offer of peace, for if Britain seemed to be fighting on for fighting's sake the war spirit would clearly be strengthened in Germany. This was one of the reasons why Balfour did not press for an early peace with Austria. As General Smuts discovered in a secret conversation in Geneva with Mensdorff, formerly Austro-Hungarian Ambassador in London, there was little chance of Austria separating herself from Germany while the war was still on. There was also, as Balfour pointed out to the War Cabinet on December 15, 1917, this danger: 'If we make proposals fully satisfactory to all our allies they will be regarded as utterly

unreasonable by all our enemies. If on the other hand we make tentative qualifications in their extreme demands, and the negotiations
nevertheless break down (as I rather think they will), then we shall
have given a most powerful instrument into the hands of our foes, for
making mischief between us and our friends.'

None of these considerations could be put before the public, and there
was no doubt about it that the public was war-weary. Certainly it
had not in Britain got to the point where there were wholesale mutinies
of troops as in France. This was why when Lord Lansdowne, coming
out of his retirement, wrote his Peace Plan letter published in the *Daily
Telegraph* of November 29, 1917, there was considerable support for
him—even from such people as Colonel House, McKenna and Walter
Runciman. This letter had a curious origin in which Balfour was
involved. Early in November Lansdowne had consulted him on his
desire to elicit a new statement of war aims from the Government by
means of a parliamentary question. At Balfour's suggestion, Lansdowne put his views in the form of a memorandum, to which Balfour
replied by saying that he did not think it was a suitable time for discussing these matters. He added that as far as he was concerned he
did not wish to see any dismemberment of Germany or Austria nor their
destruction as trading communities.

Lansdowne then decided to write a letter to the papers. He spoke
about this when he chanced to meet Balfour in the street as the latter
was about to depart to Paris for a meeting of the Supreme War Council.
Balfour, he said afterwards, did not attempt to dissuade him. Nor did
he object to Lansdowne showing the draft to Hardinge, Permanent
Under-Secretary at the Foreign Office, 'in order that he might tell me
if the letter contained any inaccuracies'. Lansdowne wrote later:
Balfour 'observed that it (i.e. the letter) was "statesmanlike" and
"would do good" '.

There was mutual misunderstanding here, as Balfour later pointed
out, for he said he had assumed that Lansdowne's letter would contain
only those parts of the earlier proposed question in the House of Lords
to which he had raised no objection. But the letter went very much
further and Lansdowne believed that Balfour had approved it. The
Cabinet at once issued a communiqué saying that Lansdowne's letter
spoke only for Lord Lansdowne himself and adding that he had not
consulted any member of His Majesty's Government before publishing
it. Lansdowne never contradicted this. Perhaps he realised later
that misunderstanding had in fact taken place. Nor did Balfour revert
to the matter. It seems, indeed, that he neither read Lansdowne's
letter in the *Daily Telegraph*, nor heard of the Government disclaimer.
He was in Paris during these days; possibly no one ever mentioned the
matter to him. This, however, is difficult to believe since the letter set

off two opposing storms; at one moment it was thought possible that Asquith might lead an Opposition movement in the House on the basis of the Lansdowne Plan. Balfour believed all discussion about 'war aims' was unprofitable. Only a decisive victory over Germany mattered in the slightest.

Lansdowne's letter to the *Daily Telegraph* reminds us that the press, much less fettered in the First than in the Second World War, played an often dangerous part in affairs. This was largely due to Northcliffe, the eccentric proprietor of the *Daily Mail* and *The Times*. During Lloyd George's controversy with the Generals, Northcliffe had supported the latter and even demanded a military dictatorship. He had early conceived a grudge against Balfour since Balfour had opposed the idea that Northcliffe should be sent, as he desired, to the United States as Chairman of the British War Mission. Northcliffe, however, was sent, was successful, and on his return, having been made a Viscount, issued a statement attacking Balfour's alleged delays at the Foreign Office and misuse of the censorship.

Another newspaper owner, Beaverbrook, also complained that the Foreign Office had frustrated him during the period when he was Minister in charge of Propaganda. When he wrote to Law about the matter at the time, he ascribed all the hindrances to Hardinge, adding that 'nothing could have been pleasanter than my relations with Mr. Balfour and Lord Robert Cecil to whom I am indebted for much kindness and wise advice'. When, however, many years later, in 1956, Beaverbrook returned to the subject he was a good deal less diplomatic than he had been to his powerful friend Law. He states frankly: 'Balfour was my enemy.'

In the reverberating events of the last year of the war, Balfour played his full part as a fairly regular attender at Cabinet meetings. But he was not deeply involved in the brouhaha that arose from Lloyd George's setting up of the Supreme War Council and the affair of General Maurice, the Pemberton Billing case, nor most of the other incidents that tended to shake the Coalition Government. But, as Foreign Minister, he was in the forefront of matters consequent upon the Bolshevik revolution in 1917, and the chaos resulting from Russia's effective withdrawal from the war against Germany. This meant, on the one hand, that Germany and her allies were no longer hemmed in; on the other hand, it meant that the axis of international political force that had been represented by Russia was no longer in existence. Balfour, the more directly concerned in the matter of Russia because of Lloyd George's immersion in military matters, urged the Soviets to honour their country's undertakings as the best way of obtaining the kind of peace they wanted: 'The only peace which could be secured by substituting argument for action,' he wrote in a Note to them, 'would be neither democratic nor durable nor Russian. It would be German and imperialistic.' The Soviets, despite the pressures upon them and the fact that they effectively ruled at this time a very small part of Russia, refused to fight the Germans and in due course they were saved by the triumph of the Allies on the Western front.

In the earlier days of the revolution, Balfour did not believe that the Bolsheviks were avowed enemies of Britain and he told the Cabinet so on December 9, 1917: 'If, for the moment the Bolsheviks show particular virulence in dealing with the British Empire, it is probably because they think the British Empire is the greatest obstacle to peace.' In reality, he thought, they were fanatics, 'dangerous dreamers'; he believed that a breach 'with this crazy system should be avoided as long as possible. . . . If this be drifting, then I am a drifter by deliberate policy.' He thus advised the Cabinet against giving aid to such anti-Bolsheviks as the Cossack general A. M. Kaledin, but the Cabinet overruled him with the result that Trotsky became angry and without any helpful results since Kaledin was militarily a man of straw.

To Balfour, as to most Allied leaders, Bolshevism was a transient phenomenon that would soon disappear. Two lines of general policy were, therefore, essential: not to alienate Russians as a whole nor groups of Russians from whom might one day come a strong government; and to persuade all Russian groups to continue the war against the Germans, thus relieving the pressure on the Western front. 'Internal affairs in Russia are no concern of ours,' Balfour said. 'We consider them only in so far as they affect the war.' Any renewal of the war on the Eastern front was, therefore, to be encouraged. He was prepared to guarantee evacuation of all Russian territory at the end of hostilities if the Soviets would agree either to fight themselves or to allow others—Americans, Japanese, British—to fight for them. If the Soviets would not agree, he was prepared to back Allied intervention on the Eastern front against the Germans without their agreement.

This led to the already confused situation in Russia becoming more confused still with British troops helping the Finnish Reds fight the Finnish Whites, with the Murmansk Soviet becoming pro-Allied and fighting the Bolsheviks, and with all kinds of splinter elements rallying to the Allied cause. It did not, however, result in any very effective fighting against the Germans. Moreover Balfour came to see that, in practice, Allied help to those Russians willing to fight the Germans would in the end mean helping those who were against the Bolsheviks since, under Lenin, the Bolsheviks were equally hostile to both English and Germans.

In due course troops were landed in North Russia and in Siberia to fight the Germans against the will of Lenin. A complete rupture of relations now seemed certain, but neither Balfour nor the Cabinet wanted a break for, if it came, it would imply that the troops were aimed against the Soviet régime as well as against the Germans. Lenin, however, hard pressed from every side and himself shot at by a would-be assassin, became desperate; in August 1918 he instituted the 'Terror', striking out wildly at any he believed (often incorrectly) might aid the Allies. The policy of non-interference in internal affairs was at an end. Meanwhile, the German front in the West had been finally turned, and the reason for sending Allied troops to Russia was no longer valid.

In London, the real nature of the Soviet revolution was at last being comprehended. Robert Bruce Lockhart, who had played a foremost part as a Foreign Office official in Russia during the days of revolution, returned home. He was called to see Balfour at the Foreign Office and discovered to his surprise that the Foreign Secretary was no longer interested in the relative strength of the Bolsheviks and their enemies. Instead he questioned Lockhart at length on Lenin's ideology and took pains to refute it point by point. The 'wind of change' he had noted with interest upon his defeat in 1906 was blowing still stronger. Policies towards Russia could no longer be treated as *ad hoc* or purely military. What had happened in Russia would reverberate through every country in the world raising both passions and fears such as had scarcely been felt since the French Revolution. In the immediate future, Balfour would no longer be directly concerned with Russia, though the problems awaiting him at the peace conferences would inevitably reflect the new factor in world affairs: militant Communism.

18

THE ARTS OF PEACE

1919–1922

In October, 1918, Law, the leader of the Conservative Party, wrote to Balfour asking what he thought ought to be the Conservative attitude to the immediate future. It was clear that there would shortly have to be a General Election since the existing Parliament had been elected in 1910. In addition, the Reform Act of 1918 had almost doubled the electorate and thus made the existing House of Commons extraordinarily unrepresentative.

The question, however, was: who should fight whom? In his letter to Balfour, Law said he believed that the Prime Minister, Lloyd George, would soon start manœuvring for an election. Lloyd George, somewhat naturally in view of his relations with Asquith, wished the Conservatives to join him on the same platform. Law, however, saw the dangers of a split in the Conservative Party as a result. On the other hand, with Lloyd George as Leader, the party might well succeed; and after a successful election it might reverse the rôles and make Lloyd George dependent on it. Law was uncertain, but of one thing he felt sure, that 'our Party on the old lines would never have any future in this country'.

Balfour agreed with his views in general terms. The responsibility of a dissolution rested with the Prime Minister of the day; but this did not remove the necessity of determining the attitude of the Conservative Party. He thought it would be most undesirable to resume Party controversy at the stage it had reached when war broke out.

In due course, therefore, Law and Lloyd George decided that they would appeal to the country as a coalition. An offer was then made to Asquith that he and some of his immediate colleagues should be included in whatever administration resulted from the election. Asquith refused. He had not recovered from the soreness and distrust of the leaders who had, as he felt, turned him out so humiliatingly two years before. Thus, the Asquith Liberals, with the Labour Party, put forward Opposition candidates in the election that followed the armistice in November, 1918.

Balfour played small part in the electioneering. In his address to the electors of his constituency, the City of London, he did, however, emphasise that the transition from war to peace was as difficult as the transition from peace to war; he believed, simply, that those who, though not possessing 'any super-human immunity from errors and miscalculations', had successfully negotiated the war were people to effect the transition.

Balfour realised, perhaps clearer than many, the peculiar difficulties of Britain emerging into peace. He said that 'to a degree unknown either in France or America, Italy or Japan, the energies of our people, when not actually engaged in fighting, were forcibly diverted from the arts of peace to those of war; and if now they have to be turned again into their former courses, the change cannot be made without difficulty, nor I fear, without some suffering.' Nor was Britain merely concerned to bring back pre-war conditions: 'While we restore, we must endeavour also to improve.' The shattering of German militarism had caused severe dislocations; and 'Russia is in a condition of septic dissolution'. It was said that this infection was already spreading to Russia's immediate neighbours, Hungary, Austria, even to Germany. There were even those 'who fear that we shall not wholly escape'.

The 'Coupon' election—so called because only the candidates to whom Lloyd George and Law sent a letter of approval were regarded as belonging to the coalition—took place on December 14. It resulted in overwhelming victory for the coalition, who gained the support of 474 members—338 Conservatives and 136 Liberals—while the total Opposition was 222 members of whom 73 were Sinn Feiners. The latter repudiated the authority of Westminster and refused to take their seats. Labour had 59 members and became the official Opposition. The Asquithian Liberals were almost wiped out. Asquith himself lost his seat.

There followed an undignified squabble over office in which, needless to say, Balfour took no part. He remained Foreign Secretary until October, 1919, when he was succeeded by Curzon. He then took over Curzon's post as Lord President of the Council. Lloyd George, of course, remained Prime Minister with Law as his deputy in the office of Lord Privy Seal. Austen Chamberlain became Chancellor of the Exchequer and Churchill Secretary for War with the Air Ministry under his control as well.

Scarcely a month after the election, Balfour was on his way to attend the Peace Conference in Paris, third man in the British delegation along with Lloyd George and Law. The evening before he departed he is said to have remarked, 'As I have always told you, it was not so much the war as the peace that I have always dreaded.' He had seen too much of the devious interlockings of international politics to set his hopes too high. One thing he was sure of: that speed was essential if the world was to return to normal conditions. Every day's delay in settling the massive problems before the Peace Conference give opportunity and encouragement for the spreading of that septic contagion he had remarked upon in his address to the electors of the City of London.

II

Balfour arrived in Paris in January, 1919. A flat had been prepared for him in the Rue Nittot, immediately above that occupied by the head of the delegation, the Prime Minister, Lloyd George. Balfour was not a principal negotiator in the discussions of the 'Council of Ten' which led up to the signing of the Peace Treaty with Germany at Versailles on June 28. That was Lloyd George's function. But there was one short period—from February 16 to March 8—when Balfour took over. President Wilson and Lloyd George had gone home, and Clemenceau was ill. During this interim it was Balfour who dominated what had rapidly become an extremely complicated situation.

The atmosphere of confusion and intrigue, into which Lloyd George had entered with great gusto, was temporarily dissipated by Balfour's sense of the urgency of getting matters settled, not least so that British troops still scattered over Europe, some of them in positions of difficulty and even danger, should be able to return home. Therefore, while he was in charge, Balfour sought to isolate the military, naval and air clauses of the German Treaty from the political and economical provisions so that they could be presented to the Germans for immediate signature. In fact, the drafts of the military terms were by no means prepared, and the proposal was defeated. Nevertheless, Balfour got the Supreme Council to resolve on February 22 that the reports of the expert committees on frontiers, finance, and economic relations with Germany should be ready by March 8. This was put into effect. 'Whereas', Winston Churchill wrote 'in the middle of February the Conference was drifting off almost uncontrollably into futility, all was now brought back in orderly fashion to the real.'

On his return from illness, Clemenceau dubbed Balfour the Richelieu of the Conference; and by the time Lloyd George and President Wilson returned to France in the middle of March, the general lines of the draft Treaty were complete. Now, as Balfour put it, came the "rough

23. A.J.B. with Lloyd George, 1922, at Lady Crosfield's garden party

Radio Times Hulton Picture Library

24. Dr. Chaim Weizmann
(1874–1952)

Radio Times Hulton Picture Library

25. Viscount Allenby, A.J.B. and Sir Herbert Samuel at the opening of
the Hebrew University, Jerusalem, 1925

By courtesy of Viscount Samuel

and tumble" stage. It was at this stage, however, that the 'Council of Ten' became the 'Council of Four', and Balfour, along with the other Foreign Ministers of the Powers, withdrew from the conferences. But though he was effectively out of the deliberations, he kept closely in touch with what went on and it was he who insisted that he must have written records of the decisions taken by the 'Four'. Moreover, his old friend Maurice Hankey was the secretary of the 'Four' and invaluable in maintaining close liaison between the Foreign Minister and his chief. Balfour and his staff were by no means unoccupied, however: they were concerned with the details of the thorny questions to be faced by the principal negotiators and Balfour himself was particularly occupied with the British Empire Delegation. This was the committee of delegates from the Dominions and India; everything that was decided by the Conference itself was open to previous expression of opinion by them.

Balfour's work behind the scenes as a member, and sometimes chairman, of the delegation was important. He and Lloyd George often found themselves having to defend their attitude and actions. When, for instance, it was pointed out that the Supreme Council was divagating from President Wilson's Fourteen Points, Balfour replied that these had suddenly been presented to Britain as the proposed basis for peace on the very eve of the Armistice; there had been little time for discussion of them; and already President Wilson himself, in one or two instances, had assented to decisions entirely opposite to his own Points. Again, on the question of the length of the occupation of German territory by Allied troops, he agreed with the Dominions that French demands should be resisted; yet, on the other hand, he pointed out that some Dominion delegates were apparently too susceptible to the pathetic appeals of the Germans, forgetting that 'the Germans were responsible for the tragedy of the whole world. She was no unhappy victim of circumstances, she was suffering and ought to suffer for her crimes.' He even opposed Lloyd George who had urged that the Allies should issue some declaration that they would not withhold commercial assistance from Germany: Balfour said that he was more anxious that the Allies should give to their own friends.

When the Treaty was at last ready for signature, Balfour went with the other delegates to Versailles on June 28. Like them he was kissed, cheered, and pelted with flowers by a delirious crowd; and he put his signature fourth on the list of British delegates, which was headed by Lloyd George, Law and Milner. He signed with a gold fountain-pen which Lloyd George had given him for the occasion. This pen he carried in his waistcoat pocket and used daily for the rest of his life. (Unlike Law, who, it appeared, gave *his* gold fountain-pen to the pilot of the aircraft in which he returned to London.)

D1jb

With the signature of the Versailles Treaty, the heads of governments left Paris, and the Foreign Ministers took charge.   Their principal task was to negotiate treaties with the remaining belligerents, Austria, Bulgaria, Hungary and Turkey.   In fact, it was the Treaty with Austria alone which Balfour himself signed on September 10, 1919; after that he returned to London and Curzon took his place as Foreign Minister, having been acting for him in that capacity during his period in Paris.   Nevertheless he took full part in the vast and complex discussions arising in the course of the preparations for the other treaties. Reading the 700 pages of the first chapter of the proceedings of the Supreme Council of the principal allied and associated powers between July 1 and September 9, 1919, one is struck by the sheer hard work that went into them, the constant swinging from subject to subject, and not least the irruption of news from Eastern Europe of countries, groups, and even battalions of soldiers who acted on the assumption that possession was nine points of the law.   It is also notable that it was usually Balfour who was asked to draft the resolutions; he had in his time been an expert drafter of parliamentary Bills, and the experience became invaluable at the peace-making.

These agreements are now dead mutton.   Yet they composed the framework of international politics in the inter-war years.   Their general drift was to 'Balkanise' Europe by giving separate sovereignty to each of the races of the old Austro-Hungarian empire—inevitably— since for many of the oppressed races the war had been one of emancipation.   No doubt it was unwise that the Tyrolese should be included in Italy for strategical reasons, and the amputation of Prussia in the east led to trouble in the 1930s.   Yet the decisions were largely inevitable. Many of the inter-war problems would, in any case, have arisen whatever frontiers had been made, for the Nazi resurgence had deeper and more complex motivations and aims than the mere rectification of frontiers.

Balfour put his finger on another radical difficulty that faced the peace negotiators when discussion arose about Hungary and the Red terrorist Government of Bela Kun which had seized power in Budapest and had no intention of obeying Allied decisions.   Hungary, Balfour believed, ought to be forced to observe the Armistice; but he could not but ask, with Clemenceau, what troops were available to compel observation and how were such troops, if available, to be financed? 'If what has been said in the Council were known outside, namely, that all the Powers had demobilised so fast under the stress of domestic necessity, it would certainly be regarded as absurd that the Powers which eight months ago, were the conquerors of the world, could not, at the present moment, impose their will on an army of 120,000 men. This inglorious situation he did not particularly mind, but he wondered

how the Conference would be able to terminate its work successfully. . . . He wished the Conference to have the authority which
power alone could give. He agreed that the economic weapon was
still available. Nevertheless, rapid demobilisation had put the Conference into a difficulty which was almost comic. His fear had been that
if Bela Kun were allowed to know that the Conference was militarily
powerless he might use his knowledge to great effect and the evil might
spread all over the world.'

Again and again it is Balfour who introduces the note of realism
into the discussions. He pointed out, for example, that all countries
of the world were in fact inter-dependent; but this should be clearly
understood and not merely accepted theoretically. There was the
Reparation Commission which had been set up under the Treaty to
deal with coal production in Central and Eastern Europe. This
Commission's terms mentioned that it should 'undertake the co-ordination of the production, distribution and transportation of coal throughout Europe'. Balfour asked: 'Did this mean the Commission would
take charge, for instance, of the Belgian coalfields and the coalfields in
Northern France? Would it attempt to regulate the conditions of
production in England? As was well known to the Council, it was
difficult to obtain coal from English coalfields even to keep British
industries going. In what manner could the proposed Commission
intervene in the internal affairs of the various countries?'

Again, he draws attention to the real nub of the Allied war debts:
'The various Allied States were mutually indebted. Their only means
of discharging their debts was by exports. Great Britain could only
pay off her indebtedness by the producton and exportation of coal.
For coal was not only one of the principal of British exports, but it was
also the means necessary for every form of manufacture. The situation
could not be solved, as during the war, by suppressing train services
and doing away with superfluities. It went to the roots of the whole
economic relations of all countries, not merely of the Allied countries
between themselves. It was not simply a question of the rich helping
the poor in any one particular commodity.'

Balfour from time to time found himself in sharp exchanges with
Clemenceau, for example over the latter's charges that General Allenby
was provoking agitation against the French in Syria. On the whole,
however, these two statesmen had considerable regard for each other,
though Balfour often felt obliged to advise the 'Tiger' to restraint.
Both the British and American delegates were, for instance, only too
anxious to relieve themselves of the large numbers of German prisoners-
of-war who were still in their hands: Clemenceau on the other hand
would have preferred to hold on to his prisoners-of-war whom he was
trying to set to work, and indeed would have happily had control of the

other prisoners-of-war in Allied hands had those Allies still been willing to remain nominally in charge of them.

The Peace Treaty with Austria, in which Balfour was principally involved, has frequently been criticised, mainly on the grounds that it left that country high and dry with no means of feeding herself and perhaps little will to do so. The Austrians of the South Tyrol, as we have seen, were handed over to the Italians, but this was due to the secret treaties made during the war in order to break Italy away from the enemy and to get her to engage in hostilities. Moreover, the suggestion that Austria should merge with Germany had been vetoed by the heads of governments in May, before Balfour took Lloyd George's place at the Conference. The French would never have agreed to such a union of German peoples; and none of the Powers wished to do anything to prevent the new-born Czechoslovak state developing, and the Czechs saw in the possible merger a danger to their existence. But early in the discussions Balfour had insisted that 'the main point was that it was desirable to set up Austria economically. She could not be left to starve. Food must be advanced to her either on such securities as existed, or she must be put in a way to earn money. She could not produce the food she required, as the territory left her by the Treaty was insufficient. . . . He thought it imperative that Austria should be fed and Czechoslovakia armed.'

Often he insisted that all the Austrian notes submitted to the Conference should be carefully examined since 'he did not think it would be proper to allow it to be said that the Austrian Delegation had never had its case properly heard, or to permit it to be thought that the immense operation of liquidating the Austrian Empire had been effected without the due consideration of all the problems involved.'

But the Austrian Treaty, like all the other treaties, was the result of a balance of powers: Balfour did not draw it up all by himself. It has to be remembered that, as far as Britain was concerned, the immediate dangers were over and done with when the German fleet was sunk. It was not so for France, since the German army was still largely intact. The more the old enemies were split up the better. The fact that the population of Austria, formerly about 22 million, was reduced by more than a half was to the French an immediate good, whatever it might bode for the future. Poland took Austrian Slavs from Galicia; Czechoslovakia took nearly 4 million of her Germans. In the end no provisions were made for Austria's economic future; she became miserably poor, and eventually in 1938 was once more united with Germany by Hitler's *anschluss*. It has been said that it would have been preferable for Austria to have been merged at once with Germany so that her un-Germanic qualities should have been a leaven in the Prussian loaf. The argument is dubious, surrounded by too many ifs and buts. It was not unnatural that there should be fears of a revived Austria, of a powerful oppressive empire; it was probably not necessary to allow the Italian frontier to be pushed right up to the Brenner Pass. But it might have taxed the wisdom of a philosopher sitting undisturbed in his study to draw the blueprints of a new Europe to arise out of the wreckage; for the representatives of nations sitting in Paris, surrounded by intrigues and the everchanging winds of opinion and by pressures from so many quarters, it was nearly impossible.

By the middle of August, Balfour himself had had enough. He was in his 72nd year and the strain of the meetings and the preparations for them, had taxed his strength. He felt that the treaties with Austria, Bulgaria and Hungary were in essence complete, though he knew that the whole problem of Turkey, Russia and the execution of the Treaty with Germany still required attention. He himself, however, was determined to have a holiday, and when Lloyd George came over to Trouville Balfour told him that he felt his holiday must be complete and that he could not undertake to resume any form of Foreign Office work. Lloyd George accepted this, persuading him only not to resign office at the moment. On October 24 it was announced that Balfour would quit the Foreign Office, where Curzon took over, and that he would become Lord President of the Council. This was, however, by no means the end of Balfour's influence upon foreign affairs; he was to play no small part in the early work of the League of Nations at Geneva, which he had mentioned in his mid-war note to President Wilson.

There is one question rising from the Paris peace talks worth mentioning. Balfour played very little part in the discussions during the talks on the question of reparation. Some years later, however, in 1924, a remarkable attack was made on the good faith of Lloyd George and his Government in this matter. The attack came from within the Foreign Office itself. One of the members of the Political Intelligence Department during the war had been James W. Headlam-Morley, a historian. After the war Headlam-Morley was officially engaged on writing a general history of the Peace at Paris. In September, 1922, he issued a confidential paper within the Foreign Office on the subject of reparation. In a footnote he asks for 'Criticism and information from any members of the Office who are in possession of special knowledge either on the matters dealt with in this memorandum or on other sections.' The paper was read by, among other people, Maurice Hankey who at once saw that Headlam-Morley was implying a serious breach of faith by Lloyd George. Hankey communicated with Balfour, and a copy of this confidential Foreign Office Paper is annotated in Balfour's own hand.

What Headlam-Morley implied was that during the Peace talks in

Paris at the beginning of 1919, Lloyd George saw that two things were absolutely essential from the British point of view: to secure the Armistice, and to stand firm on the freedom of the seas. Yet if he insisted on these matters he could not at the same time press for full reparations from the defeated for the whole cost of war. He believed on the authority of Haig that the Germans still had plenty of fight in them. He therefore deliberately confined himself to obtaining reparations for various forms of damage done, and in fact got £600 million.

Headlam-Morley, however, asserted that, after Lloyd George left Paris, there were changes substantially altering the grounds of claim. There was, for example, revolution in Germany. Britain might then have got unconditional surrender rather than armistice. The public and the Dominions were dissatisfied and at that point, Headlam-Morley alleged, Lloyd George and his colleagues tried to get out of their previous declarations that full costs of the war would not be demanded.

Balfour and Hankey discussed the matter and, though Balfour prepared the draft letter to Headlam-Morley, it was in the end Hankey who wrote on behalf of them both. The reply was that the Fourteen Points of Wilson, upon which Headlam-Morley mainly based his case, were not in any sense binding upon the governments, many of whom had in fact no chance of discussing them at length beforehand. Furthermore, the wording of the reparations reservation at the Armistice discussions in Paris 'was in fact sufficiently wide to cover pensions or even costs of war, and Mr. Lloyd George believed it to bear this interpretation'. Certainly the Fourteen Points constituted no binding or legal agreement with the defeated enemy. Lloyd George may very well have changed his mind on the subjects of reparations or total costs of the war; he may even have changed his mind under pressures from the public or elsewhere; but there was no reason why he should not do so.

Apart from the misrepresentations of the case, there were other wider problems arising from Headlam-Morley's actions. Hankey writes to Balfour on July 4, 1924: 'If confidential histories are to be written, no one is safe. There may be at this moment chapters of Mr. Headlam-Morley's history which damn your reputation or mine, of the very existence of which we have no knowledge. They may have been lying, as the reparation chapters have been lying, for two or three years in the Foreign Office without our knowledge. Some years hence they will probably be handed over to the Record Office and accepted by the world as a correct account. The obvious remedy appears to be that they should be communicated to all concerned.'

A few weeks earlier, Balfour had drawn Hankey's attention to another aspect. He wrote on June 25, 1924: 'In its whole tenor', he says referring to the Headlam-Morley paper on reparations, 'it is violently anti-Ally; and should it ever see the light of publicity, would, as far as I can

judge, do untold damage . . . it is ammunition for all the enemies—
public and private of all the Prime Ministers, and all the peoples of all
the countries concerned in fighting Germany.'

As Hankey foretold, the Headlam-Morley version of events did gain
currency, and in one form or another is to be found in many books on
this period.

III

Balfour's return to England in the autumn of 1919 did not go un-
remarked. The periodical, the *Bystander*, had a cartoon in which
Britannia addresses Balfour: 'I thank you heartily, dear Mr. Balfour,
for splendid work in Paris, but most of all for your disinterested patriotism in serving under others, having yourself held the office of Prime
Minister.' The cartoon then made gentle play with Balfour's well-
known forgetfulness: 'Mr. Balfour (with puzzled surprise): "Prime
Minister? *Was* I? Oh, ah, Yes! Quite so! Of course, I was. I
have such a poor memory for detail. Yes, yes! I *do* recall that quaint
little house in Downing Street." '

Balfour was a figure—a caricaturable figure which the public could
appreciate. He had indeed, by the last decade of his life, become
almost a father-figure, impossible though in his case such an identifica-
tion might have appeared. Another commentator in this year, Jehu
Junior in the *World* can still refer to him being known in 'certain eclectic
circles' as 'Pretty Fanny', but this comes more in 1919 from a good
press-cutting system than from current speech. Much more contemporary is Jehu Junior's further remarks:

'His sincerity, his breadth of mind, his scholarship and his geniality
won the hearts of everyone. Perhaps too much a philosophic doubter
to be a good politician, he is a great statesman and a great gentleman,
and we can thank our stars that, with the kaleidoscopic character of
some of our delegates in Paris, AJB is quietly watching over British
interests.'

Tall, lean as ever, immensely distinguished, he had the appearance
of true refinement, of a man accustomed to discriminate, yet of such
quiet charm of manner that even those prepared to criticise every sort of
celebrity could not resist. He was always a good listener, and his own
discourse had the intellect of his later philosophical writing and the
responsiveness of a man of warm sympathy. It was those who knew
him only from a distance who failed to appreciate him: to Maynard
Keynes, the Cambridge economist, for instance he appeared to be 'the
most extraordinary *objet d'art* that ever embellished statesmanship'.
There is a suggestion there that Balfour had become the prisoner of his
own *persona*. The *persona*, however, was really the man: Balfour never.

at any rate consciously, built a face to turn to the public. Yet, inevitably, a man much in the public eye, must tend as he grows old to lose a certain flexibility and spontaneity in his relations with others. To some degree, this is due to a gradual waning of interest in the future. Balfour, indeed, as his niece records, did remain interested in the future, and later preferred the company of young people; yet it was inevitably a detached interest of a man above the mêlée who, in the course of nature, would never plunge into it.

It was never easy to get below the surface with Balfour. We have seen him weeping over the death of a friend; we know of his immense sympathy and kindness to those afflicted. We know also that he was adept in the inner political game of power, and a debater able to make rings round an opponent. We know, too, that his life was beautifully balanced between public and private, between affairs and speculation; and that he was completely withdrawn (even when he ought not to have been) from concern with matters of money. This is probably why Lord Vansittart, then a senior Civil Servant, could observe: 'His detachment was unreal because he had not suffered enough to retain it.' That is almost certainly true. But Vansittart's further remarks are superficial: 'Balfour', he writes, 'was easily pleased, not easily touched, liked everybody and cared for nobody. He enjoyed eminence.' He notes that 'his sedate passion for lawn tennis gave him the thrill of a guilty conscience. His abandonment of golf for his temptress was his nearest approach to physical infidelity.' That is incorrect on two counts, the one being that he never abandoned golf. Yet more direct observations ring true: 'He was a great gentleman unaware. . . . His sliced forehand from the base-line evoked in him gleams of pale happiness. . . . (He had) a lackadaisical lucidity.' Vansittart also noticed that Balfour was always punctual for meals at his own table, no doubt because 'his food was the best ever eaten by a philosopher'. Balfour was in no sense a gourmand, nor even a gourmet; but he enjoyed good cooking and, at Carlton Gardens, had a first-class chef.

Balfour showed few signs of age. His sister, Nora, writes to him, on June 26, 1919: 'Gerald is I think decidedly well, but he is letting himself become an old man quicker than you . . . we are all getting rather old except you!' He could still enjoy the company of Lady Wemyss who, in 1918, still writes to him in this vein: 'Florence Nightingale has always been a great heroine of mine . . . I have been thinking what a pity it is that I have not always treated you as she treated Sidney Herbert!' She it is who records how Balfour 'cried about the war' in church one Sunday. Both she and Lady Desborough had lost sons in the war; both knew the quality of his comfort. 'The bitterness', he wrote to Lady Desborough after the death of her sons, William and Julian Grenfell, 'lies not in the thought that they are really dead, still less in the thought that I have parted with them for ever; for I think neither of these things. The bitterness lies in the thought that *until I also die* I shall never again see them smile or hear their voices. The pain is indeed hard to bear, too hard it sometimes seems for human strength. Yet measured on the true scale of things it is but brief; death cannot long cheat us of love . . . I am as sure that those I love and have lost are living today, as I am that yesterday they were fighting heroically in the trenches.'

He adds this, and it suggests how greatly his philosophic speculation mirrored his beliefs, perhaps led to confirmation of those beliefs: 'For myself, I entertain no doubt whatever about a future life. I deem it at least as certain as any of the hundred-and-one truths of the frame-work of the world, as I conceive the world. It is no mere theological accretion, which I am prepared to accept in some moods and reject in others.'

Yet, though to his friends his walk was as light as ever, his step as panther-like, he *was* 72: might not retirement be best? As we have seen, he had agreed to become Lord President of the Council, though retiring from the Foreign Secretaryship, and there were those in that year of 1919 who thought that Balfour might prefer some yet less onerous work still. The Mastership of Trinity College, Cambridge, had become vacant by the death of Dr. H. M. Butler. Madeline Adeane, formerly Wyndham and one of 'The Three Graces' in Sargent's picture, wrote to her sister, Lady Wemyss, to ask her to engage the support of Balfour for the claims of Professor C. D. Whetham to the Mastership against those of Sir J. J. Thomson. She adds a postscript: 'If someone outside Trinity is appointed I hear Mr. Balfour's name mentioned. But he could not take it, could he?'

There is a further hint in a letter from Charles Whibley, the littérateur, and friend of Cust, to Lady Wemyss that Balfour might have been interested in the Mastership. Lady Wemyss, it appears, had first mentioned the possibility and Whibley replied: 'It is now too late and I can only regret. A.J.B. would have been the best possible master of Trinity. His appointment would have been (I believe) agreeable to him and a splendid thing for the University . . . A.J.B. would have been free to do what he liked. For five months he would have adorned the great college in a place of dignity and no restraint. For seven months he would have lived in his own house . . . A.J.B. would have been a realised ideal, a dream of perfection come true.'

What Whibley suggests might well have appealed to Balfour with his close personal ties with Cambridge. In this same year, he was installed as Chancellor of the University (he had been Chancellor of Edinburgh since 1895), and he took his duties seriously. Through his exertions, £700,000 was obtained from the Rockefeller Foundation for the new university library in 1928, and his correspondence in the 1920s frequently concerns university matters.

But Balfour came no closer than that to university life.   No doubt, had he wished, he could have done so.   He did not.   Political life retained its attractions.   Some, indeed, said that political office was the real draw.   J. S. Sandars, his former secretary, wrote a newspaper article under a pseudonym suggesting that 'the atmosphere of departmental life, its apparatus of red boxes and private secretaries, of cyphers and memoranda, of minutes and signatures, seems to have quickened his actions and to have inspired his interest.   In truth, he enjoys place with the same spirit of philosophic satisfaction as he showed in the hour of defeat or resignation.'

As may be gathered, Sandars had parted company with his former chief.   The breach had come during the war when Balfour became First Lord and asked Sandars to return to him.   Sandars refused because Balfour had decided to allow Winston Churchill, his predecessor, to remain with his growing family in their quarters at Admiralty House. Sandars had a scarcely rational hatred of Churchill, partly, it appears, because he believed that the main object of Churchill's life of his father, Randolph, was the denigration of Balfour and Salisbury, and 'to show that his father had been infamously treated by both of them'.   Balfour, however, refused to alter his decision, and Sandars never communicated with him again.   He lived on until 1934 and died aged 81, having written a number of cynical studies of the political events in which he played a part—one study, in particular showing his bitterness at what he regarded as Balfour's betrayal in accepting the O.M. (in 1916), and later in becoming a Peer.

However, in one sense, it is probably true that his various offices in government during the war had given Balfour a new lease of political life.   We seldom come across the complaints about the tiresomeness of holding office that were frequent in earlier days.   But it is at least reasonable to suppose that, exceptional as it may be, there were in Balfour's case reasons purely patriotic: it is not always, everywhere, true as Dr. Johnson supposed, that 'patriotism is the last refuge of the scoundrel'.   Moreover, it is very likely that Balfour found himself more at ease in high office during the war because party politics, for which he had never had much taste, nor, perhaps, much talent, were in abeyance.   This was certainly one of the reasons, why, after the war, he firmly supported the idea of continuing the coalition.

All the same, when he returned to England in 1919, Balfour was ready for a rest.   He relaxed at Whittingehame, in his family circle, and saw old friends.   He went to Eton for the unveiling of his portrait by G. Fiddes Watt that hangs in the school hall there.   He read a little philosophy in preparation for the resumption of his Gifford Lectures;

no doubt, too, he indulged himself with his favourite detective fiction. He had long been a devotee of this 'living dangerously' by proxy, and friends and relatives often recommended thrillers: 'Have you', his sister Eleanor asked, 'read the detective novel by Marsh I told you of—the one that begins with a corpse in a motor-car?' He read Edgar Wallace, too. Balfour had a curious theory about the effect of reading thrillers. He told one of his private secretaries, Captain Alan Graham: 'Detective stories rest me. They affect different lobes of the brain—they draw the blood away.' A correspondent relates that travelling one day by train to Scotland, curiosity made him enter Balfour's compartment while the Lord President was in the dining-car: 'To my astonishment the author of *The Foundations of Belief* was reading *Forty Tales* by Edgar Wallace; *Red Mexico*; and *The Life of Isadore Duncan!*'

This correspondent also adds another curious observation: Balfour's top hat, he says, was on the rack and he tried it on: 'My own head is small but his hat was far too small to fit me, so his head must have been tall and narrow, for his hat was perched on my head.'

A curious sidelight on his changing taste in fiction at this time is thrown by Austen Chamberlain. Asked for his 'desert island' choice, he waved Thackeray (Chamberlain's favourite novelist) aside and said: 'Dickens, perhaps.' Of Bulmer Lytton's *My Novel* he spoke highly; Trollope was mildly interesting; Scott—well. . . . When Chamberlain asked him who was his lady-love among the heroines of romance he replied that it was the girl in the book called *The Initials*. This was a long-forgotten romance by Baroness Tautphœus, published in 1850.

IV

Before the end of the year, Balfour had embarked on his duties as Lord President of the Council, with a seriousness not always displayed by some holders of that office. It is, indeed, an office that can be made as little, or as greatly, important as its occupant sees fit. Balfour saw it as an ideal position from which to forward the policies nearest to his heart; and, since he remained Lord President for the next ten years, apart from a two-year break between 1922 and 1924, his influence was considerable and exercised in many directions. Already, at the end of 1919 he is making the Lord Presidency into a means by which the voice of science may more distinctively he heard. Science was an abiding interest. He delivers speeches on the importance of the alliance between science and industry: 'Looking at the material progress of mankind, as far as we can venture on any prophecy that, and that almost alone, is going to be the main agent of human advance.' Speaking, for example, at a Leeds University dinner he warned his hearers that 'Science itself, the acquisition of knowledge, cannot be pursued

effectively in the spirit of wealth acquisition. If you are to have
applied science, you must have pure science, because applied science
is only the particular use to which pure science is devoted, and you will
never get pure science to be that.'

At the same dinner he went further and pointed out that one could
not even omit the arts, philosophy and theology in science's wider
scope, for 'in an ascending scale, from the narrowest to the loftiest
applications of science, all hang together, all are necessary one to the
other, and none can be safely neglected'. It is worth recalling that he
had been making these points as early as 1891; and in 1908 in his lecture
on 'Decadence' he had in fact said 'science is the great instrument of
social change, all the greater because its object is not change but
knowledge'.

There were, however, other engines of human progress, and one of
these, at any rate in embryo, was the League of Nations. The drafting
of its covenant had taken place in Paris during the Peace talks under
the chairmanship of President Wilson himself. Balfour had no part
in this. The British representative was his cousin, Lord Robert Cecil.
Balfour certainly agreed at this time with the general policy of building
the peace treaties on the League and he made this clear in speeches
from the time that the League began to function at the meetings of the
Council and Assembly in London, Paris and Brussels and finally in
Geneva.

At a meeting at the Queen's Hall, London, organised by the League of
Nations Union, Balfour declared that he was 'not prepared to discuss
seriously with any man what the future of international relations should
be unless he is prepared either to accept the League of Nations in some
form, or tell me what substitute he proposes for it'. But he knew perfectly well that if even one of the great powers began to make reserva-
tions 'the future of the League will be dark indeed'. From the time
the United States withdrew from the League, Balfour knew that the
tasks it could thenceforward successfully undertake were considerably
narrowed in scope. During the discussions leading up to the abortive
Treaty of Sèvres, for example, Balfour was strongly against the League
assuming responsibility for protecting the Turkish minorities. Turkey,
he pointed out, was not amenable to public opinion and public opinion
was the only weapon the League had—it had no force at its disposal.
He may well have thought, as did others, that in due course the League
would itself have both army and finances.

Balfour did not wish the League to become a super-state; in his view
the weapons at its disposal were not fleets and armies but 'delay and
publicity'. The League, he affirmed, 'cannot be a complete instrument for bringing order out of chaos. . . . If you either allow the
League of Nations to be used as an instrument by the free nations of the

world in their own party warfare, or if they try to throw on it burdens
which it is ill-fitted to bear, on them will be the responsibility of
destroying the most promising effort in the direction of the renewal of
civilisation which mankind has ever yet made.'

Balfour twice headed the British delegation to the League of Nations
headquarters at Geneva.   He was always popular at the League meetings: his style of oratory was in great contrast to that of the French and
Italian delegates in particular; he used no gesture and he sometimes
hesitated, yet his delivery was pristine clear, and it had its own special
effect on the meetings.   Under his leadership both in 1920 and 1921,
the League discussed a great variety of problems ranging from the
traffic in women and children to the question of a plebiscite in Upper
Silesia.   As in Paris there was the question of how the Dominion delegations would act, whether they would take their cue from Britain or
not.   In all these matters Balfour played his full part, particularly in
easing personal relations between Britain and France.

Balfour's conferencing was by no means over when he returned from
Geneva in the autumn of 1921.   It had already been decided that he
should be the British delegate to the Washington conference on naval
disarmament and the problems of the Pacific which the United States
Government had called.   This was the first lead given by one of the
great nations in the movement towards disarmament.   The British
Government responded with alacrity to the invitation.

Winston Churchill, then Secretary for Air and the Colonies, wrote to
Balfour on February 26, 1921, that he was worried about Britain's
naval position *vis-à-vis* Japan, with whom the Anglo-Japanese Treaty
was still in force, and the United States: 'Britain is in danger of becoming not only second but third naval power in a few years time,' he
wrote.   He thought there was 'an overwhelming case for the capital
ships as the foundation and ultimate sanction of sea-power'.   He
wanted a programme of four capital ships to be built every year for
four or five years, 'on the lines I declared against Germany in 1912'.
There was, he thought, plenty of time to negotiate with Japan or the
United States for reciprocal reductions and retardation and to prose-
cute research and invention.   Balfour agreed with this and wrote to
Law on March 3, 1921, not proposing a ship-building programme
'of a kind which will inevitably suggest an eternal competition in armaments with the United States'; but suggesting that there was something
'between this and a continued acquiescence in a policy which would
put us in third place among naval powers'.

The Washington Conference was a time of hard bargaining; it was
also marked by Britain's wish to ban all submarines—a wish that was
defeated by opposition from the United States and Europe.   In the
end it was battleships alone that were to be restricted—and battleships

had, in any event, had their day.   Britain thus scrapped some 600,000
tons of naval vessels.

The talks with the Japanese were even more difficult.   They clung
to the Anglo-Japanese treaty, first signed by Balfour's own Cabinet;
but changes had to be made, not least to meet American objections and
fears of war.   Ultimately, a four-power treaty was substituted.   A
further treaty restored the Shantung Province to China—a China,
however, without a central government and disorganised in her relations abroad.   At the same time, Balfour announced that Britain would
hand back her lease of Wei-hai-Wei, that crisis point of a quarter of a
century earlier.

'On the whole', Balfour wrote to his sister Alice, 'the Conference has
prospered beyond anyone's expectations; and so far a very good spirit
prevails among the various Delegations.   It is true that Viviani, who
has been in charge since Briand left, has not made any particular
display either of good manners or of good temper. . . .   The pro-
British sentiment in this country appears to be, temporarily at least, in
the ascendant.'

The Washington Conference was a success, however we may regard
it now after a second World War has given a further violent shake to
the bag of conflicting interests in the Far East.   Balfour perhaps
exaggerated when he described the work there as 'an absolute unmixed
benefit to mankind, which carried no seeds of future misfortune'.   It
could equally well be said that the dissolution of the Anglo-Japanese
Treaty marked the turning-point when Japan shook off European
tutelage and began to look at the Asiatic mainland as a proper sphere
of influence for herself.

Yet in the context of the time it was a move forward; and for Balfour
a triumph.   As a shrewd observer wrote at the time, Balfour 'has
probably, in the course of his long life, had more influence on our
external relations than anyone except an actual Foreign Secretary; for,
like Cyrano de Bergerac, he has often been *celui qui souffle et qu'on
oublie*. . . .   He is conciliatory and firm; he eludes difficulties which
cannot be overcome only to obviate them in more favourable conditions,
he is courteous and unharried; he easily detects insincerity, not always
discernible to those who are themselves sincere; he has a penetrating
intellect and a very subtle mind, combined with a keen sense of
honour . . . he has been equally effective in the Chanceries of the old
diplomacy or on the platform of the new.   He responds to environment.
But his character has a moral quality which invites the best and ex-
punges the worst influences, like a highly sensitised plate that receives
light-marks but is unaffected by blackness; whereas Mr. Lloyd George's
plasticity is affected by every sort of influence that plays upon it.'

Balfour was welcomed on his return from Washington by the Prime

Minister and the Cabinet at Waterloo Station. Crowds waited to cheer. It was Balfour's second, and last, diplomatic visit to the United States, and it must be counted as one of the most successful acts of his later political career. Its success was recognised by King George V bestowing on him, later in the month of February, 1922, the Order of the Garter. At the same time it was intimated to him that an earldom would also be offered, were he ready to accept it.

Earlier Balfour's somewhat cynical view, not so much of honours, but of those who sought them out has been recorded. It is doubtful whether, for himself, he at any time wished to have a title. But in 1922 there were two reasons which inclined him to accept. One was that he had long recognised that the heir to his estates and fortunes would be the eldest son of his only surviving brother Gerald, to whom a peerage might be welcome. The second was the question of his own political future. However attractive office was, the hurly-burly of the House of Commons had lost its fascination: yet it was a big wrench to contemplate.

Balfour consulted some of his friends. One of them was Lord Derby. Derby had been a colleague in wartime cabinets and later ambassador to France. He was not an intimate, though he was a good deal more than an acquaintance; and he had sound sense, no political axe to grind and was himself the holder of an ancient title.

Derby records in his diary for March, 1922: Balfour 'told me in strict confidence that he was being pressed to take a peerage and that he would be very much guided by my advice in the matter. I strongly advised him to take it as giving him much greater opportunity than he could ever have in the House of Commons of helping our Party. I pointed out to him that we had got no leader of the Conservative Party in the Lords except Lord Lansdowne whose successor had never been appointed. That Curzon was the leader of the Coalition in the Lords but not the leader of our Party in itself. He said that the distinction had never struck him but he seemed quite prepared to consider the proposition of his becoming our leader and he said that probably now that he had discussed it with me he would accept the peerage.'

He did so some two months later, having scarcely in the meantime accustomed himself to being—consequent upon the Garter—Sir Arthur Balfour. The Earldom and Viscountcy were given with special remainder to his brother Gerald and to his heirs male and to the heirs male of his brother Eustace. He took his title, Balfour, from the cradle of the family in the County of Fife. The second title was from the name of the hill, Traprain, on the Whittingehame estate. It met with approval on all sides: for once at least the honours were equal between the title and its recipient. Only one dissenting voice was heard. His ex-secretary Sandars made the following comments in print under the pseudonym of 'Privy Councillor' in June, 1922: 'The new prefix of Sir Arthur lamentably suggested the promotion desired by a Mayor, or demanded by a Lobby suitor. And now the formal grandeur of a coronet with its modern dignity, which once he regarded with a puzzled scorn when it was his to listen to the appeal of some aspiring magnate anxious for the enlargement of his social position, completes the transformation. Into his motives for accepting ennoblement and the blue riband, it would be an impertinence to look. But the passing of Mr. Balfour, the defacement of the honoured and distinguished designation, and the exchange of the sober broadcloth of the House of Commons for the scarlet robe of a gartered earl, will long be to the minds of those who have given him their admiration and respect a disappointment and regret. *Surgit amari aliquid.*'

A peerage often marks the end of a man's active political life. It was not so with Balfour. Within the year of his entering the House of Lords, it seemed possible, for a brief day or two, that he would again become Prime Minister.

26. A luncheon given to A.J.B., when Lord President of the Council, on his return from the Washington Conference, 1922

Radio Times Hulton Picture Library

27. A.J.B., 1921

Portrait by Sir James Guthrie

19

POLITICS AND PHILOSOPHY

1922–1924

Balfour's success at the Washington Conference undoubtedly put a feather in the cap of Lloyd George's Coalition Government. But it was almost the only one it possessed. The Irish Treaty, at long last accomplished, seemed to Conservatives of dubious strength or value, and in the summer of 1922, murder and terrorism again spread through southern Ireland—this time against the Sinn Fein leaders of the provisional government. Sir Henry Wilson was shot dead by Irish fanatics in Eaton Square, London, adding fuel to the anti-Treaty flames. Then came the 'Honours' scandal, precipitated by the award of peerages to three very rich men of dubious reputation. A Royal Commission was set up. Meanwhile, unemployment had risen in 1921 to the unprecedented total of 2,100,000, although it dropped again in the following year.

In August, 1922, it fell to Balfour, deputising at the Foreign Office for Curzon who was recuperating abroad, to deal with the problem of War Debts. He wrote a note addressed to France and Britain's other European debtors, stating that Britain did not propose to ask more from her debtors than was necessary to pay her creditors. It points out also that many of Britain's liabilities were incurred for others not for Britain itself. Balfour recognised that this was a fundamental alteration in Britain's methods of dealing with loans to allies but: 'the economic ills from which the world is suffering are due to many causes, moral and material, which are quite outside the scope of this despatch. But among them must certainly be reckoned the weight of international indebtedness with all its unhappy effects upon credit and exchange, upon national production and international trade.

E1jB

People of all countries long for a speedy return to the normal. But how can the normal be reached while conditions so abnormal are permitted to prevail?'

The note expressed the obvious; but it got no support in the City of London, and American reaction was simply that this was an attempt by Britain to evade her obligations, coupled with a rebuke to herself. America went on insisting that immediate arrangements should be made for funding the British debt and this was in fact done in December, 1922. Thus the note, though sound common sense, was further damaging to the general reputation of the Coalition.

It was shortly after this, in the early autumn of 1922, that Law finally capitalised on the dissatisfaction with the Coalition Cabinet. Law himself had retired from the Cabinet owing to ill-health in the previous year; when he returned to political life he had refused Lloyd George's offer of the Foreign Secretaryship. He and other Conservatives had been alarmed by the Chanak incident when it seemed that Lloyd George was going to plunge Britain into war against the Turks. He now began to work for the break-up of the Coalition Government of which he had formerly been a member. This was partly due to his doubts about Lloyd George as a peacetime leader, partly due to the belief that a wartime Coalition ought not to survive long into the peace, and partly, no doubt, due to his own ambition.

Many Conservatives supported him; but many, and among them the most distinguished, did not. Among the latter was Balfour. Balfour recognised that Lloyd George was violently disliked by many of his fellow countrymen. This was partly, he said in a letter of October 26, 1922, because he had been long in power, but he had also been scandalously calumniated. He believed that Lloyd George still had it in his power to do more for post-war Britain than any other visible leader.

While Balfour was still in Washington, the problems of the future had been discussed by Lloyd George. He had told Lord Riddell that 'Balfour may wish to become Prime Minister. If he does, I shall support him. I am in agreement with Birkenhead and Chamberlain.' Lloyd George, however, added that Birkenhead and Chamberlain wanted him to ask Balfour for his support but he had declined: 'I shall do nothing to influence him. He must do just as he thinks best.'

But what weighed with Balfour much more than his personal support of Lloyd George was his belief in the absolute necessity of a Coalition Government in the conditions then prevailing. Almost two years before, on March 10, 1920, he had made his position clear in a letter to Lord Aldenham, the Chairman of the Conservative Committee in the City of London, Balfour's own constituency. (The letter was, in fact, never sent, for Balfour showed it to Law who discussed it with

Lloyd George, and it was decided that the time was not ripe to put into action one of the letter's proposals—namely for amalgamating the Coalition Liberal and the Conservative organisations.)

The main point of the letter, however, was Balfour's assertion that the perils of reconstruction were as great as those of the war and equally demanded a combination of parties. Balfour says that after almost half a century of party politics, he is obviously no enemy to party, 'given appropriate conditions'. The appropriate conditions, to Balfour's mind, were that the differences between the alternative parties must not be fundamental: 'If their divergencies are too pronounced, if they cut too deep into the political and social system of the country, every change of government would mean either revolution or counter-revolution; and in either case intolerable unrest, accompanied not improbably by intolerable coercion.' In the present state of things, unusual evils made unusual remedies inevitable; these remedies ought to be applied with the general consent of the community, and not become controversial weapons in the party game.

Equally, however, differences between the parties should not be too small; if that were so, it would simply mean that those who scarcely differed on questions which were vital would impair their powers of co-operation by quarrelling over differences which were trivial. He did not believe that the task of reconstruction could be satisfactorily carried through by the machinery of the two-party system. He believed that when the needs for combination were past there was no possible reason why the combining elements should not again divide. 'We need feel no anxiety lest the party system in this country should die out. It is an indigenous plant of most hardy growth.'

But at present, he suggests, 'normal methods' will provide no remedies. In Europe, work, credit and transport are all deficient. It was evident that the wreck of the modern industrial system caused by the war was having economic consequences 'undreamed of in a simpler age'. Meantime there was not enough food and coal to go round and the standard of consumption (in many countries) had risen while production was grievously crippled. It was 'impossible that, in such circumstances, there should not be industrial unrest'.

The task of restoration was complicated by the political revolution which had changed Germany, Russia and what was Austria. In all countries subversive elements were on the lookout for some way of furthering their disastrous projects. 'We are dealing with something that is new; and if we are in peril of new dangers we may meet them animated by new hopes. But if so—if we are indeed to engage in an arduous endeavour, not merely to restore what we have lost, but to restore it in a better form, can we hope to accomplish it without the friendly co-operation of men belonging to every class, working through an administration drawn from no exclusive party and organised throughout the country on broad and comprehensive lines?'

Within Coalition circles there had been even earlier an idea of establishing a new party based on the Coalition. The Liberal, H. A. L. Fisher, then at the Board of Education, had on February 4, 1920, provided some notes asked for by Lloyd George on certain propositions of this kind. Much of his thinking—and of many other people— was a result of a fear of a Labour Government coming into power. He argued that while Liberals and Conservatives agreed on many issues, there would be a danger of sharp collision between the Upper and Lower Houses if there were a Labour Government in power. A reform of the Lords, he thought, was necessary. He also suggested proportional representation, votes for younger women and several proposals to catch the Labour vote: more unemployment insurance, a universal eight-hour day, attention to supply of houses and the education of manual workers. He was even prepared to consider the nationalisation of railways ('a natural monopoly'), of the drink trade and of mineral rights, though not of collieries. He admitted, however, that the Civil Service was not formed for the management of industries, and the Government had already more on its hands than it could undertake. He was against protective taxes on food, raw materials or manufactured articles. He believed that expenditure should be reduced on military affairs, that the defence of India should be conducted on the Indian frontier not on the Persian frontier, and that former enemies should be brought into the League of Nations.

Fisher's paper was sent by Lloyd George to Balfour who commented on it to Lloyd George on February 18, 1920. It was, he thought, able and 'perfect in temper and tone'. Nevertheless, it makes Balfour hesitate. It gives in detail a programme about 'which many of your best friends are much divided'. Balfour doubts the expediency of proportional representation, Home Rule for Scotland and Wales and, though he was not in favour of 'unrestricted competition', Fisher's plan would frighten every employer in the country, he thought. To his mind what the Coalition stood for was 'reform versus revolution'. There must not be quarrels among themselves—otherwise they might wake up and find that revolution had won.

With this view Law entirely agreed, so did Lloyd George. There were further discussions among the three men. Lloyd George wrote again to Balfour: 'The gravity of the Labour onset will force us to an early decision. The Socialist movement has behind it most of the organised labour of the country. A more serious development, however, is the extent to which it is attracting the lower middle-classes; and unless there is a concerted effort to arrest this tendency, very grave consequences may ensue to the whole order of society.'

Law followed this up with a letter to Balfour on March 12, 1920, telling him that although the party were united in the Commons, they were not so in the constituencies. These proposals, therefore, came to nothing: Lloyd George's new party under the title of 'The Council of Action' was never more than a paper plan. The Coalition for which he had pleaded in 1910 was doomed to be a non-starter.

Thus when the events of early autumn of 1922 began to gain momentum, the Coalition remained what it was—wartime government lingering on into the peace. As events abroad grew more critical, Austen Chamberlain, who was Leader of the House and the party—he had taken over during Law's illness and had not relinquished office —called a meeting of Conservative M.P.s at the Carlton Club. Before the meeting, Law had again suggested to Lloyd George that he should retire in favour of Chamberlain, thus preserving the Conservative party's unity. Lloyd George refused to move. Law then decided that, whether the Conservative party were split or not as a result, it was necessary that the Coalition Government should be brought down. Balfour's attitude to this decision has been reported: 'He banged the table with his fists and shouted, "I say, fight them, fight them, fight them. This thing is wrong. Is the lead of Law and Curzon to count as everything and the advice of the rest of us as nothing? This is a revolt and it should be crushed." ' In a letter to Winston Churchill, Balfour said that he could not discover what the die-hard Conservative policy was except a dislike of coalition and a criticism of the Prime Minister: 'These provide no very satisfactory grounds for breaking up an historic party.' Furthermore he thought the result of an election might be a Labour victory or some further form of coalition. He thought it better to hang on to the end of the term if the three parties, neither with majorities, were going to get in (or Labour as the alternative).

Law, however, would not now be dissuaded. He decided, very reluctantly, that he would vote for ending the Coalition. Conservative M.P.s supported him and the motion against the Coalition was carried by 187 votes to 87. Chamberlain now consulted his Coalition friends, and it was decided to force Law to form a government. The same afternoon Lloyd George resigned.

Law was now reluctant but, having been elected Leader of the party, be began to choose his Cabinet. It was also arranged that a General Election would be held on November 15. Only four Conservatives from the previous Cabinet were willing to join Law (among them Curzon and Baldwin); Balfour and most of his distinguished Party colleagues refused and, indeed, issued a manifesto advising the Unionist party not to take a course 'which must repel powerful allies in the anxious campaign which lies in front of it'.

Between the announcement of dissolution and the General Election, three of the leading lights opposed to Law went with Balfour to his home in Scotland. A racy account of a dinner party during this visit (October 28-30, 1922) was given by Balfour's niece, Joan Lascelles, who was present, in a letter to her husband. Lloyd George, Birkenhead and Sir Robert Horne were the guests. She reports them as all being in 'great spirits'. She observed the 'disappearance of many glasses of brandy down Lord Birkenhead's throat'. Lloyd George had the table in uproar with his mimicry of Curzon. Then she turned to more serious matters: 'Sir Robert Horne thinks both Conservative Parties together will get 310 seats. Davies—Lloyd George's gaga-looking secretary—thinks it will be 375. . . . They laughed at the present composition of the Cabinet. They said that feeling everywhere showed that people in the constituencies had felt that Law had not been quite straight. Arthur said Law's conduct "had not been pretty".

'They agreed that Law was an ambitious man and that even to be Prime Minister for three weeks would mean much to him. Birkenhead was bitter about Curzon. When Curzon and he parted after Winston's dinner, before the Carlton Club meeting, Curzon's last words had been "I'm game", and then he wrote a letter reflecting at the presence there of Lord Birkenhead and Nunk (Balfour). Lloyd George was very unrestrained about Curzon. Nunk pleaded he was clever. "No", said Lloyd George, "not really and he is so weak", and then came a series of wonderful imitations of old war cabinet days. . . .

'They spoke of Winston and were nearly as funny about him. . . . Lloyd George had turned down Winston's manifesto from a Tory point of view, and had struck out sentences like—"Lord Curzon's idea of the House of Lords is a house of superior people like himself" . . . Winston had lately read the *Ethics* of Aristotle and had confided to Lloyd George that he had already thought of so much of it before for himself. They had a very low view of Amery. They asserted that Amery was the son of a Salonika Jew whose name was Hinri or something like that. Was it libellous to call him a Jew? Can it be a libel to call a man one of a nation that has produced Jesus Christ and Phillip Sassoon, asked Lord Birkenhead?'

Despite this entertaining whistling in the dark, the result of the election was decisively for Law and the Conservatives, who gained 344 seats. Labour got 138, the Asquithian Liberals 60, and the Lloyd George Liberals 57. This meant that Law had a majority of 77 over all parties combined. His Cabinet was far from impressive though he had Curzon at the Foreign Office and Baldwin as Chancellor of the Exchequer. Balfour's old post as Lord President of the Council was filled by his friend, Lord Salisbury. Balfour himself, needless to say, was not included. He remained out of office for more than two years.

II

With the fall of the Coalition, Balfour turned, as he had turned many times before in such circumstances, to philosophy. He had been elected President of the British Academy in 1921 and was responsible for getting the Academy a Government grant some three years later —ironically enough from the Labour Government. Later on, he was able to announce that the Government (this time Baldwin's) had assigned the Academy free quarters in Burlington House; when these rooms were opened in 1928 a special gold medal was presented to him, and at a luncheon the Prince of Wales proposed a toast to Balfour's health.

But his greatest—and almost his last—contribution to philosophy itself was his presentation of the second series of Gifford Lectures, under the title 'Theism and Thought' at Glasgow University in the winter of 1922–3. Inevitably, he had to cover some of the same ground as he had done a decade before in order to clarify the bases of his thought for a new generation of hearers. This he did, without, however, repeating his words, and clothing his ideas afresh. His aim is the same: to show that the values of knowledge are dependent on a spiritual outlook. Before coming to the crux of his lectures, he has a delightful passage on the uses of philosophy, in which, as always, he scarcely errs on the side of large claims.

Having dealt in the earlier set of lectures with the necessity of God in considering the 'humanities', he turns now to perception, to 'methodological doubt', and to 'I and Thou'. Here he often refers to his very first book, *A Defence of Philosophical Doubt,* and some of that work's old, sharp criticism returns. He approves, for example, of Bertrand Russell's declared philosophical scepticism but points out that Mr. Russell draws the line in the use of this instrument at the very point where his own beliefs enter into the matter. Again and again, he hammers home the point that 'We all live by faith; our inevitable beliefs far outrun any reasons which we have as yet been able to find for them. Until this state of things can be remedied (and Mr. Russell's estimate of the potentialities of the New Logic may give us hope), we must be content to adopt a provisional point of view.'

En passant, he has some shrewd things to say of Schopenhauer and Spinoza: 'Is it not obvious that Schopenhauer's metaphysic was due to his pessimism, and not his pessimism to his metaphysic?' And of Spinoza:

'When Spinoza lavishes upon this metaphysical entity every epithet of religious devotion, it is to me as when a child showers endearment upon the doll which she has tenderly adorned, yet leaves it, as she found it, a loveless and lifeless machine.'

Towards the end of the lectures, Balfour mentions that some distinguished critics have found his method of dealing with great subjects 'frankly repulsive'. He says: 'I am charged with endeavouring to rest faith on scepticism, and seeing foundations for belief among the quicksands of philosophic doubt.' This, he says, they interpret as a 'perilous attempt to disparage reason in the interests of religion'.

It is, indeed, a fresh look at the criticisms made of his first book. There, as we saw, there were some grounds for such criticism, though it was in tendency rather than in statement. In his later writing, however, Balfour carefully guards against the possibility of such imputation. As he says:

'The truth of our leading beliefs has been assumed throughout, and my only task has been to discover on what terms this great assumption (for great assumption it is), can best be justified. So far from the argument being based on scepticism, it might be described with more plausibility, though not more truth, as based on credulity. With belief it begins, in belief it ends.'

In the epilogue to *Theism and Thought*, he adds:

'I do not argue that because certain beliefs are inspired, therefore they must be true. I argue that because they are true (or on the way to truth), therefore they must be inspired.'

In 1925, Balfour gave the annual philosophical lecture of the British Academy. His title was 'Familiar Beliefs and Transcendent Reason', and he returned once more to the old problem—namely, that all men had certain beliefs in which their faith was unshakeable but which were 'ill-fitted to bear the strain of critical examination'. Among such beliefs were that I exist as a person, that others exist, that we all inhabit the same physical universe, and so on. But, says Balfour, while science is prolific in assigning causes for beliefs 'the contribution of reason to the production of knowledge seem relatively to diminish'. Causal and rational points of view seem persistently to refuse to harmonise; and 'the discoveries (embodied in scientific theory) effectively discredit the grounds on which they rest'.

Therefore, surely, we 'must assume that Reason is something more and other than one among the many agencies whose undesigned co-operation has, late in time, produced man and the beliefs of man. It must be regarded not merely as a product of evolution, but as its guide. It must be above Nature and before it, as well as in it. It must be transcendent. On no other terms can we reconcile the rational point of view with the causal and smooth away the incongruities of a naturalistic creed.'

This, with some refinements of various points, is the gist of Balfour's argument here—and, save for the more felicitous language, it could well have been his argument in his very first philosophical work.

III

Every year after the war he visited Cannes and the South of France and it was upon his return from his spring visit in 1923 that he was summoned to meet the King in London. What had happened was that Law had received such warnings of the state of his health that he felt bound to resign. He had not proposed a successor. The King, therefore, sought the advice of Balfour as a past Prime Minister and as a senior member of his Privy Council. The choice lay between Curzon and Baldwin—no one else was seriously suggested. Balfour met Stamfordham, the King's Private Secretary, on the afternoon of May 21, 1923, at Carlton Gardens. Balfour has left a memorandum of this meeting. He had two longish interviews with Stamfordham. At the first he told Stamfordham that 'the King should follow the obvious, though not the inevitable course and, in the first instance, ask the Leader of the House of Commons (Baldwin) to form a Government. If for any reason this failed, the situation would, of course, have to be reconsidered. The apparent difficulty was that Curzon was a man of greater age, greater experience and greater position than Baldwin whose experience of Cabinet work was relatively insignificant and who, so far as I was aware, had no special capacity as a Parliamentarian. But undoubtedly there were several difficulties at the present time in having a Prime Minister in the Lords: (1) because the important Cabinet offices were already held in a quite unusual proportion by Peers; (2) because to put in addition to the existing Secretaries of State, a Prime Minister in the Upper House would certainly be resented by a number of people and might make the position of the Leader of the House of Commons one of great difficulty; (3) because (though I did not mention this) the present Opposition were the Labour Party, who had no representatives in the House of Lords at all. I understood from Stamfordham that these views were probably in very close conformity with those already held by His Majesty.'

This is the first time that Balfour's memorandum has been published. He dictated it to his personal secretary the day after his talk with Stamfordham. It puts a rather different light on a situation which has been held to be dominated by Balfour's allegedly personal antipathy to Curzon. It was probably quite true that, having known Curzon and remembering the difficulties he brought to his own Cabinet in the early years of the century, Balfour did not think he would make a particularly good Prime Minister. On the other hand, his reasons for believing that it was unwise to have a Prime Minister, who was in the House of Lords, were cogent and even farseeing. Moreover, as Balfour observes in the memorandum, he understood that the King had already come to similar conclusions. But, as Blake and others have now made clear, the King's conclusions were based on advice from Sir Ronald Waterhouse, Law's Private Secretary, and Law himself had expressed himself less definitely.   All the same, there is no doubt that Law had the severest misgivings about Curzon as his successor, though he fully realised that Baldwin was a comparatively untried Cabinet member.   It was for these reasons, no doubt, that Law did not make his advice on the matter clearer.   Balfour's advice, on the other hand, was precise; its burden incontrovertible.   If personal feelings came into it—no doubt they did—it was right they should.

The decision against Curzon is by no means vitiated by the fact that Baldwin's Government, which came into power at the end of May, 1923, was, to say the least, inglorious: Curzon's might well have been disastrous.   Baldwin, faced by almost $1\frac{1}{2}$ million unemployed, decided that the only means of saving the situation was to extend the protectionist policy already in existence in the form of the McKenna duties.   But he felt it necessary to seek a mandate from the country for such a large step as he envisaged.   Balfour thought his tactics were foolish and he was scarcely surprised at the result.   The General Election in December, 1923, although it left the Conservatives as the strongest party (258 members), put them in an overall minority, for Labour had 191 seats and the Liberals 159.   It was a stalemate, and a very serious one, since the Labour representation was the key to the situation.

What was to be done?   It was clear that a Conservative Government would easily be defeated in the House of Commons by the Labour Opposition assisted by a few Liberals.   Was it better, therefore, that Baldwin should resign at once?   Was it possible that another Conservative Prime Minister could take power and hope to get Liberal support?   On December 8, 1923, Stamfordham saw Balfour.   According to Stamfordham's memorandum of the meeting, Balfour expressed the opinion that if Baldwin resigned the King would naturally turn to someone else in the Party to form a new administration, 'but no lasting government could be formed without a coalition.   He reminded me that he had always been in favour of the last coalition under Mr. Lloyd George and strongly regretted the course taken by the Conservatives which resulted in its downfall.'   Stamfordham mentioned a suggestion that he, Balfour, should become a stop-gap Prime Minister.   There was, of course, the question of a Prime Minister being a Peer, which had lately arisen in the case of Curzon.   Stamfordham goes on: 'Without actually putting a direct question as to whether he would, on the grounds of public urgency, undertake to form a government, I hinted at such a possible contingency and he did not give an absolute refusal.'   Balfour asked only that if the King should require to see him he should be informed since he had intended to go to Scotland. The King replied that he hoped he would, for the moment, remain in London.

A few days later, however, Balfour had set his thoughts in order and had come to a different conclusion. In a letter to Birkenhead on December 11, 1923, he discussed the situation at length: 'I assume for the sake of argument that it would be a national disaster if Labour came in now, even for a brief period. It would give, so the City firmly believes, a shock to our tottering credit, and might have serious electoral consequences.

'It is, of course, evident, not as a problem of high politics but as a question of simple arithmetic, that if Labour is to be kept out it can only be kept out by the joint action of the two other parties in the State. Joint action then in some shape is an absolute necessity. For reasons which we need not go into joint action cannot take the form as yet of coalition. It must be either something less than coalition, or coalition called by some other name. An arrangement between the two parties it must be—or the general feeling of insecurity will be intolerable.

'To make such an arrangement must require some little time, a good deal of patience, and the cooling of some personal animosities. I therefore am in favour of not hastening a crisis; and this can best be accomplished (as it seems to me) by the government following the very sound constitutional practice of waiting for the decision of Parliament.

'Now those who would assent to this general reasoning tell us that it cannot be applied in the present case if Baldwin remains Prime Minister. The Leaders of the Liberal party, it is said, will never consent to give even unofficial support to so unsuccessful a politician; and the suggestion is made, therefore, that by some means or other Baldwin should be excluded and Austen put in his place.

'If it were left for me to settle who should be Unionist Leader, I should not hesitate for a moment. In personal claims, in political experience, in debating power, Austen seems to me incomparably the superior. But I hope his friends will hesitate before they attempt to change horses while crossing the particular stream which threatens to overwhelm us. I have very imperfect sources of information but nothing has reached me which suggests that the party as a whole, however bitter its feelings may be about recent events, at the moment desire the change. And if it does not, it would, I am sure, be a great mistake to force a change upon it by transactions which could be misrepresented as having in them something in the nature of intrigue. Our party has been reduced by the unhappy folly of the late election to miserable proportions; it is already torn by personal divisions; and I feel that it would be still further weakened by the course which I am deprecating—even though that course were followed with the sole object of substituting the more efficient and the more experienced man, for the less efficient and the less experienced.

'But it is said (I gather) that Asquith has declared that nothing would induce him to lift a finger to keep in office any man so stupid as Baldwin. I cannot, however, believe that this represents a settled policy in the face of a grave national danger. The Unionist Prime Minister, whoever he may be, is not going to be asked to fight difficult bills, or to make great departures in domestic legislation; and I imagine that so far as the House of Commons is concerned, Baldwin, if supported by the Liberals, would get on without much difficulty.

'Nothing can be more unsatisfactory, I admit, than the prospect of a session carried on under the conditions that I have sketched. But can anybody improve upon them? Of course it would be much better that the Liberals should be "in" with Unionist support, than the Unionists should be "in" with Liberal support. But I see no possible way of securing the first of these arrangements, while the second may perhaps be within our reach.'

Over the Christmas period of 1923, agitation, not to say panic, continued at least on the Conservative side. And at the turn of the year Balfour received a request from the King for advice as to what he should do if a Minister in a minority advised him to dissolve Parliament. He replied: 'That if, after trial, it is found impossible to form an administration sufficiently stable to administer, there would be no alternative before the Sovereign but that of appealing from Parliament to the country. The King's government must be carried on, and if it cannot be carried on by any party or combination of parties in the existing House of Commons, a new House of Commons must be called into existence.'

Balfour did not, of course, think this at all desirable, particularly since there was no good reason for supposing that a new election would produce an important redistribution of party strength. He agreed, however, that there were precedents which pointed to a different conclusion, for example the election in the latter part of 1885 which gave Gladstone a clear majority, and the election following in the middle of 1886 which put the Conservatives in power for five years. But this, he thought, was largely due to the fact that in between the two elections Gladstone had started his Home Rule policy. Much the same thing had happened between the Conservative majority at the election in November, 1922, and the recent election which entirely destroyed this parliamentary predominance: this again, however, was due to the fact that in the meantime tariff reform had again become a leading issue. He, therefore, thought:

'In such circumstances, it seems to me evident that it would be the right, and probably the duty, of the King to say that unless and until it became clear that no arrangement among the existing parties could provide something like a stable administration, it was his constitutional duty to do his best with the materials provided by the recent appeal to the country.' He felt that any decision which the King might take, unsupported by clear and unmistakable precedent, might bring the prerogative into the 'region of acrimonious platform debate'. In a postscript, he wondered whether it might not be worth while to ask the Colonial Office whether the recent history of the Dominions did not provide precedence for the refusal on the part of the Governor-General to allow a dissolution asked for by Ministers: 'if such precedents exist, they should be examined with care and, if used, with caution.'

Thus, although at first Balfour may have had the idea that he could head a stop-gap government, by the turn of the year he had certainly come to the conclusion that Baldwin should meet Parliament and abide by the decision of a vote of confidence. The King's idea was also to refuse to accept Baldwin's resignation, if it came. Baldwin, who had refused any idea of coalition, perhaps knowing Asquith's feelings, therefore went forward to a vote of confidence and was in due course defeated. The King himself, indeed, it appears had realised that Labour must be given its chance; but since Labour policy included a capital levy and nationalisation, his hesitations are understandable. The situation might well have been postponed, as Birkenhead afterwards thought, if Balfour's opinion about the wisdom of the 1923 election had been heeded: 'Balfour's view of the election policy was not concealed. Had it prevailed, the Conservatives would have been in office today; the Socialists perhaps not for ten years. And tariff reform would not be dead. *Dis aliter!*'

Ramsay Macdonald formed the first Labour Government on January 23, 1924. It had Liberal support. Naturally the faulty tactics of Baldwin, which many believed had led to this dire result, came under scrutiny in party councils. On February 4, 1924, Balfour had what he described in a memorandum of the conversation 'a very informal and very confidential' talk with Baldwin, in which he pointed out that there was no comparison with Baldwin's position then and Balfour's own position in 1906. The election of 1923 was Baldwin's own act, and he had committed himself to the propositions that unemployment and tariff reform were the great pressing problems. As Balfour saw it, he could now either refuse to serve at all, or resign as leader and probably be unanimously re-elected. Baldwin said he proposed to do the latter. (Among other matters discussed was Birkenhead. Baldwin said that he thought him a liability but Balfour said his abilities were too great to ignore.)

On February 7, Balfour attended a meeting of the Conservative 'Shadow' Cabinet; and on the 13th, Conservative M.P.s met at the Hotel Cecil in London. Baldwin there agreed not to press the tariff questions, upon which Balfour proposed that the Party should agree with this. There was to be no change in Conservative leadership.

The history of the first Labour Government does not concern us. It is sufficient to say that it did not long survive and that at the election in November of the same year, 1924, the Conservatives were returned with a majority sufficient to deal with most emergencies. Baldwin again became Prime Minister and formed a strong Cabinet with Churchill at the Exchequer, Austen Chamberlain as Foreign Minister and Curzon as Lord President. Balfour commented in a letter to his sister on November 7, 1924: 'Baldwin's cabinet is a good one, except that he has made a mess of Horne, and I have a little doubt of the wisdom of putting Amery in the Colonial Office, as that now includes the South of Ireland affairs. I believe that Curzon made rather a wry face over leaving the Foreign Office.' Curzon, however, died some four months after becoming Lord President, and Balfour, at this time on a visit to Palestine, was asked to take the vacant post. He had, of course, been Lord President in the later years of the Coalition and it was a Cabinet post—perhaps at this time the only one—which attracted him because it left him free to deal with matters never far from his mind: namely, the propagation of science, and the security of the British Isles and Empire. We shall see now how in this last period of office, which extended to within a year of his death, these two ideas came together and at some points coalesced.

20

THE LIFE COMPLETE

1924-1930

It is now known that as early as 1920 the British Chargé d'Affaires in Berlin was, in his despatches, warning Lord Curzon, then the Foreign Secretary, that it seemed more than doubtful whether the Germans had learned the lessons which the war should have inculcated. He thought it by no means improbable that a strong German Government might be established. The same view came from another quarter. Field-Marshal Sir Henry Wilson, Chief of the Imperial General Staff, after a visit to the Rhineland in March, 1920, remarked that the Germans were no longer taking the overwhelming strength of the Allies for granted: 'I can well imagine a military Germany or a Bolshevist Germany, led by an outstanding figure, raising the call of clearing Germany of all foreign invaders.'

Yet, so soon after the end of the war, it was difficult to see Germany as the danger: to Balfour, it seemed more likely that the threat would come from France. There were warning signs, among them France's intransigence and determination to go her own way in keeping Germany down and making her pay for the war. More important still, however, was France's increase in aerial armaments and the disparity between the air forces of France and Britain.

Balfour had submitted a memorandum on May 29, 1922, when the Coalition Government was still in power in which he put matters very strongly indeed:

'If we had to depend solely on anti-aircraft guns and other land defences, the French air force at their present strength, or, to be precise, at the strength they would possess after rapid mobilisation, would enable them to drop on London a continuous torrent of high explosives at the rate of 75 tons a day for an indefinite period. When it is remembered that in the worst German raid only three tons were dropped on London, and that every raid was separated from its successor by a considerable period of time, the overwhelming seriousness of the situation thus revealed must be obvious to all. Day after day, and night after night, the capital of the Empire would be subject to an unremitting bombardment of a kind which no city effectively acting as the military, naval and administrative centre of a country engaged in a life and death struggle has ever had to endure. The War Office and the Admiralty would be paralysed by the destruction of the material instruments which are necessary for the conduct of their business. Lines of communication would be cut and London would be uninhabitable— probably in fact, certainly in the opinion of those who now dwell there. I say nothing about the arsenals, dock-yards, undefended harbours, nor about the shipping crowded in the port of London, for the details of the picture which I have just outlined are easily filled in.'

The Committee of Imperial Defence, as such, did not meet between 1919 and 1921, but a Standing Defence Committee, headed by Balfour, met from 1920 onwards: its most important recommendation was for an Air Ministry and an Independent Air Force.

On March 9, 1923—the Coalition Government having given way to that headed by Law—a sub-committee of the Committee of Imperial Defence, headed by Lord Salisbury, was set up to study the question of national and imperial defence in general. Balfour, though no longer a member of the Government, was on the Committee and he was also the Chairman of that part of the Committee which dealt specifically with relations between the navy and the Air Force. By this time, it was thought, the disparity between French and British forces was even greater. An interim report circulated on June 12, 1923, said that France possessed at that time about 1,200 first-line aeroplanes, of which 232 were stationed overseas and 946 in France. Of the latter about 600 were organised as an independent air force capable of being used to attack Britain. In a war between Britain and France, these 600 machines might be reinforced from squadrons allotted to the army. The Air Ministry estimated that 866 machines might be utilised to attack the British Isles unless France was simultaneously engaged or menaced on some other front.

Against this Britain, after meeting the needs of the navy, had 52 first-line machines available for home defence (only 24 were stationed in Britain), together with 24 machines attached to the army. Fifteen additional squadrons with a total eventual strength of 172 machines were being formed but would not be completed before 1925. Furthermore, the French Government contemplated increasing their air forces up to a strength of 2,180 first-line machines. Even before the completion of such a programme, the French, it was thought, could, unless opposed by an adequate air force, drop 168 tons of bombs on England during the first 24 hours of war, 126 during the second 24 hours and 84 tons for each succeeding 24 hours for an indefinite period. In other words, the weight of bombs that could be dropped on London in 1922 in a single day would be almost as great as the total weight of bombs dropped on England during the whole of the previous war.

There were certain other unpleasant conclusions that had to be drawn. One hundred and eighty of the French aircraft were stationed in North Africa: 'In time of war these must constitute a source of positive menace, both to Gibraltar and to the movements of British shipping in and out of the Mediterranean. In these circumstances, in a war with France it might be necessary to divert for a time the bulk of our shipping from the Mediterranean to the Cape route.'

The interim report remarked that the military consequences of such a situation were obvious: 'the diplomatic disadvantages, if allowed to continue must be very serious'. The Committee, therefore, recommended that in addition to meeting air power requirements of the navy, army and overseas commitments, a home defence air force should be established 'of sufficient strength adequately to protect us against air attack by the strongest air force within striking distance of this country'. The aim should be a strength of 600 first-line machines; details of the proposal should be left to the Air Staff to devise the necessary proportions of regular and voluntary or reserve proportions.

The need for a substantial increase of air power was agreed, but as Samuel Hoare, the Air Minister, pointed out in a letter to Balfour on June 5, 1923, 'as soon as the details came to be discussed, various complications and side issues arose'. There were those who thought that money spent on air would mean money saved on army and navy. There were others who thought, mainly from the point of view of economy, that greater use should be made of second- and third-line formations than Hoare had originally suggested. Amery and Curzon suggested that the scheme for expansion should be carried out by a committee, but Hoare objected that he could not carry through the details of what was a very difficult plan if he were not to be primarily responsible for it. After all, the Cabinet would have the ultimate say. His letter concluded by asking Balfour for his assistance:

'If you would throw your great weight into the scale of getting the points, to which the Committee today agreed, implemented next Tuesday, you will be giving a valuable stimulus to an immediate air expansion. I fear that without some such push we may drift back into a sea of detail and it will be months before anything effective is carried out.'

The points he refers to need not concern us very closely, although it is

F1jb

interesting to notice that Hoare was worried about the idea that the air force should be expanded by means of increasing the non-regular and in particular the civilian element.   There was a great difference in payment to skilled tradesmen in the R.A.F. and their equals in civilian life. There were likely to be difficulties with the Unions on such questions as pay, hours and overtime.   There might in wartime be a strike at the most critical moment.   He recalls that during the war, labour unrest was not infrequent in the ranks of the class of engineer and artisan who would be required for R.A.F. work.

Balfour replied to Hoare's letter on June 8, 1923.   He was then at Sheringham, Norfolk, whither, in company with many old friends, he had gone for golf.   Unfortunately, he was stricken down by phlebitis, and felt that the chances of his being at the Committee were remote. He agreed, however, that no unnecessary delay should be allowed to stand in the way of expanding the R.A.F.   He thought that the Air Minister should be responsible for the scheme, though he would certainly require outside assistance.   He believed also that the strengthening of the Air Staff was 'an absolute necessity if the air force is to hold its proper place among fighting services'.   He was much more concerned with a first-line force than with second- and third-line formations:

'A certain minimum of highly trained staff officers, officers, pilots, etc., will be absolutely necessary for a first-line force equal to dealing with an unexpected attack by a strong aerial power.   These must be, from the nature of the case, all first-line, and surely we cannot be wrong in setting to work without a moment's delay upon this minimum—the minimum required, let us say, for the first fortnight of a war at full pressure.   I do not see why this should wait till we have settled the difficult problems of reserves—vital as this element evidently is, if our position is to be made secure.   For there is here a point which must not be lost sight of: it is not merely that the issue of a war depending on the air might almost be decided in a fortnight; but that nothing would more effectively check rash councils prevailing in the cabinets of any of our neighbours, than the reflexion that the thing that might happen, in the case of hostilities, would be overwhelming damage to their own capital. They might justly think that in the short time their superiority in reserves would tell, and they might feel confident that the damage they would inflict would then be greater than the damage they would suffer.   But depend upon it, no country is going lightheartedly to embark on a war, if it knows that it would at once have to deal with an enemy not inferior to it in aerial fighting strength—knowing what bombing in the future is able to effect.'

Balfour had not come to his strongly pro-air view without asking himself and members of his sub-committee certain searching questions. Could for example, a fleet of warships, unprotected by aeroplanes successfully protect itself by anti-aircraft fire against an aeroplane attack? Has a defending air force any inherent advantage over an attacking air force whose base is at some distance? Was not final victory in the last war over the submarine peril due in large measure to the use of convoys? But would not an enemy air force find in convoys a peculiarly favourable object of attack? If our aeroplanes were overwhelmed or driven off, was there anything to prevent London being reduced to chaos by the combined effect of material destruction and inevitable panic? The answers to these questions did not presuppose a 'yes' in favour of the air force.

Nor, on the other hand, did such views as those of the General Staff which were submitted to him in June, 1923. A memorandum prepared by the General Staff and dated June 26, 1923, stated: 'The General Staff do not believe that a war with France alone, large as it appears to loom in some quarters, is either the most dangerous or likely contingency. Supposing, however, that France attacked England, is it likely that other nations would stand aside and allow France, first of all, to defeat England and then turn her attention to consolidating her power over Germany or other parts of Western Europe? May we not be forced to do more than bomb the capital and industrial towns of Northern France if we are to prevent her from using her military power on her other frontiers?' The General Staff did not agree with the First Lord that an enemy could be defeated by a series of blows at outlying possessions combined with 'pinprick stabs at his vitals by air forces'. The General Staff then made the following remarkable statement:

'We take, in short, the Great War to be not exceptional but the greatest lesson we have ever had, and that being so, foresee the possibility of our country again at some future time being drawn with all its resources into the vortex of a great struggle and when the little surface blows advocated by the First Lord will prove as ineffective and wasteful as they have in the past. Every important country of Europe is now organising for war by arranging to mobilise the whole national industry for the purpose of carrying on the war.'

The General Staff did not believe that in war any intermediate period would exist during which the control should pass to the Air Staff. There was no objective which could be attacked from the air which was not either a naval or military objective. The Admiralty had proposed attacks on 'the vital centres of national life'. The General Staff believed that this meant in plain language thickly-populated districts: it did not believe that this was either a legitimate or suitable object since the effect on world opinion would be deplorable, and they recalled that Germany's unrestricted U-boat campaign had more influence on the American people in bringing them into the war than any other single factor. They were, therefore, strongly against an

Air Staff, and felt that it should be incorporated in the General Staff so that future development could be from within the General Staff rather than as an outside competing organisation.

Balfour's report on the sub-committee on relations between the army and the Air Force, of which he was chairman, was circulated to the Cabinet on July 21, 1923. He pointed out that the Air Ministry was given control over the air forces of the country in 1917 and was thus placed on a par with the Admiralty and the War Office. Shortly afterwards, the Fleet Air Arm was severed from the rest of the Air Force. The report did not believe that complete severance was suitable. It therefore, proposed that there should be naval officers appointed to the Air Staff and Air Force officers appointed to the naval war staff, and some means should be devised by which the technical knowledge of the Admiralty should be utilised in the technical departments of the Air Ministry. The report entered into considerable detail on this question of seconding.

The report of the Committee as a whole on national and imperial defence was not circulated until November 15, 1923. By that time the recommendations for an increased Air Force had been announced as Government policy in the Houses of Parliament. In view of Balfour's views on the dangers of bombing, a report by the War Office and Air Ministry on the anti-aircraft defences of the south-east of England had been made and approved by the Committee of Imperial Defence. There had been a considerable change of view on the liability of Britain to sea-borne invasion since the years preceding the war. The report stated, on advice from the three General Staffs, that the risk of such invasion was now negligible. Before the war it was established that 70,000 men might elude the fleet: it was now thought that a raid of 10,000 men would be the maximum. There ought to be an inquiry, the report suggested, into the effects of a possible diversion of British shipping from the Channel and the Mediterranean as a result of increased air danger in time of war.

The Committee did not accept the arguments for setting up a Ministry of Defence to override Ministers at the head of Service Departments or the Combined Staffs. On the other hand, it thought that more co-ordination was necessary than was possible through the existing organisation of the Committee of Imperial Defence, and proposed that the Committee should have a permanent chairman who should be deputy to the Prime Minister. The Committee approved the already stated decision of the Government to resume the development of airships, particularly for the carriage of mails, and by means of a commercial service rather than by the State.

When it came to the signing of the report, Balfour was hesitant because, as he said, although he had done a good deal of work 'under very unfavourable conditions' in the sub-committee of which he was chairman, he had 'done no work at all in connection with the main body of the Report'. He pointed out that during much of this period he had been confined to bed. Lord Salisbury, who was chairman of the whole Committee, would not, however, agree to this. He thought that his refusal to sign the main Committee Report would occasion comment. Besides, as Hankey pointed out (October 24, 1923) in a letter to Balfour:

'You did take a substantial share in the early part of the Committee. You drafted the questions to the General Staffs on which the strategical inquiries were based, and you were the principal architect of the interim report on the strength of the Air Force which is embodied in the large report. Finally I was specially deputed to consult you, and did consult you, as to the developments of the C.I.D., and the question of a Ministry of Defence dealt with in another interim report.'

Balfour finally agreed to sign and examined the draft report with thoroughness. He, indeed, sent in seven pages of notes on the draft, mainly concerned with adding lucidity to the prose rather than altering the main tenor of it with which he was in full agreement. In due course, it was decided that the report of the sub-committee should be prepared as a White Paper for presentation to Parliament. Excisions were made of, as Hankey put it, 'matters of a most secret nature'—those specifically referring to the threats of attack on this country and its defence.

On the draft White Paper which followed, Balfour again commented in some detail, and one at least of his comments is still of interest. This is his reference to the Committee of Imperial Defence and the proposal to give it a chairman deputising for the Prime Minister. The Committee of Imperial Defence was largely Balfour's own creation. Therefore, what he has to say about the proposed change is of some historical interest. The Report suggested that the Committee of Imperial Defence had no power of initiative, that it could only advise on matters brought before it. Balfour denied this:

'The C.I.D. properly constituted with the Prime Minister in the Chair, can "initiate" any matters and any policy in matters of defence it pleases. It is quite true that it has no executive power; it cannot give orders to the Departments; but orders to the Departments are quite unnecessary if the heads of the Departments present at the meeting of C.I.D. agree with the policy which the C.I.D. recommends. Are we to understand that under the new system if the heads of the Departments differ from the policy of the C.I.D., the C.I.D. can, without appeal to the Cabinet, directly overrule (say) the Board of Admiralty? If it cannot, I see no theoretical distinction between the new system and the old; if it can, I think the new system is very bad. I quite agree, however, that in practice it is a real improvement to appoint a chairman, whose continuous duty it shall be to consider questions of defence and to carry a burden which is commonly too heavy to be borne by the head of the Government. This could have been done quite easily without change in the constitution of the C.I.D. by the simple expedient of the Prime Minister asking one of his colleagues to be his standing representative.'

Other important developments in defence planning may be briefly noted: from the Salisbury Committee emerged the important Chiefs of Staff Committee: meanwhile, the demand for a Defence Ministry grew and so did the importance of the C.I.D. secretariat which now became, also, the Cabinet secretariat—though not without much criticism. The Defence Ministry was a long time coming: and was not, in fact, made permanent until 1946. Subsequently, there have been considerable alterations in the function, powers and even title of the Committee of Imperial Defence. Some of the assumptions made by Balfour have been disproved. In the last war an enemy *did* attack Britain with overwhelming superiority in air forces, and the attack *was* resisted without utter disaster. Yet in his insistence on the future importance of air power, Balfour was undoubtedly correct. He saw, as few did then, that, as he put it in a speech to the House of Lords on June 16, 1926: 'The whole tendency of modern warlike preparation is in the direction of rapid change and extreme complexity.' He saw, furthermore, that in the future the military side of operations might not be even the major part in hostilities: 'You mobilise science, you mobilise invention, you turn your factories to purposes for which they were never intended, all your industries go in new channels, and the consequence is that the civilian side of war bears a much greater proportion to the whole energies of war than it ever did before.'

But much planning in the 1920s was vitiated by severe economy drives: and furthermore by the existence of the League of Nations, not to mention the secret Ten-Year rule laid down by Lloyd George—that no plans should be made on the assumption that World War would come within ten years. What then of the League of Nations and in particular of Balfour's enthusiasm for it? As we have seen, Balfour's hopes of the effectiveness of the League of Nations in a crisis were modified as soon as it became clear that the United States was not to be a member of it. Furthermore he observed quite early on that his enthusiasm was not shared by all departments of the British Government. He had proposed the establishment of a permanent British office at Geneva in connection with the League of Nations, but a letter from Hankey on January 15, 1921, informed him that the Treasury were against it on the grounds of expense and that the Prime Minister (Lloyd George) thought it premature.

Replying to Hankey on January 18, 1921, Balfour said: 'I do not mind being thwarted occasionally by departmental action. These incidents are inevitable. What I do object to is the dislike that certain departments have to the whole idea and spirit of the League, and their obvious satisfaction in putting a spoke in its wheel. The French are much wiser. I believe they dislike the League as much as our official friends at home; but it is there, and they set themselves to work to use it for all it is worth. They control their League representatives, but help them. They do not make small difficulties like, e.g. The Army Council. (N.B. by the Army Council I do not mean Winston.)'

There were other setbacks to the League. In 1923, Mussolini occupied the Greek island of Corfu to back up his demand for reparation from Greece for the murder of an Italian general by, it was alleged, Greek assassins. The League discussed the matter; but it was, in fact, settled by the conference of ambassadors at Paris which remained sitting until 1925. Again in 1923, the Assembly of the League generally accepted a resolution allowing each member 'to decide in what degree the member is bound to assure the execution of this obligation by the employment of his military forces'. This meant that each member would decide for himself whether his country would fight or not. By 1925 the League had still failed to produce a general system of 'sanctions', i.e. the kind of powers to enable League decisions to be enforced. Once again, protection and security were being sought by regional agreement, and the general disarmament or limitation of armaments that had been promised at Versailles and discussed at Washington seemed further off than ever. The Locarno Treaty and the Kellogg Pact achieved a certain temporary *détente*: but the delay in the preparatory work for disarmament eventually proved disastrous.

These are among the reasons why Balfour devoted some of the hardest thought of his latter years to the question of military preparations. Yet there is really no dichotomy here. He developed no cynicism towards the efforts for disarmament and peace. When Hankey asked him why it was that the nations patiently went on making treaties with each other seeing that to all appearance they broke them without the least scruple, Balfour replied (October 23, 1925): 'The answer can only be that a world in which many treaties were broken and some were kept was better than a world in which no treaties existed at all. A machinery which is always breaking down may be better than no machinery at all. . . . Treaties are certainly better kept than they used to be.' It is also worth noting that even among those whose job it was to see that Britain was kept physically secure, the idea of disarmament was never thoughtlessly dismissed. Thus, Hankey, who was secretary both to the Committee of Imperial Defence and to the Cabinet, sent a confidential paper (dated October 20, 1927) to Balfour suggesting certain measures of physical security without the use of troops or guns. One proposal was for an afforestation of frontiers. He pointed out that Genghis Khan was prevented from reaching far into Central Europe by forests. In the Great War, the lines of advance were selected to avoid forests. In future wars, tanks were increasingly bound to be relied upon, yet they were useless in forests, and air forces even in the distant future would not be great enough to subject the whole country. He, therefore, suggested that forests should be planted wherever one Continental nation could invade another. France was alarmed at the prospect, when the Rhineland should be evacuated, of having to face Germany on a common military frontier. She had an elaborate scheme of defence planned for eight or ten years hence. Could not forests be substituted for fortifications? He pointed out that the débris of a burned forest was almost as serious an obstacle as it was unburnt.

Balfour commented (October 21, 1927): 'A brilliant idea, worth probing to the bottom.' It was, in fact, an idea that France subsequently did probe and these tactical forests exist to this day in that country. Certain planting was apparently also done in England.

It is interesting to note that by 1927 the possible enemy is no longer France, as had been the case when Balfour wrote his early memorandum on air defence. The signs of German recovery and her demand for equality of rights could no longer be ignored. One aspect of it Balfour observed with anxiety in a letter to Hankey on January 13, 1926. He had been worried to learn, via the British ambassador in Berlin, that Germany was rebuilding her mercantile marine out of Government subsidies. This meant that 'a quite abnormal proportion of the new, and because new, up-to-date and, therefore, efficient tonnage of the world has been and is being built by foreigners for foreigners. This is a wholly new phenomenon and an uncomfortable one.' What he foresaw was not trade following the flag, but the flag following trade.

II

During the war, as we have seen, Balfour's lifelong interest in science had given him special insight into the work of military research, and he had set up a department during his period as First Lord of the Admiralty. While he was Lord President of the Coalition Government he had shown particular interest in its successor, the Department (then Committee) of Scientific and Industrial Research and in its counterpart, the Medical Research Council. Curiously enough when the fall of the Coalition Government broke his official connection, he almost at once made another official connection with the Medical Research Council, for he was appointed its Chairman in 1924 in succession to Lord Irwin. Thus, when he became Lord President again he was, as Chairman, responsible to himself as Lord President. His own interest in the work of these organisations extended over their whole fields.

But he saw particularly clearly that military research had to be co-ordinated with many matters which appeared to have only a civilian connotation. For example, for a country largely dependent on its food supply for imports from overseas, the problem of what was to happen during a war when supplies were likely to be cut was all important. Thus in 1921–2, the report of the Committee of Scientific and Industrial Research said: 'The problems which this Board is setting out to solve lie at the root of the economic feeding of any population dependent, as are the people of these islands, on an overseas food supply.' Therefore, in particular connection with the refrigeration and storage of food, the Food Investigation Board was established and a low-temperature research station was set up. This was in co-operation with the University of Cambridge whose Chancellor Balfour had become. Balfour was indeed instrumental in these years in establishing and maintaining the relations between the exciting work of Cambridge and its Cavendish Laboratory with the Government departments which control spending. During the economy drive of 1921, Balfour writes to Sir Eric Geddes, then wielding the economy axe, pleading for the Department of Scientific and Industrial Research as not only spending money but making it. Balfour says that the time when trade and industry languish is exactly the time to improve technical methods.

If all, or practically all, matters of civil research might well turn out to have a military bearing, it was equally true that the research departments of the fighting services had had favourable influence on the general industrial development of the country. As the report of the Committee of Scientific and Industrial Research said in 1925–6: 'The development of shipping, of transport by road and air and of wireless communications, to take only a few examples, owes much to the strenuous and "un-commercial" requirements of the fighting services. With all such developments we are in close touch through the co-ordinating boards of the departments which were set up by direction of the government in 1920.'

This co-ordination was augmented by the creation of the Committee of Civil Research. This, though it actually sprang from an idea of Haldane, Lord Chancellor in the Labour Government, had been pigeon-holed, and it was Balfour who took it up again and pressed it upon Baldwin. This Committee was analogous in constitution to Balfour's other creation—the Committee of Imperial Defence. It was to advise on broad questions of national policy involving scientific and economic research, and to co-ordinate work in which different departments of the State were concerned. Another development for which

Balfour was responsible was the formation of a research special sub-committee at the Imperial Conference over which, as we shall see, he presided in 1926.

Balfour never ceased to emphasise the need for the application of science to industry, and he was not satisfied that it was taking place as it ought to do in Britain.   In a speech on July 23, 1926, he said that if 'we look at the manner in which science is applied, let us say, in Germany or in America, and compare it with the way in which it is applied in England, I am not sure that the result of our investigation will prove wholly satisfactory'.   He pointed out that, for example, the number of professional chemists employed in great American or German works was far greater than in Britain.   He mentioned a number of inventions and pointed out that everyone of them was of foreign origin. Yet Britain's shortage of certain raw materials made such invention even more important and necessary to her.   The future, he said, 'that we look into must be a future moulded by scientific knowledge; if we lack either the imagination or the knowledge we cannot help being at a disadvantage with those who are possessed of both.'

But although he wished the State to help scientific research, he strongly resisted any attempt for the State to control it.   The best men, he said, would not be controlled.   'The State was incapable of forming a judgement on the merits of an abstruse physical or physiological inquiry.   That must he left to the genius of the men themselves.'   He did not, however, believe that it was impossible to combine with the independence of the worker some better reward for the work he was doing.

In the later years of Balfour's time as Lord President, embryo experiments on the division of the atom had already begun.   They were to culminate in the decade and a half after his death.   Neither Balfour nor the scientists themselves at that time conceived either the destructive or the constructive uses of the release of atomic energy. Balfour had certainly more than a notion of the enormous scientific advances already emerging from the experiments of Rutherford and others.   It was he who often saw that these experiments were not starved of money: as Lord President, Chancellor of Cambridge, and an elder statesman with the ear of the Prime Minister, Baldwin, he was in a unique position to help.

It is remarkable how integrated Balfour's life was.   He himself observed in his autobiography that it was a curious accident that in 1928 he should be deeply concerned in furthering the interests of two schemes of public importance, one of which was largely due to the initiation of Rayleigh, the other to Henry Sidgwick.   Both of these he had met when he was an undergraduate at Trinity College, Cambridge.   The two schemes were the National Physical Laboratory for which he was responsible as Lord President of the Council; the other was the British Academy which Sidgwick had promoted and of which Balfour had been an original member.

But Balfour was not merely the co-ordinator or the backer of scientific projects. Many of them he understood and would discuss with the permanent officials of the various departments that came under him. The late Sir Henry T. Tizard, who at this time was assistant secretary in the Department of Scientific and Industrial Research, has stated that on three or four occasions Balfour put back schemes for the Council's reconsideration and he was always right. He did not initiate scientific ideas, and certain of his own pet theories were, according to Tizard, crack-brained. Such was his belief in the possibility of extracting petrol and aviation spirit from peat by adding some fluid to water. We have already observed that these ideas cost him a good deal of money. However 'Peco' was put into commercial production at Dumfries in these years, its managing director being Nils Testrup, the chairman of the company Sir Arthur Duckham. Tizard, incidentally, speaks of Balfour's method of doing business in these years, in particular with his scientific associates. There would be lunch at Carlton Gardens. The talk would be general and the business of the day would actually be done in a brief period after lunch was over. Tizard further added that Balfour, like all true scientists, was religious, but he was extremely sceptical of an after-life or the usual ideas of heaven and hell. As far as the after-life is concerned, this is incorrect as we have seen. Even in the years Tizard knew him, there are direct statements on the matter. For example, Conan Doyle wrote to him asking for his help in asserting the fact of personal survival and spirit communion. Balfour replied (on November 1, 1919): 'I have no doubt myself of the fact of personal survival, to which it seems to me many lines of evidence conclusively point.' He did not, however, wish to enter into controversy on this subject, 'though there is no secret about my opinions'. Conan Doyle again tried to involve him in 1923, but again was stalled, Balfour telling him that his beliefs were older than scientific psychical research 'and do not depend on it'. He had, however, a hearty sympathy for scientific investigation of such matters.

III

In this last decade his great triad of interests was completed: along with strategy, and science, went the Commonwealth, and the Commonwealth Conference of 1926 was both a personal triumph and a historical landmark. The Conference was called by L. S. Amery, the Dominion and Colonial Minister, and opened in London on October 19, 1926. It was at Amery's instance that Balfour became chairman of the

Committee of Dominion Prime Ministers to discuss the future of inter-imperial relations. Such a conference had become a necessity. The League of Nations had already given an independent voice to Dominion and India representatives: they were no longer represented only by the voice of England. The Irish Free State had come into being, and had its own Minister at Washington. Canada and other Dominions, though they had co-operated throughout the war, were determined never again to be dragged into armed conflict by decisions which they could not control. Canada, indeed, exercised a strong and not entirely helpful influence at post-war international deliberations. South Africa was governed by parties not necessarily friendly to Britain; and imperial preferences, agreed at the Imperial Conference of 1923, had been killed by the Labour Government in the next year. The Commonwealth, because of the differing status and outlook of its components, appeared to be gradually falling apart.

Yet there was every reason to try and restore the links before they could be utterly destroyed. The case of the American colonies had not been forgotten. It was clear that the League of Nations was not the universal peace-bringer that had been hoped. But how was it to be done practically and how, just as important, psychologically? Balfour already in 1901 saw that the only remaining link was the Crown. The citizens of the Commonwealth, Balfour then said, knew little and cared little for British Ministries and British Party politics, but they knew and cared for the Empire, of which they were members, and for the Sovereign who ruled it.

It was this point that he went for directly, and almost recklessly, in the formula which he himself concocted after many drafts were amended and rejected. The point psychologically was expressed and agreed in these words of Balfour: '(The Commonwealth is made up of) autonomous communities within the British Empire, equal in status, in no way subordinate one to another in respect of their domestic or external affairs, though united by a common allegiance to the Crown, and freely associated as members of the British Commonwealth of Nations.'

It was a sweeping conception and one that, far from being too stringent, went almost too far for those Dominions where the feelings of kinship with the mother country were strongest. But if there was to be equality of status, there was to be diversity of functions. There might be moments in war or otherwise when decisions would have to be rapid; one of the seven self-governing communities would be obliged to take the lead and the greatest share of responsibility; as long as the centre of difficulty was Europe, it would usually be Britain who took the decisions.

On the other hand, each Dominion Government would have the right to advise the Crown on all matters relating to its own affairs and, more important and more far-reaching still, 'it would not be in accordance with constitutional practice for advice to be tendered to His Majesty by His Majesty's Government in Great Britain in any matter appertaining to the affairs of a Dominion against the views of the government of that Dominion'.

This was a giant step, but it had to be taken.   As Balfour said in his speech to the House of Lords on December 8, 1926: 'A common interest in loyalty, in freedom, in ideals—that is the bond of Empire.   If that is not enough, nothing else is enough.'

The immediate success of Balfour's formula and his brilliant steering of the committee was widely recognised.   The most dramatic evidence of this was in the completely reversed attitude of the South African Prime Minister, General Hertzog.   When he set out for England the very word 'Imperial' avowedly stank in his nostrils: on his way home he said that he no longer feared the Empire for there was no longer any question of domination or superiority over the Dominions.

Balfour in a letter to his sister, Alice, on November 24, 1926, had this to say of the fearsome Hertzog: he is 'really a very nice man; and I hope he has left these shores with somewhat different feelings about the British Empire to those which he entertained on his arrival. . . .   All the overseas people seem to me to be very pleasant and I have formed the highest opinion of them except when they are wrangling over small verbal points.'

Balfour dined with Hertzog one night and, no doubt unawares, impressed the South African leader enormously.   Birkenhead was also present and he and Balfour embarked on a 'fencing match' on the subject of the Dutch influence on Roman Law.   The display lasted from 9 p.m. until 1.25 a.m., and, wrote a fellow-diner, 'Hertzog waxed enthusiastic, and acted as second alternately to F.E. and then to A.J.B.   He said afterwards that it had been the most masterly exposition of learning and historical technique to which he had ever listened.   And A.J.B. was not a lawyer.'

As Balfour once remarked to his niece: 'I'm not erudite—but I've got a smattering of a lot of things.'

Balfour's doctrines on the Commonwealth were not incorporated into law until the Statute of Westminster in 1931.   The debates which led up to it showed that many had not realised the extent to which the doctrine of equality of status radically altered Commonwealth relations. Today, at a distance of 30 years, it can easily be seen that the formula left many things unsolved.   In 1956, R. G. Menzies, Prime Minister of Australia, asked during his visit to the Commonwealth Prime Minister's Conference, that if, for example, there was one common Crown to which common allegiance was owed, and the Crown made peace or war, could there be in a British war a neutral British nation?   Could the

Crown be at one and the same time at peace and at war with one foreign nation? Could the British Commonwealth survive the stresses and strains of completely independent Dominion foreign policies?

Menzies believed that the 'Balfour Commonwealth', as he called it, had changed in vital particulars and was now outmoded. The notion of the Crown and the common allegiance ran through it, as he said, 'like a rod of steel, creating unity out of diversity'. Up till 1948, this was true of every member nation of the Commonwealth. It was a Crown Commonwealth. But in that year India became a republic while remaining a member of the Commonwealth. The Crown ceased to have significance inside India (though India recognises the Queen as Head of the Commonwealth). At conferences of Commonwealth Prime Ministers, defence talks were confined to those nations which, in fact, regarded their defence problems as joint. Australia and New Zealand had remained champions of imperial preference, but none of the other member nations of the Commonwealth had. Whether the Commonwealth could sustain this gradual fracturing of mutual policies and interests, was in doubt, Mr. Menzies thought.

The story has been brought more or less up to date in order to put Balfour's achievement in perspective. But he himself would have been the last person to suggest that any formula had the likelihood of a long life, just as he said of his own philosophy that he hoped it might contribute something to immediate philosophical discussion but doubted whether it would have any importance for the future. Moreover, his formula did see the Commonwealth through the dangerous years of the 1930s and the Second World War. That is no small thing.

After all, Balfour's conception of Commonwealth was, however he might dress it up for the more sentimentally-minded, essentially practical. It sprang from his realisation more than a quarter of a century before, that England's unquestioned lead in supplying the world with the goods it needed could not last forever: the trade figures that he had considered, both before and after the turn of the century, were warning lights. By the end of the First World War they had turned red. That is why he hammered unceasingly at the theme that Britain should by every means in her power hold her scientific, inventive supremacy; it was why he never tired of emphasising the importance in doing so of education; it was why he saw that if Britain did not hang together with the Commonwealth she might well hang separately. Britain was a small country who, if she could not sell her goods could not feed herself; the Commonwealth could feed her, and perhaps here his interest in refrigeration is relevant. The Defence Committee, which to all intents and purposes he brought into being, had the word 'Imperial' in the middle of it. He would probably have liked to think that the Commonwealth could form one vast front, perhaps even merge with, the United States in one Anglo-Saxon federation, thus reversing the effects of the ill-starred war of the eighteenth century. He never ceased to speak and work for closer comprehension between the two English-speaking communities.

IV

Thus his basic political thinking had a lifelong coherence, not always to be found among politicians. But if the Commonwealth was one of the essentials of this coherence, it sprang not so much from any political influence—Salisbury, after all, never seriously considered the matter— but from the 'Souls': they were the forerunners of those who were exceedingly serious-minded (not jingoistically-minded) on the subject of the duties of Empire. And if such wider political attitudes had a coherence, it was modified by an innate scepticism as evident in his philosophy as in his deep-lying sense that 'The best laid schemes of mice and men gang oft agley', that in the words of Frédéric Bastiat: '*Il y a ce qu'on voit et ce qu'on ne voit pas; et ce qu'on ne voit pas est toujours le plus important.*' He knew, as George Wyndham reported him as saying, that there had been one ice-age, and there might well be another.

At bottom, philosophy was at once his solace, and a wry smile at the puny efforts of men to rule themselves or to better their estate. It was an implicit assertion, too, that there are more things in heaven and earth than are to be found in practical politics: surely he would have agreed with Gissing that practical politics is a diversion of the quarter-educated.

There is at the heart of Balfour an intuition beyond the simple evidence of the senses; this intuition was available to all, and was found not only among the religious but among scientists; this explains why Balfour had very little time for dogmatic creeds and why the religious controversies into which he was led in the 1890s and later in connection with his Education Act bored him to extinction.

To the casual eye, he seemed to be a dilettante, even a poseur; yet some basic facts of life he saw very clearly. He showed this at the National Conference on the Prevention of Destitution on May 30, 1911, when he said: 'The first rough division between the happy and the unhappy, I should put at the division of health. I should say that roughly—very roughly—it corresponds with the division between the well and the ill: and if I were asked what the next rough division was, I should say it was between those who suffered from destitution and those who, whatever their profession in life or their monetary position might be, do not suffer from destitution. The man who is ill becomes destitute, and to all the horrors of illness are added all the horrors of destitution, each acting and reacting upon the other. And then you have the third tragedy of the situation, namely, that when you have sickness and destitution combined, each one acting partly as cause and partly as effect, there is a further action and reaction upon family life in which the man or woman feels that his or her illness is the cause of suffering not merely to themselves but to those who are nearest and dearest to them.'

This did not turn him into a Socialist: we have already quoted from his substantial and convincing statements upon this subject, and in these latter years of his life he returned to it: 'You must have production before you can have distribution; and what is the use of squabbling about relations between employers and employed in cases where it may even be doubtful whether there shall be production at all?' In 1927 he spoke of 'A most ludicrous and pernicious doctrine'—namely that all our hours of work are a minus quantity in the happiness of life and all the hours of idleness are plus ones. 'I do not wish to put this too high. I am a great lover of idleness. I am always glad to hear that there are some hours of the day in which no one is going to ask me to do anything. Yet, after all, if you were to segregate 100 children, or 100 adults for that matter, in two halves of fifty, and say to one half, "You shall work your eight hours a day steadily, week in or year in, and week out or year out," and say to the other half, "You shall never do anything," then those who were ordered to do nothing would certainly commit suicide before the experiment had lasted very long.'

He emphasised in this speech, which was in support of the National Institute of Industrial Psychology, and delivered on May 5, 1927, that, as he had remarked as early as 1908: 'I do emphatically say that unless the work we do in life can be made inherently interesting—I do not say pleasurable—we have not yet got at the root of any social problem. The art of life is to make uninteresting parts into an interesting whole. No man's work—I do not care what he works on—is in itself, taken bit by bit, of an exhilarating character.'

It is difficult to connect this kind of insight with the picture of the lofty, detached aristocrat some have drawn of Balfour. When he says that the root of any social problem lies in the interest, or otherwise, of work, he is a forerunner of the industrial psychologists of the 1960s.

But destitution would not be ended tomorrow; the problems of philosophy would never be ended at all; *tout passe*, and the ways of progress, or as he would prefer to say, amelioration of the human estate, spring not from hatred but from methods parallel to those of science. He expressed this most cogently and with a beautiful lucidity in his most brilliant essay on Francis Bacon which comes nearer to the truth about that great man than anyone has yet approached: 'Bacon', he said, 'looked with "pity on the estate of man". It is true that he saw in science a powerful instrument for raising it. But he put his trust in no petty device for attaining that great end. He had no faith in the chance harvests of empirical invention. His was not an imagination that crawled upon the ground, that shrank from wide horizons, that could not look up to heaven. He saw, as none had seen before, that if you would effectually subdue nature to your ends, you must master her laws. You must laboriously climb to a knowledge of great principles before you can ascend to their practical employment. There must be pure science before there is applied science. And though these may now appear truisms, in Bacon's time they were the prophecies of genius made long before the event. I should like to ask those more competent than myself to decide the question when it was that this prophecy of Bacon began in any large measure to be accomplished. I believe myself it will be found that it is relatively recently, say within the last three or four generations, that scientific research has greatly promoted industrial invention. Great discoveries were made by Bacon's contemporaries, by his immediate successors, and by men of science in every generation which has followed. But the effective application of pure knowledge to the augmentation of man's power over nature, is I believe of comparatively recent growth. . . . In science is to be found the most powerful engine for the material improvement of the estate of man.'

Balfour's life was beautifully balanced between work and play, between politics and intellectual retirement from politics, between speech-making and committee-steering and golf, between the company of gay women and agile intellects and something so private that we barely catch a trace of it, but whose nearest description would be the word contemplation. This is why he never grew mentally old. Amery says of him in these latter years that he was 'somewhat deaf, occasionally somnolent, but with a mental edge unimpaired by the years'. The fact that he appeared to some to be the victim of his own nearly natural pose, or as Wells put it, that he 'ends in an attitude', is really a tribute to a balanced, fulfilled character. He remained endlessly interested in the variety of life. As his niece says, he was unlike an old man in that he constantly looked forward and seldom back. He rejoiced in the society of young people: 'If it were not for the young how would the world move? Whatever the old people may think of themselves, it is inevitable that they should be somewhat petrified by long experience as well as taught by it and that they should lose some of that flexibility of mind which is possessed by youth.' He was 74 when he said that.

The last four years of his life show his interest and his enjoyment scarcely abated, and his influence increased. In March, 1925, he undertook his first and last visit to Palestine. His old friend Weizmann had invited him and he says Balfour's acceptance was 'instant and enthusiastic'. The occasion was the opening of the Hebrew University on Mount Scopus. Weizmann records: 'Balfour's appearance set off a tremendous ovation, which was hushed into complete stillness as he took his place on the platform.' In Tel Aviv, the new Jewish city on the coast, women wept for joy to see him and pressed forward, as Weizmann says, to 'gently touch either the car or Lord Balfour's sleeves and pronounce a blessing on him. He was deeply affected.' Everywhere he went he talked to the settlers and said: 'I think the early Christians must have been a little like these men.' He observed with intense interest the beginning of Palestinian culture drawing its elements from every country.

Balfour later said of his tour in Palestine that 'it reminded him of a General Election tour—but with everybody on the same side'. That may have been true in Palestine, though even there incidents were caused by the Arabs. There were far more serious incidents when Balfour, wishing to visit the antiquities at Baalbeck in Syria, crossed into French-mandated territory and was the unwilling cause and horrified spectator of rioting and firing on the mob by French cavalry in the course of which three people were killed. Balfour, in fact, never got beyond Damascus.

Balfour's correspondence in these final years is not only indicative of the width of his interests, but is also revealing of certain aspects of his mind and character perhaps submerged during his more highly-charged political years. He had time to study again the question of relativity. It is, he told Sir Oliver Lodge, 'a subject which I think is at present in a very unsatisfactory condition. No living philosopher, except Bertrand Russell, and possibly Bergson, is competent to deal with the mathematical side of this; and yet I do not think it can be left entirely to mathematicians.' He exchanged letters with the newly formed B.B.C. on whose national Lecture Committee he sat, as also on the National Committee of International Co-operation, founded by Stephen Gaselee.

He delivered himself of the opinion that 'Robert Bridges was not a great poet, and certainly not a popular one.' He wrote proposing that Edith Wharton, the American novelist, should receive the Nobel Prize. He corresponded with Sir Almroth Wright, the bacteriologist, on vaccine-therapy, and he exchanged books with General Smuts (who had recently published *Holism and Evolution*); he tells him in a letter on October 18, 1926, that he has been 'driven by personal tastes and external compulsion to combine, or attempt to combine, politics and philosophy'. He revealed to John Buchan, who had written an essay about him, that 'I was taught Latin grammar though I never learned it, while as regards English grammar I neither learned it nor was taught it.' He received letters illuminated on silk from Prince Pokugawa, the former Japanese Foreign Minister whom he had known in Paris days. He corresponded with Bergson, and as the result of a complimentary reference to the work of Freud, he received a copy in German of one of that doctor's works.

There are also letters in these years from such diverse personalities as Professor A. S. Eddington, the physicist, and Baron von Hügel, the historian of mysticism. George Moore, the novelist, wrote to him on July 20, 1926, mentioning that he had spent 'many hours very pleasantly reading your quiet meditative prose, yourself always reflected in it as the landscape is in the stream'. Moore refers to Balfour's essay on Handel: 'I came upon pages that Pater would have admired as much as I do. When you mention Bach's name, the prose rises as it does in Fromentin when he speaks of Rubens.' Moore adds quaintly: 'Some thirty years ago, in a long talk with your brother I did not conceal my regret that you had not devoted your life to aesthetics instead of dividing it between aesthetics and politics. Your brother did not share my opinion.'

He expressed strong views to Stamfordham on the subject of the Order of Merit. It ought not to be given on the advice of the Prime Minister, he says: 'I see signs of the pure Whig doctrine eating into it.' Yet Balfour himself had been accused of Whiggism in his relations, as Prime Minister, with Edward VII. With King George V, however, he had established a bond of mutual esteem and indeed affection—affection that had been lacking in Balfour's relations with the King's father. He was sometimes asked to advise on the King's private problems: for example, in 1921 the King's Privy Purse had been short by something like £100,000. If he could not put more money in it, a good deal of the pageantry to which the nation had been accustomed would have to go. Should he sell some of the art treasures at Windsor? (Balfour's reply, alas, is not recorded.) In 1925, the King consulted him in his capacity as Chancellor of Cambridge University. The King, wrote Stamfordham on September 2, 1925, 'does not know whether you see the secret reports from Scotland Yard on the revolutionary organisations in the United Kingdom'. But, he continued, the King thinks you ought to know as Chancellor of Cambridge that a certain tutor there is a Communist propagandist among undergraduates and is no doubt sowing seeds of sedition. Balfour inquired into the matter, but was informed by the University authorities that the man concerned did not seem to be particularly pressing his views. He was also consulted by the University about certain undergraduate rags reported in the newspapers. Balfour, perhaps remembering his own undergraduate appearance in the Police Court, smoothed matters over.

Among the multitude of honours that came to him in these years was the membership of the Stationers' Company to which he was elected at a luncheon on July 3, 1925. What makes this event memorable is that Rudyard Kipling, who was present, wrote on the back of the programme, which Balfour retained, this verse:

> 'The Foundations of Philosophic Doubt
> Are based on this single premiss:
> "Shall I be able to get out
> To Wimbledon in time for tennis?" '

Balfour's domestic life continued on its even way. His sister Alice was still the controller of his households and they were full as always with the young members of his family. His personal secretary, W. M. Short, had resigned in 1920 after 20 years with him, mainly because he wanted more money. His new private secretary was Miss Constance Bliss. After the war, his nephew by marriage, Captain Edward Lascelles, had succeeded the disappointed Sandars.

Much of his time in his last years was spent with his niece and biographer, Mrs. Blanche Dugdale, who also assisted him in writing his autobiographical fragments by sorting through some of the voluminous papers that had accumulated in half a century. It was to Mrs. Dugdale that he made some of his most illuminating comments on the past, although she records that it was always difficult to direct him towards the past rather than towards speculation upon the future. He tells her, for example, that he is not much alarmed by Russia, whatever his earlier views had been. He did not believe that the Russians were a military danger since they had never yet succeeded in waging a big war. He supposed, however, that it was possible that, in collaboration with the yellow races, they might form some kind of economic tyranny.

Mrs. Dugdale badgered him for a statement of what the principles of Toryism really were, but she never got further than the reply that: 'I suppose the principles of common sense, to do what seems to be the right thing in a given case.' She asked him who he would like to have consider his philosophical work in the life she intended to write. He suggested Henri Bergson or his old friend, Professor Pringle-Pattison; and it was the latter, in the end, who wrote the appreciation printed separately at the end of Mrs. Dugdale's biography. It was during these talks that he made the comment so typical of him: 'I don't very much care whether there is an appreciation of my philosophy. Do not worry your head with expecting permanence for philosophic thought. Not even relative permanence. All that any man's thought is, is a contribution greater or less to the stream of thought of his own time, which flows on and turns into the thought of the next generation. There is a fashion in thought—as impermanent as a fashion in dress. Something remains —goes into the stream; but it is no use to spend time in measuring the value of the fashion itself. So do not worry your head about what need be said about my philosophy.'

Balfour had outlived many of his friends. Lansdowne, friend of his youth and colleague of his Premiership, died in 1927; he was followed by Asquith in 1929. A splendidly humorous piece of nosology occurs in a letter to his niece, Joan Lascelles, on September 24, 1927: 'All my contemporaries except those who are dead, seem to be rapidly dying; but this is of course to be expected. I fear it is also to be expected that those who survive do so in a very enfeebled condition. Most of my visitors this year have either been blind, deaf, halt or maim! I am so far only deaf, and even that, I think, is slightly better—perhaps owing to the extraction of three teeth! Otherwise aunt Nora appears to be the most juvenile of the family, though her voice is not what it was, and her walking powers, though quite good, are not what they were.

'The present inhabitants of the "Cripples Home" ' [i.e. Whittinge-hame], 'other than the family, are my dear friends the Talbots. She is completely deaf without her electrical machine, and very nearly deaf with it; moreover, she often speaks very indistinctly. The communication of spirits is not easy under these physical conditions. As for the Bishop, he has just recovered more or less from tumbling down ten stone stairs at the Deanery of York—formidable bruises in consequence and slight concussion, age 83! He also is very deaf, so that the exchange of ideas between him and Nora at meals has its difficulties. Auntie is very well, but almost a complete cripple; and I greatly fear is getting worse.

'Melco' [i.e. Lady Wemyss] '(also suffering from arthritis!) comes today, with young Lady Leconfield. I take the gloomiest view of aunt Evelyn. Lady Wolverton has just returned from the Bohemian Baths which she went to for arthritis; but I admit that I saw few signs of a disease, though she is now stouter than she used to be or ought to be. The only other cripple who has been here is Asquith who came to luncheon yesterday. He seems to me now in quite good spirits, though still lame.

'As Whittingehame seemed insufficiently supplied with invalids, I went to see Rosebery, the week before last. He was pleasant and interesting; but with no other companion than a little grandchild, whom he adores, to get to the dining room he had to be lifted bodily from his sofa on to his wheelchair, and again from the wheelchair to his seat at luncheon. I am afraid he is physically failing.

'I am sorry to say that Ruth and the children go away on October 1st—so that when you come here I am afraid you will find no one under 76 years of age!'

On July 25, 1928, Balfour celebrated his 80th birthday. He was given a luncheon by the British Academy, and the Prince of

Wales proposed his health in a speech which alluded to the 'half century in which he had maintained his golf handicap at a lower level than mine is ever likely to attain'. There were telegrams from the King and from all over the world. On the same day he received the gift of a Rolls-Royce motor-car from friends of all political parties in both Houses of Parliament. The speakers in Palace Yard were the Prime Minister, Baldwin, Lloyd George and, on behalf of the Labour Party, J. R. Clynes. It was Winston Churchill who, after Balfour's brief speech of reply, called for three cheers. This was the last time Balfour entered parliamentary precincts.

In the same year Balfour heard of the planting of the Balfour Forest at Ginegar in the Valley of Jezreel, to commemorate his work for the Jews. Somewhat previously, he had written to L. Stein, secretary of the Zionist Organisation in Britain, recalling the decade that had passed since the famous Declaration, and adding: 'Nothing has occurred during that period to suggest the least doubt as to the wisdom of this new departure. The experiment was a bold one, dealing with a unique situation in a manner wholly without precedent in history. I am, however, convinced that if it be supported by Jewish communities throughout the world its success is assured.'

In 1928, symptoms of the failure in the circulatory system which was to cause his death had appeared. This did not, however, for some time prevent his attending Cabinet meetings and being frequently asked for advice. When later he was unable to attend the Cabinet meetings, though he had moved down to his brother's house at Woking to be nearer at hand, he was kept in touch by jaunty reports of Cabinet meetings from Lord Salisbury. Such problems as whether to put a safeguarding duty on wool before the election or after, whether a Channel tunnel was wise or not (despite Churchill's advocacy), and what to do about China, then in a state of crisis, came before him and were commented upon. From Salisbury's accounts of the Cabinet, it is saddening to observe that in the year 1929 the least mentioned subject was the question of unemployment, then increasing rapidly. Salisbury observes a 'fatalistic pessimism'. He reports Baldwin as 'Oracular . . . uninformed . . . confused.'

Baldwin had something approaching veneration for Balfour, and his letters to him are not so much friendly as fawning. When, owing to increasing difficulty in walking, Balfour offered his resignation, Baldwin would not listen to the suggestion: he wished Balfour to receive Cabinet papers and to be available for consultation even though he were not able to attend the meetings. Thus when Baldwin's Government resigned in May 1929, Balfour resigned with it. On May 25, 1929, Baldwin wrote to Balfour: 'I know it is not your intention or desire to continue in office if we should be returned again, but I hope that you would not be averse from continuing your membership of the Committee of Imperial Defence which is your own child and would indeed be an orphan without you. . . . I have always been conscious of the honour you did me in accepting office under my leadership. For a generation, in a comparatively humble position, I had been an admirer and a loyal follower of you as a leader and it was with no light heart that I found myself unable to see eye to eye with you in 1922. No one could then have foreseen the course events have taken and I was deeply touched by the magnanimity and desire for further service that led you to accept my offer in 1925. It has always been a pleasure to work with you and I know that these four years of close association with you in counsel have taught me much.'

Thus Balfour's official life came to an end. He motored to Bognor, where the King was recuperating from a serious illness, to deliver up in person the Seals of his office. They lunched together and spent part of the afternoon in the garden. 'It was a moving thing', he said in the evening to Major Edward Lascelles, 'to do what one knows to be one's last public action, after fifty years of public life.'

He returned that evening to Fisher's Hill, his brother Gerald's house at Woking, and never left it again. During that summer and autumn his sitting-room was filled by family and visiting friends— Hankey, Baldwin, Lloyd George, Lord Midleton, Churchill, Philip Snowdon, the Salisburys, Lady Wemyss, Lady Desborough, Dame Edith Lyttelton, the widow of his perhaps dearest friend Alfred. He still appreciated solitude, however, and when he could no longer read easily, he allowed himself to be read to. His interest in the political scene continued and he spent many hours listening to music on the huge horn gramophone. As always it was Handel who affected him most.

It was at this time that Balfour, at last, became really worried about money. Before, when his investments flopped, and his rents ceased to be productive, he had refused to take matters seriously—he had an incurable optimism about money and pursued his even tenor of spending whatever his advisers told him.

Now, as he lay upon his deathbed, these warnings returned to him. He told his relatives that he hoped the family would be able to afford to go on living at Whittingehame House (as it turned out, they could not); and towards the end asked his nephew and heir, the present Earl of Balfour, whether the family would be able to eat after his death. This, at least, was not in doubt.

Early in March, 1930, his strength began to ebb faster, and he could speak very little, though Mrs. Dugdale who was present records that he never failed to greet his family with a smile. His last visitor was Weizmann, the Zionist leader. Mrs. Dugdale records: 'No one but myself saw the brief and silent farewell between these two, so diverse from one another, whose mutual sympathy had been so powerful an instrument in the history of a nation. The privacy of their last meeting would not be broken here except for one reason. A few days later, millions of poor Jews in the ghettoes of Eastern Europe and the slums of New York were bewailing with deep personal grief the loss of a British statesman whose face they had never seen. All over the world the ceremonial candles were lit in the synagogues, and the Prayer of Remembrance, the A'skara, was chanted. Never in living memory had this been done for any Gentile. . . . I who saw the look with which Balfour moved his hand and touched the bowed head of the other, have no doubt at all that he realised the nature of the emotion which for the first, and only time, showed itself in his sick-room.'

Shortly before the end he asked to see James Coleman, for 20 years his personal servant. Balfour took his hand and thanked him for all he had done. The last scene of all is best described by Mrs. Dugdale who was present. It was early in the morning of March 19, 1930: 'He had slept almost continuously for the two days before, but there was no reason to suppose that this state might not have gone on for some time, and no special summons had been sent to those of the family who were absent at the moment. He died holding the hands of two of his own generation who were dearest to him, his brother Gerald, and his elder sister, Mrs. Sidgwick. Gerald Balfour's wife, Lady Betty, their son Ral, with his wife, and myself were also in the room. We saw that he recognised us almost till the very last moment. When the moment came we hardly knew.'

At Balfour's own request no blinds were drawn in the house. An offer of burial in Westminster Abbey was immediately made but regretfully declined. His own wish was to be buried at Whittinge-hame in the family burial ground where were the graves of his mother and of his brothers, Frank and Eustace. Wreaths came from all parts of the world and visitors thronged to the estate in East Lothian. The service at the church was followed by the private burial whither the body was drawn across the snow on an estate cart by big Clydesdale horses.

In this manner, Balfour entered into full knowledge of those mysteries that had so long interested his speculative and inquiring mind. Though he had said that 'our beliefs must be provisional', it seems likely that he entered believing, and believing that human proof or disproof was irrelevant, in 'a God whom men can love, a God to whom men can pray, who takes sides, who has purposes and preferences, whose attributes, howsoever conceived, leave unimpaired the possibility of a personal relation between himself and those whom He has created.'

APPENDICES

I

PRINCE ALBERT VICTOR

Proposed marriage of Prince Albert Victor ('Eddy'), Duke of Clarence, and Princess Hélène, daughter of the Comte de Paris

Other material relevant to this difficult issue is to be found in the Balfour (Whittingehame) Papers:

On September 9, 1890, some ten days after Balfour's memorandum to Salisbury (quoted in the text, pp. 122ff.), the Comte de Paris refused his consent to his daughter's changing her religion, a requisite laid down for the match. General H. F. Ponsonby, the Queen's Private Secretary, wrote on September 10, 1890 to Balfour:

'The Queen asks for your opinion as to whom the succession would go if the Duke of Clarence married a papist but had children who were Protestants.

'His Royal Highness saw the Queen yesterday and was depressed at the aspect of affairs. He told the Queen that if consent to the marriage was refused he would marry Princess Hélène and lose his rights to the throne. But that his children would be Protestants and he imagined would therefore succeed.'

Ponsonby added two 'Private' *postscripta*:
'As my reply to the Queen on the succession question was different from her view and undoubtedly vague she desired me to ask you for your opinion.

'She added—"Mr. Balfour has been so kind and sympathetic that I should wish all correspondence on this subject to go only through him."' (Presumably a comparison with Salisbury's coolness.)

The second PS. read:
'If you answer my letter—direct to H.M., or through me, please say what you think of the situation as she hopes for some criticism, advice

or hope from you. I understand that the Comtesse de Paris and Princess of Wales tho' startled by the vehemence of the Count's refusal hope he will give way under persuasion and pressure.

'All I can advise is—"wait". H.M. asked why Lord S. sent for the Act of Succession? This was not to be repeated to you. The Q herself has been reading it and asks me questions on it which I can't answer. Hence this large sheet of paper for a dissertation on that measure.

'If the heir marries a papist the Crown shall descend to such person being a Protestant as would have inherited if the papist marryer was dead—now who is this? (The Queen asks.) If A.V. renounces and marries an R.C. then this question will be settled by the Act of renunciation. But if he does not renounce and marries R.C. he becomes as regards the succession as if he were dead—then when the Crown is vacant will it go to his eldest son being a Protestant—can a baby be a Protestant? I think carefully over it and wonder what lawyers would say.

'He A.V. cannot lawfully beget a child till after he is married.

'By marrying, he becomes dead. A dead man can't beget a child.

'Therefore all his children are as if they were dead—?

'What fearful controversies are in store if he marries an R.C. and has a stalwart son who is a Protestant.

'The Orleans will be a busy family pretending to both French and English thrones.

'My private opinion is that love will cool if there is no throne in the case and at any rate I can suggest no other advice than wait.

'The Prince of Wales is strongly in favour of the match if the difficulties can be surmounted.'

To these missives Balfour replied from North Berwick where he was golfing on September 11, 1890:

'You tell me that H.M. desires to have my opinion as to whom the succession would go if the Duke of Clarence married an R.C. but had Protestant children. I am afraid that my opinion is worth very little; I have not the Act with me, and in any case could only speak as a layman; but my strong impression is that under such circumstances the Duke would not only lose the Crown for himself but for his children also.

'My reasons are these—I cannot believe that the framers of the Act of Settlement can have thought that a Prince who (on their theory) was unfit to govern was nevertheless fit to educate the heir to the throne. They can hardly have been of opinion that, while the influence of an R.C. wife on her husband would be fatal, the influence of an R.C. mother on her children would be innocuous. I think, therefore, that they probably intended to exclude from the throne both the heir marrying a Catholic and the issue of such a marriage.

'It is evident that on the opposite theory grave complications regarding the succession might easily arise. For if the children were, by becoming Protestants, to regain the rights lost by the father, why not the grandchildren and the great-grand children? Let us suppose that the heir marries an R.C.: he, of course, loses the succession: his children follow the religion of the mother; *they* therefore *also* lose the succession:— but their children become Protestant—what is to happen then? According to what I believe to have been the intentions of the framers of the Act of Succession, this would make no difference. The rights originally lost could never be recovered by any reversion to the Protestant faith. But if, on the other hand, the heir *de jure* could always become the heir *de facto* by being baptised a Protestant it might be impossible to tell in what line the right to the Crown would descend and the most serious public inconvenience might consequently arise.

'I feel it almost an impertinence to give an opinion on so grave a legal question without possessing either the qualifications or the material for making that opinion of any value. But as the Queen desired to know what I thought I felt bound to state the way in which the subject presents itself to my mind. I only wish that I could be of more service in an affair which I know is causing the Queen so much painful anxiety.'

At this point, the Earl of Cadogan, Lord Privy Seal, then attending the Queen, was drawn in. He writes to Salisbury (letter undated) *inter al.*:

'The family has worked upon her feelings with great energy and some success (i.e. upon the Queen's feelings).

'I found to my horror that she (the Queen) had thought of letting the news ooze out in order to tâter le terrain, and I further found that she considered that she had to some extent sanctioned the marriage *personally*.

'I pointed out that there could be no hurry in the matter, and I begged her to consider very carefully the grave considerations set forth in your memorandum. I also urged her to maintain perfect secrecy. She promised to do both. I am afraid, from what I hear from her, there will be much difficulty in maintaining secrecy. . . .

'I may add that the Queen lays great stress on the *personal* part of the question on the ground that you wish the D. of C. to marry—that he will never marry anyone but Princesse Hélène—and that she knows of no one else whom he could marry. She therefore thinks that we ought to pay more attention to the personal question than we do. . . .'

On September 16, Salisbury, still in France, wrote to Balfour:

'Many thanks for your letter—I am afraid you must be dreadfully tired of writing me letters about this Royal Idyll. . . . I am relieved at the Comte de Paris' utterance. As to my quotation from you to the Queen, I said that I gathered from your letters (not from your opinions) that the Comte de Paris was likely to be talked round. I inferred this from the Princess Hélène's opinion that his objection would "wear off"; and from the Queen's opinion which you reported that he was "not bigotted", and that the Comtesse de Paris whose adhesion is evident was the stronger spirit of the two.

'I rather doubt its wearing off, especially if the R.C.s and French Monarchists get wind of the plan.

'Being somewhat re-assured, I have written the Queen as soothing a letter as I can. I have stated to the Lord Chancellor my apprehensions on the Act of Succession. I am a little confirmed in these by finding that two other Acts of the same period—one excluding Papists from Parliament, the other making them incapable of inheriting land—both reserve in express terms a *locus penitentice* for those Papists who are ready to declare that they do not profess the Popish religion, while in the Act of Settlement there is no trace of such a provision. This looks as if it was intentional. However, we shall see. I have also referred to him the question as to whom will succeed if Prince A.V. becomes incapable. My impression is that the Act clearly gives it to his children being *Protestants*. My . . . (word illegible) is a demand for a *declaratory* Act, making the D. of C. capable—before the General Election.'

As explained in the text, the Pope refused to agree to Princess Hélène changing her religion; a year later the Duke of Clarence became engaged to Princess Mary of Teck.

II

DYNAMITE CONSPIRACY OF 1896 (see p. 175)

Secret and Confidential Report to Sir Matthew White Ridley, 7th October, 1896, from Nicholas Gosselin

'The Solicitor for the Treasury having informed me that there was sufficient evidence to commit Ivory for trial, the Dutch Government having expelled Kearney and Haines, and Tynan's case no longer affecting the dynamite conspiracy, I think the time has arrived for a report of the part my department has played in the affair. It seems a proper time, too, to place before you in as brief a manner as possible a short history of the Secret Service.

'At the time of my appointment, the year 1890, the work was carried on openly by an agent, Mr. Monro, Commissioner of Police, in London, and in America by the Vice Consul in New York (Mr. Hoare), on both sides of the Atlantic. I very soon, in the course of six months, made up my mind that the whole system was rotten, and as a first step informed the Secretary of State that I no longer required the services of the Vice Consul in New York and asked permission to go to America and see the Informants and Sub-Agents. This was granted and I proceeded there in February, 1891, returning within six weeks. I found only one man of the whole party was a member of the Secret Societies we were supposed to be fighting; I, therefore, discharged all but this man, who soon after died; I was thus left without anyone of the old establishment and had, de novo, to build up a fresh counter organisation.

'I selected as my American agent, Mr. Gloster Armstrong, under the approval of the Secretary of State (and I may here remark he has more than justified my selection). He had been Secretary to the Mexican Land Co. in London, and under cover of this he opened an office in New York as their agent to serve as a cloak to his real work.

'I succeeded in sending him five men who were connected with the Extreme party at home, and four of these he managed to worm into the very heart of the American conspiracy. To be brief, on the 1st of August last we had seven men, every one of whom were members and some very deep in the confidence of the leaders. Death has robbed us of two men who would be invaluable now.

'When the Irish Parliamentary Party disrupted, the Extremists in America became very active, and a certain William Lyman got complete control of the Anti-Cronin wing of the Clan-na-gael, but for brevity I shall call it in future the Lyman party. This man is rich, sober, determined and a fanatic in his hatred of England. He rules with a rod of iron, and it is computed he loses personally on the 'Irish Republic' some $5,000 a year.

'Various schemes and plans have been tried and some 15 emissaries of his have visited this country in the last four years, he himself twice. I had these men under constant observation while here and in that way learned who they were in touch with and was able to inform the Police of all the most dangerous men in England, Ireland and Scotland.

'In December, 1893, he spent a great deal of money trying to do something in Dublin (murdering certain officials) by means of two men named Nolan and Merna, but I was able to foil all their plans, the result being that these men shot a fellow conspirator, a man named Read, believing he was the informant. I may say the real man is quite unknown and unsuspected.

'Lyman had a scheme to cause friction between the Governments of America and Canada by blowing up some very costly portion of the Welland Canal. This I informed the Colonial Office of. Subsequently we heard it failed owing to the agents' want of nerves.

'It was on hearing this that Lyman determined on this last affair. He sent for John Kearney, giving him $500, and directed him to proceed to Antwerp and there make dynamite, that he would be joined there by another man to help him, that Tynan and Ivory would proceed to England and Ireland and there obtain 9 or 10 men to take the dynamite to this country. It was to be carried in square india rubber bags with wiring round the neck; Tynan was to formulate the plans and superintend the campaign, assisted by Ivory.

'I must go back here for a moment. The man selected to join Kearney was Cooney ("The Fox") who helped to murder Dr. Cronin in Chicago, but meantime Lyman chose him for another job closer at hand, viz, the murder of Mr. Chamberlain, and he was given a great deal of money and provided with a complete new outfit of clothes, etc. Fortunately I got word of it by cable, and being in Antwerp, wired Mr. Anderson to inform the Colonial Office, which was done, and as a result Mr. Cooney sneaked back to New York without accomplishing anything, but one of my agents had to fly for his life. In place of

Cooney, Lyman sent a Tom Haines to assist Kearney; he was quite unknown until his appearance in Antwerp with credentials from Lyman.

'To come now to dates and hours, Mr. Armstrong cabled from New York to me on 3rd August that Kearney had gone to Antwerp and Lyman had provided him with $500. On the 11th August his letter reached me giving details of the whole plot. On receiving it I saw the dangers that surrounded the whole affair, and laid the letter before the Under Secretary and advised his calling in Sir Edward Bradford and Mr. Anderson: this was done that evening and I cabled my Agent, Mr. Armstrong, to come to England. On his arrival, 22nd August, he saw Mr. Anderson and that night he and I left for Antwerp where he remained until the men ran away.

'Seeing that Kearney and his companion were only amusing themselves I returned to London to try and find Tynan and Ivory, of whose departure from New York I had been advised. I found Ivory in the St. Pancras Hotel, and saw him myself take in a letter with a Belgian stamp on it, but fearing to betray my informant I did not put the Police on him, Mr. Anderson concurring. Although we had the locality well watched he was not picked up and as events turned out, it was just as well.

'On 5th September, Mr. Armstrong wired me from Antwerp that Tynan and Ivory were there, and with one of my own men and two of Mr. Anderson's I proceeded to Antwerp, going by different routes. On arrival I could not see the London Police officer stationed in Antwerp, as he was waiting for the boat containing the two officers sent from Scotland Yard, the boat was 5 or 6 minutes late, having got on a sand bank. When I did see him he told me the two officers were in the Hotel des Anglais and that he believed the two men I was after, Tynan and Ivory, were in that hotel. The manager had previously told him he suspected the men not to be all right.

'Everything then seemed plain sailing, as all we had to do was to bring the whole party together, and that night I hoped to do so, as the four men, Kearney, Haines, Ivory and Tynan, had passed the whole previous evening in a low sort of singing saloon with a number of women, and it was thought they would go there again. As luck would have it they did not, but Tynan, Ivory and Haines went to the Hotel des Anglais. All this happened on Sunday. On Monday, 7th, I had the police all round the hotel, the local man, Bryan, was in the office of the hotel to see men pass in and out, and the two London officers were in a bedroom looking out on the landing.

'Ivory first and then Tynan went out having informed the "boots" that they were going that day to Cologne. Sgt. Bryan got us railway guides and all went to the station, but unfortunately the guides had not

H1JB

got a train that left at 3.30 or 4, I forget which, and by that means the men slipped away unnoticed.

'I was going back to the Hotel des Anglais about 3.30 p.m. to take my man off observation when I met a carriage containing Ivory, Tynan and the "boots" driving leisurely towards the station. I made so sure our men would have seen them that I was not much concerned, but on returning found they had disappeared.

'I had a man waiting in Brussels for such an eventuality. Wired him; no contact; believe they broke journey at Malines.

'By the next train the three London policemen left for Brussels and remained there watching all trains until the 10th when they returned to London with me.

'Late on the night of the 9th I heard that a house had been taken and negotiations were going on for the purchase of materials to make dynamite. I at once made up my mind to return to London and left next morning.

'About 11.00 that night (10th) I had a wire from Mr. Armstrong that the ingredients had been delivered, and next morning I wrote Mr. Anderson and asked him to acquaint the Belgian Police which was done.

'On the 11th I heard Ivory was in Glasgow, and gave my man orders to search every hotel in it, but at last I was obliged to give the name of the hotel he was at. Eventually they "found" him and wired me. I at once, 12 noon, went to Mr. Anderson and asked him to arrest, but he declined. On hearing this I wired my Sgt. to not allow the man out of his sight till he heard further. At 5.00 p.m. I told Mr. Anderson as he would not arrest I would and that he must accept the responsibility of having me exposed, and wired my Sgt. to arrest. Meantime Mr. Anderson had changed his mind and also wired the Glasgow Police to arrest. Both parties arrived simultaneously at the hotel with this object! ! ! but as my men had instructions never to interfere they very properly allowed the Glasgow men to make the arrest.

'At this point all my duty ended, but, alas, not my troubles; I need not, however, detail them as you have a fair idea of them from other sources, and Mr. Anderson I am sure has told you of the arrests in Bologne and Rotterdam, and what the London Metropolitan Police did.

'The Secretary of State will forgive me if in making this statement I may have appeared prolix or egotistical. My excuse is that I have in my employ a large number of faithful men who work like moles, who carry their lives in their hands. If I do not speak for them, nobody can or will. It is only in human nature that it should be galling to them that all public credit and praise should be showered by the press on Scotland Yard who in this and similar matters only act, as the

Secretary of State is well aware, as the instruments in the last instance for effecting the arrests of men whose plans have been laid bare and whose whereabouts discovered by my agents at the risk often of their lives, without thanks and with what, after all, is not a high reward. This, the Secretary of State will understand, is my sole object in making a formal statement of what has occurred, that at least the Secretary of State may know though the public cannot.

'The agent who had to fly for his life I have handed over to the Treasury Solicitors.

'I sincerely hope that you will insist on the whole of the American conspiracy being laid bare by means of this man.

'Should matters go wrong for us in Antwerp or Rotterdam it will strengthen your hands most enormously to point to that hellish conspiracy in New York. . . .

'Under the circumstances of our Secret Service, when the moment of action arrives a certain amount of friction is inevitable, and when more peaceful days come I hope to be able to formulate a better system. . . . I can honestly say for nine weeks I have not known an easy hour, and have done in everything what I thought was best for the public service irrespective of how it might affect your humble servant.'

III

STATUE OF BALFOUR IN THE HOUSE OF COMMONS

Extracts from the account in The Yorkshire Post, *May 10, 1962*

A statue of the Earl of Balfour was unveiled in the Members' Lobby of the House of Commons on May 9, 1962, by Mr. Harold Macmillan, the Prime Minister. The bearded sculptor, Mr. David McFall, 42, sighed and said: 'I could not get any life into it: it is just a piece of architectural furniture.'

The applause which greeted the statue, over seven feet high and of a French limestone called Lary's Roche, was restrained. The late Earl of Balfour was revealed in bleakest white, wearing his House of Commons frock-coat, thumbs traditionally stuck into lapels.

'I wanted to do it in bronze,' explained Mr. McFall, who has done two bronzes of Sir Winston Churchill, one for The Fishmongers' Hall and the other for Sir Winston's constituency of Woodford Green. 'Bronze is a far better material and you can do more with it.' He gestured to the statue and sighed again. Apparently the committee did not think Balfour was historically important enough for bronze. 'It is more expensive than French limestone though you can work more quickly with it. I tried to give the statue versimilitude, but the material was against me. Look at it—it has no life, has it?'

Mr. McFall did a model for the statue in bronze, with Lord Balfour wearing a golfing cape. But the House of Commons Committee rejected it. 'They said it was too fancy,' said Mr. McFall. 'But I felt it was the true Balfour: he was very fond of dressing up.'

Other statues in the Members' Lobby are done in marble. 'I told them I disliked marble—it makes the place look like Genoa Cemetery,' said Mr. McFall. 'The committee were reasonable. They let me have the French limestone, even though they refused to let me have bronze.'

Sir Godfrey Nicholson, M.P., Chairman of the Memorial Committee, told *The Yorkshire Post* later that though Mr. McFall wanted to work in bronze, the Committee felt that the statue should match the statue of Asquith standing next to it. The Asquith statue is in white marble. 'They had to be a pair,' said Sir Godfrey. He called the Balfour statue 'A good work of art and a good statue and I am sure it will grow on us.' Although he had not known Lord Balfour, he had seen many photographs and was certain the statue represented 'an essential aspect of Balfour, though, of course, there were others.'

The £800 block of French limestone used was originally earmarked for Epstein's statue of Lloyd George, but Epstein died before he could begin it. 'Now it has been decided that both the Churchill and the Lloyd George statues are to be done in bronze,' said Mr. McFall. His fee for the work was £10,000. It took him three years, of which one year was spent on plans and consultations with the Committee.

Before he unveiled the statue, Mr. Macmillan said that Lord Balfour stood somehow above the turmoil of party politics as a figure who had been through all the battles without ever being soiled in temperament and character. "I had the good fortune to know him in his later life after his devoted work in the First World War and the succeeding years. For us, in that Indian summer of a statesman, he seemed partly a stately survival from the older battles and partly an inspiration to new endeavours. One of his most endearing qualities was his kindness to and interest in younger men. Nevertheless, Balfour still stands in that slightly hazy penumbra between the confusion of our times and the clearer, sharper light of history. Although there are happily many still alive who knew him either by personal contact or by repute, it is strange to reflect that he was born in the first half of the 19th century, in the year indeed of the Communist Manifesto. As a young man he attended the Congress of Berlin as a member of Lord Salisbury's staff, under the brilliant leadership of Lord Beaconsfield, and there he met Count Bismarck. There he witnessed the signature of the Treaty of Berlin. As an old man, he took a leading part in the Paris negotiations. He signed the Treaty of Versailles and subsequently led the British delegation to the Washington Conference. Altogether his work in public life covered a span of over 55 years. He enjoyed an almost automatic intellectual pre-eminence, yet this was so tempered by modesty and courtesy that it had in it no element of arrogance.

'Indeed, it is difficult to convey to those who cannot remember him, his extraordinary charm . . . elusive yet pervasive. His conception of political life allowed him a reasonable leisure to pursue his wide interests . . . in music, in science, in philosophical speculation and in games. "Even games," he said, "are not to be regarded as wholly serious." But in this House of Commons Lobby it is pre-eminently as a House of Commons man that he is remembered. It was Baldwin who said that if Asquith was the last of the Romans, Balfour was the last of the Athenians. It seems appropriate to recall that typical aphorism here where Balfour's statue now stands opposite that of Asquith.

'His acceptance in 1887 of the post of Chief Secretary for Ireland caused some surprise. But his tenure of that office soon showed that underneath the outward charm lay the hidden steel . . . moral and physical courage to a rare degree. In 1891, Balfour became the leader of the House, a House of which Gladstone was still a member. He led the House for 12 years, a remarkable performance at any time.

'Nothing that we have seen in our own time can match the turbulence of parliamentary life at the end of the last century and the beginning of this. In those days a determined band of obstructionists was able skilfully to exploit all the possibilities of parliamentary procedure without being contained by the counter-measures which governments have subsequently evolved for their own protection. Of course, Balfour knew something about parliamentary tactics from the days when as a young member he had placed his debating powers at the disposal of Lord Randolph Churchill's "Fourth Party". But his mastery as leader of the House was acquired by patience, tolerance and humour, by judicious balance of firmness and flexibility. Then there came the crushing defeat of 1906, followed by reactions familiar to many a politician before and since. However, Balfour survived. Indeed, his apparent eclipse proved a few years later to be no more than a prelude to further achievements. His contributions to the deliberations of the War Cabinet have been vividly described in the memoirs of his colleagues. As Foreign Secretary he was responsible for the Balfour declaration on the Zionist question and all that has followed from it in the history of our own times. His tenure of the Foreign Office also showed his profound understanding of the importance, transcending temporary chances and changes, of an enduring association between this country and the United States of America. The man who forged the Anglo-French Entente went years later to Washington to lay the foundations of that Anglo-American understanding which has ever since served the free world so well. It was not until less than a year before his death at the age of 80 that he finally left ministerial office.

'All of us today join in the recognition of his right, by character, intellect and achievement, to this signal place of honour in the House of Commons which he loved and served so well.'

Present at the ceremony, were the Earl of Balfour—the statesman's nephew—and Lady Ruth Balfour, Lady Evelyn Balfour, and Lady Kathleen Oldfield, the three nieces of the statesman. Lord and Lady Salisbury were also present with the Speaker of the House of Commons,

Lord John Hope, Minister of Works, who supervised the arrangements for the statue to be erected in the Lobby, Sir Godfrey Nicholson, Chairman of the Memorial Committee and Committee members, Mr. Hugh Gaitskell, Leader of the Labour Party, Sir Kenneth Pickthorn, Mr. Jo Grimond, Lady Megan Lloyd George, Mr. D. R. Grenfell and Lord Bridges.

The Committee was first set up after a House of Commons resolution in 1957, under the chairmanship of the late Mr. Walter Elliott, M.P.

Foreign Office,
November 2nd, 1917.

Dear Lord Rothschild,

I have much pleasure in conveying to you, on behalf of His Majesty's Government, the following declaration of sympathy with Jewish Zionist aspirations which has been submitted to, and approved by, the Cabinet.

"His Majesty's Government view with favour the establishment in Palestine of a national home for the Jewish people, and will use their best endeavours to facilitate the achievement of this object, it being clearly understood that nothing shall be done which may prejudice the civil and religious rights of existing non-Jewish communities in Palestine, or the rights and political status enjoyed by Jews in any other country".

I should be grateful if you would bring this declaration to the knowledge of the Zionist Federation.

Y. ing
Arthur James Balfour

THE BALFOUR DECLARATION

NOTES

MANUSCRIPT SOURCES

The main *MS*. sources have already been described on pages xxi-xxii. They are referred to in these Notes as 'BM' and 'Whitt'. The other principal source of *MS*. material is to be found at Stanway, Winchcombe, Gloucestershire. This material is chiefly concerned with Balfour's correspondence with Mary Wyndham, who married Lord Elcho and in due course became Countess of Wemyss on her husband's succession to the title. These papers are referred to in the Notes as 'Stanway'.

Details of the early and pre-A.J.B. history of the Balfour family are in two main unpublished manuscript sources:

(1) *The Balfour Family*, compiled by Charles Barrington Balfour (A.J.B.'s uncle) in 1886. A number of copies of this were made; the one I saw is in the possession of Lady Ruth Balfour (A.J.B.'s niece) at Balbirnie, Markinch, Fife. It comprises two volumes, bound in leather, and goes in some detail into all the branches of the Scottish families bearing the name, Balfour.

(2) 'A Record of the Balfour Family of Whittingehame', written largely from the memories of Alice Balfour (A.J.B.'s sister) by the present Countess of Balfour, wife of the 3rd Earl, A.J.B.'s nephew. This *MS*. is in one copy only, in the possession of the Countess of Balfour, whose personal knowledge of the family is invaluable. *In the Notes, this MS. is referred to as 'Family Record'*.

It is not clear how far use was made of these two sources in Mrs. Blanche E. C. Dugdale's two-volume biography, *Arthur James Balfour: First Earl of Balfour, K.G., O.M., F.R.S.* (1936)—subsequently *referred to herein as 'Dugdale I' or 'Dugdale II'*. But Mrs. Dugdale's work is a supplementary source for the family history.

'Family Record' is a prime source for A.J.B.'s own life, supplemented by his unfinished *Chapters of Autobiography, by Arthur James, First Earl of Balfour*, edited by Mrs. Edgar Dugdale [i.e. Mrs. Blanche E. C. Dugdale], published in 1930—subsequently *referred to herein as 'Auto.'*

Other details about the Balfour family and A.J.B.'s early years are in *The Dictionary of National Biography, 1922-30*, edited by J. R. H. Weaver, published 1937. The article concerning A.J.B. is by Algernon Cecil, a distant cousin.

CHAPTER 1

Page 2. l. 27 James Balfour's portrait is at Whittingehame House, East Lothian.

Page 4. l. 32 Pamphlet writers: 'Men of the Moment: A. J. Balfour', by Edward Rogers and Edmund J. Moyle (London: Treherne & Co., 1902).

Page 5. l. 16 *Auto.*, 2.

Page 5. l. 32 *Family Record.*

Page 6. l. 10 *Auto.*, 1.

Page 6. l. 19 'Dominated': *Family Record.*

Page 6. l. 29 Lady Waterford: *Dugdale* I, 16-18.

Page 7. l. 5 Cess-pools, etc.: G. M. Young, *Victorian England* (1936).

Page 7. l. 12 Eleanor ('Nora') Sidgwick: *Family Record.*

Page 7. l. 24 Robertson Memoir: *Memoir of Lady Blanche Balfour*, by Dr. Robertson, Minister of Whittingehame Parish, 1865–1918 (privately printed).

Page 7. l. 29 Macaulay: *Auto.*, 12-13.

Page 7. l. 40 Jane Austen: *Auto.*, 39: v. also *Novels of the 1840s*, by K. Tillotson (1954).

Page 8. l. 14 French novels: *Auto.*, 11-12.

Page 9. l. 16 Inner eye: 'Religion in her teaching was closely connected with conduct'—*Mrs. Henry Sidgwick. A Memoir* by her niece, Ethel Sidgwick (1938).

Page 9. l. 32 Evangelicalism: G. M. Young, *Victorian England* II, 416, 434, 438.

Page 9. l. 39 Bagehot: *Literary Studies* (1858), ii, 190.

Page 10. l. 1 Distress in Lancs.: *Dugdale* I, 19.

Page 10. l. 19 Condemned: *Family Record.*

Page 10. l. 26 Debt to mother: *Auto.*, 68.

Page 10. l. 37 Sisters: *Family Record.*

Page 11. l. 15 Delicacy: *Auto.*, 6.

Page 11. l. 20 Tired legs: Cynthia Asquith, *Haply I may Remember* (1950).

Page 12. l. 3 Percys: *Auto.*, 5.

Page 12. l. 22 Tennyson: *Auto.*, 6.

Page 12. l. 25 Passion for Pope: Cynthia Asquith, *Remember and Be Glad* (1952), 30.

Page 12. l. 33 Debt to Chittenden: *Auto.*, 6.

Page 12. l. 36 Chittenden's description: *Dugdale* I, 21f.

Page 13. l. 12 Pretty Fanny: *Mr. Balfour*, by E. T. Raymond (1920).

Page 13. l. 14 Flavour of effeminacy: Asquith in letter to Margot A.: *Life of Lord Oxford and Asquith*, by J. A. Spender and Cyril Asquith (1932), I, 102-3.

Page 14. l. 18 Salisbury's talk: *Auto.*, 22-3.

Page 14. l. 37 Thackeray and Cory: According to a letter in *The Times*, Mar. 22, 1930, his tutor was never Cory (William Johnson) but the Rev. Francis St. John Thackeray. Cory was one of his masters. *Auto.*, 21-3.

Page 15. l. 31 Philosophy: *Auto.*, xii.

Page 16. l. 11 Lady Blanche and science: *Auto.*, 17-19.

Page 17. l. 1 Eton, 'scarcely rational': *Remember and Be Glad*, op. cit, 31.

Page 17. l. 5 Essence of Eton: Speech at unveiling of his own portrait in the School Library by Lord Curzon, June 4, 1921. Reprinted in *Opinion and Argument from Speeches and Addresses of the Earl of Balfour, K.G., O.M., F.R.S., 1910–27* (1927)—subsequently *referred to as 'Op. & Arg.'*

Page 17. l. 12 Italy: Ethel Sidgwick, op. cit.

Page 17. l. 19 Symbolic gateway: *Auto.*, 23-4.

Page 17. l. 21 Fellow Commoner: *Auto.*, 25f.

Page 18. l. 21 Séances from 1875: v. Conan Doyle letter to *Times*, Mar. 29, 1930.

Page 18. l. 33 Strutt: *John William Strutt, 3rd Baron Rayleigh*, by R. J. Strutt, 4th Baron Rayleigh (1924).

Page 19. l. 19 Classical Tripos and maths.: v. *A History of Technology*, Vol. V (1959), 780.

Page 19. l. 24 Reading J. S. Mill: *Auto.*, 52.

Page 19. l. 27 Sidgwick: *Auto.*, 34f. Ethel Sidgwick, op. cit.

Page 19. l. 41 'Cared not a jot': *Theism and Humanism*, 138.

Page 20. l. 26 'Subject the universe': *Auto.*, 60.

Page 20. l. 31 Keynes: *Keynes* by R. F. Harrod (1953).

Page 20. l. 42 Metaphysical Society: v. *The Metaphysical Society. Victorian Minds in Crisis, 1869–1880*, by Alan Willard Brown (New York, 1947)—subsequently *referred to as 'A. W. Brown'.*

Page 21. l. 5   Apostles: *A. W. Brown*, 1-9, 17, 300.

Page 22. l. 9   Durnford: *Dugdale* I, 28.

Page 22. l. 43   Skye escapade: *Auto.*, 41ff.

Page 23. l. 10   Tennis: *Auto.*, 36.

Page 23. l. 18   Darwin: *Auto.*, 36-7.

Page 24. l. 38   Tripos: *Auto.*, 60.

Page 25. l. 12   Appetite for work: *Men of the Moment*, op. cit.

Page 25. l. 19   Case against exams.: v. Speech under auspices of Edinburgh School Board, Nov. 2, 1886, reprinted in Wilfrid M. Short's *Arthur James Balfour as Philosopher and Thinker: A Collection of the more important and interesting passages in his non-political writings, speeches and addresses, 1879–1912 (1912)*—subsequently referred to as '*Short*'.

Page 25. l. 22   Love for Cambridge: v. *Short*, 188-9, 192, 197-8.

CHAPTER 2

Page 27. l. 1   Description of A.J.B.: from scrutiny of portraits, photographs, etc. No detailed physiognomical description seems to exist.

Page 27. l. 23   Open doors: *Dugdale* I, passim; *Auto.*, passim.

Page 28. l. 17   Lady Airlie, Burne-Jones, Leighton: *Auto.*, 233-4.

Page 28. l. 38   Handel: *Essays and Addresses*, by A. J. Balfour, M.P., F.R.S., D.C.L. (1893; 3rd edition, with additions, 1904, published in Edinburgh), 111-84.

Page 29. l. 27   At Crystal Palace: *Diaries and Letters of Mary Gladstone (Drew)*, edited by L. Masterman (1930).

Page 29. l. 34   Lyttelton children: *M. Gladstone Diaries*, op. cit.

Page 30. l. 27   'Old person of Whittingehame': Balfour papers at Whittingehame (subsequently *referred to as 'Whitt'*). The verses are probably in Alice Balfour's hand. They are pinned to an envelope, inscribed 'Composed by A.J.B., Mary Gladstone and others at Whittingehame, combining names of places in East Lothian with some of A.J.B.'s favourite expressions underlined. First visit of Gladstones to Whitt.'

Page 31. l. 9   Sunday evening prayers: information from 3rd Earl of Balfour.

Page 31. l. 26   Mary Lyttelton: from her unpublished diary. I have not seen the whole of this diary which may no longer be extant. The items used here were those copied from her diary after her death at A.J.B.'s request and found by me among his papers at Whittingehame. They will be *referred to here as 'M. Lyttelton diary'*. One item (see below) has a comment in A.J.B.'s hand.

Page 31. l. 42   Strutt: *M. Lyttelton diary*, op. cit.

Page 32. l. 17   Tyndall: *M. Lyttelton diary*, op. cit. Tyndall, a physicist and professor of natural philosophy at the Royal Institution, was a colleague of Faraday whose life he wrote. He was one of the first climbers of the Matterhorn; his researches were on heat and light (he discovered the 'Tyndall effect'). He was an excellent lecturer and a pioneer in popular scientific writing.

Page 32. l. 20   Neville Lyttelton: *Dugdale* I, 32.

Page 32. l. 25   'Quaint boy': *Mrs Gladstone. Portrait of a Marriage*, by Georgiana Battiscombe (1956).

Page 32. l. 30   Strathconan and Gladstone episode: *Auto.*, 70-1.

Page 33. l. 23   'Mein Heer Van Dunk': *Auto.*, 74.

Page 33. l. 35   Breakfast with Gladstone: Battiscombe, op. cit.

Page 33. l. 45   Lady Horner: letter, to Mrs. Dugdale, 1932-4 (Whitt.).

Page 34. l. 35   'Feeling of frivolity': *Dugdale* I, 49.

Page 34. l. 45 Salisburys' suggestion: *Auto.*, 86.

Page 35. l. 23 Tea with M. Lyttelton: *M. Lyttelton diary*. This entry has a note in A.J.B.'s hand, 'This is the last time'. He presumably meant the last time they were alone together since it is clear they met at the Cheshams.

Page 35. l. 29 Lavinia: letter from Lavinia Talbot to A.J.B., Dec. 27, 1876. (Whitt.).

Page 35. l. 39 *M. Gladstone diaries*.

Page 36. l. 14 Edward Lyttelton: letter to A.J.B., Mar. 23, 1875 (Whitt.).

Page 36. l. 23 'Staggered': *Dugdale* I, 34.

Page 36. l. 39 Anniversary with Talbots: private information from 3rd Earl of Balfour.

Page 36. l. 45 Despair: *Family Record:* 'From this passion his heart never seems to have been free, and I fancy that that profound grief re-echoed for him in every tale of irremediable sorrow, so that as far as possible he appeared successfully to ignore such things.'

Page 37. l. 21 Shares expenses: letter H. Sidgwick–A.J.B. undated (British Museum —subsequently *referred to as BM*).

Page 37. l. 22 Snow: letter A. Snow–A.J.B., Jan. 19, 1872 (BM).

Page 37. l. 44 Christchurch gift: letter Archdeacon Henry W. Harper, Canterbury, N.Z.–A.J.B., May 22, 1880 (Whitt.).

Page 38. l. 8 Spencer Lyttelton notes: *Dugdale* I, 37ff.

Page 38. l. 40 Metaphysical Society: v. *A. W. Brown*, op. cit.

Page 39. l. 8 A.J.B–Edward Talbot (Whitt.).

Page 39. l. 44 Frank Balfour: *Family Record*.

Page 40. l. 19 Nora's marriage: *Family Record*.

Page 40. l. 33 Return: *Auto.*, 91.

Page 40. l. 36 First speech: *Auto.*, 93.

Page 41. l. 23 Hicks-Beach: *England 1870–1914*, by R. C. K. Ensor (1936), 33— subsequently *referred to as 'Ensor'*.

Page 43. l. 1 Beresford Hope: *Auto.*, 117f.

Page 44. l. 29 'Glorious Bohemian': *Journals and Letters of R. Brett, Viscount Esher*, ed. M. V. Brett (1934) II, 55.

Page 44. l. 30 Lord Derby: A.J.B. Memorandum, May 8, 1880. This extract is also printed in the *Auto.* with the exception of the one word 'alcohol'.

Page 45. l. 12 Gesture: *M. Gladstone diaries*, May 21, 1878.

Page 45. l. 22 Cypher: *Auto.*, 106.

Page 45. l. 35 Disraeli's deafness: *Life of Lord Salisbury* by G. Cecil, II, 287.

Page 46. l. 13 Borrowed clothes: *Men of the Moment*.

Page 46. l. 21 Bismarck: *Auto.*, 110.

Page 47. l. 21 Wyndhams: *Auto.*, 234.

CHAPTER 3

Page 48. l. 19 'Immortal work': frequently referred to thus in letters to Lady Elcho.

Page 48. l. 22 Altered title: *Auto.*, 65, also *A Defence of Philosophic Doubt, being an Essay on the foundations of Belief* (1879; reprinted 1920), viii. All references are to the 1920 reprint of which, however, Balfour remarked in his 1920 preface: 'The re-issue has been paged so as to correspond with the original edition. I have made no attempt to revise the text, or in any way to bring it up to date; but I have found in an old copy some trifling verbal alterations and a few notes.

These were written very soon after the book was published, and I have inserted them without substantial alteration'. The original edition of the *Defence* is now rare. It should be noted that the second part of the title is confusing, since it is the title also of his second major philosophical work, *The Foundations of Belief*, (1895).

Page 49. l. 7   *Familiar Beliefs and Transcendent Reason*, 10. This was the British Academy annual philosophical lecture under the Henriette Hertz Trust, and was printed in 1925.

Page 49. l. 17   Most useful philosophy: the quotation is from his long review of *Bishop Berkeley's Life and Letters* published in the *National Review* of March and April, 1883, and reprinted in *Essays and Addresses*, 51.

Page 49. l. 38   Destructive: *Defence*, vii.

Page 49. l. 41   'No desirable goal': *Defence*, 295.

Page 50. l. 3   Jaspers: from Karl Jaspers's book, *Nietzsche*, quoted by Walter Kaufmann in introduction to *Existentialism from Dostoevsky to Sartre* (1957).

Page 50. l. 9   'Habits of thought': *Defence*, 298.

Page 50. l. 19   'Sceptical attack': *Defence*, 298.

Page 50. l. 21   Mansel footnote: *Defence*, 327.

Page 50. l. 33   'The Immediate Problem of Philosophy: A lecture delivered to the Edinburgh University Philosophical Society on 3rd November 1880 by A. J. Balfour, M.P.', 3. The booklet was privately printed in paper back. The printer's name, unusually, is not given.

Page 50. l. 35   Section on Darwin, Lyell, etc., is compiled from many sources, including *A. W. Brown*, op. cit. I found specially useful *Evolutionary Theory and Christian Belief. The unresolved conflict*, by David Lack (1957). To Balfour himself there is one reference, 99.

Page 51. l. 25   'Pretensions of Science': *Immediate Problem*, op. cit., 10.

Page 51. l. 30   *A. W. Brown*, 301.

Page 51. l. 36   Consistency: *Defence*, 323.

Page 52. l. 7   'Would not be freed': *Defence*, 320.

Page 52. l. 11   Grounds of belief: *Defence*, 8.

Page 52. l. 17   'How Came I?': *Defence*, 6.

Page 52. l. 19   Innate, connate; *Defence*, 5.

Page 52. l. 21   'Ordinary view': *Defence*, 13.

Page 52. l. 25   Shock of Mill: *Theism and Humanism* (1915), 138.

Page 52. l. 37   *Immediate Problem*, 31.

Page 53. l. 1   'Pure empiricism': *Defence*, 73; see 15-72.

Page 53. l. 6   'Mankind observing': *Defence*, 71.

Page 53. l. 15   'Ultimate premises': *Defence*, 75.

Page 53. l. 21   'Scepticism possible': *Defence*, 84.

Page 53. l. 21   Optical illusion: *Defence*, 84; also v. Part III, chap. xii.

Page 53. l. 25   'Persisting universe': *Defence*, 81.

Page 53. l. 30   'Natural convictions': *Defence*, 84.

Page 53. l. 35   'Convert philosophy': *Defence*, 293-4.

Page 53. l. 42   Kant: *Defence*, Part II, chap. vi, 85-137.

Page 54. l. 25   'Three popular arguments': *Defence*, Part II, chap. vii, 138-54.

Page 54. l. 34   Uniformity of nature: *Defence*, 145.

Page 54. l. 39   Experience proves nothing: *Defence*, 145.

Page 54. l. 41   Balfour accepts: *Defence*, 146.

Page 54. l. 44   Mill, Reid, Hamilton, Spencer: *Defence*, Part II, chaps. viii-xi.

Page 55. l. 3   Reserved for Spencer: *Defence*, 240-1.

Page 55. l. 9   *Defence*, Part III, chap. xii: also 249.

Page 55. l. 36   Confidence in science: *Defence*, 303.

Page 56. l. 4 Philosophy the judge: *Defence*, 293.

Page 56. l. 15 Sceptical uneasiness: *Defence*, 261-2.

Page 56. l. 29 *Foundations of Belief*, 30f.

Page 57. l. 25 Bacon: speech at tercentenary celebrations, Gray's Inn, London, 1912, reprinted in *Essays Speculative and Political*, by Rt. Hon. A. J. Balfour (1920), pp. 148-165—subsequently *referred to as 'Essays Speculative'*.

Page 57. l. 31 J. G. Piddington: *Family Record*. (Piddington not traced.)

Page 57. l. 33 Margot Tennant (Asquith): *The Autobiography of Margot Asquith*, Vol. I (1920), v. refs. to Balfour.

Page 58. l. 6 'Distilled through . . .': Ben Jonson on Shakespeare.

Page 58. l. 11 'Inward inclination': *Defence*, 317.

Page 58. l. 20 'Religion . . . no worse off': *Defence*, 315, 319.

Page 58. l. 22 Living share: v. also *Defence*, 326.

Page 58. l. 24 Need for religious truth: *Defence*, 320.

Page 58. l. 29 H. G. Wells: *Experiment in Autobiography* (New York, 1934), 664. Subsequently *referred to as 'Experiment'*.

Page 58. l. 41 Letter to Pringle-Pattison: (Whitt.). Andrew Pringle-Pattison (*né* Seth), 1856–1931, graduated from Edinburgh University in 1878. He was professor of philosophy successively at Cardiff, St. Andrews and Edinburgh. He wrote on Scottish philosophers, Hegel and *The Idea of God in the Light of Recent Philosophy* (1917).

Page 59. l. 4 Pringle-Pattison's summary: *Dugdale* II, 420ff. (Appendix, Notes on Lord Balfour's philosophy.)

Page 59. l. 26 Prof. Clement C. J. Webb: v. *Arthur James Balfour* (*Earl of Balfour, K.G., O.M., P.B.A.*), *1848–1930*. Paper-back from the *Proceedings* of the British Academy, Vol. XVI (undated). Also contains notes by Sir Frederick G. Kenyon on A.J.B. and the British Academy.

Page 59. l. 39 *Foundations of Belief*: Authority, Part III, chap. 2, 194ff.

Page 60. l. 26 Pollock–A.J.B.: July 1879 (BM).

Page 60. l. 37 Pringle-Pattison: v. supra.

CHAPTER 4

Page 62. l. 5 'Hurricane': *Auto.*, 127-8.

Page 62. l. 13 Hertford: *Auto.*, 121.

Page 62. l. 22 Midlothian: *Auto.*, 123.

Page 62. l. 24 Call at Hatfield: *Auto.*, 122.

Page 62. l. 29 Disraeli picturesque: *Dugdale* I, 54.

Page 62. l. 33 No despairing view: *Auto.*, 124f.

Page 62. l. 43 Brazen mask: v. *Memoirs of Sir Almeric Fitzroy* (2 vols., 1925).

Page 63. l. 13 Gladstone's secretary: *Rambling Recollections*, by Sir Henry Drummond Wolff (1908), Vol. II, 253.

Page 63. l. 19 Dreadnought: *Auto.*, 141.

Page 64. l. 6 Wolff: *Auto.*, 43.

Page 64. l. 15 Cunning: *The Fourth Party*, by Harold Gorst (1906), son of J. E. Gorst.

Page 64. l. 22 Gorst at Central office: *British Political Parties*, by R. T. Mackenzie (1956), 262-3.

Page 64. l. 27 Good mathematician: *Auto.*, 135.

Page 64. l. 38 'Superior': Gorst, op. cit., 61.

Page 65. l. 21 Lord Midleton quotation: NOT in his book, op. cit., but from a *Times* article, 'Fifty Years', Feb. 1, 1932.

Page 65. l. 37 Ensor: *England, 1870–1914*, by R. C. K. Ensor (1936), 66-7.

Page 66. l. 16 Tartly replied: *Lord Randolph Churchill*, by Winston S. Churchill. (1906; edition used here, one-vol., 1951), 119.

Page 66. l. 24 Lucy: *A Diary of Two Parliaments, 1880–1885*, by Sir Henry Lucy (1886).

Page 67. l. 7 A.J.B–Salisbury, Sept. 29, 1880 (BM Vol. 6).

Page 67. l. 20 Name is a joke: *Rambling Recollections, II,* 259.

Page 67. l. 34 Dissatisfaction with Northcote: A.J.B.–Salisbury, Aug. 25, 1880 (BM Vol. 6).

Page 68. l. 32 Efficiency: Salisbury–A.J.B., Sept. 2, 1880 (BM Vol. 6).

Page 68. l. 44 Voting the other: A J.B.–Salisbury, quoted in *Lord Randolph Churchill*, by Robert Rhodes James (1959), 82.

Page 69. l. 6 Gorst–A.J.B.: 1880 (no further date) (BM Vol. 109).

Page 69. l. 10 A.J.B.–Salisbury: Sept. 29, 1880 (BM Vol. 6).

Page 69. l. 35 Cool proposal: *Auto.*, 146f.

Page 70. l. 9 Bashi-Bazouks: *Auto.*, 150.

Page 70. l. 26 'One of my dreams': Mackenzie, op. cit., 23.

Page 70. l. 31 Queen Victoria: *Queen Victoria's Letters*, 2nd series, Vol. III, 219.

Page 70. l. 38 Constitution: *Auto.*, 152-3.

Page 71. l. 2 Churchill's fitness: Rhodes James, 108.

Page 71. l. 16 Balfour's critics: Rhodes James, op. cit.

Page 71. l. 24 F. H. O'Donnell: E. T. Raymond, op. cit.

Page 71. l. 35 Balfour 'ghastly': *Rambling Recollections*, Vol. II, 259.

Page 74. l. 4 Forster: *Life of Forster*, by P. Wemyss Reid, Vol. II, 441.

Page 74. l. 8 Scene with Forster: *Records and Reactions*, 60.

Page 74. l. 24 Balfour's speech: *Dugdale* I, 60f: v. E. T. Raymond, op. cit.

Page 75. l. 4 Gladstone–A.J.B. (BM Vol. 10).

Page 75. l. 11 'Infamy' letter: *Dugdale* I, 69.

Page 76. l. 3 Clash noted: W. S. Churchill, op. cit., 175-6.

Page 76. l. 39 Gladstone–Queen: *Queen Victoria's Letters*, 2nd series, Vol. III, 510.

Page 77. l. 5 Redistribution: A.J.B.'s query to Gladstone and Gladstone's reply (taken down by Lord Hartington) are in one envelope in Whittingehame papers: v. Ensor, op. cit., 88.

Page 77. l. 26 Whiggism: E. T. Raymond, op. cit.

Page 77. l. 32 *Communitates: Ensor*, 88.

Page 77. l. 39 Chamberlain quote: *Ensor*, 87.

Page 78. l. 16 'Averse to changes': *Dugdale* I, 87.

CHAPTER 5

Page 79. l. 8 Letters G. W. Balfour–A.J.B. (BM Vol. 149).

Page 79. l. 14 Depression: *Dugdale* I, 70ff.

Page 79. l. 25 Laura: *Some Hawarden Letters, 1878–1913, written to Mrs. Drew.* Ed. L. March-Phillipps and B. Christian (1917), 173ff.

Page 80. l. 10 Mary Gladstone–A.J.B. (BM Vol. 112, undated).

Page 80. l. 21 Laura's will: M. Asquith *Auto.*, Vol. I, 50.

Page 81. l. 7 Lady Betty Montgomery: memorandum to Mrs. Dugdale (Whitt.).

Page 81. l. 29 M. Wyndham–A.J.B.: Aug. 7, 1883 (Whitt.).

Page 81. l. 34 'If only you had married me': Extract from letter, Mary Elcho (née Wyndham), Aug. 7, 1896 (Whitt.).

Page 81. l. 38 'Such fun': *Some Hawarden Letters*, op. cit., 178-9.

Page 83. l. 12 Cynthia Asquith, *Remember and Be Glad*, 9.

Page 83. l. 38 L. Lyttelton-Frances Balfour letter (Whitt.).

Page 85. l. 14 Salisbury–A.J.B., Jan. 15, 1881 (BM Vol. 6).

Page 85. l. 27 A.J.B.–Lady Elcho: one of large numbers of letters retained by Lady Elcho and now in the possession of Lady Violet Benson at Stanway, Winchcombe, Glos., subsequently *referred to as 'Stanway'*.

Page 86. l. 18 Lady Frances Balfour; from her book *Ne Obliviscaris* (1930).

Page 86. l. 32 Arthur furious: *Ne Obliviscaris* (letter to G. W. Balfour).

Page 87. l. 17 Avoid rows: *Dugdale* I, 80.

Page 87. l. 24 Salisbury–A.J.B. (Whitt.).

Page 90. l. 2 'Foolish' Churchill: Rhodes James.

Page 91. l. 1 Asquith, *Life*, op. cit., 102-3.

Page 92. l. 7 'S': July 8, 1893 (BM Vol. 8).

Page 92. l. 12 MacColl: *Ensor*, 92.

Page 92. l. 44 Eaton Hall: *Auto.*, 209-12.

Page 93. l. 17 A.J.B.–W. S. Churchill (BM Vol. 12).

Page 93. l. 41 *After Thirty Years* (1928), 396-8.

Page 94. l. 14 A.J.B.–Salisbury: *Dugdale* I, 94-5 (BM Vol. 6).

Page 94. l. 43 Defence of Union: *Auto.*, 213.

Page 95. l. 35 'Most vindictive': v. above (letter of Dec. 23, 1885).

Page 95. l. 43 Chamberlain discussions: *Auto.*, 215ff.

Page 96. l. 26 'Slippery Whig': *Auto.*, 221.

Page 97. l. 32 A.J.B.–Salisbury: March 24, 1886 (Whitt.).

Page 97. l. 37 38th birthday: *Dugdale* I, 105-6.

Page 98. l. 3 A.J.B.–Lady Frances: *Dugdale* I, 107f.

Page 98. l. 23 Cranborne's reply: *Dugdale* I, 108-9.

Page 98. l. 39 Near kinsman: Rhodes James, 278.

Page 99. l. 4 Counterpoise: A.J.B.–Salisbury, Nov. 17, 1886 (BM Vol. 6).

Page 99. l. 15 A.J.B.–Salisbury: Dec. 21, 1886 (Whitt.): v. Rhodes James, 292.

Page 99. l. 28 Thwarted Chancellor: Rhodes James, 296-7.

Page 100. l. 12 A.J.B.–W.H. Smith: Dec. 22, 1886 (Whitt.).

Page 100. l. 26 Country saw appointment with 'Stupefaction' (*D.N.B.*, 1922–1930, 46-7).

Page 101. l. 17 Asquith: *Life*, op. cit., 102-3.

Page 101. l. 33 Health: *Dugdale* I, 126-7 (from uncompleted chapter of *Auto.*).

Page 102. l. 20 Told Morley: *Recollections*, by John Viscount Morley, 2 vols. (1917), Vol. I, 228.

CHAPTER 6

Page 103. l. 1 Lord G. Hamilton: *Parliamentary Reminiscences and Reflections, 1886–1906*.

Page 104. l. 1 Morley, op. cit., I, 226-9.

Page 104. l. 21 Time to cool: Morley, op. cit., I, 227.

Page 104. l. 29 Salisbury policy: *Life of Salisbury*, by G. Cecil, Vol. 3, 303.

Page 105. l. 12   Sentimentality: Memo of talk made by Mrs. Dugdale, Aug. 26, 1928.

Page 105. l. 14   P. S. O'Hegarty: *A History of Ireland Under the Union, 1801–1922* (1952).

Page 106. l. 25   Chamberlain–A.J.B. (BM Vol. 91).

Page 106. l. 25   Coercion: v. *The Chamberlain Tradition*, by Charles Petrie (1938), 71.

Page 106. l. 32   Churchill–Hicks-Beach: quoted Rhodes James, op. cit., p. 325.

Page 107. l. 40   Attack on police: *Dugdale* I, 143.

Page 108. l. 33   Carson: *The Life of Edward Carson, Lord Carson of Duncairn*, by H. Montgomery Hyde (1953), 71.

Page 108. l. 38   'Carson had nerve': *Dugdale* I, 147.

Page 109. l. 3   'Life or . . .': Aug. 7, 1896 (Stanway).

Page 109. l. 8   Scotland Yard: Apr. 3, 1888 (Irish Letter book, 87-88. BM).

Page 109. l. 29   Bloody Balfour: Press cuttings book at Whittingehame (kept by Alice Balfour).

Page 109. l. 35   Healey: E. T. Raymond, op. cit.

Page 109. l. 40   Go to Hell: Lady Elcho–A.J.B. Jan. 12, 1890 (BM).

Page 110. l. 8   Cousin in gaol (Stanway).

Page 110. l. 26   Salisbury–A.J.B.: Oct. 26, 1887 (BM Vol. 6).

Page 110. l. 28   Wyndham dinner: *George Wyndham*, by J. A. Biggs-Davison (1951).

Page 110. l. 44   Gatty: *George Wyndham Recognita*, by C. Gatty (1917).

Page 111. l. 6   Abominable place: Jan. 26, 1889 (Stanway).

Page 111. l. 14   Lady Frances Balfour: *Dugdale* I, 154.

Page 111. l. 18   Buller: Memo. A.J.B.–Mrs. Dugdale, Aug. 26, 1928 (Whitt.).

Page 111. l. 40   Pillow policy (BM Vol. 6).

Page 112. l. 6   Balfour order: *Dugdale* I, 171.

Page 112. l. 9   Balfour report: A.J.B.–Salisbury, Jan. 8, 1889 (BM Vol. 7).

Page 112. l. 18   S.–A.J.B.: Jan. 10, 1889 (BM Vol. 7).

Page 112. l. 27   Hopkins: v. *Sermons and Devotional Writings of G. M. Hopkins*. Ed. C. Devlin (1959).

Page 112. l. 38   S. H. Butcher: *Dugdale* I, 165.

Page 113. l. 36   Unproclaim: *Dugdale* I, 170.

Page 114. l. 2   Salisbury–A.J.B.: Oct. 26, 1887 (BM Vol. 6).

Page 114. l. 14   Churchill rose: Lucy, op. cit., 53.

Page 114. l. 25   Podsnap: Rhodes James, op. cit., 339.

Page 114. l. 34   A.J.B.–Smith: Hambledon MS., Dec. 22, 1886.

Page 115. l. 34   Balfour denied: *Dugdale* I, 162-4.

Page 116. l. 25   Carson recalled: H. Montgomery Hyde, op. cit., 87.

Page 118. l. 5   O'Shea–A.J.B.: *Dugdale* I, 182-3.

Page 118. l. 15   Difficult choice: *Ensor*, 185.

Page 118. l. 38   Golf like Wagner: Lucy, op. cit., 434-6.

Page 119. l. 15   Speech of 1913: *Op. & Arg.*, 63ff.

CHAPTER 7

Page 121. l. 4   A.J.B.–Elcho: July 18, 1891 (Stanway).

Page 121. l. 26   Note from Ponsonby: *Royal Papers, Victoria*, Vol. I, Oct. 29, 1891. BM Balfour Papers.

Page 122. l. 8   Duke of Clarence (Whitt.): v. Appendix I.

Page 124. l. 20   If Smith goes: A.J.B.–Salisbury, Nov. 23, 1888 (BM Vol. 7).

Page 125. l. 7   Hicks-Beach to Akers-Douglas: Chilston Papers. Akers-Douglas became Viscount Chilston. His papers were deposited at the County Hall, Maidstone, Kent, in 1956.

Page 125. l. 22   Salisbury's doubts: G. Cecil, op. cit., Vol. IV, 219.

Page 126. l. 14   Verses (Whitt.).

Page 126. l. 39   Jackson: A.J.B.–Salisbury, Aug. 27, 1891 (BM Vol. 7).

Page 127. l. 4   Really Leader: Rhodes James, op. cit., 352-3.

Page 127. l. 26   Lucy, op. cit., 455, 459.

Page 128. l. 3   Press Fund: v. *Short*, op. cit., 407.

Page 128. l. 15   Irish Letter Book (BM).

Page 129. l. 17   Talk with Joe (BM Vol. 7).

Page 129. l. 21   Told Lady Elcho: Mar. 15, 1892 (Stanway).

Page 129. l. 37   Gladstone letter (Whitt.).

Page 130. l. 23   Margot letter (BM Vol. 112).

Page 130. l. 27   Balfour reply: From Dublin.   Copy at Whittingehame.

Page 130. l. 43   Sir Frederick Ponsonby: *Recollections of Three Reigns* (1951).

Page 131. l. 28   Lady Eve: a broadcast, v. *The Listener*, Oct. 25, 1956.

Page 132. l. 26   Berwick landscape: *Auto.*, 229.

Page 132. l. 38   Remorse: *Auto.*, 228.

Page 133. l. 16   C. Elcho (Asquith): *Remember and Be Glad*, op. cit., 177-8.

Page 133. l. 41   Lowlands (Stanway).

Page 135. l. 11   Lady E.–A.J.B.: Jan. 12, 1890 (Whitt.).

Page 135. l. 21   Letter from Austria: Lady E.–A.J.B., undated (BM Vol. 149) (Joan Lascelles group).

Page 137. l. 31   A little pain: Jan. 3, 1894 (Stanway).

Page 138. l. 25   Oscar Wilde: A.J.B.–Lady E. (Stanway).

Page 138. l. 37   Fitzgerald: Jan. 17, 1890 (Stanway).

Page 139. l. 36   Fortune teller: Aug. 20, 1892 (Stanway).

Page 140. l. 32   Verses (Whitt.).

Page 141. l. 14   Name of Souls: *Auto.*, 232.

Page 141. l. 25   Names of Souls: Margot Asquith, *Auto.*, 176.

Page 142. l. 8   For Souls: v. Lord Midleton, op. cit., H. G. Wells, op. cit., and *The Glitter and the Gold*, by Consuelo V. Balsan (1952).

Page 142. l. 29   Wells: *Experiment*, op. cit., 427.

Page 142. l. 41   Esher, *Journals*, op. cit., Vol. I, 183.

Page 143. l. 6   Lady B. Montgomery: private memo. to Mrs. Dugdale, 1928 (Whitt.).

Page 144. l. 11   Wells: *Experiment*, op. cit., 427.

Page 145. l. 15   No history complete: Margot Asquith, *Auto.*, Vol. I, 139.

CHAPTER 8

Page 146. l. 1   Balfour–Sidgwick: Nov. 21, 1892 (BM Letter Book, Nov. 11, 1892–Apr. 11, 1893).

Page 146. l. 16   Psychical matters: *A. W. Brown*, op. cit.

Page 147. l. 3   Presidential Address: Society for Psychical Research. Presidential address to 63rd General Meeting, Westminster Town Hall: v. *Short* extracts, 424ff.

Page 149. l. 14   Victoria Univ. speech: v. *Short*, op. cit.

Page 150. l. 5   Cambridge Univ. Local Lectures: v. *Essays and Addresses*, 315ff. Esher v. supra, I, 183.

Page 150. l. 37   *The Foundations of Belief, being Notes Introductory to the Study of Theology*, by the Rt. Hon. Arthur James Balfour. (1895). References below are to the second edition, which appeared in the same year.

Page 151. l. 4   Humour: *Foundations*, 21.

Page 151. l. 7   Side glances: *Foundations*, 48-50.

Page 151. l. 26   If they survive: *Foundations*, 48

Page 151. l. 34   Perishing world: *Foundations*, 265.

Page 151. l. 37   Infinite Truth: *Foundations*, 277.

Page 152. l. 6   All these statements: *Foundations*, 278.

Page 152. l. 17   C. C. J. Webb: v. British Academy *Proceedings*, Vol. 16 (quoted above).

Page 152. l. 30   Kant: *Foundations*, 137f.

Page 153. l. 3   Authority: *Foundations*, 194ff.

Page 153. l. 16   Open minds: *Foundations*, 197.

Page 155. l. 2   James FitzJames Stephen: v. *A. W. Brown*, op. cit., 133, 185, 332.

Page 155. l. 12   Russell Kirk: *The Conservative Mind* (1954), 342.

Page 155. l. 25   Conservative doctrine: *Essays and Addresses*, 238-9.

Page 156. l. 5   Political science: v. *Essays and Addresses*, 241f. (Also Notebooks, 'Introduction to science of politics', BM Vol. 261, §2).

Page 157. l. 6   Kirk: v. supra, 337-45.

Page 157. l. 35   Unlovely Germ: *Foundations*, 325.

Page 157. l. 38   Beauty: *Foundations*, 326.

Page 158. l. 17   A. J. B.–Mary Gladstone: v. *Some Hawarden Letters*, op. cit., 250.

Page 158. l. 6   Esher: op. cit.

Page 160. l. 17   A.J.B.–Oliver Lodge (BM Vol. 116).

Page 160. l. 38   A.J.B–Wilfrid Ward: Dec. 7, 1895 (Letter Book 16, BM): v. also *The Wilfrid Wards and the Transition*, by Maisie Ward (1921).

Page 161. l. 4   Gore on Sidgwick: v. *A. W. Brown*, op. cit.

Page 162. l. 9   A.J.B.–Lady E.: Mar. 3, 1895 (Stanway).

Page 162. l. 22   C. C. J. Webb, op. cit.

Page 163. l. 23   A.J.B.–Betty Balfour (BM Vol. 149).

Page 163. l. 30   Landseer: *Essays and Addresses*, op. cit., 320 (Inaugural address to Cambridge Univ. Local Lectures, Aug. 2, 1900).

CHAPTER 9

Page 165. l. 14   Fourth Party: Midleton, *Records and Reactions*, 87ff.

Page 166. l. 5   Cabinet making: *The Life of J. Chamberlain*, Vol. III, by J. L. Garvin, 4f.

Page 167. l. 23   Agriculture: *Ensor*, 284.

Page 168. l. 9   Writing to Queen: Feb. 25, 1896 (Stanway).

Page 168. l. 28   Balfour the hinge: Garvin, III, 7.

Page 168. l. 37   Salisbury–A.J.B. (BM Vol. 8).

Page 169. l. 38   Charles Tennant letters (Whitt.).

Page 170. l. 22   Salisbury–A.J.B.: July 31, 1895 (BM Vol. 8).

Page 170. l. 32   A. S. T. Griffith-Boscawen: *Fourteen Years in Parliament* (1907).

Page 170. l. 40 Balfour described: *Men of Moment,* op. cit., 33.

Page 171. l. 30 Grover Cleveland: *Ensor,* 229f.

Page 171. l. 36 President's words: quoted *Old Diplomacy and New, 1876–1922 from Salisbury to Lloyd George,* by A. L. Kennedy (1922).

Page 172. l. 7 Manchester speech: *Dugdale* I, 225.

Page 172. l. 38 A.J.B.–Goschen (BM Vol. 92).

Page 173. l. 27 Lady F. Balfour: *Dugdale* I, 121.

Page 173. l. 44 No harm in inquiry: J. Chamberlain–A.J.B., Feb. 21, 1896 (BM Vol. 92).

Page 174. l. 6 Hercules Robinson: marked 'Received Feb. 10 or 11' (BM Vol. 92).

Page 174. l. 26 Wyndham–A.J.B.: Sept. 19, 1896 (BM Vol. 121).

Page 174. l. 37 Irish Peers: A.J.B.–Lady E., Aug. 16, 1896 (Stanway).

Page 175. l. 17 War: (Stanway).

Page 175. l. 21 *Recollections of Three Reigns* (1951).

Page 175. l. 26 Brains: Bigge–A.J.B., Jan. 2, 1900 (BM Vol. 1).

Page 176. l. 10 Army achievements: Midleton, 98.

Page 176. l. 15 No plan: *Ensor,* 292.

Page 176. l. 30 Pooh-poohed: v. *Life of the Rt. Hon. Sir C. W. Dilke, Bt., M.P.,* by Stephen Gwynn, completed by G. M. Tuckwell (1917), 2 vols. I, 268, II, 451.

Page 177. l. 5 Defence Committee: v. *The Defence Committee: A Forerunner of the C.I.D.,* by Zara Shakow (*Canadian Historical Review.* Toronto. xxxvi, No. 1, Mar. 1955): also v. *Defence by Committee. The British Committee of Imperial Defence, 1885–1959,* by F. A. Johnson (1960).

Page 178. l. 11 Chamberlain–Devonshire: Garvin, II, 15.

Page 179. l. 25 A.J.B.–Chamberlain: Garvin, III, 154.

Page 179. l. 42 Haddington speech: v. *Short,* 70f.

Page 180. l. 10 A.J.B.–Edward Talbot: *Dugdale* I, 284.

Page 180. l. 24 A.J.B.–W. T. Stead (BM Letter Book No. 2, Vol. 6).

Page 180. l. 29 Boredom: Griffith-Boscawen, op. cit.

Page 182. l. 7 Chamberlain–Hatzfeldt: Garvin, III, 231ff.

Page 182. l. 25 A.J.B.–Salisbury: Apr. 14, 1898 (BM Vol. 8).

Page 182. l. 29 Salisbury–A.J.B.: Apr. 9, 1898 (BM Vol. 8).

Page 182. l. 44 Salisbury–A.J.B.: Apr. 26, 1898 (Whitt.).

Page 185. l. 17 Chamberlain–A.J.B.: Jan. 7, 1900 (BM Vol. 91).

Page 186. l. 3 A.J.B.–Alice (BM Vol. 150) (Date '4 . . . 1899').

Page 187. l. 9 A.J.B.–Salisbury: Dec. 18, 1899 (BM Vol. 8).

Page 187. l. 33 Balmoral: A.J.B.–Lady Elcho; Nov. 2, 1898 (Stanway).

Page 188. l. 1 A.J.B.–Salisbury: Jan. 1, 1899 (?1900) (BM Vol. 8).

Page 188. l. 19 A.J.B.–Chamberlain: Jan. 4, 1900 (BM Vol. 91).

Page 188. l. 29 Bigge grievances: *Dugdale* I, 296.

Page 189. l. 2 Famous words: *Ensor,* 254.

Page 189. l. 28 A.J.B.–Sidgwick: Jan. 15, 1900 (BM Vol. 150).

Page 189. l. 34 Blunders: *Dugdale* I, 306.

Page 190. l. 19 Politics in bed: *Dugdale* I, 218.

Page 190. l. 29 A.J.B.–G. Wyndham (BM Vol. 121).

Page 191. l. 12 Akers-Douglas: v. Chilston Papers, op. cit.

Page 192. l. 4 Julian Amery: *Life of Chamberlain,* Vol. IV (continuation of J. L. Garvin's work): subsequently *referred to as 'Amery'.*

Page 192. l. 11 C. T. Ritchie (BM Vol. 9).

Page 192. l. 32 Salisbury relations. S.–A.J.B.: Dec. 9, 1900 (BM Vol. 9).

Page 193. l. 44 A.J.B.–King: Feb. 6, 1901 (BM Vol. 1).

Page 194. l. 39   W. S. Churchill–A.J.B. (BM Vol. 12).

Page 195. l. 2   A.J.B.–Betty B. (BM Vol. 149).

Page 195. l. 10   A.J.B.–Lady E.: Aug. 29, 1900 (Stanway).

Page 195. l. 14   A.J.B.–King: Aug. 26, 1903 (BM Vol. 1).

Page 195. l. 23   Salisbury's influence: v. *Salisbury: Portrait of a Statesman,* by A. L. Kennedy (1953).

Page 195. l. 33   Passion and prejudice: Midleton, 109ff.

Page 196. l. 19   Equalise down: *Op. & Arg.,* 107f.

Page 196. l. 35   M. Asquith: *Auto,* Vol. I.

Page 197. l. 11   Vanderbilt: v. *Glitter and Gold,* by Consuelo Vanderbilt Balsan (1952).

CHAPTER 10

Page 198. l. 5   Unanimity: v. *British Political Parties,* by R. T. Mackenzie (1955), 28.

Page 198. l. 11   Esher: *Esher* I, 340.

Page 198. l. 23   Chamberlain sick: *Amery,* 460-1.

Page 198. l. 25   Hicks-Beach: July 11, 1902 (BM Vol. 13).

Page 199. l. 13   Told Chamberlain: *Amery,* 469-70.

Page 200. l. 24   Petrie: *The Powers behind the Prime Ministers* (1959).

Page 200. l. 34   W. S. Churchill, *Great Contemporaries* (1937), 257.

Page 201. l. 3   Brainpower: *Ensor,* 343.

Page 201. l. 20   World of letters: A.J.B.–Knollys, July 18, 1899 (BM Vol. 1).

Page 201. l. 30   *Life of Lord Lansdowne (1925).*

Page 201. l. 40   Peerages (v. BM Vol. 3).

Page 202. l. 1   Cabinet papers: A.J.B.–Sandars, Feb. 27, 1904 (BM Vol. 80).

Page 202. l. 15   King's admiration (BM Vol. 1).

Page 202. l. 19   Civil List (BM Vol. 2).

Page 202. l. 27   Told Lansdowne: Jan. 11, 1915 (v. *Life of Lansdowne*).

Page 202. l. 34   Civil Servants (BM Vol. 3).

Page 203. l. 1   White (BM Vol. 3).

Page 203. l. 36   Secondary education: *Ensor* 355f.

Page 204. l. 42   Evesham: v. *Experiment,* 662.

Page 205. l. 18   Chamberlain cared: *Amery,* 486.

Page 205. l. 21   Chamberlain–Balfour (BM Vol. 92).

Page 206. l. 44   Balfour pleads: *Dugdale* I, 326.

Page 207. l. 13   Lloyd George: v. *My Brother and I,* by W. L. George (1958), 173.

Page 207. l. 37   Halèvy: *History of English People,* Vol. I, Epilogue, 207.

Page 208. l. 21   Lodge (BM Vol. 116).

Page 208. l. 23   Presidential: v. *Essays and Addresses,* 385.

Page 208. l. 25   Lodge–A.J.B.: July 23, 1904 (BM Vol. 116).

Page 208. l. 36   A. S. Eve's *Rutherford, Being the Life and Letters of the Rt. Hon. Lord Rutherford, O.M.* (1939), 113.

Page 210. l. 39   Registration tax: Amery, 523.   *Dugdale* I, 340, *Ensor,* 372.

Page 211. l. 17   On high seas: *Amery,* 516f.

Page 211. l. 34   W. S. Churchill–A.J.B. (BM Vol. 12).   Also A.J.B.'s reply.

Page 212. l. 42   A.J.B.–the King (BM Vol. 1).

Page 213. l. 22   L. S. Amery: *Dugdale* I, 348.

Page 214. l. 19 King's suggestion: 9 June 1903 (BM Vol. 1).

Page 214. l. 22 A.J.B.–Lady E: *Dugdale* I, 351.

Page 214. l. 28 Notes on Insular Free Trade: published 1903 as 'Economic Notes on Insular Free Trade'. v. also *Essays and Addresses*.

Page 214. l. 36 Told King: *Dugdale* I, 352-5.

Page 216. l. 6 *Life of Oxford*, 53.

Page 216. l. 15 Austen heard: *Great Contemporaries*, 245.

Page 217. l. 14 Derby jumped: v. *Lord Derby, King of Lancashire*, by Randolph S. Churchill (1960) subsequently *referred to as 'Derby'*.

Page 217. l. 27 Balfour furious: v. E. T. Raymond, op. cit.

Page 217. l. 39 Muddle: *Dugdale* I, 361.

Page 217. l. 43 Duchess and Ritchie: v. *Derby*.

Page 218. l. 10 Liked Brodrick: Chilston Papers, v. supra

Page 218. l. 38 A.J.B.–Hicks-Beach (BM Vol. 13).

Page 219. l. 10 Sandars wrote (BM Vol. 130).

Page 219. l. 24 A.J.B.–W. S. Churchill (BM Vol. 12).

Page 220. l. 4 A.J.B.–King: Nov. 6, 1903 (BM Vol. 1).

Page 220. l. 15 Esher and Brodrick: Esher II, 59. Midleton, 267.

Page 220. l. 26 Lucy: *Dugdale* I, 413-14.

Page 220. l. 33 Nightmare: Midleton, 267.

Page 220. l. 38 Chamberlain wrote Feb. 12, 1905 (BM Vol. 92); also reply.

Page 221. l. 19 A.J.B.–Lyttelton (BM Vol. 93).

Page 221. l. 30 Half sheet of notepaper: text in *Dugdale* II, 23n.

Page 221. l. 36 Lyttelton (BM Vol. 92).

Page 222. l. 7 A.J.B.–Lady E. (Stanway).

CHAPTER 11

Page 223. l. 10 Defence: v. *The Supreme Command, 1914–18*, 2 Vols, by Lord Hankey (1961), *Defence by Committee : The British Committee of Imperial Defence, 1885–1959*, by F. A. Johnson (Princeton, 1960).

Page 224. l. 40 Borden: Dec, 4, 1903 (BM Vol. 1).

Page 226. l. 1 Dilke: v. supra, *Life of Dilke*.

Page 226. l. 4 Sandars–Short (BM Vol. 136).

Page 226. l. 44 Esher reminded: *Esher* II, 432.

Page 227. l. 6 Report on raid (Whitt.).

Page 227. l. 19 Knollys–Sandars (BM Vol. 2).

Page 227. l. 24 Balfour decided: Feb. 27, 1904 (BM Vol. 2).

Page 227. l. 36 A. Chamberlain: *Down the Years* (1935), 207-8.

Page 228. l. 22 Battlefields: *Esher* II, 62-3.

Page 228. l. 31 Esher prophecy: *Esher* II, 179-80, 183.

Page 228. l. 44 Balfour wrote July 1907: v. *My Political Life*, by L. S. Amery (1953), I, 215.

Page 229. l. 8 Cabinet report (BM Vol. 1).

Page 229. l. 32 St. John: Feb. 27, 1903 (Stanway).

Page 230. l. 12 Arnold-Forster: v. *The House of Cassell*, by S. N. Smith (1958), 166.

Page 230. l. 20 Reply on Haig: July 25, 1905 (BM Vol. 40).

Page 230. l. 23 'Not a gentleman': Knollys–A.J.B. (BM Vol. 2).

Page 230. l. 25   Sandars–A.J.B. (BM Vol. 82).

Page 231. l. 6   Brodrick claim: Midleton, 161.

Page 231. l. 24   Roberts left: *Esher* II, 44.

Page 231. l. 29   Prestige: A.J.B.–Knollys, Sept. 18, 1905 (BM Vol. 2).

Page 232. l. 23   Told Mrs. Dugdale: based on note by Mrs. Dugdale, not included in her biography: v. *Dugdale* I, 424.

Page 233. l. 4   Fisher–Esher: v. *Fear God and Dread Nought*, Correspondence of Fisher of Kilverstone, ed. A. J. Marder, Vol II (1956).

Page 233. l. 20   Fighting for existence: *Dugdale* I, 371.

Page 233. l. 40   King's cipher (BM Vol. 1).

Page 234. l. 20   King writes privately (BM Vol. 79).

Page 234. l. 30   B.'s reply: Dec. 28, 1903 (BM Vol. 1).

Page 235. l. 32   Fisher to wife: v. *Fear God*, Vol. II, op. cit.

Page 236. l. 1   A.J.B.–King: June 9, 1905 (BM Vol. 3).

Page 236. l. 10   A. Chamberlain: *Down the Years*, 209.

Page 236. l. 28   Draft memorandum: 'Memorandum on the Military Question': (BM Vol. 75).

Page 237. l. 32   India not always friendly: Midleton, 198.

Page 237. l. 40   Knollys–Sandars: Jan. 6, 1903 (BM Vol. 1).

Page 238. l. 5   Curzon's behaviour: May 29, 1903 (BM Vol. 1).

Page 238. l. 30   A.J.B.–King (BM Vol. 1).

Page 240. l. 31   A.J.B.–King: July 19 and 25, 1905 (BM Vol. 3).

Page 241. l. 23   Unpleasantness: *Esher* II, 103.

Page 241. l. 32   Knollys–Sandars: Sept. 9, 1905 (BM Vol. 3).

Page 242. l. 1   A.J.B.–Sandars (BM Vol. 82).

Page 242. l. 13   Telegram (BM Vol. 2).

Page 242. l. 21   Curzon deserves (BM Vol. 3).

Page 242. l. 36   Knollys–A.J.B.: Feb. 24, 1905 (BM Vol. 2).

Page 243. l. 11   Lord Ronaldshay: *Life of Lord Curzon*, III, 39-40 (1928).

Page 244. l. 28   Wyndham warned: *Dugdale* I, 416-7.

Page 245. l. 12   MacDonnell–Knollys (BM Vol. 2).

Page 245. l. 28   Sandars–A.J.B. (BM Vol. 80).

Page 245. l. 43   Wyndham's nerve: v. *G. Wyndham*, by J. Biggs-Davison, op. cit.

Page 246. l. 19   Wyndham–A.J.B. (BM Vol. 123).

Page 247. l. 20   Balfour's tribute: *Short*, 521.

Page 248. l. 3   Delcassé (BM Vol. 2).

Page 248. l. 19   Salisbury–A.J.B. (BM Vol. 75).

Page 248. l. 38   Three achievements: *Down the Years*, 207.

Page 250. l. 33   A.J.B.–J. Chamberlain: Nov. 2, 1905 (BM Vol. 92).

Page 251. l. 23   A.J.B.–Gerald Balfour (BM Vol. 149).

Page 252. l. 12   Distress (BM Vol. 82).

Page 252. l. 20   G. Balfour–A.J.B. (BM Vol. 149).

Page 252. l. 28   Chinese labour: Nov. 16, 1903 (BM Vol. 1).

Page 252. l. 42   A.J.B.–Lyttelton: Oct. 20, 1905 (BM Vol. 93).

Page 253. l. 11   A.J.B.–Chamberlain (BM Vol. 92).

Page 253. l. 43   King regrets (BM Vol. 2).

Page 254. l. 23   Sober electioneers (BM Vol. 75).

Page 254. l. 44   Writer in *Times*: R. T. Mackenzie, op. cit., 267.

Page 255. l. 5   Salisbury–A.J.B.: Jan. 28, 1906 (BM Vol. 75).

Page 255. l. 14   Balfour–Lady Salisbury: *Dugdale* I, 438-9.

Page 255. l. 25 Undismayed: *Dugdale* II, 20.

Page 255 Section VII: Sources include *Dugdale, A Jewish Pilgrimage*, by Israel Cohen, and *The Balfour Declaration*, by Leonard Stein (1961).

CHAPTER 12

Page 259. l. 15 Salisbury–A.J.B. (BM Vol. 75).

Page 259. l. 23 A.J.B.–Chamberlain: *Dugdale* II, 23.

Page 260. l. 7 Mackenzie, op. cit., 71.

Page 260. l. 39 Chamberlain stated: J.C.–A.J.B., Feb. 7, 1906 (BM Vol. 92).

Page 260. l. 43 J.C.–A.J.B.: Feb. 10, 1906 (BM Vol. 92).

Page 261. l. 15 In circles: *Dugdale* II, 27.

Page 262. l. 26 Warhorse: *Dugdale* II, 30.

Page 262. l. 40 Sandars–A.J.B.: Jan. 13, 1907 (BM Vol. 82).

Page 263. l. 36 To plain speaking: *Dugdale* II, 44.

Page 264. l. 11 Esher reports: Esher II, 222.

Page 264. l. 43 A.J.B.–Lansdowne: Apr. 13, 1906, v. *Life of Lansdowne*, op. cit.

Page 266. l. 2 Manchester speech: *Dugdale* II, 33.

Page 268. l. 3 Haldane (BM Vol. 82).

Page 268. l. 16 Letter from Roberts (Whitt.).

Page 269. l. 15 Esher–King: *Esher* II, 316-17.

Page 269. l. 38 A.J.B.–Asquith: Nov. 5, 1908 (BM Vol. 10).

Page 270. l. 35 Murray's paper: *Esher* II, 364.

Page 271. l. 10 A.J.B.–Lansdowne (Whitt.).

Page 271. l. 38 Sea power: *Dugdale* II, 53.

Page 273. l. 23 Garvin: *The Observer and J. L. Garvin 1908–14. A Study in a Great Editorship*, by A. M. Gollin (1960), 130.

Page 273. l. 43 Beresford gas-bag: v. *Fear God*, Vol. II, op. cit.

Page 274. l. 23 *Decadence* (1908): reprinted in *Essays Speculative and Political* (1920).

Page 277. l. 24 Roosevelt letter: (BM Vol. 5).

CHAPTER 13

Page 287. l. 11 A.J.B.–Eve Balfour (BM Vol. 149).

Page 287. l. 20 Balfour's tactics: v. passim *Mr Balfour's Poodle*, by R. Jenkins (1954)—subsequently *referred to as 'Jenkins'*.

Page 287. l. 42 Illegality of Valuation: *Dugdale* II, 56.

Page 288. l. 9 Grey said: *Jenkins*, 58

Page 288. l. 29 Saintsbury: *A Last Scrapbook*, 155-8.

Page 289. l. 41 Garvin: v. Gollin, op. cit., 113.

Page 290. l. 11 Garvin wrote: Gollin, 115.

Page 290. l. 27 Hicks-Beach (BM Vol. 13).

Page 290. l. 33 Lord Birkenhead: *Frederick Edwin, 1st Earl of Birkenhead*, Vol. 1 (1933), 198.

Page 291. l. 29 Knollys told Clerk: *Jenkins*, 68.

Page 291. l. 31 Asquith moved: *Ensor*, 417.

Page 292. l. 36 Vote black: *Dugdale* II, 59.

Page 294. l. 13 Balfour at Lansdowne House: *Jenkins*, 97.

Page 295. l. 3 Asquith–King: v. *King George V: His Life and Reign*, by H. Nicolson (1952), 131.

Page 295. l. 8 Asquith–A.J.B. (BM Vol. 10).

Page 296. l. 10 A.J.B.–Lyttelton (BM Vol. 93).

Page 296. l. 28 A.J.B. Memo: *Dugdale* II, 62-3.

Page 297. l. 6 Asquith to wife; v. *Life of Asquith*, Vol. II, 291, op. cit.

Page 298. l. 6 Garvin appeal: *Gollin*, 216.

Page 298. l. 32 Ensor suggests: *Ensor*, 424.

Page 299. l. 20 Lloyd George *War Memoirs*, 39.

Page 300. l. 20 Sandars–Garvin: *Gollin*, 309f.

Page 301. l. 19 I should resign: *Lord Derby, 'King of Lancashire'* (1960), by R. Churchill, 126-7.

Page 301. l. 24 King later said: *Jenkins*, 121.

Page 301. l. 33 A.J.B.–Stamfordham (BM Vol. 4).

Page 302. l. 11 King's minute: v. Nicolson, op. cit.

Page 302. l. 25 Final straw (BM Vol. 4).

Page 303. l. 28 Sandars–Derby: *Derby*, 119.

Page 303. l. 43 To dissolve or not (BM Vol. 4).

Page 304. l. 20 Knollys complains (BM Vol. 4).

Page 304. l. 30 Knollys replied (BM Vol. 4).

Page 305. l. 7 Short–Alice (BM Vol. 85).

Page 305. l. 12 'My dear Ettie': *Derby*, 119.

Page 305. l. 42 Shocking scandal: July 16, 1911 (Stanway).

Page 306. l. 8 Stamfordham–Salisbury: July 28, 1911 (BM Vol. 4).

Page 307. l. 6 Letter to *Times*: *Dugdale* II, 81.

Page 307. l. 19 Stamfordham, two letters (BM Vol. 4).

Page 308. l. 17 A.J.B.–Salisbury (BM Vol. 75).

Page 308. l. 29 King resentful: v. also *Esher* III, 65.

Page 308. l. 36 Salisbury–A.J.B. (BM Vol. 75).

Page 309. l. 24 Lord Newton: *Life of Lansdowne*, 422-3; *Jenkins*, 153.

Page 310. l. 4 Unsent memo: *Dugdale* II, 69-70.

Page 310. l. 31 A. Chamberlain: *Jenkins*, 157.

Page 311. l. 8 Lady Elcho's son: *A Family Record*, by Lady Wemyss (1932; privately printed, but copy in London Library).

Page 311. l. 14 Wilfrid Blunt: *My Diaries, 1888-1914*, 770-1.

Page 311. l. 27 Reynold's: Whittinghame cutting book.

Page 311. l. 37 Balfour moved: *Jenkins*, 167.

Page 312. l. 1 Asquith sacrificed: *Dugdale* II, 82.

Page 312. l. 5 King disturbed: *Jenkins*, 169.

Page 312. l. 18 King grateful: *Nicolson*, 149f.

Page 312. l. 37 A.J.B.–Lady Wemyss (Elcho): Aug. 11, 1911 (Stanway).

Page 313. l. 4 Sandars note (BM Vol. 85).

Page 314. l. 1 A. Chamberlain: *Mackenzie*, 81.

Page 314. l. 7 *Derby*, 147.

Page 314. l. 24 Told Derby: *Derby*, 130.

Page 314. l. 26 London speech: *Mackenzie*, 81.

Page 314. l. 44 Margot (BM Vol. 10).

Page 315. l. 8 A.J.B. Speech: *Op. & Arg.*, 15.

Page 315. l. 20 Lyttelton letter, Oct. 21, 1911 (BM Vol. 93).

Page 315. l. 25 Wells: *Experiment*, 661.

Page 315. l. 44 Sandars–A.J.B. (BM Vol. 85).

Page 316. l. 14 *Short* (BM Vol. 85).

Page 316. l. 37 *Jenkins*, 187.

Page 317. l. 1 Speech: *Op. & Arg.*, 20.

CHAPTER 14

Page 318. l. 1 Baccarat: March, 1913 (Stanway).

Page 319. l. 14 Elgar (BM Vol. 4).

Page 319. l. 32 Pringle-Pattison (BM Vol. 116).

Page 320. l. 20 Lady Betty (BM Vol. 149).

Page 320. l. 38 Lady Betty: May 8, 1911 (BM Vol. 149).

Page 321. l. 9 Financial affairs: mainly from 3rd Earl of Balfour.

Page 322. l. 19 Told Alice: Aug. 25, 1911 (Whitt.).

Page 322. l. 23 Bergson: *Essays Speculative and Political* (1920).

Page 323. l. 27 Hugh Redwood: *Bristol Fashion*, 97-8 (pointed out to me by F. T. Scott of Wimbledon).

Page 324. l. 13 The Lecture: It exists in two printed forms, very different in content. (1) *Criticism and Beauty. A Lecture Rewritten. Being the Romanes Lecture for 1909* by the Rt. Hon. A. J. Balfour (1910). This is the text used here. (2) *Questionings on Criticism and Beauty*, by the Rt. Hon. A. J. Balfour. *Delivered in the Sheldonian Theatre, November 24, 1909. Verbatim Shorthand Report.*

Page 326. l. 36 Gifford: *Theism and Humanism, being the Gifford Lectures delivered at the University of Glasgow, 1914*, by the Rt. Hon. A. J. Balfour, M.A., F.R.S., LL.D, D.C.L., Hon. Fellow of Trinity College, Cambridge (1915).

CHAPTER 15

Page 332. l. 8 Margot wrote (BM Vol. 112).

Page 332. l. 26 Asquith's nerve (BM Vol. 86).

Page 333. l. 6 *Derby*, 170.

Page 333. l. 13 Blake: *The Unknown Prime Minister. Bonar Law* (1955), by Robert Blake, 140—subsequently *referred to as* 'Blake'.

Page 333. l. 24 Braithwaite: *Lloyd George's Ambulance Wagon. The Memoirs of W. J. Braithwaite, 1911–12.* Ed. H. Bunbury and R. M. Titmuss, 188, 252.

Page 335. l. 8 Balfour memo: *Dugdale* II, 100-1.

Page 336. l. 25 Stamfordham: Oct. 7, 1913 (BM Vol. 4).

Page 337. l. 12 Balfour prophesied: *Mutiny at the Curragh*, by A. P. Ryan (1956), 68. Subsequently *referred to as* 'Ryan'. Balfour–Law: *Blake* 176-7.

Page 338. l. 22 Brass bands: *Ryan*, 162.

Page 338. l. 40 Roberts delighted: *Ryan*, 182.

Page 339. l. 4 A.J.B.–Churchill: *Ryan*, 188-9.

Page 339. l. 5 Balfour speech 1913: *Op. & Arg.*, 78-80.

Page 340. l. 34 Defence co-operation: v. Sandars–A.J.B., Jan. 11, 1912 (BM Vol. 136).

Page 341. l. 12 House told: *Ensor*, 484.

Page 341. l. 32 Sandars: Jan 11, 1912 (BM Vol. 136).

Page 341. l. 42 Law's biographer: *Blake*, 228.

Page 342. l. 2 Member of sub-committee: v. Hankey, *The Supreme Command, 1914–18* (1961), I, 151.

Page 342. l. 42 A.J.B.–W. S. Churchill (BM Vol. 12).

Page 343. l. 11 To Fisher on dreadnought: v. *From the Dreadnought to Scapa Flow. The Royal Navy in the Fisher Era, 1904–1919. Vol. I. The Road to War, 1904–14*, by A. J. Marder, 332.

Page 343. l. 13 German Navy Law (BM Vol. 12).

Page 343. l. 17 Balfour's misgivings: A.J.B.–W. S. Churchill, Mar. 22, 1912 (BM Vol. 12).

Page 344. l. 30 Churchill–A.J.B. (BM Vol. 12).

Page 345. l. 8 Nord und Sud: reprinted in *Essays Speculative and Political*.

Page 345. l. 24 Grey charlatan: *My Brother and I*, by W. L. George, op. cit., 238.

Page 345. l. 33 Bulford: *A Family Record*.

Page 345. l. 40 Veritable rock: *World Crisis*, Vol. I, 218, by W. S. Churchill.

Page 346. l. 1 Park Crescent: *Dugdale* II, 113.

Page 346. l. 3 Lady Wemyss writes: *A Family Record*.

CHAPTER 16

Page 348. l. 1 Telling Grey: *Blake*, 220.

Page 348. l. 6 Official message: *Blake*, 222.

Page 348. l. 17 Stated to Churchill: *Dugdale* II, 114.

Page 348. l. 35 Lichnowsky: *Dugdale* II, 119.

Page 349. l. 27 Haldane's argument: *Dugdale* II, 117.

Page 351. l. 10 Sandars' glee (BM Vol. 136).

Page 351. l. 27 Prince Louis: Oct. 30, 1914 (BM Vol. 136).

Page 351. l. 33 A.J.B.–Alice (BM Vol. 150).

Page 352. l. 18 Asquith thanks (BM Vol. 10).

Page 352. l. 23 From Asquith: *Dugdale* II, 125.

Page 352. l. 31 A.J.B.–Sandars (BM Vol. 136).

Page 353. l. 6 William Balfour: May 15, 1915 (BM Vol. 149).

Page 353. l. 34 A.J.B.–Gerald (BM Vol. 149).

Page 356. l. 1 Balfour warns Churchill (BM Vol. 12).

Page 356. l. 25 Fisher regrets: *Blake*, 224.

Page 356. l. 30 Postponement (BM Vol. 12).

Page 357. l. 22 A.J.B.–Alice (BM Vol. 150).

Page 357. l. 38 General Staff Paper: see below (Whitt.).

Page 358. l. 33 Lord Durham (BM Vol. 181).

Page 359. l. 28 Tougher, says Hankey: *Dugdale* II, 140.

Page 360. l. 32 Sir Arthur Wilson: *The Supreme Command* I, 317—subsequently referred to as 'Hankey'.

Page 360. l. 42 Sir Henry Oliver: v. *A Great Seaman*, by Adml. Sir W. J. Witherby (1956).

Page 363. l. 4 Report to Cabinet: *Dugdale* II, 150.

Page 365. l. 9 Northcliffe (BM Vol. 112).

Page 365. l. 16   Stamfordham called: Oct. 18, 1915 (BM Vol. 4).

Page 365. l. 24   Margot accuses (BM Vol. 112).

Page 366. l. 2   A.J.B.–Salisbury (BM Vol. 85).,

Page 367. l. 15   Balfour's memo: *Dugdale* II, 172 (and Whitt.).

Page 368. l. 3   Not as Blake: *Blake*, 339.

Page 368. l. 30   Lloyd George: *War Memoirs* II, 999.

Page 368. l. 44   Moment's consideration: *Blake*, 337.

Page 371. l. 12   *Derby*, 239.

Page 372. l. 2   Asquith's almost unbelievable: Joan Lascelles letter (BM Vol. 149).

CHAPTER 17

Page 374. l. 22   Diplomatic activity: v. *Studies in Secret Diplomacy during the First World War*, by W. W. Gottlieb (1957).

Page 375. l. 15   *Life and Letters of Walter H. Page*, by B. J. Hendrick (1924), 259—subsequently *referred to as 'Page'*.

Page 375. l. 32   Grey replied: v. Private Memorandum circulated to Prime Minister and Mr. Balfour from Grey.   Foreign Office, Feb. 10, 1916.

Page 376. l. 4   Dec. 4: Private Memorandum from Grey.   F.O. Dec. 4, 1916.

Page 376. l. 36   Page note: *Dugdale* II, 188.

Page 376. l. 44   Northcliffe: *Page*, 207.

Page 377. l. 6   Page reports Cecil: *Page*, 209ff.

Page 377. l. 28   Belligerents: MS. note (Whitt.).

Page 377. l. 43   Spring Rice: *Dugdale* II, 189.

Page 378. l. 11   Roosevelt: Oct. 25, 1915 (BM Vol. 5).

Page 378. l. 24   *The Zimmerman Telegram*, by B. W. Tuchman (1959).

Page 379. l. 13   Shook his hand: *Dugdale* II, 195.

Page 379. l. 38   Told Col. House: *Intimate Papers of Col. House* III, 236.

Page 380. l. 10   Dumfries incident: *Auto.*, 238.

Page 380. l. 31   Ian Malcolm: *Lord Balfour* (1930).

Page 380. l. 35   Told Sims: *Page*, 274.

Page 381. l. 14   Balfour a Tory: *Page*, 257-8.

Page 382. l. 2   Polk: *Page*, 263-4.

Page 382. l. 37   Coughed: *Page*, 264.

Page 383. l. 36   Spring Rice: *Dugdale* II, 208.

Page 385. l. 23   Pilgrims' Dinner: *Op. & Arg.*, 267.

Page 385. l. 43   Told Cabinet: *Dugdale* II, 210.

Page 386. l. 16   Loved that man: *Page*, 403.

Page 387. l. 3   Samuel: *Viscount Samuel*, by J. Bowles (1957).

Page 387. l. 15   Lords speech: *Op. & Arg.*, 245.

Page 388. l. 3   *Conflicts* (1942), 157.

Page 388. l. 19   New psychology: *Op. & Arg.*, 254.

Page 389. l. 5   Asquith remark: v. *Trial and Error*, by C. Weizmann (1949).

Page 391. l. 10   A.J.B.–Weizmann: v. *The Balfour Declaration* (1961), 154—subsequently *referred to as 'Stein'*.

Page 391. l. 42   Montefiore: v. *A Jewish Pilgrimage*, by Israel Cohen.

Page 392. l. 21   Declaration: *Stein*, 547.

Page 392. l. 32   National home: *Stein*, 552.

Page 394. l. 8   Small notch: *Op. & Arg.*, 233.

Page 394. l. 29 Hebrew Univ. speech: *Op. & Arg.*, 255.

Page 397. l. 21 On Lloyd George: *Dugdale* II, 284-5.

Page 401. l. 18 Beaverbrook: *Men and Power 1917–18* (1959).

Page 402. l. 6 Details of relations between Britain and the Bolsheviks: v. *Intervention and the War. Anglo-Soviet Relations 1917–21*, by Richard H. Ullman (Princeton, 1961).

CHAPTER 18

Page 404. l. 1 Law–A.J.B.: *Blake*, 384.

Page 405. l. 8 Address to electors of the City of London: *Op. & Arg.*, 270-3.

Page 406. l. 5 Dreaded peace: *Dugdale* II, 263.

Page 406. l. 35 Churchill wrote: v. *The Aftermath*, V, 190.

Page 408. l. 1 *Documents on British Foreign Policy.* 1st Series, Vol. I, 1919. Ed. E. L. Woodward and Rohan Butler (1947).

Page 408. l. 33 Hungary: *Documents*, 207-8.

Page 409. l. 18 Belgian coalfields: *Documents*, 328.

Page 409. l. 25 Coal: *Documents*, 218.

Page 410. l. 14 Czechs: *Documents*, 118-19.

Page 410. l. 23 Austrian notes: *Documents*, 432.

Page 411. l. 33 Headlam-Morley: *Reparations. A Chapter of a History of the Peace Conference.* Foreign Office 11984.

Page 412. l. 16 Balfour's annotations (Whitt.).

Page 412. l. 32 Hankey–A.J.B. (Whitt.).

Page 413. l. 8 Bystander: Whittingehame cuttings book.

Page 413. l. 38 Keynes: v. The Economic Report, June–Sept, 1945 (courtesy of R. F. Harrod).

Page 414. l. 17 Vansittart: *The Mist Procession* (1955), 218.

Page 414. l. 33 A.J.B.–Eleanor (BM Vol. 150).

Page 414. l. 37 Lady Wemyss–A.J.B.: Aug. 8, 1918.

Page 416. l. 6 Sandars: *Studies of Yesterday*, by 'A Privy Councillor' (1928).

Page 416. l. 15 Sandars and Churchill: v. *The Powers behind the Prime Ministers*, by Sir C. Petrie (1959).

Page 417. l. 18 Books choice: *Down the Years*, 245f.

Page 417. l. 37 Material progress: *Op. & Arg.*, 135.

Page 417. l. 40 Leeds Univ: *Short*, 112.

Page 418. l. 15 League: *Op. and Arg.*, 289.

Page 419. l. 24 W. S. Churchill–A.J.B. (Whitt.).

Page 419. l. 35 A.J.B.–Law (Whitt.).

Page 420. l. 29 Shrewd observer: *Old Diplomacy and New, 1876–1922*, by A. L. Kennedy (1922), 366.

Page 421. l. 23 *Derby*, 429.

Page 422. l. 1 Privy Councillor: *Studies of Yesterday*, 182.

CHAPTER 19

Page 423. l. 16 Debtors: *Dugdale* II, 351-2.

Page 424. l. 32 To Riddell: *Dugdale* II, 346.

Page 424. l. 42 Aldenham (Whitt.).

Page 427. l. 22   A.J.B.–W. S. Churchill: Sep. 14, 1922 (Whitt.).

Page 427. l. 42   Balfour manifesto: *Blake*, 461.

Page 428. l. 3   Dinner party (Whitt.).

Page 429. l. 12   *Theism and Thought. A Study in Familiar Beliefs. Being the second course of Gifford Lectures delivered at the University of Glasgow 1922–23*, by Arthur James Balfour, Earl of Balfour, K.G., O.M. (1923).

Page 430. l. 23   *Familiar Beliefs and Transcendent Reason*. The British Academy. Annual Philosophical Lecture Henriette Hertz Trust (1925).

Page 431. l. 3   Meeting with King (Whitt.).

Page 433. l. 2   A.J.B.–Birkenhead (Whitt.).

Page 434. l. 19   A.J.B.–Stamfordham: Jan. 2, 1924 (Whitt.).

Page 436. l. 8   A.J.B.–Alice (Whitt.).

CHAPTER 20

Page 437. l. 7   Henry Wilson: v. *Documents on British Foreign Policy*, 1st Series, Vol. 9 (1960).

Page 437. l. 20   Memorandum.   Committee of Imperial Defence.   Sub-committee on National and Imperial Defence.   Interim Report.   June 12, 1923.

Page 439. l. 26   Hoare (Whitt.).

Page 442. l. 4   Balfour's report: ND 60.   C.I.D. National and Imperial Defence Committee.   Sub-committee on relations between Navy and Air Force.

Page 442. l. 17   Report as whole: ND 68.   C.I.D. sub-committee on National and Imperial Defence.

Page 442. l. 43   Hesitant to sign: A.J.B.–Hankey, Oct. 23, 1923 (Whitt. copy).

Page 443. l. 25   Notes on C.I.D. Report, Jan. 9, 1924.

Page 444. l. 21   House of Lords: *Op. & Arg.*, 155.

Page 444. l. 42   From Hankey (Whitt.).

Page 445. l. 1   Reply to Hankey (Whitt.).

Page 445. l. 35   A.J.B.–Hankey: Oct. 23, 1925 (Whitt.).

Page 446. l. 1   Physical security (Whitt.).

Page 446. l. 39   Medical Research: v. A.J.B.–S. Baldwin, Mar. 12, 1925 (BM Vol. 12).

Page 447. l. 20   A.J.B.–Geddes: Oct. 21, 1921 (Whitt.).

Page 448. l. 6   Speech: July 23, 1926: *Op. & Arg.*, 169.

Page 448. l. 39   *Auto.*, 29.

Page 449. l. 28   A.J.B.–Conan Doyle (Whitt. copy).

Page 451. l. 18   A.J.B.–Alice (Whitt.).

Page 451. l. 24   Dining with Hertzog: v. *Private and Official*, by Nourah Waterhouse (1943).

Page 451. l. 40   Menzies: v. *Times*, June 11 & 12, 1956.

Page 453. l. 32   Destitution: *Short*, 214.

Page 454. l. 9   Socialism: *Op. & Arg.*, 146ff.

Page 454. l. 26   Industrial Psychology: Smart, 89.

Page 454. l. 43   Bacon: reprinted in *Essays Speculative and Political*, 148ff.   Also *Short*, 222-3.

Page 455. l. 29   Amery: *My Political Life* III, 299.

Page 455. l. 32   Wells: *Experiment*, 666.

Page 455. l. 36   The young: *Op. & Arg.*, 36.

Page 456. l. 34   Bridges: A.J.B.–Stamfordham, Nov. 10, 1928.

Page 456. l. 38   Smuts (Whitt.).

Page 457. l. 4   Freud: letter from Edward Jones to K.Y.

Page 457. l. 8   Moore (Whitt.).

Page 457. l. 19   O.M.: A.J.B.–Stamfordham, Apr. 22, 1927 (Whitt.).

Page 458. l. 17   Dugdale talks: *Dugdale* II, 407.

Page 459. l. 6   Joan Lascelles (Whitt.).

Page 460. l. 43   Baldwin wrote (BM Vol. 12).

Page 461. l. 37   Asked nephew: 3rd Earl of Balfour–K.Y.

Page 462. l. 14   James Coleman: *Daily Telegraph*, Mar. 20, 1930.

Page 462. l. 40   Final quotation: *Theism and Humanism*, 19.

INDEX